America's Switzerland

ALSO BY JAMES H. PICKERING

~

Frederick Chapin's Colorado:
The Peaks About Estes Park and Other Writings (1995)

"This Blue Hollow": Estes Park, The Early Years, 1859–1915 (1999)

Mr. Stanley of Estes Park (2000)

In the Vale of Elkanah: The Tahosa Valley World of
Charles Edwin Hewes (2003)

The Ways of the Mountains:
Thornton Sampson, Agnes Vaille and Other Tragedies in High Places (2003)

Early Estes Park Narratives (2004)

The MacGregors of Black Canyon: An American Story (2008)

Joe Mills of Estes Park: A Colorado Life (2013)

Estes Park and Rocky Mountain National Park: Then and Now,
Revised Edition (2019)

America's Switzerland

~

Estes Park and Rocky Mountain National Park, the Growth Years

JAMES H. PICKERING

University Press of Colorado

© 2005 by University Press of Colorado

Published by the University Press of Colorado
245 Century Circle, Suite 202
Louisville, Colorado 80027

 The University Press of Colorado is a proud member of
the Association of University Presses.

The University Press of Colorado is a cooperative publishing enterprise supported, in part, by
Adams State University, Colorado State University, Fort Lewis College, Metropolitan State
University of Denver, Regis University, University of Colorado, University of Northern Colorado, University of Wyoming, Utah State University, and Western Colorado University.

∞ This paper meets the requirements of the ANSI/NISO Z39.48-1992 (Permanence of Paper).

Library of Congress Cataloging-in-Publication Data

Pickering, James H.
   America's Switzerland : Estes Park and Rocky Mountain National Park, the growth years /
James H. Pickering.
      p. cm.
   Includes bibliographical references and index.
   ISBN 978-0-87081-806-6 (hardcover : alk. paper) — ISBN 978-1-64642-064-3 (pbk : alk.
paper)
   1. Estes Park (Colo.)—History. 2. Rocky Mountain National Park (Colo.)—History. I. Title.
   F782.L2P53 2005
   978.8'68032—dc22

                                                                    2005005433

Cover illustration from the postcard collection of Bobbie Heisterkamp

Jim Pickering, Eddie Hoppe, and Dove Hares motored from their homes in Lincoln, Nebraska, arriving in Estes Park on Sunday night and they plan to spend the next two weeks at the National Park Hotel.

Mr. Pickering . . . spent several weeks in the Park last summer and will be remembered as the young artist, who painted so many clever advertisements for the Riverside Amusement Park.

—*Estes Park Trail* (August 16, 1929)

And so it began. . . .
This book is dedicated to the memory of my father.

Contents

~

List of Figures		*ix*
Introduction		1
Chapter 1.	Estes Park in 1915—New Beginnings	7
Chapter 2.	The Growth of "the Village"	23
Chapter 3.	F. O. Stanley and the Development of Estes Park	53
Chapter 4.	Building a Community	89
Chapter 5.	Rocky Mountain National Park: The First Years	119
Chapter 6.	Publicizing Park and Town: The "Eve of Estes" and Winter Sports	147
Chapter 7.	The Transportation Controversy: Rocky Mountain National Park, 1919–1921	179
Chapter 8.	Rocky Mountain National Park: The Toll Years, 1921–1929	209
Chapter 9.	Growth and Maturity: Estes Park in the 1920s	253
Chapter 10.	Hard Times Come to Colorado: Estes Park in the 1930s	281
Chapter 11.	The Years After Roger Toll: Rocky Mountain Park, 1929–1941	327
Chapter 12.	Estes Park and Rocky Mountain National Park: The War Years . . . and After	363
Notes		387
Selected Bibliography		431
Index		437

Figures

~

1.1. Estes Park in 1915. Map by Fred Clatworthy   8
1.2. Rocky Mountain National Park dedication, September 4, 1915   9
1.3. Rocky Mountain National Park dedication. *Left to right:*
     publicist Robert Sterling Yard, Enos Mills, F. O. Stanley,
     Colorado representative Edward Taylor, park booster Mary
     Belle King Sherman, and Colorado governor George Carlson   12
1.4. The Corners (Elkhorn and Moraine), Estes Park, 1903.
     Community building and John Cleave house in foreground;
     post office across the street   19
1.5. The Corners in summer, ca. 1903   19
1.6. Estes Park and Rocky Mountain National Park: Lodges and
     Resorts, ca. 1940   21
2.1. Abner Sprague's plat of the Town of Estes Park, dated January
     1906   24
2.2. Cornelius H. Bond   26
2.3. Fred Clatworthy's Ye Little Shop, ca. 1910   29
2.4. Original Hupp Hotel (renamed Estes Park Hotel), ca. 1913   31
2.5. Josephine (Josie) Hupp   32

2.6. First issue of *The Mountaineer*, Estes Park's first newspaper,
      June 4, 1908   36
2.7. Manford Hotel, ca. 1910   37
2.8. Estes Park, 1908   39
2.9. Estes Park, ca. 1910   39
2.10. 1919 Panoramic Photograph of Estes Park   40, 42–45
2.11. Estes Park Post Office, built in 1914   46
2.12. Ralph Macdonald's Steam Laundry   47
2.13. J. Edward Macdonald's "Popular Shop," ca. 1910   48
2.14. J. Edward Macdonald's new store and adjacent home, ca. 1914   49
2.15. Monroe's Livery (later Hupp Livery), upper Elkhorn, ca. 1910   51
3.1. Reconstructing the North St. Vrain Road, 1907   57
3.2. The Stanley Hotel, ca. 1915   59
3.3. Estes Park Transportation Company depot and offices on
      Elkhorn Avenue, ca. 1915   66
3.4. Stanley Steamers at the railroad station in Lyons, ca. 1915   67
3.5. Taking the Stanley Mountain Wagon to Estes Park   68
3.6. F. O. Stanley during the 1930s, with Byron Hall on left and
      his niece, Dorothy Emmons on right   86
4.1. Reunion Dinner at community building, ca. 1903   91
4.2. Estes Park Fish Hatchery, ca. 1910   96
4.3. "Sunbeam"   99
4.4. Bringing the elk up from Lyons, 1913   102
5.1. Park supervisor Charles Russell Trowbridge, 1915–1916   120
5.2. Dixie MacCracken, first park ranger, on the Fern Lake Trail   127
5.3. Chief ranger in charge and superintendent Lewis Claude Way,
      1916–1921   129
5.4. Rocky Mountain National Park, first administrative office
      in Estes Park village, July 27, 1923   130
5.5. Automobile on Fall River Road   137
5.6. Camping at Aspenglen Campground   139
5.7. Tourists on the trail   142
6.1. Advertising Estes Park. Burlington Railroad brochure, 1913   149
6.2. Advertising Estes Park. Float on Stanley Mountain Wagon,
      ca. 1915. Byron Hall on running board, Enos Mills in passenger
      seat   150
6.3. The "Eve of Estes," shaking hands with Enos Mills; Superin-
      tendent Way stands at left   153
6.4. Colorado Mountain Club at Fern Lake   163
6.5. Winter skiing at Elkhorn ski course on Oldman Mountain   173

6.6. Summer ski festival on Oldman Mountain, June 24, 1934   176
7.1. Enos A. Mills, ca. 1920   180
7.2. Map showing Roe Emery's "Circle Tour" beginning and
     ending in Denver, 1922. Published by Union Pacific Railroad 187
7.3. Coded telegram to Superintendent Way, August 18, 1919.
     "Infidel" refers to Enos Mills   194
7.4. Clem Yore   197
8.1. Superintendent Roger Wescott Toll, 1921–1929   210
8.2. New RMNP administration building, September 25, 1924   220
8.3. Rocky Mountain Parks Transportation Company garage and
     offices on Elkhorn Avenue, 1924   221
8.4. First transportation company bus being hauled through the
     Big Drift on Fall River Road, June 20, 1923   223
8.5. Steam shovel handling twenty cubic feet of snow on the Big
     Drift, June 9, 1927   224
8.6. Colorado Mountain Club at Boulderfield Shelter Cabin,
     July 31, 1927   230
8.7. Early Cheley camp brochure   244
8.8. Olinger Highlanders at Glacier Basin, July 1, 1927   247
9.1. Estes Park and Rocky Mountain National Park in 1927. Map
     by Richardson Rome   252
9.2. Sanborn Map of 1926. Upper Elkhorn Avenue to Moraine
     Avenue   255
9.3. Sanborn Map of 1926. Middle Elkhorn Avenue, from Moraine
     Avenue to Riverside   256
9.4. Sanborn Map of 1926. Lower Elkhorn Avenue, from
     Riverside east.   257
9.5. Joe and Ethel Mills and their two children, early 1920s   261
9.6. Riverside Amusement Park from rear   267
9.7. Ted Jelsema's Romancers performing at Riverside   268
9.8. The Dark Horse Tavern at Riverside with its famous
     carousel barstools   269
9.9. Lower Elkhorn Avenue in the 1920s: J. Edward Macdonald
     store; the Josephine Hotel; William Tallant shop; transportation
     company and offices; and original Hupp Hotel   275
9.10. Upper Elkhorn Avenue: Fred Clatworthy's store, the
      Sherwood Hotel, and the Community Church are the three
      most visible buildings   277
10.1. Construction at the Rock Cut on Trail Ridge Road,
      August 1932   299

10.2. Early view of the Big Thompson road 301
10.3. Parade in Estes Park celebrating the completion of the new Big Thompson Highway, May 29, 1938. Estes Park Library and Auditorium in background 305
10.4. Map of the new South St. Vrain Highway, 1939 308
10.5. Parade celebrating completion of the new North St. Vrain Highway, June 4, 1939. Transportation company building in background 311
10.6. Parade, June 4, 1939. Reviewing stand in front of Jay Building 312
10.7. Ceremony marking the start of drilling at East Portal, June 23, 1939 321
10.8. "Holing Through" the two ends of the Alva Adams Tunnel, June 16, 1944 323
11.1. Rocky Mountain National Park in 1934 328
11.2. Superintendent Edmund P. Rogers, 1929–1936 331
11.3. CCC Camp in Little Horseshoe Park, May 1933 336
11.4. Robert Fechner, founding director of the CCC, addressing recruits in Little Horseshoe Park, 1934 339
11.5. CCC Camp in Hallowell Park 341
11.6. Noted guide Shep Husted, foreman at Camp NP-4-C 343
11.7. Park naturalist Dorr Yeager 350
11.8. Arapaho exhibit, Moraine Park Museum 353
12.1. Map of Estes Park and Rocky Mountain National Park, ca. 1950 364
12.2. Scrap drive in Estes Park 368
12.3. Abner Sprague and Charles Reed, June 1939. Reed has just flipped with Sprague for the "right" to purchase the first annual entrance permit for RMNP 369
12.4. Ryoji and Yaye Kato 373
12.5. Kato Tea Garden on the Bear Lake Road 374
12.6. The Y-junction: Big Thompson entrance to Rocky Mountain National Park 384

America's Switzerland

Introduction

~

... and yet I am greatly mistaken if the verdict of more familiar acquaintance by the American people with America is not, that here,—among these central ranges of continental mountains and these great companion parks, within this wedded circle of majestic hill and majestic plain, under these skies of purity, and in this atmosphere of elixir, lies the pleasure-ground and health-home of the nation.

—SAMUEL BOWLES, *The Switzerland of America: A Summer Vacation in the Parks and Mountains of Colorado* (1869)

As EDITOR BOWLES OF THE *Springfield Republican* made his way through Colorado's parks and mountains during his memorable 1868 visit and recorded his impressions, the comparison he repeatedly made was to the Swiss Alps. "We saw enough of it in our stage ride across the Continent in 1865," he wrote in his preface, "to suggest that it would become the Switzerland of America . . . ; and now, after a new visit . . . we find our original enthusiasm more than rekindled, or original thought confirmed." Not surprisingly, such a prediction struck a responsive chord in the popular imagination of the nation and, in the years that immediately followed, Bowles's book played an important role in promoting the scenic wonders of Colorado and the Rocky Mountain West.

Within a decade of Bowles's visit, Colorado's parks became a favorite destination for those seeking pleasure and health. For many of these visitors, the destination of choice was not Colorado Springs and nearby Manitou Springs—the "Saratoga of the West," where the fashionable found, or at least pretended to find, a social scene comparable to anything in the East or even Europe—but the upland valley of Estes Park, some seventy miles northwest of Denver. The Denver press had decided by 1880 that this valley was "the gem of the mountains," a place easy of access and without social pretension

1

where Americans of all ranks could feel at home. This has not changed. For nearly a century and a half the Estes Valley has been one of Colorado and the West's most visited places. For ninety years the village of Estes Park has served as the eastern gateway to Rocky Mountain National Park, from its beginning the most popular national park west of the Mississippi. This book is concerned with this special region of north-central Colorado—town, valley, and national park during their years of greatest growth and development, from 1903 to 1945—a story I began in *"This Blue Hollow": Estes Park, The Early Years, 1859–1915* (1999) and *Mr. Stanley of Estes Park* (2000).

Occupying an area of nearly six square miles, Estes Park, Colorado, is a world apart. The town sits at 7,500 feet above sea level in a semi-arid 32-square-mile upland meadow that also bears its name. To the east across twenty miles of undulating foothills and winding valleys and canyons are the historic railroad towns of Lyons and Loveland. Fort Collins, the county seat, lies forty miles to the northeast. The Estes Valley is watered by two major rivers and their tributaries, Fall River and the Big Thompson River, which rise in the high country to the west.

The geologic story of Estes Park is a complex one. Yet, thanks to the forces of uplift and erosion that created the Rocky Mountains, Estes Park is surrounded by scenic beauty that few North American towns can rival. To the south towers 14,256-foot Longs Peak, flanked by Mount Meeker and Mount Lady Washington; to the west and the northwest along the Continental Divide are the spectacular peaks, jagged knobs, and rugged projections of the Front Range and the Mummy Range. The sub-alpine portion of this mountain world is one of U-shaped valleys, rocky amphitheaters, and crystal clear lakes. Its flowering meadows are separated by heavily wooded stands of ponderosa and lodgepole pine, douglas fir and engelmann spruce, intermixed with aspen and willow of shimmering green or gold. Since 1915 some 417 square miles of this wilderness west of Estes Park has been set aside in Rocky Mountain National Park, a full third of which lies above 11,500 feet in harsh, wind-swept tundra. Across the Divide, on the park's western slope, rise streams that form the Colorado River.

My narrative begins on September 4, 1915, with the dedication of Rocky Mountain National Park, a day of new beginnings, and provides a brief summary of the discovery and early development of the Estes Valley and the beginnings of its tourist industry. The modern history of town and region properly dates from June 1903, when Freelan Oscar Stanley, a consumptive from Newton, Massachusetts, brought his small steam car up the North St. Vrain Road and down into Estes Valley. Stanley's arrival, in the words of his friend Enos Mills, was an "epoch making event," establishing a relationship and presence felt for more than four decades. After chronicling Estes Park's early growth, the community that developed around it, and the critical role that F. O. Stanley played in both, I take up the early, formative years of Rocky Mountain National Park, the efforts made at its promotion, and the decade-long controversy over roads and transportation that shaped and retarded its development. Subsequent chapters trace the history of town, park, and their relationship chronologically through the expansive years of the 1920s and the difficult years of the 1930s and early 1940s. The book concludes with V-J Day in August 1945, which brought to an end the austerities of war and ushered in a yet another era of growth and development.

Beginning in 1915, the relationship between Rocky Mountain National Park and the village of Estes Park has been an interdependent one, and for this reason I have resisted the temptation to write two histories rather than one. As in *"This Blue Hollow,"* I have tried to place their shared history in its larger regional and national context. What happened in Estes Park and in Rocky Mountain National Park between 1903 and 1945 are part of a decidedly "American" story involving an increasingly mobile, affluent, and leisure- and recreation-oriented nation, its discovery of western tourism, and its continuing love affair with national parks and the Colorado mountains.

As I discovered long ago while researching the Estes Park region, comparatively little exists in the way of reliable published material. This is particularly true for the town of Estes Park where for the period in question no history currently exists. The situation is somewhat better with respect to Rocky Mountain National Park. Here, Curt Buchholtz's *Rocky Mountain National Park: A History* (1983) provides a useful overview. But his is a relatively small, selective book, which in 228 pages takes on the formidable task of telling the history of both Estes Park and Rocky Mountain National Park from Native American times to the date of publication. Of necessity, Buchholtz devotes less than fifty pages to the period under discussion here—enough to make its outlines clear but not enough to provide the kind of informed detail that its history deserves. Also helpful is Lloyd Musselman's older *Rocky Mountain National Park, Administrative History: 1915–1965*, published by the National Park Service in 1971. Musselman's mimeographed paperbound book is organized topically rather than chronologically, however, and it develops its themes selectively, often with little regard for the larger context in which the events took place, including the evolving history of the National Park Service itself.

Fortunately, the literature that frames my study is far more robust. Particularly useful is the expanding body of scholarship on tourism and travel, their role in shaping American values, and the ways they have affected development west of the Mississippi, including the development of national parks. These works allow us to better understand the history of places like Estes Park, where for nearly 150 years taking care of tourists has been the economic focus of community life. I have in mind full-length studies like Hal K. Rothman's *Devil's Bargains, Tourism in the Twentieth-Century West* (1998) and the essays contained in his *The Culture of Tourism, The Tourism of Culture* (2003), both of which explore the impact of tourism on western communities; David Wrobel's *Promised Lands: Promotion, Memory, and the Creation of the American West* (2002) and *Seeing and Being Seen* (2001), the former a study of the ways in which promoters contributed "to the process of identity formation among westerners and to the construction of a 'West' in the national imagination," the latter an important collection of essays on various aspects of western tourism, including the influence of the automobile; as well as more general studies like Marguerite S. Shaffer's *See America First: Tourism and National Identity, 1880–1940* (2001). These works expand the insights offered by Earl Pomeroy in his pioneering *In Search of the Golden West: The Tourist in Western America* (1957) by demonstrating not only how tourism became part of America's consumer culture and redefined our relationship to nature but also how tourists and tourism have contributed to the larger dialogue about our national identity. As demonstrations of the ways in which the once neglected (or looked down upon) study of tourism has become a subject for serious inquiry, such works offer important perspectives on the story I wish to tell here.

I have also used a wide variety of primary sources. These include local, county, state, and federal records; letters; diaries; journals; oral histories; reminiscences; and photographs, some of which remain in private hands. All provide bits and pieces of this complex story. For the history of Rocky Mountain National Park I have made extensive use of park archives that contain the unpublished monthly and annual reports of successive superintendents, letters, legal files, documents, maps, photographs, and other materials as well as a wide variety of specialized studies and reports, most of them unpublished. The completeness of these records—and their ease of access, particularly with respect to the cede jurisdiction controversy and the lawsuits it generated—limited the need to use the archives containing National Park Service documents in Denver, Kansas City, and College Park, Maryland.

As in my earlier books, I have found Colorado newspapers—particularly the *Estes Park Trail* and those published in Denver and the valley towns along the Front Range—to be an invaluable and largely untapped resource. Throughout the first half of the twentieth century as in the last half of the nineteenth, these papers demonstrated an ongoing interest in events taking place in Estes Park and later in Rocky Mountain National Park and are particularly valuable for the years before 1921, when Estes Park had no permanent year-round newspaper.

Once again my indebtedness is great. The materials that have gone into this book, collected over a period of almost two decades, reflect the help of literally hundreds of people, many of whom have become friends. I cannot possibly acknowledge them all here, although I trust that each will recognize his or her contribution and approve of the way in which it has become part of a larger narrative. Some debts, however, are simply too great and extend over too many years to be allowed to pass unnoted. These include my indebtedness to Frank Hix and Pieter Hondius of Estes Park, who have been gracious enough to read and comment on the manuscript and who have done so in the context of the history of their families whose roots in Estes Park predate the twentieth century. Betty Kilsdonk and the staff of the Estes Park Museum (Lisel Goetze Record, J. J. Rutherford, and Robin Stitzel) have been of great help, as have Judy Visty, Joan Childers, Christy Baker, and Ferrel Atkins at Rocky Mountain National Park, where I have had ready access to the park's library in McLaren Hall and to the materials in the Museum Storage Facility. Many hours have also been spent at the Estes Park Public Library, the Colorado Historical Society, and the public libraries in Denver, Boulder, Longmont, Loveland, and Fort Collins, and their staffs have been of great help. Sybil Barnes, who is the local history librarian at the Estes Park Public Library as well as park librarian, has been an invaluable day-to-day resource. At the University Press of Colorado I am greatly indebted to both acquisitions editor Sandy Crooms, who made important suggestions about revising and strengthening the original manuscript, and project editor Laura Furney, who meticulously copyedited the final manuscript and prepared it for publication. I would also thank Dan Pratt of the University Press of Colorado for his skillful handling of both layout and design. There is also Patrick Sartorius of Westminster, Colorado, a friend since my Michigan days, who has read every word of the manuscript, made corrections, and offered the suggestions of a good editor.

Special thanks are due to the Charles Redd Center for Western Studies at Brigham Young University and the Martha Gano Houstoun Research Fund at the University of Houston, which provided funds to help underwrite the cost of publication.

Of equal importance have been my encouragers: those in Estes Park who have invited me to speak and then listened to my talks in a variety of venues; my good friends and trail companions Alex Drummond, Terrell Dixon, and Tom Collingwood; and my sister Nancy Pickering Thomas, whose efforts in helping the national park to arrange, catalog, and preserve its materials has greatly facilitated my own work. Above all there are the members of my immediate family to whom I owe so much for their interest, support, and forbearance: my wife, Patricia; my son, David; my daughter, Susan Pickering Byrd; and my son-in-law, Richard Byrd. One writes books for many reasons. This one allows me to give back to those who care about the history of this remarkable mountain region in partial exchange for what Estes Park has given to me and to my family over what is now a half century.

JAMES H. PICKERING
ESTES PARK AND HOUSTON

Chapter 1

~

Estes Park in 1915—New Beginnings

AS THOSE BRAVING THE UNCERTAIN WEATHER TO ATTEND the dedication ceremonies were well aware, the afternoon of September 4, 1915, was a watershed event in the life of Estes Park. Rocky Mountain National Park was at last a reality. With the passage of the park bill, signed into law by President Woodrow Wilson on January 26, 1915, came significant changes to town and region, including the continuing presence of the federal government. Although the size and impact of that presence were at first small, both would inexorably grow, and the history of Estes Park would be shaped accordingly.

Despite the gray and glowering weather, the dedication was a festive affair. Many arrived early to visit, picnic, and take full advantage of the day's offerings. Estes Park residents and those staying at local ranches and hotels came on foot and on horseback, as well as by bicycle, carriage, wagon, and automobile. By mid-morning a steady stream of cars from the valley towns had begun to arrive. The road coming up Fall River from Estes Park village was steep and narrow, creating something of a logistical problem. But by the time the official ceremonies began at 2:00 P.M. some 267 automobiles and a large, enthusiastic gathering of spectators and guests—by one count numbering as many as 2,000[1]—had managed to crowd into Horseshoe Park near

7

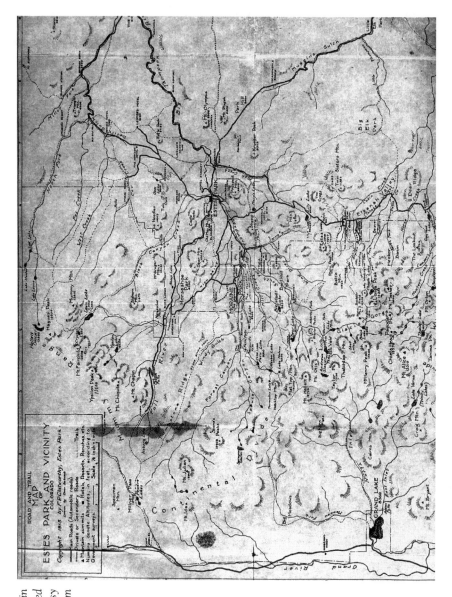

1.1 Estes Park in
1915. Map by Fred
Clatworthy. Courtesy
Estes Park Museum

1.2 Rocky Mountain National Park dedication, September 4, 1915. Courtesy National Park Service–Rocky Mountain National Park

the eastern portal of the new road being built up and over the Continental Divide. The "horizon was one vast rainbow effect of automobiles," the reporter for the *Denver Times* noted, "the black cars and yellow and white and red and brown being so closely parked as to create the effect of a bit of scenery all their own."[2] It was, the *Rocky Mountain News* added, "the greatest automobile demonstration ever seen in Colorado."[3]

Not surprisingly, the largest contingent of visitors was from Denver, but other towns were also well represented. For the Denverites the day had begun early with a 7:30 A.M. rendezvous at the Majestic Building at 16th and Broadway, headquarters of the Denver Motor Club. There club members queued up drivers for an automobile procession to the park, led by shiny new Packards carrying Colorado governor George Carlson, congressman Edward Taylor, Assistant Secretary of the Interior Stephen Mather, his young deputy Horace M. Albright, and other notables. Additional autos joined enroute, including a number of big Stanley Mountain Wagons, whose introduction to the mountain roads of Colorado in 1908 had done much to improve the transportation of tourists to and from Estes Park and other towns. The vehicle attracting most attention, however, was the "unaphone" touring car belonging to George E. Turner of the Turner Moving and Storage Company. Its built-in bell organ regaled spectators along the way with sprightly music.

Although the speakers of the day would talk of Colorado and the nation, local competition and boosterism were decidedly in the air. Not wanting to be outdone by Loveland and Lyons, each poised to declare itself "the gateway to the park," the Fort Collins press urged its readers to put pennants and banners on their automobiles and get an early start so that it is "evident to Denver that Fort Collins is on the job and that the National park is not owned by Denver." Residents of the county seat apparently needed little encouragement. Despite the dedication ceremonies' conflicting with the closing of the Larimer County Fair, "no less than 400 people, including the city officials and other prominents, went to the exercises."[4] Two hundred more came by auto caravan from Loveland.

To the knowledgeable observer, the presence of so many automobiles in Horseshoe Park was an instructive reminder of the way in which the automobile and automobiling had revolutionized tourism, offering an increasing number of middle-class Americans the ability to see the wonders of the West. Once a plaything for the rich, automobiles had improved in size and comfort and decreased in cost, making possible a leisurely and flexible travel experience. Automobiles encouraged an individualized relationship with place. Introduced into national parks as early as 1908, automobiles not only quickly broadened and democratized access but became the chief means by which many Americans would come to experience and understand nature. By 1915, motorists and the organized clubs and associations they belonged to were well on their way to becoming a powerful force in national park affairs. In the years that followed these motorists and their automobiles would influence, in turn, the ways in which the nation's parks, struggling to reconcile use and preservation, developed their infrastructures. Automobiles would also significantly affect the way in which gateway towns like Estes Park conducted the business of tourism.[5]

The new arrivals were greeted by the ladies of the Estes Park Woman's Club, whose members distributed button souvenirs and provided picnic-style box lunches and hot coffee. Their husbands, members of the Estes Park Protective and Improvement Association, handed out ice cream cones to the children. The coffee was particularly welcome for the day was cool. Serenading close by was the 25-piece Fort Collins concert band, which had arrived in Estes Park the day before. Robert Sterling Yard, who Stephen Mather had persuaded to give up his job as editor of the *New York Herald*'s Sunday magazine to help publicize the nation's parks, circulated among the crowd with his photographers to capture the moment on film. He had been in the new park for a month gathering information. Particularly visible were the newsreel cameramen from the Denver offices of Pathe Studios, with whom Yard had arranged "to film the run of the motorists and the dedicatory ceremonies so that they may be shown in every state in the Union."[6]

At the appointed hour the band from Fort Collins struck up "The Battle Hymn of the Republic," and the ceremonies began on a small knoll, near what is now the Lawn Lake Trailhead. Overhead, suspended between two tall pines, hung a banner proclaiming the occasion. A fortunate few found seats in front of the low bunting-draped platform reserved for dignitaries and special guests; most stood. Enos Mills, chair of the "Celebration Committee," the man whose tenacious advocacy had already earned him the title "father of the park," presided over the day's program. It began with a chorus of "America" sung by the schoolchildren of Estes Park accompanied by the band, the crowd patriotically joining in on the second and third verses, and included the reading of congratulatory telegrams, the introduction of special guests, and a number of speeches focussing on the future prospects of park and region. "We should enlarge this park," Mills told the audience with his customary expansiveness. "It ought to extend from Wyoming on the north to the Pike's [sic] Peak highway to the south. I am sure all here want to do their share toward bringing that about."[7] When his turn came, Secretary Mather, who within a year would head a newly created National Park Service, congratulated the people of Colorado "upon a work so well begun" and briefly outlined the government's plans for the new park, expressing his hope that it would help increase the number of tourists in the West and awaken Americans "to a realization of the wonders of their own land.[8] As he spoke there was a deluge of rain: "an absolute downpour washed over his bared, silver haired, tanned face, and almost worthless raincoat." Because of the weather, Governor Carlson "cut his speech short and graciously backed up to his seat in a hastily contrived canvas shelter."[9]

The program of the day, made available in advance, listed the names of nine speakers (each "limited to five minutes"). Of the nine only one declined. This was sixty-four-year-old F. O. Stanley, the owner-builder of Estes Park's largest hotel and a man who had invested heavily during the previous decade to build and expand the infrastructure of the village. When his turn arrived, the self-effacing Stanley quietly told Mills "to make a bow for him." Mills did as told, making the "the bow so nicely that he received a round of applause."[10] Within an hour the ceremony was over. Because of the rain the crowd dispersed quickly.

Despite the drizzle, a number of brave souls stayed behind to inspect the new Fall River Road. Although the road as yet covered only some three

1.3 Rocky Mountain National Park dedication. Left to right: *publicist Robert Sterling Yard, Enos Mills, F. O. Stanley, Colorado representative Edward Taylor, park booster Mary Belle King Sherman, and Colorado governor George Carlson. Courtesy National Park Service–Rocky Mountain National Park*

miles and five switchbacks, its completion promised a further boon to re-gional tourism by opening "one of the most wonderful roads in the world" directly linking Estes Park to Grand Lake and Middle Park. "The view is a grand one indeed," one participant from Fort Collins noted, "as the splendid timber below you adds a wildness to the scene that thrills you."[11]

Not everyone's thoughts that day were focussed on the future and its prospects. For Charles Boynton, the veteran editor of the *Longmont Ledger*, the dedication ceremonies brought reflections that took him backward in time. In March 1877 Boynton had come to Longmont from Denver, where three years later he incorporated the *Ledger*. As he listened to the various speeches, Boynton found his attention wandering to the slopes of Deer Moun-tain across the valley and to thoughts of just how much Estes Park had changed in the last two decades before. The vista, he wrote two days later, brought

> back old time memories when we camped near the spot now made
> famous by this gathering, in 1885 and 1887: when the cattle were wild

and when an occasional bear would make a sensation that shook the waves of sound to Longmont. Those were days worth living. We remember that we had to put four horses to our empty wagons to get them over the steep and rocky roads. Now the autos glide over better grades.[12]

Editor Boynton was surely not alone in his reflections. Others photographed in Horseshoe Park that day had similar reasons to be retrospective, among them sixty-five-year-old Abner Sprague and his eighty-four-year-old mother Mary, the oldest of the spectators and said to be the oldest resident in the park district. The Spragues, mother and son, could see the many changes that the last half century had brought to Joel Estes's valley. Save, perhaps, for the introduction and quick dominance of the automobile—an event that Enos Mills suggested in 1912 was "probably the most influential thing in the development of Estes Park"[13]—most of those changes were incremental and imperceptible; so much so that those who came back year after year were hard-pressed to tell the difference. But for authentic pioneers like the Spragues the differences were obvious and in some cases dramatic, even profound.

⁓

Mary Sprague first saw Estes Park in the fall of 1864—the same year she and her husband, Thomas Sprague, together with their three children, including fourteen-year-old Abner, crossed the prairie by ox-team from Illinois to settle in a sod-roofed cabin in the Big Thompson Valley, below the future site of Loveland. Within a decade Mary and Thomas Sprague would establish themselves on a ranch in Willow (Moraine) Park, where she would become Moraine Park's first postmistress—a position she would occupy for 30 years.

The Estes Park that she encountered was a virtually empty valley. The only signs of permanent settlement were the crude log buildings and corrals that Joel Estes and his sons had erected on lower Willow Creek (now Fish Creek) to house themselves and their ranching operation. Although the Esteses, who had taken up residence the previous year, found few signs of Indian life, Native Americans and their ancestors had inhabited the park on a seasonal basis for more than 10,000 years. Later residents and visitors would discover projectile points, scrappers and other tools, and pottery shards at various places, as well as the remnants of game-drives (low stone walls following the contour of the land behind which hunters crouched in ambush) on the tundra of Trail Ridge and Flattop Mountains, providing clear evidence of use by the indigenous Northern Ute and Northern Arapaho

Indians, the latter latecomers who arrived sometime after 1800. Cheyenne, Shoshone, and Apache Indians may also have been occasional visitors. As late as 1914, in fact, the Northern Arapaho told stories about a spirited fight with a band of Apaches who had taken refuge behind rock walls of a hillside "fort" at the upper end of Beaver Meadows.

It was not that the Esteses lacked occasional visitors, some of whom became temporary lodgers. In August, 1864, just weeks prior to Mary Sprague's arrival, the Estes family had been visited by William Byers, the founding editor of the *Rocky Mountain News,* who spent the night at their ranch with three companions on their way to attempt to climb Longs Peak. That effort proved an almost comic affair. After stumbling around the slopes of Longs Peak and adjacent Mount Meeker for the better part of two days, the party gave up in disgust, Byers assuring readers of the *News* that "not a living creature, unless it had wings to fly . . . would ever stand upon the summit." In the process of recounting their adventures he named the valley after his host, confidently predicting that "Eventually this park will become a favorite pleasure resort."[14]

The Esteses entertained a variety of other visitors, including prospectors, who periodically arrived in hope that the great mineral belt of Colorado—which had brought so much wealth, excitement, and scarring to Boulder and Clear Creek counties to the south—extended into the picturesque valley. Although signs of their efforts were visible in various places, the prospectors invariably departed disappointed, fortuitously leaving the natural mountain world much as they found it.

Abner Sprague first came to Estes Park four years later, in 1868, the year that saw one-armed Civil War veteran John Wesley Powell and six others, including the ever-determined Byers, make the first successful ascent of Longs Peak. Sprague, now a young man of eighteen, arrived with two school chums, who, having ridden their ponies westward following a cart track through the foothills into the mountains, stumbled upon Estes Park. "We pushed our ponies to the Divide," Sprague would later write, groping for words adequate to express the memory of the view from Park Hill. "The surprise of it made us speechless. Thousands of people have seen this view of Estes Park but . . . only a few came onto it unexpectedly as we did."[15]

Joel Estes was gone, having left two years before in April 1866. Seven years of solitude and isolation were enough. After the rigors of a particularly hard winter, he abandoned his squatter's claim to seek a more temperate climate, leaving behind his crude log buildings and his name. But as Sprague and his two youthful companions soon discovered, the valley was not empty. Descending from the crest of Park Hill, they came across Estes's successors—

two rather surly and initially uncommunicative mountaineers—setting posts for corral fences. One was Griff Evans, a usually jovial Welshman who had taken possession of Estes's ranch and buildings. The other was James Nugent, a small-time rancher who made his home in a crude cabin in nearby Muggins Gulch. Nugent would soon gain worldwide fame through the pages of Isabella Bird's *A Lady's Life in the Rocky Mountains* (1879) as the "desperado Rocky Mountain Jim." The two were not expecting visitors. "To our questions," Sprague later admitted, "Griff and Jim answered freely enough after they found out we were not looking for Estes Park, but had stumbled into the place."[16]

Any lingering ambivalence, let alone hostility, toward outside visitors of the kind Sprague and his friends encountered would change quickly in the next decade as Estes Park opened to the nation and the world. It began with the arrival of the Windham Thomas Wyndam-Quin, the fourth Earl of Dunraven, who came up from Denver during the 1872 Christmas season to hunt. Dunraven had money from coal and other interests and like so many of his wealthy English countrymen found good investment opportunities in post–Civil War America. Although his initial visit was brief, the unspoiled beauty of Estes Park appealed to the Earl, and he soon began planning to make a large part of it his own.

These plans advanced rapidly during the winter and spring of 1874 as the valley was surveyed and opened for settlement. Foreigners could not directly file homestead claims, but they could own land. To that end Dunraven secured the services of Theodore Whyte, a young and talented Irish Canadian mining engineer. And it was Whyte, using means that were clearly questionable if not patently illegal, who within months helped the Earl of Dunraven gain effective control of almost 10,000 acres of the best land in Estes Park.

In the years that followed the story would be repeated—so often, in fact, that it soon was considered historical fact—that the Irish earl had acquired Estes Park as an exclusive hunting preserve for himself and his aristocratic friends. Had this been Dunraven's motive, by 1874 he was too late, and by at least a decade. By then the recreational and scenic attractions of Estes Park had been well reported in the press as far away as London, and each summer since the late 1860s had witnessed ever-larger groups of summer vacationists. Although the existing roads were roads in name only, that did not stop the influx of visitors coming up from the hot and dry towns along Colorado's Front Range and, increasingly, from places further east and even Europe. In August 1873, for example, almost a year before Theodore Whyte had actually set in motion Dunraven's plan to acquire land in the park, a reporter for the *Larimer Press*, enjoying the hospitality of Griff Evans's ranch, found among his fellow guests "representatives of Chicago, Philadelphia and New York, and our own towns of Denver, Longmont and Greeley."[17]

Far from seeking exclusivity—which had all but passed out of the valley with Joel Estes and his family—it seems much more likely that Dunraven, like those who followed him, saw Estes Park not as a place to keep and hunt wild animals but as a place to raise cattle and accommodate tourists. The surprisingly mild winter climate seemed conducive to the former; the cool, if short, summers conducive to the latter; and for a time the Earl of Dunraven seemed to have both the capital and the will to invest in both. Whatever his initial motives, by August 17, 1876, the date he incorporated the Estes Park Company, Limited, as a holding company for his Estes Park investments, Dunraven was using precisely the same language that would be employed during the next three decades by cottage and resort companies to describe their intentions. The Estes Park Company, Limited, intended to

> purchase . . . certain lands and to improve and develop the resources of the same, etc. to establish hotels, houses, shops and store[s], to make and provide telegraphs, roads and all other works and means of transport for improvement of property of said Company, to aid, encourage and promote immigration into the property of the Company, to develop and preserve the sporting and fishing, etc. and to sell, lease, exchange, mortgage or otherwise deal with all of the property of the Company.[18]

This is not the language of a would-be owner of a private game preserve but the familiar language of an entrepreneur and developer.

Having fenced his land, one of Dunraven's first acts was to bring in a sawmill and begin cutting lumber to build the Estes Park (or "English") Hotel south of the old Estes ranch along Fish Creek. Completed and opened with considerable fanfare during the summer of 1877, the three-story hotel, with its manicured lawns, artificial lake, and nine-hole golf course, would provide a significant presence in the Estes Park resort industry for more than thirty years.

The Earl of Dunraven never, in fact, had the park to himself. Within a year of the survey, Estes Park's other early settlers—the so-called "pioneers of '75"—had entered the valley to take up homesteads on land that Whyte had either overlooked or misfiled upon. Although they came to ranch, farm, and raise families, by the end of the decade the Spragues, Jameses, MacGregors, Fergusons, Hupps, Rowes, Lambs, and one or two others had all discovered that, whatever their original inclinations and intentions, their lives in Estes Park, and in many cases their livelihoods as well, would depend upon their willingness and their ability to cater to tourists.

"The hotel business was forced on us," Abner Sprague recalled. "We came here for small ranch operations, but guests and visitors became so numerous, at first wanting eggs, milk, and other provisions, then wanting lodging, and finally demanding full accommodations, that we had to go into the hotel business or go bankrupt from keeping free company!"[19] The Spragues' experience was typical. Their first boarders were passersby from the English Hotel on a trip up Windy Gulch, who told Mary Sprague that if she would fix a chicken dinner they would return to eat it. Soon others were stopping in for dinner, then two people asked if they could spend the winter, and so it began.

Theodore Whyte became the Earl of Dunraven's resident manager. Initially there were minor conflicts and skirmishes between Dunraven and the other early settlers. Annoyed by the presence and persistence of Sprague and the others who were impediments to the Estes Park Company's clear and open use of Estes Valley, Whyte and his cowboys tried bluff and intimidation. When the pioneers of '75 stood firm, peace and accommodation followed.

For the next two decades and more the Spragues and their fellow pioneer families, together with the Earl of Dunraven, had the tourist business in Estes Park pretty much to themselves: the Jameses on Fall River, the MacGregors at the mouth of the Black Canyon, the Fergusons above Marys Lake, the Spragues in Moraine Park, and the Lambs up in the Tahosa Valley at the foot of Longs Peak. Having quickly found ways of turning a profit from scenery, they helped to make Estes Park—the "Gem of the Rockies" as the newspapers soon began to refer to it—one of Colorado's and the West's favorite vacation destinations. In so doing they established a tradition of local, family-dominated businesses—one that not only acknowledged a commitment to local community and its values but had a keen sense of the need to protect the wilderness on which so much of their livelihood depended.

Although the roads to and from the valley remained a trial even for those who came prepared, Estes Park's close proximity to Longmont, Fort Collins, Lyons, Loveland, Boulder, and Denver helped. So did the fact that visitors to Estes Park encountered little of the exclusiveness and pretentiousness identified with Manitou, west of Colorado Springs, Colorado's most famous resort community. In Estes Park accommodations of some sort, indoors or out, were varied and available. Many, in fact, preferred to forgo the routines of boardinghouse life and erect a tent near the MacGregors or Spragues or in some remote and less congested spot and rough it for the season, only occasionally, if ever, taking their meals with the regular guests. It did not matter. The summer activities and lifestyle of Estes Park were casual, relaxed, and welcoming. And most agreed that the prices were reasonable.

Of course changes came with the passage of the years. Each year brought a new cottage or two, an enlarged dinning room, "improvements" of one kind or another, just as each year brought more people into Joel Estes's valley. But for the most part summers in Estes Park remained consistent and predictable and returning visitors anticipated and relished this continuity. This leisurely pace continued throughout the 1880s and 1890s, and was still very much in evidence in late June 1903, when Flora Stanley, the wife of automobile pioneer F. O. Stanley, arrived with her Swedish maid to nurse her tubercular husband through a summer of convalescence.

Descending Park Hill from whose crest she later confessed to have been "spellbound by the beauty of the scene," Flora passed by the barns and corrals of the Dunraven Ranch, built on the site of Joel Estes's squatter's claim, and then followed the meandering Big Thompson westward. Ten minutes later Flora's stage had arrived at "The Corners" near the confluence of the Big Thompson and Fall Rivers, a small group of buildings that in 1903 was the extent of the hamlet of Estes Park.

Within a span of a single decade all of this would change. Where there had once been a quiet crossroads at the Corners, there was now a bustling and rapidly growing, if nondescript, mountain town; while to the west and south, in place of a remote and largely inaccessible mountain wilderness was the new national park. For the creation of the national park there was Enos Mills to thank, together with the broad coalition of individuals and organizations that organized public support and saw the park bill through Congress. Credit for the creation and growth of the town of Estes Park and the expansion of the local resort industry that accompanied it belonged to other equally farsighted men, who within a short period of time concluded land transactions that opened for subdivision and development two major parcels of land long in private hands. The first of these involved the quarter section surrounding the Corners at the confluence of the Big Thompson and Fall Rivers, purchased in March 1905 from postmaster John Cleave by Cornelius H. Bond and three longtime friends for the purpose of laying out a town. The second, and substantially larger transaction, took place three years later, in June 1908, when Burton D. Sanborn, an irrigationist and developer from Greeley, and a fully recovered F. O. Stanley succeeded in gaining title to the Earl of Dunraven's Estes Park holdings, some 6,000 acres in all, including buildings and cattle. Stanley and Sanborn divided the land between them, Stanley ultimately taking title to the acres lying north of an imaginary line across the northern slope of Prospect Mountain and Sanborn retaining those to the south.

In the years that followed, Bond, Stanley, and Sanborn would all invest heavily in Estes Park and its future. Bond would use his Estes Park Town

1.4 *The Corners (Elkhorn and Moraine), Estes Park, 1903. Community building and John Cleave House in foreground; post office across the street. Courtesy Lula W. Dorsey Museum, YMCA of the Rockies*

1.5 *The Corners in summer, ca. 1903. Courtesy Estes Park Museum*

Company to develop a town. Sanborn, who already owned Bear and Bierstadt Lakes, would become involved in several short-lived irrigation and power-generation schemes. F. O. Stanley, who apparently financed most of the

Dunraven purchase himself, had major plans for Estes Park as well. Over the next decade he would use his considerable wealth not only to build the finest resort hotel in northern Colorado but to invest again and again in Cornelius Bond's new town, providing a growing Estes Park with the infrastructure it needed to become a modern community.

~

The creation of the village of Estes Park and the growing anticipation after 1907 of the coming national park fueled still additional expansion of the local resort industry. Turn-of-the-century visitors could stay at Dunraven's well-appointed Estes Park Hotel, Horace Ferguson's Highlands Hotel by Marys Lake, the Elkhorn Lodge just west of the Corners, or the outlying guest ranches operated by the Spragues, MacGregors, and Lambs.[20] By 1915 their choices had widened considerably. Four new hotels—the Hupp (1906), the Manford (1908), and the Sherwood and Prospect Inns (1915)—were located in the village itself. Just beyond and within walking distance were three more: the magnificent Stanley Hotel (1909), the Crags Hotel (1914) on the northern slope of Prospect Mountain built by Enos Mills's younger brother Joe, and A. D. Lewis's Lewiston Hotel (1914) on the bluff overlooking Elkhorn Avenue. Beyond the village were still other new establishments. These included Willard Ashton's picturesque Horseshoe Inn, built on a gentle knoll at the mouth of Endovalley, and Harry Bintner's equally rustic Columbines Lodge in the Tahosa Valley, which opened in 1908; Mary Imogene McPherson's Moraine Park Lodge above Abner Sprague's old ranch (now operated by James Stead) and Abner Sprague's new lodge in Glacier Basin, which opened two years later in 1910; the Brinwood, at the west end of Moraine Park, built by the son and son-in-law of pioneer Horace Ferguson, and the Rockdale Hotel at Marys Lake, soon be moved up the hill and expanded to become the Lewiston Chalets, which opened in 1913. In 1914 there were still other new resorts: Charles and Steve Hewes's Hewes-Kirkwood Hotel, Ranch & Store near the Longs Peak trailhead in the Tahosa Valley and Burns Will's Copeland Lake Lodge near the entrance of Wild Basin. A year later, in July 1915, Minnie and Dan March opened their Fall River Lodge in Horseshoe Park, strategically located on the as-yet-to-be-completed Fall River Road within a stone's throw of the park's dedication site.

Yet another round of new building followed the establishment of the park, climaxing with America's entry into World War I two years later. Over the next two decades there would be further changes, but these, on the whole, would be far less dramatic. The face of Estes Park would remain much

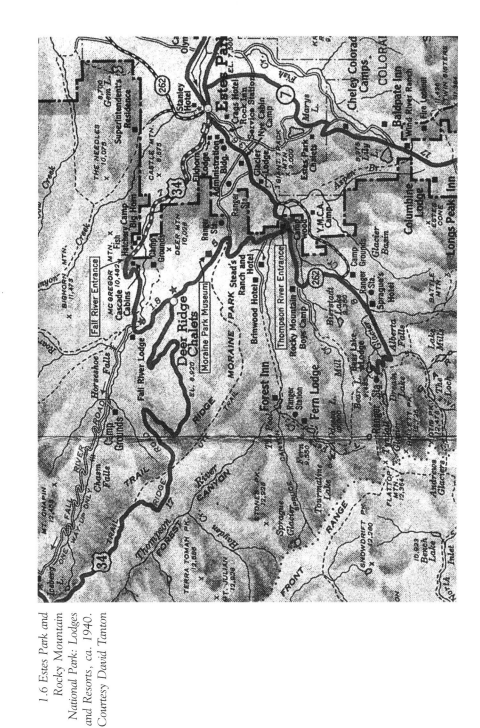

1.6 Estes Park and
Rocky Mountain
National Park: Lodges
and Resorts, ca. 1940.
Courtesy David Tanton

the same until the hectic years of the late 1930s and 1940s and the Colorado–Big Thompson Project, which flooded the valley and created Lake Estes. But beneath the apparent sameness of things, there were significant changes and transformations. It is these events—the growth and development of the town of Estes Park and its new national park during the years from 1903 to 1945—that are the focus of the chapters that follow.

Chapter 2

~

The Growth of "the Village"

The towns here are a good deal like asparagus, for, figuratively, where you see naught but the bare ground at night, you the next morning behold a healthy and rapidly developing centre of business.

—J. G. PANGBORN, *Rocky Mountain Tourist* (1877)

A S PANGBORN SUGGESTS, Colorado towns tended to spring up quickly. An unplanned assortment of houses and commercial structures claimed the vacant land, and seemingly overnight—"asparagus-like"—a community had put down roots. Such was the case with the village of Estes Park. In little more than a decade, the town had established a visible footprint that would be recognizable to visitors returning fifty or seventy-five years later. Further growth and change came slowly and incrementally, scarcely disrupting the face of the known and familiar, and giving residents and returning visitors alike a reassuring sense of stability and permanence. Aesthetics scarcely mattered. Estes Park's quickly earned reputation as a quaint and attractive resort community was clearly due to its picturesque mountain setting, not the architectural tastes, talents, or vision of its early builders.

Although Estes Park did not become an incorporated village until 1917, its origins as a town can be clearly identified. That history began on April 20, 1905, when the principals of the newly-formed Estes Park Town Company—Cornelius H. Bond, Joseph R. Anderson, and William Beckfield of Loveland and John Y. Munson of Berthoud, all friends of long-standing—exercised their option to purchase John Cleave's 185-acre ranch at the confluence of the Big Thompson and Fall Rivers for the purpose of establishing

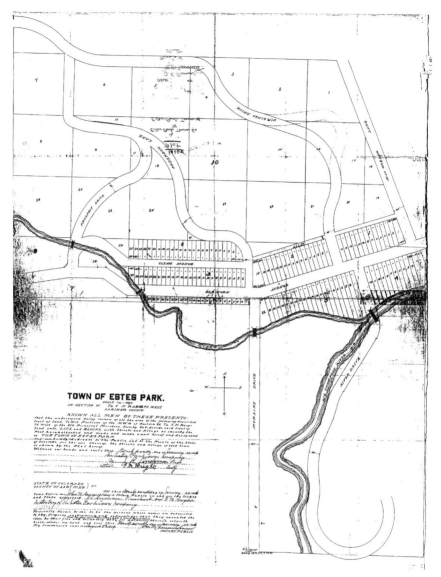

2.1 *Abner Sprague's plat of the Town of Estes Park, dated January 1906. James H. Pickering Collection*

a town. The price paid was $8,000.[1] Although the negotiations were completed with little public attention, and proved more difficult than anticipated,[2] Bond and his partners knew precisely what they were doing.

The site, though limited on the north, south, and west by the ruggedness of the terrain, was geographically-speaking a natural one. Others had thought so too, for adjacent to the Cleave house, clustered around the Corners, was the small nucleus of buildings that since before the turn of the century had served as the center of the valley's community life. These included John Cleave's post office; several small stores; a cabin and iron pump used by photographer Henry Rogers; and a long, narrow forty-by-twenty-two-foot building that served as school, church, and general meeting hall. To the west bordering Fall River were Frank Cantwell's stage barns. Although busy enough throughout the year, summers transformed the Corners into a place of general rendezvous for visitor and resident alike. "During the season, " Flora Stanley wrote, in describing her experiences during the summer of 1903,

> the "Corners" is a scene of life and gayety, when at nightfall, the stage comes in with the mail and passengers. The whole Park pours forth to meet it—ranchmen on their broncos, rigs from the scattered hotels, young men and maidens, usually on horseback—all chattering and laughing.[3]

In January 1905, the Corners had become busier still with the announcement from Washington that as of February 1 Estes Park and Moraine Park would receive year-round daily mail service from Lyons.[4]

Once their purchase had been made public, the partners wasted little time in advertising their intention to create "one of the prettiest resorts in the west." "Many new buildings are contemplated and will be built," the *Loveland Register* informed its readers on March 29, 1905,

> Estes Park is one of the world's noted summer resorts, and the piece of land secured by these gentlemen is one of the most valuable in the park. It is said that a splendid offer has been made the fortunate purchasers on which they could have already realized a nice profit.[5]

Adding to expectations, a week later, was the "possibility" of "an electric road . . . to the park."[6]

Cornelius H. Bond, the company's president, was the driving force behind the new enterprise. Hardworking and entrepreneurial, Bond had arrived in Loveland from Ohio on March 7, 1879, at twenty-two a brand-new graduate of Muskingum College come west because of lung disease. That summer, taking to the mountains, Bond made his first visit to Estes Park, camping for a few days in Willow Park in a spot not far from the Spragues' small resort. Having established himself as a successful grocer in Loveland, the popular Bond then entered Republican politics and in November 1895, without any previous

experience in public service, was elected sheriff of Larimer County.

During his five years as sheriff Bond came to know the region well. His official duties took him across much of the county's mountainous terrain on horseback, providing firsthand knowledge about the needs and prospects of his constituents. That knowledge stood him in good stead in the years that followed, beginning in 1902 when Bond was instrumental in getting the county commissioners to replace the old Bald Mountain–Pole Hill road to Estes Park with a new road up the Big Thompson Canyon. Larger opportunities soon beckoned. Three years later he organized the Estes Park Town Company and began negotiations with John Cleave. Cleave had been a resident of Estes Park for thirty years, and Bond and his partners found the sixty-five-year-old Englishman ready to sell and move on. To underscore his own commitment, Bond moved his family up from Loveland and installed them in Cleave's small house, while he himself assumed the duties of postmaster. Bond then turned his attention and considerable talents to the development of Estes Park.[7]

By mid-May county surveyor Abner Sprague had completed his platting, and within weeks the Estes Park Town Company was offering its first lots to the public. The site plan was clearly optimistic. Following the contours of the land along the banks of the Big Thompson and Fall Rivers were lots occupying a full seven blocks—some 264 lots in all—as well as several new streets, euphemistically described as "scenic driveways." Most of the lots lay along both sides of Elkhorn Avenue, then little more than a dusty wagon road bordered by pastures and barbed wire fences, winding its way along the river. Others lay on the north side of a new street, paralleling Elkhorn, to be called Cleave Street after the now-departed postmaster.

As was often the case in the mountain towns of Colorado and the West, the local topography (two intersecting streams and the narrow valley surrounding them) complicated Sprague's task and prevented anything resembling the kind of a simple open-and-level grid pattern preferred by surveyors and long-accepted as part of the tradition of American town planning. Fortunately, however, Sprague had considerably more open, unencumbered ground to work with than his counterparts in the contiguous mining towns of Black Hawk and Central City to the south, where, it was said, there wasn't "enough level ground in these two cities to accommodate a circus tent."[8]

Every available piece of ground in Sprague's platting was occupied with a numbered lot, leaving no open space for park or school. This oversight was quickly noted and remedied. On the "Second Amended Plat of the Town of Estes Park," dated April 7, 1908, the fourteen lots in what had been Block 1 on the north side of lower Elkhorn were removed and the word "Park" inserted. Although efforts would be made that same year to have the park moved to the "beautiful triangular tract of ground between the Thompson and Fall Rivers,"[9] nothing came of the attempt. The open area, since 1944 known as "Bond Park," not only remained the village park but as the subsequent site of the post office, town hall, library, and fire station became the civic center of Estes Park. Land for a new schoolhouse, within the village and just north of the park, would also be forthcoming, although not for almost a decade.

Here as elsewhere in the West, despite its mountainous terrain, the layout of new town was functionally oriented along a central street destined to become its commercial center. Twenty-five-foot lots on upper Elkhorn were offered for $50, those further east for $35; and sales were brisk. Some prospective buyers were so eager to purchase property and get into the tourist business, and so afraid of missing out, that they camped nearby in tents waiting for their opportunity, while Sprague finished his work. By early June, twenty-five lots had been sold with "demands for more."[10] Buildings quickly followed.

As might be expected, most of the wood-frame structures raised that spring and summer were of hasty design, built of boards and logs cobbled together by saw-and-hammer, with little or no attention to anything beyond simple utility. Many of the logs came from the "Pole Patch," a burned-over area in Mill Creek Basin, where the Forest Service gave local residents free access to cut and haul out timber. Built without basements, some buildings were little more than tent platforms given the appearance of permanency with board or log sides and a roof. "We were willing to build "anything that would shed water and hold a business name or sign," photographer Fred Payne Clatworthy later admitted. The important thing was to be ready for the tourist season.[11]

The Ohio-born Clatworthy, in many respects, was typical of the new-comers. He had discovered Estes Park with his mother and sister the previous summer, coming up by covered wagon over the new Big Thompson road from Loveland, where he owned part interest in a ranch, taking pictures along the way. Captivated by the natural beauty of the place, Clatworthy decided to make his home and his living in what he immediately recognized as a photographer's paradise.

When the opportunity came the following spring, the twenty-nine-year-old bachelor was ready. Purchasing two $50 lots with borrowed money, Clatworthy hired carpenter Frank Alderdyce, who agreed to charged him $3.50 for ten hours of work. Bringing in a load of lumber, the two men went to work and within a month had completed a 30-by-14-foot wooden building, boasting "the first real store window in town, . . . a single glass 4 x 5 feet in size." By July 4, 1905, Clatworthy's Ye Little Shop was open for business. With as yet no clear title to the land he purchased, Clatworthy hedged his bet. "We put skids under the building," he later explained, "so that in case of no title, it could be moved." Although this precaution proved unnecessary, in the spring of 1907 Clatworthy would relocate his business further up the street to a larger and more permanent structure, behind which he constructed a red-tile building for use as a darkroom.

For the next quarter century Fred Clatworthy maintained a presence on Elkhorn Avenue under a big sign that read "Everything for the Tourist." This was scarcely an exaggeration. Over the years Clatworthy had the town's first soda fountain and the first laundry agency (which dispatched bundles of cleaning to Denver by way of Lyons). He was also the first seller of leather souvenirs, Spaulding sporting goods, and Lowney's chocolate creams; had the first picture studio, stocked with his own black-and-white and hand-tinted park and valley views; sold Kodak cameras and film as an Eastman Kodak Agency; and handled rustic willow furniture, camping equipment, eggs and fruit. When Clatworthy finally closed his doors in 1930 to devote himself to wholesaling autochromes, a technique that he pioneered, his was the oldest continuing retail establishment in Estes Park. By then he had gained a nationwide reputation as a landscape photographer, regularly drawing large audiences to his illustrated lectures on western scenery.

That summer Clatworthy did not lack company. "Hammers could be heard from one end of town to the other," he recalled, "all getting ready for the first big business season." Among the other new businesses were Charles and Ed Johnson's log butcher shop on the north side of upper Elkhorn, Joe Ryan's shoe repair shop, and a restaurant operated by the West brothers of Loveland near the post office. By September 1905 a two-inch water system

2.3 Fred Clatworthy's Ye Little Shop, ca. 1910. Courtesy Estes Park Museum

nearly three miles long was being put in, covering the entire length of the property and connected to Black Canyon Creek. "The town is coming right along," the Town Company's J. R. Anderson told the *Loveland Reporter*, "There will be quite a village there before another year."[12] Anderson was right and early comers like Clatworthy were amply rewarded—within a year the price of village lots in many cases had doubled. Although not everyone found the new business opportunities to their liking, those who gave up soon found others willing to take their place.

This was only the beginning. By the following summer whatever seasonal peace and quiet the Corners once enjoyed was for the most part a thing of the past. The largest of the new buildings and clearly the most ambitious was the twenty-three-room Hupp Hotel, built by Josephine (Josie) Hupp on the southwest corner of Elkhorn and Moraine Avenues.[13] Featuring verandas on two sides, a good-size dining room, steam heat, and hot and cold running water, the Hupp was the first building in the new town to have a basement. Particularly well-sited, the hotel was constructed across four lots, which included the land formerly occupied by both John Cleave's post office and the small general store owned by the "efficient and business-like" Elizabeth Ann Foot. Both tenants were obliging. Cornelius Bond, no doubt only too willingly, transferred his responsibilities as postmaster to Josie Hupp. Miss

Foot, who had been doing a brisk summer business in everything from needles to Sloan's liniment and lemons at that location since 1891, was equally agreeable. She relocated her Mercantile Company to a new building directly east, at the southeast corner of Elkhorn and Moraine, added a fifteen-cent-a-book circulating library, and was ready as usual for summer business.

Other new businesses opening in 1906 included the combination restaurant, bakery, and ice cream store located just south of the Hupp Hotel operated by Josie Hupp, her niece Ellen Hupp, and her husband Henry "Hank" Hupp; William Tallant's art studio (to which he would soon add a residence next door) east of the hotel on Elkhorn; William "Billy" Parke's photography shop and curio store across the street; and Louie Corbelle's barbershop at the southwest corner of Elkhorn and River Drive. Corbelle, who like many early residents had first come to Estes Park as a health-seeker, needed help in starting up his new enterprise thus his barbershop became something of a community project. Sam Service hauled logs in from one of the outlying mills, and one Sunday other villagers turned out to help erect Corbelle's building in the manner of an old-fashioned barn raising. At the upper end of Elkhorn George Johnson erected a building to use as a baggage room and express office for his Loveland Stage Company.[14] That same summer Dr. Roy Wiest, who would become Estes Park's first resident physician, brought his family up from Hygiene and opened a drugstore.[15]

Apart from the Hupp Hotel, the most prominent of these new structures was Sam Service's big general merchandise store at the corner of Elkhorn Avenue and Virginia Drive.[16] Service's store with its extended frescoed front would anchor the Estes Park business district for more than two decades. Lest one mistake the nature of the establishment or the services offered, the owner had the words "Sam'l Service General Merchandise" painted billboard-fashion in white block letters across his sloping roof. Another large sign, in equally large black letters across the side of the yellow building, read "Hay & Grain & Camper's Supplies Gasoline." Both legends, like the peaks of the Front Range framing the rest of the scene, quickly became a familiar sight to resident and visitor alike.

By 1905 Sam Service was no stranger to Estes Park, or to the world of general merchandising. A native of County Antrim, Ireland, Service had come in 1901 to Estes Park from Lyons, where he owned a grocery business and quarry and briefly served as the town's mayor. Purchasing William Parke's general store, the first Estes Park business to be open year-round, Service was soon joined by his brother-in-law, Jim Boyd, a blacksmith. Service's store stood on the south side of Elkhorn, across from the future park; and Boyd operated a good-sized blacksmith shop immediately to the west. Ser-

2.4 Original Hupp Hotel (renamed Estes Park Hotel), ca. 1913. Courtesy David Scarbrough

vice soon discovered that Parke's building, which housed Estes Park's first telephone, was much too small for a growing town with prospects. When the Town Company provided the opportunity, Service promptly relocated the business to the corner lot across the street. This new location would prove even more ideal in the years after 1914 when the Estes Park post office was moved to the adjacent village park.

Construction on the new building began in fall 1905 and continued into the following spring. In contrast to his old store, Service's new building was large and commodious, with gas illumination and a large pot-bellied stove. The stove quickly became a favorite gathering place for the town's male residents, particularly in colder weather. One early photograph, taken by flashlight about 1906 or 1907, shows twenty-seven village "notables" crowded together around the stove, enjoying the social camaraderie made possible by the genial Irishman.[17]

Service also purchased the lot immediately adjacent to his store for a substantial log home with a wide front porch and five upstairs bedrooms, also completed in 1906. Like a number of other private residences along Elkhorn, the house was fronted along the street with a picket fence—in the

Services' case with one painted sky blue.[18] The two lots were of sufficient width and depth to accommodate not only store and residence (said at the time to be "about the biggest dwelling in the park") but a bakery and much larger warehouse and storage building, which Service soon erected at the rear. Sam Service was not through. In 1919, with the automobile firmly established as a fixture of western tourism, he briefly expanded his business interests to include a "modern filling station" located further east on Elkhorn in the building that had once housed William T. Parke's original store.[19]

Although the Hupp Hotel and the Service store gave the new town the beginnings of a look of permanency, many new structures not only looked temporary and transportable but were. Such flexibility initially had advantages in a community where much of the business was decidedly seasonal. But once Estes Park became an incorporated town in 1917, the village fathers began to worry about such things. Precedent, nevertheless, remained powerful, and as late as October 1919, the town trustees granted photographer-merchant F. J. "Pop" Francis permission "to move [his] portable [tent] store building . . . located on lot 1, block 5 [the corner of MacGregor and Elkhorn] for the winter months and erect the same on said location at the beginning of the summer season of 1920."[20]

As Francis and other early business owners quickly learned, the greatest problem in Estes Park was the sudden vagaries of wind. Even presumably "permanent" structures like Sam Service's store proved vulnerable. "During the storm of last Friday afternoon," the *Lyons Recorder* noted on June 28, 1906, "the new store building of Sam Service in Estes Park was moved twenty-one inches from its foundation by the heavy wind, and three large panes of glass in the front windows were broken."[21] Service, it turned out, was fortunate. The "miniature cyclone" lifted the house that J. R. Anderson was building "completely off its foundation and deposited [it] on the ground, while a pile of slabs was distributed generously over the street."[22]

Not all the new in-town building was for trade and commerce. Within a relatively brief time, Sam Service, William Tallant, Sidney Sherman, and Jim Boyd, followed by Julius Schwartz and Josie and Henry Hupp, had all constructed new residences within easy walking distance of their Elkhorn Avenue businesses. Merchant J. Edward "Ed" Macdonald, who arrived in Estes Park in the summer of 1908 to visit his brother-in-law William Tallant and decided to stay, took up residence on Elkhorn, purchasing and remodeling the log building originally built by the Forest Service as district headquarters. It had been available since May when those offices were removed to Fort Collins. Before 1910, others resided in town, including Estes Park's first resident preacher Elkanah J. Lamb, his wife Jane, and S. B. Harter of Loveland. The Lambs, who had sold their Longs Peak House to Enos Mills in 1902 and then built a new residence, "Mountain Home," at the head of Wind River, were both well into their seventies thus a house in the village, which they built in 1906, offered relief from the harsher winters of the Tahosa Valley. The Harters, by contrast, built their small cottage in 1907 on a lot next to the Service home strictly as a summer residence.

Although neither the Lambs nor the Harters lived in Estes Park for long, others did. The Lamb house, located near William Tallant's home and gallery, became Fluta Ann ("Flutie") Ruple's arts goods and millinery store shortly after she purchased it in 1910, a business she would operate on that site until 1938. The Harter house, which sold about the same time for $2,000, remained a residence for another decade, then was converted to commercial uses. Purchased by Anna Wolfrom Dove, it was reopened as an Indian curio shop in the summer of 1920, and then, in 1937, acquired by the enterprising Harriet Byerly, who incorporated it into the new addition for her National Park Hotel.

The Estes Park Town Company actively encouraged such close-in home and cottage building by platting an additional quarter section on the adjacent hillside known locally as "Bond Hill," which offered some "of the finest cottage sites in Estes Park."[23] Among those who quickly took advantage of the location and its views were William Beckfield and Joseph Anderson of the Estes Park Town Company, who built on adjoining lots; former postmaster John Cleave, who decided not to leave Estes Park after all; and English architect-photographer Henry "Lord Cornwallis" Rogers. Later they would be joined by Walter Fulton, a sawmill operator, and Frank Grubb, whose big red livery barn was a short walk down the hill. Cornelius Bond would also build a new home near the village, but his was located on the south side of the Big Thompson. During the winter of 1906–1907, according to the *Longmont Ledger*, some ten houses were erected in a sixty-day period with another ten projected for the coming spring.[24]

Given the hasty wooden construction and the vagaries of the wind, fire posed a constant danger that even the establishment of a volunteer fire department as early as January 1907 did not totally allay.[25] Clatworthy and others justifiably worried that the new town had become "a firetrap," and when fire randomly struck, as it did periodically, the results were often devastating. One of its first victims was the recently completed house of *Denver Post* newspaperman Al Birch, perched spectacularly on the rocky ridge a short distance north of Elkhorn Avenue, diagonally across from the town park. On the night of December 21, 1907, "Jacob's Ladder," the house so-named because the colored leaded glass door reminded Birch of Jacob's biblical coat, caught fire and burned to the ground. Subsequent investigation revealed that the builders and stone mason had done their work well. But "the carpenter who did the interior wood-work," Birch explained years later, "was not an experienced man. He left the floor joists running right under the fireplace—with just four inches of cement above the timbers."[26] The ends of those joists, heated by the firebox, caught fire, leaving the house a blackened ruin. Although Birch began work almost immediately on a small log cabin below the ruins on Black Canyon Creek, Jacob's Ladder was never rebuilt (because "I could not live up there enough to justify the expense"). A century later Carl Piltz's skeletal stone work still remains largely intact, a familiar and historic landmark above the town.

~

The changes of these years, and the pace at which they were accomplished, was not lost among returning summer visitors. "There is lots of new building here in Estes Park since you were here," one young woman wrote to her cousin shortly after her arrival in May 1907.

> They have moved the Post Office back towards Cantwell's [livery and freight] barn, and have built a big Hotel on the corner where the P.O. was. They have also built a residence, a drug store, and a barber shop between the barn and where the Post Office used to stand. There are 8 or 10 new houses going up now and one steam laundry and one Livery Barn right here on Main St. or rather Elk Horn Ave. as the people out here call it.[27]

Commercial building along Elkhorn continued at the same "remarkable rate" over the next two years. By 1908, in addition to the Estes Park Bank, the first brick building in town, completed and opened in mid-June, there was George and Ben Johnson's livery barn and harness shop on upper Elkhorn at the bridge over Fall River; Roy Wiest's drug store; Fred Adams's corner bakery, which carried "a complete stock of goods in its line and handles fresh vegetables" and offered to furnish lunch to travelers[28]; Harry Boyd's meat market; George Wagner's Kandy Kitchen with soda fountain and cigar cases[29]; and a pool hall and confectionery store opened by an enterprising young man from Loveland named Raymond Wild.

The year 1908 also saw the opening on upper Elkhorn Avenue of "an up to date bath house with four nice bath rooms" and "2 separate rooms for ladies and a spacious dining room in front" operated by the Coulter-Boettcher Plumbing Company[30] and Julian Johnson's Estes Park Steam Laundry, whose false front made the building seem somewhat larger than it actually was. Johnson's laundry was particularly welcome among Estes Park's resort owners, for it released them from the arduous task of washing towels, sheets, and table linen, and of maintaining facilities and help to do so. Occupying a specially constructed building with a cement floor at the east end of Elkhorn, Johnson advertised that he studiously avoided customary bleaches while promising to "return everything but the dirt."[31] Not to be outdone, that same year Sam Service completed the large warehouse behind "his already large store."[32]

The two largest projects of 1908, however, were the construction and opening of Estes Park's new community Presbyterian church, built by subscription at a cost of $4,000,[33] and the village's second downtown hotel, the twenty-one-room Manford House. Both new buildings were located on the north side of Elkhorn Avenue, the Manford on the northeast corner of Elkhorn and Moraine diagonally across from the Hupp Hotel, the church a half block to the west. Bigger than its rival, the Manford House contained a large dining room and kitchen, parlor, gentleman's smoking room, and office on the first floor with guest rooms on the second. On the south and east exteriors were open verandas. In anticipation of overflow business a row of tents were erected immediately adjacent to the hotel.[34]

All of these new establishments, like their predecessors, were erected on lots purchased from Cornelius H. Bond's Estes Park Town Company. Bond would enjoy a long career in Estes Park insurance and real estate and be remembered as a village icon. His role in town affairs from the beginning was an active one, and he was clearly the kind of master salesman and promoter that the new town needed. Much of his success, the Fort Collins *Evening Courier* pointed out in June 1908, tongue-in-cheek, was due to "the energy of his new partner in business." "Said partner," the *Courier* went on to explain,

2.6 *First issue of* The Mountaineer, *Estes Park's first newspaper, June 4, 1908. James H. Pickering Collection*

is a mountain sheep, which Mr. Bond has trained so that it browses on the top of the cliffs over any particular locality in which he wishes to sell town lots. When prospective buyers come into the park, the sheep gets into action and five or six of Bond's friends come out into the road with field glasses to take a look at the sheep. Of course, the visitors are astonished at the sight and astonishment gives way to delight when they are informed that town lots are to be had at reasonable rates at the foot of the cliff whereon the sheep is perched. The rest is easy. The tenderfoot buys the lot, takes a snap shot of the scene with the sheep in the background and goes home happy. The sheep is then moved on to the next convenient height to await another load of tenderfeet.[35]

Whatever his techniques, they were effective, and more than one "tenderfoot" decided to pursue his fortune in Bond's new village. Bond, like many early residents, was, as the *Courier* intimated, keenly aware of wildlife and the attractions that fish and game held for summer tourists. While the town was in the process of being platted in May 1905, Bond, with the help of Greeley parties, assumed half the expense of stocking the Big Thompson with fifty thousand trout to ready the stream for the coming season.[36] Bond

2.7 Manford Hotel, ca. 1910. Courtesy Estes Park Museum

later took the lead in seeking to reintroduce elk to the Estes Park region, a species all but wiped out by the profligate hunting of the previous century.[37]

Although the establishment and building out of Estes Park village was the work of two decades, from 1905 to about 1925, the frenzy of new construction probably reached its zenith during summer 1908. Much of this was chronicled in the pages of Estes Park's first regular newspaper, the short-lived *Mountaineer*, put out that season in an eight-page format by veteran Loveland newspaperman J. Gordon Smith, using a portable press. Work on F. O. Stanley's as-yet-unnamed hotel complex had reached its critical stages. Everyone in Estes Park who wanted a job had one, and workers from Denver and the other valley towns, and in some cases from as far away as Chicago and Boston, crowded the village. Even then, labor, particularly of the skilled sort, was in short supply. The roads to and from the valley towns were also crowded. Not only was there the usual flow of summer visitors, many of whom now arrived aboard the Stanley Steamers operated by the two competing auto stage lines, but a seemingly endless stream of horse-drawn supply wagons brought up tons of construction supplies from the railheads at Lyons and Loveland. Rough lumber could be harvested and planed locally; but everything else, from bathtubs and flagpoles to the huge generator for the new power plant, had to be brought in and over roads that in places differed little from their nineteenth-century counterparts. For all the confusion, signs of progress were apparent everywhere. "There is more building going on in Estes Park at this time than ever before in its history," the *Mountaineer* announced that June. "No matter which way you look, you will see a new building going up, a hotel, a cottage, or a business house. The world is catching up."[38]

Living accommodations for out-of-town workers, especially during the tourist season, were at a decided premium. Most were housed in tents, giving areas around Stanley's hotel and elsewhere the appearance of a military camp. Departing workers simply sold their tents to the newly arrived and such transactions were of sufficient interest to attract the notice of those reporting the local news (including one involving the painters that Stanley had brought in all the way from Boston). By the end of October 1907, Estes Park hotel man Charles Lester reported that 342 people were getting mail at the post office and estimated that the town's resident winter population had reached 500, an increase of some 350 from two winters before.[39]

Those numbers were easily surpassed the following spring and summer when work resumed once again on Stanley's hotel and the tourist season arrived. "There were more autos in town Saturday than there are in Kansas City, Mo.," the *Longmont Ledger* pointed out on June 19. "No panic here. Estes Park against the world."[40] "Estes Park should be called the tent city," the *Ledger* noted that same month. "There are more tents set up in town than in any past season."[41] Merchants like Sam Service did so much business that beginning in March he hired Steve Mattox to make three round trips to the valley each week to keep his store supplied with goods. Given the hubbub, the town's future prospects seemed assured. "There is a demand for more houses here, and more people are going to spend the winter here than ever before," the *Mountaineer* editorialized that summer. "We repeat our statement of last week: Estes Park is just getting started."[42]

Although the streets of the village would remain unpaved for several decades, dusty or muddy depending on the weather, and the sidewalks, where they existed at all, were made of boards in the time-honored fashion of most western frontier communities, by 1912 electric lights had come to Elkhorn Avenue.[43] First-time visitors were impressed. "The surprising thing here," a Philadelphian wrote of his week-long visit four years later, in 1916,

> is that all things are so new. It surely is up to date in every possible particular. There are traffic regulations and a bonded indebtedness, antiseptic drinking fountains and a fire department, a high school and a motion-picture palace, churches and manicure parlors—and garages. . . . This village has about five hundred permanent residents, most of whom care for the comfort and pleasure of the hundred thousand visitors who are visiting the Park this summer.[44]

2.8 Estes Park in 1908. Courtesy Estes Park Museum

2.9. Estes Park, ca. 1910. Courtesy David Scarbrough

~

Documenting with certainty the growth and development of new towns is
never easy. It is particularly difficult in the case of Estes Park where until
1921 there was no year-round newspaper to report such things—if only to
satisfy local boosterism and cultivate civic pride. Period photographs, therefore, are particularly helpful. One of the best to survive is the panoramic
view of Estes Park village (reproduced here) taken about 1919 by an unknown photographer from the Miller Studio in Baltimore, who stationed
himself on the lower slopes of Little Prospect Mountain. The photograph
captures virtually the entire town—from Moraine Avenue on the left to the
length of Elkhorn Avenue in the center and on the right—providing for
historians an invaluable snapshot in time.

2.10 Panoramic Photograph of Estes Park, 1919. James H. Pickering Collection

Given the position of the camera, the buildings along middle and lower
Elkhorn Avenue are the ones most clearly visible and detailed. They include
the stream-cobble-and-stucco school building behind the vacant lot reserved
for a park. Built in 1916 at a cost of $25,000 to specifications drawn up by
local architect and builder Al Cobb, it replaced the village's second school,
built of logs on the same site in 1907. That building had been periodically
enlarged until by 1914, having reached its capacity, it was torn down and
replaced. The new school would house all grades until 1925, when the first
four grades were shifted to classrooms in the town auditorium built that year
across the street to the south and east.[45]
    Clearly visible on the sloping hill behind the schoolhouse is the white
steeple of Estes Park's first Catholic Church, St. Walter's, built in 1915.[46]
Several hundred yards to the right of that building, framed by the rocks of
Lumpy Ridge, are the Stanley Hotel, the Manor House, and the Casino.
Immediately to the school's left, separated by private houses, is Prospect
Inn, also completed in 1915. It consisted of a 30-by-34-foot dining room, a
large lobby, and seven bedrooms on the second floor.[47] By 1919 this "pleas-

ant little hostelry" was advertising itself as "just on the edge of the village, ten minutes to golf links, fishing, livery and auto centers that will take you anywhere in the park region."[48]

Sam Service's store and his adjacent home and storage warehouse dominate the center of the picture. Directly across the street, with white façade clearly visible, is the building housing the offices of Rocky Mountain National Park. To the right of the Service building, occupying part of the area set aside in 1908 by the Town Company, is the Estes Park post office, erected in 1914 on land donated by C. H. Bond and then leased by the town to the federal government.[49] Directly across the street is the "Big Red Barn," owned by Frank Grubb. By the year this photograph was taken two other good-sized livery operations also directly fronted Elkhorn Avenue, although neither Elijah "Lige" River's Stanley Livery and its adjacent blacksmith shop on lower Elkhorn or the Hupp Livery, which stood on upper Elkhorn near the bridge over Fall River, is visible here. Immediately to the left of Grubb's livery, separated by a street first called River Drive (now East Riverside) is a building with a façade (only partially visible in the photograph). This is Jim Boyd's blacksmith and wagon repair shop, which by 1919 was repairing automobiles as well. Much more visible is the Boyd house, set back from the street and immediately behind the national park building. Not visible in the photograph except for its roof and façade, is the building on lower Elkhorn between the Grubb and Stanley liveries containing Julian Johnson's original steam laundry, since 1914 owned and operated by Ralph Macdonald.[50]

Further up Elkhorn Ave at its intersection with Moraine, the Hupp Hotel (now known as the Park Hotel) and the Manford Hotel (now known as the Hupp) are clearly visible diagonally across the street from one another. The Estes Park Bank and E.M.A. Foot's mercantile store occupy the other two corners. By this date these two hotels had been joined by two others, both visible in the photograph: the Brown Tea Pot Inn, located three doors west of the bank and two doors down from the community church, and the Josephine Hotel, half way down Elkhorn in the middle of the block.[51]

The largest structure in this photograph, actually a series of structures joined together, is the long building dominating the right center portion of the photograph. Those familiar with contemporary Estes Park will easily identify this structure as the Park Theatre Mall. (The actual theater is the large white building standing nearby, as yet without its distinctive tower, built and opened in 1913.)[52] In 1919 and for a number of years thereafter these buildings housed the depot, storage facilities, workshops, dormitory space, and offices of Roe Emery's Rocky Mountain Parks Transportation Company. The building had grown by stages. Originally erected by F. O. Stanley

2.10 B (left) and A (right) Panoramic Photograph of Estes Park, 1919. James H. Pickering Collection

to house his auto stage line, in 1916 they had been turned over to Emery, who enclosed under a single roof what had originally been separate structures. Needing more space, Emery had extended the building back across Fall River, using for landfill, it was later said, the chases of the Stanley Steamer Mountain Wagons which he had purchased and then junked in favor of White touring busses.

Three other buildings in the 1919 photograph are also noteworthy because of their visibility and their residents. The first is the house built in 1908 by Sidney Sherman, standing directly east of the theater. The second is the original home of postmaster John Cleave, which had been moved to a lot on Anderson Lane (today's Bighorn Drive) directly behind the Hupp Hotel. The third is the log home of Estes Park merchant J. Edward Macdonald, two doors east of the Josephine Hotel on east Elkhorn. The Macdonald home, which he had remodeled, still stands and today's visitors may recog-

nize the back porch as the entrance to Macdonald Book Shop, to which the house was converted in 1928.

J. Edward Macdonald, a native of New Jersey, had arrived in Estes Park with his family in 1908 and had gone into the general merchandise business with his son the next year by purchasing the stock and goodwill of E.M.A. Foot in the building at the corner of Elkhorn and Moraine then owned by Homer James. Their sign read "The Popular Shop Macdonald and Son." In the late winter of 1910, the building was sold to Miss Foot, who preferred not to renew the lease. Macdonald hired Al Cobb to erect a building of his own on two lots further down Elkhorn,[53] which he continued to occupy in partnership with his son Ralph until the spring of 1915. That same year the Macdonalds began a wood, hay, and grain business, utilizing the good-size storage facility that stands behind house and store. Macdonald's dry goods, grocery, and general merchandise store, which Ed Macdonald operated until

2.10 D (left) and C (right) Panoramic Photograph of Estes Park, 1919. James H. Pickering Collection

his retirement in 1932, is clearly visible in the photograph. It stands directly east of the Josephine Hotel. Also visible are the stone ruins of Al Birch's Jacob's Ladder. They stand on the rocky bluff directly east of the schoolhouse above the street platted as MacGregor Lane.

∽

For all the talk of growth and progress Estes Park still had the problems of most new towns. Sanitation was the most pressing. For the first three years of its existence, the Town Company largely ignored the issue, assuming that individuals and businesses would address the matter in appropriate ways. By September 1909, however, there was sufficient concern to occasion a "mass meeting" of Estes Park citizens to organize an association able to deal with sewerage disposal and the installation of a proper sewer system. The result

Panorama View Of ESTES PARK VILLAGE, Colorado

was the formation of the Estes Park Sewage Association, with C. H. Bond of the Town Company elected as chair and Roy Wiest, the town doctor, as secretary-treasurer. Two actions followed: Dr. Wiest was immediately authorized "to take the necessary steps to find out whether any legal obstacles stand in the way of using the Big Thompson River to carry off the sewage of the park" and a committee consisting of F. O. Stanley, Homer James, and Sam Service was appointed to "select the best route for the sewer."[54]

Despite the fact that the meeting obviously had been called to address a matter of pressing public concern, someone, presumably C. H. Bond, a bit disingenuously assured attendees and the press that

> The disposal of the sewage here is taken up so that the town may remain in the same sanitary condition as at present, and not wait until necessity demands action be taken. It is the intention of the association to push

2.11 Estes Park Post Office, built in 1914. Courtesy Estes Park Museum

the matter to a successful conclusion and thus protect the interests of everyone in the park.[55]

Such optimistic assurances notwithstanding, Estes Park did have a problem. A lawsuit had been filed the previous year by the City of Loveland against the Hupp Hotel to protect the town's water supply by halting "at once sewerage from flowing the into the Big Thompson." *The People of the State of Colorado vs. the Hupp Hotel* was heard first in county court. There the hotel prevailed, but Loveland appealed and by January 1911 the case had reached the Colorado Supreme Court. The high court subsequently reversed the ruling of the lower court, remanding the case for retrial. Whether the sewerage system that Stanley and his colleagues were charged with investigating was ever installed is unclear. Presumably it was, for all the individuals given responsibilities at the inaugural meeting of the Estes Park Sewage Association were prominent local businessmen[56] and had a stake in arresting an issue that could badly jeopardize the reputation and the health of the young community. Even so, by fall 1910, with the Hupp case still before the high court, there was widespread agreement that new steps to safeguard the community as well of residents along the lower Thompson would have to be taken.

By January 1911, Bond and others had decided that, as with water and electricity, a municipal entity was needed. On January 19, 1911, Bond and

2.12 Ralph Macdonald's Steam Laundry. Courtesy Paula Steige

four others incorporated the Estes Park Sewer Company, with a capital stock of $5,000, for the purpose of building, owning, and operating a sewer system. This decision and the planning that preceded it were clearly undertaken in consultation with the Loveland authorities. Not only did James McMullen, the sitting mayor of Loveland, agree to serve as one of the company's incorporators, but the evening before the official papers were signed in Estes Park the Loveland City Council, in a show of good faith, voted to "donate" the sum of $500 in exchange for stock in the new Estes Park Sewer Company "to aid in the building of a water system for that town, to cost probably about $3,000." In return for Loveland's contribution, it was "understood that the mountain town is to at once check its sewerage from flowing into the Big Thompson which was the cause of the suit against the latter municipality."[57]

The Estes Park Sewer Company took what it saw as the necessary steps to address the problem by constructing a system connecting the Hupp Hotel and most of the businesses and private dwellings of the village with a pipeline that emptied into a gravel bed in Stanley Meadows far enough north of the river to prevent contamination. Whether that ditch was adequately constructed, or constructed in the right place, is unclear. What is clear is that for several years the system apparently working as planned, and periodic checks of water quality revealed little or no need for concern.

2.13 J. Edward Macdonald's "Popular Shop," ca. 1910. Courtesy Estes Park Museum

The problem of sanitation, aggravated by the continuing growth of the village of Estes Park, had not in fact been permanently resolved. Matters came to a head once again four years later, in September 1915, at a time of near hysteria in Loveland and the Big Thompson Valley over cases of typhoid. Tipped off by a report from a Loveland resident who had worked in the park that summer and who claimed that raw sewerage was being discharged directly into the Big Thompson, Mayor T. R. Norcross, several Loveland aldermen, and the accuser himself motored to Estes Park to investigate. What they discovered was that the "sewer built by the park development company [sic] had not been made to empty into the gravel pit, as was promised, but was allowed to find its way into an open ditch, less than a hundred yards from the river, and then flowed directly into the river."[58] Alderman Gifford, a member of the inspection party, was far more graphic. "The slime and filth pours directly into the stream," he told the *Loveland Daily Herald*.

> The outlet to the sewer is located approximately one-half mile below the village and within 100 yards of the river. From the pipe-line it discharged into a stagnant slough which borders the river and is carried

2.14 J. Edward Macdonald's new store and adjacent home, ca. 1914. Courtesy Paula Steige

in an open ditch to the bank of the river where it is diffused thru the waters and offers contamination of a serious nature.[59]

Such inflammatory reports with their "startling disclosures" brought immediate response from the Loveland authorities. Amidst talk of prosecution and the failure of the Estes Park Sewer Company to live up to its agreement of 1911, city attorney Ab Romans was dispatched to Estes Park to confer with officials of the sewer company, and state health officials were notified. Within days, Mayor Norcross returned to Estes Park with a state health officer, who made his own investigation. Both men then attended a public meeting of Estes Park citizens, chaired by Alfred Lamborn, manager of the Stanley Hotel, where a number of recommendations were made, including the need to clean up the banks of Fall River in the very center of the village. "It was found," The *Loveland Daily Herald* reported on September 24, "that the banks of this stream back of the Hupp hotel and extending to the Monroe livery this side of the bridge is a veritable dumping ground and is a menace to the health of those who derive their water supply from the river."[60]

Although there was little that could be argued in defense of conditions along Fall River, "leading citizens of Estes Park were considerably wrought up . . . over the charges that they had not lived up to the agreement with the

city of Loveland for disposal of sewage four years ago." Cornelius Bond, as
one of the principals of the Estes Park Sewer Company, was among those
most stung and felt the need to defend both himself and the company. Tele-
phoning the *Loveland Reporter*, Bond assured the editor that the sewer had
been built exactly as planned and had then been approved by a committee of
the Loveland City Council. "The city sent a committee up here to inspect
the site," the *Reporter* quoted Bond as saying,

> and the sewer was built as recommended. I measured the length of the
> waterway from the sewer outlet to the river yesterday and it was 950
> feet. We had the water analyzed at various times and I do not believe
> Estes Park can be blamed for the trouble Loveland is having with the
> water. I believe the main trouble will be found farther down, right in the
> city's storage and filter basins. I was on the city council when the water
> system was built and I contended then and have since that sooner or
> later they would have trouble with the water.
>
> At the same time we stand ready up here to do our share in making
> conditions right, but we insist that Loveland do the right thing also. Dr.
> Morgan [the Colorado public health officer] thinks that there should be
> a septic tank built here for disposal of sewerage of the village. That can
> probably be done at a moderate expense, but this is not an incorporated
> town and there are comparatively few here to bear the cost.[61]

With little or no choice, the company immediately set about to address
the issue. Although a septic tank was installed at Stead's Ranch in Moraine
Park to safeguard the waters of the upper Thompson, Bond and his colleagues in Estes Park chose a simpler and cheaper expedient by cleaning the
filter in Stanley Meadows and constructing a second filter basin so that one
filter would always be in use, even when the other was being cleaned. The
cost to the company was said to be about $2,000.[62]

For all of Bond's assurances, the fact of the matter was that in its unin-
corporated state the village of Estes Park was ill-prepared to address many of
the challenges and responsibilities that came with becoming a "modern"
town. As the *Loveland Daily Herald* astutely, if somewhat snidely, noted in
discussing the crisis of 1915, "The lack of sanitary conditions are attributed
to a lack of organization, there being no town government to restrict and
enforce rulings. In the past this has been left to civic pride, which in many
instances has apparently not been a factor in bringing about the desired
results."[63] That civic pride should not extend to sanitation is hardly surprising. Yet when the 317 permanent residents of Estes Park finally decided in
April 1917, by a vote of 73 to 12, to incorporate the three-quarters of a
square mile village—creating what was said to be "the richest town of its size

2.15 Monroe's Livery (later the Hupp Livery), upper Elkhorn, ca. 1910. James H. Pickering Collection

in the state of Colorado"[64]—it was precisely because of the community's inability to address such issues without taxing power.

Incorporation did not, however, bring the sanitation issue to an end. In late June 1917, Dr. J. H. Morgan of the State Board of Health engaged the town's newly elected trustees in a "Discussion of sewer question."[65] Improvements clearly needed to be made, and the only question was whether to "enlarge the present method of sewerage disposal" or to install a new system in Stanley Meadows.[66] In either case, F. O. Stanley's concurrence was needed and he was invited to attend a special meeting of the village trustees on October 11, 1917. In this, as in most things civic, Mayor Wiest and his colleagues found Stanley agreeable. Determined to resolve the issue and now having access to public funds, the trustees passed a motion to correspond with Dr. Morgan of the State Board of Health in regard to construction and size of additional septic tanks to serve the town, as well as with the Elkhorn Lodge and the Crags Hotel, which made use of the system, and to ask Dr. Morgan to recommend an engineer to draw up plans for approval of the state board.[67] Deliberations continued through the fall, much of it focusing, evidently at Dr. Morgan's suggestion, on the installation of a new Imhoff tank, a system whose two-story construction allowed for the anaerobic disintegration of sludge and that was then widely used at military posts, including the Army's recuperation camp in nearby Denver. Nevertheless, by the end of the year a final decision had not been reached either in regard to which system to install or just how the town was to pay for it.

These discussions were materially assisted in early January 1918 with a sudden visit to Estes Park on January 4 by members of a Larimer County Grand Jury "to see whether or not the demands of the City of Loveland regarding the disposal of sewage and the state laws governing exits on build-ings are being complied with in this section." Two jurors spent "upwards of an hour and a half" inspecting the sewerage disposal system in Stanley Mead-ows, while others toured most of the area's hotels and resorts. Their findings were to be reported at the beginning of the March term.[68] The village trust-ees chose not to wait. At their meeting on February 25, 1918, they voted not only to purchase the holdings of the Estes Park Sewer Company for $95 and bring sanitation exclusively under their control, but to go ahead and install the Imhoff tank and pay for its construction through a $9,000 bond issue.[69] A week later, on March 4, 1918, they passed Town Ordinance #9 calling for a bond election on April 2, authorizing sewer improvements owned and managed by the town,[70] and then, following its passage, quickly established a series of sewer assessments for properties outside the incorporated limits of Estes Park, including the Elkhorn Lodge and the Crags Hotel.[71] By mid-July work on the new system was far enough along to satisfy Loveland, Larimer County, and State of Colorado officials, putting the matter of legal action finally to rest.

In later years concerns about the sanitary conditions of the campgrounds and liveries along the Big Thompson and Fall Rivers would reoccur. But never again would the people of Estes Park be faced with the specter of grand jury indictments, mass protest meetings, and the threat of county and state sanctions over the sanitary conditions of its rivers and streams. Other is-sues, of course, would arise to occupy the attention of the new village.

Chapter 3

~

F. O. Stanley and the Development of Estes Park

F. O. STANLEY'S DRAMATIC AND UNEXPECTED ARRIVAL in Estes Park on the morning of June 30, 1903, gave notice of a man with every intention of leaving his mark upon the place. From Billy Welch's hotel-resort on the North St. Vrain above Lyons, where he had spent the night, Stanley drove his small steam automobile up the narrow, rutted wagon road to Estes Park, a trip of nearly twenty miles. He did so alone. According to legend the Oxford-educated Welch was so skeptical of the undertaking that he declined to loan Stanley a companion for the trip. If true, Welch clearly underestimated the determination of his guest. An hour and fifty minutes later Stanley was in front of Sam Service's store. His arrival, Enos Mills would note a decade later, was "the epoch-making event in the history of the Park."[1] In terms of F. O. Stanley's role in shaping and securing the future of Estes Park, Mills was scarcely exaggerating. No other individual looms larger in the development of the town and region. As to determination, his would never again be a matter of question.

Before that summer was over Stanley had purchased 8.4 acres just to the north of what would become the center of the new village of Estes Park. There, on a hillside of huge boulders with a splendid view of Longs Peak and the Front Range, Stanley began to construct a 5,240-square-foot Georgian house to serve as a summer home. Its cost, reportedly $7,000, was a princely sum for the time and place. But the "cottage at Rockside," to which F. O. and Flora Stanley would return each summer for nearly forty years, was but the prelude to even larger investments.

Stanley made those investments quickly. Moreover, prior to June 1903 F. O. Stanley knew little or nothing about Estes Park. Yet, within less than a decade, this middle-aged Yankee from Kingfield, Maine, would commit himself and a considerable portion of his financial resources to developing Estes Park and the surrounding area. He designed and built the Stanley Hotel and its eleven buildings. He improved, not once but twice, the North St. Vrain Road up from Lyons, and then organized a transportation company to help tourists make the trip. He was responsible for constructing Estes Park's first power plant, helped establish its first bank, and was instrumental in improving the town's water and sewerage system. He gave his support and influence to Enos Mills's plan for a national park and vigorously defended the right of private citizens to travel its roads. For the better part of four decades until his death in October 1940, F. O. Stanley's commitment to Estes Park remained undiminished. By so doing he become a community legend.[2] Stanley did not die broke, as has sometimes been said.[3] But the modest size of his residual estate, both in Colorado and in Massachusetts, underscores the extent of his involvement.

~

Making these events all the more remarkable and improbable was the fact that when F. O. Stanley came to Colorado and Estes Park in 1903, he was the victim of recurring tuberculosis with a doubtful prognosis. Dr. Baker, the family physician, made his diagnosis on February 27, 1903. Five days later, on March 4, F. O. and Flora Stanley were in Denver.

Challenges and the willingness to confront adversity and seize upon opportunity were nothing new to Freelan Oscar Stanley (1849–1940). Having begun his career as a schoolteacher in rural Maine, Stanley had long-since demonstrated the capacity to try new things and the ability to adapt to new situations. An example of the latter included his response to a fire in 1882 that destroyed the small factory in Mechanic Falls, Maine, where he was successfully manufacturing school supplies, and left him almost penniless. In the aftermath, new opportunities beckoned. His big chance came in October 1884 in the form of an offer from his identical twin brother, Francis Edgar Stanley (1849–1918), to return to Maine from Boston, where F. O. had been working as an assistant cashier at a safe company, and join his brother's expanding dry plate photography business at Lewiston. Stanley assayed his brother's prospects and his own, and then accepted. Prosperity returned. In a matter of a few years, aided by Stanley's ability to conceptualize, design, and build a new dry plate coating machine, the brothers Stanley had developed the Stanley Dry Plate Company into one of the leading firms in the competitive field of dry plate photography. Then came their even more stunning success with the automobile, making the Stanley Motor Carriage Company *the* household name in steam cars.

While regaining his strength and stamina in Colorado, F. O. Stanley discovered still other opportunities. His instincts directed him to what he knew best. Among the things that Stanley brought west was his understanding of the role automobile transportation was destined to play in the development of tourism. Moreover, given the funds provided by George Eastman, who completed purchase of the Stanley Dry Plate Company in January 1904, and the cash flow provided by the Stanley Motor Carriage Company, Stanley had the resources to lead rather than follow. In Estes Park, a resort community without the advantages of immediate railroad access, he found an ideal place to make the demonstration.

Roads came first and, as Stanley quickly learned, those outside of Denver, particularly in the mountains, were in deplorable condition. There were exceptions. The new road up the Big Thompson Canyon from Loveland had opened with considerable fanfare in spring 1904, and it was therefore not surprising that Stanley should turn his attention to the road from Lyons to Estes Park, an important "gateway" for people arriving from the East.

Stanley personally invested in the Lyons road twice, in 1904 and again in 1907. Initially, at least, his motives seem to have been altruistic. His efforts in 1904 came at a time when his summer cottage in Estes Park had not yet been completed, before the village of Estes Park had been platted, and well before Stanley himself could have seriously contemplated the building of a major hotel in the remote mountain valley, more than twenty miles from a railroad. What Stanley did understand, however, was that the future of the automobile demanded better roads.

Raising the funds, it turned out, proved the easy part. Stanley found the hotelkeepers of Estes Park, long-since used to contributing to road projects serving their community, agreeable enough. So too were businessmen in Lyons and Denver and officials of the Burlington Railroad. A foreman and five crews were quickly hired to install new bridges and improve various sections of the old wagon road with the expectation that maintenance and upkeep could then be turned over to the commissioners of Boulder County.

Although the Stanley-led efforts left the North St. Vrain Road "in better shape than it ever has been before," Boulder County did not come forward. It was a lesson in the politics of road building that Stanley would factor into his subsequent plans.

Not satisfied by what had been accomplished, in fall 1904 Stanley hired fifty-eight-year-old John B. Hall of Lyons to locate a better road to Estes Park by making a reconnaissance of the valley of the Little Thompson River as far west as Muggins Gulch. Hall's report of January 17, 1905, was hardly encouraging and underscored just how daunting mountain road building could be. The "cost of putting a good road through," Hall concluded, "would be enormous."[4]

Stanley was undeterred. By now there was more at stake, for when Stanley again turned his attention to the North St. Vrain Road in the winter of 1906–1907, he had decided to build a large and truly modern hotel in Estes Park and to establish an auto stage line to provide speedy and dependable transportation for his future guests. On March 7, 1907, he announced that he had made arrangements with the Burlington Railroad to organize an automobile company and to construct a new road to Estes Park at a cost of $50,000.[5] Whatever his initial agreement with the railroad, when the *Longmont Ledger* reported further news on March 22, 1907, there was no mention of the Burlington. Instead, the new road from Lyons to Estes Park would be a public-private partnership between the State of Colorado and F. O. Stanley of Boston and Estes Park.[6]

Stanley, once again, had little trouble securing financing, beginning with a pledge of $5,000 of his own money. Of the $15,000 total needed, the State of Colorado agreed to appropriate $3,250; private subscribers put up the rest.[7] Of equal, if not greater importance, Boulder County agreed to take over its section of the completed road.[8]

To supervise construction Stanley turned once again to John Hall and his twenty-eight-year-old son Chester Byron Hall, both of whom, as residents of Lyons since 1882, were intimately familiar with the terrain and its problems. The Halls, in fact, lived just east of Welch's North Fork resort, where the road to Estes Park left the river to ascend Rowell Hill, and where much of the important work laid out by surveyor Abner Sprague was to take place. Construction began on April 15, 1907. At the Lyons end, the Halls built what amounted to a new road. It began above the town and the redstone cliff known as Steamboat Rock, where the existing road turned right to enter the foothills, and continued on to reconnect with the existing road a quarter mile above the Meining ranch in Little Elk Park (now Pinewood Springs). Sprague's specifications called for a road "no less than fourteen feet wide" that would "give ample room for the machines and vehicles to pass

3.1 Reconstructing the North St. Vrain Road, 1907. Courtesy Byron Hall

each other."[9] The road built by the Halls was even better: eighteen-feet wide with "plenty of room to pass anywhere."[10]

Perhaps the most important new section of road came through Welch's resort and redirected traffic along the North St. Vrain away from Rowell Hill, whose near-legendary steepness had terrified stagecoach travelers for years. This one-mile bypass was so important to the entire project that Stanley personally negotiated the easement, paying Welch $3,000.[11] The other major section of new road, some 2.5-miles in length, required substantial blasting, for it ran along a mountainside strewn with rocks and boulders. Its completion required that the sides be "built up with rock for a good base, then finished by hand work."[12]

The Halls made excellent progress, considering the extent of the work and the terrain, and by late June 1907, Stanley was able to make a tour of inspection by driving the entire road.[13] Two months later, with the tourist season underway, he notified the commissioners of Boulder County that the road to the north line of the county was ready for acceptance.[14] It was not a moment too soon. Hall immediately relocated his workers to Estes Park, where work on Stanley's big new hotel was underway and where Byron Hall had the contract for excavation.

The news that F. O. Stanley intended to build a resort hotel in Estes Park had first become public on January 25, 1907—almost two months prior to the announcement that "all the preliminaries" had been completed for the new auto road from Lyons to Estes Park." The *Longmont Ledger* ran the initial story, reporting on "good authority that F. O. Stanley, of the Stanley Automobile fame, is planning to build a $200,000 hotel at the head of Big Thompson Canon, as it enters Estes Park."[15]

The location that Stanley chose was perfect, a quarter section north and east of the growing village platted two years before—a location with much the same view of the Front Range that he had come to enjoy from the porch of Rockside, half a mile to the west. Behind the site to the north, forming an equally stunning backdrop for future photographs, were the granite knobs of Lumpy Ridge and its famous outcropping, the Twin Owls.

Site and setting were critical to the purpose that F. O. Stanley had in mind. Convinced about the future of Estes Park as a summer resort, Stanley had decided to build a large, luxurious hotel, one fully in keeping with the classic resorts of his native New England. Cost was never more than a secondary consideration. What F. O. Stanley wanted was a self-contained facility, not unlike the grand lodges built by the railroads at Glacier, Yellowstone, and the Grand Canyon, complete with amenities that would make it the first wholly modern summer resort in northern Colorado and one of the best in the West.

Stanley also wanted grace and dignity, and to achieve them he chose the same Georgian revival architecture used so successfully for the cottage at Rockside three years before and, a decade earlier, for his home in Newton, Massachusetts. Although the conception, design, and preliminary plans for the new hotel were Stanley's own, he required architectural help, particularly with respect to the engineering of large structures in a mountain setting. For this he engaged the services of T. Robert Wieger of Denver, whose prior experience with such projects, like much about the man himself, is largely unknown.

Construction of the hotel and its outbuildings required a project manager. For this role Stanley (or probably Wieger acting on his behalf) engaged Frank Kirchoff of Denver, owner of Denver's Kirchoff Lumber Company, who had previously worked for Wieger and whose home in Denver Wieger himself had designed. Kirchoff and Wieger together, with Stanley's counsel, chose the subcontractors, most of whom were based locally in Denver, although some came from as far away as Chicago and Boston. For on-site day-

3.2 The Stanley Hotel, ca. 1915. James H. Pickering Collection

to-day supervision they hired Al Roenfelt of Denver, a twenty-three-year veteran of the construction business. Additional advice was also available close at hand through Henry Rogers of Estes Park, an English architect and photographer, whose company Stanley had enjoyed since his first summer in the park. Rogers drew up the plans for the Casino (or Stanley Hall as it is now called),[16] and was, apparently, officious enough to make his authority unpopular with some of the workmen.[17]

Ground for the 217-by-107-foot main building was broken in fall 1907. Although construction was suspended during the winter, Kirchoff and Roenfelt made good progress. By the end of May 1908 the steel framing was complete, and in early June work on the third story had begun. By July the first wagonloads of finished lumber for floors and siding began to arrive from the Kirchoff Lumber Company in Denver. Fortunately, given the logistics of mountain transportation, most of the lumber used for framing and sheathing could be cut locally. It came either from Bierstadt Lake, where the Reverend Albin Griffith and his sons operated a sawmill on land leased from the Forest Service, or from Hidden Valley, where Stanley himself set up a mill.[18]

Work went on briskly through the summer. By the time the first bad weather brought work to a halt for 1908, only interior work on the hotel remained. Preliminary construction on other structures had also begun. These included quarters for hotel employees and an ice house adjacent to the main hotel, the new garage and machine shop (the Carriage House) to the east of the Casino, as well as a large cement reservoir near the crest of the hill behind the hotel to serve as its water supply. Outdoor labor continued into December, with construction of the laundry adjacent to the hotel building begun as late as mid-month. By the time work closed down till spring, the entire project, with the exception of the Manor House, was underway.

The Manor House, immediately adjacent to the central building, would take longer. This scaled down thirty-two-room replica of the main hotel, with its own dining room, kitchen, parlors, billiard room, and heating, while clearly conceived as an integral part of the Stanley complex, was not begun until October 1909. The success of the hotel's first season encouraged Stanley to move ahead with the Manor House, which provided additional guest capacity and could be occupied during colder weather.

Just how much F. O. Stanley spent on the entire project is unclear. He was among those rare individuals who settled his debts immediately and in cash. And in the absence of state or federal income taxes and partners or shareowners to satisfy, the keeping of formal records was unnecessary. The Stanley Hotel no doubt had books to provide subsequent owners, but none apparently have survived. Estimates of the Stanley Hotel's final cost vary dramatically, from $150,000 to $1,000,000, with the true figure probably somewhere in the vicinity of $500,000, a princely sum for 1909.[19]

Early visitors were impressed. "The new Stanley hotel in the Park is something great," J. N. Gordon, secretary of the Loveland Commercial Association told the local press in July 1908. "It surprised me to see such a magnificent and modern structure. . . . It will be the means of a class of trade going to the Park that they have heretofore been unable to provide for."[20]

Labor difficulties were few and short-lived. The only serious controversy, in fact, involved the new hotel's name. Newspaper reports, following the progress of construction, referred to the "big hotel" alternately as the "Stanley" or the "Dunraven," causing confusion, and in the case of the name "Dunraven," consternation. The name resulted in so much confusion that in August 1908 the *Longmont Ledger* sought to resolve the issue for its readers once and for all. "We have been making a mistake all summer by calling the new hotel the Stanley," Charles Boynton confessed. "It is the Dunraven. So we will call it the new Dunraven in the future."[21] On whose authority Boynton made his pronouncement he did not say.

Editor Boynton's attempt at clarification did not help matters, especially in Estes Park. "If it was left to the people of the Park to name the new Hotel," the town's new summer paper, *The Mountaineer*, editorialized that same month, it would be called "The Stanley." The name Dunraven does not call up pleasant memories. About the only thing Dunraven suggests is a land-grabber who tried to convert the Park into a game preserve for his own use. Mr. Stanley's name will always be associated with the upbuilding of the Park, making it a place delightful for all the people. Give the splendid structure a fitting name.[22]

Sensitive to public sentiment, F. O. Stanley quickly let it be known that he was offering a prize of ten dollars "to the person suggesting the most appropriate and fitting name."[23] The community responded as one. As the *Loveland Reporter* explained several months later, "Mr. Stanley had intended to name the hotel the Dunraven, but a petition signed by nearly every one in the park was presented to him this week asking that the hotel be named the Stanley, and he has acquiesced."[24] The actual petition came to Stanley on a large leather buckskin, which for many years hung in the hotel lobby:

> Mr. Freelan O. Stanley, Greeting: We, the undersigned, appreciating the good work you have done in Estes Park, hereby petition that the building which will stand as a monument to its founder, shall be called "The Stanley Hotel."[25]

Beneath this inscription were some 180 signatures, including those of every hotel and resort keeper in Estes Valley.

The hotel that Stanley opened on June 22, 1909, was impressive, if not stunning. Boulder's *Daily Camera* was effusive in its description:

> The parlors are handsomely carpeted with imported English fabrics woven especially for this house. The lobby, 100 by 40 feet, is furnished with special design, soft green leather chairs and settees and the walls are finished in soft crimson and white, with carpets to match.
> The banquet hall is done in dull mahogany and will seat 250 persons. The main drawing and music room is of Louis XVI design damask, bright frost and gold, and has a sweet toned grand piano. The smoking and billiard rooms are paneled in solid mahogany, with heavy beamed ceiling, and the smoking room has a monster fireplace of native lichen-covered gneiss. Large sun parlors open on the rear of the hotel and the front is serrated with a series of broad verandas. Two electric passenger elevators connect the three floors.[26] The house has a telephone in every room and in every way is modern and complete.[27]

The *Camera's* enthusiasm for Stanley's new hotel in Estes Park is inter-esting, even generous, in light of the fact that less than six months earlier, on January 1, 1909, Boulder had opened with great fanfare its own new and long-awaited luxury hotel, the seventy-five-room, five-story Boulderado, the "pride of the city" and Boulder's grandest building. Although their appearance was dramatically different inside and out, Colorado's two new luxury hotels did have one thing in common: neither would consistently, if ever, make money for their owners.

Some two thousand Boulderites had toured their new hotel during a grand public open house held on New Year's Eve 1908. The Stanley Hotel marked its opening on June 22, 1909, with a similarly appropriate, if somewhat less public, occasion: the arrival from Denver of 125 members of the Colorado Pharmacal Association for their twentieth annual meeting. The special coaches of the Colorado and Southern brought to the depot in Loveland "as jolly a bunch of druggists as ever constructed a pill or reached for a bottle of soothing syrup."[28] The train was met by Stanley himself and a fleet of twenty-two gleaming Stanley Steamers. After a brief parade through Loveland, Stanley and his steamers set off caravan-fashion up the Big Thompson road for Estes Park, a journey repeatedly interrupted by a man in a bear costume who was just as repeatedly shot dead by the drivers. The next morning the association held its opening session in the Casino with Stanley delivering the welcome, during which he accepted the invitation to become "a member in good standing of the Colorado Pharmacal Association." The much-anticipated era of the Stanley Hotel had begun.

F. O. Stanley would retain direct ownership of the hotel until 1926, when he sold it (unsuccessfully as it turned out) to a syndicate of Milwaukee investors.[29] During its heyday and before the Great Depression years made it difficult for any hotel to turn a profit, the Stanley Hotel served as a model of the complete mountain resort: a self-contained world that included a nine-hole golf course, facilities for tennis, lawn and indoor bowling, croquet, trapshooting, and billiards—the last, its owner's preferred form of recreation. The Stanley boasted "a thoroughly equipped garage, with expert mechanic in attendance," a laundry "fully supplied with every known appliance for turning out first-class work," a "private water plant, at a considerable elevation in the mountains" fed by the "pure, undefiled, sparkling, life-giving water of mountain springs," an "abundant supply of fresh cream . . . furnished from the ranch belonging to the hotels," and a "well-equipped livery."[30]

There was also a 200-acre, mile-long airfield below the hotel, "one of the finest in the west," marking Stanley's brief flirtation with the airplane. The maiden flight took place on August 8, 1919, when a "huge crowd" gathered to watch the arrival over Mount Olympus of a red Curtiss Oriole biplane from Denver with a special "extra" edition of the *Denver Post*: "AIRPLANE SETS NEW RECORD, TAKES DENVER POST TO ESTES PARK, HEART OF THE ROCKIES."[31] Regular flights into "the blue ethereal" for tourists and residents willing to pay a dollar-a-minute to see the park and its "snow-capped peaks" by air began the following summer. These abruptly ended in August, when just after takeoff on a flight bound for Denver the usually reliable engine suddenly cut off, forcing the pilot to make an emergency landing. The plane descended fifty feet, hit a fence, and came to rest on a hillside, breaking the jaw of its passenger Alberta Yore, wife of the owner of the Big Thompson Hotel, and leaving her seriously cut and bruised.[32]

Accident notwithstanding, Stanley's hotel had everything to attract the well-heeled tourist willing to pay $5 a day, giving Estes Park the kind of resort facilities previously available only in places like Colorado Springs and Manitou. The two decades following its opening were the "great years" of the Stanley Hotel, with a routine that included Saturday dances ("high-class-balls") in the Casino and Sunday evening concerts in the Music Room, good food prepared in an "all-electric" kitchen and leisure amenities equal to any to be found in the West.

~

Although Stanley automobiles would revolutionize mountain travel on the roads of Colorado, it was David Osborn of Loveland, who together with his three sons, Will, Otto, and Estes, pioneered the way. Beginning in the summer of 1907 their Loveland–Estes Park Transportation Company placed in service five Stanley Model F 20-horsepower touring cars, each capable of carrying four passengers plus the driver. Charging $3.50 for the daily three-hour trip (slightly more if the traveler's destination was Moraine Park), that first summer the Osborns, making two trips a day, carried an estimated three thousand people.

As the supplier of their vehicles, Stanley was quite aware of what the Osborns were doing and of the capacity (and no doubt the profitability) of their operation. It would later be said, in fact, that with his own stage line about to begin, Stanley tried to eliminate his competitors by approaching the commissioners of Larimer County, promising to lend them funds to improve the road up the Big Thompson Canyon in return for an exclusive franchise. Rebuffed, so the story goes, Stanley backed away, conceding the automobile transportation business from the Loveland–Fort Collins–Greeley area to the Osborns and others, and limiting his own to Longmont and Lyons.[33]

In 1908 the Osborn enterprise did even better, adding three new nine-passenger Mountain Wagons to their fleet and transporting as many as one hundred passengers a day. Throughout the next decade travelers arriving at the Colorado and Southern depot at Loveland could count on being greeted by a row of gleaming red automobiles, with drivers calling "Take the Stanley Steamer to Estes Park." The cars often traveled up the deep-walled canyon in caravan fashion, weaving their way through the scenic wonders of the Narrows at the mouth of the Big Thompson to the Forks Hotel (at what is now Drake), crossing and re-crossing the river along the way. At the hotel passengers alighted for lunch, while the cars replenished their water supply from the river by siphon. "Easy as a Rocking Chair," the *Loveland Herald* enthused in March 1908: "No innovation of modern methods of transit has been so acceptable, so pleasing and so universally popular with the pleasure-seeking people who live in or visit Colorado, as the line of passenger automobiles operated between Loveland and Estes Park."[34]

Every trip up the gorges of the Big Thompson, where in places the road-bed was only a foot or so above the river, provided passengers with potential adventure. Meeting an oncoming car forced one of the vehicles to give way and back up to a turnout. Adding to the trials was the fact the Osborn steamers initially lacked the amenities of tops, windshields, and side curtains. Veteran travelers came prepared with goggles and slickers or capes, buttoned to the neck. The uninitiated all too often paid a price. "Coming with Derby hats and high-wing collars, spats, and wearing neatly pressed suits," one experienced early visitor noted with scorn, "you can well imagine their appearance when they arrived at their destination over dusty roads or through rainstorms."[35]

The technology of the Stanley Steamer was marvelously adapted to the curves, hills, and surface of the Big Thompson road, performing effortlessly even on daunting stretches like the Rapids, the long, precipitous grade just beyond the Forks Hotel, which slowed most gasoline cars almost to a stop. It was, in fact, to meet the challenge of just such roads that F. O. Stanley used his summer experiences in Estes Park to design the celebrated nine-passenger Model Z Stanley Mountain Wagon, first introduced in 1908 with a price tag of $2,000. The Stanley Mountain Wagon, enlarged into a "long and bulky and sturdy" twelve-seater with a low gear ratio and large wheelbase, had a dramatic impact on tourist travel in places like Colorado whose mountain roads not infrequently posed problems for transportation of any kind. The huge 30-inch boiler of the Mountain Wagon was the largest the Stanley Motor Carriage Company ever made, while its equally large 30-horsepower Stanley engine was the one that had been developed for speed trials on the beach at Ormond-Daytona, Florida, where in 1906 and 1907 Stanley racers set world records. In both the standard version, whose seats and top could be removed to accommodate steamer trunks, or the flatbed Express Wagon, which used the same chassis, the Stanley Mountain Wagon proved an ideal vehicle to haul large loads over Colorado roads.

The Mountain Wagon quickly became the vehicle of choice not only at the Stanley Hotel but at such resorts as the Elkhorn Lodge; at Longs Peak Inn and the Columbines Lodge in the Tahosa Valley; at the Brinwood and Stead's in Moraine Park; at the Western Conference of the YMCA; and at Lester's Hotel (formerly the Rustic) in the north end of Estes Valley. A surprisingly large number of Estes Park residents also drove Stanleys.

Lyons and Longmont, Loveland's rivals to the south, were as aware as F. O. Stanley of the instant success of the Osborn operation. During summer and fall 1907 their newspapers fretted about the loss of business. Both were over-joyed to learn in early February 1908 that Stanley intended to establish a stage line up the North St. Vrain, beginning in Longmont where it would connect with the trains of the Colorado and Southern. Stanley himself added to expectations by predicting that during the coming summer "an auto will go through Longmont on the average of one every ten minutes."[36]

The Estes Park Transportation Company was incorporated on June 16, 1908, with capital of $15,000. The first of the new Mountain Wagons reached Denver and Longmont during the first week in June; and the inaugural trip to the park followed on Thursday, June 11. Regular service began with six red and yellow passenger cars and one express car—two cars being stationed at each of the three major points of destination. The schedule that first summer was a limited one: a single three-hour trip each day, leaving Longmont at 10 A.M. and arriving in Estes Park by way of Lyons at 1:00 P.M. The return trip left Estes village at 2:00 P.M.

Stanley had prepared for his new auto venture carefully. As early as December 1907, he purchased three lots on Elkhorn Avenue to serve as garage and office headquarters. Until they were completed Stanley shared the tent buildings across the street that the Osborns had put up the previous spring.[37] Both facilities were destined to outlive their original uses. The buildings of Stanley's Estes Park Transportation Company have long since been incorporated into what is now the Park Theatre Mall. The Osborn garage, on the north side of Elkhorn Avenue near the Fall River bridge, was completed in 1909 and by summer 1915 had been enlarged to a 130-by-50-foot brick and cement block building with concrete floor and plate glass front, covering a full three lots.[38] Today it exists as a series of shops, whose new façades mask, but do not totally hide, the original roof line and con-struction.

Stanley, who owned most if not all of the Estes Park Transportation Company's capital stock, would continue to be principal owner until May 1,

3.3 Estes Park Transportation Company depot and offices on Elkhorn Avenue, ca. 1915. Courtesy Estes Park Museum

1916, when, for reasons which undoubtedly had to do with the Stanley brothers' plans to give up ownership of the Stanley Motor Carriage Company, F. O. Stanley sold his interest in the transportation company to another early transportation pioneer, Roe Emery. Emery almost simultaneously bought the Osborn line, merged the two, and then absorbed both into his newly incorporated Rocky Mountain Parks Transportation Company, gaining in the process some twenty twelve-passenger steamers and six trucks for hauling freight. Ten days later, on May 11, Emery further consolidated his control of regional transportation by purchasing Grant Glover's Fort Collins–Estes Park Transportation Company and its fleet of Stanley Steamers. This was not Emery's last business transaction with Stanley. In 1929 he would purchase the Stanley Hotel as the centerpiece of what had already become a highly successful hotel and transportation empire.

During its eight years of operation Stanley's Estes Park Transportation Company was a financial success. In 1928 Stanley recalled with pride that "I received about $22,000.00 for what cost me only $10,000.00, and the pur-

3.4 Stanley Steamers at the railroad station in Lyons, ca. 1915. Courtesy Estes Park Museum

chase price was based on an inventory of actual property value, nothing being added for good-will, and we had declared a dividend each year."[39] What Stanley might have added was that the Estes Park Transportation Company was also the most profitable of all of his Colorado business ventures—including the Stanley Hotel.

~

In 1907 a reconstructed road from Lyons to Estes Park was essential to the success of Stanley's evolving plans. Of equal importance was the infrastructure of the new village of Estes Park. Stanley again was more than equal to the task. Stanley's interest in technology and how things worked extended far beyond photography and steam cars—such things came to him naturally. It was therefore hardly surprising that while work on the new hotel went on, Stanley should step forward to help Estes Park meet its need for a bank, an improved water supply, and a plant to generate electricity. Later, Stanley would help Estes Park improve its sewer system and establish it first public golf course.[40] The first three of these projects came within months of one another in 1908, the others within a decade. Still later, there would be other

3.5 Taking the Stanley Mountain Wagon to Estes Park. Courtesy Byron Hall

demonstrations of Stanley's civic-mindedness, including donating land for a new school building and the recreation area now known as Stanley Park. Most of these initiatives were accomplished with surprising ease. Unfortunately, the most ambitious of Stanley's plans, was not accomplished at all.

The Estes Park Bank was the first of these ventures and although Stanley was willing enough to lend his name to give the new institution the appearance of strength and stability, his role was a secondary one. By summer 1907, the village of Estes Park was two years old, and the need for a locally chartered bank to serve its expanding business community had become obvious. The chief organizer was not, however, one of the town fathers, but rather forty-six-year-old Sidney Willis Sherman, who had come to Estes Park earlier that year with his wife and son from Grand Rapids, Michigan, seeking improved health. Among Sherman's assets was experience as a bank cashier.

Sidney Sherman was bright, capable, and hardworking—the kind of man who appealed to Stanley. Sherman knew how to get things done and his efforts, first on behalf of the bank and then on other projects quickly brought him into a close working relationship with Estes Park's leading citizens, whose trust and confidence he clearly enjoyed. Although by 1908 he had built a comfortable six-room log home on Moraine Avenue within easy walking distance of the bank and had announced his intention of making "this house a home for many years to come," [41] Sherman's stay in Estes Park was unexpectedly brief. By the end of 1912 he had left the village, leaving others to carry out the tasks he had so willingly undertaken and so ably performed.

Sherman actively promoted the bank project both in Estes Park and in the neighboring valley towns. Some thirty-six individuals agreed to purchase stock. Of these, twenty were residents of Estes Park, while eleven lived in Loveland.[42] The other four, although non-residents, all had strong ties to Estes Park: hotel men Charles Lester and Charles Reed of Longmont, wealthy landowner Frank W. Crocker of Denver, and F. O. Stanley. Sherman's organizational efforts moved quickly. By early 1908 he had received sufficient commitments toward the bank's initial $12,000 capitalization to call an organizational meeting to elect directors and officers. It took place in the dining room of the Hupp Hotel on February 20, 1908. By that date, 119 of the original 120 shares of stock, each with a par value of $100, had been sold. That Sherman himself had agreed in advance to play a permanent role in the bank's operation is suggested by the fact that he himself subscribed for twenty shares and became the major shareowner.[43] C. H. Bond, then perhaps Estes Park's leading citizen, subscribed for nine, but no one else took more than five

Although Stanley, then wintering in Newton, was not at the meeting, his absence scarcely mattered. He was elected president, J. D. Stead and C. H. Bond first and second vice-presidents, and Sidney Sherman as cashier. Stanley initially tried to refuse the honor, informing his fellow directors by letter that he would serve as a director but not as president. The newly elected directors were insistent, and F. O. Stanley served as honorary bank president for the next eleven years.[44]

The one-story 20-x-40-foot brick Estes Park Bank was erected in the heart of the growing village, on the northwest corner of Elkhorn Avenue and Anderson Lane. Directly across the street were Estes Park's first two downtown hotels, the Hupp and its new rival, the Manford, which opened that same summer. The land on which the bank was located, two lots purchased from the Estes Park Town Company on February 15, 1908, for a price of $800, had been the site of Estes Park's original community building and schoolhouse. The construction contract went to local builder Guy Smith, the lowest bidder, for $1,627, a price that included the bank's reinforced concrete vault. By late May, Smith had finished the project, and on May 26 the bank building was formally accepted by the directors. Although a grand opening was confidently announced for Monday, June 1, 1908, it was delayed by the late arrival of specially made polished oak, ground glass, and iron grill work fixtures, and the desks and counters. On June 16, with everything in place, the Estes Park Bank, the third chartered bank in Larimer County and thirty-seventh state bank in Colorado, opened its doors to customers. First-day deposits totaled more than $4,000.[45]

Sidney Sherman managed day-to-day affairs. He also found time to act as ticket agent for both the Osborn and Stanley auto stage lines, sell fire insurance for three different companies, and serve as a real estate agent ("See me for bargains") and a notary public.[46] Sherman retained his position as cashier until 1912 when he suddenly resigned and was replaced by A. D. "Gus" Lewis.[47] Quickly profitable, the Estes Park Bank paid its shareholders an annual dividend of between 6 and 12 percent almost every year between 1910 and 1930.

Equally pressing that summer was the question of water and how an adequate supply could be obtained and distributed to the growing community. Here Stanley played a more direct and self-interested role, for he needed a safe and secure water source for his new hotel. By that summer when he put in a temporary line to tap the town's system so that Roenfeldt's workers could mix plaster and cement, it was evident that the original two-inch line, laid down from Black Canyon Creek in 1905, could no longer meet demand. The original system, consisting of nearly three miles of black iron pipe, had been expected to last "for at least five or ten years." At their July meeting at the Manford Hotel, the officers of the Estes Park Town Company voted to replace the original main with a new six-inch pipe and to build an enlarged diversion dam and reservoir in the Black Canyon above the village.[48]

This was but a stopgap measure. The Town Company, however adept at selling lots and promoting and developing the new town, was ill-equipped to assume responsibility for such long-term issues. What was needed was an independent utility capable of dealing with this problem and future ones. Here, as on any number of occasions where forward thinking and action was required, Bond turned to Stanley for guidance. On September 17, 1908, Bond and two of his fellow Town Company officers, John Y. Munson and J. R. Anderson, invited Stanley and Howard James to meet with them. From that meeting came the Estes Park Water Company, incorporated three weeks later on October 7, 1908, with capital stock of $20,000[49] and both Stanley and James as directors. By early November the Estes Park Water Company had acquired the Town Company's water system at a cost of $8,000[50] and installed Sidney Sherman as secretary, suggesting just how valuable the bank cashier was becoming to his adopted community.

By the date of the Estes Park Water Company's incorporation, Donald MacGregor had replaced J. R. Anderson as director. MacGregor, the second son of pioneers Alexander and Clara MacGregor, was ranching the family holdings in the Black Canyon, where the town's water supply was located, and his presence on the board, like Howard James's and F. O. Stanley's, was thus dictated as much by necessity as by expertise or even interest. The directors, no doubt with outside opinion, had determined that the best way to increase the holding capacity of the town system was through the construction of two new concrete reservoirs—one 30-feet square on the hillside south of the Jameses' Elkhorn Lodge, the other 20-feet square, above and to the north of the new Stanley Hotel—connected by a four-inch pipe. Like the original system, water would be drawn from Black Canyon Creek on the MacGregor ranch, where a new reservoir was to be built, requiring continuing long-term access to Donald MacGregor's land. The new storage system, it was projected, would allow 6,000 to 7,000 feet of new main to be laid down throughout the town.[51]

F. O. Stanley's position at the head of the certificate of incorporation was more than honorary. He was to be the major and controlling shareholder of the Estes Park Water Company, and over the next two decades, as the system was expanded to meet increasing demand, Stanley would play an active role. His participation lasted until he divested himself of the Stanley Hotel. In December 1928, the company and its 331 shares of stock were sold to Albert Hayden, Ralph MacDonald, Frank Grubb, and Charles Hix—four prominent Estes Park businessmen—for $33,900. They, in turn, almost immediately sold the company to the Town of Estes Park to operate as a public utility.[52] Remarkably, the entire system would continue to be served by the eight-inch main from Black Canyon Creek until 1940, when the town secured another source on Glacier Creek, five miles from the village.

The Estes Park Electric Light and Power Company represented Stanley's third and most important early contribution to securing the infrastructure of Estes Park. As was the case with the water company, his involvement was more than a matter of courtesy and convenience. A well-constructed and efficient hydroelectric plant was absolutely critical to his plan for an "all-electric" hotel. Once put into service, the facility on Fall River quickly became critical to the expanding needs of the village of Estes Park as well.

Stanley could, of course, have used coal to generate electricity. But the amount required for daily use, if only for hot water, would have been large. Moreover coal was expensive. In 1907–1908 it cost $12 a ton and had to be brought up from the valley by wagon over roads that were often problematic, particularly in winter and early spring. Water, by contrast, was economical, and although it posed problems of its own, in 1908 these seemed less significant than the cost and logistics of coal. Hydropower, moreover, was in vogue. In the decade after 1879, the year when the Niagara River falls were first tapped for electricity, the number of hydro-plants rapidly expanded in response to the rising demand for direct current. By 1890, thanks to the machinery and technology pioneered by Westinghouse and General

Electric, some two hundred electric plants across the United States were using waterpower, including a small plant at Telluride. That Stanley, who had already learned how to harness the energy in water for steam cars, should choose hydroelectric power for his new hotel seems, in retrospect, almost inevitable.[53]

The 80-acre site Stanley chose on Fall River, some four miles beyond the village, was located amidst a sequestered grove of ponderosa pines and douglas firs immediately west of the new fish hatchery. Byron Hall and his workers broke ground for the new plant on October 9, 1908. There, on a terrace some 10 to 15 feet above Fall River, Stanley erected a concrete-floored one-story 28-foot-by-26-foot-9-inch wood-frame building to house a turbine and generator.

Although Stanley needed the plant to open his hotel on schedule, the contract for construction was not awarded until early October 1908 and the company that Stanley organized to oversee its operations was not incorporated until October 28. There were four directors: Stanley, John Y. Munson, Cornelius H. Bond, and Sidney W. Sherman. Capital stock in the new corporation was set at $20,000.[54] Although Stanley provided the funds for the project and retained financial control, the involvement of Munson and Bond was significant. Both men were principals in the Estes Park Town Company, a fact suggesting that from the beginning the Fall River plant was probably designed to serve local residential and commercial needs as well as those of Stanley's hotel.[55] Once in operation, news that the new plant would make electricity available to the entire village spread quickly.

Stanley had gotten outside help from a Denver consulting engineering firm for the power generating equipment, but when it came to the building itself Stanley was on surer ground. Not surprisingly, the architectural style of both the plant and the adjacent two-bedroom operator's cottage was once again Georgian, matching the style of Stanley's summer home and the buildings of the Stanley Hotel. The original color of the buildings, we now know, was green rather than the mustard yellow of the hotel. This may well have been a mistake. If so, it was rectified in 1921 when they were repainted the same color as the hotel.

The equipment that Stanley selected, like everything he had put into his hotel, was state-of-the-art. It consisted of a 200-kilowatt/2300-volt horizontal shaft Western Electric generator, powered by a Denver-built HUG water wheel. The adjacent switchboard was made of elegant slate and marble with brass controls. For the water supply, Stanley had Byron Hall construct an earth-and-log dam and diversion some 5,300 feet upriver (at what later became known as Cascade Lake). It was completed by the third week of

October 1908.[56] Water for the turbine was brought down from an intake pipe and head-gate located on the north bank of the diversion through a buried 18-inch riveted steel pipe, a drop of some 400 feet. At the time of construction, it was estimated that the "minimum summer fall of the stream" would produce 400 horsepower of energy.[57]

The total cost of the power plant, an estimated $69,000,[58] did not, apparently, pose much difficulty for Stanley. Its completion, however, proved more problematic. Hall and his workers had made a late beginning, and by early June 1909, with the hotel scheduled to open for the druggist convention in less than two weeks, workmen were still installing the generator and waterwheel.[59] The logistics proved formidable. When the new generator was brought from Loveland up the Big Thompson road on May 1, 1909, it required four teams of horses, including one team at the rear to prevent the end of the wagon from swerving and overturning at curves.

The deadline was met. On the first night of the state pharmacal convention the lights of the Stanley Hotel were turned on for the first time. The "effect was marvelous," the *Loveland Herald* later reported, "so numerous are the lights. They will be turned on at Elkhorn Lodge and over the whole city in a short time."[60] The power plant with its handsome buildings and well-kept, manicured lawn, soon itself became something of a tourist attraction, "one of the sights of the park."[61]

F. O. Stanley's new hotel was planned to be electricity intensive. Electricity was used not only to generate light but to power virtually every "roasting, frying, broiling and toasting" appliance in Stanley's all-electric kitchen, down to an automatic egg boiler with three heating units. The same electrical system operated a 120-loaf-capacity oven in the hotel's basement and provided steam and hot water for the laundry, kitchen, bathrooms, and other purposes. Like so much of Mr. Stanley's hotel, the laundry was said to be unique: "the only steam laundry in the world where all the power is electrically produced."[62] Steam for the washing machines and mangle came from a six-foot-high copper boiler, specially constructed for the hotel by the General Electric Company—"doubtless the largest similar apparatus ever built." There were four other boilers in the hotel basement, the largest capable of not only providing enough hot water for 120 baths but piping water to small hot-water radiators in the private bathrooms for use on chilly mornings.[63]

For all the praise showered upon Stanley's Fall River power plant, there were problems, a number of them intractable. Some became chronic irritants to local residents who quickly became used to the having their homes lit by electricity. The first had to do with load. Although initially the plant served only the Stanley Hotel, the Elkhorn Lodge, and eight customers in the village and during its first summer operated for only twelve hours a day, demand steadily grew. By 1912 there were forty-five customers and by 1920 some one hundred. While most of the early consumers were located in the village, during summer 1915 a line was extended to Stead's Ranch in Moraine Park and, in 1920–1922, to the Estes Park Chalets, up High Drive, and north toward Devils Gulch, bringing the service load to about 150 customers.[64]

The major problem, however, was the cold of winter, which so greatly reduced the flow of water in Fall River that service from the plant was limited to a few hours a day. At times, the weather was so severe that operations ceased altogether. "Coal lamps have come into use again here, "the local correspondent of the *Loveland Reporter* noted with frustration in January 1910. "We find it pretty hard to fall back onto the old lamps again. When we were using the oil lamps all the time we were satisfied with them, but now we find it hard to go backwards. The spirit of the Park is to go forward."[65]

In point of fact, as the consulting engineers whom Stanley hired from Denver should have told him, the plant itself was poorly sited, particularly since electricity was to be made available beyond the summer months and the growing demand from permanent residents was not limited by season. Had it been "located in the village," the *Estes Park Trail* observed in 1924, "it would have ten times the water for operation over its present location, and if it was located where Loveland's new plant is to be located [at the mouth of the Big Thompson Canyon] it would have nearly twenty times the water for operation."[66] There was also Stanley's generosity, for prior to 1917 when Estes Park was incorporated, Stanley provided electricity to light the streets of the village for free.

Stanley did what he could, for the Stanley Hotel was also affected by unsatisfied demand. As early as 1913, only four years after the power plant's opening, Stanley found himself faced with the choice of either enlarging the existing plant or installing a separate new one at the hotel. He chose to do the latter for the price of coal had dropped and a dedicated steam plant located at the hotel itself now made better financial sense. This new plant, complete with tall metal smokestack and piercing whistle, was constructed to the west of the main hotel building. It provided steam heat and hot water for all the buildings at the Stanley complex, reducing significantly the reliance on electricity from Fall River.

The new steam plant at the hotel did nothing, of course, to address the deficiencies of the original plant. Alterations and improvements began as early as 1919, when Stanley replaced the original 18-inch steel penstock carrying the water from Cascade Lake with a 24-inch wooden stave line wrapped tightly with coiled wire to increase the amount of water reaching waterwheel and generator. Two years later, in late summer 1921, Stanley purchased a second hydroelectric unit—a 680-kilowatt General Electric generator powered by a 900-horsepower Worthington Francis turbine. This equipment, which was installed the following April, required that the original plant building be extended by some 16 feet on its northwest side. Although the new generator had a capacity far larger than the water source that turned the turbine's blades and, therefore, could only generate power from May through September, it did for a time meet the lighting needs of both hotel and town because the peak usage months matched those of the plant's greatest capacity.[67]

The problems of winter nonetheless remained. In June 1921 Stanley's manager Alfred Lamborn insisted that the new generator "will supply sufficient current for all the needs in the Park for many years to come,"[68] but by mid-November the water in Fall River had dropped so low that it was feared the plant would have to be shut down from midnight to 5 A.M. each day.[69] The next year, with demand and complaints about "miserable service" in winter still increasing, Stanley invested an additional $48,000 in the Fall River plant, enlarging the dam at Cascade Lake to a height of seventeen feet with reinforced concrete to create more storage capacity and submerging the intake of the penstock to nine feet to increase water pressure. The same year he rebuilt the transmission lines linking plant and village to make them more efficient. In spring 1927 a new voltage regulator was installed to maintain the level of current regardless of load. These efforts proved stopgap measures. Insufficient electrical production persisted seasonally through the 1920s and into the 1930s and long after the plant had been sold to the Public Service Company of Colorado.

A general survey of the plant made in 1927 indicates the dollar amount of sales between 1916 and 1926. What it shows is that exclusive of the Stanley Hotel, total yearly electricity sales increased almost six-fold, from $5,820.02 in 1916 to $28,236.91 in 1926. In 1926 the plant served 18 hotels and 525 cottages, a number far larger than anyone would have dreamed less than two decades before.[70]

Despite demand, the Public Service Company of Colorado, which purchased the plant on June 1, 1928, made no additional effort to improve winter service until January 1931, a month that saw no precipitation. Then, as part of a series of improvements said to cost $40,000, a 50-horsepower diesel engine and a 32-kilowatt generator was brought on line to supplement the two hydro units. That fall the company made another $12,000 worth of improvements, which included enlarging the dam on Fall River to prevent power outages during the winter.[71]

The periodic crises plaguing the plant were not over. Two years later, in February 1933, at the beginning of the driest year in Estes Park history, the water level of Fall River once again dropped, making it impossible to run the two hydro units for more than a few hours a day. Even the new diesel engine proved inadequate. As yet another stopgap measure, the Public Service Company secured the YMCA Camp's permission to make use of its old unused steam plant.[72] Later that same year, the cement dam at Cascade Lake was once again reconstructed, bringing its height to twenty-four feet and its thickness to twenty-two feet at the base and four feet at the top, doubling the capacity of the reservoir.[73] Yet, the problem of winter freeze-up remained. When this occurred in January 1937 during a particularly hard winter that saw the village's water pipes freeze for the first time since 1911, a gasoline engine was brought to the plant to provide power, only to have it quickly burn out because it was run too long at top speed.[74]

During the years of Stanley's ownership it is doubtful that the Fall River power plant, like the Stanley Hotel itself, ever made much money, even with its successive alterations. Byron Hall, who helped construct the original plant and served as its manager for many years, later indicated that before 1916 income did not cover taxes and the interest on Stanley's original investment, let alone the cost of operating and maintaining the plant itself.[75] During his years of ownership, Stanley quietly swallowed his frustrations and made up the difference out of his own funds.

~

F. O. Stanley arrived in Estes Park as a man with established tastes and standards. And, like other village leaders, he was only too well aware that the aesthetics of the village, with its melange of wooden buildings, its dusty streets, and its partially completed board walkways, were far from attractive. "There is much that might be done to make the village look less like a cabbage patch," John Y. Munson, one of the partners of the Estes Park Town Company, editorialized in the September 7, 1912, issue of his new summer weekly village paper, the *Estes Park Trail*:

> The street might be sprinkled from Elkhorn to the Stanley hotel, cans provided for waste paper and garbage, which could be removed daily and all droppings on the streets cleaned up every morning, and grass plots and a color scheme adopted that would make the village a fitting introduction to the Park. There is a lot more to be done than both associations [the Business Men's Association and the Estes Park Protective and Improvement Association] can do, but, certainly the village

demands the urgent attention of the business men that it may develop in attractiveness as the Park grows in popular esteem.[76]

Such statements were not lost on Stanley. By 1912 he had long-since returned to making Newton, Massachusetts, his winter home and knew first-hand how a public-spirited community, albeit an affluent and somewhat complacent one, could cultivate local pride for civic purposes. Moreover, Stanley himself had already demonstrated in the elegant Georgian architecture of his Estes Park home, hotel complex, and power plant how a sense of beauty, indeed elegance, could be superimposed on a raw western mountain community. And he was prepared to do still more. That same month he responded to the spirit of Munson's editorial while chairing a meeting called to promote a new road up and over the Continental Divide. Stanley turned the conversation to the need to beautify the village of Estes Park and when it was suggested "that a committee of ladies would be most influential in bringing about the desired conditions," Stanley immediately appointed a committee of five.[77]

Over the intervening winter Stanley did not forget his committee. Before leaving Newton for Estes Park the following June, he wrote to Dorothy Schwartz, wife of lumber dealer Julius Schwartz, to thank her for a progress report of the committee's accomplishments. "I felt confident when the movement was started last fall at the meeting we had," he wrote,

> that if we could get the ladies interested, that we should have a new era of cleanliness in Estes Park, and I am of course more than delighted to learn that the movement is so successful.
>
> Nature has made Estes Park one of the most beautiful places in the world, and we should fall short of our duty and responsibility if we failed to make it the cleanest pleasure resort in the world. With the pure air and perfect water supply, we could make Estes Park as famous for health conditions, as it is for its scenery.[78]

Part of what Dorothy Schwartz surely had to report to Stanley was the organization of the Ladies Improvement and Development Society on October 5, 1912. Although the name of the organization was changed at the second meeting to the Estes Park Woman's Club, the emphasis on local "improvement" and "development" remained. By June 21, 1912, a date that coincided with Stanley's letter, the Woman's Club had donated $100 toward the purchase of a sprinkler cart "to be used chiefly to lay the dust" along the length of Elkhorn Avenue as a "means to make the first impression to visitors a favorable one."[79]

Progress for Stanley meant more than sprinkler carts and clean streets. Looking down from his home at Rockside or from Stanley Hotel's veranda, he remained distressed about the general appearance of his adopted summer home. By fall 1916 he was determined to do something about it. His plan, characteristically, was bold and imaginative. He would purchase as much as possible of the lower section of town—the area east of Riverside and Virginia Drives, excluding the park—and remove all the existing structures, including the Grubb and Stanley liveries and Ralph Macdonald's steam laundry. In their place he would erect a "new model town," built "on the picturesque lines of Tyrol Alps hamlets," anchored by a new headquarters building for Rocky Mountain National Park and the "new Stanley," a 140-room downtown hotel that would "cater to summer tourists who can afford only moderate priced accommodations."[80] The first hints of what Stanley had in mind became public in late December. According to Boulder's *Daily Camera*,

> Plans have been perfected and negotiations started for a right-of-way for a railroad into Estes Park, according to a rumor, which attributes the plan to F. O. Stanley. . . . Mr. Stanley . . . recently purchased a quarter of the town of Estes Park and is trying to buy the greater part of the remaining town with a view to razing the buildings and constructing a picturesque model town.[81]

Tactful and private, Stanley was disinclined to discuss plans not matured or to disparage anything or anyone in public. The latter most certainly included criticisms of the town of Estes Park, whose residents held him in great respect and near veneration. But as his statements of 1912–1913 suggest, Stanley was also keenly aware of the responsibilities of stewardship. His feelings on this subject ran deep. He, more than anyone, was aware of the growing disparity between the elegant buildings that he had built between 1905 and 1909 and the cheap, utilitarian, poorly designed and constructed structures that made up so much of the rest of the village. Although the ensuing years did little to change his mind, in public at least, Stanley held his tongue. What is most remarkable about his "grand design" of 1916, therefore, is that although his plans quickly came to the attention of the press and were widely reported, their details remained sketchy and general, and Stanley's own voice remained curiously absent from the conversation.

There was, however, one exception: a lengthy article that appeared in the December 3, 1916, issue of the *Denver Post*. Detailed and knowledgeable, it speaks to Stanley's beliefs about the shortcomings and unsightliness of Estes Park and his plans to remedy them in ways that suggest that the nameless reporter—who may well have been longtime *Post* employee and Estes Park resident Al Birch—had direct access to Stanley himself. "For several years," the story begins, it has been his hobby, but conditions never became such until the last few weeks that he could make an actual start toward a realization of his ambition. He now has agents at work in an endeavor to purchase every foot of land in one-half of the present village of Estes Park. . . .

If Mr. Stanley succeeds in purchasing the land he desires—and the prices he offers indicate very strongly that he will—he will raze every house, every stick of lumber, every fence on the property and build from the ground up. . . . His idea is that the present village of Estes Park, being of a straggling mushroom growth, developed with no general eye to civic beauty or picturesqueness, makes a decidedly unfavorable impression upon every visitor who enters it for the first time—an impression that requires several days of rambling thru the magnificent scenery of the surrounding mountains to efface. He wants the first glimpse of Estes Park to be favorable, pleasing, imparting a sense of the picturesque—just as so many Swiss and Tyrol villages are charmingly unique and picturesque.

Recently Mr. Stanley completed purchase of about one quarter of the land property—absolutely barren land without even a fence. On part of this plot he will erect a 140-room hotel, which will have a bath to every sleeping room.

Now he is trying to get an equal amount of land on the opposite side of the main street—from the new post office east—which is now occupied by several big livery stables, a steam laundry, several prosperous stores, several residences and other buildings. . . .

The present owners of the land are being offered more land a little farther out of the heart of town for their businesses, as well as exceedingly handsome cash bonuses for the change. Mr. Stanley's idea is that in a model town big, unsightly livery stables should not front on the main street or even be right in town at all. He advocates placing the stables out of sight of tourists and mostly having neat, clean offices downtown, to which visitors can apply for horses. If—as is the case here—about 600 horses are required each day to supply the needs of the tourists, those 600 horses can be hired as well by telephone as by pointing to the whole herd "milling about" in a muddy, unsightly corral.

And the same holds true of garages, machine shops and the like, Mr. Stanley believes the big transportation company can remove its mechanical departments a short distance out of town—off behind some hill—and handle its town business thru a comfortable, up-to-date, sightly office on the main street.

Neither does this man of wealth and big ideas think summer visitors should be forced to run the gauntlet of scores of cheap, side show looking curio shops, peanut stands, ice cream parlors, picture post card racks, loud smelling cafes and the like. . . .

If Mr. Stanley gets the land he is after, he will start building his model city as early as possible in the spring, and will have enough men on the

job to finish it by early June, when the tourist season starts. He will
allow no person who locates in his community to own a lot or a
building; he will rent stores at a reasonable rental, and will allow only a
certain number of men in each line to rent buildings. If any renter
attempts to "soak" visitors exorbitant prices, out that renter will go, bag
and baggage, at a moment's notice.

Streets that are nothing more than streets will have no place in this
model community. The highways there must be things of beauty—
something to attract attention and impress one with their beauty. Mr.
Stanley wants visitors to go away PRAISING the town of Estes Park, not
roasting it for its unsightliness. He wants them to tell their friends that
Estes Park has absolutely the prettiest and most novel town in the
United States.

Men of vision in this community say there is no question of Mr.
Stanley's success in obtaining the land he wants, and most of the
residents here are waking up to the necessity for improving the looks of
the village. And they say that if success comes with this model town on
one-half the present townsite, it merely is a question of two or three
years before the owners of the land and buildings in the other half of the
town will rebuild their community or will sell out to Mr. Stanley and let
him complete his work thruout [sic] the whole village. . . . [82]

Stanley's plan, allowing for the *Denver Post* writer's enthusiasm and hyperbole, did have substance. The 1916 season, the first since the dedication
of Rocky Mountain National Park, had been an exceptionally busy one in
Estes Park. So busy, in fact, that Steve Hewes, co-owner with his brother
Charles of Hewes-Kirkwood Inn in the Tahosa Valley, estimated that some
2,500 would-be visitors had been forced to cancel their plans for lack of
accommodations. To Hewes's remarks, the *Morning Express* added a note of
its own, confidently predicting that "there is going to be a veritable building
boom in Estes Park."[83]

Stanley was, of course, well aware of the prospects of Estes Park and, for
a time at least, he seemed prepared to superimpose his own vision upon the
town. Not only did he purchase two acres of undeveloped property on Elkhorn
for a reported $15,000, a price considered at the time outlandish,[84] but that
same fall personally approached L. Claude Way, the recently appointed chief
ranger in charge of the new Rocky Mountain National Park. Having explained his intention to erect a new colonial-style hotel east of the town
park and perhaps his larger plans as well, Stanley presented Way with an
intriguing proposition. Would Way and his superiors in Washington be
interested in constructing a new headquarters and residence facility within
town limits? The location, he told Way, was in the village park, just east
of the post office and west of the site of his new in-town hotel on land

to be donated to the federal government by the Estes Park Business Men's Association.

Way's response was immediately enthusiastic. The space being leased by the government in the small white frame building on Elkhorn Avenue was inadequate. By early October Way had sent Stanley's proposal to Robert B. Marshall, then serving in Washington as superintendent of the new National Park Service on loan from the Geological Survey. In contacting Marshall, Way and Stanley could not have placed the project in more knowledgeable hands. Four years earlier, in September 1912, Marshall had spent extensive time in Estes Park (where he undoubtedly was introduced to Stanley) studying the feasibility of locating a new national park in the region. It was, in fact, Marshall's report of January 1913 with its enthusiastic recommendation that not only gave Rocky Mountain National Park its name but led within weeks to the introduction of the first park bill in Congress.

Marshall's response of October 16, 1916, was anything but pro forma. "I am sending you herewith a much marked-up sheet of paper. . . ," he began. "The drafting is of course [not] the very best: It will, however, give you a rough idea of my plan to appropriately develop the lot for the proposed administration building."

Marshall then went on to explain precisely what *he* had in mind:

> I rather think that the office and the house should be connected by a porte cochere, and that the house should be one-story with the flooring not more than two steps above the ground.
>
> We must try to get an artistic effect. The exterior should blend with the general scenery and the roof should be tile: with considerable pitch. The tiles, of course, should not scare the rest of the scenery! The house, office, garage, and stable should all blend.
>
> Now if you are too busy to do much with this, I think if you would turn the matter over to Mr. Stanley, giving him an idea of what is wanted, his architect could plan the buildings so as to blend with the new Stanley Hotel. Incidentally[,] he could give us some idea of what the cost of the buildings I have indicated on this sketch would be. We do not want anything too expensive but the buildings should be artistic, neat, and comfortable.

Marshall's final suggestion was that Way contact Cornelius H. Bond to get "a rough estimate of the value of the lot and a diagram or plat of Estes Park showing the location of the lot in relation to its surroundings." Having clearly allowed his own enthusiasm to race ahead, Marshall concluded by placing the project back in Way's hands:

> Of course the suggestion that I have given you for the inside of the house is just a rough idea, as I am not a bit of an architect. Therefore mark it up

in whatever way seems best to you. We want something that will be a
credit to the national parks, but you and Mrs. Way have to live in it.[85]

Marshall quickly had the requested response from the Business Men's
Association. On October 26 association trustees J. Edward Macdonald, Pieter
Hondius, and Samuel Service notified Marshall that "we are much in favor
of this plan and will gladly take the necessary action towards deeding this
property to the Park Service providing you secure an appropriation to erect
the buildings."[86] Way enclosed this letter in one of his own, indicating that
Bond had valued the 200-square-foot lot at $10,000, and that he had fol-
lowed Marshall's earlier advice with respect to Stanley:

> I had a conference with Mr. Stanley and his architect regarding building
> plans and they promise to submit sketches the latter part of the week.
> The architect does not approve our plan for two separate buildings, his
> argument being that it will present a crowded appearance and make it
> impossible to get an artistic effect. He will however submit plans
> following his ideas for one building and ideas for two, for our consider-
> ation. After talking the matter with him I am inclined to his argument.[87]

In early November the first cautionary note was sounded, one that had
it been directly communicated to Way, Stanley, and others in Estes Park
would undoubtedly have slowed down, if not halted, the entire project.
Marshall had informed his superior, Stephen T. Mather, then still assistant
to the Secretary of the Interior for national parks, of the discussions going
on in Estes Park. Mather was in Chicago, and on November 4, 1916, Marshall
sent him a letter regarding the commitment he had received from Macdonald,
Hondius, and Service and the fact that Way had met with Stanley and his
architect. Mather did not, apparently, respond directly to Marshall. But there
is a brief, one-sentence handwritten signed notation at the bottom of
Marshall's own letter, evidently in the hand of a clerk or secretary, which
ought to have put all parties on notice: "Mr. Marshall: Mr. Mather doesn't
think it advisable to do anything with this now." The letter, returned to
Way, became part of the official file.

There were other complicating factors. As we now know, at the time of
this correspondence between Washington and Estes Park, Mather and his
deputy Horace M. Albright were having second thoughts about Robert
Marshall. These were critical days. The new National Park Service, established by law on August 25, 1916, was awaiting the passage of the appropriation bill that would allow the bureau to organize itself. Mather had been
counting on Marshall to become the first director of the new agency. But
Marshall, although hardworking, had already demonstrated his lack of tact

in dealing with the public and had gotten himself in trouble in Yellowstone National Park. He had closed the popular park two weeks early, reacting impulsively to a possible railroad strike. Even more significantly in terms of his discussions with Way and people in Estes Park, Marshall had dismayed his superiors by approving changes in the plans for a new Yellowstone power plant, changes that raised the cost substantially beyond the appropriation Mather had obtained only with great difficulty. By late December 1916 Marshall would be informed that he was being transferred back to the Geological Survey.[88]

Although it is unclear whether Marshall ever saw Mather's scrawled response, discussions in Estes Park between Way and Stanley and between Estes Park and Washington continued as if he had not. On November 30 Way sent Marshall a lengthy two-page letter indicating that he was sending on Wieger's plan for the administrative building, together with a village map showing the proposed site. "Mr. Wieger present[ed] several arguments in favor of one building among them," Way informed his superior,

> The crowded appearance which would follow the erection of two buildings on this site; the additional cost of constructing two buildings; and the fact [that] by ground floor bed rooms, we would lose the privacy desired due to the location and contemplated erection on [sic] new Stanley Hotel.

"As a preliminary plan I think this is a good one," Way concluded, "and with a few minor changes, made to meet our needs."

At the end of Way's letter of November 30 is a comment, added after the letter had been typed: "Reference enclosed letter from Mr. Wieger also cost sheet which is enclosed. Building was not to exceed $10,000. Enclosures received today's mail."[89] Wieger's hasty note, written by hand from Denver, is apologetic: "I sent you yesterday the drawings & blue prints & enclose the description estimate of cost. It runs higher than I had thought due to the comparative inaccessibility of Estes Park, no doubt."[90]

Although the blueprints alluded to in this correspondence, like those of the Stanley Hotel, have apparently not survived, the four-page memorandum "Describing the Drawings Submitted by T. Robert Wieger, Architect," and Wieger's one-page "Schedule of Costs Main Building–Stable and Garage" have. What they suggest is the extent to which the project had quickly evolved under the unchecked enthusiasm of Way, Marshall, Wieger, and Stanley:

> *Location*: The building is to be placed in the centre of a small public square, situated in the heart of the village of Estes Park, and bounded by four important roads. It faces the main thorofare [sic] to the South, the

new post office to the West, the village school to the North, while a large new hotel is contemplated on the East. . . .

The Grounds: A wide semi-circular gravel driveway gives direct communication, both East and West, from the main road to the office and exhibition room is connected with a service driveway to the rear entrance, stable, garage and the North road. Graveled promenades unite the office and residence entrances. At the end of the promenade, in the Northeast corner, a concrete fountain with a large basin, to contain mountain trout, is designed. . . .

Arrangement: The South half of the first floor is devoted to the administration features of the building, comprising a large exhibition room containing suitable display cases and tables, a public office, clerk's office, private office, filing room and toilet. A glass partition divides the exhibition room and office, so that one clerk has full observation of all public spaces. The private office gives the one direct interior connection between the office and residence portions.

The North half of the first floor contains the living rooms for the supervisor. A good sized living room, dining room, pantry, kitchen and toilet are provided with ample hall ways and porches . . .

The second floor contains four large bed rooms with large clothes closets, and a good tiled bath room. In addition to the basin, closet and tub, a shower bath is also installed. . . .

Stable and Garage: The garage will be of ample size for one automobile. The stable will contain three stalls with modern sanitary stable fittings and harness case. . . . A fenced paddock, inclosing a manure pit and ash pit, adjoins this building.

Design: The buildings are designed in the Colonial period of architecture, harmonizing with adjacent structures and giving a lasting and stately style and attractive appearance.[91]

The remainder of Wieger's narrative has to do with the exterior appearance (clapboarded walls, painted light gray with white trimmings); a poured concrete foundation faced with native granite fieldstones; a green, asbestos-shingled roof; and a tiled entrance. The schedule of costs, which as Wieger made clear were for building construction only, came to $17,300.[92]

On December 4 Robert Marshall wrote Way acknowledging the receipt of the plans for the administration building. "It looks pretty good to me," he told Way "—better than the sketch you sent, and better than the one I sent you! As soon as we can get down to real business I will take this up with Mr. Mather. Please thank Mr. Stanley for his interest in the matter."[93] Whether by this date Marshall had yet to receive Wieger's cost sheet, or simply chose to ignore it, is unclear.

Save for one additional piece of surviving correspondence, a letter from L. C. Way to F. O. Stanley in Boston, dated December 11, 1916, reporting to

Stanley the substance of Marshall's letter of December 4,[94] nothing more is heard of the administration building project. Clearly Wieger's estimate of cost was a major reason. In 1916 the entire appropriation for Rocky Mountain Park was only $10,000. But there were other factors operating as well, including the departure of Marshall during December and the general uncertainties during the first months of 1917 as the newly authorized National Park Service awaited its first appropriations and established its priorities. When funding came in mid-April, the bill placed a limit of $19,500 on salaries for the director of the new bureau and his entire staff, little more than the cost of Wieger's building before landscaping.

Of far greater regret, little more is heard of Stanley's plans for a new "colonial-style" hotel and the "new model town" to which it was to give architectural direction, although both projects were evidently alive and well in early 1917. Others, however, took them seriously. Not the least of these was Al Hayden, who in filing a petition on behalf of forty-two fellow citizens on January 17 to allow Estes Park to become Larimer County's fifth incorporated town, told the *Fort Collins Express* that the "impending plan for the beautification of the village and its transformation into one of the most sightly resort villages in the nation make its incorporation imperative."[95]

Beyond this date the record is silent about Stanley's ambitious projects. Perhaps he was disappointed by the slow reaction and the probable negative response of the National Park Service, or perhaps his decision not to push ahead had to do with the increasingly precarious financial situation of the Stanley Motor Carriage Company in Newton, which the Stanley brothers were even then making plans to dispose of. There was also the mounting friction with Germany over the resumption of unrestricted submarine warfare in the North Atlantic, which on April 6, 1917, would provoke Woodrow Wilson to sign a proclamation of war. Whatever the cause, by the time winter turned to spring Stanley had turned his attention to other things.

The two lots east of the park intended for the site of the new hotel remained in Stanley's hands until September 1925 when, following the approval by the voters of a $71,000 bond issue, Stanley donated one of them, then valued at $8,000, to the Town of Estes Park as the site for a new auditorium.[96] Twelve years later, on March 31, 1937, for a reported price of $8,000, Stanley sold the other lot, a 2.49-acre parcel, to Larimer County School District 30 to provide Estes Park with a new school building.[97] That piece of land, bordering Elkhorn Avenue, is where the Estes Park Municipal Building is now located.

Rocky Mountain National Park would continue to maintain its administrative offices in the small white frame building on Elkhorn Avenue until

3.6 F. O. Stanley during 1930s, with Byron Hall on left and his niece, Dorothy Emmons, on right. Courtesy Byron Hall

1923. That October they were transferred to a new headquarters building on what was then the outskirts of Estes Park, on the southern slope of Davis Hill where Moraine Avenue swings west along the Big Thompson.[98] The 26-by-45-foot masonry and lumber building, occupying land donated to the Park Service in May 1921 by the Estes Park Woman's Club, was of the thoroughly functional, nondescript governmental sort, painted dark brown—a far cry from the gray clapboard colonial-style building that Wieger had suggested. Across the street for many years was Harold Arps's Blue Ribbon Livery—not one of the picturesque buildings of the "new model town" that was to transform Estes Park into an American Tyrol.

Urban renewal of the sort Stanley visualized would come to Estes Park but not for more than six decades and then by way of a man-made disaster rather than through purposeful planning and design. On July 15, 1982, a wall of water some 25 feet high, unleashed by the failure of a gate valve at the farmer's cooperative dam at Lawn Lake, raced down Roaring River, through Horseshoe Park and the valley of Fall River, flooding and devastating much of the village of Estes Park. Three lives were lost and the damage to property in Estes Park exceeded $26 million. From the disaster at Lawn Lake nonetheless came new beginnings. Under the aegis of the Estes Park Urban Renewal Authority, created in 1983, came an ambitious plan to revitalize and beautify the central business district. It included the construction of a park and a river walk—both of the sort that Stanley and his architect would have been among the first to appreciate.

~

Despite the setbacks of 1916, Stanley's contributions to the growth and improvement of Estes Park continued for more than four decades. Although Stanley declined to take credit, others took note. The *Loveland Reporter*, in calling attention in October 1909 to the many "improvements . . . that Mr. Stanley has been back of," was equally explicit about the result: "it was Mr. Stanley that brought new life into the park six years ago, and now it is pushing right to the front every day."[99]

Estes Park would have developed without Stanley's initiative, money, and participation. Unquestionably, however, the expectations that Stanley brought with him were instrumental in doing for Estes Park what Estes Park, left to its own devices and to those of lesser capacities and vision, would have done much less well or not at all. What historically took place in most western mountain communities was largely a matter of happenstance. Thanks to Stanley's attentiveness, Estes Park was clearly more fortunate than most.

Chapter 4

~

Building a Community

Wɪᴛʜ ᴛʜᴇ ʙᴜɪʟᴅɪɴɢ ᴏᴜᴛ ᴏꜰ ᴛʜᴇ ᴠɪʟʟᴀɢᴇ ᴏꜰ Eꜱᴛᴇꜱ Pᴀʀᴋ in the years after 1905 came a slow but steady expansion in the number of residents. Between 1890 and 1900 the year-round population increased from 125 to 218. By 1910 the population of Estes Park had grown to 396; a decade later in 1920 it reached 539.[1] In the nineteenth and early twentieth century, this population had been widely dispersed among outlying ranches and resorts. Now it was geographically centered in and around a village of clustered homes and businesses whose inhabitants found themselves bound together not only by economic fortune but, increasingly, by a strong and widely shared sense of community.

Part of this feeling was the legacy of Estes Park's pioneer days. Despite frontier conditions and the vagaries of mountain life, the park's earliest residents quickly learned that their interests and concerns, like their livelihoods, were intimately linked to those of their neighbors. At first, what brought them together was their opposition to the attempts by Theodore Whyte and the Earl of Dunraven's cowboys to drive them from their land; later it was by the common discovery that their futures, and the future of Estes Park, would be determined not by their success in ranching and farming but by their willingness to accommodate themselves to tourists. These relationships, and the identity they provided, inevitably deepened with the passage of the years, enriched by shared memories of difficulties overcome, of hard times endured, and, increasingly, by an awareness of having been part of a common story. By the turn of the century these traditions, together with a strong attachment to place, had solidified and Estes Park had its own history, some of it already elevated to the level of myth and legend.

For those arriving in Estes Park in 1905 and for a number of years afterward, the closeness of village life and the knowledge of being part of a new and growing town hastened the process of community-building. That this socialization took place in a remote and still relatively isolated mountain setting among individuals who differed but little in their ethnic stock, background, education, religion, politics, and wealth created a sense of similarity and comfort that made close personal relationships both easy and inevitable. Ties of friendship were increasingly cemented by ties of marriage,[2] adding through kinship yet another layer of homogeneity to a place where each year eight months of much-welcomed peace and quiet replaced the last departing tourists. As in many small towns, much of what happened in Estes Park would be determined by the strength of these relationships, by the measure of social control that accompanied them, and by the effectiveness of the organizations and institutions that they made possible and sustained. It can be surmised that an economy focused on satisfying the needs of tourists had fewer internal tensions, initially at least, than a community whose economic survival depended on residents dealing largely with one another. That most tourist activity, particularly in the early years, was decidedly seasonal provided the opportunity to build and sustain a sense of community life.

"Those who live in Estes park in winter have tranquil and happy times," the special Estes Park correspondent of the *Fort Collins Weekly Courier* reassured readers in February 1903:

> The tourists are all gone and people work quietly and enjoy life
> thoroughly. They read abundantly and visit to their heart's content. The
> ground is generally free from snow and but a few days are extremely
> cold. First one family and then the other invites everybody to "come
> over and spend the evening and have something good to eat." From
> fifteen to fifty come, and a royal social time follows.[3]

Although there is something almost defensive in this bucolic description of how a mountain community passes the winter, it is undoubtedly accurate. From the 1890s on, the valley papers are filled with personal items about card and dinner parties, holiday celebrations and gatherings, turkey shoots, oyster suppers on New Year's Day hosted by the village bachelors, and the surprise serenading of newlyweds. When blacksmith Jim Boyd brought his

4.1 Reunion Dinner at community building, ca. 1903. Courtesy Estes Park Museum

new wife Fannie back to Estes Park after their wedding, the two were subjected to "a rousing tin pan serenade . . . by the bachelors (and a few old maids)." The Boyds were evidently prepared. "They bore their martyrdom with great fortitude and returned good for evil by treating the crowd to candy, fruit, and cigars."[4]

There were also the reunion Thanksgiving dinners at the village schoolhouse, which brought together residents from throughout the valley. Like "the old time log rollings," Enos Mills later remarked, this annual event "produced friendships and sympathetic neighborly feelings; occasionally they promoted marriage."[5] Residents also remembered a much-celebrated "literary society" organized early in the century by John Adams and Louise Tallant. Meetings, held at the schoolhouse, featured songs, dances, and recitations performed by such local residents as Enos and Joe Mills and Warren Rutledge, an Irishman from Sligo who brought along his own phonograph.[6]

Summers brought an expanded agenda of social activities, most of them staged for those staying at the valley's guest ranches and resorts. "Resting is the principal object for which tourists come to Estes park," a visitor wrote in August 1881, "but that does not interfere with general good times, an informal hop, a music party, a charade party, and an occasional evening devoted to tableaux or amateur theatricals serve to make life gay."[7] The Fourth of July was formally celebrated in Estes Park as early as 1876, when some thirty residents and visitors gathered in a small grassy cottonwood grove on Fall River to mark both the nation's birthday and Colorado's entrance into the Union with a picnic.[8] During the early 1890s fireworks had become part of the festivities, and by 1899 the day featured three hours of organized events, with published program, including an address by Enos Mills followed by "Happy Hours" at 2 P.M. and fireworks at 8.[9]

From an early day there were bronco-busting and other rodeo-type events recalling the cowboy traditions of the West, such as the one attended near the Dunraven Ranch on Fish Creek by F. O. and Flora Stanley during their first visit in 1903. More authentic activities associated with cattle raising were equally visible at any number of the valley's working ranches, including those operated by the MacGregors in the Black Canyon; Pieter Hondius in Horseshoe Park and Beaver Meadows; and Theodore Whyte and his successors, who ran large herds on the Earl of Dunraven's lands. As authentic ranching waned in the new century and what remained of the Old West disappeared or became mythologized, Estes Park resorts, even the upscale Stanley, increasingly stylized their social activities to reflect the western outdoor experience, offering a dependable menu of trail rides, cookouts, campfire talks, and cowboy dances designed to convey a sense that the tourist guidebooks were correct: the West was a place where visitors were made to feel at home and, however briefly, part of a genuine community.

The new century, of course, brought other substantial changes. "The automobile, better mail service, the telephone and the increase of land owners," Enos Mills later noted, "all combined to make changes in the customs of the Park."[10] Nevertheless, even with the development of the village after 1905, much of this informal "old-time" socializing not only continued but intensified. It was also focused: tourism had become the lynchpin of the valley's economic life.

During its first critical decade, in the absence of incorporation, less formal organizations defined life in Estes Park as they did in communities throughout the West, and their impact upon town and region was significant. Some of these were simply social and fraternal—the Presbyterian Women's Association organized to support the new church in October 1908[11]; Odd Fellows Lodge 163 founded in March 1910 and its sister lodge, the Rebekas, founded less than a year later in January 1911; a PEO sisterhood chartered in June 1918, and the Estes Park Post of the American Legion formed by fifteen ex-servicemen in June 1920. By 1912, the Odd Fellows had their own hall on Elkhorn above Roy Wiest's doctor's office and drugstore, and the new building served as a convenient and needed venue for meetings, dances, and other events.

Three other organizations had far more important roles to play. For more than a decade the Estes Park Protective and Improvement Association, the Estes Park Woman's Club, and, to a lesser but still significant extent, the Estes Park Business Men's Association, in effect, took the place of town government. Separately and collectively, they helped Estes Park address many of its most important and pressing civic problems and by so doing established a tradition of community action and a set of precedents and expectations that lasted into and beyond the 1920s. Membership in these organizations tended to overlap and represent the social and business hierarchy of the town itself, factors that gave their efforts stability, continuity, and a sense of legitimacy. For the individuals involved, membership was also a way of establishing and maintaining status.

Much of the success of these organizations had, of course, to do with the individuals who stepped forward to assume leadership roles and their ability to marshal the human and financial resources of residents behind their projects. So successful were these organizations in promoting and directing the spirit of volunteerism within the Estes Park community and in visibly discharging many government functions, that they made formal incorporation unnecessary for almost a dozen years.

$\sim$

The Estes Park Protective and Improvement Association was not, in fact, a new organization. It had initially been formed in 1895, "to prevent the destruction of fish in the rivers of the Park, the illegal killing of game, and the destruction of the timber by campfires."[12] This concern was more than justified. By 1880, the indigenous elk, which in the previous decade had attracted sportsmen—including such celebrities as the Earl of Dunraven—from as far away as England and Ireland, had been hunted nearly to the point of extinction. The fish population was scarcely in better shape thanks to the enthusiasm of anglers who descended upon local streams and lakes each spring and summer, often with the encouragement of local resorts that held contests to see who could catch the largest number, without regard to size. The carelessness of campers was also a significant and increasing problem. One need only gaze at the charred remains of the great fire of August 1900, which swept the Glacier Gorge, Loch Vale, Bierstadt Lake, and Bear Lake regions—in many places to timberline—to be reminded of the fragility of nature when confronted by human folly.

The elected officers of the first Protective and Improvement Association, as might be expected, were all prominent resort owners and first-generation pioneers. Abner Sprague was chosen president; Ella James, the widow of William E. James, founder of Elkhorn Lodge, treasurer; and James Ferguson, the son of Horace Ferguson, who was then operating the Highlands Hotel near Marys Lake, secretary. Of the activities of this early organization we know little, other than the fact that it posted signs in various parts of the park "forbidding fishing and hunting without permission" and warned visitors of the fines to be imposed on those who violated them.[13] Its most important legacy was its precedent. By calling attention to the need to protect the diminished wildlife population, Sprague and his fellow officers helped establish a level of environmental concern that would continue and intensify in the decade that followed.

The Estes Park Protective and Improvement Association (EPPIA) was formed anew on September 22, 1906,[14] with an initial membership of twenty-one, each of whom agreed to pay a one-dollar annual fee. Thanks to the efforts of its predecessor, the need to preserve "the beauties of the park" was taken for granted. What was now needed in Estes Park, its members decided, was some sort of broad-based local organization that, without resorting to taxation, was capable of meeting various needs—a "system," as one "old resident" elliptically wrote in 1912, "in which all could have a voice to conserve energy and resources rather than waste, yet be relieved of irregular, uncertain and non-related attempts such as would occur in the absence of some general policy undertaken by all concerned."[15] Enos Mills called the first meeting to order and then turned it over to Frank W. Crocker,[16] who served as temporary chairman. Following the adoption of a formal printed set of "Statements and Stipulations," the new group elected Stanley president; Cornelius Bond secretary; and an executive committee consisting of Stanley, Bond, James Stead, Pieter Hondius, and eleven others to serve as directors. As in the case of its predecessor, the choice of leadership made sense for both Stanley and Bond, the successful businessman from the East and the moving force behind the Estes Park Town Company, were widely perceived to be at the center of village development. EPPIA membership quickly expanded to include virtually every resident property owner.

The association's charter was an exceedingly broad one: "to suggest, provide for, and maintain improvements, such as roads, trails, fish hatcheries, tree planting, forestry, and any like attempts intended to be of use and benefit."[17] All of these improvements, of course, were rooted in the economic realities of Estes Park, and although the document's preamble pointedly insisted that the association's activities were "for further beautifying of said Park, and not for pecuniary profit," there was from the beginning the unspoken assumption and expectation that helping nature would also materially help in developing tourism. Another and equally important purpose was a quasi-political one. By serving as a forum in which citizens could discuss issues of local importance, the EPPIA served the community in the manner of the venerable New England town meeting.

The organization quickly gathered momentum. The establishment of a fish hatchery on Fall River Road in 1907 was the project that served as the catalyst and focus for the EPPIA's activities, but there were others as well. Over the next decade the EPPIA was responsible for the construction of a new trail from the Big Thompson bridge up the north side of Prospect Mountain and then south to Marys Lake; the building of trails to Ypsilon and Fern Lakes; the installation of a concrete bridge over Black Canyon Creek; and for protecting the purity of the town's water supply. The association also assumed much of the local responsibility for advertising Estes Park regionally and nationally by sponsoring the publication of an attractive booklet of William Parke's picture views showing local hotels and their surroundings and by subsidizing an early travelogue. In addition the EPPIA took credit for posting signs warning against the indiscriminate picking of wild flowers; for arresting and convicting individuals on charges of poaching deer and beaver; and for apprehending two others who broke into cottages during winter 1911.[18] Still other efforts were directed at discouraging the leasing of private land for camping, shooting, picnicking, and fishing. Many of these activities required money, and by August 1912, the association could report that in six years it had raised some $12,000 for its various projects.[19]

The building and opening of the fish hatchery was the EPPIA's greatest accomplishment, although the idea itself was not new. Such a project had been discussed locally since at least 1902, particularly among those who were familiar with the Denver hatchery, the first in Colorado, established two decades earlier nine miles north of the city on the Brighton road. What now gave the idea of a hatchery for Estes Park its impetus was the concerted backing of a group like the EPPIA, whose tourist-conscious members realized all too well, as hatchery superintendent Gaylord Thomson later put it, "that if our streams were filled with fish it would be one of the greatest advertising features of the park."[20]

Considering the time, place, and resources required, the fact that the Estes Park Fish Hatchery was completed and ready for inspection on July 22, 1907, less than a year after its conception was remarkable. It was made possible because a handful of individuals immediately stepped forward with major contributions. Chief among them was Pieter Hondius, who offered to lease the association a site on property he owned along Fall River, four miles west of the village. The other early supporters we can only surmise, but from the subsequent record we can safely assume that they included Stanley, Bond, and Frank Crocker.[21]

Other than perhaps Stanley and Bond, the Dutch-born Hondius (1871–1934) was the EPPIA's most active and important member. He had originally come to Estes Park by way of Denver in 1896 because of chronic asthma, and then decided to stay on to ranch and farm by purchasing some 2,000 acres of

4.2 Estes Park Fish Hatchery, ca. 1910. Courtesy Estes Park Museum

land in Horseshoe Park and in Beaver Meadows. The Hondius barn, built adjacent to his ranch house at the upper end of Beaver Meadows, was said to be the largest in Larimer County. Ranching in Estes Park was never easy— particularly when it involved driving as many as 350 cattle to winter pasture in Loveland over the torturous hills of the Bald Mountain–Pole Hill road. Cattle gradually gave way to other interests beginning in 1904, when Hondius, now a U.S. citizen, married Eleanor Estes James, the daughter of the original owner of Elkhorn Lodge. This event, together with other ventures such as the construction of the six-mile Hondius Water Line in 1906, which sold water from Buck Creek in Upper Beaver Meadows (later expanded by tapping Beaver Creek itself) to cabin owners in the High Drive area south of Deer Mountain, brought him into contact with the valley's tourist industry.

Hondius was soon involved in town affairs, leading the effort to raise money for the new fish hatchery. Lacking tax revenues, the town fathers of Estes Park, like their counterparts in other frontier communities, turned to subscription as a way of mobilizing enthusiasm and money behind efforts directed at local improvement. Public subscription had a number of well-understood virtues. Chief among them was the fact that it minimized the need for government, an institution that Westerners tended to view with suspicion. Promoting the public good through voluntary association was eminently democratic, a fact that appealed greatly to communities that relied on broad participation and a sense of civic responsibility. Raising money through subscription worked for another reason as well. It permitted (and encouraged) wealthier members of the community to assert their standing, generosity, and leadership in advancing the public good while, simultaneously, demonstrating a lack of self-interest and their commitment to an egalitarian society.

The surviving records of the EPPIA indicate, not surprisingly, that Stanley's contribution of $250 made him the largest single subscriber to the fish hatchery, but the total effort was broadly based. On the list of 148, James Stead gave $50, and eleven others gave $25 each, the remainder making much smaller contributions, many in the amount of one dollar.[22]

Not all funds were collected locally. Some money came from Longmont and Loveland, whose residents had long enjoyed Estes Park as a retreat from summer heat. As late as mid-May 1907, with construction about to begin, Pieter Hondius wrote to Charles Boynton, editor of the *Longmont Ledger,* to call his attention to the project, indicating that the $1,387 contract cost of building "will greatly exceed our first estimate" and reminding readers that "a greater Estes Park is also worth much to Longmont." In a separate letter published with Hondius's, one J. C. Garett chided his fellow residents "that residents in the Park and Loveland have subscribed as liberally as could be expected while Longmont has yet to subscribe her share."[23]

When individual subscriptions fell short, additional funds were raised through dances and other benefit events held at local resorts throughout the valley both before and after the project's completion. These included a vaudeville show featuring a one-act farce in August 1908 and an equally memorable costume ball, complete with grand march, held four years later in the Stanley Hotel's Casino. The vaudeville show, staged in the village park in a "monster" circus tent, attracted an audience of some two hundred. The sums raised by such occasions were relatively small (about $100 in the case of the vaudeville show), and, like many of the sums pledged by subscription, were probably less important in the end than the feeling of participation they created among residents and tourists alike.

Of the $3,352 it cost to build and equip the hatchery, $712 came in the form of donated labor, including the grading. The remaining $2,640 was raised in cash.[24] Work began on Sunday, May 25, 1907, when nine men, six shovelers, and three surveyors, showed up on the selected site, a level piece of wooded ground well back from the riverbank. Pieter Hondius, Henry Rogers, and Bert Merriman did the surveying, while Henry and Charlie Hupp and Howard James went to work digging a 635-foot ditch, 12 inches deep and 3 feet wide, to bring water from a spring on the Hondius property to the hatchery site. "The day was cold and the shovelers had to work hard to keep warm."[25] Construction nevertheless moved ahead quickly, not only because of the approaching tourist season, but because in their enthusiasm the orga-nizers had ordered 600,000 eggs scheduled to arrive any time after July 4. On Sunday, June 30, Pieter Hondius, Henry Rogers, and a gang of men began flooring the building, and two days later, on July 2, Bert Merriman com-pleted laying the pipe from spring to hatchery.[26] Within weeks all was ready for tourists and eggs.

The new hatchery was an immediate success and quickly became one of the park's chief tourist attractions. By the end of the 1907 season it was reported that 620,000 eggs had already been hatched and that large numbers of eastern brook trout and rainbow trout eggs were expected to arrive during the coming winter and spring.[27] "There is no other hatchery in the west that can approach it," J. C. Garrett assured his Longmont neighbors that Sep-tember. "Everything is good, substantial and practical. The outside appear-ance of the building is neat and attractive. Further improvements are planned, such as ponds for keeping the fish until considerable size is attained."[28]

Those improvements came two years later, following yet another round of fund-raising. Four sizing ponds, of the kind Garrett had mentioned, were constructed. Peter J. Pauly of St. Louis, who had run a sizable cattle opera-tion in the park in the 1880s and retained an active interest in local affairs, donated funds for two small ponds. Bruce Eaton of Greeley, a summer resi-dent of Moraine Park, and Stanley contributed the larger ones. At the same time the association built a cottage to house superintendent Gaylord Thomson and his family at a cost of $1,944. A small portion of the funds required came through donations and benefits, but the rest was borrowed and carried by the EPPIA on its books as an encumbrance.[29] Sixteen hundred dollars was raised from eight individuals—F. O. Stanley, Cornelius H. Bond, Pieter Hondius, Howard James, Burton D. Sanborn, Charles Bache, Frank W. Crocker, and Frank W. Stover—each of whom took notes to be repaid at some indefinite later date.[30]

No small part of the hatchery's success was the attention of its resident superintendent, Gaylord H. Thomson, an experienced and well-read pisci-culturist, who initially came on loan from the Denver hatchery but stayed on to preside over the facility for some twenty-two seasons. Thomson was an engaging fellow, filled with enthusiasm for his subject, who made himself readily available to explain the niceties of the artificial propagation of trout and their spawning seasons, habitats, and habits. He created further interest by offering visitors a look at his display of "freaks" and oddities, which he

4.3 "*Sunbeam.*" *James H. Pickering Collection*

kept in jars of alcohol "for study."[31] For a number of years there was also "Sunbeam," Thomson's pet fish, brought to Colorado in 1908 as an egg, placed in the water upon hatching, and then returned to the hatchery as a sick fish. Cured of his fungus but remaining undersized, Sunbeam was put on display for visitors, becoming so tame that he could be lifted from the water in a glass jar and handled. A widely distributed postcard, "a plea for the fish," owed its existence to practical demonstrations of the handling of Sunbeam, a performance seen annually by thousands of visitors. When Sunbeam died after the close of the 1915 season by jumping into a trough without water, his demise was reported in the papers as a story of interest.[32] By 1920 Thomson's daily lectures, even without his pet fish, "had grown so popular, and their reputation spread so far," that it took "the capacity of the building to take care of the crowd attending."[33]

The Estes Park Fish Hatchery never managed to become self-supporting as its architects had hoped, and by 1912, after a series of negotiations, control was turned over to the State of Colorado under a three-year lease agreement with the association. The hatchery continued to serve its purpose well into the 1920s. Beginning in summer 1921, its work was supplemented by the efforts of the Estes Park Fish and Game Association, a new organization formed by a group of local men concerned by the continuing scarcity of rainbow trout in a region touted as "a fisherman's paradise" and by the fact that many of the fry placed in streams were being prematurely devoured by larger fish.[34] By that October this group had established a sizable nursing pond near the Chapman house in Moraine Park, which Superintendent

Thomson pronounced "the finest pond of its kind he has ever been privileged to see."[35]

One of the Fish and Game Association's major goals was to stock at least one new lake each year. To carry out its program Ed Andrews and other association members developed a special packboard to allow the transportation of cans of fish, each weighing some forty-five pounds, up to the lakes within the park. "These packs are so comfortable," Roger Toll noted in his monthly superintendent's report for June 1922, "that they make carrying fish a pleasure."[36] The Fish and Game Association's work continued and over the next five years it constructed five semi-permanent retaining ponds and planted nearly six million trout fingerlings in local waters. It also offered rewards for the arrest of anyone killing elk, deer, or bighorn sheep.

The efforts of the Fish and Game Association were needed for by the spring of 1928 the lease on the fish hatchery site had expired and the original buildings had become antiquated, all but abandoned as far as fish propagation was concerned. "Estes Park has been piddling along at the job of keeping the streams stocked," the *Estes Park Trail* had warned the previous October, with its usual nod at the tourist trade. "Let's quit dilly-dallying and get busy and give Estes Park and [the] Big Thompson canyon region the finest fishing to be found in the state. When this time comes Estes Park will find itself unable to take care of the crowds."[37] To make this happen a new facility was needed, and for a time there was a debate about whether the association should secure permanent ownership of the Fall River location or build a new facility in Moraine Park, where James Stead offered the use of his spring and agreed to deed property to the state for a hatchery and sizing ponds.

That November a committee of the Chamber of Commerce, headed by Joe Mills, visited the Colorado Fish and Game Commission in Denver to discuss the matter. They returned with a commitment to build a modern facility on the old site, providing that the 1909 notes encumbering the property taken by Stanley and others would be retired and donated with their water rights to the state.

Renovation took place in the winter and spring of 1928–1929 and was extensive. At a cost of some $40,000, the old building was dismantled and a new one, roughly twice the size, built on the same site. The superintendent's house was thoroughly remodeled and new shelter buildings and equipment were added, increasing the total capacity of the facility to some four million eggs a year. To reduce the necessity of seeding undersized fish into lakes and streams, eight-by-twelve-foot concrete nursing and retaining ponds were also built.[38] The enlarged facility reopened with a new superintendent, John

Mitchell, former assistant head of the Denver hatchery, who replaced the now-retired Gaylord Thomson. For the next half century, until July 15, 1982, the new Estes Park Fish Hatchery remained a landmark. That morning, in a matter of minutes, water from the breached dam at Lawn Lake swept through the Fall River Valley rendering the hatchery, like the nearby Stanley power plant, inoperable. It was never reopened.

~

Two other significant projects of the period, both with lasting impact, may also be linked, at least indirectly, to the interest and support of the Estes Park Protective and Improvement Association. The first was the reintroduction of elk into the park in 1913. This effort, like so many others, seems to have originated with C.H. Bond, who four years earlier, in the spring of 1909, was reported to have taken out an option "on a bunch of elk that he is going to try to get parties interested in and have them kept in a private preserve here in the park."[39] The idea was revived in 1913 by a group of citizens led by Pieter Hondius,[40] who raised sufficient funds to bring twenty-nine young elk (five or six males, the rest females) from the Jackson Hole region of Wyoming to Estes Park. The herd was brought to Gardner, Montana, by the Bureau of Biological Survey, the government agency charged with overseeing the thinning of the local elk population through a nation-wide dispersal program that included Colorado. From there, under the direction of the Forest Service, which paid the freighting charges,[41] the animals were transported to Lyons by the Burlington Railroad. There Hondius and other Estes Park people assumed responsibility. The elk were transferred to cages attached to Stanley Mountain Wagons for the trip to the village, where they were unloaded in the corral of Frank Grubb's livery before being herded into a temporary barbed-wire enclosure near the Stanley Hotel. "One of the interesting sights for tourists in Estes Park, which will be new even to former visitors," the *Estes Park Trail* pointed out in June 1913, "is a herd of about twenty-five elk, which can be observed any day grazing in what has been rechristened the Stanley Elk Park."[42] The elk were then herded into Horseshoe Park and released. Two years later, in 1915, twenty-four additional elk (all two-year-old cows) were brought in to join them. This second herd was placed in the corral of the Elkhorn Lodge, west of town, from where they "apparently broke from their confinement soon after arrival and escaped into the mountains."[43]

Pieter Hondius did much of the negotiating with local Forest Service officials on how the elk were to be transported and released. In the process

4.4 Bringing the elk up from Lyons, 1913. Courtesy National Park Service–Rocky Mountain National Park

he kept Stanley, who had undoubtedly contributed financially, informed of his progress. One of the ironic and prophetic footnotes of history is contained in the letter that Stanley wrote Hondius from his winter home in Massachusetts on March 20, 1913. "From what I learn about the elk," Stanley warned, "I am afraid Estes Park will be overrun with animals of that kind, and we may have to get Roosevelt up there to help reduce the number."[44]

The other project bearing the imprint of the association was the campaign for the creation of Rocky Mountain National Park. The idea had first been floated in October 1907 by Herbert N. Wheeler, the new head of the Medicine Bow National Forest, who had recently established his headquarters in the village. Invited by his neighbors to address the EPPIA, Wheeler had a suggestion. "If you want to draw tourists," Wheeler told them, "you should establish a game refuge where tourists can see the wild life."[45] He then produced a map on which he pointed to an area of more than 1,000 square miles west of the village extending across the Continental Divide. Although Enos Mills was not present that evening, the idea fitted perfectly with his own widening wilderness agenda, and Mills soon made Wheeler's plan his own.

The idea of a national park also struck a responsive chord among the members of the association, for such an attraction, particularly one maintained and operated at government expense, promised to greatly expand tourism. As a hotel owner with a growing interest in transportation, Stanley was immediately interested, and within a year Stanley and Mills were reported by papers in Loveland and Greeley to be "actively working" together on the project.[46] In June 1909, the "park idea" was formally brought before a special meeting of the Estes Park Protective and Improvement Association, and a committee of two appointed: Enos A. Mills and F. O. Stanley.[47] Two months later, the EPPIA unanimously adopted a resolution supporting the Wheeler-Mills plan to secure a park of some 600,000 acres under rules and regulations similar to those governing Yellowstone. The following year the association voted to "secure funds to pay the expenses of Mr. Mills in his work in trying to secure the National Park" and to send Mills and Stanley to Washington to work on behalf of the park bill.[48]

During the six years that followed, Stanley and others helped subsidize Enos Mills's promotional efforts, including the frenetic cross-country lecture swings that brought him before virtually any group that would give him a platform and hearing. The Estes Park Protective and Improvement Association also helped. As one of the coalition of groups that Mills, Denver lawyer James Grafton Rogers, and others assembled in support of the project, the EPPIA assisted Mills with his travel expenses and helped him defray $400 of the costs "connected with the appearance of pictures and articles about Estes Park in many of the leading papers and magazines of the country."[49]

The Estes Park Protective and Improvement Association existed until the eve of the town's incorporation in 1917, but by 1913 interest and activity had peaked. That year the annual August meeting stipulated in the bylaws was immediately adjourned for lack of a quorum. The officers and directors for the preceding year, which included stalwarts Pieter Hondius, C. H. Bond, Enos Mills, F. O. Stanley, Howard James, William. T. Parke, and Sam Service, were simply held over for another term.[50] The lack of enthusiasm was understandable: much of the program that the EPPIA had articulated for Estes Park had been completed.

Of equal, if not greater, importance was the precedent established for community action. Its members would in later years contribute to civic projects through other organizations, and the legacy of the EPPIA continued to provide in memory a source of strength and reassurance. As the anonymous "Old Resident" wrote prophetically in September 1912, "When the time comes for Estes Park people to assume the dignity of municipal government, they will remember with pride, and be prepared to plant in the larger field of good-will and high standards given a start by the Estes Park [Protective and Improvement] association."[51]

Nor was the lesson lost on outsiders. On June 26, 1915, veteran Denver newspaperman Arthur Chapman, best known for his popular poem "Out Where the West Begins," devoted an entire *Denver Times* story to the phenomenon of Estes Park, "the model of progressiveness" though lacking "a mayor, a council, a commission, or anything else in the form of a governing body." Citing directly the "on the job" work of the EPPIA, Chapman extolled Estes Park and heralded the fact that both the fish hatchery and the village's new post office had been built not by government "pork barrel" but by public subscription. Estes Park, he continued, was an example for state and nation. "How greatly the moral atmosphere of the country would be cleared, and how much actual money would be saved," Chapman rhetorically asked, "if all communities followed the Estes Park example." Chapman's two-page article cataloged the town's "amazing . . . material progress" and then concluded:

> Meantime, if there be any eminent student of sociology among those who visit Rocky Mountain National park during its first season, let him stop and make a study of Estes Park village—the community without a government. It will provide him with a striking class illustration of the Jeffersonian theory that the least governed community is the best governed.[52]

Ironically, what Chapman failed to understand, or was not told during the visit that preceded his article, was that talk of incorporation was very much in the air. As early as August 1914, the EPPIA, the very group that Chapman credits with making incorporation unnecessary, had appointed a committee to examine the issue.

The last meeting of the Estes Park Protective and Improvement Association for which minutes exist took place on September 14, 1915. Incorporation of the town of Estes Park followed some eighteen months later. For those entrusted with guarding the official record of government in Estes Park, the line of descent is perfectly clear. The surviving minutes of the EPPIA reside in the office of the Town Clerk of Estes Park. Bound together in a slender volume titled "Pioneer Book of Estes Park" they are shelved directly next to the first volume of "Minutes of the Board of Trustees of the Town of Estes Park."

In the absence of surviving minutes we know rather less about the early activities of the Estes Park Woman's Club and the Estes Park Business Men's Association. What we do know, however, is that both groups, like the EPPIA, focused their efforts on projects that directly benefited Estes Park's tourist economy.

The Woman's Club began as an auxiliary arm of the EPPIA, charged by the male members with raising funds for association projects. It became its own organization by default. In pursuing its goal of a fish hatchery on Fall River, Mary Belle King Sherman later recalled, the EPPIA

> found itself without sufficient funds to meet the running expenses. Further contributions were out of the question and it was at the end of its resources. At this point the women were appealed to and soon became actively interested. And although they were not included in the membership of the association they zealously set to work to raise money. . . . The men found the assistance given by the women very valuable and depended on their cooperation. Finally, to show their appreciation, they invited them to a meeting of the association and suggested that the little band of women workers be thereafter known as the Woman's Auxiliary of the Estes Park Protection [*sic*] and Improvement Association.[53]

During the auxiliary's first season, which was probably 1907, the year the hatchery opened, members raised some $800 through a series of "bazaars and dances and other entertainments."

The success of the bazaar as an annual event quickly caught on and for a number of years served as a convenient way to tap tourist dollars and provide a centerpiece for the village's summer activities. Because no building in Estes Park was large enough, on several occasions a large circus tent was brought up from Denver and set up in the village park. For a number of summers Flora Stanley, who Mary Sherman describes as the group's "acknowledged leader," not only played a key role in planning and organizing the annual event, but together with Carrie Sanborn, the wife of Stanley's partner, dressed as a gypsy and told fortunes by reading palms with cards.[54] By August 1914, the bazaar, now referred to as the "event of the season," had become an all-day affair lasting till midnight. Among its attractions were a wildflower display, a raffle of photograph albums with "characteristic Estes Park views," fortune-telling, a fish pond, and booths selling candies, needlework, paintings, autographed books (some no doubt contributed by Enos Mills), baskets, preserves, and household articles. Tea, lunch, and dinner were served, together with "refreshments at all hours." All this raised some $800.

The ever-available F. O. Stanley contributed to the success of the summer bazaars as well. In 1914 he furnished electricity from his power plant to illuminate the tent, which had been transformed by pine and spruce branches into a "bower of green."[55] In August 1908, he enlivened the event, dedicated that summer to the fish hatchery, by bringing down to the village the two bear cubs he had purchased in June and had on display near his cottage at Rockside. "The Teddy Bears were . . . in a tent by themselves," the *Mountaineer* reported. "Of course everybody had seen them before, but it was for the hatchery this time, and the dimes were gladly paid. The bears felt their importance and were on their best behavior."[56]

The arrangement between the EPPIA and its auxiliary worked well for a time. But once the fish hatchery was taken over by the state in 1912 to the "great relief to all concerned," the women of the auxiliary decided it was time to focus their fund-raising on other projects. At this point there was controversy. In Mrs. Sherman's carefully chosen words:

> Mountain roads and trails appealed to them, and when they took their next season's contribution to the association they asked that it be used for this particular purpose; but the association, while it approved in general of roads and trails, had a policy of its own and could not see its way clear to grant the request for the Woman's Auxiliary. . . . Thereupon the women decided to have an organization of their own and the Woman's Auxiliary went out of existence. It was not hampered by formal requirements of dissolution. . . . With no by-laws or records, all that remained was a name, which was dropped, and the Woman's Auxiliary came to an end.[57]

In her memoirs Eleanor James Hondius tells the same story, although with the greater detail and directness of a central participant.

> That summer [1912] we decided to raise money for roads and trails. . . . I went to the last meeting of the Protection Society to hand over the $300 or $400 we had raised that summer. I was told it was kind of us to have raised the money, but we were only an auxiliary, and could not dictate to the Association the use of the money. I refused to hand over the money.[58]

The individual to whom Eleanor Hondius refused to tender their hard-earned money was her husband, EPPIA treasurer Pieter Hondius.[59]

The dissolution of the auxiliary almost immediately followed Eleanor Hondius's report and rebuff, and by that October a new women's organization, dedicated to the "advancement and improvement of Estes Park," had been formed to take its place. Founded on October 5, 1912, the Woman's Club of Estes Park set to work raising funds for the construction of a trail into Horseshoe Park. Personally laid out by Eleanor Hondius—with the help of Fred Clerc and Johnny Adams—from the hill behind Elkhorn Lodge and then west over the long ridge of Deer Mountain to the High Drive, the "Eleanor Hondius Deer Mountain Trail," as it was officially designated in 1917, was completed the following summer at a cost of $308.85.[60]

The Woman's Club pursued an active civic agenda. In 1922, toward the end of its first decade of existence, the editor of the *Estes Park Trail* in cataloguing the club achievements deliberately—and correctly—placed the role of that organization within the historical context of the developing town:

> During the early years the Woman's Cub was the mayor and town council, for Estes was an unincorporated village—then it was that it bought a street sprinkler and maintained it; inaugurated clean-up day, serving free and bountiful lunch to the workers; arranged for the disposal of garbage; protested against automobiles speeding thru the village and posted warning to auto drivers; removed disfiguring tobacco signs, and fenced the village green. The Woman's Club advocated the establishment of the first tourist bureau for tourists, and made it possible by giving $10,000 toward it. The Woman's Club also fought a furious if apparently futile fight against roaming stock. It was perhaps this last nuisance that made members see the necessity of incorporating the village, and they marshaled their forces toward that end, for lo! the women of Colorado were voting potentialities for politicians to reckon with.[61]

So proficient, in fact, were the women of Estes Park in raising money that by summer 1914 they were able to purchase two lots on Davis Hill on which to build a library and clubhouse. For reasons unclear, that facility was never built. Instead, in October 1921 the property was donated to the Department of the Interior to provide a site for Rocky Mountain National Park's new administration building.

Given the problems it had encountered with the EPPIA, it is interesting to note how quickly the Estes Park Woman's Club made common cause with the Estes Park Business Men's Association, many of whose members, of course, also belonged to the EPPIA. Although both of these almost exclusively male organizations were dedicated to the advancement of tourism, the Business Men's Association, founded in 1910 or 1911, from the beginning focused on expanding the commercial interests of its members. As might be expected, the early agenda of the Business Men's Association, which by May of 1920 had become the Estes Park Chamber of Commerce in name as well as fact, included advertising and publicity. But it also included trail building, an interest apparently sufficient to bring the two newer organizations together as allies.

By September 1912, according to merchant Ed Macdonald, the Business Men's Association had a membership of about forty. It also had a direction and purpose, which Macdonald outlined that month in a letter to the *Estes Park Trail* in his capacity as association president:

> As the town of Estes Park is unincorporated and has no form of village
> government, no officers of any kind to represent or look after public
> interests, the feeling was general that there should be some organization
> whose functions would be that of a chamber of commerce, and whose
> officers should be in intimate touch with the business affairs and general
> welfare of the town of Estes Park.

Moreover, there was progress to report. The previous year the association had raised and expended some $300 in producing and nationally distributing 10,000 copies of a "booklet designed to acquaint the public with the many advantages of a visit to the Park in the fall, and so prolong, in the interests of our hotels, stores and liveries, the usually very short tourist season." It also had erected a concrete watering trough near the center of the village "for the convenience of horse-back riders, teams and autos" (by which he meant, of course, Stanley Steamers) and was then contemplating the construction of new trails in the Loch Vale and Bear Lake regions of the future park.

But, as Macdonald apologetically made clear, the Business Men's Association had problems. The first was financial. "That the association has so little to show in the way of accomplishments," Macdonald confessed, "is due almost wholly to the lack of funds. Having no ladies' auxiliary to provide money, it has been seriously handicapped."[62] The other was equally serious, especially in a place as small as Estes Park, and had to do with image and perception. "There seems to be an impression in certain quarters," he continued,

> that the Business Men's Association is antagonistic to the Estes Park
> Improvement association. There is absolutely no ground for this belief.
> The work of the two associations is along different lines, although both
> are working for the same end—the growth and prosperity of the Park,
> and there seems to be no good reason why both associations should not
> work in perfect harmony, and in some enterprises, as for instance in the
> improvement of roads and trails, actively cooperate. That the phenom-
> enal growth of the town, the splendid roads we have so much reason to
> be proud of, are due largely to the efforts of the Estes Park Improvement
> association, are facts no one can gainsay, and then there is their crown-
> ing achievement—the fish hatchery—which has benefited the Park in
> an almost incalculable degree.

In conclusion, Macdonald credited the past efforts of Stanley and Bond and offered his hope that the Business Men's Association "can supplement the work" of the EPPIA without friction: "The Business Men's Association has no axe to grind, no special interests."[63]

Trail editor John Yale Munson, one of Bond's colleagues in the Estes Park Town Company, could not let Macdonald's letter pass without comment, which he provided in a page-one editorial. Acknowledging the fact that many local residents were members of both associations, Munson offered some suggestions:

> The Business Men's association [should] confine its activities to the village of Estes Park and leave the larger field to the Improvement association. There is so much that might be done to make the village look less like a cabbage patch. The street might be sprinkled from Elkhorn to the Stanley hotel, cans provided for waste papers and garbage, which could be removed daily and all droppings on the streets cleaned up every morning, and grass plots and a color scheme adopted that would make the village a fitting introduction to the Park. There is a lot more to be done than both associations can do, but, certainly the village demands the urgent attention of the business men that it may develop in attractiveness as the Park grows in popular esteem.[64]

Munson's permanent residence was the valley town of Berthoud, incorporated since 1888. Yet pointedly absent from his suggestions is an acknowledgment that the tasks he so briskly assigns to Macdonald's Business Men's Association are those that local governments are organized and financed to address. In Estes Park that time had not yet arrived.

Macdonald's comments about "antagonism" between the Business Men's Association and the EPPIA, even if correct, had nothing to do with the women of Estes Park. In fact, by late spring and early summer 1912 the Business Men's Association and the Ladies' Auxiliary of the EPPIA (soon to become the Estes Park Woman's Club) had begun cooperating as co-sponsors of the village's annual Fourth of July celebration, an elaborate affair of races and a baseball game climaxed by a grand ball at the Stanley Hotel.[65] The joint sponsorship of this tourist-oriented event continued in 1913 and 1914, by which time it featured not only a picnic and the usual games and contests but a grand parade of horseback riders, carriages, and automobiles, gaily decorated with flags and red, white, and blue ribbons, which proceeded up Elkhorn Avenue to the Elkhorn Lodge, from there to the Stanley Hotel and then back to the village.[66]

The alliance between the Business Men's Association and the new Woman's Club, of course, made perfect sense. The agenda of the Woman's Club, with its emphasis on village improvement, had a great deal in common with the tourist-oriented goals of the Business Men's Association, while the latter found in the women's organization the fund-raising mechanism whose absence Macdonald so lamented. It is tempting, of course, to speculate that the decline and eventual dissolution of the EPPIA resulted from the defection of its fund-raising arm, making it difficult, if not impossible, to mount new projects. It is nonetheless true that in the months that followed the auxiliary's break with the EPPIA the Business Men's Association moved increasingly to the center of community life and became, together with the Woman's Club, the recognized focus for efforts to meet village needs. To be sure, many of the members of the EPPIA simply shifted their time and attention to the newer organization, allowing wounds to heal without further irritation.

When five years later, in spring 1917, Al Hayden and his fellow businessmen filed incorporation papers, not a single woman is listed as a co-petitioner. It was not necessary. In July 1916, with talk of incorporation in the air, a motion was made that the Woman's Club should "suggest to the Business Men's Association that they [*sic*] take steps toward incorporation." After some discussion "the motion was tabled for further attention after the matter was discussed in the homes," and that October "the Club was asked by the men to appoint a committee to confer with the Business Men's Association about incorporation."[67] Although no record of this conference exists, it does no damage to the historical record to suggest that the men were told to proceed immediately.

The decision to incorporate ushered in a new chapter in the life of Estes Park. With the affairs of government in the hands of a taxing authority much of the weight and force in directing village affairs naturally shifted. The Woman's Club and the Business Men's Association, nevertheless, continued to play important roles in lobbying for village improvements and raising funds to pay for them. In spring 1920 the Business Men's Association formally became the Estes Park Chamber of Commerce, when some seventy-three men reconstituted the old organization under a new charter and then elected hotel man James Stead as its first president. Voicing a concern that past "advertising of Estes–Rocky Mountain National Park had been . . . desultory," the chamber took immediate steps to redouble those efforts. Although it operated without a salaried employee until 1925, when it opened an information bureau in the front end of the newly built town hall, the chamber would claim that year that it had become "the envy of all similar organizations in Colorado."[68]

~

The minutes of the new Estes Park Board of Trustees, carefully taken by Charles Hix, are largely a record of official actions and provide only scant information about the actual ebb and flow of village life and how issues faced by the expanding town were taken up, addressed, and resolved. They say even less about the differences of opinion, conflicts, and controversies that from time to time must have lurked beneath the surface. There are, to be sure, exceptions. We know, for example, that Julius Schwartz, who had purchased Homer James's lumberyard on Fall River west of the village, came before the council at a special meeting on April 28, 1920, to explain that his refusal to sell the town cement to complete the new steel bridge across the Big Thompson at Riverside Parkway was because he took "exception to the manner in which certain supplies had been ordered." In short, Schwartz had not received the business that he expected—a difficulty that was neatly resolved when trustee Ed Lindley "moved that the rest of the material needed in construction of the bridge be purchased from Mr. Schwartz and he be given the opportunity in the future to furnish supplies in his line needed by the town." Lindley's motion passed unanimously.[69]

The manner in which council resolved the Schwartz complaint—which today would smack of cronyism and probably be illegal—tells us a great deal about the close-knit structure of small town life and the values and attitudes which held the community together. So too does the amazingly stable and self-perpetuating nature of the city's all-male government. Between 1917 and 1935, a period spanning nearly two decades, only twenty-seven individuals served as mayor or trustee. Of the seven mayors during those years, Frank Bond, the son of pioneer C. H. Bond, served for seven years and grocer Sam Service for four. Only two of the other five mayors failed to succeed themselves in office for a second term. The staying power of the twenty-three individuals who served as trustees was equally remarkable. Realtor-developer Al Hayden, the town mayor in 1921 and 1922, served another ten years as trustee. Clyde Low served as a trustee for eleven years, Elijah R. "Lige" Rivers for ten, Casey Rockwell for nine, Byron Hall for seven, and Ed Lindley and Frank Bond for six each. Only three elected trustees failed to serve two terms. Without exception, these individuals were part of Estes Park's business establishment. As such they were prepared to view complaints like the one voiced by Julius Schwartz as legitimate and to act accordingly.

Although they come from the early 1940s, at a time when life in Estes Park had become more complex, it is unlikely that the attitudes regarding the responsibilities of local government expressed in April 1943 by Mayor Glen H. Preston as part of his "state of the town remarks" differed substantially from those of his predecessors a decade or two before:

> Just one year ago this month this council took office, and accepted the serious responsibility of managing the affairs of our town. . . . I read recently that Thomas Jefferson, the great leader of Democracy . . . said, "Where the law of the majority ceases to be acknowledged, there good government ends, and the law of the strongest takes its place, and life and property are his who can take them."
>
> You, Friends, are that majority and it is the earnest desire of your Mayor and Council to see that this local government is for the majority and that no strong individual or group of individuals get control of your Town. I have said, and the Board has heard this before [,] that I like to think of this Town as an Enterprise or a Big Business (for it is) with Assets of something over $270,000.00, with the Taxpayers as the stockholders, and we the Council as the Board of Directors, entrusted with the job of expending some $40,000 of your money each year. The profits of this concern to be efficient government, and good municipal services.[70]

As a statement of the role of limited and businesslike government and how it should be operated, few could have framed it better.

By 1920, if not before, candidates for election to mayor and council were decided by the caucus of a quasi-political organization called the Citizens Party, a group that more often than not recommended and ratified incumbents. Candidates for office in Estes Park ran unopposed until the election of April 1921, when, during the height of the transportation controversy involving the national park, a group of individuals that included C. H. Bond, Enos Mills, Clem Yore, L. E. Grace, and Stanley Hotel manager Alfred Lamborn placed another slate of candidates before the voters under the banner of the Taxpayer Party in an attempt to make the election a referendum on the issue. Although these men were community leaders and sent out a statement of their position, the response was negative. In the race for mayor, Citizen Party candidate Al Hayden received 157 votes to 8 for his challenger, justice of the peace Joseph. J. Duncan. The Taxpayer Party candidates for the three council positions fared somewhat better although in each case they were beaten by margins of more than two to one.

Its protest over, the Taxpayer Party did not make another appearance until March 1936, when it made no attempt to identify itself with its predecessor of fifteen years before. "There are no hard feelings connected with the formation of this party," its backers announced: "We simply want to give Estes Park the chance to hold an election on election day." Although the new party did not try to nominate a candidate for mayor, it did, as the *Trail* put it, upset "predictions of a quiet election."[71] If there was a distinction between "citizens" and "taxpayers" in a decidedly Republican town, it was one that the *Estes Park Trail* did not, or could not, describe. Estes Park residents were not impressed either: in the election the Citizens Party, "the old guard," won five of the six seats being contested. The lesson of those years, where local politics was concerned, seems clear. In a town whose interests were focussed on tourists and tourism, local government in Estes Park throughout the 1920s was perceived to work well, if at times by fit and starts.

~

Isolation helped. "Perhaps . . . being off the beaten path," the *Estes Park Trail* suggested as late as 1934, "gives us a feeling of unity that makes us work together better than most communities."[72] Except for a three-month period, running from roughly the first of June to the first of September when the town was filled with visitors, Estes Park was usually free to concentrate on its own affairs with little in the way of outside distraction. In times of national crisis and need, on the other hand, remoteness mattered little. In 1917 and again in 1941, Estes Park and its citizens responded like similar communities across the United States.

For Estes Park, as for the rest of the nation, the upheavals in Europe that began in 1914 initially seemed far away. The Denver papers, of course, were filled with war news, particularly the *Denver Post,* which indulged its love of sensationalism by illustrating its reporting with maps, photographs, and cartoons of the Kaiser and his Huns. During the years of neutrality, 1914 to 1917, most U.S. citizens chose to ignore the growing evidence of Germany's calculated outrages, preferring to enjoy the economic boom that accompanied "the last days of innocence." As one nation after another turned to the United States for food, particularly wheat, and for tungsten and molybdenum, the key ingredients for manufacturing steel and alloys, Colorado's farmers and miners prospered. So did Estes Park, where aided by the new national park the tourist business reached new records, encouraging the expansion of existing hotels and resorts and the building of new ones.

Wilson's declaration of war on April 6, 1917, gradually brought complacency to an end as the United States mobilized for war. Beginning that fall a million draftees and volunteers marched off to hastily constructed training camps, and before Armistice Day in November 1919 brought an end to it all, five million U.S. citizens had served in the military, including some 43,000 from the state of Colorado. No community was spared. Moreover, as Wilson and the government made clear from the beginning, the burden of winning the war, financially and otherwise, was one to be shouldered by the American people. In Estes Park, with its tradition of community support and volunteerism, the Wilson program for the war effort struck a responsive chord.

In spring and summer 1918, the town came together for war. By the end of June a local Council of Defense, chaired by Joe Mills, had been organized to protect property and conserve resources,[73] and park superintendent Louis Claude Way, a former army captain and war veteran, together with John Baker, "the champion rifle shot in the world," had begun to teach rifle marksmanship to local men subject to the draft, some sixty out of a population of 200, at a range constructed on the outskirts of town.[74] Not to be outdone, the older men of the village organized the Estes Park Guard, "designed along the lines of the state and national guard," and elected Captain Way to lead them. Julian Hayden and Lawrence E. Grace were chosen as first and second lieutenants. This home guard, which was soon converted to a National Guard unit as the supply company of the Third Colorado Infantry, numbered about forty, and included many of the village's best-known residents or members of their families.[75]

Enthusiasm ran high, and by late July guard members were planning to build a log armory, "modeled on the plan of one of the most famous frontier forts" and set "on a commanding eminence . . . surrounded by a stockade." Captain Way offered to supply the logs for the new building from the park,[76] with guard members pledging to do the construction. Not to be left out, some twenty patriotic village women organized themselves under the captaincy of Hattie Carruthers as the Women's Defense Club of Estes Park, said to be "the first of its kind to be formed in the United States."[77]

To the extent that homegrown patriotism needed encouragement, it came from the family of hatchery superintendent Gaylord Thomson, who sent three sons off to war—the twins Laurence and Clarence and their brother Homer. By early March 1918 Thomson was publishing their letters home in Loveland and Fort Collins newspapers, each bearing the careful marks of wartime censorship.[78] The letters from Laurence and Clarence Thomson graphically brought the war back to the mountains of Colorado. Laurence, a member of the Twentieth Colorado Company, Third Battalion of the Fifth American Expeditionary Force Regiment was badly wounded in the fighting at Belleau Woods in June 1918, an engagement long-remembered for its carnage. News of his injury made the front page of the *Loveland Daily Herald*.[79] Caught in machine gun fire in a wheat field—shot twice in the right leg and once in the left, splintering five inches of bone—young Thomson lay wounded for more than nine hours before being taken to a field hospital. Months of convalescence in a Paris hospital followed before he was well enough to be shipped home in November 1919 to face sixteen more operations. In June 1920 Laurence Thompson came back to Estes Park a war hero, well enough to celebrate by crossing Flattop Mountain to Grand Lake on crutches.[80]

His twin brother, Clarence, in France with the Marines, also had a story to tell. "Paris was surely great and I enjoyed it," he wrote home to his parents on July 3, 1918, "but what a sight we made; my uniform was so badly torn from trench life that where women were I had to keep my overcoat on." A victim of the infectious diseases that ravaged the Allied armies, Clarence spent twenty days in one military hospital with measles only to be quarantined in another for diphtheria.[81]

Not all letters back to Estes Park were so grim. Charles Hix, on leave from his job at the Estes Park Bank and serving with the American Expeditionary Force in France, wrote his mother on April 26, 1919, patriotically using AEF stationery, saying he had "gone to two dances this week. At one were French Mademoiselles and at the other Irish Y.M.C.A. canteen girls. The latter are from an English canteen about 25 kilometers for [sic] here."[82] The nineteen-year-old Hix does not mention if he danced but the dances were undoubtedly welcome distractions.

Most wartime activity in Estes Park was focused on the local chapter of the American Red Cross, which set up headquarters in a small building in the village. In deference to its needs, the Estes Park Woman's Club patriotically "abandoned the fundraising field" for the duration.[83] By the end of March 1918, through a series of teas, bazaars, and at least one recital, the women of the Red Cross were able to purchase and ship overseas more than $1,200 in supplies.[84] By early April that figure had surpassed $2,400—"none of the contributions coming from the summer population of rich tourists."[85] Others in the village aided the Red Cross by cutting and finishing garments to be sent to the war front, while the Ladies Aid of the church contributed hemmed bandages.[86]

Despite the war, summer of 1918 brought the usual influx of tourists. In June Charles Lester, proprietor of the Rustic Hotel in the north end, by then renamed Lester's Hotel, reported that the eighteen hotelmen of the park had signed an agreement to use no wheat flour during the coming season. Lester also offered the opinion that "there is a feeling that in these war conditions some at least of the wealthy want to get their families out of the busy world for a time," meaning, of course, that with the heat of summer, war or not, tourists would be back in Estes Park.[87]

Home front efforts were also financial. "Estes Park is ablaze with patriotic fire," the *Rocky Mountain News* reported on June 30, 1918.[88] Although
the statement smacks of the verbal excesses of the day, it is clear that village
residents rose to the task of financing the war. As J. Edward Macdonald
recalled in 1923,

> To the first loan [which carried a 3.5-percent tax-exempt return] we
> subscribed $6,000 before Uncle Sam had a chance to ask for it. The
> second loan we were given a quota of $10,000 and every one said we
> could never make it and the answer was $12,500. For the third . . . our
> quota was $15,000 and we subscribed $21,000. Uncle Sam thought he
> had us stumped when he gave us $30,000 for the fourth loan and we
> didn't do a thing to that, only $42,500. . . . And of the War Savings
> Stamps we only absorbed about two or three times as many as our
> quota.[89]

Funds in smaller amounts were raised as well. In April 1918 a Thrift
Stamp dance was held at the Odd Fellows Hall. That evening 38 five-dollar
War Savings Stamps were sold, together with 144 twenty-five-cent Thrift
Stamps. The admission fee was four Thrift Stamps with a five-dollar War
Savings Stamp entitling the purchaser "to all the dances of the evening."[90]
The Liberty Loan program of which Ed Macdonald speaks was deliberately
aimed at the well off and financial institutions. Its success in Estes Park
attests to the fact that by 1918 many residents had become prosperous, even
affluent, a prosperity they were patriotically willing to share.

By summer 1919 the war was over, and life in the United States and
Estes Park had begun to return to something resembling normalcy. Once
again the Woman's Club was ready. Because "so many summer visitors . . .
regretted the lack of summer activities" by early July the club announced
that for the coming season it had organized a program of "remarkable entertainment for tourists":

> card parties will be given at the beautiful Estes Park Golf and Country
> club, Stead's old-time cowboy dance will once more hold sway and a
> regular camp fire fish fry will be held. An Indian play written by Miss
> Anna Wolfrom will be staged outdoors with the mountains for back-
> ground and the river and meadow for setting. A nature talk on the
> Rocky Mountain national park, illustrated by his natural colored
> photography, will be given by Joe Mills.[91]

The season began with a two-day celebration over the Fourth of July weekend, during which the town hosted an elaborate reception for returning
soldiers on behalf of all of Larimer County. It was, according to the *Loveland
Daily Herald*, "the biggest celebration Northern Colorado has ever seen."

Despite inclement weather, a crowd of between eight and nine thousand crowded into the village to watch an elaborate program that included a military parade up Elkhorn; speeches; races of various kinds, including a free-for-all climbing contest on Oldman Mountain; and a performance of "fancy shooting" by Johnny Baker, all culminating in a reception and "Welcome Home" ball at the Odd Fellows Hall. "The road to Estes Park was lined with autos from early morning. . . . The hotels were crowded to capacity, and you were lucky to find a place to eat . . . and the campgrounds were crowded to overflowing."[92] As the weekend made clear, the war was over, and as in years past there would be no "slow time" in Estes Park.

Chapter 5

~~

Rocky Mountain National Park: The First Years

E VEN BEFORE THE OFFICIAL DEDICATION CEREMONIES in Horseshoe Park the new national park had begun to organize itself under acting supervisor Charles Russell Trowbridge (1865–1937).[1] Like many other early superintendents, Trowbridge, a native of New York, had a military background. A veteran of the Philippine insurrection during the Spanish-American War, Trowbridge had chosen a career in government. For some years he worked with the Secret Service and then, in 1913, became one of eight "inspectors" assigned by the Department of the Interior to keep an eye on its far-flung activities, including the nation's thirteen parks. Trowbridge arrived in Estes Park on July 1, 1915, with a first-year appropriation of $3,000,[2] but without ranger or support staff. Although Trowbridge loved the outdoors, he knew little about park management. He knew even less about the wilderness area of which he was now in charge. Having located space in the village for summer headquarters and purchased furniture and fixtures, Trowbridge opened his office on July 10. He then set off by horseback to inspect roads, trails, and in-holdings.

Although Trowbridge had been selected because of his previous performance in the field,[3] his was not an easy assignment. With the post came an unusual set of conditions. In their eagerness to get the much-delayed legisla-

5.1 Park supervisor Charles Russell Trowbridge, 1915–1916. Courtesy National Park Service–Rocky Mountain National Park

tion through Congress, its supporters had accepted the arbitrary provision limiting total park expenditures for "maintenance, supervision, and improvement" to $10,000 per year. Although Colorado representative Edward Taylor explained that the amendment was "merely precautionary, . . . owing to the present financial condition of the country," and that $10,000 "will in all probability be sufficient for the maintenance of the park for several years to come,"[4] such a sum barely covered the salaries of Trowbridge and his rangers and left little or nothing to address the needs of the area Trowbridge was now called upon to supervise.

In the glow of victory, supporters like Enos Mills tried to put the best face on the matter. When questioned closely by Charles Boynton of the *Longmont Ledger* in March 1915, Mills appeared satisfied. "No roads can be constructed until surveys are made," he told Boynton, "and it will take a good deal of surveying to lay out the roads which are wanted. . . . Next year they may ask for $100,000 and get it."[5] Although this was, no doubt, a reasonable expectation, these were not reasonable times. Not only were troubles brewing in Mexico and Haiti and a war in Europe, but in some congressional minds the appropriation for the new national park in Colorado quickly became identified with the state's apparent unwillingness to complete the Fall River Road to Middle Park. The restriction on funding remained in force until March 1, 1919, when, thanks to intense lobbying efforts by Colorado interests, it was repealed by Congress. Even then, park officials had to wait for the beginning of the new budget year for the additional funding.

As a result, for the better part of five years, Trowbridge and his successor were forced to make do with budgets that allowed for little more than the status quo. Given that fact, it was perhaps fortunate that the 358.5 square miles making up Rocky Mountain National Park were far less than the nearly 1,000 square miles for which Enos Mills had originally campaigned. They were was also substantially less than the 700 square miles that Robert B. Marshall of the U.S. Geological Survey had recommended in his January 1913 feasibility report. The challenges facing Trowbridge were nonetheless formidable: how to administer with limited resources the entire wilderness area between Estes Park and the village of Grand Lake some sixteen miles across the Continental Divide.

As Trowbridge quickly learned, only five miles of the fifty-five miles of roads within the park fell under federal jurisdiction; the rest belonged to the state or county. Moreover, these roads, built by pioneers over four decades, were almost all in fair to bad condition. Some, in fact, were little more than wagon roads, like the one to the "Pole Patch," the area of lodgepole pine near Mill Creek, over which local residents hauled out timber. Existing roads included the road constructed by Abner Sprague from the grounds of the YMCA encampment to his resort on Glacier Creek, some mile and a half in length, running parallel to the creek; a private road extending two miles beyond Sprague's to within a mile of Bear Lake; and a road into Wild Basin that began near Copeland Lake and extended into the park for approximately a mile and a half. This road from Copeland Lake, "passable for horse-drawn vehicles only," led to the Wild Basin trail system. It had been built a decade before by the Arbuckle Reservoir Company in order to develop reservoirs at Pear and Bluebird Lakes. There was also the Beaver Creek Road, starting at the High Drive (above what is now Beaver Point) and extending about a mile and a quarter into the park, built around 1910 to remove timber. The park road in the best condition was, ironically, not in the vicinity of Estes Park at all, but on the far less frequented west side of the park, extending a mile and half north of the village of Grand Lake, recently completed by Grand County using convict labor.[6]

Of greatest interest and concern to Trowbridge was the much-publicized Fall River Road being constructed by the State of Colorado. By 1915 this road, designed to provide the long-sought direct link between Estes Park and Middle Park, already had a lengthy and troubled history. The idea of building such a road had been talked about since at least the mid-1880s and for a brief time in 1892–1893 seemed likely to become a reality when Abner Sprague was hired to locate a road from Loveland to Middle Park by way of the Big Thompson Canyon and Fall River. Milner Pass, where both Fall River Road and, later, Trail Ridge Road would cross the Continental Divide, recalled an even earlier transmountain route. It was named for railroad engineer T. J. Milner, who in 1881 surveyed the area for a route to the Pacific that would run up through Fall River Pass, around the Poudre Lakes to Milner Pass, and then west into Utah.[7]

Although the first section of route surveyed by Sprague became a reality in 1904 with the county's completion of the road up the Big Thompson Canyon, it took almost another decade for work on the extension up Fall River to begin. It was, moreover, a modest start. In summer 1913, following the acceptance of a petition by landowners deeding the previously surveyed right-of-way, Larimer County commissioners finally approved the first mile and three-quarters of "a new public highway" in Horseshoe Park.[8]

The commissioners' action was immediately controversial. It came in the face of an injunction previously granted by the district court in Fort Collins on behalf of a group of Larimer citizens who insisted that any road to Middle Park must be built by way of the Poudre River, arguing their case in terms of the economic benefits that such a route would bring the county.[9] The commissioners, for their part, dodged the issue by insisting that they were simply acting on the merits of the local constituents' petition, which applied only to the first mile and three-quarters of the proposed road and not the entire route across the Divide.

Construction began that August, with the arrival of thirty-eight convicts from the Colorado State Prison at Cañon City (state warden "Tom Tynan's Boys"). The men, who were housed in a series of crude log cabins built in Endovalley, had been made available to the county under an 1899 state law permitting convicted felons to shorten their sentences for good behavior while constructing roads—an experiment, its proponents argued, that increased highway dollars through the use of free labor while exerting "the moral and physical influence upon the convicts of an outdoor life and a camp managed entirely on the honor system."[10]

By early September 1913, making use of horses, the convicts had completed some 3,000 feet of road. Most of this was "easy work" that simply followed the existing trail to the log homestead erected by Dan and Minnie March in 1911 and enlarged the following year, located not far from today's Lawn Lake Trailhead. Although camp superintendent Thomas Lancaster announced that his crews had now reached "difficult rock work," he still expected to be finished "before snow flies." Even by 1913 standards the taxpayers of Larimer County were getting their money's worth: "The total cost per capita," a paper in Fort Collins reported, "was 75 cents per day."[11] Fortunately for Lancaster, the weather remained good into December. Nevertheless, the hard granite encountered in September slowed the work appreciably and so greatly increased the cost that on December 23, with four feet of snow already on the ground, the chairman of the board of commissioners ordered the convicts off the road and withdrew the county from the project because available funds were not only exhausted but overdrawn by $600.[12]

Meanwhile, in an attempt to resolve the issue of the injunction and the "unpleasantness" it had created, political negotiations between state and county officials were taking place, and by the end of the year a compromise thought satisfactory to Colorado governor Elias M. Ammons had been proposed. Both the Fall River and Poudre Canyon Roads would be completed, with the expense shared by county and state: the county would provide $7,600 for the Fall River Road and half the cost of the road up the Poudre Canyon, then estimated at $30,000.[13]

Although final ratification of the agreement did not come until the first week of February 1914, by January Superintendent Lancaster's men were back on the job. Given the winter hardships, with an unprecedented snowfall—the December blizzard of 1913—that left remnants on the ground until June, work continued to be slow. "Cold weather with deep snow and high winds drifting the snow kept the men from hitting the rock and dirt and when they did work they found it hard."[14] Despite these conditions, an additional 1,200 feet of road was built. This was progress, yet by late March not more than a mile of new road had been completed west of the March homestead.[15] The arrival of spring and summer helped. Governor Ammons inspected the road in June and expressed his enthusiasm. By late July the road had reached Upper Horseshoe Falls (or Chasm Falls as it was by then known),[16] while on the west or Grand Lake side the Forest Service had allocated $3,000 to begin work on the connecting road north of the village, making use of part of the old wagon road to the abandoned mining camp of Lulu City on the banks of the Grand (Colorado) River.[17] Construction work on the road's eastern section continued until late October 1914 when the convict camp was shifted to the Poudre. Here matters stood when Trowbridge arrived the following summer.

The acting supervisor was dismayed. Work on the road was continuing under a $18,000 state contract that had begun on July 2, but at the time he wrote his annual report for 1915 in early fall, the road-head remained somewhere in the vicinity of Chasm Falls. Still, Trowbridge noted, the contractor expected that he would complete his work by November and reach the county road above Grand Lake. What bothered Trowbridge was not only the slow progress but the condition of the two-mile portion already "completed." Although in "fair condition," he wrote,

> It is entirely too narrow, in some places being only 8 and 10 feet in width. The point known as the second "switch back" which is reached

by a 12% grade, was not sufficiently wide for the average vehicle to change direction without a "see saw" movement which made the point extremely dangerous, there being no protection to prevent a vehicle from going over the embankment.[18]

The convicts, as it turned out, had constructed no culverts to restrain erosion, and now these needed to be added at certain grades. Trowbridge, in short, found the completed portion decidedly problematic, and he recommended to the Department of the Interior that it halt work and undertake a new survey of the entire route because "the survey which was made in 1912, was a preliminary survey only."[19] That summer Trowbridge personally went over the Fall River Road some ten times to learn firsthand what he could. In his annual report for 1915, he recommended not only the new survey but that $50,000 in supplemental federal funds be appropriated for the road's completion.[20]

Trowbridge also spent considerable time evaluating the existing 128.5-mile trail system that made accessible most of the "interesting parts of the National Park." By 1915 techniques of trail building were well established and, fortunately, several of the major trails were new and thus in relatively good condition. These included the Bierstadt Lake and Storm Pass Trails, which intersected at Glacier Creek and extended 1.5 miles and 4 miles respectively. Both had been built by the Forest Service in 1914. There was also the 6.5-mile trail, leading from Moraine Park past Fern and Odessa Lakes to Lake Helene, also built in 1914 with contributions from local resort owners; and the 3.5-mile trail from Glacier Basin to Loch Vale, constructed in 1913 by members of the EPPIA. Most of the park's other trails, like the roads, were in need of repair and reconstruction.[21]

Trowbridge was not alone in this concern. The citizens of Estes Park remained vitally interested in the progress of "their park" and were not shy to offer their opinions. The main problem with the trail system, Pieter Hondius told the *Rocky Mountain News* in January 1916, is that most of the existing trails are Western trails, which "Eastern people cannot follow" because their only signage or "indication of a direction" is " a blaze on a tree or some other mark that only can be followed by experienced woodsmen." What was needed in the park, he explained, were "Eastern Trails, five feet in width, built for safety and comfort."[22]

Trowbridge was well aware that part of his assignment was to establish a base line for future park development. As a result, he was determined to make his 1915 annual report, which he submitted only a month after the park's dedication, as comprehensive as possible. To that end he visited and surveyed the condition of each of the four existing ranger stations built by the Forest Service. The closest station was at Mill Creek and the other three were located on the Fall River Road, some five miles inside the park and about half a mile from what was then the road's terminus; on the Flattop Trail, eleven miles from Grand Lake and fifteen miles from Estes Park; and at Poudre Lakes near Milner Pass. Only two of the buildings, he discovered, were even partially furnished, making them useful only for emergencies.

Trowbridge also visited the park's private resorts. These in-holdings included the tent and cabin camps run by the Higby brothers (Cliff, Reed, and Lester) at Fern Lake and the Pool on the upper Big Thompson River, the latter consisting of only two walled tents, one of them with a cookstove, used by travelers on their way to Fern Lake and beyond; Abner Sprague's lodge on Glacier Creek and its adjacent twenty acres of man-made trout ponds; the small cabin resort that Willard Ashton operated for camping and fishing parties at Lawn Lake; and Timberline Cabin, on the Longs Peak Trail below Jim's Grove, built by Enos Mills in 1908. There was also the small resort camp at Bear Lake, then still considered remote, operated by A. E. Brown. "In my opinion," Trowbridge subsequently wrote, "the rates heretofore made by the Forest Service for permits for resorts were entirely too small." In 1915 these ranged between $10 and $25 for the season.[23]

In addition Trowbridge somehow found time to put together a rough appraisal of the park's wildlife. The deer and elk populations, he estimated, numbered herds of 600 and 30. Beaver were "plentiful" and "the big horn sheep are found in considerable numbers and some of them are exceptionally tame, tourists having approached within a few yards them." "From what information I have been able to obtain," Trowbridge added, "the increase for the last year has been exceptionally large."[24] Although he had no idea of their numbers, Trowbridge also noted that there were mountain lions and coyotes roaming the park and "if they increase to any extent, will become a detriment to the preservation of other animals, when action will be necessary looking toward their destruction."[25] Common black bears, on the other hand, were "only a few" and posed no threat.

Because of limited time and manpower Trowbridge could not survey and report on the existing irrigation reservoirs in Wild Basin and the irrigation ditches scattered throughout the park, many of which were held in the name of private parties and corporations. The same was true of "several so-called mineral claims," the largest of which was the Eugenia Mine on Battle Mountain.[26]

Help arrived on August 10, 1915, a month before the park's scheduled dedication, with the hiring of Richard T. ("Dixie") McCracken, a twenty-two-year-old structural engineer from Washington, D.C. McCracken was no stranger to Estes Park. His father, Robert McCracken, was the brother-in-law of Frank Crocker and had a summer home near the Crocker Ranch. In Dixie McCracken's telling, his decision to apply for a job as ranger was some-thing of a whim. "In my younger days," he recalled in July 1959, "I had shinnied up and down the mountains all the way from the Mummy Range to the south of Longs Peak and when this park was being talked of being cre-ated I thought I ought to be pretty good at living up there and because of my love for the mountains I decided to apply for the job. Much to my surprise, after a few months I was notified by the government that I was appointed ranger in the National Park."[27]

McCracken was soon joined by two other men, Frank Koenig and Reed Higby, to fill out Trowbridge's ranger staff of three. None had much in the way of preparation or training. In the years before the park service began to professionalize the ranger corps, rangers were selected for their practical ex-perience in outdoor life and for their ability to demonstrate a variety of frontier skills, including the ability to work long hours and endure hardships in remote and difficult places. From their annual salary of $900, each man had to pay for the feed and maintenance of his horse. These salaries, Trowbridge knew—the same salary paid to year-round assistants at Yellowstone more than thirty years earlier—were much too low for the kind of work the job required, let alone to attract the type of individual that Stephen Mather wanted to bring into the national parks. But until the establishment and organization of the National Park Service to regulate such matters, all that supervisors like Trowbridge could do was to make suggestions.

To his credit, he tried. "There are only three rangers provided for this park at a salary of $900.00 per annum," he reminded his superiors in his annual report, "which salary, I do not consider sufficient to attract the right kind of men, for this class of labor. This is an expensive locality to live [in]."[28] Fortunately McCracken and Higby were local boys with friends and family nearby.

For most assignments undertaken that first summer and fall—which included the posting of rules and regulations, fire warning signs, and bound-ary markers and the supervising and general policing of some 350 square miles—the size of Trowbridge's ranger force was just barely adequate. In times of emergencies like forest fires, however, there was risk of being overwhelmed. Early on Trowbridge struck a deal with the residents of Estes Park, offering them continued free access to the fire-killed and dead-and-down timber of the Pole Patch "with the understanding that they are to volunteer their services when necessary to suppress forest fires."[29] As a result when a fire broke out in Hidden Valley on Halloween night 1915 in the sawdust pile of an abandoned sawmill, a band of citizens, which the *Rocky Mountain News*

5.2 Dixie MacCracken, first park ranger, on the Fern Lake Trail. Courtesy National Park Service–Rocky Mountain National Park

estimated numbered more than a hundred, seeing a glow in the sky and massive clouds of smoke billowing eastward, left their partying and rushed in evening clothes and costumes to fight the fire. "There in the light of the fire the bizarre costumes of the masqueraders mingled strangely with the uniforms of the foresters, the evening clothing of men and women," the News reported the next day in a page-one story. "Romeo and Satan worked side by side with the kaiser [sic] and a Chinese dragon."[30] The fire at Hidden Valley burned for nearly twenty-four hours, leaving some 400 to 500 acres of spruce and pine timber "a barren stretch of charred ashes." By the following evening, aided by a shift in the wind, the blaze had been contained, and "a ragged, blackened band, dressed in ruined panoply of Halloween, came straggling back to Estes Park."[31]

Supervisor Trowbridge was just as fortunate the following Fourth of July, when shortly after noon a careless motorist started a fire by throwing firecrackers into the forest near Lily Lake. A call for help was put out and quickly responded to. Among the first to arrive on the scene were Mrs. John D. Sherman—by now conservation chairman of the General Federation of Women's Clubs, who was making her home on what is now Wind River

Ranch—and novelist Edna Ferber, who came down from Longs Peak Inn where she was a regular summer guest. They were soon joined by Charles Mace, who with his brother Gordon had homesteaded across the road near the future site of Baldpate Inn; Enos Mills; and C. R. Trowbridge. "Only prompt action by a large group of volunteers," the *Rocky Mountain News* observed five days later, "prevented . . . [the fire] from sweeping over a wide territory and doing great damage."[32]

To Trowbridge's satisfaction, local support for the park remained strong. In October 1915, the month after the dedication, residents staged a mass meeting at the Hupp Hotel that sent Enos Mills off to Washington armed with three petitions, one of which asked Congress for an appropriation of $125,000 to be spent on roads and trails through Rocky Mountain National Park. The two others were of equal local importance. One requested that the administrative offices of the national park remain in the village of Estes Park rather than be relocated to Fort Collins (as had apparently been rumored); the other that Gem Lake, the tops of the Twin Sisters and Deer Mountain, and the heavily wooded Miller Fork region, the natural northern boundary of Estes Park, be brought within park boundaries. On two of these fronts Mills and his supporters in Estes Park were successful. Headquarters for Rocky Mountain National Park remained in Estes Park and on February 14, 1917, 25,265 acres, although not the area surrounding Miller Fork, were added to the park.

On August 14, 1916, Trowbridge was replaced by Louis Claude Way (1877–1943). Although Way, like his predecessor, was a military man, a veteran of the Spanish-American War, he brought to his new assignment considerable managerial and forestry experience. Way had served as a Forest Service ranger in the Santa Catalina Forest north of Tucson, in a forest preserve on the Mexican border, and, most recently, at the Grand Canyon National Monument, which he had supervised for the previous three years. He had been recommended by Stephen Mather's personable young deputy Horace Albright, who had taken time from his honeymoon at the Grand Canyon in December 1915 to mush through the snow to visit with the ranger and his wife in their rustic cabin. Way made a favorable impression, and when the time came to appoint a permanent superintendent, the thirty-nine-year-old Way got the post.[33] His appointment initially carried the title of Chief Ranger in Charge—a title changed a year later, once the new National Park Service had been organized and funded, to Superintendent.

5.3 *Chief ranger in charge and superintendent Lewis Claude Way, 1916–1921. Courtesy National Park Service–Rocky Mountain National Park*

Captain Way, like his predecessor, was strapped for funds, and despite evidence of Rocky Mountain National Park's increasing popularity, when it came to both repairing and improving park infrastructure, Way found his options limited. For fiscal year 1917, for example, after putting aside $7,440 for salaries and $1,042 for livery and office expenses, Way's budget contained only $300 for the construction of a single new three-mile trail, $918 for the repair and maintenance of existing trails, $100 for repair and maintenance of telephone lines, and $200 for fighting forest fires. That same year, by contrast, Way's counterpart at the far smaller and less-visited Mesa Verde National Park had $83,568.20 to spend, including $8,000 to erect a new administration building and museum.

It would later be charged that Way brought with him an authoritarian style that at times smacked of arrogance and that he often failed to communicate with Estes Park residents on matters having to do with the park and park policy.[34] Such allegations, which arose principally during the transportation controversy that dogged Way's final years, were probably unfair. The record indicates in fact that quite the opposite was true: by every indication Way was an energetic and capable administrator who took up his new assignment with enthusiasm, determined to engage the citizens of Estes Park in the same spirit of cooperation as his predecessor.

Like Trowbridge, Way spent his first several months on the job actively surveying the park to learn firsthand all he could about the area under his jurisdiction. On these reconnaissance journeys, carefully documented in his monthly reports, Captain Way was sometimes accompanied by his wife, a

5.4 Rocky Mountain National Park, first administrative office in Estes Park village, July 27, 1923. Courtesy National Park Service–Rocky Mountain National Park

noted horsewoman, who gained local notoriety in her own right through her encounter with a "certain famous movie star, whose chief stock in trade as an actor . . . [was] his ability to ride horses and do fancy 'stunts' in the saddle." The visitor made the mistake of challenging Mrs. Way to a 16-mile race from Grand Lake to Estes Park over the notorious Flattop Mountain Trail. Unknown to the actor, the vivacious and beautiful Mrs. Way had once been a trick rider for Buffalo Bill's Wild West Show and routinely made the trip across Flattop in five hours. "When they pulled into Estes park, Mrs. Way in the lead, the movie actor was as limp as a rag, his horse was played out, and he ached in every bone, while Mrs. Way and her mount were fresh and strong and ready to start over."[35]

Way proved a quick study. By late November 1916 when he visited Denver for the first time since his appointment, Way had learned enough about the park to formulate a number of priorities that he willingly shared with a writer for the *Denver Times.* As might be expected, road improvement—both widening the access roads to the park and completing Fall River Road to the Grand Valley—was high on his agenda. So too was the park's trail system. "Above all," Way told the *Times,* "trails must be broken to allow the sightseer to penetrate on foot into the fastnesses of the hills. Too much emphasis

. . . cannot be laid on the importance of making every corner of the park accessible to the pedestrian."[36]

There was also the matter of winter sports, an activity that his predecessor had largely ignored, but one which Secretary of the Interior Franklin Lane would shortly make clear to Mather that he wished to see implemented, where practical, as park policy.[37] "I am developing the idea of using the park in winter," Way expansively told his interviewer, clearly warming to the subject.

> We are putting in two ski courses at Fern Lake. . . . There is room for every kind of winter sport, snow-shoeing, tobogganing and hockey, and the air is never too cold. Why, we play golf all winter in Estes Park. When I get the program of winter sports arranged we expect to make the park one of the best-known winter resorts on the continent.

During his interview, Way also touched on the issue of concessions in a discussion that reveals that the new chief ranger was a man with strong opinions:

> There has been a lot of discussion about establishing concessionaires in the park. . . . I went thru the free-for-all system at the Grand canon [sic] and found that concessions which you can regulate, fix charges for and hold to their responsibilities are best. . . . With a concession you can fix rates and require enough equipment in horses and machines to accommodate all who come.[38]

Way was clearly not press-shy where park matters were concerned and, in the months that followed, anyone in Estes Park claiming that they did not know what Captain Way was up to, or why, simply had not read the *Denver Times*.

The next month, during another interview in Denver, he went to some lengths to correct "statements made by various persons" that there were no suitable sites "within the big playground" for new tourist hotels. By way of illustration he suggested three: one in Horseshoe Park to take advantage of the new Fall River Road; a second in Wild Basin, near the junction of Cony Creek and the North St. Vrain (apparently in the vicinity of Calypso Cascades); and a third at Bear Lake. The Wild Basin site, he suggested, would provide access to a "section of the country . . . of especial beauty" that "few tourists have visited . . . because of the lack of accommodation," while a hotel at Bear Lake would open up the Glacier Gorge country, "including Black and Blue lakes, a region of unexcelled wildness and beauty . . . considered by some the most beautiful region within the national park."[39]

As Way had suggested to the reporter for the *Denver Times*, the maddening delays in completing the Fall River Road, whose construction was by now into its fourth year, had become a chronic concern. Problems continued. Three miles of new road had been constructed in 1915, and by spring 1916 $42,326 had been spent on the thirty-six-mile project, the lion's share, more than $31,000, coming from the state under the agreement hammered out with Governor Ammons two years before. Despite high expectations, progress nevertheless remained frustratingly slow, so much so that in May of that year, in response to a letter of inquiry, state highway commissioner Thomas J. Ehrhart confirmed that only 7.5 miles of road had been completed on the eastern side and that an additional $91,000 would be necessary to finish the remaining 28 miles—fully $79,500 more than the State of Colorado had appropriated for that purpose.[40] Complicating the matter, even after the new survey completed in 1916, was the lingering threat of injunction proceedings by some Larimer County residents if further attempts were made to expend state funds on a road within the park.[41]

Alarmed at the prospect of yet more delay if state dollars alone were to be used, the Denver Civic and Commercial Association through its Good Roads Committee mounted an attempt to gain $25,000 in federal dollars to finish the job. Before preparing a draft bill to be submitted in Congress by members of the state delegation, the committee, which included Denver tourist-conscious mayor Robert Speer, wisely decided to solicit Mather's views on the likelihood that such legislation would be approved. Mather's response came within two weeks and was politely negative. "I do not see how the department of the interior can, in any way, do anything toward facilitating the progress of the construction work," Mather told them, citing as justification the "understanding . . . given . . . by the governor of Colorado [at the time of the park bill] that the state would build the Fall River road out of its own funds and that no demand would be made for a federal appropriation to aid this project."[42] Lest there be any mistake about federal intentions on the matter, on May 20, 1916, Mather gave Way "verbal instructions" that Fall River was to be "considered a State road until completed and that no park funds were to be expended for maintenance."[43] Given such circumstances, further delays became inevitable.

Thanks to pressure from concerned groups like the Denver Civic and Commercial Association, substantial progress was made by the state during 1917 with vague, although no doubt sincere, promises that the road would be completed the following year. Compared to the previous two years "in which no additional mileage was opened to the public, and very little rock work done," Way wrote in his annual report,

> Work on the Fall River Road above Horseshoe Park has progressed
> rapidly. . . . This year . . . the completed portion has been extended a

little over a mile above the road end of this spring, and four to six weeks' work will complete the road to Chapin Creek Pass. Work on the Western Slope has also made rapid progress this year, and two or three week's work should carry the completed road-way to Poudre Lakes, leaving from four to seven miles, (depending upon which route is accepted) of way upon which no work has been done, to connect up Eastern with Western ends.[44]

On the Western Slope, the 1917 contract called for the construction of a five-and-a-half-mile section extending from the North Fork of the Colorado River to the Poudre Lakes. The contractor was Richard W. McQueary of Granby, who began his work with a crew of thirty men and sixteen teams. The work was laborious, most of it accomplished by hand with shovels, picks, and augers. Explosives were used, and this too required a great deal of hard drilling to place the charges. Despite Way's optimism, by late November only two miles had been completed. "My work has been most difficult," McQueary told the *Denver Post*. "First there was a shortage in men and then when we did get the men there were many natural obstacles to overcome, such as walling up portions of the road with granite to furnish a suitable roadbed and protection at the turns."[45] If he needed further proof of the difficulty of his task, McQueary added, he had only to lift his eyes from the foot of Milner Pass and survey the seven rugged switchbacks above him, all completed that season.

By summer 1918, the project's end was still nowhere in sight. Base camps were established by breaking through deep snow drifts in June, and an enlarged force of workmen was soon at work cutting trees and removing the rubble of large boulders that had been dynamited. Construction on the roadbed moved forward, and with McQueary and his men finally approaching Poudre Lakes, a critical decision had to be made on how the two ends, then still some seven miles apart, should be connected above timberline. The original route laid out by Grand County surveyor Frank Huntington called for the road to follow the old Forest Service trail and continue by way of Chapin Pass, down Chapin Creek, to a junction with the Cache la Poudre River. The road would then follow the river to the Divide at Poudre Lakes and Milner Pass. This route, covering a distance of nine miles, would allow a future extension to the Poudre River Road and access to Fort Collins.

But equally feasible was the higher and more scenic six-mile route over Fall River Pass. On August 10, 1918, in an effort to decide, a party from the Denver Civic and Commercial Association was taken over the road. "Mr. Enos Mills talks for upper route," Way noted in his monthly report; "Mr. [Roe] Emery and myself for either upper or lower. . . . I making it plain that we are not advocating either one route or another, but that we want a road across the continental Divide at the earliest possible date, regardless of which route is chosen."[46] The visitors from Denver, according to Way, were "unanimously in favor of the upper route."[47] Mills, forever an advocate for scenery, who as early as 1913 had gone on record with his belief that automobiles were better than horses for seeing the outdoors, felt strongly enough about the "Highline" route, as it was called, to travel to Washington to lobby on its behalf.

Although Way claimed neutrality, the National Park Service quickly made up its mind. Within weeks Director Mather had received a report from his assistant and confidante Horace Albright, who had been dispatched to Colorado to "study" some of the park's problems, recommending the Highline route. "This . . . very scenic route . . . is according to all accounts, the best route from every other standpoint," Mather wrote in his 1918 annual report.

> The alternate route, and the one selected by the State, follows Chapin Creek down a wooded valley to its junction with the Cache la Poudre River, thence it follows this larger stream through its wooded valley to Poudre Lakes. This route is longer than the other, it has no scenic qualities worthy of mention, it will cost more to build the road on this survey, and it will be very expensive to maintain after it is constructed.[48]

Mather also suggested, as a way of mollifying northern Colorado, that the Department of the Interior "vigorously prosecute" the development of a road linking the Fall River Road to the road up Poudre Canyon using Chapin Pass, making "possible the circle trip through the park between Estes Park and Fort Collins."[49] This would also, Mather well knew, give Fort Collins its long-desired road to Middle Park.

The issue of Highline or Lowline almost immediately generated new controversy, with the State Highway Commission arguing that the Fall River Pass route would cost an additional $50,000 to construct despite the fact that it was three miles shorter. The decision in favor of the Highline, which the *Denver Post* attributed to Mills's lobbying,[50] came from Washington on November 26, 1918, in a letter from Secretary of the Interior Lane to Colorado Governor Gunter. "Construction work . . . has been conducted very slowly," Lane told the governor, clearly betraying frustration and annoyance.

> Nearly four years have passed since the park was created, and the road is still quite far from completion. Each year some work has been done, and invariably promises have been made that the following year would see the highway finished. A year ago we were assured that the last link would be built this year, and that automobiles could cross the park in

August at the latest. It now appears that at least another working season must be utilized to finish the project and perhaps longer. I can only infer from the delay that the state is taking slight interest in the Fall River road and that other projects are being advanced while this important highway not only remains incomplete, but actually falls into a serious state of disrepair.

It has been the policy of the department to patiently wait the connecting of the sides of the park by this much needed thorofare, [sic] and to refrain from insisting upon any changes in route or construction plans or in other directions advising a course of action by the state. The time is at hand, however, when we must insist that the Fall River road be rushed to completion and that it follow the shorter and more scenic route across the Mummy range and the north end of the Trail ridge to Poudre lakes.[51]

Lane concluded by asking for Gunter's "assurance" that the road would be completed in 1919 "along the route that the government has approved," which, he pointedly noted, would "place Rocky Mountain national park in an entirely different light" when asking the appropriation committee to remove the $10,000 limitation on park funding.

Colorado's response came two weeks later with news that the State Highway Commission had recommended to the governor that $150,000 be appropriated for 1919 to improve the Big Thompson Canyon Road and complete the Fall River Road over the Highline route.[52] In June Mather visited Denver, where he received fresh assurances that Fall River Road would be completed by September. Although substantial progress was made that summer despite a labor shortage caused by the war in Europe, by fall 1919 the two ends of the road still had not reached Fall River Pass. "While it is disappointing that this road will not be completed this fall, according to promise," Way wrote in his annual report, "the work has been pushed vigorously." The contractors, he noted, were now estimating a completion date of July 15, 1920, by which time state highway commissioner Elmer E. Sommers had promised to "place the entire road in first-class condition, before asking the Government to accept [it]."[53]

The contractors were wrong again. July 1920 came and went and by early September, with the road still incomplete, the chief engineer reported that given the size of the crew at his disposal and the imminent approach of winter weather the road could not be finished that season. Highway Commission Chairman Sommers was now clearly on the spot over what appeared to be yet another round of promises proved empty. He immediately ordered additional crews into the field and by the end of September 1920, the road to Grand Lake was at long last a reality. On September 14, 1920, in anticipation of the event, contractor McQueary drove his car from Grand Lake to Estes Park. That same day Captain Way made the journey in the opposite direction, negotiating with some difficulty the "long and deep mud holes" that left the last five miles before Grand Lake still "in deplorable condition." From Grand Lake village, Way continued on to Denver by way of Berthoud Pass before returning to Estes Park, having completed what would soon become known as the 240-mile "Circle Route."

Public events helped to dedicate the new road. On Saturday, September 27, 1920, McQueary hosted a fish fry on top of the range, on a stretch as "straight as a gun barrel," for state and county officials and invited guests.[54] McQueary followed this with a second celebration on the sagebrush flat west of Grand Lake, where a large crowd enjoyed still another a fish fry, this time with a rodeo and baseball game added. Two days later, on September 29, Superintendent Way and a party of businessmen made "the first official motor car trip" in four automobiles provided by the Rocky Mountain Parks Transportation Company, repeating his circle trip of two weeks before "without trouble."[55]

Some of the curious could not wait. Even before these official events, Loveland merchant C. B. Powell, with wife and daughter, and accompanied by Mark Ellison, publisher of the *Loveland Daily Herald*, and his wife, made the first private automobile trip. Powell negotiated his big Haynes automobile over the double-tracked road "without difficulty and without a mishap or slightest damage to the car," despite encountering a heavy hailstorm at Poudre Lakes on the return trip. Ellison confirmed Way's enthusiastic predictions of the previous four years of what the road would mean to the park and its visitors:

> It is difficult to describe the beauty and the scenic wonderland of the
> new highway, starting at Horseshoe park, and climbing up the valley
> over sixteen switchbacks until you reach the summit of the range, at
> nearly 12,000 feet. The Grand valley, as viewed from the summit, is one
> of the most inspiring that can be found in any country and in many ways
> equals, if not surpasses, any view from this side. . . . A trip over this
> wonderful highway will bring many far nearer Heaven than most
> mortals get here on earth. . . . Viewed from the top of the range, just
> before you descend to the valley floor, over twenty-six switch backs, the
> coloring of the landscape in connection with the Poudre lakes and the
> headwaters of that river, together with the beaver dams and smaller lakes
> which furnish waters for the Grand river are beyond description.[56]

This was but the first of such descriptions. Some early travelers like *Longmont Ledger* editor Charles Boynton, who made the trip with family and friends

5.5 *Automobile on Fall River Road. Courtesy National Park Service–Rocky Mountain National Park*

from his cabin near Allenspark in July 1922, commented on the steep drop-offs encountered along the way, with views "straight down the mountain" and from which "a fall will mean instant death." Survival assured, Boynton pronounced the trip "wonderful" with "no car trouble and no accidents," cautioning his readers that "gasoline in Longmont was 27 cents, in Estes Park 36 cents and in Grand Lake 45 cents."[57]

~

Although Fall River Road and its delays absorbed much of his attention, L. C. Way was active on other fronts. Way did well with the meager resources available to him and found ways to stretch his limited funds. During the 1917 season he greatly improved communications between the supervisor's office and his district rangers by completing a twenty-five-mile telephone line from Estes Park across the Divide to Grand Lake by way of Flattop Mountain. Mindful of the still-unsolved mystery of the Reverend Thornton R. Sampson, who had disappeared two years before while crossing Flattop to attend the park's dedication,[58] Way had several telephones installed at strategic points along the way "for the accommodation of travelers." In addition, he reconstructed the existing nine-mile telephone line to the shelter cabin on Longs Peak and the fifteen-mile line up the Fall River Canyon. That same year ten miles of existing automobile roads were worked over, seventy miles of trails rebuilt, a mile of new trail constructed toward Nanita and Nakoni Lakes, and a new shelter cabin built at Poudre Lakes. Way also constructed a small supervisor's residence not far from the village of Estes Park behind MacGregor Ranch, complete with water and sewer systems and "other modern features."[59]

Of perhaps greatest importance in meeting the needs of the rising stream of visitors was the opening during summer 1917 of the park's first campground. Way was acting just in time, for adding to the popularity of automobiling in Rocky Mountain National Park was enthusiasm over "autocamping," a form of recreation that offered motorists who loved the outdoors an easy and comparatively inexpensive way to see the wonders of the sparsely populated West. Autocamping took the new mobility one step further, by making possible sustained, leisurely, and restorative contacts with nature. The nation's park system was one of its primary beneficiaries. Autocamping, extolled in the pages of magazines like *Outdoor Life* and in a series of books dedicated "to the good fellows of the road," took many forms. At its simplest, motorists brought along a tent to pitch by the side of the road or in a campground in "the real gypsy way." For those not content with standard equipment, by the early 1920s cars could be ordered with such special features as built-in food boxes or duffle carriers, kitchenettes that attached to the back seat, or a device that converted front and rear seats into a comfortable double bed. Also available were a variety of car-supported tents.[60]

Such campers were hardly roughing it, and not surprisingly their demand for campground accommodations, having spawned a new industry in small towns and cities across the nation, also became a focus of attention in the national parks. Some municipalities offered free camps with amenities such as water, toilets, showers, laundries, and stoves to lure travelers to stop and spend a few dollars. In 1915 Denver established its first auto campground in City Park, which had to be expanded because its seventy-five spaces were always quickly filled.[61] One of those visiting City Park that summer was Assistant Secretary of the Interior Stephen Mather, soon to become head of the National Park Service. Impressed by what he saw, Mather took measurements so that similar facilities could be installed in national parks to make them "accessible to the tourist of moderate means or [to] those who prefer to avoid the accommodations of hotels and live as much in the open air as possible in their tour of the scenic attractions of the country."[62] Many of the autocampers in City Park that summer were bound for Estes Park, a short seventy miles away, and one of the parks that Mather surely had uppermost in mind was the soon-to-be-dedicated Rocky Mountain National Park.

5.6 *Camping at Aspenglen Campground. Courtesy National Park Service–Rocky Mountain National Park*

For the site of his new campground Captain Way chose Bartholf Park, as Glacier Basin was then known, where he laid out one hundred campsites and installed campstoves, garbage pits, and a half-mile of trail. Way assigned a ranger to the facility to look after sanitation and to respond to the questions and needs of visitors. The enterprising Way then raised money by private subscription to extend the Glacier Basin Road to the campground. It became an instant success.

Way received help toward the development of other areas of the park as well. That summer the Arbuckle Reservoir Company of Longmont hired Hank Hutcheson from Allenspark to construct a wagon road, useful to hikers, from a point two miles above Copeland Lake up the North St. Vrain past Copeland Falls and Chickadee Pond to reach Arbuckle No.3, or Pippit Lake, where the company had a reservoir.[63]

Although ecology and interpretation were low priorities on Mather's agenda for the nation's parks, 1917 saw the beginnings of a naturalist program of sorts. In response to an initiative from Washington, Way appointed four young women collegians as "nature guides . . . to accompany camping parties . . . and give lectures upon the trees and flowers as well as the birds and animals of the region." Way, who himself prepared the government examinations to qualify the four, was pleased with the result, indicating to the press that they filled "a long term need." "Few young men," he added, "could qualify so well as lecturers on nature subjects." In deference to their sex, Way restricted the activities of his lady guides to day trips below timberline unless they were accompanied by a "first-class" male guide, selected from a group of local young men who the park examined and licensed but did not directly employ. Although there was nominal charge for these guides, Way was pleased to note that "Almost from the hour that their appointments were announced they have been swamped with applications for their services."[64]

Despite Way's enthusiasm, there is no record that the program was repeated in 1918, although during the next two years Way had printed and distributed a list of the park's birds and plants drawn up by ranger Dean Babcock. It was not until the 1923 season that his successor, Roger Toll, hired a naturalist and reintroduced nature guiding of the sort that Enos Mills championed as a way of bringing nature to the uninitiated.

~

The 1918 summer season was unusually cold and rainy. For the first time, the number of visitors to the new park dropped, a decrease attributable to not only the weather and the news from abroad about Americans fighting and dying in the trenches and forests of France, but because of the wartime restrictions that placed railway travel in the hands of the U.S. Railroad Administration and banned all railroad advertisement. Captain Way forged ahead as best he could. The highlight of the season was the opening of a new road connecting the Mill Creek and Glacier Basin Roads, made possible by funds Way raised through private subscription. This short one-mile stretch not only allowed safe and easy access to the free campground in Glacier Basin, but eliminated the steep grades of the original Bear Lake–Sprague Lake Road, which ran through the YMCA grounds, over the shoulder separating Emerald Mountain from Bible Point, and created annoying congestion. The new Glacier Basin Road also greatly shortened the distance to Sprague's resort, Loch Vale, Bear Lake, and the whole Glacier Gorge country. That summer and fall Way also persuaded resort owners in Moraine Park to contribute private dollars toward the construction of a mile-long road west along the Big Thompson with the expectation that it would one day "extend to the Pool and Fern Lake."[65]

The continuing success of the campground in Glacier Basin, coupled with the fact that property owners along Fall River Road east of the park had all but excluded the possibility of camping by fencing and posting their land, not surprisingly led to discussions about establishing additional sites within the park itself. For a time in late winter 1918, Superintendent Way considered building a campground in the Tahosa Valley on the side of Twin Sisters Mountain about half a mile south of the new Baldpate Inn on a site offering "spacious grounds and ample water." Such a facility, Way reasoned, would serve the needs of those hiking to the summit of the Twin Sisters, whose upper trail and fire lookout were now part of the national park, and those of more serious hikers and climbers on their way to Longs Peak and Mount Meeker to the southwest.[66]

Although the crippling limitation on the park's appropriation was finally lifted in March 1919, increased funding was still a fiscal year away. This handicap was made all the more difficult by the number of visitors to Rocky Mountain National Park. During the park's early years, these numbers were hard to count for the park operated no entrance stations. From May 30 to October 1 the visitor count was obtained from checkers hired by the Tourist and Publicity Bureau of the Denver Civic and Commercial Association and stationed on the Longs Peak and Estes Park Roads; in the off-season the visitor count was gleaned from hotel registers. In 1919 the number of visitors counted rose dramatically from 101,497 to 169,492, making Rocky Mountain National Park the top "tourist resort" in the entire park system with a total that nearly equaled the numbers in Yellowstone, Yosemite, Sequoia, and Glacier National Parks combined.

Repairs and improvements, nevertheless, quietly went on. The Mill Creek Road, from its junction with the Moraine Park Road at the entrance to Hallowell Park to the Mill Creek Ranger Station, was greatly improved, allowing autos to reach the ranger station. The newly reconstructed road, Way noted in his annual report, also facilitated hiking access to both Bierstadt Lake and Flattop Mountain and gave Estes Park residents better access to the fire-killed timber of the Pole Patch. This accessibility increased wood sales and made it easier for Albin Griffith, who still had timber sale rights at Bierstadt Lake, to haul out dead timber and cordwood, thereby improving the beauty of the lake's wooded shoreline.[67]

In 1920, for the first time, Way had money. For the fiscal year beginning July 1, 1920, the appropriation for Rocky Mountain National Park was increased four-fold to $40,000, still far short of what was required to take care of the backlog of needed work but large enough to launch a series of new initiatives. Most of the new funds went to road repair and construction and

5.7 Tourists on the trail. Courtesy National Park Service–Rocky Mountain National Park

to the acquisition of new and badly needed tools and equipment. The Glacier Basin Road was significantly widened, improving access to the campground as well as to the trails of the Loch Vale and Bear Lake regions. That summer also saw the replacement of many of the park's bridges, which Way believed were without exception unsafe for travel, and the long-deferred maintenance and restoration work on the Fern Lake Trail ("in the worst condition of any trail in the Park"), the Flattop Trail, and the trail on Longs Peak. The trail system as a whole, however, remained deplorable. "Our entire mileage of existing trails," Way wrote in his annual report, "should be rebuilt to make them adequate for foot or horse travel." They are "absolutely unsafe for travel with the exception of [the] Fern Lake and Flattop trails."[68]

Private generosity continued to play an important role in enhancing the park. In spring 1920, with the expectation that Fall River Road would be completed within months, the park installed a new and long-needed gate to mark its eastern, or Fall River, entrance. It was located on the road to Horseshoe Park directly south of the summit of Castle Mountain about a mile and half west of the village. Designed by ranger Dean Babcock and built on land donated by Dr. Homer James, the ornamental "rustic style" gate was the gift of Frank L. Woodward, a prominent Denver lawyer and a longtime park supporter and Estes Park summer resident. It consisted of two 16-foot square weathered-log cabins, one of which served as ranger quarters and the other as an information bureau and lounging shelter, joined by a timber portal above the road.[69] James and Woodward were not alone in their generosity. By August, thanks to funds furnished by resort-owner Frank Byerly, it was possible to drive a car to within approximately one-half mile of Bear Lake and Byerly's Bear Lake Lodge, which in 1920 was still a small, primitive complex consisting of several log buildings and a number of tent cottages.[70] Although the road itself was still "more in the nature of a wagon road" and was officially posted as "closed," Way subsequently reported that "automobiles use it without a great deal of discomfort to the passengers."[71] The Bear Lake Road would not be significantly improved through reconstruction until 1926–1927; yet one June afternoon in 1923, rangers counted twenty cars at the lake—a precursor of things to come.[72]

Although the 1919 and 1920 tourist seasons were record ones, it was generally agreed that both would have been larger still had it not been for a continuing lack of adequate lodging. As Way assured his numbers-conscious superiors in Washington in his 1919 annual report,

> A canvas of three hotels and the Tourist Bureau of Denver shows that, in Denver alone, from 100 to 150 persons per day, during July and August, or a total of between 6,200 and 9,200 persons, could not secure accommodations here, and hence did not visit the Park. Each day, a list of available rooms, if any, was telephoned to the Denver Tourist Bureau, the average number of rooms available per day being three or four, to supply the demands of hundreds in Denver alone. I have not heard of one hotel in this region that was not booked to capacity for the entire season by June 1.[73]

Estes Park's hotel and resort owners were as aware as Captain Way of the new demand on the local tourist economy and expanded their facilities to meet it. In 1919 alone accommodations for four hundred new guests were added in Estes Park village and its immediate vicinity. That year the Lewiston Hotel (by now part of the Lewiston Hotel Company), on the bluff overlooking upper Elkhorn Avenue, added some sixty rooms and enlarged its dining room—an expansion that made it second only to the Elkhorn Lodge in terms of capacity. The Lewiston also added a dance hall and billiard room.[74] At about the same time, the Lewiston Hotel Company's Chalets at Marys

Lake increased its capacity by 70.[75] Joe Mills increased his capacity at the Crags to 190,[76] and Harriet Byerly opened her new National Park Hotel on Elkhorn Avenue with room for 85.

Although the new Fall River Road was not completed until the season was effectively over, on June 15, 1920, Rocky Mountain Lodges, Inc., the parent company of A. D. Lewis's Lewiston Hotel Company opened Grand Lake Lodge. Located within the national park at its western entrance, Lewis's new facility had a capacity of 150 and consisted of a large 50-by-150-foot central rustic building with a circular open fireplace and one- and two-room cottages. The porch and dining room of the main lodge offered guests a panoramic view of Grand Lake below and equally stunning mountain vistas to the south, east, and west. Way was extremely pleased. "The appearance of this building far exceeds my expectations," he wrote in his May 1920 monthly report:

> It appears to me to fit in well with the surrounding country, and does not
> have as bare and unbroken an appearance as we had feared it would
> have from a study of the plans. . . . I think, however, that it would
> detract from, rather than add to, the general appearance, to construct an
> "L" in front of the building, as the plans call for, and I have suggested to
> Mr. Lewis that he hold his plans in abeyance . . . [for] to place it in front
> would detract from the magnificent view.[77]

Lewis was persuaded. Generations of visitors would agree with Way's judgment.

The expansion of the two Lewiston properties in Estes Park and the addition of the Grand Lake Lodge across the Continental Divide was particularly significant for tourism in Rocky Mountain National Park. The increased capacity and the amenities they provided made it possible for Roe Emery's Rocky Mountain Parks Transportation Company to enter into season-long agreements to book all-expense tours with the railroads for the first time. "Heretofore," Way explained in is monthly report for April 1920, "we have been unable to handle all this business, for the reason that no hotels would take the transient trade." The railroad companies "make the statement that the number of people for the all-expense tours of the Rocky Mountain and Yellowstone Parks depends solely upon the accommodations available."[78] Way and Emery were correct. By March 1, 1920, with the nation's railroads once again under private control, it became possible to negotiate the kind of tourist packaging on which Emery and his company would thrive. Summertime activity soared. During the 1920 season Rocky Mountain National Park received 240,966 visitors, an enormous 42 percent increase—a number more than three times larger than either Yellowstone or Yosemite. There was so much business, in fact, that even with the increased accommodations demand outstripped the supply. "All of the hotels did a capacity business during the season," Way noted in his annual report, "and a majority of them had to turn some people away, as they did last year, though no records of numbers have been kept."[79]

The 1920 season marked a turning point for Estes Park tourism, bringing to an abrupt end the rapid period of hotel and resort expansion that had begun in 1908 and continued steadily through the war years. Although visitors increased again in 1921 by more than thirty thousand, establishing yet another record, there was a sudden and totally unexpected change in the demand for accommodations. As Way noted at season's end, "The kind of accommodations desired has changed from last year, when hotel accommodations were in great demand, and showed a shortage. This year the demand has been for summer cottages and camping grounds and while hotels, with the exception of three, in so far as we can ascertain, have been filled, there has been ample of this class of accommodations."[80] Way's observation was echoed the following year by his successor Roger Toll. "The class of accommodations demanded by the traveling public has changed considerably during the past few years. Two years ago, hotel accommodations and the more expensive class of cottages were in great demand. This year the great demand has been for camping grounds and inexpensive cottages."[81]

This was not a temporary phenomenon. With the completion of Fall River Road, for many tourists Estes Park and Rocky Mountain National Park became a place of transit rather than a final destination. Thanks to Emery's circle tours and the automobile, from this time on Fall River Road would dictate the way and the pace in which many people would visit and come to know Rocky Mountain National Park, with the road itself serving as a kind of guidebook. For most it was a thoroughly positive experience, one that enhanced rather than diminished tourist perception, if only because entering and traveling the park by machine encouraged tourists to recognize that "they were in a special landscape." As historian David Louter has noted, "The contrast of machines in such a setting alone, it seems, triggered this response."[82] Such tourists, on the other hand, were not inclined to linger.

What Way and Toll were witnessing was by no means a collapse in Estes Park's hotel industry. Rather what was happening was a broadening and democratization of the tourist market as more and more people of average means jumped into the family car and headed for the mountains, many to camp and rough it in the outdoors, often to come and go in a single day, while others boarded Emery's busses in Denver at 8:00 A.M., enjoyed lunch at the Estes Park Chalets and a two-and-a-half hour stop beginning at noon, and by dinnertime were in Grand Lake. By 4:30 the next day Emery's passengers, having completed the "Grand Circle Tour," were back in Denver, having paid $25.50 for the experience. Only on tours of three days or longer was a night spent in Estes Park. Unlike parks like Yellowstone, which finally admitted cars in 1915 and where the transition to auto tourism was made difficult because of the railroads and their control of travel and tourist facilities,[83] the triumph of motorized transportation in Rocky Mountain National Park came easily. Fall River Road made its success complete. Given what appeared to be an ever increasing number of visitors, there was, however, little concern. As it had done in the past, Estes Park adjusted its tourist economy accordingly.

Chapter 6

~

Publicizing Park and Town:
The "Eve of Estes" and Winter Sports

"I F THE HON. STEPHEN T. MATHER OF CHICAGO were in the movie-picture business instead of the department of the interior," the *Rocky Mountain News* editorialized on July 14, 1916, "we would suspect him of press-agenting work of the 'circusing' variety." The *News*'s concern was not the widely circulated *National Parks Portfolio*, a handsome clothbound view-book put together by Mather's publicist Robert Sterling Yard and issued to coincide with the introduction of the bill creating the National Park Service. Rather, what provoked the editorial was the release of a publicity photo article, presumably approved by Yard, titled "Bandit Holds Up Stage in Yosemite," which depicted a masked highwayman "who lined up the passengers, boosted up their hands and went thru their clothes in old wild western fashion." The *News*'s attitude toward the event was ambivalent, if not admiring. "Were Secretary Mather other than he is," the editorial concluded,

> we would suspect him of sicking that road agent onto the Yosemite coaches. And even if he did do it, we would not feel harshly toward him. There's a reason. In his national parks he has the only show ever staged in America, which surpasses anything and everything that the most ebullient press agent in the world could say about it.[1]

As the *News* suggests, thanks to Yard and his own instincts as a former New York newspaperman and magazine editor, Stephen Mather proved to be brilliant in selling the nation's park system. Beginning in 1915 Rocky Mountain National Park, with its rising tide of visitors, understandably became a central focus of attention. Yard made sure that photographers were on hand to record the dedication ceremonies in Horseshoe Park, and in the months that followed Yard saw to it that the park was showcased in as many news and feature stories as possible, some of which were published under his own byline.[2]

Other groups helped as well. The Denver Tourist Bureau played an active role as did the railroads serving Colorado, whose advertising departments circulated slides and motion picture films featuring the state's scenery through much of the East, Midwest, and South. Western railroads, which owned many of the great "log palace" hotels within the national parks, not only underwrote much of Mather's publicity, including the $43,000 *National Parks Portfolio*, but seasonally utilized lecturers, among them several residents of Estes Park. The Union Pacific sent photographer Frank Byerly on tours of towns and cities in the Midwest, where he gave stereopticon lectures, using his own photographs "to arouse wholesome interest and curiosity in Estes Park and Rocky Mountain National park district" by informing them "of the wonderful natural playground awaiting them in Colorado."[3] The Union Pacific made good use of former journalist and author Clem Yore and the equally colorful mountain guide Shep Husted. In fall and winter 1917 the two men visited some thirty-six towns and cities including Chicago, Fort Worth, Washington, and New York, bringing back with them $35,000 worth of advertising, in the form of thirty pages of feature stories and 175 news stories.[4] That same winter the Santa Fe Railroad sent Joe Mills on a month-long lecture tour, armed with 160 lantern slides of animals and scenery, to tell of his own mountain experiences while promoting the Estes region.[5]

"Selling" Estes Park and its attractions was, of course, not new. It had begun well before the turn of the century, especially on a state and regional basis, and then intensified after 1905, when it became part of the campaign spearheaded by the emerging U.S. tourist industry to make seeing the scenic wonders of the West a matter of patriotic duty. By 1912, the Burlington Railroad was circulating *Beautiful Estes Park, Colorado*, a twenty-page booklet with foldout map and Fred Clatworthy and L. C. McClure photographs that extolled Estes Park, "the playground of playgrounds," offering "everything to the vacationist that the heart of man could ask." After 1915, such publicity was extended to Rocky Mountain National Park, "the finest grouping of mountain scenery in the Colorado Rockies."

6.1 *Advertising Estes Park, Burlington Railroad brochure, 1913. James H. Pickering Collection*

6.2 Advertising Estes Park. Float on Stanley Mountain Wagon, ca. 1915. Byron Hall on running board, Enos Mills in passenger seat. Courtesy Byron Hall

As part of the federal government's commitment to tourism Mather's park superintendents also had a role to play. Kept aware on a regular basis that their annual appropriations depended upon visitor headcount, they were expected to make themselves available to the local and regional press and to participate in the promotional activities that Mather and Yard inspired. They were also expected to initiate publicity efforts of their own. Way, sensitive both to Washington's needs and his own, was more than happy to oblige.

Most of Way's subsequent encounters with the press were routine and predictable, often to the point of being innocuous. But as in the case of the Yosemite highwayman, on one occasion Captain Way made a tactical error in judgment. In agreeing during summer 1917 to participate in the misguided publicity scheme surrounding the so-called "Eve of Estes," inspired and carefully choreographed by Al Birch, assistant city editor of the *Denver Post*, Way soon found himself caught up in an embarrassing situation that not only brought down the wrath of his superiors but cost him the respect of one of his own rangers.

The idea of sending an attractive young woman (or man) into the wilderness to live off the land was scarcely original. It had been tried several times in the "sedate and civilized" East with varying amounts of publicity success, including an episode involving one Joe Knowles, "the Maine woodsman, who went into the wilderness naked and empty-handed, to come forth again two months later—clothed, vigorous and an infinitely finer man physically than when he went in."[6] But Birch, a summer resident of Estes Park, saw in the mountains of his own Colorado, where nature was to be taken rather more seriously, the opportunity to grab a few headlines for his paper while helping to publicize the beauty and outdoor opportunities of the new national park. The story also promised to provide stay-at-home readers a bit of welcome relief from the rising tide of war news from Europe, whose indignities and horrors the *Post* was adept at reporting.

Just how, or when, Birch approached Way with the project he had in mind we do not know. What we do know, as Way apparently did not, was that Birch was a consummate stuntsman, who had already made a career out of thinking up and executing outrageous ways to call attention to the *Post* in its ongoing circulation battle with the *Rocky Mountain News*—sometimes with unintended consequences. On one occasion Birch managed to release eight "escaped" monkeys onto the coping of the dome of the state capitol building, with the intention of having them "captured" by the Denver police and fire departments using extension ladders before a big crowd of onlookers, an episode that ended with the cavorting monkeys pelting a delegation that had come to visit Colorado governor Elias Ammons with exploding light bulbs unscrewed from the dome's ribs. Although publicizing Rocky Mountain National Park as a Garden of Eden no doubt initially sounded innocent enough, Superintendent Way clearly failed to understand just how far Al Birch and the *Post* were prepared to go in pushing their stunt. In point of fact, in involving himself with a newspaper that operated a circus; fed itself on contests, promotions, and sensational journalism; and whose part-owner was a friend and sometime business partner of Buffalo Bill, Captain Way was a man in over his head.

The escapade began with the selection of an attractive young woman to play the role of the "Modern Eve." Birch did not have to look far. At DeLux Studios, located at 1230 Sixteenth Street in Denver, which the *Post* frequently used to produce its photographs, Birch found a receptionist named Hazel Eighmy, who he persuaded to assume the role of Agnes Lowe of Ann Arbor, Michigan, a young coed from the University of Michigan in Colorado on holiday. Birch introduced her to the world on July 29, 1917, with a story in the Sunday edition of the *Denver Post* written under his own byline.

"Agnes Lowe," a young woman of twenty in Estes Park, together with her mother and her brother, Richard, was preparing that very morning to

> go off into the wilderness alone and attired in as primitive fashion as was the First Woman, without food, weapons or shelter, to subsist seven whole days thru her skill in woodcraft. She will pick or kill her own food, cook it over a fire made after the fashion of prehistoric man, and fashion a bed and its covering that will protect her against the cold of lofty mountain nights. And at the end of one week she will return to civilization in as good physical condition as when she left, without having lost a single one of her 116 pounds of weight. That is, she will TRY to do all this.

Accompanying Birch's article were several photographs of the blonde-haired Miss Lowe, which the *Post* explained had been taken especially for *The Denver Post* by Bert Blasing of DeLux Studios.

Birch went on to explain that Agnes Lowe was determined "to do what Knowles had done." For at least a week, she had been "hitting the trails" in preparation, and her mother and brother, knowing the "phenomenal woodcraft" learned from her lumberman father who had taken her as a child into the "trackless woods," had at length consented to let her go. Miss Lowe had selected the Thunder Lake region of Wild Basin, "a vast area almost virgin to the foot of man," so remote and trail-less that "even the oldest inhabitant of the region—Enos A Mills himself—knows it only hazily."

Lest anyone wonder, Birch assured his readers that

> No advertising "stunt" has impelled Miss Lowe to adopt this "back to nature" outing. She is no actress. She is no candidate for the "movies." She is no writer, about to spring a new book upon a weary public. Neither is she a notoriety-seeking suffragette. Instead she is just a wholesome, level-headed, healthy young college girl, a University of Michigan co-ed, with a passion for the out-of-doors and an inherited aptitude, wonderfully developed for woodcraft.

With a concluding comment that "The trackless woods are open books to her sympathetic mind,"[7] as far as the *Post*'s Sunday readers were concerned the stage had been effectively set.

The follow-up story the next day was once again front-page news. It featured a photograph (by DeLux) showing the "Modern Eve" waving goodbye to mother, brother, and girlfriends before departing into the forest, having promised to communicate back in some way.[8] Captain Way and Enos Mills were both on hand for the carefully arranged send-off. That Mills, an avowed enemy of "nature faking," had also become one of the cast of players speaks worlds about the skill and persuasiveness of Birch.

6.3 The "Eve of Estes" shaking hands with Enos Mills; Superintendent Way stands at left. Courtesy Lulabeth and Jack Melton

To the surprise of everyone, although clearly planned to stir still greater interest, Agnes Lowe was quickly back. After some thirty-six hours in the woods, "hungry, drenched and nearly frozen" she suddenly appeared at the Babcock cabin on the ledges north of Longs Peak Inn, tearfully asking to be cared for until mother and brother could come for her. By the time of the article, Agnes Lowe, pneumonia avoided by effective home remedies, had been re-united with family and friends at Clem Yore's recently opened Big Thompson Hotel, where "if sufficiently recovered" she was expected to address the Colo-rado Campfire Club the following evening about her "adventure."[9]

Post readers opening their papers the next day, August 1, 1917, found the "Modern Eve" once again front-page news. Agnes told of her Sunday night ordeal in the rain near Thunder Lake where wet wood prevented a fire. Beginning to get a cold, the "level-headed" college girl "decided to give up and go back to civilization. I trust I am not fool enough to stay out in the wilderness when common sense says to come in." With a hint, unmistakably placed in the story's headline that the "'Modern Eve' May Try Again Life of Primitive," Agnes Lowe then briefly disappeared from the *Denver Post.*[10]

This was Wednesday. On Saturday, August 4, Way arranged his work schedule so that by 3 P.M. he was at his office in Estes Park village to greet the returning Agnes Lowe. The second arrival of mother and daughter had been carefully designed by Birch to provide the carnival-like atmosphere missing the week before. The previous evening both Miss Lowe and her mother were "royally entertained . . . at various hotels in Estes Park," includ-ing the Stanley Hotel where they were given a dinner, and later at the Big Thompson Hotel where they were guests at a dance at which "Mr. and Mrs. L. C. Way and other park officials were present." The next day, "the 'movie' operator insisted upon Mayor Roy L. Wiest and Supervisor Way, with C. H. Bond, Samuel Service and other leading citizens, getting out in the center of the main street in front of the post office and posing shaking hands with Miss Lowe." From the village the Lowes were then taken to Longs Peak Inn to spend the night, where Enos Mills was expected to devote "most of his time to final coaching of the girl for her arduous and risky adventure." Lest anyone fail to understand that the doings of the "Eve of Estes" were by now big-time news, Birch referred to "the sizable and energetic press delegation" that had attached "itself temporarily to her household" and to the fact that the "translation of her resolve into action is being telegraphed to every cor-ner of America, and every handshake and smile are following by special delivery post to periodicals everywhere."[11]

By now Way was no doubt becoming increasingly uncomfortable with the fraud he was being asked to help perpetuate. He had been forced to pose for any number of contrived photographs, attend a dance where Miss Lowe was the center of attention, and play the onlooker as Miss Lowe's "mother" and "brother" expertly supervised the public relations surrounding the young woman's every move and kept her on schedule. The whole affair—innocent as it must have at first seemed—was getting out of hand.

The second departure was carried in Monday's *Post* with two farewell photographs: the first, the one taken on Saturday in the village, showing Miss Lowe alighting from her automobile to greet Superintendent Way and Mayor Wiest; the second, taken a day later against the background of Longs Peak Inn, showing the smiling, skin-clad "Eve of Estes" saying goodbye before plunging into the wilderness. According to the story accompanying the photos, a crowd of "nearly 2,000," including L. C. Way and Enos Mills, together with a "battery of cameras" had turned out for the event.[12] Birch's prose was becoming increasingly more purple and tongue-in-cheek, no doubt to make sure that even the most trusting readers were now in on the game.

Birch was by no means through. As was the case with his Denver monkeys, Birch had a knack for knowing how and when to ratchet up his promotions to the point of absurdity. "Well, folks—here's Adam!" he began his story the following day, August 7, introducing a letter purportedly received by the *Post*, written from Greeley the previous day:

> Dear Sirs—You think you have did a smart thing sending "Eve" such far into the mountains but such shall avale you nothing. I must find her. These national park policemen shall not keep me from this fare young Eve were there numbers as mighty as the sunbeams, for I have had a vision from heaven while I sleep directing me to what I shall do. Go find Eve, if you do not I shall. Vision says so. Tremble and obey heaven's vision. This command comes from heaven, in the vision—tell fare young Eve I am coming. I am onto you. Before you get this I shall be in Rocky Mountain National Park. These devils, park policeman cannot stop me. I send picture of myself in ceremony robes as directed by vision.
>
> Yes sir,
> George Desouris
> Adam the Apostle

With the article was a photograph of "Adam (Himself)" and a "dispatch" from Rocky Mountain National Park to the effect that "park officials will not tolerate the girl being molested" and that "if captured [Adam] will be hurled out of the park upon his ear." A determined Way is also quoted as announcing: "Adam won't think he's in the Garden of Eden if he comes up here."[13]

Much to Birch's delight, the story of Miss Agnes Lowe was being picked up nationally by a press amused by the goings on in Colorado. To illustrate Birch's column of August 8 the *Post* reprinted a cartoon from the *New York Evening Telegram*. It showed a group of middle-aged males lined up to make travel arrangements, one saying, "Hey I want one to Estes Park in hurry. Physician's Orders." According to Birch, "Papers from every section of the United States and Canada, from Portland, Maine, to Portland, Oregon, from Hudson's Bay to Key West, Florida, have been publishing 'Miss Eve's' adventures, and have been telegraphing frantically to Denver and to the national park for photographs of Miss Lowe and her primitive costume." As if to mollify Captain Way and his Park Service bosses in Washington, who were by now decidedly not amused by the high jinx in the most popular of their parks, Birch assured his readers that "The Rocky Mountain National park—and for that matter, the whole of Colorado—received more advertising from the exploit of this pretty young girl than this region has received from every other source in many years. The eyes of the whole of North America are upon Colorado. The story of the 'modern Eve' has given that essentially human note to this state's advertising that nothing before has contained."[14]

Despite Birch's claims, in Colorado at least, the saga of Miss Lowe was becoming a bit stale. For all the story's supposed nationwide importance, it was now being carried by the *Post* as page-13 news. Not content simply to report his own success, Birch kept the story alive by inserting into his story of August 8 two additional pieces of information. The first indicated that Miss Lowe had kept her promise to communicate. A message written in charcoal on "three bits of aspen bark" had been found by tourists (miles from Thunder Lake) near the Longs Peak Trail:

1—Nearly froze last night.
2—Tempted to give up, but didn't.
3—Have fire now. Feeling Fine.
　　　　—A. L.

The second bit of news had to do with George Desouris, the self-styled "Modern Adam." He had been captured by rangers after a "strenuous fight" as he was trying to enter the Thunder Lake region clad "in a moth-eaten bear hide." There were no photographs of the capture or its purported aftermath when the rangers escorted Desouris down to Estes Park village and handed him over to the town marshal who, before the jeers "of a great crowd on the main street," hustled him out of town "on a big automobile stage filled with New York tourists."[15]

Although onetime *Post* writer Gene Fowler, in his 1933 history of the newspaper and its famous owners, Frederick Bonfils and Harry Tammen, would claim that Desouris was a telegrapher on vacation from Omaha who Birch corralled into being photographed in a bearskin before being dispatched into the national park, there is no actual record that the "Modern Adam" was anything more than a photograph and a brief story. Fowler has Way calling down to Denver to inform a startled Birch that "There's a nut up here . . . who claims you appointed him as Adam to find your Eve. I tried to argue with him and he put up a fight."[16] Fowler's story, like others in his book, is apparently apocryphal, and seems to have been largely constructed from the details of Birch's original story.

Captain Way and Enos Mills were not through participating in Birch's escapade—in name if perhaps not in fact. According to yet another story, two days later on August 10, both men "ran across" Miss Lowe near the trail along the Roaring Fork (a small stream near Longs Peak Inn). They were promptly invited to her "den" for an impromptu lunch. Because Birch identifies her camp as being about a hundred feet above Thunder Lake, the ten or so mile walk deep into Wild Basin that followed no doubt allowed the two men to work up sufficient appetite to attack the luncheon that Miss Lowe "quickly prepared" and served. Consisting of pine bark soup, mountain trout, mushrooms, chipmunk peas, wild honey, and choke berries, it was a meal, Way and Mills admitted, fully "the equal of some meals they have paid good prices for in city hotels." By now Miss Lowe had "adroitly" solved the problem of clothing and was wearing "crude but serviceable" sandals made of aspen bark tied on with cords of "wire grass" and, in apparent deference to the sensibilities of her male guests, a pair of leggings made of "tough" leaves. Birch also indicated that park rangers were having a difficult time keeping curious tourists ("both men and women") from "penetrating the Wild Basin section of Thunder Lake to get a glimpse of the 'modern Eve.'"[17]

Agnes Lowe returned from her "adventure" on cue, arriving back at Copeland Lake at noon two days later, where she was photographed and quickly taken away. By mid-September Birch had his sequel ready, a long three-part Sunday magazine-section article written by Agnes Lowe herself providing a detailed day-by-day record with photographs of "How I Proved to Science that Modern Woman Can Live Like Mother Eve." The first installment was accompanied by a shorter piece by Mrs. H. R. Lowe, titled "Why I let My Girl Go Back to Nature." There was, of course, the obligatory bear story featuring "one of the big brown bears that inhabit the Rocky Mountain heights, the most vicious of all the bear family." This bear had been encountered in a cave where Miss Lowe had sought shelter from a lightning storm on the second night. Before she escaped by playing dead, "he bushed and snuffed at every inch of my body" and, "with a grunt, thew me over on my back."[18]

The first of these articles appeared on September 16, 1917; the second and third on successive Sundays. In the third, written with the same kind of histrionics as its predecessors, Miss Lowe told of her encounter with the original Adam, the Greek from Greeley named George Desouris. She had been warned of his approach by a note "written on the back of a ranger's notebook," telling her that the "religious fanatic" had been sighted in Estes Park where, after having frightened tourists "into an embryo panic" with his ravings, he disappeared into the wilderness. Their encounter, which reads like a chapter from a pulp novel of the cruder sort, gives way to a madcap "panic-stricken" chase that ends with a second note informing her that a search party led by "Mr. Mills, the naturalist; L.C. Way, the park supervisor[;] and chief ranger Frank Kennedy" have "rounded up" Adam and taken him to the "Estes calaboose" (a convenience that, in 1917, did not yet exist). The story ends with a brief paragraph recounting her return from "voluntary exile":

> A great cheer went up. I saw my mother stand in an automobile to wave her handkerchief. It seemed *so* strange they should be glad to see me. If they knew how unhappy I was at the thought of the gown and corset and shoes and stockings and furbelows with which I would have to go into the hotel for dinner, they would be as downcast as I was at heart.[19]

To this final chapter of Birch's publicity hoax was appended a photo of Mills and Mrs. Lowe welcoming Agnes back to civilization, accompanied by a three-paragraph note "by Enos Mills (The World-Famous American Naturalist)" stating, incredibly enough, that "I wish other girls could take a leaf from the record of Miss Lowe's experiences and go and do likewise."[20]

Whatever their degree of actual involvement in the episode of the "Eve of Estes," it was not Mills's or Way's finest hour. Mills, of course, was answerable only to himself and perhaps a sense of humor allowed him to dismiss without regret Birch's humbuggery, some of which had clearly been at the expense of his own reputation as a respecter of nature's integrity. After her brief moment of fame, which was followed by an invitation from the Fort Collins Commercial Club to attend the annual Labor Day Poudre River Picnic,[21] Hazel Eighmy returned to receptionist duties at DeLux Studios, where she remained at least through the following year. Way, on the other hand, was not his own agent. Within a week of Birch's first *Post* columns, he had been called on the carpet by Washington and asked to explain his participation in this "frame-up for publicity purposes." Way weakly responded that he felt that the *Post* stories and those that they had triggered "will result in very valuable publicity . . . bringing hundreds of people to this park." Birch had already preempted that argument and Horace Albright, speaking for the Park Service in Mather's absence, responded that Way's involvement would "surely bring adverse criticism upon park management" and that "a national park is not the stage for even this sort of thing."[22]

Equally incensed was ranger Dixie McCracken, who had been detailed to meet Agnes Lowe on the trail near Longs Peak Inn and deliver her clothing. Following orders, McCracken found himself "right in the middle of it." Realizing that Way and Birch were in "cahoots," he confronted the superintendent and angrily accused his superior of advertising the park "by something that wasn't so." "I blew my stack," McCracken later recalled. "We didn't need that kind of stuff." According to McCracken, that incident "for some reason" soured their relationship, and from that moment on Way didn't like him. Soon afterward McCracken resigned his post and spent nearly two years in southern France as a volunteer scaling lumber in the forests near the Pyrenees. When he returned to Estes Park after World War I and found Way still in charge, McCracken decided not to take up his old job, although he stayed close to Rocky Mountain National Park for the rest of his life, because "I just had to see a pine tree grow up somewhere."[23]

As is so often the case, there was a sequel. It involved a publicity-seeking Dutchman named Van Den Enden, an author who reportedly had spent the previous three years giving lectures across the United States on his "experiences and adventures." Shortly after Agnes Lowe's return on August 12, Van Den Enden arrived in Wild Basin where he immediately set off for Thunder Lake, ostensibly in search of new experiences for his repertoire. He had obviously heard of the Modern Eve and was determined to use her notoriety to enhance his own. Unfortunately, Van Den Enden's first foray into the wilderness turned out to be as unlucky as Miss Lowe's. A heavy rock fell on his ankle and he was forced to return to the Copeland Lake Lodge where he recuperated and gave a lecture. A week later, on the afternoon of August 21, Van Den Enden, "clad in lion's skin with sandals made of wood," again went off to live "the prehistoric life." More successful this time, he returned on schedule the following Sunday with the announcement that he would "tell his experiences at the Boulder County Fair next week."[24] A few days later, in passing through Loveland, Van Den Enden, now referred to as "Prof. Von Elden of Brussels," confessed that

> he did not go into the mountains for the publicity he would gain by
> such an act, but to regain his physical strength. He has been a champion
> wrestler of European rings for several years. Since his arrival in the

United States nineteen months ago, he has mastered the English
language and is now on tour of the cities of 25,000 or over in the
United States.[25]

Perhaps this was so; but in a world where a receptionist can be easily transformed into the "Eve of Estes," who can tell.

∼

Fortunately in terms of his own career prospects, Captain Way was having
greater success on other, less controversial, fronts. One of these was his plan
to implement a winter sports program. The timing was right. By 1916, recreational skiing, snowshoeing, and tobogganing were well established throughout much of Colorado, where the use of snowshoes and skis for transportation and communication dated to mining days.[26] As far back as the early
1860s Methodist minister John L. "Father" Dyer regularly strapped on a pair
of "Norwegian snowshoes" (as skis were called until about 1900) and made
himself famous by delivering sermons and packages of mail to scattered mining camps in Breckenridge, Fairplay, and Alma in spite of blizzards that
made travel by other means impossible. Other early mail carriers also resorted to skis, most of them homemade, as did miners engaged in winter
prospecting. Recreational skiing for fun and competition soon followed, and
by the 1880s clubs with both men and women were active in a number of
mining districts.

Enos Mills also popularized and romanticized the use of skis, while adding substantially to his reputation as a mountaineer. During the winters of
1903 to 1906, while serving as Colorado's State Snow Observer, Mills traversed the upper slopes of the Rockies along the Continental Divide by ski
and snowshoe, measuring snow accumulation at the headwaters of streams
to anticipate spring and summer runoffs. His adventures in high and remote
places with avalanches, mountain lions, and snow blindness subsequently
provided subject matter for some of his most famous essays, in which with
his characteristic enthusiasm he sometimes spoke as if, like Father Dyer, his
winter wanderings were something of a holy calling. "Snow observers," Mills
told a reporter for the *Denver Times* in January 1904, "must go beyond the
trails, climb the heights and traverse the wilds through all kinds of weather.
. . . The work has roughness and its dangers, but there is an abundance of life
and fun in it."[27]

For all its early and widespread popularity, recreational skiing as an organized activity in Colorado declined with the mining industry toward the end
of the century. Its revival began in fall 1911 with the arrival in Hot Sulphur

Springs of the "Flying Norwegian," Carl Howelsen, who by the time he left his native country for America in 1904 had won every major cross-country and ski-jumping championship. Later, touring with the Ringling Brothers and Barnum Bailey Circus, Howelson further enhanced his reputation by sliding down a wooden chute and jumping (or "flying") over the backs of two elephants, a career that ended with a back injury. Coming to Hot Sulphur Springs as a stonemason, Howelsen could not stay off skis. By December 1911 he had formed a winter sports club whose first project was a two-day ski carnival held the following February featuring a variety of skiing, jumping, sledding, and cross-country events. Howelsen then moved on to Steamboat Springs, where he built a jump and in 1914 organized the town's first winter carnival. By the time he left to return to Norway in 1922, organized winter sports were once again firmly established in Colorado.

In both Denver and Estes Park the impetus for winter sports came from the Colorado Mountain Club (CMC), a group of socially prominent Denverites who organized themselves in April 1912 to promote mountain recreation and preserve "forests, flowers, fauna, and natural scenery" (the latter, most specifically, by providing leadership and support to the campaign to create Rocky Mountain National Park). Among its twenty-five charter members were two future park superintendents, Roger Toll and Edmund B. Rogers; lawyer James Grafton Rogers, who helped draft the park bill; and Enos Mills, who for many symbolized the spirit of mountaineering and conservation that the CMC sought to encourage. Much of the idea for the CMC had, in fact, come from Mills himself. During the summer of 1911, Mills had urged James Grafton Rogers to form an advocacy group along the lines of John Muir's Sierra Club, and although Mills, citing the press of other duties, had declined to help with the organization or hold office, his presence was thought to be so essential that at its first meeting the club voted to "consider him present" anyway and added his name in ink to the original charter. "We cannot," James Grafton Rogers wrote, "form a club without you."[28]

Most early members of the CMC were familiar with Estes Park, and during the club's first decade many of its outings brought members to the Longs Peak region, then as now a magnet for mountaineering. Particularly memorable was the CMC's 1913 outing, during which members climbed Flattop, Hallett, Taylor, Otis, and Thatchtop Mountains before descending Odessa Gorge to Fern Lake Lodge where they rode catamaran boats across the lake. The "crowning joy of this outing" was a moonlight ascent of Longs Peak, where CMC members were photographed at 4:30 A.M. against the hint of first light.[29] Summer outings within Rocky Mountain National Park were repeated in 1914, 1916, and 1919.

Winter outings on ski and snowshoe were popular among CMC members as well, many of whom learned the basics of the sport on the grounds of the John Evans estate, which overlooked the Denver Country Club. In 1919 the CMC laid out a thousand-foot ski run at Genessee Mountain, the City of Denver's first mountain park, which subsequently played a key role in the evolution of skiing and jumping in Colorado. But when winter fun was to be had, CMC members turned to the Fern Lake region of Estes Park.

The first CMC outing to Fern Lake took place in February 1916, when members spent three days at Fern Lake Lodge, then owned by the Higby brothers. They came at the invitation of the newly formed Outdoor Club of Estes Park, organized the preceding month "to look after a regular program of winter sports" and to help develop the new park. Not incidentally the Outdoor Club also wanted to increase the tourist business in Estes Park, where a number of hotels were now open for the winter season.[30] The program of the local group was an ambitious one. In addition to installing a skating pond in the middle of the village, by late January members had completed a half-mile toboggan run that began on Prospect Mountain near the Crags Hotel and finished "almost at the doors of the Hupp and Park hotels," at the corner of Elkhorn and Moraine. The new run lay close to Davis Hill, used by local residents for skiing and sledding. Given a good run, it was possible to sled down Davis Hill and then keep going along Fall River. To add to the excitement the Outdoor Club also constructed a number of large bobsleds and imported a couple of "real" Canadian ones.[31]

The members of this new club had even larger plans in mind. Keenly aware of the success of the annual winter carnivals at Hot Sulphur Springs and Steamboat Springs, they wanted one of their own. That February, in order to underscore their seriousness and "to get pointers on the handling of the show and to lend their support to such affairs in Colorado," a number of Outdoor Club members made arrangements to attend the Hot Sulphur Springs event, some, including a number of women, going and coming on snowshoe by way of 13,000-foot Flattop Mountain, pulling their gear and provisions on light sleds and camping two nights along the way. They arrived in Hot Sulphur Springs just in time to watch competitions featuring the "Flying Norwegian," Carl Howelsen; future U.S. Olympians Lars and Andres Haugen from Minnesota; and other champions. The roundtrip journey, Cliff Higby later recalled, consisted of "ten miles by auto, twenty by train, thirty-two by bobsled stage and sixty on snowshoes," concluding with a memorable night spent in a snowbank half way down Forest Canyon.[32]

To mount a mid-winter event attractive enough to rival those in Middle Park the members of the Outdoor Club, working on behalf of a community

6.4 *Colorado Mountain Club at Fern Lake. Courtesy National Park Service–Rocky Mountain National Park*

that numbered only some five hundred year-round residents, needed help. Given the well-developed ties between the CMC and Estes Park, it was logical that this new Estes Park group should turn to its friends from Denver to serve as co-sponsors. "There has been perfected the organization of the Estes Park Outdoor Club for the promotion of all outdoor sports in their season," Cliff Higby wrote CMC secretary George Barnard in late January 1916.

> Committees are at work on skating, skiing, tobogganing, and snowshoeing. Considerable interest and enthusiasm is being shown everywhere. We want first to enlist the interest and support of the best bunch of outdoor enthusiasts in the state—the Colorado Mountain Club. We appreciate their love of the beautiful, the noble and the rugged and admire their whole-souled participation in those forms of endeavor which alone give one the fullest enjoyment of these things. . . .
>
> To this end the Estes Park Outdoor Club invites the co-operation of the Colorado Mountain Club thru the outing committee. Early in February we will be glad to have as our guests members of the Mountain Club in a few days of "phrenzied phun and phrolic."
>
> At the conclusion of this tournament plans will be formulated for an annual winter carnival on a scale to attract visitors from all over the country.[33]

Barnard was immediately receptive. "One can scarcely realize how interest in the Estes Park region has advanced since it was made a national park," he enthusiastically told the *Rocky Mountain News*, echoing Higby.

> We have had inquiries concerning the attractions of the place in winter. Perhaps we have been jealous in guarding the secret of the charm of the region in winter, but we have known it and appreciated it. Now that the area has become a national playground it is presumed that thousands will be initiated into the charms and the mysteries of the region, not alone in summer, but in winter.
>
> It is a magnificent place for a winter carnival. There is no winter sport that cannot have the best of facilities with a little trouble and pains to bring it about.[34]

On Saturday morning, February 12, 1916, eleven officers and directors of the CMC—including George Barnard, Robert Collier, Agnes Vaille, Edmund Rogers, and Morrison Shafroth—left Denver for Estes Park. Arriving in Longmont, the party boarded steamers from the Estes Park Transportation Company for the trip to Estes Park where they were immediately introduced to the new toboggan run near the Crags Hotel. When driven inside by darkness, the guests from Denver were served a meal of wieners, buns, and coffee by the ladies of the Estes Park Woman's Club.[35] The next morning the group was taken to Stead's resort in Moraine Park, where donning snowshoes they set off for Fern Lake, a location chosen because of its accommodations, accessibility, and snow, although then seldom if ever "visited in winter except by a few old-time residents of the Estes Park region."[36]

The events that follow over the next two days showed the same care and attention as those on the previous day. Joe Mills, Dixie McCracken, and Cliff Higby had taken provisions up to Fern Lake Lodge several days earlier, where they partly dug out cabins from the drifted snow and cut and stacked an ample supply of firewood. In the main lodge a roaring fire was ready to welcome the party, which had been expanded to include members of the Estes Park Outdoor Club. Much of the next two days was spent skiing, snowshoeing, and tobogganing on the heights surrounding the lodge, taking photographs of the country and of themselves, and hiking to such destinations as Lake Odessa, Spruce Lake, Tourmaline Gorge and beyond, while strictly observing the CMC rule "No party less than four." Climaxing it all was a warm dinner followed by an evening of songs and stories around the massive stone fireplace in the lodge's north room. The date had been chosen, as it would be in future years, to get the benefit of a full moon.

The return trip turned out to be something of a surprise. Instead of going down the winding trail they had ascended on Sunday, their Estes Park hosts led the "long jolly line of red cheeked snow-shoers" directly down Fern Creek to the top of Marguerite Falls. "Here all snow shoes were loosed and pitched over the falls; then everyone let loose all holds and plunged down pel-mel [sic] over and over to drop nearly out of sight in the snow at the bottom." Fern Falls further down Fern Creek posed less of a problem: "each person squatted on the trail of his 'webs' and coasted down the falls in the narrow granite-bound canon without difficulty—except when someone's snowshoes suddenly stuck in the snow and precipitated him, or her, head-long into the snow." After stopping briefly at the Pool, where Fern and Spruce Creeks meet to form the Big Thompson, they completed the trip back to Moraine Park and the waiting steamers, stopping just long enough at the gigantic boulder known as Balanced Rock to build a fire and enjoy a quick lunch of chocolates, raisins, crackers, and bacon roasted on a stick. The final compulsory snowball fight followed.[37] That night, by way of a concluding celebration, there was a big dinner at the Crags Hotel.

The Fern Lake outing, widely proclaimed a success, was followed almost immediately by a series of articles in the Denver papers, complete with photographs. These included a long, well-illustrated feature piece in the *Rocky Mountain News* by Estes Park resident John King Sherman, who predicted that "These few days spent in the mountains in winter will be epoch-making in their importance."[38] There was also the joint announcement that

> The Colorado Mountain Club will join the Outdoor Club of Estes Park in arranging a big snow carnival, to be held in the park the whole of the week beginning Feb. 20, next year. An effort will be made to interest the government officials of the national parks department in the project so that the carnival will be given nation-wide advertising.[39]

Superintendent Way needed little encouragement. Having arrived in August 1916, amidst plans for the 1917 carnival, Way immediately saw the activities of the high-profile CMC and its Estes Park counterpart as a way of implementing and publicizing his own program of winter sports. Winter or summer the number of visitors mattered, and if Estes Park was to become a recreational center for winter activities, he wanted Rocky Mountain National Park involved.

As proof of his intentions, by early December 1916, Way had laid out four ski runs, two at Fern Lake and two at Lake Odessa, which he then had tested by a party of nine men and nine women that he personally conducted to the site on snowshoes. The courses above Lake Odessa made use of the natural contour. Skiers would climb the slope as far as they dared and then come rushing down over the broad expanse of snow. Although only two of the women making the excursion had used snowshoes before, none found the going particularly difficult, leading Way to comment to the *Rocky Mountain News* that "it is about a third as difficult to travel in the mountains this time of year . . . if one wears snowshoes. . . . There are no rocks on any of the ski courses we picked out, and absolutely no danger to any novice who uses them. By the time we reached Odessa Lake the women as well as the men had become snowshoe and ski experts."[40]

Two months later, on February 10 and 12, 1917, the Outdoor Club staged its promised winter festival, using the Fern Lake outing of the previous year as precedent to advertise the event as the "second annual Carnival of Winter Sports." A special invitation was again extended to the CMC and its members. The site chosen by carnival chairman Joe Mills and his committee was just south of the fish hatchery on Fall River, a location that "in spite of the solid covering of snow and ice on the course" could be "still easily reached by auto."[41] The program of ski jumping and snowshoe, ski, and toboggan races for both men and women drew 463 participants, including 85 members of the Outdoor Club and the CMC. Prizes were awarded by businesses in Denver and Estes Park.

Although the promoters had announced their intention "to secure some of the country's best ski jumpers," with the exception of Herman von Beust, a Swiss who won the ski jumping contest, most of the other winners were local. Only one serious accident marred the festivities. In the lady's toboggan race, held in the late afternoon, the three-man sled carrying Eleanor Hondius overturned, fracturing her left leg above the knee. Despite the accident, the Estes Park carnival—which Enos Mills made sure was recorded on several thousand feet of film by a movie operator from Denver—was pronounced "an otherwise highly successful and quite spectacular event"[42] and, in Superintendent Way's words, marked "a new departure in National Parks."[43]

In order to underscore his interest in the development of winter sports, Way made it a point several weeks later to attend the rival carnival in Steamboat Springs, where, according to Cliff Higby, he "studied every detail of these winter activities, even taking measurements of the jump hill.[44] He then persuaded four champion ski jumpers, including Henry Hall who had just established a world's record, to "tramp on snowshoes . . . from Routt County across the continental divide . . . to Estes Park, to look this region over with a view to developing winter sports in the great national playground . . . and [to] make suggestions for increasing the success of the local affair."[45]

In Estes Park, organized activities for winter 1917 were not yet over. Following the conclusion of the carnival on Fall River, some forty members of the Outdoor Club and the CMC made their way on snowshoe and ski back to Fern Lake for several more days of "jollification" and races. Fern Lake continued to be the destination of choice through 1934, with the exception of 1930 and 1931 when the CMC elected to go elsewhere. By general consensus these long-remembered events with their rituals and traditions, beginning with a dinner at the Brinwood Hotel near the Fern Lake Trailhead, marked the highpoint of the winter season both for the CMC and Rocky Mountain National Park.[46] New initiates were impressed. "Say, old man," one first-timer was quoted as saying in 1920 as he gazed up at the Little Matterhorn, "I want to thank you for dragging me up here. I hadn't an idea it was like this. I'll never forget these days, not if I live to be a hundred. And believe me, I'll be back."[47]

What began as a three-day weekend affair was expanded beginning in 1922 to one that lasted a full ten days over two weekends, allowing members to come and go as their situations allowed. In 1918, despite the war, it took twenty automobiles to bring some sixty CMC members up from Denver. One of the participants was Agnes Vaille, a CMC regular whose name would become forever associated with tragedy when she died on her descent from Longs Peak after becoming the first woman to climb its East Face in winter. That year she posed for a photograph, snowshoes in hand, that appeared in the *Denver Post*.[48]

Adding interest to the event in 1922 was the presence of both national jumping champion Lars Haugen and Lieutenant Marquis d'Albizzi, chief ski instructor of the Italian army, who during World War I had trained hundreds of soldiers in the Austrian Tyrol in the art of traveling by skis. Albizzi had become a popular figure in Colorado skiing circles the previous year after being engaged by the Denver Ski Club to coach its members at the run on Genessee Mountain.[49] As Way's successor Roger Toll noted in his monthly report for March, "His demonstration of the many uses of skis in going up hill, and in taking cross country trips, was a revelation to those who heretofore considered that the only use of skis was to slide down hill, or jump on artificial courses."[50]

To sustain the CMC's participation in the annual Fern Lake event, which Way and Toll realized was a means of simultaneously publicizing the park and maintaining the interest and political support of an influential group of Denverites, both men went out of their way to make improvements. In 1920 a new ski course was opened up through the timber. Running back 125 yards from the lake with a slope of 15 to 20 degrees, special care was taken to make sure that the stumps left by cutting were not more than six inches from the ground. On a trial run, a toboggan with two men slid nearly across the lake.

To facilitate the CMC's visits of 1923 and 1924, new cross country ski trails marked by enameled signs were constructed from Fern Lake to Spruce Lake and from Bear Lake to Fern, a ski jump-out onto the lake was built, and a new hiking and snowshoeing trail was completed from the Brinwood Hotel to the Pool.

Concessionaire Frank Byerly did his part. Fern Lake originally was strictly a summer camp, which housed many of its guests in tents. During the outing's first years, people slept wherever they could find a place. The storehouse was turned into a dormitory with two-deep bunks and more bunks were improvised in the lodge building's living room. Gradually, Byerly saw to it that well-chinked log sleeping cabins were constructed. In 1922, to handle larger parties, which for several seasons included contingents of the Olinger High-landers, a boy's club from Denver, Byerly added a new dinning room to the lodge, featuring a large round table with a built-in lazy susan. By that date lodge and outbuildings were able to accommodate about fifty-five people in reasonable comfort. A telephone line from the Mill Creek Ranger Station to Fern Lake allowed communication with Denver and other places. Highlight-ing the 1925 visit, by which time as many as eighty were taking part, was bear steak brought back by Byerly from a hunt in the San Juans.[51]

The Outdoor Club of Estes Park (which would shortly change its name to the Estes Park Group of the Colorado Mountain Club) continued to hold its own carnivals into the 1920s, with the active support of local businesses, which saw their potential for developing a new stream of tourist income. By 1918 these activities had gained sufficient state and national attention to attract contestants from the Steamboat Springs carnival, including the cel-ebrated Haugen brothers who specialized in setting world's records in jump-ing.[52] In 1923 the date was changed to better fit the realities of Estes Park's tourist economy. A ski tournament was held on Saturday and Sunday, June 30 and July 1, on the Continental Divide near Fall River Pass, an area now accessible because of the completion of Fall River Road.[53]

Such events certainly offered a welcome relief from the tedium of win-ter. But by 1923–1924, local sponsors had come to understand that if Estes Park was to attract the winter sports–minded to the village, where they could be fed, housed, and otherwise entertained, facilities must be developed to make the village itself, rather than Fern Lake or some other remote site, the focus of activity. Davis Hill was suitable for amateur skiers and children, but the toboggan run that the CMC members had so enjoyed before their first Fern Lake outing necessarily closed Moraine Avenue to regular traffic and as such was only suitable for use on special occasions. Rudimentary ski and toboggan runs already existed on Deer Mountain by winter 1916–1917.

Way, who visited them in February, found the toboggan course in "dangerous condition" and supervised the laying out of new ski jumps there the follow-ing month.[54] Beyond these facilities there was little within easy walking or driving distance of Estes Park village to make the winter visitor stop and stay.

There was also increasing local competition. It came from the hamlet of Allenspark some 16 miles to the south where by 1921 there was a ski club and where in 1922 Johnny "Mack" McCollister laid out a quarter-mile course with a 3 percent grade. The course was a rudimentary one, but it had one decided advantage. Its relatively easy accessibility to Denver and the valley towns by way of the scenic and comparatively good and well-maintained South St. Vrain Road made it a popular alternative to traveling all the way to Estes Park. As the often-perceptive Charlie Hewes, looking on from Hewes-Kirkwood Inn in the adjacent Tahosa Valley, noted in his journal on March 16, 1922, "Valley people . . . are now flocking in swarms every Sun-day to use it. . . . People can leave right after breakfast, even in Denver, and motor to Allens by noon, use the course for several hours, and get back home for a late dinner. Thus the whole proposition is working wonderfully and the fame of Allens is spreading far and near as a great winter recreation area."[55]

Hewes, of course, was not alone in understanding the possibilities of Allenspark. Later that same year Lyons surveyor L. H. Deiterich laid out a new half-mile course a few hundred yards beyond the old one, with parking nearby for as many as eight hundred cars. Although both courses could be used free of charge, the old one was quickly turned over to the "amateurs who find the new one a little too fast for learning."[56] That same year, to advertise its new winter sports facility, the Allenspark Ski Club hosted the first of a number of well-attended annual tournaments. The club scored a major success the following year, 1923, when despite blizzard-like conditions more than five hundred spectators showed up in the tiny village to watch a jumping display by international champions Lars Haugen, Hans Hansen, and C. L. Hopkins. "Haugen's leap of 101 feat [sic] was the best seen in this part of the country," the *Longmont Ledger* reported, "while the loop-the-loop by Hansen, and Hopkins' spectacular riding were revelations to those who thought ski riding was a form of children's amusement."[57] Interviewed after the event, Hansen and Haugen were emphatic that a course could be laid out on nearby Cowbell Hill, site of the old Clarabelle Mine, "that would be equal at least of any in the world, and with its accessibility would eventually be-come the skiing center of the country."[58] Such stories put the people of Estes Park squarely on notice.

The growing popularity of Allenspark was, no doubt, a major catalyst for the sudden burst of near-frenzied enthusiasm for winter sports that consumed the people of Estes Park during a two-year period beginning in fall and winter 1923–1924. There was also the visit to the village in November 1923 of National Park Service director Stephen Mather and his deputy Horace Albright, who met with village mayor A. D. Lewis, transportation company president Roe Emery, and park superintendent Roger Toll (who also happened to be president of the Estes Park Group of the CMC). Although most of their public utterances were well-worn statements on the need to use sports to stimulate travel and publicize the park through the winter season, the visit brought new talk about the possibilities of an enhanced and more widely visible winter program.[59]

What made the difference, however, was the formation of a new local organization. It came in late January 1924 at a dinner meeting at the Stanley Manor, where some fifty-five members of the Estes Park Group of the CMC turned out to discuss how best "to take up the work and carry it forward in the development of a winter sports season in the Estes Park region." The result was the Colorado Ski Club, with officers, a board of directors, and a committee system that, as in the days of the Estes Park Protective and Improvement Association, put the Estes Park business establishment firmly in control of things. Village government was represented as well. Mayor Lewis, president of the Lewiston Hotels, was chosen president, and other officers and directors included realtor Albert Hayden; banker Charles Hix; Frank Haberl, manager of the Stanley Hotel; businessman Glen Preston; former or present resort owners Clifford Higby and Abner Sprague; and chief ranger Thomas J. Allen. In matters concerning the Stanley Hotel, Haberl spoke for the absent Stanley, while Allen brought with him the authority of Superintendent Toll for matters involving the national park.[60]

Membership, which cost a dollar a year, was made a matter of hometown pride. "Surely every loyal Park resident will want to have a part in the unique work the Club is doing that is already giving it publicity in nearly every part of the United States," the *Estes Park Trail* intoned in the issue announcing the club's formation, speaking as if on behalf of a well-established organization. "You are a mighty poor booster if you do not become a part of it and assist in its work to the best of your ability."[61] Within a week the new organization had 84 local members from a town of five hundred, with additional members drawn from other towns in northern Colorado and, remarkably, had already sponsored the organization of a similar club in Loveland.[62] Less than a week later, Mayor Lewis, who had gone east on a trip to confer with railroad officials about ways of "building up still greater travel to Colorado," announced "that 100 additional hotel guests were registered at Estes Park village over the last weekend, drawn there by the carnival sports." Many of these, he pointedly noted, were from other states.[63]

In the weeks that followed, news of winter sports and the "community spirit" that was building its "great future" dominated the *Estes Park Trail*, at times pushing most other news off the front page. "It is often said and generally understood," the new club's Outing Committee observed in the February 15 issue, "that Estes Park knows how to go after what it really wants and what it goes after in dead earnest it usually gets."[64] Much of the news, not surprisingly, had to do with the establishment of new facilities close to, or within easy driving distance of, the village. That winter a ski run was opened on the north side of Deer Mountain, near Deer Ridge Chalet,[65] where operator Orville W. Bechtel conveniently served lunches and refreshments and sold photographs. The course ran down onto Ashton Flats in Little Horseshoe Park, so named because Willard H. Ashton, builder of the Horseshoe Inn, had a cabin there. Although well out of town, the Rocky Mountain Parks Transportation Company quickly established a regular schedule to haul skiers and their equipment up and back.[66] By November 1924 the Deer Ridge course had been enlarged. Intended now for experienced skiers, the run into Little Horseshoe was made fully 100 feet wide and 1,200 feet in length, with a toboggan run at one side. At the top Bechtel provided a shelter cabin with a fireplace.[67]

Much closer to town, on the northwest side of Prospect Mountain, Joseph Liebman offered the use of his property and an outbuilding for a beginners' ski course. A new bobsled run was laid out on the northeast slope of Little Prospect Mountain, while in the heart of the village the southeast corner of the park was flooded to create a skating pond. The 400-foot long Liebman course (referred to as "Liebman Hill") was laid out in November 1924 under the expert direction of Cesar Tschudin, a former Swiss army ski instructor, hired at the beginning of the year to offer free lessons in any and all sports from January 15 until April 15—the period now officially designated "Winter Sport Season."[68]

The most impressive addition of the season—and the one on which the members of the Colorado Ski Club pinned most of their future hopes—was the new ski course, toboggan run, and jumping course on the north-facing slope of Oldman Mountain, just west of Elkhorn Lodge. The site, which enjoyed a relatively level outrun and space for parking on both sides, was one that had been personally selected by Lars and Anders Haugen and Henry Hall, who had trekked over the Divide from Middle Park in February 1917 at Way's invitation to give advice on where and how to develop a ski industry in Estes Park. Built by voluntary labor at a cost of $72.50[69] and finished in January 1924, the course was intended to provide the kind of jumping facility needed to compete with those at Hot Sulphur Springs, Steamboat Springs, and Denver's Genessee Mountain. Howard James of the Elkhorn Lodge leased the site to the club for a period of five years for one dollar.

The highlight of the Colorado Ski Club's first year, an event that set the tone and expectations for years to come, was the first annual All-Colorado Tournament held on Saturday and Sunday, March 15 and 16, 1924. This free day-and-a-half event, made possible by the new ski run and jump on Oldman Mountain, attracted a number of nationally known jumpers, including Barney Riley ("the Wild Irish Rose of Skidom"), the Haugen brothers, and Henry Hall, as well as amateur participants from virtually every ski center and ski club in the state. There was also a sprinkling of collegians from the State Agricultural College at Fort Collins and from the universities in Boulder and Denver. The crowd on Sunday numbered more than eight hundred, despite the fact that a three-day storm in the valley had closed many of the lower roads. "This attendance proves the possibility beyond a shadow of a doubt," the *Rocky Mountain News* concluded in its summary story on the tournament, "that Americans can and will have winter sports in the Colorado mountains that are equal to and easier of approach than those staged in Switzerland."[70]

Amateur winners in the various categories received prizes given by local and regional businesses. That year the all-round national amateur competition, which brought with it the silver loving cup put up by the Stanley Hotel, was won by seventeen-year-old Lewis Dalpes of the Denver Ski Club, who would continue to compete in Estes Park into the late 1930s. Dalpes's jump of 105.5 feet beat out Lars Haugen, who fell. In the cross-country event two local men, Norton Billings and Barney Laycock, finished first and second. Billings would go on to enjoy considerable success and fame on the Colorado ski circuit and, together with fellow Estes Park resident John Steele, compete in the 1932 Winter Olympic Games at New York's Lake Placid.

Four local hotels—the Stanley, Lewiston, Hupp, and National Park—opened for the event and offered special rates. On Saturday evening, at the end of the first day, a banquet and reception for visitors was held at the Lewiston Hotel, a site not far from the ski run on Oldman Mountain. That evening visitors and residents with energy to expend skied on a lighted ski slope in the village. Among the special invited guests were the commissioners of Larimer County, who pledged that the roads would remain open "regardless of snow and in first class condition."[71] To the delight of its organizers, the moment galvanized the entire community, even the young, who were

6.5 *Winter skiing at Elkhorn ski course on Oldman Mountain. Courtesy National Park Service–Rocky Mountain National Park*

not only encouraged to compete for prizes but to write letters to the *Estes Park Trail* on the subject "What We Think of the Art of Skiing."

Anxious to capitalize on what all agreed was a "decided success," on the day after the tournament members of the Ski Club invited Lars Haugen and Barney Riley to inspect the ski run and jump on Oldman Mountain and make recommendations for its improvement. Much to the delight of event organizers the two offered the view that with some additional work "it will be possible to equal and even exceed the records of any known jumping course anywhere." Haugen further suggested that there was "no possible reason why Estes Park can not become nationally known as a winter sports center." To that word of encouragement, the *Trail* added a challenge of its own:

> The world is rapidly hearing of Estes Park as a winter resort and it is only a matter of time until winter activities will surprise those who know only of the Park as a summering place. Only as we make much of our possibilities, will the outside work [world] come in and enjoy. We can be the St. Moritz of America—will we?[72]

In an effort to make that happen before the next season the bottom of the hill below Oldman Mountain received additional grading and smoothing so that jumpers would not find it as difficult to stand following a jump. Also a fence was installed at the landing area to catch and hold as much snow as possible.

Jumping tournaments on Oldman Mountain highlighted the winter seasons of 1925 and 1926. The 1925 event, held on the very day that the intrepid Agnes Vaille froze to death on the Boulder Field of Longs Peak, took place in a snowstorm that kept the Sunday crowd gathered at the base of the run down to about 1,000 spectators.[73] The 1926 tournament, by contrast, set an attendance record. On the second day some 3,500 people gathered to watch Erling Strom, a native of Norway and member of the Rocky Mountain National Park Ski Club (as the Colorado Ski Club was now known), win the featured race. It was said to be the largest crowd of people ever to come to Estes Park to attend a single event.[74]

The 1926 carnival marked the climax of Estes Park's drive for preeminence in winter sports. Thereafter, the popularity of the mid-winter event began to decline. In 1928, despite the heroic efforts by volunteers who spent an entire day hauling more than 100 tons of snow down from drifts on Fall River Road to make the course useable, only a few hundred spectators turned out to watch. The low turnout was attributed to lack of advertising, but part of the reason no doubt had to do with the absence of big name jumpers, who had decided to go elsewhere.[75] In 1929 and 1930, with Colorado and much of the nation mired in the first years of the Depression, the event was cancelled entirely, although a "local" contest was held in Horseshoe Park in February as a warm-up for the annual ski tournament in Allenspark, where far more modest expectations and a more reliable snowpack kept the event alive and well, if intermittently, into the 1930s.

Competitive ski events in Estes Park were revived in 1931, when not one but two tournaments were held. The first was staged, as usual, in midwinter with considerable success, stimulated in part by reduced admission prices and an improved field of athletes. The crowd was estimated at 2,000 people.[76] Among those in attendance was Secretary of the Interior Ray Lyman Wilbur, who was presented with a lifetime membership in the Rocky Mountain National Park Ski Club. The second tournament, the first Annual Mid-Summer Ski Meet, was scheduled at the end of June to coincide with the beginning of tourist season. Its proceeds were dedicated to sending four members of the local ski club to the Olympic trials at Lake Placid. Twenty trucks and a crew of one hundred volunteers worked through the night of June 27 to bring some 500 cubic yards of snow down from the top of Fall River Pass and spread it by hand on the Oldman Mountain course.[77] This laborious chore was greatly facilitated in 1933 when a miniature railroad was permanently installed to haul snow by cable car up the 200-foot mountain. These arrangements had the desired effect. That first year a crowd of some 5,000 visitors gathered on nearby hillsides and the flat below to watch while Fox Movietone News cameras captured on film the unusual sight of daring young men riding gracefully through the warm summer air. For one day at least Estes Park, if not the "St. Moritz of America," had become "the summer capital of winter sports."

Winter and summer ski tournaments were repeated between 1932 and 1935 (although the winter meet in March 1935 was shifted to the Park Service's new facilities in Hidden Valley). In 1932, in fact, there were two fairly well-attended winter events in January and February, the second to honor the town's two Olympic competitors, Norton Billings and John Steele, recently returned from the winter games. Ice statues, flags, and evergreen-laden ornamental gateways similar to those at Lake Placid were installed at the entrance to the ski jump, whose take-off chute was elevated to send the jumpers shooting higher in the air than ever before.[78] The jumping events featured the return of Denver's Louis Dalpes, who won for the third time to retire the Stanley trophy.

The mid-summer event that June and those that followed were planned with the hope of stimulating tourism during the Depression years. As a result, the atmosphere of the "annual frolic" became increasingly elaborate

6.6 *Summer ski festival on Oldman Mountain, June 24, 1934. James H. Pickering Collection*

and carnival-like with the addition of such attractions as a "Queen of Ski-Land," a series of novelty races and stunts, and appearances by the Boulder Municipal Band and the orchestra from Ted Jelsema's Riverside Amusement Park, which entertained with popular tunes between events.[79] Paid attendance nonetheless slipped to something like 1,000 in both 1933 and 1935. The June 1934 carnival, for which volunteers from the park's Civilian Conservation Corps (CCC) camps helped prepare the course, fared slightly better. Some 1,500 spectators turned out despite a rain that fell before and during the meet. Profits in those years, if any, suffered accordingly.[80] This was not because of a lack of advertising. Two days before the 1935 carnival, heralded by daily announcements over Denver's radio station KOA, a truckload of snow accompanied by a "bevy of Estes Park's fairest beauties" was hauled through the streets of the capitol city.

In 1934, with the opening of four new ski courses in Hidden Valley, the focus of regional winter sports activities shifted to Rocky Mountain National Park, bringing to an end the promotional hoopla and entertainment that the village site had provided.[81] Thereafter, where winter sports were concerned, the local business community and its newspaper seemed more or less content to express periodic gripes about the Park Service's "obstructionist" unwillingness to develop Hidden Valley into a first class winter recreational area that would help the economy—albeit without local expense. Successive superintendents countered by insisting that any development must utilize only the natural topography. The Park Service did, however, open the beaver ponds near Hidden Valley for skating, where it installed a warming shed, and kept the road to Bear Lake Road and Fall River Road to Willow Park open for use by skaters and skiers. Superintendent David Canfield, who arrived from Crater Lake as a self-proclaimed "winter sports enthusiast" in 1937, stated the park's position emphatically: "There will be no construction of artificial facilities such as ski jumps and ski tows nor will any professional meets be encouraged. Every effort will be made to make park snow sports attractive to novices as well as experts in the use of sliding facilities available very much as nature made them."[82]

Although CCC workers help lay out a new toboggan run in 1938 and a new two-mile downhill course with a drop of 1,000 feet in 1939, and there was talk in 1939 and again in 1940 of opening a second ski facility in Mill Creek Basin to alleviate crowding and other inadequacies,[83] the only other "improvement" in Hidden Valley before the end of World War II came in March 1941, when local high school boys constructed and installed a primitive ski tow, making use of an automobile engine capable of pulling skiers 600 feet up the mountain in a matter of minutes.[84]

Jumping on Oldman Mountain resumed in 1939 and 1940, when a tournament was held in June as part of festivities celebrating the Silver Jubilee of Rocky Mountain National Park. For that occasion the hill was improved, making jumps of up to 170 feet possible. After World War II, in June 1949 and 1950 and August 1951, the summer event was revived once more for what its promoters hoped would be "an annual affair." For a time it seemed to work. Some 3,000 spectators turned out in 1949 to watch Olympic star Gordon Wren of Steamboat and other competitors and stunt events featuring two skiers riding one pair of skies and Al Huebner of Estes Park descending the hill backward ("the first time it's been done in this part of the country"). In 1951 snow was generated by a machine. Huebner was back, this time jumping through a flaming hoop before a crowd of 4,000.[85] The 1951 event was the last. Beyond that date the course down what had once been a vision quest site for Native Americans gradually lapsed into decay, leaving Rocky Mountain National Park to handle the demand for winter sports as best it could.

In point of fact, despite the hard work and enthusiasm of the mid-1920s and a brief revival in the 1930s, Estes Park would never become the kind of winter sports mecca its supporters hoped. The climate was against it and so was geography and historical circumstance. Estes Park winters were too mild— mild enough in most years to support herds of grazing cattle. And at elevations above 9,000 feet, where the winter snowpack was deep enough for skiing, the National Park Service with its mandate to protect the environment was in charge, a fact that precluded the towering ski jumps and open slopes necessary for big-time skiing. Hidden Valley was acceptable enough for a time, although of limited appeal even during its best years, but its attractiveness decreased as more glamorous and challenging sites at Aspen, Breckenridge, Vail, and elsewhere developed after World War II. All this despite the winter dreams of the CMC's hearty members, who for nearly two decades made the woods above Fern Lake ring with sounds of the "Doxology," "America," and the "The Star Spangled Banner" as they trekked by full moon toward Lake Odessa.[86] For all their hopes, and the hopes of many others, Estes Park and its mountain world would remain for most a summer destination, one far more suited to the escapades of a "Modern Eve" than a Barney Riley, "the Wild Irish Rose of Skidom."

Chapter 7

~

The Transportation Controversy:
Rocky Mountain National Park, 1919–1921

A T 9:00 A.M. ON WEDNESDAY, AUGUST 16, 1919, Enos Mills phoned
L. C. Way from Longs Peak Inn to inform him that he had dispatched
one of his two touring cars on a sightseeing trip into Rocky Mountain National Park. The car's destination, he told Way, was the end of the not-yet-
completed Fall River Road. It is unlikely that Mills's driver, Edward Catlett,
or his paying passengers, three tourists from Illinois on holiday, knew about
the phone call. But Catlett knew the trip was illegal and in direct violation
of the park's new policy that for the past two months placed such business
solely in the hands of Roe Emery's Rocky Mountain Parks Transportation
Company. Catlett nonetheless followed his employer's instructions.

Way acted at once. Mills's cars had been seen in the park before and the
"Father of Rocky Mountain National Park" had been warned. Way drove up
Fall River Road to the first switchback near Chasm Falls and waited. Catlett
stopped on command and, although Way later reported he became "imperti-
nent" and pointedly intimated "that Enos Mills was a bigger man than the
United States government," he obeyed the superintendent's order to leave
the park. When Way called Longs Peak Inn to inform Mills of what had
happened, Mills responded "that he would notify me as to his next action."[1]
Elliptical though it sounded, there was nothing mysterious about the message:

7.1 Enos A. Mills, ca. 1920. James H. Pickering Collection

Enos Mills intended to challenge in court the legality of the park's new concessions policy and he now had his test case.

Although no one could have known it at the time, the issue of concessions in Rocky Mountain National Park, once joined, would mushroom into a controversy that would linger over park and region for the better part of a decade. Beginning with the opposition of only a handful of individuals, initially dismissed by Way as "undesirables," the issue soon escalated into a seemingly intractable legal and political confrontation between the State of Colorado and the federal government over who had the right to police roads within the national park. The issue would not go away and, before it was finally settled by legislative action in 1929, the political, economic, and personal costs had been enormous. Thanks to a series of protracted lawsuits and the efforts of Enos Mills and those who succeeded him, the "cede jurisdiction controversy" attracted widespread public attention, making Rocky Mountain National Park a point of heated contention throughout the state and consuming the time and attention of public officials at all levels. The Estes Park region suffered most. The dispute retarded the development of Rocky Mountain National Park during a period of general prosperity, shortened the tenure of one of its superintendents, and, for a time, even raised questions about whether the park itself should be abolished.[2]

~

The question of concessions in the nation's parks was one that Stephen Mather and his new National Park Service were forced to grapple with from the first. And well before 1918, when he drafted an official directive on the subject for Secretary of the Interior Franklin Lane to issue, Mather had made up his mind. Traditional business thinking argued that opening the parks to free competition would keep prices down and improve service. Mather had already learned from experience that quite the opposite was likely to be true. At Yellowstone, Yosemite, Glacier, and elsewhere where it had been encouraged, a policy of unrestrained competition turned out to be both chaotic and uneconomical. As one concessionaire lowered prices to meet and then undercut the competition, the level of service suffered and standards were relaxed.

It was not a pretty picture. Yellowstone, the nation's oldest park, where concessions operating under ten-year leases had been written into its enabling legislation, had suffered years of private exploitation. By 1916, the year the Park Service was created, Yellowstone had become a nightmare of competing businesses, whose facilities and offices were eyesores, cluttering the landscape and taking up valuable park land—businesses that not only failed to cooperate with one another but whose prices and aggressive methods of soliciting customers were confusing and often questionable. As chief assistant Horace Albright later recalled, when Mather took "over the parks, Yellowstone had one concessioner running the five hotels, two lunch stations, and one stagecoach line, two others running permanent camp systems, another two concessioners running stagecoach lines, and several running traveling camps."[3] Tourist visitors, ill-served and often-abused, were the losers. Yosemite and Glacier had long histories of similar troubles. Mather found Glacier, which had been established as recently as 1910, so riddled with steam and electric railroads, power and irrigation projects, concession leases of up to 20 years, and ongoing timber sales that, in the words of one historian, "Glacier Park was not really a national park, in the proper sense of the word, but a sort of hybrid national forest with a few park features, and it was at first administered as such."[4]

In fall 1916, even before he had an appropriation for his new bureau, the energetic Mather had begun to consolidate concessions in Yellowstone, putting into practice the policy that he would apply elsewhere. The future of the nation's parks and adequate congressional funding to maintain and improve them, Mather believed, directly depended on their ability to attract an ever-increasing number of visitors. Getting people to the parks and keeping them there as long as possible became a major goal—a goal that could only be achieved if the concessions encountered provided a level and quality of service that made visitors lifelong "friends of the parks" who would want to return. This was best achieved, he decided, by what he called a "regulated monopoly," an arrangement allowing single concessionaires, operating with assured government contracts, to attract outside capital to maintain and improve facilities and services.

As a successful laissez-faire capitalist, who had made a fortune as "the king of Borax," there was a great deal of irony in Mather's position. As it would later be frequently pointed out, such views were not only antithetical to the accepted business culture of the day but were at odds with Mather's own practices. Stephen Mather accepted such contradictions. The free enterprise system might work in businesses like borax, but when it came to parks too many small enterprises invariably led to squabbling and misguided competition. Mather's models were the regulated public utilities that served U.S. cities, where exclusive franchises were exchanged for governmental oversight and regulation.

It was to achieve such ends that the new concession policy was drafted and implemented. In the case of Yellowstone, Mather took away the franchise of one of the three permanent camp operators, forced three others to merge, and then resisted the political pressure that followed from members of Wyoming's congressional delegation.[5] Secretary of the Interior Lane, sensitive to the shabby record of his predecessors, fell in line, and the consolidation of concessions in Yellowstone continued. By 1924, Harry W. Child's Yellowstone Park Transportation Company with the firm financial backing of the Burlington Railroad enjoyed an absolute—and very profitable—monopoly on the park's hotel and transportation facilities. Mather succeeded in Yellowstone not only because he was able to withstand the political pressures of a small state but because he had clear jurisdiction to intervene. Unfortunately, in Rocky Mountain National Park, the question of jurisdiction was not nearly so clear.

～

Although Mather told the *Rocky Mountain News* at the time of Rocky Mountain Park's dedication that "there had been no general plan prepared for the development of the park, and not much can be done until more money is available,"[6] by December 1916 when he returned to the city, which advertised itself as the gateway to all the western parks, Mather's thoughts had crystallized. Well aware of the political and financial advantages of marshalling the broadest possible coalition of business, commercial, and civic groups in the promotion of national parks, Mather used a luncheon address to the business community at the Shirly Savoy Hotel, to urge "Denver business men and men of means throughout the state . . . to go into partnership with the federal government in the development of the national playgrounds located in Colorado" in order to raise "the necessary home capital . . . to pay the expense of constructing hotels, chalets, and inns in the Rocky Mountain National Park." Fresh from his victory over the Yellowstone concessionaires, Mather spoke expansively on what was to become a favorite theme: "If a company is formed to construct hotels in the Rocky Mountain or Mesa Verde parks," he told the *News* in an interview before his Savoy speech, "it will obtain exclusive hotel and transportation facilities in the park for a term of five years, after which it will continue in the concession with the government as a partner."[7]

Mather's message was well received. According to the *Rocky Mountain News*, Denver's capitalists left "inspired." In the aftermath, the *News* praised the assistant secretary as "a practical realist" and urged the people of Denver to "work with Mr. Mather and his staff."[8] The Denver business community rallied in support. The powerful Denver Civic and Commercial Association called a meeting of its executive committee to consider the Mather proposition and three days later the directors of the Denver Tourist Bureau passed a resolution in support of "a movement to organize a local corporation to finance hotels, chalets, camping grounds and other improvements in the Rocky Mountain National Park."[9]

For all the enthusiasm in Denver there were grumblings in Estes Park. The agitation came from a small group of local businessmen, most notably liverymen, who, citing what they claimed to be the failure of concessions-planning in Yellowstone and Yosemite, were said to be "up in arms" over the government's proposal "to bring in a lot of rich men from the outside, give them tight monopoly on all business and freeze us out competitively." Other rumors had it that private automobiles, rigs, and horses were to be banned from the park. Superintendent Way, to his credit, acted quickly, convening a meeting in the village to explain exactly what Mather had in mind and how Estes Park businessmen might approach the opportunity. "All you liverymen, including the hotel keepers who own and rent horses," he told his audience, should

> form a company: put in each of your horses and rigs for so many shares of stock. Keep your stock in your own stables, just as you do now and go on doing business without change. But divide your profits according to the stock each holds. With such a central company the government can have ONE outfit to do business with and to hold responsible. The fakers and the jitney bus robbers cannot come in and touch you. . . .
>
> You hotel men get together. Organize a company to build hotels yourselves within the national park, so it will not be necessary for the

government to bring outsiders in here. You have operated your own
hotels with success; you can run these others in the national park in the
same way.

To underscore the point, Way, now sounding every bit like Mather, went on
to accuse the critics of being disgruntled by their own failure to "get monopolies in the national playground and freeze out rival business men" and
declared his confidence that "the majority of the Estes Park residents . . . are
entirely in favor of the proposed concessions."[10]

Way apparently left his audience mollified. But he was nonetheless sufficiently concerned to take time, coming down from Estes Park on his way to
the National Parks Conference in Washington, where concessions were on
the agenda, to address the issue for the Denver press and "emphatically"
deny "numerous reports that the government favors an absolute monopoly
for national park concessions," by which he apparently meant a single concessionaire to handle all services. He also explained that Mather's term "regulated monopolies" meant only "direct supervision by the government officials in the park, so that tourists will be given the best possible service for
the least possible money and no one will be 'gouged' in the rush season by
greedy hotel men or liverymen." As an example of what he had in mind,
Way cited the jitney bus outfits that had handled the transportation between Boulder and Nederland the previous summer and "made life a burden
for those persons unfortunately compelled to make the trip." More graphically, Way recalled his own experience at the Grand Canyon where

> a flock of liverymen would come in during the rush season with rigs
> some of which were so dilapidated they were held together with bailing
> wire, and with harness that was half rotten rope. These conveyances
> were not safe for women to travel in. Furthermore, when business was
> slack, the liverymen cut prices and fought over tourists until the visitors
> were disgusted and no liveryman made money. In rush season, when rigs
> were too few, these men would bargain to take persons on a certain
> drive for, say $4, and after getting their passengers out of town would
> refuse to drive them back unless they were paid $8 cash.[11]

Although grumblings continued to be heard,[12] in the absence of any
government initiative to revive the fears of the Estes Park and Denver business communities, the issue dropped from sight. The *Denver Post*, which
carried Way's disclaimer, left no doubt where it stood with respect to the
superintendent of Rocky Mountain National Park in late 1916. The *Post*
accompanied its lengthy article with a photograph of Way and his wife "on
one of their many mid-winter snowshoe trips across the Continental Di-

vide" and then used the caption to praise the superintendent as a man who "turned down a much higher salary to accept the post of supervisor of the Rocky Mountain National Park, because he loves his work. He is an endless worker for the development of Colorado's scenic attractions for the most good of all the people."[13]

There the matter rested for more than two years, until May 13, 1919, when without warning Secretary of the Interior Lane announced that he had awarded an exclusive transportation concession under a twenty-year contract to Roe Emery and his Rocky Mountain Parks Transportation Company. The delay in implementing Mather's program of regulated monopolies, given all the discussion in fall and early winter 1916, is somewhat hard to account for. Doubtless it had to do with Washington's increasing preoccupation with the war in Europe, as well as with Stephen Mather's own personal situation. Almost immediately after the close of the National Parks Conference, which Way had attended, Mather was hospitalized for depression and did not return to full duty until spring 1918. His temporary replacement, Horace Albright, chose not to pursue the issue of concessions, and when Mather returned to duty, the United States was at war and there were other, more pressing, matters to occupy his attention.

The choice of the forty-five-year-old Emery and his Rocky Mountain Parks Transportation Company was hardly surprising. Since acquiring the Stanley and Osborn transportation lines in 1916 and melding them into his own growing regional transportation empire, Emery provided service to Estes Park and Rocky Mountain National Park summer and winter, and his company had gained a solid reputation for its dependability, modern equipment, and low cost. Equally important to both Mather and Lane was the record that Emery had earned as a concessionaire at Glacier National Park beginning in 1914, where with the support of Louis Hill, president of the Great Northern Railroad, he had greatly improved transportation by introducing comfortable White Motor buses and touring cars. The popularity and financial success of Emery's Glacier Park Transportation Company inevitably brought him to Mather's attention, and in a short time Roe Emery was not only a member of Stephen Mather's inner circle but a close personal friend.[14]

Taking notice of his accomplishments at Glacier were the Western railroads serving Denver and the Front Range and they asked Emery to survey what could be done to improve transportation in the Estes Park–Rocky Mountain National Park region with an eye to putting in place a similar system. Emery's plan involved coordinating existing service from Denver, Fort Collins, Loveland, Longmont, Lyons, and Greeley. The railroads were impressed. In April 1916, with a number of contracts in hand and financial help once again from Walter White and the White Motor Company, Emery incorporated the Rocky Mountain Parks Transportation Company.

Although in time Emery would gain a stranglehold on regional transportation, it was, at first, tough going. As Mather explained in his 1919 annual report to the Secretary of the Interior, tourists came but not in sufficient numbers. Despite a solid reputation for good service and fair prices, during its first four years company lines lost some $65,000, and friends in Denver urged Emery to abandon the enterprise as hopeless. Unable to make money in the face of what the Park Service referred to as "unrestricted and irresponsible competition," by early 1919 Emery's company was brought "face to face with the alternative courses of continuing its operations to the point of financial breakdown or withdrawing its equipment and disposing of it in the automobile market. . . . It naturally chose the latter," Mather noted, "and it was to secure the continuing maintenance of its efficient service that we decided to make it the official transportation line, under contract."[15]

Thanks to Mather and the new franchise things began to change. By the end of his first decade of operation, which included the best years of the heady 1920s, Emery owned not only the state's largest and most financially successful transportation line but a chain of mountain hotels that included the Lewiston Hotel, the Estes Park Chalets, and the Stanley Hotel in Estes Park; the Grand Lake Lodge in Grand Lake; and the Hot Springs Hotel and Placer Inn in Idaho Springs—all of them operated in conjunction with "circle trips," package tours that took passengers from Denver through Rocky Mountain National Park and then back by way of Grand Lake, Berthoud Pass, and Idaho Springs, with stops for meals and overnight stays along the way. Emery and his Rocky Mountain Parks Transportation Company were so successful that in 1927 he surrendered the franchise at Glacier to concentrate exclusively on his Colorado operations.

"I made them look," Emery would later comment, and for more than three decades until he exited the business entirely in 1952, Roe Emery quite literally shaped the way that hundreds of thousands of people would encounter and understand Rocky Mountain National Park. His tours, ranging from two to twelve days, promised a "real vacation because the escort eliminates every vexatious element . . . and leaves you free to sit back and enjoy every minute of your vacation."[16] When historian David Louter writes of how automobiles and busses transformed the way in which Americans experienced nature within national parks, he was thinking of transportation pioneers like Roe Emery.[17]

Even with the coveted franchise in hand, celebrated by the purchase of $100,000 in new equipment, Roe Emery needed all the staying power he

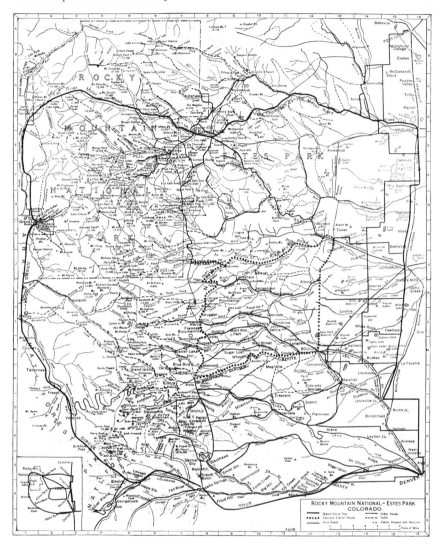

7.2 *Map showing Roe Emery's "Circle Tour" beginning and ending in Denver, 1922. Published by Union Pacific Railroad. James H. Pickering Collection*

could muster, for almost immediately there was controversy. It began slowly and almost without warning. The *Denver Post*, the self-proclaimed watchdog of the peoples' interest, often sounding the alarm in such matters, initially adopted a positive position, enthusiastically greeting news of Mather's concession as "One of the biggest boosts that has been given Colorado tourist business in a number of years. . . . By letting a transportation concession in the Estes Park region," the *Post* editorialized in its page-one story, "the government has assured tourists of safe, comfortable, frequent and moderate-priced access to the park. This has been the custom in all other national playgrounds."[18]

The concessions arrangement with Emery went into effect on June 10, 1919, and during the next month Way made a point to meet with commercial clubs in Boulder, Fort Collins, and Loveland to explain the park's new policy. In Estes Park the initial response was one of confusion rather than opposition over whether or not the concession was, in fact, an exclusive one that would keep all rent-car drivers from entering the park. Way promised to find out. Having taken the pulse of things, Way was able to report to Washington at the end of May that

> All and all, there is practically no opposition or objection to the
> granting of a concession to the Rocky Mountain Parks Transportation
> Company. Personally, I have had no protest, even from jitney drivers.
> While I have been informed indirectly that three undesirable parties,
> whom I have mentioned in former correspondence regarding this
> subject, are doing considerable talking, so far as I can judge, this is the
> only opposition. All the responsible automobile livery people accept
> the condition with good grace. They are very anxious, however, to learn
> whether or not the Park will be closed to them this coming summer.[19]

Whether Way himself was in fact confused about the ramifications of the new policy is unclear (although surely by now he knew enough about Mather's regulated monopolies to strongly suspect what the answer would be). Within a week, however, he delivered an official statement of clarification: "All such for hire vehicles will be rightly barred from Rocky Mountain National Park."[20]

The new policy, as Mather explained it, sounded eminently reasonable. It did not seem at all reasonable, however, to Enos Mills, who immediately saw in the new concession the hydra head of governmental monopoly about to crush entrepreneurs like himself who expected free access to the park. Mills had already made his position clear. Absolutely convinced of the correctness of his position to the point of self-righteousness, by summer 1919 Mills was a man spoiling for a fight. The announcement of Emery's new concession provided a more than adequate occasion.

∼

To outsiders Enos Mills's growing disaffection with Mather, Albright, and the National Park Service was undoubtedly difficult to understand. In spoken word and in print Mills had been one of the new organization's earliest and most ardent supporters, and like so many other wilderness preservationists he had rhapsodized over the appointment of the charismatic and high-energy Stephen Mather as its first head. During the first months of 1916, when Mather was launching his all-out campaign to establish the Park Service and crafting its enabling legislation, Mills was in fact considered an insider, one of a small group of congressmen, writers, editors, and other park supporters who gathered in strategy sessions held in the Washington homes of congressman William Kent and park publicist Robert Sterling Yard.[21]

By the following January, however, the seeds of discontent were unmistakably there. At the Fourth National Parks Conference held early that month in Washington, a showcase event designed by Mather to publicize parks and gain adequate funding for the recently created National Park Service, Mills used his address "The National Parks for All the People," delivered on the first day before a distinguished gathering of senators and congressmen, to denounce concessions within the parks. Mills would later view his speech as a defining event—the moment "I launched my campaign against transportation and other monopolies in National Parks." Mills was adamant: "Concessions are a bad feature in any Park. . . . Why should private concerns reap profits by exploiting the visitors to National Parks?"[22]

Enos Mills had other, and equally compelling, reasons to part company with Mather and the National Park Service. His own agenda for the wilderness of Colorado was unfinished, and here, he suspected, it was the National Park Service itself that stood in the way. In the years after 1915, flush with success, Mills had launched yet another crusade. His new goal—one that he vigorously pursued through his usual program of speeches, writing, and personal lobbying—was park status for both Mesa Verde and Mount Evans. More expansively, Mills wanted to extend the borders of Rocky Mountain Park south to Pikes Peak and north to embrace the entire Front Range and the forest sections of Colorado and Wyoming, a distance of some two hundred miles—a plan that would take in Mount Arapaho and the Arapaho Glacier, the largest in Colorado, both eliminated from the final park bill of 1915. Such proposals, not surprisingly, drew opposition from mining, cattle, and timbering interests in places like Boulder and Fort Collins, which strenuously objected to the withdrawal of so much land from public use and whose press concluded that Mills had gone "park mad."[23]

Headway was slow and Mills blamed the Park Service for not moving forcefully and publicly enough, particularly with respect to Mount Evans. Mills was largely correct. Although Stephen Mather was a park enthusiast, he was decidedly against "proliferating" new parks, especially "when the established ones required so much to bring them up to his standards." When the subject arose, Horace Albright recalled, the politically astute Mather "lavishly praised the areas being promoted and assured their backers that he would keep them in mind."[24]

Moreover, as Mills surely knew, Mount Evans posed a particularly difficult problem for the Park Service, for its 100,000 acres were squarely in the middle of a national reserve managed by the Forest Service. Albright, left in charge throughout 1917 while Mather was convalescing, knew all too well the sensitivities involved in the interagency rivalry and wanted to move slowly and behind closed doors. Mills, on the other hand, had long ago made up his mind about the Forest Service and its utilitarian polices. An "aggressive and conspiratorial" Forest Service, Mills believed, had secretly fought the creation of Rocky Mountain National Park and now it was opposing the addition of Mount Evans. Mills wanted Mather and Albright to publicly say so and to fight the battle out in the open where he himself could play an active role.

Horace Albright visited Denver in June 1917. After briefly touring the Mount Evans area, he headed north to Estes Park to meet with Mills and confer with Way. It was, Albright recalled, "a difficult, unpleasant meeting." Mills hectored Albright and the Park Service for permitting grazing in national parks and for not "fighting" hard enough for the Mount Evans expansion and the removal of the $10,000 funding limitation for Rocky Mountain National Park. He then raised the issue of concessions. In Albright's retelling, Mills "wanted to ban all transportation and lodging concessions while still retaining his own inn and his other property within the park. His adamant attitude seemed to leave no room for reasoning."[25]

Although Mills agreed to pose for a photograph with Albright and park supporters Mary and John Sherman, in the aftermath of his visit Mills went directly over Albright's head, sending a letter to Secretary of the Interior Lane attacking Albright on the subject of Mount Evans. With his customary hyperbole, Mills accused Albright and publicist Yard of using their official positions "to screen the insidious work of the Forest Service"[26] and of being "a menace to the entire cause of national parks."[27] Albright allowed a recuperating Mather to answer for him, and Mather's anger clearly showed. "Your charges are not worth discussing," he wrote Mills, "but I simply will not stand by in silence and have slanderous statements go by without a protest."[28] Mills, aroused, was as usual implacable and unrelenting. Several weeks later, during a public meeting and in the presence Albright's assistant, Arthur E. Demaray, Mills charged that Albright was a "crook" who had "sold out to the Forest Service" to further "his own cheap political interests" and "abandoned the principles of national parks."[29] Albright's views on Mills were just as strong. "Enos Mills," he wrote years later, "was one of the meanest, most cantankerous, most fascinating men I ever knew."[30]

Albright's investigation of Mount Evans was, in fact, a thorough one. He returned to Colorado once again in October 1918, where, at Mather's request, he personally spent five days exploring the region with Way and two experienced mountain climbers. He then traveled to Estes Park. This time, however, he deliberately avoided Enos Mills until the eve of his departure. Then he had Way send Mills a message: if he would come to the Park Service office in the village, Albright would see him briefly. "Well, I think he must have done the one-minute mile from his place," Albright recalled,

> for he rushed in with tie askew and panting like a hound after a fox. Of course, he was anything but gentle and contrite. He ranted on about the park, but mainly confined himself to chastising me for not paying attention to the Mount Evans region. He said I was in cahoots with the Forest Service to let them keep that area, and on and on. I didn't have the time or the inclination to listen to much of this, so I cut him off with a few curt sentences about my recent trip up Mount Evans and the possibility of recommending its inclusion in our service.[31]

Reporting the meeting to a colleague a few days later, Albright closed with the statement that "I am done with the fellow, unless he comes around with an apology."[32] Mills, of course, seldom if ever apologized, and from that point on the issues dividing the two took on a decidedly personal note. Mather fared little better. Albright and Mather were both younger than Mills—Albright, in fact, was not yet thirty—and with their college degrees and fraternity-nurtured self-confidence they were the kind of men that the self-educated Mills instinctively disliked. Nor was Mills alone. Mather, whose New England roots went back to Puritan divines Increase and Cotton Mather, rubbed some of his contemporaries the wrong way with his authoritarian attitude; and Albright appeared at times a bit too brash and sure of himself for a man of his age and experience. In any case, as far as Mills was concerned, both men, acting in league with the hated Forest Service, had capitulated on parks.

~

Despite the apparent calm surrounding the new transportation policy, Way remained cautious. He sent letters to newspapers in the valley towns containing the Rocky Mountain Parks Transportation Company's local service schedules and attempted to address "conflicting stories" by making it clear that "private automobiles may enter the park as heretofore, no restrictions being placed upon them other than traffic regulations, for the safety and comfort of all." Much of the remaining confusion had to do with the complexity of the transportation company's posted schedule of trips and fares. The schedule for the 1919 season included four sight-seeing trips beginning and ending in Estes Park, forty-three different rates for touring car destinations beyond the village (sixteen of which contained provisions for multiple stops), not to mention totally separate schedules of "Special Service" for picnicking and shopping, with hourly rates for "running time" and "waiting time." To those used to spur-of-the-moment trip-taking, this no doubt seemed like bureaucracy run amuck.[33]

By July there were problems to report. Serious questions had been raised, presumably by Mills, about the fact that jurisdiction over state and county roads within the park had never formally been ceded to the federal government—questions that threw open to question the legality of Mather's new transportation policy. Way took up the matter directly with Horace Albright, when he briefly came through Estes Park on his way north to Yellowstone, where he had recently been appointed superintendent. They decided that the best way to proceed was to initiate the process of taking over legal control of the roads. To that end Way secured a resolution from the Colorado State Highway Commission, which had been empowered by legislation two years before "to make agreements on behalf of the State of Colorado with the United States Government . . . in any manner affecting the public highways of the state." That resolution, dated August 13, 1919, transferred "control, management, maintenance, and supervision" of the public highways within Rocky Mountain National Park. Exempted from the resolution was Fall River Road, still under construction by the state, although the commission's resolution provided that upon completion, maintenance, control, and supervision of the road would pass to the federal government.[34]

How many of these backstage maneuverings Enos Mills was aware of is uncertain. Even if he had been, it probably would not have mattered. Convinced of the moral and legal correctness of his position, Mills determined that there must be a test case and then deliberately set about to create one. To that end he sent a letter, marked "personal," to Superintendent Way, in which he leveled a series of charges against Emory's transportation company and the Estes Park business community, reiterated his own position on concessions, and then concluded with a veiled threat. "I am also aware," Mills wrote, that

> the hotel and business men of the Estes Park region are practically
> unanimous in encouraging the transportation company to give inferior

service to this region. This atmosphere has been in existence for a number of years. . . . As you know, I have always taken a stand against concessions. I have repeatedly called attention this summer to the fact that there is much said for concessions, but on the other hand, watching as I have carefully the working out of this concession, I am now willing to go to bat in opposition to it.[35]

That same day, well before Way could have seen the letter, Mills sent Edward Catlett and his passengers into the park. Way not only ejected both, but, given clear evidence of provocation and Catlett's attitude, barred Catlett from entering the park again until further notice. Mills had long since discovered the press's power in forming and shaping public opinion. Way's act, however correct and necessary, gave Mills the occasion to portray his employee as the martyred victim of government tyranny and abuse. Ignoring his own role, Mills publicly defended his chauffeur as "a law-abiding citizen . . . respected for his industry and integrity. . . . Therefore, I am asking" Mills concluded, "if you will not join with me in preventing an honorable man from being stamped with dishonor by a Prussianized park official who is acting in collusion with the Rocky Mountain Parks Transportation Company."[36]

Way informed Washington of his actions by telegram and asked for guidance. "Will I make arrest of Mills, driver, or both, and take before Commissioner? Or secure warrant for Mills, in event case is pushed?"[37] Clearly understanding that he was being provoked and tested, Way urged the Director in a letter written the same day to push the case against Mills "to the limit," "for it has been rumored in the Village by other jitney drivers that we are favoring Mr. Mills and permitting him to violate the regulations, when we will not permit others to do so."[38]

Arno B. Cammerer, a career civil servant who had taken Albright's place as assistant director of the Park Service, responded immediately by telegram. His office had consulted its lawyers, and they advised that, until the legal issues could be resolved definitively, the prudent course was one of compromise and delay. Even with the Highway Commission resolution in hand (and a similar one from the Board of County Commissioners of Larimer County), the question of police jurisdiction was far from clear. This was particularly true with respect to the unfinished Fall River Road, already a tourist favorite, which had been deliberately excluded from the resolutions. Speaking for the usually aggressive Mather, Cammerer instructed Way to use extreme caution. He should continue to intercept and eject violators, but no arrests should be made, or even warrants secured for arrest, because "it would be decidedly dangerous to let the case get into courts at the present time."[39]

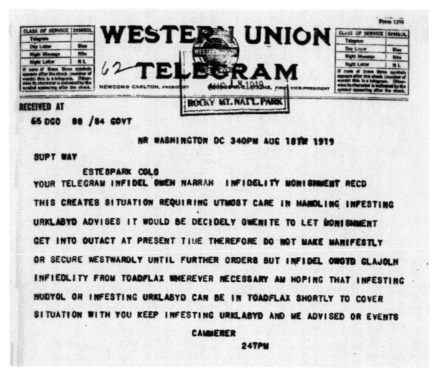

7.3 *Coded telegram to Superintendent Way, August 18, 1919. "Infidel" refers to Enos Mills. Courtesy National Park Service–Rocky Mountain National Park*

"What the Service hopes," Cammerer wrote Way in a follow-up letter, "is to keep these matters quiet, until complete jurisdiction over both Park and roads has been granted by the State, and if you can hold Mills over the present season, we can push this matter to conclusion before next."[40] So serious was the perceived threat that Cammerer had his telegram forwarded to Way in code, with Mills, by now clearly the enemy, identified as "Infidel."

Way followed orders and tried to placate Mills. An exchange of letters followed. Way patiently explained to Mills what Mills already knew and could not accept. Mills's response largely skirted the issues Way raised. Instead, he threw Emery's regular scheduled trips back in Way's face: "one of the charms of this region and a vacation is to avoid these mathematical and exacting schedules which compel you to make reservations in advance to see a certain sight that is said to be good, without waiting until on the ground and then acting accordingly."[41] Way was patient and resourceful. He again approached Mills, this time with a plan that would allow independent drivers to use park roads if they would furnish a bond guaranteeing adequate service. By now Mills surely sensed that Way, Mather, and the Park Service were on the defensive.

Within a week of the Cammerer telegram there were new provocations. "Mills Attorney called yesterday about forcing case," Way wired Mather on August 25. "His car reported in Park on the High Drive. Other jitneys following his example. Ejecting when found, by us. Situation acute."[42] As a military man used to prompt action, Way clearly felt the frustration of his position. But, given his instructions, he could do little more than wait to see what would happen next. Anxious to help resolve the legal issues, Way spent time investigating the ownership status of the roads within the park, becoming convinced that most had been developed years before as right-of-ways over public domain lands and as such could be claimed by either county or state. Of far greater significance was the legal opinion he now received: jurisdiction over those roads would have to come from the state.[43]

Enos Mills filed a formal complaint against Way in the U.S. District Court of Colorado, citing his rights under the enabling legislation of the park and seeking a temporary injunction preventing interference with his "common rights as a citizen of Colorado in traveling over the park roads" held in "state ownership." The hearing, called in Denver on September 4, 1919, did not last long. In deciding not to grant the injunction, Judge Robert E. Lewis refused to hear Mills's witnesses, stating from the bench "that it was ridiculous for any person to set up litigation that the United States Government did not have power to regulate traffic and business for the benefit of the people, within the Rocky Mountain National Park."[44] The government responded on September 24 with a motion to dismiss.

Although Mills would insist that his position had broad backing in Estes Park, Way was no doubt correct that the number of his supporters was small and that with only two or three exceptions they did not include local hotelkeepers. Among Mills's allies, however, were two of the most influential men in the village, F. O. Stanley and C. H. Bond. Both were men of principle, wealth, and influence, who as lifelong Republicans embraced free enterprise as a way of life. The other well-known citizen joining Mills's cause was forty-four-year-old Clem Yore, a quixotic author and former journalist, who following his arrival in Estes Park in June 1915 had quickly intruded himself and his opinions into the life of the community.[45] Yore could also lay claim to make common cause with Mills as the owner of the Big Thompson Hotel, opened in 1917. Although Yore cut a formidable figure, many found him something of a braggart, given to demonstrations of self-promotion and willing to throw his weight around in their assertion. He was, in short, a man who Way, in any other circumstances, would have been correct in largely ignoring. But Bond and Stanley were different: both were to be taken seriously. That Way largely dismissed the influence of all three was, in the end, a tactical mistake he would regret.

Almost immediately after the hearing before Judge Lewis, Stephen Mather arrived in Denver to attend an open meeting in Estes Park, convened by Way on Sunday, September 6 to address the concerns of a group of local businessmen. Confident of his ability to persuade, Mather was particularly interested in engaging those supporting Mills's position, most notably Stanley, Bond, and Yore. Mather also wanted to meet Mills face-to-face on his home ground and to draw him out on his complaints so that they could be publicly responded to. Although Way sent a car to Longs Peak Inn to bring Mills to the meeting, Mills refused to attend, saying only, Way later reported, that he "would have Mr. F. O. Stanley speak for him." The subject of Mills's attendance would itself shortly become an issue, Mills contending to California congressman John E. Raker that Mather "did not, nor did anyone connected with the National Park Service, send me word that he actually was to come and when. Nor did he or anyone phone me after his arrival. . . . Mr. Mather made not the slightest attempt to have a conference with me."[46]

The meeting took place in Way's office in the village. Undaunted by the presence of the Park Service director or those who he knew disagreed with him, Stanley directly raised the subject of the transportation monopoly and his opposition to it. Stanley, Way later wrote, "stated that 90 to 98 percent of the people of Estes Park, also 90 percent of the visitors to the Rocky Mountain National Park, were opposed to the concession" and " that the principle was wrong":

> About seven people applauded Stanley's speech, while the rest re-
> mained silent. Stanley concluded by stating that the people of Estes
> Park did not want the park administered by officials in Washington,
> who did not know anything about the needs of the Park, etc., insisting as
> has always been done, that the Estes Park people should take over the
> management of this park and run it for themselves.[47]

On the basis of his presentation before Mather, Stanley became irrevocably linked in Way's mind with the absent Mills. "It is singular," he later told Mather, enjoying the irony,

> that of the 28 hotels served by the concessioner's machines, Mr. Mills
> and Mr. F. O. Stanley are the only ones, so far as I can learn, who
> claimed that the concessioner gave poor service, was indifferent to the
> desires of the public, and that the drivers were mostly poor. . . . It is also

7.4 Clem Yore. Courtesy Estes Park Museum

singular that neither Mr. Mills nor Mr. Stanley has yet reported one
specific case to me for investigation.[48]

The meeting of September 6 and the entrance of Stanley and Bond onto
the field, marked what, in retrospect, was an increasingly murky, unpredictable, and legally intractable situation. Given the legal questions raised by
the Park Service's own attorneys and the statement that Way had received
from Colorado's assistant attorney general about the need to seek a legislative remedy, Mather would have done well had he reminded himself and his
subordinates of Cammerer's advice of less than three weeks before: that the
Park Service should try "to keep these matters quiet" by whatever means
necessary until the jurisdiction issue had been resolved once and for all.

Such an approach would probably have worked. The 1919 tourist season
was over and the jitney drivers had disbanded, leaving winter transportation
uncontested in Emery's hands. Mather and his associates had nine months
to pursue a definitive remedy. To publicly suspend the concessions policy, if
only temporarily, and do whatever was necessary to make Emery financially
whole was well within Mather's power and resources. Mather had done such
things before and would do them again, whether by adding personal
subventions to Yard's and Albright's government salaries or providing a
$200,000 personal loan in 1925 to the Yosemite National Park Company to
keep that foundering concession afloat until it could be absorbed into the
more successful Curry Company. Had he taken action to appease Mills and
his supporters, the cost to the Park Service, Way, and Mather himself would
have been small—perhaps a little loss of face, but surely nothing more. But
by the end of the decade the cost of not having done so was incalculable.

The 1919 season ended without further incident. Way's annual report
waxed enthusiastically about the popularity and reliability of Emery's transportation service. By the end of September it even seemed that a legislative
resolution might be forthcoming. On September 25, Way met with governor
Oliver H. Shoup to discuss the state's ceding of jurisdiction. The meeting
ended with "the Governor promising to do everything in his power to have
this bill passed during the Special Session."[49]

Mills aside, local opposition seemed to have entirely faded. Joe Mills of
the Crags Hotel, who had been appointed with fellow owners Charles Reed
and A. D. Lewis by the Hotel Men's Association "to inquire into the working of the [auto] livery concession, and to gather complaints," reported in
October that none had been received."[50] Mather's annual report to the Secretary of the Interior was similarly serene. Speaking of the transportation
contract with Emery, Mather dismissed the opposition out of hand: "Certain

parties have not been satisfied with this arrangement, and have sought to restore the old conditions, but these efforts have been unavailing."[51]

~

The apparent quiet was deceptive, for as Superintendent Way soon learned, as fall turned to winter Mills and his colleagues remained active. Early in the new year, on January 15, 1920, some forty representatives of the commercial clubs and chambers of commerce of Loveland, Fort Collins, Longmont, Lyons, Greeley, and Boulder met at the YMCA in Fort Collins to discuss how to abolish the transportation concession. The meeting was apparently called by Stanley's surrogate and manager of the Stanley Hotel, Alfred Lamborn, and Clem Yore, for they were the chief speakers. Yore, who was increasingly acting as a kind of stand-in for Enos Mills, clearly relished the role. Displaying a map, he dominated the meeting, charging Emery's company with inadequate service and unreasonable prices and claiming that "existing conditions" were "making Estes Park unpopular thruout the United States." These were, of course, Mills's charges. But Yore went further. "It is the belief of Mr. Yore," the *Loveland Daily Herald* reported, "that if the transportation company is allowed to continue with the only concession, hotel, horseback, camping, and other concessions would follow, which will spoil Estes Park as the peoples' playground." A resolution was unanimously adopted by those in attendance that their parent bodies should petition their legislators to have Emery's concession abolished.[52]

Although Enos Mills chose not to attend, he was very much aware of the meeting, for he followed up the resolution with a lengthy letter to the *Daily Herald* in which he inveighed against the "inexcusable and unjust" transportation monopoly with its "royal and privileged cars." "Of course it is inevitable," Mills wrote, echoing Yore and underscoring his belief in conspiracies, "that so powerful a monopoly seeks to secure its existence and to grow. The monopoly is bound to become a meddler in all legislation, national as well as state, and through politicians, whom it can reward, and industries which it can control, this aristocracy will be a menace of justice. Already it is trying its hands in politics."[53]

The very fact that such a meeting could be held and attract a large audience was ominous. What soon became obvious was that Mills and his allies had significantly widened the public stage, setting in motion a series of meetings in various towns along the Front Range, with their inevitable press coverage, which Way and the Park Service had neither the time nor means to prevent or control. From these meetings came a series of charges, many of them outrageously and even knowingly false about the transportation company's fares, services, and policies, delivered with inflammatory rhetoric and then repeated and re-repeated until they assumed the status of accepted fact. At the center of it all, although often out of sight, was Enos Mills.

Oddly enough, Way remained unconcerned. In his monthly report for January 1920, written some ten days after the meeting in Fort Collins, he seemed philosophically resigned, strongly convinced that for all the talk "no such action will be taken. . . . It is obvious," he wrote, that

> we will continue to have annoying cases of this kind from time to time, due to the fact that there are a few in this section who are actuated by motives of personal gain and interest. While this is regrettable, I can not see why it should have any detrimental effect. There is an old saying that one braying ass will make more noise than a hundred nightingales.[54]

Unfortunately, for a time at least, Way acted on these convictions. When in late February the Allenspark Commercial Club, where Mills was an active member, decided to debate the monopoly issue and invited Way to present his side in person or submit a written argument, the superintendent chose to do neither. With Mills in attendance, the organization took note of Way's refusal, declaring "that evidently the leading champion of the monopoly did not have much of a case." Listening to a tirade against monopolies, it promptly voted several "uncompromising resolutions," including an "unqualified" condemnation of

> the present transportation concession in Rocky Mountain National park, as monopolistic, unnecessary, unjustifiable, unlawful, unjust, unreasonable, undemocratic, un-American, corrupt, vicious and iniquitous; as autocratic favoritism conceived in secrecy; as the incubator of a dangerous political machine; as an invitation and license to exploitation and blackmail; as an alliance of bureaucratic politicians and profit-grabbing special interests; as an assault upon the people's rights; and as a betrayal of trust by public servants.[55]

Perhaps regretting that in Allenspark he had yielded the field to Mills by default, Way suddenly reversed course and decided to carry the debate to his critics. In March, initiating what quickly became a seemingly never-ending round of fatiguing public appearances, Way spoke to the Longmont Lions Club and a week later accepted a similar invitation from the Lyons Commercial Club before going on to Denver to a meeting of the American Travel Development Association. In Lyons, with Roe Emery at his side to "set forth the facts of his business," Way proceeded to deliver what the editor of the *Lyons Recorder* called "one of the most able presentations of a governmental policy we have ever heard."[56] A week later Way was back in Lyons before the commercial association, this time to take on Clem Yore in face-to-face debate.[57] Despite Way's efforts, however, most of the press coverage was becoming increasingly one-sided and negative.

Way had now narrowed his principal opponents in Estes Park to six— Enos Mills, C. H. Bond, Clem Yore, Alfred Lamborn, Charles E. Lester, and Donald MacGregor—and had identified to his own satisfaction the motives of each, which in the case of all but Bond and Lester he imputed to self-interest. Mills and Yore wanted to operate their own machines for profit. Lamborn was merely "the mouthpiece of Mr. Stanley, who is no doubt influenced by the failure of the Rocky Mountain Parks Transportation Company to continue the use of the Stanley steamers." MacGregor would like to run cattle in the park and saw the monopoly as a threat to his ranching interests. Bond and Lester, on the other hand, were speaking for the old-time Estes Park residents who resented changes in "old accepted policies." Toward such individuals Way was philosophical. "During the summer months they are too busy to give thought to these questions; during the winter months they have nothing to do but look up trouble."[58]

As summer 1920 approached and seasonal jitneys renewed their opposition, there had been sufficient talk for Way to add two more local residents to his list of troublemakers as probable "ringleaders"[59]: Charles Robbins, a painter-decorator, and Lawrence E. Grace, owner of the Gracecraft Shop. The provocations of both men were obvious. Robbins had erected a large billboard advertising trips into the park on Stanley property at the juncture of the Big Thompson and North St. Vrain Roads where tourists approaching the village could not fail to see it. Grace had gone farther and was particularly confrontational, advertising in the local phonebook that his National Park Service Auto Company had touring cars available day or night to "see the Park in comfort and safety." He also placed a sign with similar advertising in the window of his shop. Not content with simply soliciting business, Grace attached a blank telegram to the window with a note suggesting that people step inside, register their protest, and "rid the country of the possibility of the Prussianized control of the National playground." Robbins was only slightly more circumspect in passing out cards listing trips to the fish hatchery and Fall River Road.[60]

Despite the fact that Emory more than doubled his fleet of touring cars to 53 for the 1920 season, by the end of June the village was crowded with rent-car drivers. Although Superintendent Way was still operating under the constraints imposed the previous summer and was determined to act prudently, another incident was inevitable. It came less than two weeks later, on July 13, 1920, and involved Charles Robbins. That afternoon, ranger Dwight S. McDaniel stopped Robbins's car and its passengers on Fall River Road between Horseshoe Inn and Fall River Lodge. McDaniel warned Robbins that if was stopped again he would be arrested. That same afternoon a defiant Robbins re-entered the park, was again intercepted by McDaniel, and just as promptly ejected. Way did not immediately attempt to make good on McDaniel's promise of an arrest. He had learned that Robbins, Grace, and Mills had sworn out a warrant charging assault and battery, to be served when an arrest was made of one of their drivers. Armed with the news, Way tried to engage the issue directly with those involved—to no avail. "I have endeavored in every way to handle this situation without going to the extreme," he wrote Cammerer on July 17, 1920. "I have talked with Robbins on the street, and have received nothing but ridicule. I have also had a conference with Robbins and Grace in this office, and was laughed at and sneered at; and urged to take action."[61]

It was Robbins who forced the issue. On the day of his letter to Cammerer, Robbins filed a complaint against Way and McDaniel in Larimer County Court, asserting, as Mills had done, his right as a citizen to travel freely "and without molestation" over public roads. He contended that McDaniel's actions in stopping and ejecting him "were attended by circumstances of insult and a wanton and reckless disregard" for his rights, and asked for $1,000 in damages.[62]

These legal skirmishes, together with Way's failure to make arrests, only heightened tensions in Estes Park, where the audacity of the Robbins suit gave many the impression that Way and the Park Service were powerless to enforce the transportation policy. As incidents multiplied, so did the level of provocation. On July 20, temporary ranger Maye M. Crutcher, returning to the village from the top of Fall River Road, met and stopped a for-hire driver named Harry McMahan, who not only refused to give the names of his passengers and leave the park but who, on his return when Crutcher again intercepted him, "threw on more power and yelled for me to get out of the road which I had to do to escape being run down."[63] Two days later McMahan, again operating in the park illegally, did virtually the same thing, this time in the presence of three government witnesses.[64]

Way once again sought instructions. On June 24 Cammerer wired his superintendent to station additional rangers at the park entrances, keep careful track of all violators, and post in conspicuous places copies of his telegram with its clear reference to U.S. penal law.[65] A less dedicated man might simply have waited. Whatever charges would later be leveled against Way and his performance as superintendent, lack of dedication, determination, and energy were not among them. Anxious to prevent further episodes if at all possible, Way summoned to his office the next morning the one individual who, next to Enos Mills, he had come to identify as closest to the center of the opposition. Way was determined to explain personally to Clem Yore his instructions from Washington. He also no doubt suspected that, once summoned, the egotistical Yore would be likely to respond, as Enos Mills, just as probably, would not.

Yore arrived at 10 A.M. He responded in much the way the superintendent expected, posturing in the manner of the town bully in one of his western novels. Should the instructions in Cammerer's telegram be carried out, Way was told,

> we would get into trouble, that the rent car drivers (by inference Robins [*sic*], Grace, Thomson and Mac Mann [*sic*] and Kerr) would use force[;] that they were in a killing mood: that he had used his influence to keep them in hand in the past but that now they were getting beyond his control and that there was likely to be a killing if we attempted to carry out our instructions. He talked as tho he was the ringleader and adviser of this crowd and stated that in the event we did carry out our instructions they would start criminal case against myself and rangers. I told him that we were Federal officers under oath to do our duty and carry out instructions and that we would therefore be compelled to do so regardless of consequences.[66]

After making these threats, Yore left, only to reappear two hours later. He had "instructed the boys to go ahead as before but not to use force."[67]

During the next three days Ranger Crutcher, armed with high-powered binoculars, recorded six more instances of illegal entry. Such hands-off tactics, of course, only emboldened the jitney drivers and made inevitable the kind of incident that Yore said he would try to prevent. It occurred the day after Yore's meeting with Way. On the morning of July 26, 1920, one of Yore's confidantes, Grace, was driving a car with two women passengers and a maid along Fall River Road. At approximately 10:30 A.M., as Grace's car reached a point about halfway between the fish hatchery and Horseshoe Park, it was stopped by ranger Dwight McDaniel. What happened next became a matter of hotly contested debate. According to the passengers—Mrs. John F. Thomey, the wife of a St. Louis manufacturer, and her traveling companion, Mrs. George Howell—Grace stopped his car on demand, telling McDaniel that he had no right to halt their trip until after the Robbins and Mills cases had been decided by the courts. Then, without further provocation Grace and his passengers maintained, the ranger jumped onto the running board of the open touring car and grabbed Grace around the neck, "stating that the Government had given him the privilege of using force, and he would use it."[68]

Ranger McDaniel had a decidedly different version. Having been informed by Way of Yore's warning that there was likely to be a killing and that he should therefore be on the lookout, McDaniel maintained that when Grace reached toward his back pocket he assumed that he was going for a gun and that the act of grabbing the driver was, therefore, an act of self-defense.[69] Grace immediately filed a complaint with local justice of the peace J. J. Duncan, charging McDaniel with willful assault. The case was heard six weeks later on Wednesday August 11, 1920, in a makeshift courtroom at the Odd Fellows Hall in Estes Park village.

Before this date there had been further developments in the legal actions brought by Charles Robbins and Enos Mills. Harry B. Tedrow, representing the Department of the Interior, was successful in having Robbins's damage suit moved from state to federal court. Tedrow also received from federal judge Robert E. Lewis a permanent injunction barring Robbins from operating a passenger business within the park. Robbins's lawyers, the Fort Collins firm of Lee and Shaw, which also represented Mills, immediately appealed the decision to remand the damage suit. But this did not prevent Judge Lewis from handing down the requested injunction against Robbins. Lewis then announced that a final decision in the case of *Mills vs. Way* would be withheld until the Robbins appeal was heard by the Circuit Court of Appeals.

The trial of ranger Dwight McDaniel trial did not go well for the National Park Service. The Odd Fellows Hall was packed with some one hundred visitors, who witnessed proceedings that Way characterized as "decidedly a farce" and a "frameup."[70] Grace's passenger, Mrs. Thomey, it turned out, was a personal friend of Yore, and the former lawyer, to Superintendent Way's annoyance, was a visible presence in the courtroom where he offered "his usual advice" to Mrs. Thomey and others while calling attention to himself. The state district attorney, acting for the prosecution, acknowledged the government's right to make the arrest, choosing to focus attention on McDaniel's excessive use of force. Four witnesses were called: Grace, Yore, Mrs. Thomey, and fellow passenger Mrs. Howell. Grace insisted that after stopping the car he had reached down for the gear shift and not a gun, while Yore denied under oath that he had ever told Way "that there was liable to be a killing" (even though, as Way subsequently noted, "he told the same story to several other people in the village the same day").[71] Despite the fact, as Way later observed, that all the witnesses but Grace were seated in the rear seat and had no way of seeing Grace's action, their testimony was sufficient to convince Judge Duncan that McDaniel had used force that went beyond his official capacity. The ranger was convicted on the charge of assault and battery and fined $50 and costs. Given the circumstances, the government's attorneys decided that an appeal would be useless, leaving McDaniel, who could not legally be reimbursed, "to take the count."[72]

The court's decision was, of course, well publicized, and Way and the Park Service once more found themselves on the defensive. Mills had continued his verbal attacks, including a "red hot circular" titled "Politicians and Profiteering in the National Parks" in which he repeated his increasingly shrill litany about "poor service, overcharging, incompetence, neglect, and actual collusion of park officials with monopoly favorites." He followed this diatribe with yet another published attack, this time in Estes Park's summer newspaper, *Trail Talk*, asserting that the "vicious transportation monopoly" was simply "acting as a political machine for the director of the National Park Service." Their goal, he warned, is "to have the Estes region added to the Rocky Mountain National Park, so as to give this monopoly and the park officials the power to wreck the private holdings in this region and pluck the visitors who come to it."[73] Even those accustomed to Mills's hyperbolic prose must have shaken their heads.

Given the manner of their assertion, refuting such accusations was impossible, and Way wisely did not try. Mills, undeterred, was back in the news as the 1921 tourist season began when he used a luncheon debate before the Denver Civic and Commercial Association to repeat in Way's presence his accusations of collusion, "blackmail," and "doubled and trebled transportation rates," which during 1920 "deprived at least 10,000 persons from entering the park."[74] "Mr. Mills made some most astounding statements," Way wrote about the event in his monthly report. "It is my opinion, and the opinion of many others present, that Mr. Mills was practically laughed out of the debate."[75]

Way's confidence that public opinion had turned decidedly against Mills and his followers did not waver. As proof he cited the lack of further trouble with rent-car drivers and, the ease with which he secured sixty-foot right-of-ways from Pieter Hondius and other property owners along the High Drive, in Horseshoe Park, and along Fall River from Horseshoe Park to the park's entrance that fall in anticipation of the need for formal ceding of the state and county roads within the park. The following spring there were further signs of support. In the March 1921 town elections, opponents of the Park Service (who Way listed as "Messrs. Yore, Lamborn, Grace, Church, Bond, [and] Mills") attempted to make a referendum of the transportation issue by introducing an alternative slate of candidates, supporting for mayor none other than justice of the peace J. J. Duncan, the man who had fined Ranger

McDaniel in his altercation with Grace. The fact that Duncan received but eight votes Way took as yet another sign that "the bulk of the people of Estes Park appreciate the work we are doing and are favorable to our policy. . . . Needless to say," he told Washington, "I have taken no part in this election."[76] Way had further good news to report that May when the Estes Park Woman's Club passed a resolution by a ballot vote of thirty to four to gift its lot in the village to the park for an administrative site.

Although the 1921 summer season was relatively quiet, by early fall there were signs that the government was becoming tired of the issue and the controversy surrounding it. Coming through Estes Park during a visit to Yellowstone and other western parks in late September, Albert Fall, the latest in a quick succession of Secretaries of the Interior, in a speech before the Woman's Club told his audience, with Mather at his side, that "the controversy about concessions in the Rocky Mountain Park must cease or he would feel compelled to go before congress and secure the repeal of the act creating the Park." In answer to a question about the effect such an act would have on the railroads and their advertising of the Estes Park region, the passenger traffic manager of the Union Pacific, who happened to be a member of Secretary Fall's party, "stated emphatically [that] further attention to the region would necessarily cease" and that the five railroads, which spent $500,000 advertising the park, would devote their attention—and their dollars—to Yellowstone and other places.[77]

Fall's comments about abolishing the park were not lost on the Estes Park business community. Within weeks the Chamber of Commerce "passed a resolution by a vote practically unanimous, endorsing in strong language the present policy of the National Park Service and its management."[78] "The future of the Park is of grave importance to the State," the *Estes Park Trail* editorialized in reporting the meeting, "and the local Chamber felt it high time to let the government and the people know their true opinion of the trouble a few persons have sought to stir up concerning the concessions feature, which is in common with the other National Parks."[79]

Although the following months did not bring the resolution Secretary Fall had demanded, they did witness two major changes among the leading combatants. On October 24, 1921, without warning and under a set of circumstances that surprised everyone, Way resigned his position as superintendent. Way had been offered and accepted the superintendency of the national park in Hawaii and had wired Washington that he would be ready to sail by November 4. Then, having left Denver for Arizona on vacation, Way suddenly decided to purchase a 2,400-acre ranch on the San Pedro River near Mammoth and enter the cattle business.

Eleven months later and with equal suddenness came the death of Enos Mills. Mills, who had spent much of the previous year lecturing across the nation, died on September 21, 1922, following treatment for a severe abscess that required removal of a portion of his jaw and several teeth. He was only fifty-two and left behind him a wife of four years and a three-year-old daughter. At his well-attended funeral at Longs Peak Inn there were only generous words. In death the memories were kind ones—memories of the colorful, animated, and genial innkeeper whose friends and admirers included some of the great names of his generation, and memories of the naturalist and mountaineer whose enthusiasm and near childlike capacity for wonder came through clearly in print and in person. He was once more the "Father of Rocky Mountain National Park," not the angry, hypersensitive, outspoken critic of the Park Service and its managers, unwilling or unable to compromise issues or to meet opponents halfway. Fortunately for posterity, the less pleasant side of Mills was converted by family, friends, and apologists into a kind of martyrdom or simply overlooked and forgotten.[80]

Not so with Louis Claude Way. Way, it is has been said, had few admirers, and Dixie McCracken, one of the park's original three rangers who had parted with Way over the stunt involving the Eve of Estes, maintained that when Way left Estes Park in October 1921, he did not leave a single friend in town.[81] Such an assessment is untrue. The *Estes Park Trail*, speaking on behalf of "Mr. Way's friends in Estes Park," extended him "best wishes for every success . . . in his new venture," and on the eve of his departure both Way and his successor were guests at a meeting of the Estes Park Chamber of Commerce, "one of the most largely attended meetings of the year."[82] There was, to be sure as his official Park Service photo portrait suggests, a certain rigidity about Way, the legacy perhaps of his military career and a less-complex world in which orders were given and obeyed without the need to explain or justify. Way deserves better than the judgment that McCracken and others have delivered on his years in Estes Park. With inadequate resources and beset with intractable issues and problems that none of his successors had to face, Captain Way served the National Park Service and Stephen Mather well. In retrospect, his sudden departure from Estes Park is not difficult to explain. Like Enos Mills, he had worn himself out pursuing a calling to which he was passionately committed.

Chapter 8

~

Rocky Mountain National Park:
The Toll Years, 1921–1929

L. C. Way's successor, Roger Wescott Toll (1883–1936), was superbly qualified for his assignment. A member of the first generation of Stephen Mather's Park Service, he was among the remarkable group of rising professionals whose sense of pride and purpose would mark them forever as "Mather's Men." Of equal, if not greater, importance, Toll was a Coloradan, the son of a wealthy and socially prominent Denver family with long-standing ties to the Estes Park region and to Rocky Mountain National Park.[1]

Mountains and mountaineering were Roger Toll's first loves. "A climb in the mountains," Toll would later write in an idiom reminiscent of John Muir and Enos Mills,

> builds up one's strength and adds new thoughts, new interests, and new information. It gives one a feeling of accomplishment in the very fact of having overcome the difficulties that intervened between the foot of the mountain and its summit and it affords many pleasant recollections for the afterdays. . . .
>   In the open, one learns the character of his companions with more rapidity and certainty than in the more conventional life of cities. A friend is defined as one with whom you would like to go camping again. Strong and weak characteristics rapidly develop. Selfishness can not be hidden. True and lasting friendship is often built up in a short time.[2]

8.1 *Superintendent Roger Wescott Toll, 1921–1929. Courtesy National Park Service–Rocky Mountain National Park*

Toll had begun early. Boyhood summers were spent with his three brothers, Charles, Henry, and Oliver, near Tolland west of Denver, where his father, Charles Hanson Toll, a prominent lawyer who served as Colorado's attorney general, owned land and had a mountain retreat. The Toll brothers also came to Estes Park. On August 22, 1894, at age eighteen, Roger Toll added his name to the registry at Lamb's Longs Peak House before, presumably, hiking the Longs Peak Trail. Even in winter, the mountains were not far away. From the windows of the large family home on Race Street overlooking Cheeseman Park were views of Longs Peak, Mount Evans, and Pikes Peak, the state's most prominent "fourteeners."

Like his brothers, Roger Toll went east to college. Then, after receiving a civil engineering degree from Columbia in 1906, Toll embarked on a romantic interlude during which he spent a year traveling the world with his brother Carl, stopping off in Switzerland long enough to climb Mount Rosa and several lesser peaks. There was also a six-month tour of duty with the Coast and Geodetic Survey, which sent Toll to Alaska to help chart and survey the coastline in the southern half of Cook Inlet. By fall 1908 Toll was back in Denver where he worked for the next seven years for the Denver City Tramway Company, one of his father's clients—the last three as chief engineer.

Toll was also a charter member of Colorado Mountain Club and before going off to World War I became one of its most active participants. Among Toll's earliest contributions was the CMC's famous mountain register, a weatherproof cast-bronze cylinder with a hinged top and spring fastening, holding pencil and registration book, which he invented in 1915 and then helped to place on many of Colorado's peaks. Four years later, in 1919, Toll took the lead in culling CMC records and gathering other information for *Mountaineering in the Rocky Mountain National Park*, the park's first modern climbing guide, published in 1919 by the National Park Service. It would later be said that Toll was "probably the only person who has climbed all of the 50 mountain peaks in Rocky Mountain National Park."[3]

Given his background and inclinations, it was perhaps inevitable that Toll should give up the often sedentary life of an engineer for a career with Mather's new National Park Service. While stationed in Washington as a major with the Ordinance Department during World War I, the personable Toll happened one day to drop by the Department of the Interior to talk about parks. Horace Albright was in. The two met, liked each other, and kept in touch. When a vacancy at Mount Rainier National Park opened up in September 1919, Albright suggested that Mather contact Toll. The two men met in Hawaii where Toll and his wife were vacationing and Toll was climbing mountains. Mather was impressed and Toll was hired for the job.[4]

Two seasons at Mount Rainier were enough to convince Mather and Albright that Roger Toll was among the best and brightest of the Park Service's young superintendents, and in fall 1921, they brought him home to Colorado. To what extent the troubles in Rocky Mountain National Park, where the situation seemed only to be getting worse, suggested that a change in superintendents was necessary is uncertain. Whatever the reasons, Toll's eight years as head of Rocky Mountain National Park more than justified their confidence. Contributing to Toll's success was his familiarity with place, together with his temperament and personality. It was said of Roger Toll that he never let differences rise to the level of antagonism.[5] That fact alone distinguished him from his immediate predecessor. But the thirty-eight-year-old Toll, like his boss Stephen Mather, had something more: the easily recognized poise and self-assurance of one born to lead. These qualities, taken together with the advantages and connections of his Colorado background, his interests, and his organizational skills, made Toll uniquely suited to the job that was now his.

As Washington surely expected, the news of Toll's appointment was well received in Estes Park and throughout the state. "Mr. Toll knows every foot of Estes and the Rocky Mountain National Park," the *Estes Park Trail* told its readers, "is . . . a member of the Colorado Mountain Club, and last but not least, is a perfect gentleman."[6] Toll undoubtedly found such endorsements helpful, for the challenges that Way had confronted, particularly with respect to the transportation controversy, immediately became his own. Although the death of Enos Mills removed the Park Service's most outspoken critic and reduced the level of public acrimony in Estes Park, the issue itself did not go away; but the nature of the debate changed as did the arenas in which the drama played itself out.

Of those in Estes Park prominent enough to make a difference after Mills's death, only Bond and Stanley seemed interested in pursuing the matter, and both were generally content to allow resolution through the state and federal legal system. Of the two, Stanley was the most publicly outspoken. In early December 1921, he authored a lengthy letter to the *Denver Post*, soon reprinted elsewhere, in which he strongly criticized the government's willingness to grant an exclusive franchise over roads "built by the people for public use." The *Post* treated Stanley's letter with deference, using its subheadline to capture succinctly and accurately the thrust of his argument: "F. O. Stanley Has No Criticism for Firm Operating Line, but He Declares Principle of Giving Exclusive Franchise over Public Property is Wrong."[7]

By the time of Toll's arrival in Estes Park, the issue of jurisdiction had advanced beyond individual lawsuits. While the Robbins appeal was still pending before the appellate court, Governor Shoup suddenly decided to enter the arena. Aware that most state roads passed through federal forest reserves or national parks, Shoup became concerned that the federal government might widen its claims to exclusive jurisdiction over roads other than those in Rocky Mountain National Park. To head off such action, he instructed the state attorney general's office to intervene directly in the Robbins case by assisting Robbins's Fort Collins lawyers in arguing the case before the U.S. Circuit Court of Appeals in St. Louis.

That decision, handed down on October 9, 1922, was in favor of the federal government on all points. Before that date, however, Governor Shoup had decided upon a new tactic. Because his initial attempt to introduce a brief on behalf of the state had been denied by the circuit court, Shoup now believed that direct action in the form of a new and separate state suit against park officials might be necessary to settle the jurisdictional issue once and for all. Before instructing Colorado attorney general Victor Keyes to move ahead, Shoup convened a meeting of interested parties in Denver on June 27, 1922. Toll, of course, was present; so too were Robbins's lawyers, Paul Lee and George Shaw of Fort Collins; Attorney General Keyes; and Governor Shoup.

As Toll reported in a lengthy, five-page letter to the director of the National Park Service two days later, the meeting was short but polite.[8] When called upon to comment, Toll had outlined the courses of action open to the government, among them the return of the entire park to state jurisdiction as Secretary Fall had suggested the previous fall. Keyes spoke of a compromise that included moving park boundaries to exclude privately owned land and resorts like those in Moraine Park, thereby providing rent-car drivers freedom of access. Governor Shoup said little during the meeting, although he remarked with a smile that he was in favor of federal control so that more visitors would come to Colorado. When the discussion ended, Shoup called aside George Shaw and later Victor Keyes for a few minutes in private. The hour-long meeting then adjourned "without having reached any stated decision."

Toll stayed in Denver to lunch with Keyes and Paul Lee. Keyes told Toll, apparently on the basis of his brief conversation with the governor, that he expected written instructions within a day or two to initiate a suit in the name of the State of Colorado. That afternoon, Toll sought out Shoup himself, so that he could "correctly report the situation" to his superiors in Washington. Given his remark about the desirability of federal control that morning, Shoup's response was surprisingly vague and noncommittal. That information, Toll was told, should be obtained from George Shaw because the governor "wanted to be fair to him." Toll followed up with Shaw the next day, only to be told that Shaw "did not believe any change in the regulations could be made that would be satisfactory." More to the point, Toll learned that a suit would be brought in Federal District Court and as park superintendent he would be the defendant. Should the suit be lost, Shaw told him, it would be appealed directly to the Supreme Court.

Before leaving their meeting, Toll pressed George Shaw on just "who was urging action on his part." While Shaw did "not definitely reply," Toll wrote in his letter of the next day that

> I assume that Mr. Stanley and Mr. Mills are the two most actively interested. I am inclined to believe that politics is one of the leading considerations in Shaw's action, rather than any unusual activity on the part of Mr. Stanley or Mr. Mills. Mr. Shaw told me that three of the Democratic candidates for Governor had stated that one of their platform planks would be in opposition to the Park Service regulation in this Park. It is quite possible that Mr. Shaw, who is Chairman of the State Republican organization, wishes to forestall this action, and it may be that the Governor is also influenced by political considerations. He has declined to become a candidate for re-election this fall, although it is generally understood that if he is sufficiently urged he might run again. I am unable to see that it is a good political move.[9]

Noteworthy about Toll's letter to Washington is not only its author's willingness to engage personally the principals involved but the way in which his knowledge of Colorado and its politics allowed him to depersonalize the issue by placing it in a different and larger context.

Attorney General Keyes was correct. On August 5, 1922, Lee and Shaw instituted a suit in the name of the State of Colorado against Roger W. Toll.

The federal government was excluded as a party, Lee later explained, "because the state complained only of the acts committed within its bounds by Mr. Toll and those under his direct authority."[10] Granby Hillyer, U.S. district attorney for Colorado, who had been joined in the case by James Grafton Rogers's Denver firm on behalf of Roe Emery's transportation company, moved to dismiss.

On October 9, 1922, before Hillyer could argue his motion, the Robbins case came to an end in St. Louis. The decision by the Circuit Court of Appeals to dismiss the suit was soon followed by the dismissal of Enos Mills's original suit against Way, leaving only Lee and Shaw's new action against Toll to be decided. The hearing on the motion to dismiss that case was held in the U.S. District Court in Denver on December 27, 1922, where it was taken under advisement by Judge J. Foster Symes, who had replaced Judge Lewis. On August 7, 1923, Symes granted the government's motion to dismiss, on the grounds that because the U.S. government was involved, the court was without jurisdiction unless so given by a special act of Congress.[11] Symes's decision was immediately appealed to the U.S. Supreme Court just as George Shaw had predicted.

Although active opposition to the transportation franchise in Estes Park had quieted considerably after Mills's death in September 1922, it was revived within weeks of Judge Symes's ruling. On September 2, 1923, Esther Burnell Mills used the first anniversary of her husband's death to host a midday dinner at Longs Peak Inn, where she announced the formation of the Colorado chapter of Friends of Our National Parks, an organization dedicated to "carrying on the fight of the late Enos A. Mills, against the power granted by the government to the superintendents of parks and the monopolistic control of transportation into the parks."[12]

Esther Mills's new organization attracted little attention, even locally, and by summer 1925 Toll reported that apart from "Mrs. Enos Mills, Mr. F. O. Stanley, Mrs. Anna Wolfrom Dove, Burns Will and probably a few others, there has been comparatively little recent agitation among the local people on the subject."[13] In point of fact, on the matter of the transportation company and the park's concessions policy the great majority of Estes Park's citizens had long-since made up their minds.

Much to the disappointment of the Department of the Interior and the National Park Service, the Supreme Court ruling handed down on May 11, 1925, proved inconclusive. The court decided simply that the District Court of Colorado had erred in its dismissal of the suit against Toll and remanded the case back to that court so that it could be retried on its merits. The government's attorney, George Stephan of Denver, now urged compromise.

The government's position, he told Toll, was "not a strong one," and an adverse ruling "would have an unsettling effect upon transportation franchises in other parks, particularly where the State has not ceded jurisdiction."[14] Although Toll dutifully reported Stephan's cautionary warnings to his superiors, he was probably not displeased when the Park Service decided to push ahead rather than temporize. "We have taken our stand and should adhere to it until the question is finally disposed by the court," acting director Arno Cammerer wrote Toll on June 17, "—then we must abide by the decision. . . . If the case is decided against us, then the question as to policy for the future administration of the park will be squarely up to us."[15]

The continuing role of the law firm of Lee and Shaw following the dismissal of their clients' cases and Enos Mills's death continued to perplex both Toll and the Park Service. While he lived, Enos Mills, with possible help from supporters like Stanley and Bond, had presumably been paying for much, if not all, of the litigation. The government now wanted to know just who was financing the opposition. In an effort to learn, Secretary of the Interior Hubert Work personally convened a meeting of all the interested parties in the Denver office of U.S. district attorney George Stephan on June 20, 1925. In attendance besides Secretary Work were Roger Toll, Paul Lee, and George Shaw, and three representatives of Emery's transportation company, including its lawyer. George Shaw refused to divulge the names of his clients or their motives, leaving Toll to conclude his report to Washington with the comment, "Apparently there is no present action to be taken, and things will just drag along for another year or so until the legislature meets, at which time the question of jurisdiction can be referred to that body."[16]

Frustrated, Secretary Work returned to Washington, now determined to force the issue politically through good old-fashioned arm-twisting. Enlisting Colorado senator Lawrence Phipps and congressman William N. Vaille as intermediaries, Work made it clear to the governor's office that unless the state withdrew its suit against Toll, Colorado would lose "at least $140,000" in federal appropriations that had been earmarked for road maintenance and construction in Rocky Mountain National Park. Congressman Vaille followed up Work's message with one of his own, restating the government's intention in a telegram to attorney general William L. Boatright. The result was yet another meeting of the principals, this time in the offices of Colorado's new governor Clarence J. Morley. On January 8, 1926, with Senator Phipps himself in attendance to reinforce the seriousness of Vaille's message, Attorney General Boatright, acting on behalf of the State of Colorado, agreed to dismiss the case against Toll, and Governor Morley agreed to submit to the

Colorado legislature a bill ceding the state highways in Rocky Mountain National Park to the United States.[17]

During the nearly six years that the jurisdictional issue remained largely a legal one, safely lodged in the federal courts, public interest in the matter had slowly waned. But once Governor Morley placed it in the political arena, inviting scrutiny and comment from every legislator and newspaper in the state, the ceding issue, predictably, became emotional and divisive once again. A bill to cede jurisdiction of the roads in both Rocky Mountain National Park and Mesa Verde National Park, drafted by James Grafton Rogers, was introduced in the Colorado State House of Representatives in January 1927.

The official posture of the Department of the Interior, Toll judiciously told the *Rocky Mountain News* in late December 1926, was a neutral one. "The government does not intend to enter into controversy or litigation with the state," he is quoted as saying, "but if the state wishes to cede jurisdiction, the government will accept it and assume obligation for road development."[18] There was also news from Washington: should the state refuse, $199,000 in federal appropriations for road work in Rocky Mountain National Park might well be forfeited.[19]

Once the cede bill was referred to the House Committee on Federal Relations, there was immediate opposition. Most of it came from mining interests in Boulder County and from northeastern Colorado that vehemently argued, as they had more than a decade before, that the new legislation would jeopardize irrigation and power projects desperately needed along the Front Range. At times the rhetoric, much of it framed in terms of states rights, became heated and hyperbolic with references to federal blackmail and intimidation. Some of it invoked the memory of Enos Mills. Typical was the response of the editor of the *Boulder News-Herald* who on February 5, 1927, told his readers, "This State does not surrender to threats. . . . Czarist Federal encroachment on the rights and property of States must stop!"[20]

The heavy-handed role of the state's congressional delegation proved counterproductive. Finding the state's apparent dallying an increasing source of embarrassment, it weighed in with a published telegram to Colorado's new governor William Adams citing "positive information that if jurisdiction is ceded, congress . . . will authorize expenditure of additional $1,435,000 for roads in Rocky Mountain National Park during next few years."[21] Such a message was easily converted by opponents into yet another instance of federal blackmail. Much the same was true of the speech given the following month by Secretary of Interior Hubert Work before both houses of the state legislature in which he threatened, like his predecessor, to abandon the park entirely. "If the state doesn't want the park enough to fulfill its promise to cede control," the Colorado native told the legislators, "let it go back to what it was before and let's forget it."[22]

Officials in Denver through the tourist-conscious Denver Civic and Commercial Association, the leading business and professional organization in the state, quickly rallied behind the new legislation, which also gained the endorsement of the Chambers of Commerce in Estes Park, Lyons, Longmont, Fort Collins, Allenspark, and Grand Lake, those communities most directly effected. The *Rocky Mountain News* lent its editorial support, rejecting the arguments of mining and irrigation groups. Nevertheless, the state legislature remained deadlocked. As the 1927 session came to an end, a joint house and senate committee agreed to a bill ceding jurisdiction to Mesa Verde but took no action on Rocky Mountain National Park.

The consequences of legislative inaction were soon evident, much in the way Secretary Work and others had predicted. Some $500,000 in funding originally earmarked for road construction in Rocky Mountain National Park was divided among eighteen other national parks, and a five-year, $1,237,500 federal road-building program within the state was "indefinitely suspended."[23] Roger Toll soon went on record as saying that the loss of expected revenue meant abandoning plans to build or reconstruct forty miles of roads and ninety miles of trails.[24]

When the manager of the Denver Civic and Commercial Association telegraphed congressman Edward Taylor to see whether the park's funding was actually to be distributed elsewhere, the response was immediate, to the point, and curt. "I am surprised that any one in Colorado doesn't know that," Taylor wrote, clearly giving vent to his frustration and annoyance.

> Because Secretary Work and both of our senators and Chairman Crampton of the Interior Department Appropriations committee that handles all appropriations for all the parks, and I, as the ranking minority member of that committee, have hundreds of times told its press and the legislature and all business men's associations that the Rocky Mountain National [Park] would never get any money for road building this year or any other year or at all until the Colorado legislature sees fit to pass a law giving the Federal Government the same jurisdiction over the roads it builds as every other state having a national park has freely given to its Federal Government. . . . .[25]

One paper put it even more succinctly: "No cede: no money."[26]

Despite continuing opposition of northeastern Colorado towns, by late summer and early fall 1928, with a new legislative session about to begin, the economic realities of the sort that Congressman Taylor had predicted had crystallized Denver's support of yet another attempt at ceding legislation.

"There's no sense in Colorado seeking to fight Uncle Sam," the *Rocky Mountain News* editorially advised the legislators on January 4, 1929, "it's like butting the head against a stone wall."[27] News out of Washington further strengthened that resolve. Senator Phipps let it be known that $457,000 for road building and park maintenance would be available if a cession bill cleared the legislature by March 4, 1929. The Department of the Interior and the Park Service also evidenced a new flexibility. In late January came word from Taylor that the Secretary of the Interior had agreed to a clause in the new legislation reserving for the state and its citizens water rights on existing streams within the park, removing what was for many along the Front Range a crucial sticking point—one that the Park Service itself feared might lead to further litigation.

In the end the passage of a new cede jurisdiction bill came quickly and with surprising ease. Despite predictions in the press that heated debates "will rage in the legislature again this winter," on February 7, 1929, the house passed the bill by a vote of 54 to 7. Senate concurrence followed. A relieved Governor Adams signed the bill, which was then sent on to Washington where Taylor quickly arranged for congressional legislation accepting Colorado's cession. The bill was signed into law by outgoing president Calvin Coolidge on March 2, 1929. Almost simultaneously, Horace Albright, Stephen Mather's successor as director of the Park Service, announced a ten-year, $1,750,000 road-building program, to begin with the construction of a new $650,000 "wonder road" across Trail Ridge to Milner Pass.[28]

∽

Roger Toll's role in the cede jurisdiction controversy, however important in securing the future of Rocky Mountain National Park, was far less visible than his day-to-day accomplishments as superintendent, particularly in the face of resources that remained limited. As late as 1927, Toll's permanent staff consisted of himself, assistant superintendent Thomas J. Allen, four rangers (including one chief ranger), and three support personnel. This staff was supplemented by a temporary clerk-stenographer, a clerk assigned to the information bureau at park headquarters, and fifteen temporary rangers employed for the summer season. Additional workers, hired for construction or maintenance work on road, trails, buildings, and for other assignments, brought the summer workforce to as many as a 125.[29]

The road and trail systems were constant and nagging concerns. Despite periodic attempts at repair and improvement, most of the roads within the park remained in deplorable condition—one-track affairs without passing lanes, quagmires, or dusty rutted trails depending on season with sharp turns, steep grades, and poor drainage. All but a few of the park's original wooden bridges also needed replacement.[30] Excluding Fall River Road, the park Toll inherited consisted of less than thirty miles of road, all of them within ten to twelve miles of Estes Park, making summer congestion inevitable. As Toll remarked in his 1923 annual report, in clear recognition of how the automobile now defined the tourist experience, "In less than a day an automobile party can cover all of the roads on the eastern side of the park, and on the following day they are apt to depart, feeling that they have seen everything that is accessible to them."[31]

Budgetary increases helped, although until 1926 appropriations for Rocky Mountain National Park, despite clear evidence of its popularity, continued to lag behind those of Yellowstone, Yosemite, and Glacier. In 1924 Congress authorized a three-year program, beginning with the 1926 fiscal year, to spend $7,500,000 on road improvement and construction within the national parks. Some $445,000 of those funds was earmarked for Rocky Mountain National Park, and Toll quickly made his priorities clear. More than two-thirds of the new monies, or $300,000, he explained in June 1924, would be used "to improve our present roads to a satisfactory condition before undertaking new construction."[32]

In 1924, however, these funds were still two years away. Toll's budget for that year contained only $18,750 for road maintenance and improvement. Toll used a portion of those monies to open the increasingly popular Glacier Basin region to automobile traffic by improving the "barely passable" road to Bear Lake, whose attractions now included Frank Byerly's recently enlarged Bear Lake Lodge, the first buildings of Frank Cheley's new summer camp, and the ranger station constructed in 1923. Visitors to Bear Lake that summer could also take advantage of a new three-mile trail into Odessa Gorge and Lake Odessa. That fall the Colorado Mountain Club and Frank Byerly helped pay to extend this trail to Fern Lake in anticipation of the CMC's annual winter outing to Fern Lake Lodge.

The 1925 budget was only marginally higher. Toll used his road funds to have crews widen two dangerously sharp curves on Fall River Road and improve the surface of its roadbed east of the Divide with the aid of a recently purchased portable rock crusher. He also widened and improved the grade on the Big Thompson entrance road (then located on the southwest side of Eagle Cliff near the Y junction) so that autos were able to pass one another. On Fall River Road at Chasm Falls, where since 1922 a plank bridge allowed visitors to cross the falls, a new parking area was created to unblock traffic. The parking facilities at Bear Lake were enlarged as well to handle the cars

8.2 New RMNP administration building, September 25, 1924. Courtesy National Park Service–Rocky Mountain National Park

coming to that increasingly popular area of the park. Toll also replaced the old and inadequate log-stringer bridge across Fall River near the fish hatchery. The new stone and masonry bridge, the first of a permanent type to be constructed in the park, made use of seven thirty-foot steel I-beams to reinforce a concrete slab floor.[33]

When the new funds finally came in 1926, Toll used the first installment to begin two major road projects. The first, which took two years to complete, reconstructed the Bear Lake Road, much of it on new alignment. This seven-mile project was planned and supervised by the Bureau of Public Roads, an agency of the Department of Agriculture with whom the National Park Service by now had an inter-bureau agreement, giving it access to state-of-the-art engineering. Work began above Tuxedo Park, where the road was redirected to eliminate the steep section climbing Glacier Creek Hill. The new route (the one traveled today) left the old road at the upper end of Tuxedo Park and followed the north side of Mill Creek for three-quarters of a mile to the lower end of Hallowell Park and the foot of Bierstadt Moraine. There it crossed Mill Creek, swung around the moraine, and climbed to the top of the hill where it rejoined the old road, keeping to the north bank of Glacier Creek all the way to Bear Lake. In order to allow travelers to reach

8.3 *Rocky Mountain Parks Transportation Company garage and offices on Elkhorn Avenue, 1924. Courtesy National Park Service–Rocky Mountain National Park*

the Glacier Basin campground, Toll constructed a spur road and bridge across Glacier Creek.[34] By June 1927 the first two-mile section above Tuxedo Park was open for use.

The second road project of 1926 was equally important. This was a 1.8-mile road at Deer Ridge linking the High Drive to Fall River Road in Horseshoe Park. Its completion facilitated tourist travel between Moraine and Horseshoe Parks and their resorts, eliminating the old road whose narrowness and excessive grade prevented passing. The section of this road descending into Horseshoe Park, which crossed a new 24-foot masonry-faced concrete bridge over Fall River, made possible the building of a scenic lake near Horseshoe Inn.

Toll's road maintenance problems were further reduced in 1926, with the relocation of the eastern boundary of the park, which returned to county responsibility some seven to eight miles of the Fall River Road, several miles of the Longs Peak Road, a short section of the High Drive, and all of the roads in Moraine Park as far as Stead's Ranch. The elimination of so much private property from the park would, it was hoped, make it easier for the state to cede jurisdiction.

Because of its popularity and use, Fall River Road also received attention. The road was a chronic concern. Even before its formal completion, it

had become obvious that many of its curves needed widening to allow automobiles and busses sufficient clearance. Retaining walls were also a problem.
Some as large as sixteen feet high and one hundred feet long were regularly
collapsed by winter snows and spring thaws. To make matters worse, because
of inadequate drainage, mudslides could close the road in any season. The
two slides created by a single cloudburst in July 1925 "practically washed out"
five miles of road and stranded one bus and ten cars that had the misfortune
to be trapped between them.[35]

Opening the road in the spring through five miles of snow on each side
of Fall River Pass posed yet another challenge. Compounding the task was
pressure from the railroads, transportation company, and private automobile drivers, all of whom wanted the road open for summer travel as soon as
possible, and certainly no later than the regularly advertised date of June
15. New technologies helped. During the years immediately following the
road's completion in 1920, snow removal was largely accomplished by crews
with hand shovels laboriously attacking the huge drifts in Fall River Valley,
which on the "Big Drift" just east of Fall River Pass could be as deep as
twenty to twenty-five feet. In some years it took a month or more of work
on this stretch alone to open a passageway for cars and busses. To facilitate
the task, in 1923 Toll took steps to improve the park's major road camp in
Little Horseshoe Park by widening its access road, installing a 600-gallon
gasoline tank, improving its buildings, and connecting its cookhouse to a
nearby spring. As funds allowed, additional equipment was brought in to
help, beginning with tractors and scrapers. In May 1925 the Park Service
began to use a specially constructed 17-ton steam shovel capable of handling one-and-a half cubic yards of snow at a single bite.[36] Six years later, in
1931, an early rotary-type plow—the "Snow-Go"—was purchased, which
saw service for many years.[37] Even with this new equipment, much of the
work still required hand labor, often under conditions of extreme wind and
cold with workers subjected to the constant danger of snow blindness and
frostbite.

During his first spring in the park, Toll used two tons of ordinary dynamite to expedite the process of snow removal. The following spring, in an
attempt to decrease time and expense, Toll called in representatives of the
DuPont Powder Company to demonstrate the use of its new instantaneous
detonating chord, known as Cordeau, a ribbon of powerful TNT encased in
lead pipe. Set off by a blasting cap, the entire length of ribbon exploded
simultaneously. Toll was impressed. That October, he placed 650 pounds of
Cordeau in fifty-pound sealed boxes at intervals of twenty-five feet along the
road east of Fall River Pass where the winter's heaviest drifts were anticipated.[38]

8.4 *First transportation company bus being hauled through the Big Drift on Fall River Road, June 20, 1923. Courtesy National Park Service–Rocky Mountain National Park*

8.5 Steam shovel handling twenty feet of snow on the Big Drift, June 9, 1927. Courtesy National Park Service–Rocky Mountain National Park

Successfully detonated on May 24, 1925, the explosion removed about one thousand cubic yards of snow and opened a trench some fifteen to twenty feet wide and three hundred feet long to an average depth of six feet.[39] Toll estimated that his experiment cut the cost of snow removal on the Big Drift by nearly three-fourths. That year the road was opened a full six days ahead of schedule.

This technique and the new steam shovel made possible a snow removal system on Fall River Road that the Park Service would follow for a number of years. Removal on the east side of the Continental Divide began around the first of May, with the steam shovel slowly moving up the road toward the Big Drift on the top of Fall River Pass. If weather turned bad crews could find comfort and protection in the 14-by-18-foot stone building, Timberline Road Camp, that Toll had built in 1925 just east of the pass itself. By the end of the month the dynamite along the Big Drift had been exploded and a path cleared, allowing the steam shovel to move west where by mid-month it would meet hand crews from Grand Lake working their way east. The formal opening of the road for summer travel, always a special and well-photographed event, was achieved by having a horse-drawn team pull a transportation company bus or some other vehicle through the remaining snow. Toll noted in his monthly report for July 1926 that the entire job that year involved the removal of 119,359 cubic yards of snow, more than a third of which still had to be removed by hand.[40]

Opening the roadway, however laborious and time-consuming, was only half the spring battle. There were also annual snowslides to contend with. These came down from the south slopes of Mount Chapin in three well-identified places within less than a mile of one another. So predictable were these slides that two of them were assigned names—the one closest to village was called "Fan Slide," the one next to it "Middle Slide" (or "Old Faithful"). They presented a formidable challenge. In 1926 Fan Slide ran about the first of May, bringing down some thirty feet of snow along nearly five hundred feet of road. Two years later, in spring 1926, Old Faithful closed the road six times; on one occasion nearly taking the life of a Park Service worker who had stopped his truck to remove snow from the road ahead.[41] Victory against the elements on Fall River Road was always short-lived. By mid to late October, if not earlier, the first winter snows had closed the road once more, sealing off the alpine world of Trail Ridge until the spring ritual began again seven months later.

~

Toll was equally worried about the condition of the park's one hundred miles of trails, all but a few miles of which predated the park itself. He was particularly concerned about the longer trails because of their obvious importance to those who came for extended stays and spent their vacations roaming the backcountry on foot or with saddle horses. Such visitors, Toll realized, were far more likely to form a special attachment to the park and return than those who casually inspected the mountain scenery from the safety of their automobiles or one of Roe Emery's touring busses and then motored on in search of new sights and stimulation. "These have opportunity to see much more of the park, and to see it in a more leisurely manner that brings a higher degree of enjoyment and appreciation," he noted in his 1923 report. "For this class of visitor the trails should be improved. . . . Rocky Mountain [National] Park will never be fully opened up by automobile roads, but it has great possibilities as a delightful trail park."[42] A "trail park," of course, required good trails.

The Longs Peak trail system with its increasing number of hikers and climbers, two-thirds of whom were now routinely attempting the summit without a guide, demanded major attention. Two months before the park's dedication in 1915, the CMC had placed the first weatherproof bronze canister of the kind that Toll himself had designed on the summit to allow climbers to record their achievement. When the record book was replaced fourteen months later, on October 1, 1916, it contained 883 names, representing visitors from thirty-five states and three foreign countries.[43] By 1923 that number had grown dramatically.

The three existing trails to the Boulder Field also left much to be desired. The most popular and crowded of the three came up from a trailhead in the Tahosa Valley, not far from the Hewes-Kirkwood and Longs Peak Inns. This trail had been built originally in 1882 by Elkanah Lamb and his son Carlyle, who used it in connection with Longs Peak House, then becoming a popular way station for those bound for the peak. This trail, which replaced a much steeper and more difficult pony trail built four years earlier, brought climbers to Timberline Cabin, a small frame bunkhouse, near the sheltered trees at Jim's Grove, that Enos Mills had built for overnight use in 1908. The second, or North, trail to the Boulder Field began in Moraine Park. This trail, built by Abner Sprague's brother, Fred Sprague, in 1885, climbed along the west branch of Wind River and the west side of Battle Mountain, joining the Tahosa Valley Trail at Granite Pass. A third and lesser-used trail, built in 1910 by Abner Sprague, connected his resort at Sprague Lake in Glacier Basin to the North Longs Peak Trail.

The trail from the Tahosa Valley was the most critical, yet nothing was done until summer 1921, when Way had a survey made to reconstruct a major portion of the original Lamb trail. Although the National Park Service would not establish its first standards for horse and bridle trails until 1934, the trail that rangers Dean Babcock, Tex Eddins, and their crew laid out that summer was a step in the right direction. It decreased the grade of much of the existing trail—which in places was as high as a fatiguing 30 to 40 percent—to a more manageable 15, and relocated it away from ravines with their drainage problems. The only disadvantage, more than compensated for by the improved grade and condition, was that the new trail was a bit longer than the old. It followed heavy forest along the ridge most of the way, breaking timberline on Mills Moraine to the east of the peak and close to what is today the junction below Jim's Grove. This new trail was so accommodating that chief ranger Lloyd McDaniel was able to ride his motorcycle all the way to timberline.[44] Even mountain veteran Cliff Higby was complimentary, if in a backhand way. "I think it is now the best trail in the Park," he noted in August 1922—adding, "which by the way, is not saying much."[45] That same month Toll had ranger Mac Dings paint "yellow discs with red centers" to mark the remainder of the route from the Keyhole to summit, creating what generations of climbers have come to know as the "fried egg route."

After the death of his cousin, Agnes Vaille, on the Boulder Field in January 1925, following the first successful winter ascent of the East Face, Roger Toll took a number of steps to increase safety on Longs Peak in the hope of avoiding future tragedies and facilitating rescue efforts. Toll's efforts were also motivated by the decision of Enos Mills's widow to close Timberline Cabin for the coming 1925 season and abandon the now-dilapidated structure to the custody of the Park Service. Located at an elevation of some 11,050 feet, the frame 12-by-24-foot building with its two small tiered bunkrooms had been used by climbers and vacationers for almost two decades and, most recently, had served as a shelter for the party sent out to locate and recover Agnes Vaille's body and find her missing rescuer Herbert Sortland. As a stopgap measure, Toll had a telephone line, connected to the Estes Park exchange, strung on ten-foot poles from Timberline Cabin through Jim's Grove to the Boulder Field. Had such a system been in place the day of the tragedy, Toll later told the press, aid for "Miss Vaille and Walter Kiener, her companion, . . . could have been summoned in time to save the life of Miss Vaille and greatly lessened the suffering of all who participated in her attempted rescue."[46]

The new telephone line was installed by ranger Jack Moomaw and a small crew, which cut and packed in the poles, together with wire and hardware. The poles were particularly cumbersome. Because a large part of the line was located above timberline and exposed to the elements, summer lightning flashes miles away "would sometimes cause the wires to pop and sparkle long before the thunder was heard." On one occasion a worker who had the misfortune of standing just under the low wires "was knocked sprawling when a charge bounced off."[47]

During summer 1925 Toll also laid out a new trail from Timberline Cabin and Jim's Grove to the middle of the Boulder Field. The old trail from Jim's Grove to Granite Pass ran almost directly uphill (parallel to the new phone line), and because of its steepness was a constant victim of erosion. The new and more scenic trail was constructed by Moomaw and seasonal ranger Curtis Skinner. It ran south from Jim's Grove to Mills Moraine and was partially achieved by reconstructing the existing trail to Chasm Lake. From there an entirely new trail, beginning at approximately 11,600 feet, crossed the face of Mount Lady Washington to Granite Pass where it joined the old trail and then ascended to the Boulder Field by means of a series of gentle switchbacks. The new trail and its "spectacular" views, Toll predicted, will become a popular trip "for many who do not intend to climb Longs Peak" and "one of the most important trail trips in the park."[48]

Prior to 1925, the Longs Peak Trail ended at the north side of the Boulder Field near a flat rock with steel rings installed by the Estes Park Woman's

Club as a hitching rack. As Moomaw recalled, their aim was to make the new horse trail into the center of the Boulder Field "look as though it has always been there."[49] This took more than two tons of dynamite, all of which had to packed up by horse. Despite the difficulty of the task and the fact that when it came to trail-making Moomaw was self-taught, the gently winding new trail, constructed over a relatively smooth and stable surface of small rocks and gravel, was open for use on July 14, 1925. The following year a new three-quarter mile trail was built from the Longs Peak Trail to Chasm Lake, where five years later a shelter cabin was erected from which to conduct rescue operations on the East Face and elsewhere on the mountain.

The Sprague Trail to the Boulder Field, the so-called North Longs Peak Trail, was also reconstructed. During summer 1928, Moomaw and a crew began the project by building three miles of trail above Alberta Falls and completed the task two years later by reaching the junction with the trail coming up from the Tahosa Valley. This trail climbed steadily east and then south, passing through the visible remains of the Bear Lake fire of 1900, and joined the Boulder Brook Trail from Sprague Lake before ascending the flanks of Battle Mountain to Granite Pass.

During summer 1925 Toll also decided to open a new route to the summit by installing cables on the ledges of the North Face above Chasm View, near where Agnes Vaille had fallen during her descent. Such a measure, he believed, would reduce congestion on the regular Keyhole route where on a summer day climbers could be found strung out all along the back of the mountain, often dangerously crowding each other in the Trough and on the Narrows and Homestretch.

Although plans for installing the cables were presented to Toll in August 1925 by a recovering Walter Kiener, Agnes Vaille's Swiss-born guide, the actual task of installation fell to the dependable Moomaw. The task proved prodigious. The five-eighths inch galvanized-iron cable was 200 feet long and far too heavy and cumbersome for the back of a single packhorse. Moomaw solved this logistical problem with the help of seasonal rangers Glenn Walker and Harry Simpson. They loaded the cable on two horses with a few feet of slack between them, and by that means brought it to the end of the horse trail. There the cable was uncoiled, then lugged on the shoulders of a trail crew across the granite face of the cliff like a long snake. During the week-long installation, it was decided to cut off some thirty feet of cable and install it in two sections, the upper cable some forty feet above the lower and more difficult one. The cables, capable of sustaining five tons and fastened to eyebolts embedded in six inches of concrete and secured by clamps, were ready for use by September 2, 1925. They were almost immediately christened by guide Robert Collier Jr. and a party of six (including four women), who then returned by way of the regular Keyhole route, establishing a pattern that climbers would follow for years.

Moomaw and his team did their work well. The cables, although never very popular with guides, lasted without need for major repair until 1973, when they were removed to turn the North Face back into a technical route.

~

Thanks to Roger Toll the summers of 1925 to 1927 were the busiest in Longs Peak history. His efforts were helped by Agnes Vaille's father, Frederick O. Vaille, who donated funds for a small granite and cement shelter hut to be constructed on a narrow ledge just below the Keyhole at an elevation of 13,200 feet. Designed by Denver architects, the cylindrical building, with its beehive roof, narrow door, and two deeply set windows, was said to have been inspired by ancient dwellings in the Apulia region of southern Italy.[50]

Toll's major project of these years was built five hundred feet below the Vaille shelter in the Boulder Field itself. This was the story-and-a-half rock building officially named the Boulderfield Shelter Cabin, but more widely known as the Boulderfield Hotel, which together with its adjacent stable were intended to replace the now-abandoned Timberline Cabin. Although Toll originally wanted to locate both structures on the saddle between Longs Peak and Mount Lady Washington near Chasm View, for strategic reasons the site was changed to the Boulder Field itself.

Construction on both the Vaille shelter hut and the Boulder Field Shelter Cabin began in August 1926 under the direction of Denver contractor Lars Laursen. His task was formidable. The sand to make concrete had to be packed up by horse and burro from the Longs Peak campground, over a trail that rose some 3,000 feet, and then carried in sixty-pound bags to the two building sites. In the case of the Vaille shelter, this meant crossing the entire Boulder Field with its great slabs of granite and climbing an additional 500 feet. The rest of the materials, tools, and supplies, including the timber, had to be brought up the same way. There was also the weather, unpredictable in any season. Not surprisingly the work went slowly. Guide Harold Dunning, who watched construction progress during his goings and comings, recalled that even on the warmest days it was necessary to keep gasoline torches going under the mixing boxes so that the cement would not freeze. On many days, because of wind, rain, or sleet, the men could not work at all.[51] "It was hell," Moomaw recalled two years later. "Horses came in nearly every day covered with ice. I packed the rest of the lumber myself and froze the tips of

8.6 *Colorado Mountain Club at Boulderfield Shelter Cabin, July 31, 1927.* Courtesy *National Park Service–Rocky Mountain National Park*

my fingers one day. But we finished everything we were supposed to do and came out in a blizzard the last day of September."[52]

Given these conditions and the shortness of the season, construction on the cabin, its adjacent stable, and the Vaille shelter hut was not completed until early July 1927. Built of native boulders, the eighteen-foot square shelter cabin—which Robert Ripley's syndicated "Believe It or Not" column later dubbed the "highest hotel in the world"—was designed to be impregnable to the elements, with its concrete floor and massive corner-buttressed double walls strengthened on the interior by tie rods. The inside consisted of a single room with a double-deck bunk, table, benches, storage boxes, and coal and kerosene stoves. Above was a low unfurnished attic or loft used for sleeping and reached by ladder. Access to the building was through a strong plank door looking out at the North Face, so located to prevent the accumulation of drifted snow. On each of the other three sides metal-paneled windows offered views of the Boulder Field approach route, the Keyhole, and Storm Pass.

Despite the care taken to build floor and walls, its timbered roof proved problematic. Winds sweeping across the amphitheater below the Keyhole are legendary. Dunning compared their power and ferocity to dynamite, for they "can blow things all to smithereens and then stop and be as quiet as if nothing ever happened."[53] On three occasions after completion the winds tore the roof off completely, scattering it in bits and pieces across a wide area of the Boulder Field. The problem was finally solved by imbedding the great roof timbers in rock and cement across the top of the building, then wiring and nailing the roof to the timbers and piling tons of rock on the roof itself. The roof of the nearby 85-foot-long stone stable—substantially larger than the shelter cabin and resembling a five-car garage—presented a similar problem. By the time of its construction, however, the shelter cabin had been completed and the lesson of the wind learned. As a result the roof of the stable was made so it could be taken off and stored over the winter. Although that solved one problem, it caused another. Digging drifted snow out of the roofless stable at the beginning of each season proved a considerable task.

Toll had originally planned to leave the shelter cabin unattended and open for free public use. But as it neared completion he was approached by thirty-four-year-old Robert Collier Jr., a longtime summer resident of Estes Park and an active climber, who asked about operating the building as an inn or small hotel under a concession agreement. The fact that Collier was also an experienced guide, and agreed to provide a guide service for approved and posted fees, appealed to the safety-conscious Toll.

This arrangement worked well for the better part of a decade. Collier outfitted the shelter and took care of the business side of things, while his wife, Dorothy, a well-known climber in her own right, helped prepare and serve meals.[54] Her outgoing personality, it was said, served to compensate for the more serious demeanor of her husband. For all their efforts, the Colliers made little if any money running their hotel, even after Dorothy was added to the park payroll as a fireguard. That fact scarcely mattered, however, to the hardy souls who came to stay, and during its brief existence the Boulder Field Hotel enjoyed great popularity. Not the least of its attractions was the companionship of the healthy young men who Collier recruited to be his guides. It was demanding assignment: the guides worked seven days a week for a salary of a dollar a day, taking tourists to the summit and back for a fee of two dollars.

Collier's guides nonetheless considered their summer experiences on Longs Peak as among the most memorable of their lives. One of them was a young man named Merrill Mattes, who had been recruited by Collier in his hometown of Kansas City and would go on to enjoy a highly successful career with the National Park Service. "While the standard scheduled climbing time began right after breakfast and ended at noon," Mattes recalled, the guides were on standby for those who wanted to get to the summit in the afternoon. Frequently, therefore, we led climbing parties twice during the day. This was no strain on us, once adjusted to the rarefied altitude. In fact, at times, when business was dull, we would scramble up and down the North Face by ourselves—between the hotel and the summit— to see who could make the round trip by that route in the fastest time. I don't know who holds the record for this non-Olympic event, but in a letter sent home at the time I reported doing it in a little over an hour.[55]

Mattes and his fellow guides slept with the overflow guests from the hotel in a small shed at the end of the stable, a space intended as tack room, which they dubbed the "bridal suite." Days began early with a 4:30 A.M. wake up call from Robert Collier, delivered in a voice that "seemed loud enough to echo off the East Face. . . . Sometimes," Mattes added, "this routine failed to penetrate the ears of the guides sleeping in the neighboring 'bridal-suite.' Then he would wake up these delinquents by throwing a handful of rocks on the top of the shed's tin roof."[56]

The esprit de corps of Collier's Longs Peak guides of the late 1920s and early 1930s is perhaps best reflected in a surviving piece of memorabilia: an undated series of "Don't Ask" questions and answers, written by hand on Boulderfield Shelter Cabin stationary, which poke good-natured fun at the tenderfeet who invaded their mountain domain.

1. *Do you live here all winter[?]*
   No—the inclemency of the weather makes it impossible. We usually spend the cold months in warmer climes.
2. *Don't you ever get lonesome up here in the rocks[?]*
   No indeed. We meet so many interesting people from all over the world and they ask such intelligent questions.
3. *Where do you get the fresh veg.[?]*
   All fresh veg. are grown in a garden patch on the other side of the Keyhole & the freezing temp. keeps them crisp at all times.
4. *How did that stove get way up here[?]*
   It was packed between two horses. At every switchback it was necessary to stop & repack the animals in order to get them around the turns.
5. *What do you use the rope for[?]*
   When people fall off the east face we use it to measure the distance they fall.
6. *Do people die many times during the summer[?]*
   Only once, Madam.[57]

As their questions and answers suggest, the guides had ample time on their hands, for which a wheezy wind-up phonograph, their major source of entertainment, only partially compensated. "Songs by Rudy Vallee were played so often that they squeaked," Mattes noted, "and would drive me out into the night to contemplate the starry heavens."[58] It could, however, be exciting. On more than one occasion Mattes and his fellow guides were pressed into service to help rescue climbers in trouble. In August 1934, they were needed close to home when Dorothy Collier fell and suffered a concussion, after which she was unconscious off and on for the better part of two days. Guide Hull Cook, who was also a medical student, used the telephone line to consult with doctors in Denver because it was felt she should not be moved.[59]

There were other duties as well. One that Mattes remembered vividly came on July 4, 1929, when he was called upon to help with the fireworks display sponsored by the Estes Park Chamber of Commerce and set off from the summit of Longs Peak. This event had begun two years before, in imitation perhaps of the New Year's displays staged atop Pikes Peak, when Collier and his young assistants detonated some thirty-six flares just after dark. A similar display was repeated in 1928, attracting considerable attention. In 1929, the chamber wanted to improve the show by using 100,000-candle-power magnesium flares that would be visible for miles around. Two hundred pounds of fireworks were transported to the shelter cabin by burro. From there the cases of combustibles, some weighing upwards of sixty pounds, were taken to the summit on the backs of the guides. "We scrambled up the mountains," Mattes recalled, "blithely indifferent to the fact that none of us had ever handled big, professional-type rockets. The result was several scorched fingers and eyebrows as well as a glorious display that could be seen, presumably, from all over central Colorado."[60]

The Boulderfield Shelter Cabin operated for nine years, from 1927 through the 1935 season. Despite the fact that it was built to be airtight so that snow would not blow in, each winter the building would fill up with ice and within a matter of years the walls themselves had begun to show cracks. A study by Denver architects in fall 1935 confirmed that the building was "rapidly collapsing." What Toll and the architects did not know, and what we are today only beginning to appreciate fully, is that the Boulder Field itself is composed of debris atop a massive glacier whose movement over time is capable of destabilizing any structure on its surface.[61] By 1936 the structural deterioration in the shelter cabin had become so serious that it was closed. A year later it was dynamited into oblivion to prevent collapse and accidental injury, ending yet another chapter in Longs Peak's colorful history.

Although the Boulderfield Hotel has been gone for more than sixty years, the Agnes Vaille Memorial still stands at the Keyhole above. But as

Harold Dunning noted many years ago, the Vaille hut with its stone bench and open door and windows "is of little use [as a place of refuge] because it is too small and a very cold, undesirable place to even think about staying in." Had it been built on the south side of the Keyhole, Dunning continues, it would have been in the sunshine and therefore have been a better shelter. As it is, the six-foot in diameter structure never sees sunshine and remains remote and cold, a grim reminder of mountain tragedy rather than a place of refreshment and cheer.[62]

~

Roger Toll's improvements to the Boulder Field and its approaches were timely. Not only were climbers attempting Longs Peak in record numbers but during the first three decades of the century were finding new, and ever more dangerous, ways to make the journey. Enos Mills in his younger years was responsible for several of these historic climbs, including a June 1903 descent of the East Face to Chasm Lake. He also made two important new ascents: one from a place two hundred feet east of the Keyhole, about midway between the Keyhole and the Trough; the other from the summit of neighboring Mount Meeker by way of the Notch. Unfortunately for mountaineering historians (although perhaps fortunate to the extent they discouraged others from attempts to repeat them), Mills recorded his exploits only in the vaguest of terms or left their reporting to others.[63]

More recent was the ascent of the North Face made by Willard T. Day on July 1, 1916. Having left his party at the Keyhole, Day made a "hard and perilous" climb along the east side of a snow patch at the edge of the chasm and from there worked his way directly to the summit with the aid of a four-inch crack in the rock. His time from Longs Peak Inn was three hours and fifteen minutes. "It is strenuous," Day noted in the aftermath, "and should not be attempted unless one is in good condition, physically and mentally, and willing to take a chance."[64] The following year, on September 23, 1917, Roger Toll and a party of three made a similar ascent of the North Face. They too found the going difficult, concluding that "the north side of the peak is too steep and too frequently icy to make a safe or practical route."[65]

Far more remarkable was the first recorded climb of the rugged East Face. This was accomplished on September 7, 1922, by James Wadell Alexander, a thirty-four-year-old assistant professor of mathematics from Princeton and guest at Hewes-Kirkwood, who made the trip alone. According to the original plan, it was to have been a joint effort. Alexander, a member of the Colorado Mountain Club, was to have been accompanied by

Jack Moomaw, and the two men spent several days in preparation, scanning the East Face with binoculars to pick out a feasible route. On the appointed morning, because his wife's riding horse was missing, leaving the ranger without a way to get above timberline, Moomaw did not go. Alexander decided to make the attempt by himself despite the fact, he later told Moomaw, that "since early boyhood he always had a terrible fear of high places; and that the first time he climbed Longs Peak, by the regular trail, he almost 'gave up' at the Key Hole [sic]."[66]

Alexander left Hewes-Kirkwood at 8:30 A.M. and by 2:30 that afternoon was standing on the summit where he was greeted by a party of four telephone men. Reaching the base of the East Face above Chasm Lake, the plucky professor crossed the snowfield by cutting seventy-four steps across the ice with a borrowed axe. From there he reached and traversed the ledge known as Broadway, which he had the honor of naming, and then by climbing through accessible chimneys made his way to the top. In his descent Alexander followed the narrow ridge on the southwest corner of the peak that leads from the summit to the top of the Trough, thus bypassing both Narrows and Home Stretch.

Two days later Alexander repeated his feat, this time in the company of Moomaw who took a number photographs, several of which quickly found their way into newspaper and magazine articles. On this attempt Alexander was wearing tennis shoes, which became wet and so battered by the scrambling and jumping over scree that they actually peeled off, leaving him incapacitated to spend the rest of his vacation mostly "playing cards with the women at Hewes-Kirkwood Inn."[67]

Other historic climbs of Longs Peak's East Face followed and by a variety of new routes. These included an ascent of the North Chimney leading from the top of Mills Glacier to Broadway by William F. Ervin and Colonel Bruns three years later, in 1925, and the first successful winter ascent and descent, using Agnes Vaille and Walter Kiener's route, by Clerin "Zumie" Zumwalt and Charles Hardin in January 1934. On September 10, 1922, Elmira Buhl became the first woman to climb the East Face, when she duplicated Professor Alexander's exploit with a party made up of seven members of the CMC.

The other notable achievement of the 1920s belongs to Joe and Paul Stettner, two brothers who had climbed extensively in the German and Austrian Alps before immigrating to the United States. In September 1927 the Stettners made their way to the summit of Longs Peak using a route to the right of Alexander's Chimney, then "perhaps the most difficult climb in the country" and "certainly the most advanced, not only on the face, but in all of Colorado, until after World War II."[68] The Stettners had come from Chicago that summer on their motorcycles over dusty, unpaved roads, bringing with them the pitons and carabiners they had used so successfully in Europe. Locating 120 feet of half-inch hemp rope in a village store after someone at Longs Peak Inn refused to lend them one (because he thought it too late in the season and the brothers too young and inexperienced), the Stettners spent the night in the abandoned Timberline Cabin, by then in a "powerful state of disorder." The next day they made their way to the foot of Mills Glacier beyond Chasm Lake, from where they scanned the East Face for a route to the summit.

Although they knew about Alexander's route, the Stettners were determined to find something new, choosing a course that led by means of a series of plates, cracks, and ledges to Broadway where the wall of the East Face begins. There they changed from hobnailed boots to felt-toed climbing shoes. With younger brother Paul in the lead and snow falling around them, they renewed their ascent, negotiating their way to the summit over the series of ledges that now bear their name. At one point Joe fell and was left dangling in space. Fortunately Paul had a good belay and the rope held, allowing his brother to find a good hold on the wall below. So difficult was their route that it would be repeated only twice in the next two decades, on the second occasion, in 1942, by Joe Stettner himself.[69]

~

In addition to the work on the Boulder Field, Toll devoted considerable attention to the trails of Wild Basin. Although the amphitheater-like region of glacial valleys with its forests, peaks, and tributaries of the North St. Vrain was but little known to early tourists, it quickly became popular once the park was established. The CMC helped by making Wild Basin and its thirty square miles of wilderness the site of its annual summer outings in 1913, 1916, and 1919. For the 1916 event ranger Cliff Higby built a footbridge across the St. Vrain at the junction of Cony Creek and a trail south along the river. This allowed campers to enjoy the beauties of Calypso Cascades (or Calypso Falls, as they were then called) and provided the first step in linking the Ouzel Lake and Pear Lake Trails. These two trails and others received regular use, and by the time of Toll's arrival virtually all of the trails in Wild Basin, like those elsewhere in the park, were in need of repair or reconstruction. This included the long trail to Thunder Lake, built by the Forest Service sometime before 1912, which then terminated on a ridge a mile east of the lake itself.

The watersheds of Wild Basin, on the other hand, were well-known and had already been exploited by water interests in Longmont, Lyons, and other valley towns. By the early years of the century, in fact, there were trails of sorts leading to reservoirs at Sandbeach, Blue Bird, and Pear Lakes, originally constructed to bring in equipment and supplies for dam building. Sandbeach Lake, filed on as early as 1902 and possibly used for storage purposes even earlier, was reachable by two routes: one by a road along the north side of Horse Creek's south branch coming from Meeker Park; the other, by means of a more traveled four-mile trail leading from the northeast side of Copeland Lake through the forest. The original dam at Sandbeach Lake had been unreinforced and its 1903 breaching sent a wall of water cascading below, wiping out the bridge across the St. Vrain near Copeland Lake and doing considerable damage. This dam was replaced by a ruble and masonry structure in 1906 and by a concrete one in 1911. Beyond Sandbeach there was a trail leading to the Homestretch on Longs Peak, blazed by Jack Moomaw in 1921. This trail, good enough for horses to travel well above timberline, was used in early August 1922 to bring out the body of J. F. Kitts, who had been killed by lightning on the summit.

The filings on Bluebird and Pear Lakes also dated from 1902. These were made by the Arbuckle Reservoir Company, which had built the original mile-and-a-half road that entered the park near Copeland Lake. In 1915 the company received approval from the state engineer to build a dam at Bluebird Lake, then reached by a trail that stayed on the north side of the North St. Vrain until it had crossed both Cony and Ouzel Creeks. From there this trail headed south to climb the increasingly steep moraine to timberline and into the narrow, walled valley where Bluebird Lake (Arbuckle Reservoir #2) is located. Material to build the fifty-seven-foot high dam, completed in 1923, was brought up over this trail, including the bars of reinforcing steel. These were chained in bundles to an axle beam connecting two wagon wheels, with one end of the load dragged along the ground behind a team of four horses. Sacks of cement were brought in more conventionally by donkeys, as was the disassembled rock crusher used to make sand for the cement and the old automobile engine that powered the crusher.[70] By contrast, the original bridle trail to the Pear Lake Reservoir (Arbuckle Reservoir #4), cut by contractor Henry H. Hutcheson in 1910 to haul in cement, entered Wild Basin from Allenspark and not along the North St. Vrain from Copeland Lake.[71] The Pear Lake dam was completed in 1916.

As money became available Toll went to work improving the Wild Basin trail system. The scenic Pear Lake Trail was extensively reconstructed during summer 1924. It took hikers around Finch Lake and along the top of Copeland

Moraine through forests and glacial debris to the rockbound reservoir below Mount Copeland. In 1926, at the suggestion of the Allenspark Chamber of Commerce, a new three-mile trail was constructed from the Pear Lake Trail along the north side of the moraine to cross Cony Creek at the foot of Calypso Cascades. It then continued on past Ouzel Falls to connect with trails to Ouzel, Blue Bird, and Thunder Lakes. As Toll noted in his annual report that year, the trail "increases the accessibility of points in Wild Basin, helps to unite the trail system in that region, and offers an attractive circle trip."[72]

Between 1928 and 1930, the old Thunder Lake Trail through the depths of Wild Basin was extensively rebuilt in expectation that it would eventually be extended across the Continental Divide by way of Boulder Grand Pass. By 1930 a shelter cabin had been constructed at the lake. The desirability of such a trail was clear. It would allow hikers coming from Wild Basin to reach Grand Lake by way of the East Inlet Trail. Although the Hewes brothers and three of their guests from Hewes-Kirkwood marked a possible route with cairns as early as August 1913 and Jack Moomaw later had the route surveyed, the expense was prohibitive and this trail was never built.

Perhaps the most dramatic trail work during the Toll era, however, occurred in Horseshoe Park and in Glacier Gorge—on the trail to Lawn Lake and the trail that led to Mills Lake and Loch Vale. The existing trail to Lawn Lake was not new. It had been in use for many years, particularly after 1907 when Willard Ashton, builder of Horseshoe Inn, erected a cabin at the lake for use by guests interested in fishing. Four years later, in 1911, Hugh Ramsey and his workers substantially enlarged this trail into a wagon road up Roaring River to bring in the equipment needed to reinforce the earthen dam at the lake's outlet built in 1902 and 1903 by the Farmers Irrigating Ditch and Reservoir Company—the dam whose collapse some eighty years later would wreak so much damage along Fall River and upon the village of Estes Park.

The major reconstruction of the Toll years began in August 1928 and altered much of the existing trail by relocating both its beginning and end. Some 1.6 miles of new trail was added above Horseshoe Park by moving the existing trailhead away from Roaring River to its present location, a spot then just east of the Fall River Lodge power plant. New and old trails met where the old trail crossed Roaring River at its intersection with the trail to Mount Ypsilon. At the Lawn Lake end, there was another mile of new trail, making the approach to the lake less exposed by keeping it closer to the trees. Once completed, the new trail made it possible to reach the northern part of the park without having to use Fall River Road, whose narrow switchbacks could scarcely accommodate cars and horses and therefore posed a danger for hikers using the road. Three years later, in 1931, the Lawn Lake Trail was extended to Little Horseshoe Park and Deer Mountain, where at Deer Ridge it intersected with the trail to Hidden Valley, completed in 1923. The present Lawn Lake parking lot was not added, however, until 1936.

Toll's alteration of the existing trail leading to Mills Lake and the Loch in 1927 was even more spectacular. Although it made the trip to those lakes a bit less direct, hikers now were introduced to lovely Alberta Falls, named by Abner Sprague in honor of his wife. The original trail, built in 1913 by the Estes Park Business Men's Association under Sprague's direction, avoided Alberta Falls entirely. That trail remained on the east side of Glacier Creek until the falls were passed and then turned southwest between the Glacier Knobs and Half Mountain to enter Glacier Gorge. In 1921 L. C. Way had this trail shortened, reducing the distance from Glacier Gorge to the Loch to some two and a half miles. Way's trail (which today exists as a sparsely-used fire or emergency trail) begins a short distance above the trailhead at Glacier Gorge Junction and follows the terrain on the west side of the Glacier Knobs.

Toll's attention to the trail to Loch Vale was part of a larger plan to open up the entire Glacier Gorge region for greater use. Abner Sprague helped by swapping his ownership of the two 80-acre tracts on which Mills Lake and Loch Vale were located, receiving in return title to the 160 acres containing his Glacier Basin resort. Toll relocated Way's 1921 trail to the east of the Glacier Knobs so that it enjoyed a series of unobstructed views looking toward Sprague Lake and Bierstadt Moraine before and after reaching Alberta Falls. This required the building of a long eighty-foot bridge to cross the swampy area just above Glacier Gorge Junction. In Toll's day the trail above Mills Lake to Black, Green, and Frozen Lakes was scarcely used. As late as 1933 park naturalist Dorr Yeager noted that the trail beyond Mills Lake leading to Black Lake was "faint (often only blazes)" with "No trails above Black Lake."[73]

~

In addition to the new administrative headquarters building near the village completed in October 1925, Toll also oversaw the development of a badly needed utility area to house the repair and storage facilities for maintenance and construction operations. As in the case of the administration building the issue was one of funding, and it was not until fiscal year 1923 that Toll's budget permitted him to negotiate for a suitable site. Accessibility to Estes Park was a major consideration. Toll soon found a desirable twenty-acre tract located south of the High Drive near Beaver Creek, some two miles southwest of the village and less than half a mile inside the park's eastern boundary, a site sufficiently hidden from public roads to make its buildings inconspicuous. Its owner, the Estes Park Development Company, agreed to a price of $100 an acre, and that October the sale was concluded.

Construction began almost at once. The first buildings erected were a machine shop, a nine-stall garage to shelter the park's motor equipment, a warehouse, and a mess house for road crews operating within the park. The new 30-by-78-foot machine shop, which allowed for overhauling motor equipment during the winter months, was completed by 1924 and by the end of the following year a total of seven peeled-log buildings had been erected within the new compound. The buildings, stained dark brown with green-shingled roofs to blend and harmonize with their surroundings, were designed by the National Park Service's landscape architects, making use of the style known affectionately as "Park Service Rustic," which called for decorative exterior stonework and extended pole rafters to improve the appearance of structures otherwise aesthetically nondescript. By the late 1920s a series of six small frame residences for Park Service employees had been added to the site. Construction continued into the mid- to late 1930s, and most of the current buildings date from that period.

~

Roger Toll's years at Rocky Mountain National Park fortunately coincided with the best economy that Colorado and the United States had seen since before World War I. For most people this meant a higher level of affluence and discretionary spending than they had ever known. Part of this new-found wealth was invested in family vacations to places like Rocky Mountain National Park and in automobiles to get there. Many of these vacationers came to camp, straining the existing facilities at Glacier Basin beyond capacity. For a time private campgrounds, where the standard charge was 50 cents per night, relieved the pressure. By the time of Toll's arrival these included O. P. Low's campground just east of the village post office, which accommodated more visitors than any other private campground inside or outside the park, F. O. Stanley's campground at Tuxedo Park, and the campgrounds operated by Daniel March and Charles Bryson along Fall River.

Adding to the challenge were the habits of autocampers who chose to dispense with campgrounds altogether and park and camp on public roads or on adjacent private property, often without permission. By summer 1922, as

Roger Toll noted in his monthly reports for both July and August, this practice, particularly prevalent along scenic Fall River Road west of the village, had become cause for considerable alarm.[74] This came not only from local residents concerned by the number of incidents involving defaced trees, refuse-littered campsites, and the careless use of fire, but from county health authorities and officials of the City of Loveland who feared that the Big Thompson was again being polluted. In response to what Toll referred to euphemistically as "a careless or destructive tendency," many property owners simply fenced their land and posted "keep out signs," prompting a spate of newspaper letters about the unfriendly attitude toward tourists in Estes Park. Making matters more difficult was the fact that the free campground at Glacier Basin was a long way from town and could be reached only over a steep grade.

Toll was able to address at least part of the problem by establishing new campgrounds. The first of these facilities, Aspenglen, was laid out on a forty-one-acre tract off Fall River Road purchased from Pieter Hondius and opened during summer 1924. Two other sites were acquired, one of nineteen acres in Endovalley at the upper end of Horseshoe Park on land purchased from homesteader Minnie March; the other, called Pineledge, south of the High Drive near the utility area, two miles from Estes Park. By 1925 both the Aspenglen and Endovalley campgrounds had been connected to Fall River Road. Beginning in 1925, thanks to a right-of-way secured from Pieter Hondius, the Park Service was able to obtain water for both utility area and campground by constructing a cut-off dam on Buck Creek above High Drive. Pineledge Campground was first used during summer 1926. By 1932, however, because of the need for housing and its location, Pineledge had been taken out of service and its road system incorporated into the utility area's new residential section.

These new campgrounds were particularly welcome, for Estes Park in the 1920s did not repeat the building boom of the previous decade. That same demand helped places like the Western Conference of the YMCA, or "Y Camp," with of its wide range of family-oriented facilities and activities and its reasonable rates—rates low enough to draw complaints from local hotelmen about unfair competition. By World War I most of the Y's original sleeping tents of the 1908 era had been replaced by more substantial tent houses and wooden housekeeping cottages, and its reputation as a summer destination had been firmly established.[75]

Under able and businesslike executive director Ira Lute, who assumed that position in February 1918, the Y embarked on a decade of expansion. Lute began by streamlining his administrative operations and recruiting professionals to staff them. That fall, in order to eliminate the Y's trouble-some debt and pay for needed improvements, Lute mounted a fund-raising campaign chaired by Estes Park summer resident William Sweet, a longtime supporter of the Denver YMCA who was about to be elected governor of Colorado. Although the goal of $100,000 was an ambitious one for the place and time, the Western Conference had important and influential supporters like A. A. Hyde of Wichita, Kansas, owner of the Mentholatum Company, and the Reverend John Timothy Stone, the energetic pastor of the largest Presbyterian church in Chicago, each of whom pledged $10,000. Through Stone's efforts, the Rockefeller Foundation made a similar pledge.

While the campaign was still in progress Lute and his board began to invest in the future, starting in 1919 when the grounds were electrified by means of a 10-horsepower generator and an existing steam engine. Other improvements followed, including staff housing, stone entrance pillars, a stone bridge across Wind River, a grocery store and post office building, a new stable, a bathhouse, and a major enlargement of the original 1902 Wind River Lodge. The first truly modern cottages, each with two bedrooms, kitchen, living room, and bath, also belong to this period. So does the area known as Fellowship Park, the 78-acre tract bounded by Glacier Creek, the Big Thompson, and Wind River purchased by Hyde from F. O. Stanley in December 1921.[76] Although, like the resorts and hotels of Estes Park, the Western Conference of the YMCA would soon find itself struggling with the effects of regional and national recession, these were good years during which the Y achieved a level of fiscal stability that it had not known before. Lute also made peace with the Y's for-profit neighbors by joining the Estes Park Hotel Association and inviting several local businessmen, including pho-tographer Fred Clatworthy, to join his board of directors.

~

Another phenomenon of the Toll years, one encouraged by the affluence of the times, was the establishment of a number of private camps for boys and girls in the Estes Park region, some within Rocky Mountain National Park itself. Park Service administration in Washington gave its blessing to such enterprises as it did in older parks like Yellowstone, Glacier, and Yosemite. While Frank Cheley's Bear Lake Trail School—a name later changed to Cheley Colorado Camps—was the best known and most enduring, a number of other camps in their day enjoyed a similar popularity if not the same longev-ity. What they shared was the belief of park proponents like John Muir, Enos Mills, and Stephen Mather that bringing young people—particularly youth raised in hectic cities and suburbs—into contact with outdoor life in an unspoiled and uncrowded wilderness setting encouraged clean living, developed appropriate Christian values, and promoted respect for nature, parents, God, and country. In the case of the Bear Lake Trail School, this form of wilderness education was guided by a man "acknowledged to be the foremost leader of boy work in this country."[77] The Cheley recipe worked, as attested to by generations of former campers who remembered into adulthood its traditions and rituals—a heady mixture of wrangled horses, hiking boots and backpacks, campfire songs, honors and awards, tents pitched in the rain, and sourdough flapjacks deftly flipped in the cool of a mountain morning over an outdoor fire. For many, Cheley became an intergenerational experience, eagerly passed on to children and grandchildren.

However famous, the Cheley camps were not the first. That honor belongs to the Rocky Mountain Boys Camp, established in August 1919 on a 120-acre site on the south lateral moraine above Hallowell Park in Mill Creek Basin by the Reverend Harrison Ray Anderson, pastor of the First Presbyterian Church in Wichita, Kansas, and two others. Fellow Presbyterian John Timothy Stone, who had originated the idea and owned the site, served as the camp's principal advisor. That first season the only two buildings on the property were an old shack and corral, the remnants of George Hallowell's ranching days in the 1890s. New buildings were soon added, and by 1921 Anderson's camp included five log cabins and four smaller structures. The largest served as lodge and library and was furnished with stuffed furniture, Navaho rugs, mounted skins, a piano, and a Victrola. Camp property also contained a livery, baseball diamond, tennis and basketball courts, and a swimming pool, said to be the only one within the national park. Water piped in from Mill Creek provided hot and cold showers. For entertainment on rainy days and evenings a wireless radio—a concession to civilization—was installed on the hillside.

The number of campers at the Rocky Mountain Boys Camp was small—only some twenty in 1921 and apparently never more than forty—but the range of outdoor activities made possible by the camp's own motor transportation included a five-hundred-mile six-day camping trip to the Medicine Bow Mountains of Wyoming, highlighted by a visit to the Frontier Days Rodeo in Cheyenne.[78] The camp's backers were not constrained by money. By 1923 the Rocky Mountain Boys Camp was advertising itself as "The Only Riding Camp in America": "If Staying in Estes Park, If Going to the Coast, Or Going Abroad—Leave That Boy With Us."[79] That season, thanks to Stone's recruiting, "the sons of many a wealthy Chicago family" were numbered among the campers in Hallowell Park.[80]

8.7 *Early Cheley Camp brochure. Courtesy Estes Park Museum*

The camp and its director, John H. Stevens, an insurance man from Chicago, offered no apology for the exclusivity of its clientele. As Stevens told the *Estes Park Trail* in July 1923,

> The progress of this Camp is being watched carefully all over the Country by educators, who are interested in the work with a special group such as this (these boys being the sons of the more wealthy) in the belief that the so call rich boy has need of natures [sic] most sublime lessons, and the mental and moral background offered by the now fast passing old West of the days of the range.[81]

Noble experiment or not, by November 1924 Stevens had sold his interest to a syndicate composed of Frank Cheley, David Primrose, and Cliff Higby.[82] Primrose, longtime athletic director and coach at Minnesota's Macalaster College, had come to know John Timothy Stone in Chicago while serving as director of physical education at Stone's church. Under Primrose's leadership the Rocky Mountain Boys Camp flourished. By 1928, with tuition set at $400 for the eight-week season, campers departed from Chicago's Union Station for Denver in a special car on the Burlington. Camp was divided into two "ranches"—the "Diamond Bar" outfit for older boys and the "Quartercircle T" for younger ones. Each camper was assigned his own horse and during the season was required to work on an "Attainment Plan" aimed at earning either the "Wrangler's" or "Cowpuncher's" degree (with their accompanying blue or red bandana) by demonstrating "proficiency in riding, hiking, campcraft, first aid, and general mountaineering activities." That year ten of the boys were taken on a post-season nine-day trip to Yellowstone at a cost of an additional $100.[83] Primrose continued to direct the camp until 1951, when the entire enterprise was sold to the National Park Service, which for a time used its buildings for seasonal housing and then razed them.

~

If the Rocky Mountain Boys Camp was for the sons of the well-to-do, the Olinger Highlanders drew from the other end of the social and economic spectrum: city youth from Denver's far from affluent north side. The Olinger Highlanders, a club founded in 1916 by Denver mortuary owner George Olinger, was initially made up of some one hundred boys ten years old or older, then playing baseball in the Highland section of Denver. Although the stated purpose of the organization was physical fitness and character-building through "instruction and entertainment" and mandatory church attendance, the Highlanders from the beginning had a decidedly military orientation: the boys appeared in distinctive military dress and were taught to drill, a skill that they frequently demonstrated in public. By 1922, the Olinger Highlanders, five to six hundred strong, were holding their annual camp at the Glacier Basin campground. A smaller winter camp took place at Fern Lake, where, like the members of the CMC, they made use of the lodge and its facilities. Prior to their 1923 summer camp, a company of Highlanders, together with the sixty-member Olinger Highlander Boy's Band demonstrated their well-disciplined talents by putting on a close order military drill and concert before an illuminated grandstand in Estes Park village for residents and tourists.[84]

For a time in 1922 George Olinger entertained the idea of establishing a permanent camp of his own at Fern Lake or Spruce Lake. The next spring, with membership in the organization now in excess of 1,200, he decided on the latter site and secured a permit from Roger Toll to build a camp for summer and winter use, plans soon abandoned because of the high construction cost at such a remote location. Glacier Basin was far more accessible and the Highlanders continued to use the site with the Park Service's blessing. "We are more than glad to have the Park utilized for this purpose," Toll wrote Olinger on May 18, 1923. "I would also like to say that your camp of last year was a splendid example of a systematic, orderly camp, and that everything was done by your organization to leave the grounds in good condition for the summer visitors that followed."[85]

The military nature of the Olinger organization was readily apparent, from the layout of the camp to its daily program of activities. The *Longmont Daily Times* described the arrangements for 1922 in some detail:

> The boys will sleep in tents, eight boys or a squad in a tent, and each company will have their own street, about 40 boys to a company. At the head of each company street, the captain's tent will be placed, where he will be in command. Directly behind the captain's streets will be the three majors' tents who are in command of each of the three battalions, the East, South and North. Directly behind the majors' row will be the colonel's tent with his staff, who is in command of all military activities. Headquarters will be established nearby for the adult leadership. . . .
> The whole camp will be patrolled by sentries, a company of 40 boys going on guard each twenty-four hours. A guard house tent will be provided for the boys on guard for their accommodation away from the rest of the camp, and any unruly boys are placed in this guard house under supervision.[86]

Adult leadership, as the description suggests, was small. Most of the actual day-to-day supervision came from sixty of the older boys, who as non-

8.8 Olinger Highlanders at Glacier Basin, July 1, 1927. Courtesy National Park Service–Rocky Mountain National Park

commissioned boy officers had attended a special two-day Highlander officer's training camp (or H.O.T.C.) prior to the arrival of the other 480 Highlanders, whose average age was eleven. In order to make the summer experience affordable, the fee was kept to five dollars for the week, which included a thorough physical examination with results delivered to parents in the company of their sons. While the afternoon regimen of outdoor sports resembled those of other camps, morning activities were decidedly military, beginning with 6 A.M. reveille and "the morning bomb," followed by breakfast, an hour of Bible study, and "straight military drill and tactics, band practice, etc."

Although there was no encampment for financial reasons during the Depression summers of 1933 and 1934 and again during the summers of 1945 and 1946, the Highlanders returned to Glacier Basin in 1947 as they had done for more than two decades. Highlander camp lasted into the 1950s when it was discontinued. By then, the military aspect of the Highlander program had became increasingly controversial among visitors and Park Service personnel, who objected to seeing boys as young as nine or ten marching in the meadows near the campground with heavy rifles as punishment for some violation of regulations.

~

The most successful and enduring youth summer camp in the park was the one begun by Frank Howbert Cheley at Bear Lake in 1921. Cheley (1889–1941), a proponent of growth into manhood through firsthand experience with the outdoors, came straight from the YMCA tradition. Born in Colorado Springs, where he briefly attended Colorado College, Cheley worked for the Y in South Bend, Indiana, and later in St. Louis, Missouri, where he directed summer camping programs. While in St. Louis, Cheley became acquainted with Lansing F. Smith, a Y board member, who was also president of the University Society Publishing Company, and it was Smith who helped launch Cheley's career as a writer, first as editor and author of the company's two 22-volume sets of books, "The Father and Son Library" and "Modern Boy Activity," and then as the highly successful author of his own books, more than forty in all, the majority of them directed at boys and their dads.

Returning to Colorado to further promote his "boy camp idea," Cheley worked briefly for George Olinger and his Highlanders organization and then for several summers directed the Denver Y's Chief Camp Ouray at Granby, which had opened in 1907. Cheley by now had fully developed his own camping philosophy, one that stressed learning by doing and the physical, social, moral, and spiritual development made possible through outdoor recreation. His goal for every camper became what he called "Fun-Plus," a motto that Cheley visualized in a logo copyrighted in 1934, showing the letters "F-U-N" inside a coiled lariat rope with a plus sign in the middle of an open letter "U." Not surprisingly, Cheley wanted a camp of his own.

Cheley began his Bear Lake Trail School—"an alpine summer camp for boys" between the ages of 10 and 17—in 1921 under a lease agreement with Frank Byerly. Construction on the first of what would be a small group of buildings began almost at once. These included a 36-by-45-foot headquarters lodge, Tipi-Waken, which contained a large second floor assembly room with great stone fireplace and bath and shower rooms, office, library, museum, and activity rooms below. It was built, like neighboring Bear Lake Lodge and its various outbuildings, of burnt trees salvaged from the fire of 1900. The elevated veranda offered a fine view into the wilderness of Glacier Gorge. That first summer there were nine campers, a number of whom attended on scholarship; in 1922 there were thirteen. That same year, perhaps to signal his commitment to the region, Cheley became a director of the Front Range Lodge Company formed by Frank Byerly and his wife Edna Bishop and which owned and operated both Bear Lake Lodge and Fern Lake Lodge.

As the number of campers increased, other buildings were added, including two dormitories. Meals continued to be taken at Bear Lake Lodge, which enlarged its kitchen. An active camp agenda was established early. According to one of Cheley's first camp brochures,

> The boys are awakened at 7:00 A.M. for a brisk setting-up exercise. Promptly at 7:15 there is a dip in Bear Lake, then assembly for flag raising, followed by breakfast. Next comes inspection of quarters and camp duties. Two and one-half hours of the forenoon are devoted to definite field instructions in campcraft, woodcraft, geology, birdcraft, forestry, botany, horsemanship, simple surveying and mapping, handicraft, knife and hatchet, etc. At 11:45 comes the daily swim, for Bear Lake is a spring-fed lake and is somewhat warmer than the mountain streams formed by the melting snow. At 12:00 comes dinner in the big dining lodge, followed by a rest period of reading, writing, chatting and quiet games. The entire afternoon is given over to activity by choice to innumerable beautiful spots—horseback trips, fishing jaunts, hikes, nature rambles, the construction of camp furniture, shelters, shacks and shanties. Supper will be served at 5:00, followed by an hour of group games. With the coming of darkness the campfire will be lighted, on the hill or by a lake as fancy may direct. After short vespers, conducted by the boys themselves, taps will sound, lights out for nine hours of refreshing sleep.[87]

By 1926 the capacity of the Bear Lake Trail School, now renamed Camp Haiyaha, had reached sixty. That summer Cheley and his staff of fourteen, which included Ernest Altick who would remain associated with the Cheley operation for many years, served a total of eighty-four different boys. It also saw the beginning of Cheley's Camp Chipeta, "A Vigorous Camp for Vigorous Girls," with an initial enrollment of twenty-five. Camp Chipeta made use of buildings located at Scott's Heights above the YMCA, with the two Cheley camps sharing a string of horses.

Frank Cheley became the victim of his own success. Increased enrollments, together with the fact that by 1925 the touring cars of the Rocky Mountain Parks Transportation Company were bringing ever-larger crowds of visitors directly to Bear Lake over the new road instead of terminating service three miles below, made it difficult to maintain an appropriately restful environment. "Do you know," Cheley is said to have told Ernie Altick, "one day we'll have 50 cars a day coming up here."[88]

During that memorable 1926 summer Cheley located a new 160-acre site for Camp Haiyaha at the head of Fish Creek, in a heavily wooded upland valley on the northern slopes of Twin Sisters Mountain. Later an adjacent 75 acres was obtained from Jacob Christian, who had used the land for his ranch and dairy operation. Borrowing money from Lansing Smith, Cheley began constructing a series of distinctive lodge and dining room buildings in preparation for an expanded camping operation that began in the summer of 1927. These included the buildings for two new Cheley camps for younger boys and girls, Ski Hi and Chipeta, as well as new facilities for Camp Haiyaha, which was transferred from Bear Lake in 1928 and relocated above the other two. The camp's former buildings at Bear Lake were converted to guest facilities for Bear Lake Lodge.

Although all Cheley's camps, or "Cheleyville" as they were dubbed by the *Estes Park Trail*, were an immediate success, the Depression left Frank Cheley so deeply mired in debt that in 1932 he could not meet his final payment to Lansing Smith. Despite record enrollments even during the worst of these years, that indebtedness lingered over the Cheley family for the better part of a decade and was finally discharged after Frank Cheley's death in 1941. By then, with Frank's son, Jack, and Ernie Altick serving as co-directors, the Cheley operation had been further expanded beyond the "Land O'Peaks Ranch" through the acquisition in February 1937 of 80 acres on Fox Creek near Glen Haven to create Trails End Ranch for Boys and for use as a base camp for backpacking and horseback trips. The remote site encouraged, in fact made necessary, a more rustic camping experience—one without electricity, flush toilets, and telephone and where the boys slept in covered wagons constructed out of old wagon beds. Four years later, in 1941, another 80 acres was acquired further to the east, some three miles up Dunraven Glade along the North Fork of the Big Thompson. This became the new site for Trails End Ranch for Boys; the old site on Fox Creek became Trails End Ranch for Girls, offering the same rugged outdoor experience as its brother camp. An additional 140 acres adjoining the main Land O'Peaks Ranch camp to the west and south, the former homestead property of sometime-poet Amanda Blocker Byrd, was acquired in fall 1944. The Cheley camps ran at full capacity during the years of World War II and by 1945, the year that Cheley celebrated the camp's twenty-fifth anniversary, young people from twenty-eight states had been exposed to the Cheley experience.

Other camps[89] and summer schools in the Estes region, including those operated by the Western Conference of the YMCA,[90] marked the decade of the 1920s. Most, however, were too small and too financially fragile to survive the general austerity of the 1930s and are now all but forgotten. Those that did, like Frank Cheley's camps, did so with difficulty even with their attractive settings and reputations. Although the 1930s by no means brought an end to boys and girls camps in and around Rocky Mountain National Park, the level of activity of the 1920s would not return until the years after World War II.

⁓

Roger Toll was transferred to Yellowstone National Park as superintendent on February 1, 1929, to replace Horace Albright. Stephen Mather had suffered a massive stroke the previous November and Albright, the man clearly most qualified to carry on the Mather tradition, had been called back to Washington to take his place. Toll, now highly regarded in park circles, was personally recommended by Albright to head the nation's oldest, largest, and arguably most prestigious national park. His confidence was well placed and for the next seven years, despite the difficulties of the Depression, Toll carried on the program for Yellowstone that Albright had begun.

Roger Toll died prematurely at age fifty-three. On February 25, 1936, he was killed in an automobile accident in New Mexico while on his way to Mexico City to negotiate the formation of an international park area along the U.S.-Mexican border. Toll's future with the Park Service was bright: in 1936 he seemed destined for even greater things. Nowhere was his loss felt more strongly than in Estes Park, where he had so often come in his younger days on CMC outings and where his seven-year tenure as superintendent was fondly remembered. That legacy is recalled today at the Toll Memorial erected by the National Park Service in his memory in 1941. The site was chosen with care. It stands on a rocky promontory of Sundance Mountain, high on the tundra above Trail Ridge Road, with a clear view of many of the mountains that Roger Toll had once climbed and named. Equally fitting is the metaphor with which George Barnard and Ellsworth Bethel, fellow CMC co-founders, concluded their brief April 1936 eulogy in the club's magazine, *Trail and Timberline*: "Remember the yellow discs which he marked the winter trails in Rocky Mountain. All unconsciously he has marked for us the best trail through life with golden markers—sincerity, devotion, kindness."[91]

9.1 Estes Park and Rocky Mountain National Park in 1927. Map by Richardson Rome. Courtesy National Park Service–Rocky Mountain National Park

Chapter 9

～

Growth and Maturity: Estes Park in the 1920s

BETWEEN 1919—WHEN THE PANORAMIC PHOTOGRAPH WAS TAKEN from Prospect Mountain—and 1926 the growth and development of Estes Park continued. Our understanding of how the village looked in that year rests on firm ground. Thanks to Sanborn fire insurance maps created from a survey completed in May and June 1926, we have a set of scaled drawings that provides us with an exact footprint of Estes Park, showing every hotel, residence, structure, and water line within the town limits and in much of the surrounding area as well.[1] Of additional help to historians are two volumes of insurance records which supplement the Sanborn maps and use a similar base line.[2]

What these maps chiefly show is the extent to which, in a period of seven years, the village had built itself out to become a busy commercial center dedicated to tourism. Dominating an increasingly congested Elkhorn Avenue were liveries, hotels, and garages, including the sprawling warren of interconnected structures that housed the freight and passenger operations of Roe Emery's Rocky Mountain Parks Transportation Company. In 1919 vacant lots and private residences were still found along Elkhorn Avenue. By 1926, the vacant lots were almost totally occupied with most of those remaining being used for miniature golf courses (there were three on Elkhorn by 1930) and other tourist amusements. Along upper Elkhorn from the Fall River Bridge to the Estes Park Bank only one private residence remained, the Homer James house, while in the block to the east, the number had been reduced to about four, including the homes occupied by the Service and Macdonald families. Much the same was true along Moraine Avenue, where the sturdy log home built in 1908 by banker Sidney Sherman had already been razed to make way for a local telephone exchange.[3]

Among the newer businesses on lower Elkhorn was Frank Rollins's garage and campground, a visible reminder of the way in which the automobile had now become a central part of the tourist experience. Located just east of the village park on the site of what is now the Municipal Building, these popular facilities had been originally opened by Oscar Peter (O. P.) Low in 1921 on land owned by F. O. Stanley. Rollins had taken over Low's operations in fall 1924 under a five-year lease that included free fuel and oil for Stanley's automobile. Rollins renovated and enlarged the business by installing a playground, fireplaces and picnic tables, and a new comfort station with hot and cold running water. He also painted the surrounding fences to match the colonial yellow, white, and red of Stanley's nearby hotel. By 1927 the Rollins campground, staffed with uniformed attendants, was being hailed as "one of the best equipped of such in the West."[4]

Across the street in the village park two new buildings, a library and town hall, had joined the post office, making the park—which for some years also contained a bandstand—seem rather un-park-like. The Estes Park Public Library, a neat stucco, wood, and stone structure, was designed to blend architecturally with the adjacent post office and school building. It had been built by the Estes Park Woman's Club in spring and summer 1922 at a cost of about $5,000, much of the actual construction done by village men who hauled in thirty loads of stone, logs, and sand.[5] Two years later, in fall 1924, the town hall was completed, a project under active discussion since at least 1919 when the town fathers briefly considered purchasing the movie theater on Moraine Avenue and converting it to civic purposes.[6] The new building, constructed of moss-covered granite and roofed with slate tile shingles, was sited back-to-back with the post office, its entrance facing west toward Virginia Drive. In addition to a meeting room for the village trustees, the town hall contained a jail cell "for scoffers of the law" and a garage large enough to house both a drying rack for a fire hose and the town's new White Motor fire truck (purchased the year before at a cost of $5,640, more than half raised by subscription). The town hall was soon serving other needs. By the following summer the Chamber of Commerce had been invited to establish an office in the front end.[7]

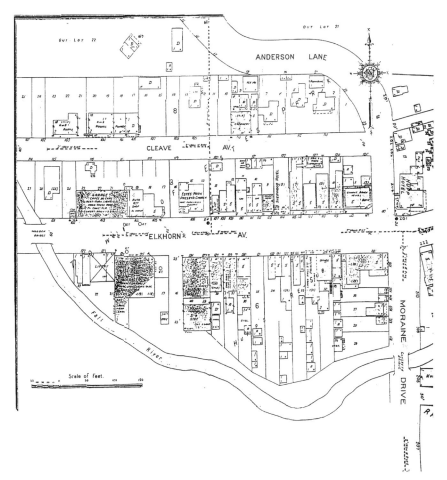

9.2 Sanborn Map of 1926. Upper Elkhorn Avenue to Moraine Avenue. Copyright 1926, The Sanborn Map Company, The Sanborn Library, LLC. All Rights Reserved. Further reproductions prohibited without prior written permission from The Sanborn Library, LLC

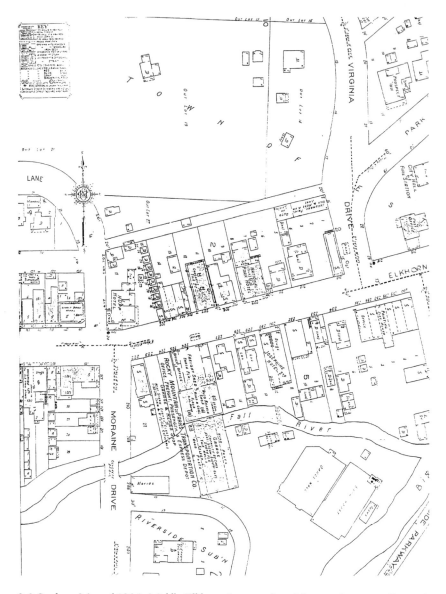

9.3 *Sanborn Map of 1926. Middle Elkhorn Avenue, from Moraine Avenue to Riverside. Courtesy The Sanborn Map Company. Copyright 1926, The Sanborn Map Company, The Sanborn Library, LLC. All Rights Reserved. Further reproductions prohibited without prior written permission from The Sanborn Library, LLC*

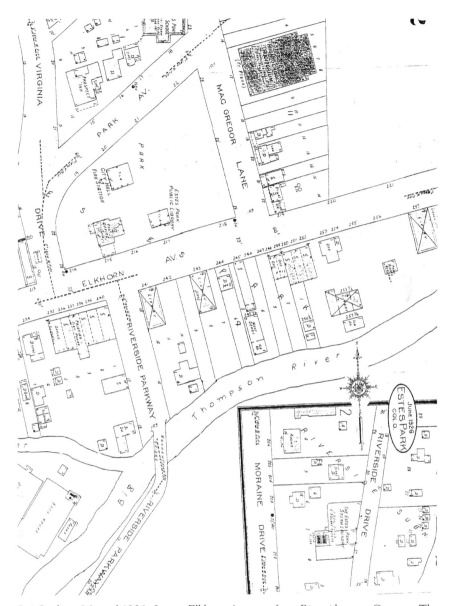

9.4 *Sanborn Map of 1926. Lower Elkhorn Avenue, from Riverside east. Courtesy The Sanborn Map Company. Copyright 1926, The Sanborn Map Company, The Sanborn Library, LLC. All Rights Reserved. Further reproductions prohibited without prior written permission from The Sanborn Library, LLC*

The town's maturity was signaled by halting attempts at "modernity."
Some of this was purely cosmetic, such as the new stucco veneer given the
Hupp Hotel in fall 1926 during a renovation that significantly increased the
number of rooms. The most visible signs of progress were several recently
constructed buildings on Elkhorn Avenue designed to house multiple businesses and provide the kind of permanency and fire safety that the rest of the
village so plainly lacked. Although fire posed a constant danger, especially
because of the mountain wind's strength, the town had been fortunate. The
two most dramatic fires of recent memory—those that razed Al Birch's home
in December 1907 and the Estes Park Hotel in August 1911—had occurred
in places without adjacent structures and therefore failed to touch off the
kind of conflagration that had devastated other Western towns. As a result,
few preventative steps were taken. As recently as 1921, the year when the
town finally passed an ordinance prohibiting additions to existing wooden
buildings, only four structures in the entire village could lay claim to being
safe from the threat of fire.[8]

The first of these new multi-occupant block buildings was erected by
Byron Hall and George ("Many") S. Billings in spring 1923. Located directly
across the street from the Presbyterian Church and east of the Johnson
Garage, the concrete and tile structure, fifty feet wide and seventy feet deep,
was designed to house three stores and featured a "modern" front of tapestry
brick, paneled columns, peacock quartz art ornaments, and plateglass windows. At the rear of each store were living quarters, consisting of a small
living room, kitchen, and bath.

Even more impressive was the Boyd Building, a block of seven stores
down the street at the corner of Elkhorn and Riverside. Built in spring 1925
of brick and tile, the one-story building with its 118 feet of street frontage
covered almost five existing lots. Two of the new stores had already been
leased by the *Estes Park Trail* and C. H. Bond and Company. For reasons that
are no longer clear (perhaps because of the wishes of their lessees) the stores
were not made uniform, varying in depth from sixty to eighty feet. No doubt
because of difficulties encountered in excavation, there was only a partial
basement. The Boyd Building provided downtown Estes Park with one additional sign of "progress": unlike its neighbors to the west, it was set back
eight feet from the property line. It also had a concrete front sidewalk and
gutter, the latter the first to be laid in the village.

In order to make room for the new building, Jim Boyd had to move
three others, including his own residence. His blacksmith shop on Riverside
was moved closer to the river and the original National Park headquarters
building, then still occupied by C. H. Bond, was moved to approximately

where the blacksmith shop had stood, no doubt so that Bond's customers would not be unduly inconvenienced by Boyd's clientele of horses, wagons, and cars. The third building on the property, the Boyd home, was moved to what was then the village outskirts.[9]

Three other fireproof buildings of the period reflect the town's growing concern with its own vulnerability. The earliest of these, the first brick and steel building in town, was located on upper Elkhorn Avenue just to the east of the future site of the Hall and Billings building. The 25-by-62-foot structure was built during fall and winter 1922–1923 by Jennie (Mrs. Homer) James at a cost of some $10,000.[10] The other two were further down the street: a tile and stucco building to the east of Frank Grubb's livery, built in 1923 by the brothers Al and Julian Hayden to house their realty office and one other business; and the Service Block, a brick building with room for three businesses, located next door and erected the same year. Its first occupant was the much-traveled C. H. Bond and Company, which by 1927 was sharing its office space with the Estes Park Water Company and the light and power department of the Stanley Corporation, which then owned and operated both the power plant and the Stanley Hotel.[11]

~

Two of the largest new buildings on the Sanborn map were the Estes Park Auditorium on MacGregor Avenue, adjacent to the schoolhouse and facing the park, and the complex known as Riverside built behind Elkhorn Avenue on the triangular piece of land that marked the confluence of Fall River and the Big Thompson. Although neither survives, both were village landmarks in their day, each with a distinctive history.

The auditorium, although designed and built to serve the purposes of village and school, had its origins in the hope for something far grander. It began with the dream of Enoch Josiah "Joe" Mills (1880–1935), the younger brother of Enos Mills, who had come to Estes Park in 1899 from the family farm in eastern Kansas. Working summers at Longs Peak Inn, Joe Mills attended the agricultural college at Fort Collins, where he excelled at intercollegiate athletics, a talent that carried him south to Texas to coach and serve as athletic director at several schools, including Baylor University in Waco.

By 1911 the younger Mills was back in Colorado to stay, coming first to the hamlet of Drake where he managed the Forks Hotel, a popular halfway stop in the Big Thompson Canyon, and then to Estes Park, where in July 1914 he opened the Crags Hotel on Prospect Mountain overlooking Moraine

Avenue and the village. Although for the next decade he divided his time between Estes Park and Boulder where he coached and served as director of athletics at the University of Colorado,[12] Joe's popularity and contagious enthusiasm made him a natural leader where civic undertakings were concerned. One of these—a project that he seems to have single-handedly inspired—was for a large conference center auditorium to improve the town's ability to attract new business.

It had to do with bringing rotarians to Estes Park, a town as yet without a Rotary chapter of its own.[13] An active member of the Boulder Rotary, Mills had been impressed by the organization's commitment to community service. He was also aware of the amount of money that the delegates to its annual convention brought into the economy of any city or town fortunate enough to be its host. In spring 1922, Mills approached a number of fellow members of the Estes Park Chamber of Commerce. Why not, he asked them, bring a Rotary International Convention to Estes Park?

Mills's proposal struck a responsive chord. That June he paid his own way to the west coast to attend the Rotary International Convention in Los Angeles, not as a delegate but as a man with a mission: to confront as many of the conventioneers as possible with the slogan "An International Convention for Estes Park in 1925." Mills brought home an encouraging report: his overtures had met a "hearty acceptance."[14] The Estes Park Chamber of Commerce quickly made the project its own. On June 12, 1924, only three days after the Los Angeles convention, the chamber appointed a committee chaired by C. H. Bond to study the issue. Within weeks the committee's authority had been considerably expanded: it was "given full and complete power" to prepare plans and locate a site for a building capable of seating four thousand people. Given the size and population of Estes Park, the challenge of such a project was enormous. But so was the enthusiasm that Mills had inspired and plans were racing ahead. That same evening Bond was able to announce that his committee had already secured almost $25,000 in pledges toward the building and that in just a "few hours' time."[15]

Bond and the chamber leadership were in earnest. The very next night, June 27, 1922, sixty-five members of the Loveland Rotary invited Estes Park's leading businessmen to meet with them at the Crags Hotel for "a splendid chicken dinner." As soon as the meal was over, both groups adjourned to the Crags dance hall where, following "many a merry song and toast," Mills and his fellow chamber members got to the business at hand. The Loveland delegation left with chapter president Hugh Scilly promising to do everything in his power "to assist in landing the Rotary convention for Estes Park in 1925."[16]

9.5 Joe and Ethel Mills and their two children, early 1920s. Courtesy Patricia A. Washburn

What gave the project credence and urgency was the widespread belief among local hotel owners and merchants that Estes Park was annually losing convention business to other places for lack of "an up to date and commodious convention auditorium." Plans to remedy the deficiency advanced steadily over the following winter. On April 30, 1923, the chamber hosted a dinner at the Lewiston Hotel for 116 people, including some 50 representatives from every Rotary Club from Denver to Cheyenne. Its purpose was a pointed one: to help the Estes chamber learn what must be done to secure the 1925 convention. The hosts heard what they wanted to hear. As the *Estes Park Trail* happily reported within days, "All of Northern Colorado was unanimous in its belief that if Estes Park will provide sufficient auditorium capacity she has the opportunity of becoming the convention city of the West as Atlantic City is to the east."[17]

Two weeks later, now thoroughly convinced that a sizable auditorium made good business sense, the Chamber of Commerce reaffirmed its commitment to push ahead by appointing yet another committee. Joe Mills, Homer James, and Roy Wiest were charged "to prepare plans for the building and to raise funds for the building." In support, architect Charles Levings offered "the opinion . . . that a convention hall with all the modern arrangements and that would have a seating capacity of 3,500, up-to-date heating plant, lighting system, etc. could be built for $70,000 or less." Hedging its bets, the chamber voted that the money should be raised before a site was selected.[18]

Although the *Estes Park Trail* chose to ignore the fact, there were scoffers who doubted that such sums could be raised. To counter this pessimism, Ed Macdonald wrote a lengthy two-page letter to the *Trail* pointing out the village's success during World War I in not only meeting but oversubscribing its quota in Liberty Bonds and War Savings Stamps. Macdonald had other opinions to share as well, including the view that a civic center of the dimensions suggested by Charles Levings be sited in the village park, "Or would you prefer to see it in its Autumn and Winter setting, a pasture for Cows and Donkeys, a tangle of rubbish and weeds? The arguments against this location are not worthy of serious consideration."[19]

For all the early enthusiasm, fund-raising soon became a significant problem, particularly because it was generally agreed that a sizable portion of what was needed, perhaps as much as half, would have to come from outside Estes Park.[20] In early June a private corporation, the Estes Park Auditorium Company, was organized with capital of $100,000 to take charge of the project with Joe Mills as president. Shares of stock would be issued with a face value of ten dollars in the expectation that, as Mills said, "every resident and property owner of the region will take as much of the stock as they can afford."[21] At its meeting on June 6, the chamber assured Mills that it would make available "funds . . . for the necessary expenses of the work."[22]

Progress was made. By early August Mills was able to tell the chamber that six individuals, one of whom no doubt was F. O. Stanley, had committed a total of $18,500 for a facility costing "in the neighborhood of $50,000" and capable of handling "any convention up to 5,000 people without crowding."[23] Other donors stepped forward, and on September 7 Mills announced that his committee now had pledges totaling $30,280, some 60 percent of the whole. On that basis—with success now seemingly within grasp—the chamber passed a formal resolution asking the Seventh District Rotary to tender Estes Park's invitation to host its Sixteenth Annual Rotary International Convention in 1925.[24]

By October, with $43,000 reportedly in hand, the Auditorium Company was ready to consider possible sites. Two pieces of land were offered. The first, two acres located at Beaver Point on the Moraine Park Road, came from Anna Wolfrom Dove, the owner of several local businesses, including the Wigwam Tearoom on Wind River Trail. The second came from F. O. Stanley, who offered to gift the company six lots in the heart of the village, facing the park—the very property on which seven years before he had planned to erect his new downtown hotel. In return Stanley asked only that "a strictly high grade building be built." His offer was immediately accepted as the more preferable, providing "sufficient funds could be secured to build that type of building."[25]

By this date, however, and for reasons never reported, the entire project had been significantly reduced in scope. When the Auditorium Company updated its plans for the chamber on October 15 the 3,500-seat convention hall had been reduced to a 1,200-seat auditorium, with the understanding that the building could, if necessary, be made to seat an additional 400 and that a 600-seat balcony could be added at a later date. The auditorium would have a stage of "standard size" for theatrical purposes.[26]

Over the next seven months there was little additional news about the convention auditorium, perhaps because its scaled-down version had somewhat dampened local enthusiasm. Nevertheless, hopes to land the 1925 Rotary Convention remained alive and well. In May 1924, the Chamber of Commerce voted to send Joe Mills to the June Rotary Convention in Toronto and pay for a booth from which he could pass out literature and postcards advertising Estes Park as a site for the following year. Ten days later, on May 26, the Estes Park Auditorium Company's board of directors announced that the building would be erected the following fall and that a drive for funds, beginning in Denver, "will be launched shortly to finance the building" with the drive in Estes Park to "be made a little later."[27] The discussion of a new local fund-raising drive was, of course, odd given the periodic announcements of the previous year about money already subscribed. Nevertheless, near the end of July, Joe Mills wired a check for $5,000 to Rotary District Seven president Dr. John Andrew of Longmont, then attending a site-selection meeting in Chicago, to guaranty Estes Park's invitation.[28]

Resolution came quickly. The next month, to the dismay of Estes Park, it was announced that Cleveland, Ohio, would be the site of the 1925 Rotary International Convention. To the extent that explanations were offered, it was that the site had been "taken away from Estes because of the fact that the place does not have an auditorium of sufficient size to accommodate the convention."[29]

One can only surmise that the failure to erect a convention facility during winter 1924–1925, well in advance of the Rotary meeting, had to do with money that was not forthcoming. There was also the fact that Mills and his colleagues, flush with enthusiasm, had advanced a timetable that was far too optimistic. There was, after all, nothing magical about 1925 as opposed to 1926, 1927, or even later as a target date. But once announced, that date seems to have taken on a life of its own, and no one appears to have suggested, at least in public, that the invitation be delayed until the necessary facilities were in place. Ironically, Rotary International did come to Colorado in 1926 for its Seventeenth Annual Convention. But it came to Denver, not Estes Park.

On February 1, 1926, Joe Mills, as president of the Estes Park Auditorium Company, posted a notice of dissolution that included the certification that "all debts owing by said corporation have been fully paid." The *Estes Park Trail*, once so outspoken in its support of the convention hall, duly published the notice in its April 3 issue. It appeared buried on page nine without editorial comment.[30]

The project was not yet dead. It was revived in June 1925 by the Chamber of Commerce, which announced that, with assurances that "those who had made financial pledges in the past [had] agreed to let their pledges stand," a new committee had been appointed "to decide on the site and the style of building to be erected."[31] Hotelman James Stead quickly stepped forward to offer "from ten to twenty thousand running feet of logs" for the construction of a building on "the rustic order."[32]

By that October, however, these plans too had changed dramatically. Estes Park would have its auditorium. It would occupy a piece of land facing MacGregor Lane, 200 feet north of Elkhorn Avenue—land to be donated by

Stanley. But the auditorium would no longer be a convention facility built by a private corporation or the town. Rather, the new building would be a combination auditorium and gymnasium erected by Estes Park School District 30 and financed by $71,000 in voter-approved bonds, precisely the kind of public financing that the Estes Park Auditorium Company had been designed to make unnecessary. The cost, moreover, was in line with Charles Levings's estimate of two years before. "The new building is exceedingly beautiful," George Patterson, editor of the *Trail*, told his readers (without a hint of irony), "and will be of such usefulness that it can be used to advantage by the entire community twelve months a year."[33]

Completed in summer 1926 in time to occupy a prominent place on the Sanborn fire insurance map, the new brick and tile auditorium-gymnasium building was designed to seat 893 people in opera chairs on the floor. By using the stage, which was constructed as a basketball court seating 500, the new facility could hold as many as 1,500. The building was decidedly utilitarian: to relieve congestion in the school across MacGregor Avenue it contained three large classrooms—two beside the large foyer on the first floor and one more on the second. In the basement were locker rooms and a bowling alley.

As with F. O. Stanley's plan for a new model town, we can only imagine what might have been had the convention hall been built as originally planned. How different the appearance and ambience of downtown Estes Park might have been—and with what long-term impact on its tourist-based economy—had there been an attractive convention hall capable of seating 3,500 or more, across the street from a Georgian style 140-room hotel and surrounded by the "charmingly unique and picturesque" buildings of a "Swiss village"? On such missed opportunities no one seems to have publicly reflected.

～

The second major footprint on the 1926 Sanborn map was the complex of buildings known as Riverside Dance Hall and Amusement Park. Located at the confluence of the Big Thompson and Fall Rivers, Riverside was built during fall and winter 1922–1923 by two entrepreneurial young men, Ted Jelsema, a twenty-nine-year-old Michigan native, and his partner Frank Bond, the eldest son of Cornelius H. Bond. Jelsema was a relatively recent arrival. He had come to Estes Park in 1916 or 1917 and entered the tourist business in a modest way with a tent bowling alley, shoeshine shop, and dry cleaning service before turning to more substantial projects.[34] In September 1921, Jelsema was enterprising enough to win the contract to install 2,700 feet of sewer line connecting residents on Bond Hill with the existing system. Later that year he completed a private fish hatchery and reservoir system on property he had purchased south of Marys Lake.[35] But Jelsema clearly had larger things in mind, and when the opportunity arose he formed a business partnership with Bond, reportedly with financial backing from Harriet Byerly, owner of the National Park Hotel.[36] The property on which their new venture was built was obtained from C. H. Bond, who may have provided financial help as well.

As originally constructed, Riverside consisted of a wooden 160-by-60-foot recreation pavilion, containing a lobby with a large stone fireplace, ice cream and lunch parlor, and dance hall with rustic booths against the west wall, capable of accommodating upwards of two hundred couples. Immediately adjacent to the east Jelsema and Bond constructed a 40-by-80-foot steam-heated swimming pool, enclosed on three sides by changing rooms and lockers and later covered with a canvas roof to protect bathers from sun and rain. At the south end of the pool, which was large enough for racing contests and water carnivals, was a sand beach. With the installation of a new boiler in 1925, the temperature of the water taken out of Fall River could be kept at a tropical 84 degrees. Additional attractions included a merry-go-round, bowling alley, and shooting gallery. The main entrance to Riverside, gaily illuminated after dark, was to the north by way of a six-foot cement sidewalk that crossed Fall River over a rustic log bridge. It opened directly on Elkhorn Avenue next to the Josephine Hotel beneath a large sign. On the south side of the river was an auto entrance and fenced parking lot with a lighted gate.

Riverside opened on July 4, 1923, with the *Estes Park Trail* assuring its readers in a tone that even then sounded a bit defensive that "the boys plan to run a strictly clean and up-to-date place and will cater to the high-class trade that will be glad to come under those conditions."[37] High class or not, Riverside barely survived its first year. On October 23, 1923, an early snowstorm dumped between two and three feet of snow on the village, collapsing the roof of the dancehall and doing serious damage to both floor and walls. Repairs were quickly made and Jelsema and Bond had Riverside ready for the 1924 season.[38]

Riverside, for all the attractions it offered summer tourists, was not, even in its heyday, a particularly attractive place, at least in light of day. Across the back of the drab wooden dance hall and the adjacent pool, facing the parking lot, signs were installed reading "Dancing," "Refreshments," and "Swimming," all in large, rather garish, white letters. The pool, once its canvas top had been added, resembled from the rear the tent of a traveling

9.6 Riverside Amusement Park from rear. Courtesy Estes Park Museum

circus that had come to stay. The rest of the site was dirt parking lot, almost completely covering a piece of land that had once been coveted by residents as the site for the village park. "No prettier spot could be imagined," the *Mountaineer* had editorialized on August 6, 1908, "and even without public authority this place is being used every day by people seeking rest and shade." Such a park, the paper continued, would give the town "something to be proud of."[39]

This, of course, did not happen, and with the establishment of Riverside a new era of carnival and honky-tonk arrived in Estes Park, creating an atmosphere of vibrancy and fun that was new, exciting, and hitherto absent. Because it brought people into the village after dark and made it profitable for the businesses along Elkhorn Avenue to extend their hours, Riverside was good for everyone, despite its appearance.

Under the management of Jelsema, who bought out Frank Bond's interest in late 1924 or early 1925, Riverside flourished. Despite his youth, Jelsema was a true impresario. Each summer he installed a resident band usually made up of young collegians from neighboring states, among them the seven-piece Nebraskans, a popular group from the University of Nebraska that

9.7 Ted Jelsema's Romancers performing at Riverside. Courtesy Estes Park Museum

played Riverside during the 1924 and 1925 seasons. For three summers, 1927–
1929, Jelsema put together his own group, the Romancers. By June 1929 the
sounds of the Riverside orchestra were being "piped by wires" to speakers
located above the gateway on Elkhorn Avenue. That same year Jelsema gave
his establishment a more "rustic look" by pine paneling the walls of the
dance hall. He also put in a retaining wall along Fall River. The Elkhorn
Avenue access to Riverside remained little more than an alley until spring
1938 when Jelsema purchased the old J. E. Macdonald store building, remodeled its west wall, and moved it several feet to the east to provide a wider
entrance.[40]

A distinctive and favorite longtime feature at Riverside were its Wednesday night theme dances, repeated season after season by popular demand:
the Indian Pow Wow Dance, the Circus Dance (with peanuts, Cracker Jack,
and "numbers of trained and untrained animals"), the Pirate Dance, the
Hard Times Dance (first held in 1928), the mid-August Christmas Dance,
the Plantation Dance, the Rodeo Dance, the Inter-Fraternity Dance, and
the Balloon Dance (balloons were tied "to the lady's ankle and the one who
keeps their [sic] balloon the longest wins a handsome prize. Oh, boy, great

9.8 The Dark Horse Tavern at Riverside with its famous carousel bar stools. Courtesy Estes Park Museum

sport!"). For some years there was also a Pan-Hellenic Ball, at which fraternity and sorority members, old and new, were invited to rekindle friendships while listening to the latest dance music interspersed with medleys of college and fraternity songs. Visitors, it was said, drove in from Denver, Cheyenne, Fort Morgan, and from as far away as North Platte for the occasion. Jelsema awarded a loving cup to the fraternity or sorority with the best turn out. For the 1930 season Jelsema began to circulate his own *Riverside News*, "a weekly review of the events taking place at Riverside Amusement Park."

The well-publicized Cowboy Dance held at Riverside in late June 1930 was among the most memorable. That afternoon cowboys, Indians, covered wagons, stagecoaches, and that summer's resident orchestra, Hub Else and his Jayhawks, dressed "in wildest attire," paraded up and down Elkhorn Avenue. Attendees that evening, which included the usual mixture of "locals" and tourists, found the dance hall appropriately decorated with bales of hay providing seats for the orchestra. The *Estes Park Trail* was uncharacteristically colorful and detailed in its coverage:

> Clem Yore, author, was the deputy sheriff and looked as though he
> might be one of his own famous characters such as "Hard Riding Slim

McGee," come to life. Jiggs Miller was bartender and Ed Kitchell of
Maplewood, Missouri, was the southern plantation owner, dressed in
frock coat with goatee, etc. Ted Jelsema was the dance hall owner, Buck
Washburn the manager, and Tiny Mills was the hard character. A real
bloody battle was staged, lights went out; fire belching forth from guns
was the only thing seen; and when the lights were turned on, Buck
Washburn lay on the floor.[41]

Showman that he was, Ted Jelsema was ever on the lookout for ways of
attracting new patrons and encouraging old ones to return. In 1931, for
example, he brought six Sioux Indians down from Cheyenne's Frontier Days
Rodeo to dance at Riverside.

From the beginning Riverside was a financial success. Jelsema plowed
much of the money directly back into the community by making real estate
investments. In 1925 he built a group of six cottages in the village to house
his summer employees and added another eight in 1927, the latter conveniently located south of Riverside. Jelsema's major new investment of the
period, however, was the three-story Josephine Hotel at the entrance to Riverside, purchased from an overextended Josie Hupp in 1930. Jelsema promptly
renamed the hotel the Riverside to match his amusement complex and then
applied a coat of ornamental stucco to give his property a new look.[42]

~

On November 5, 1926, shortly after issuance of the Sanborn maps, the *Estes
Park Trail* published a disquieting essay by a woman named Marie Richmond.
This essay had recently been awarded second prize in a contest sponsored by
the Chamber of Commerce. Richmond's prosaic title, "Estes Park Improved,"
belied the content. The story she tells is one of blight and neglect and the
apparent inability, or unwillingness, of the town to do anything more than
sponsor an annual Cleanup Day to remove winter trash from yards and premises. "Estes Park could be made a very ideal little village with but a few
improvements," the author innocently begins, "most of which are due to the
failure of people who see them daily to notice the need. . . . People coming
into Estes Park from outside notice them readily."

What residents refused to see makes up the balance of Richmond's pointed
essay. These include "gaudy, unnatural sign boards that blur the real mountain scenery," buildings whose colors fail to harmonize with one another and
detract from "the rustic effect," and numerous "unkempt yards" of which
"the village should be ashamed." "When walking in any part of Estes," she
continues,

you find back yards looking more like a trash pile than where anyone lives. Tin cans are scattered everywhere along with pasteboard boxes, paper, and other rubbish. . . . Ashes are scattered everywhere, killing the grass and flowers that struggle to grow and beautify your yard. . . . A neat little house is built on the hillside and would be a place to be proud of, but upon one side of the house is nailed an old ragged piece of canvas and held out from the house by a crooked dirty structure; under this is the wood, not even neatly piled. Near this is an old piano box in which the supply of coal is kept, coal is scattered all over the ground. Against the box leans an old shovel and beside that sets [sic] a coal bucket. Some of the ashes are in a can, but it has evidently not been noticed that the can is full for ashes are piled high around as well as scattered over the yard. A broken down fence encircles a patch of weeds that might once have been a garden.

Marie Richmond does not limit her inspection, or her comments, to private dwellings:

The gutters on Elkhorn Avenue are piled half full of dirt, cigarette stubs, papers, gum wrappers and other filthy articles. . . . Donkeys running loose are the worst of nuisances. Nothing can be left even [on] your porch but what some donkey must see what it is and if it is eatable eat it, if not, scatter it all over or break it. . . . How can Estes be made beautiful with such pests running loose[?] . . .

Stables on Main Street are very unsightly as well as very unsanitary. The stables are only a few feet from the river and people down below use the water not knowing, or at any rate, not realizing what is upstream and are fully unaware of the danger. . . .

Her grievances cast a wide net, and before concluding Richmond even takes on the Chamber of Commerce, sponsor of the contest:

Estes Park is widely advertised as an ideal summer resort. In all the pictures no trash is visible and in some mysterious way make Estes Park look very neat and clean. Even the most dilapidated houses are made to look like modern dwellings. Reading material lifts Estes Park above the present condition. Advertising pays, but we should live up to what we advertise. . . . Let's not disappoint the tourists.[43]

One thing not mentioned, although others did, was the unsightliness of late fall and winter, when shop windows boarded shut with raw lumber or simply papered over gave the appearance of a town all but abandoned.

Although she might not have been aware of it, Richmond was reacting to the fact that for all its popularity and success Estes Park village had architecturally changed but little over its first two decades. In this respect at least, Estes Park was atypical. Although it was never as raw-looking as the average Colorado town, particularly those in mining districts, the village of Estes Park gave little evidence in fall 1926 of the kind of substantial stone and brick construction so often found in American towns by their second or third decade, as their inhabitants became concerned with their towns' appearance and wanted their towns to display wealth and stability. There were exceptions, most notably the Estes Park Bank, the new multiple-occupant brick buildings along Elkhorn Avenue, the new auditorium, F. O. Stanley's hotel and summer residence, and a handful of other homes in or near the village. But where other Colorado towns had a brick or stone opera house to proclaim their sophistication, taste, and affluence, Estes Park was content with its white-frame Park Theatre and Riverside Amusement Park.

This, of course, was precisely Richmond's point. Estes Park was a resort town, reflecting the consumer needs of the U.S. middle-class tourists who traveled west to the Colorado mountains during the first decades of the twentieth century. In the absence of architectural intervention of the sort that Stanley had contemplated a decade before, it was these visitors, arriving in droves in late June and decamping by Labor Day well before the aspen turned, who dictated with their tastes, expectations, and purchases Estes Park's economy and landscape. Unlike other mountain destination towns such as Aspen and Georgetown—both of which were originally mining communities—Estes Park was created as a tourist town. America had fallen in love with nature and the region. Estes Park and its residents provided what was necessary to make the tourist experience possible.

∽

Knowing nothing about Marie Richmond except her name, it is difficult to assess the accuracy of her statements and descriptions, although one suspects from what we know from other sources, including photographs, that they do not greatly miss the mark. What is interesting and telling is that the Chamber of Commerce, an organization unashamedly committed to demonstrations of civic pride and boosterism, saw fit to single out her essay for recognition and that the *Estes Park Trail*, the chamber's mouthpiece on most issues, chose to publish it without comment before those of other prizewinners.

Although her criticism went unanswered in the pages of the *Trail*, Richmond had struck a responsive chord. Public statements about the need for cleanliness and civic pride, although usually muted, were scarcely new. Richmond's disquieting criticisms were, in fact, shared by many. Relying on his own pocketbook and the town's volunteer spirit, Stanley had tried and failed to clean up and remodel the village. A decade later, even with the new school auditorium, "Beautifying the Village" remained a more or less constant theme of the *Trail* and its readers, and editor George Patterson periodically used his position to suggest tactfully what the town might do to improve its appearance. Like Stanley and Richmond he suggested that the livery barns lining Elkhorn might well be removed to other sites so that their choice locations could be put to better use.[44]

It was precisely that need to exert a measure of order and control over the affairs of a village that had grown for more than a decade without either that led in spring 1917 to the decision to incorporate the three-quarters of a square mile that was the town of Estes Park. Shortly after the April vote for incorporation there was a second election, this time for mayor and village trustees. Although it had been expected that Cornelius Bond would be the town's first mayor, by the time the uncontested slate of candidates was announced Bond had withdrawn his name in favor of Dr. Roy Wiest.

Expectations for the newly incorporated town were high. As the *Denver Post* announced just prior to the April vote,

> Estes Park is to have cement sidewalks, storm sewers, better fire protection, adequate electric lighting system and restricted advertising on store fronts. Everything will be done to develop the whole settlement along the lines drawn up by F. O. Stanley for making a "model town" of half the village. Glaring and inartistic signs will not be permitted on stores. All livery barns will be moved off the main streets. Stock will be kept up in a "town pasture."[45]

The *Longmont Call* offered the additional opinion that "one object the board of trustees will have will be the control of automobile travel. The congestion is greater in the park and on the roads to the park in the summer months than it is in Denver."[46]

The first meeting of the Estes Park trustees took place on June 5, 1917, with Charles F. Hix, cashier of the Estes Park Bank, chosen as clerk and recorder. Within weeks the council had hired the Longmont firm of Secor & Secor to provide legal advice, ordered an assessment of taxable property, and proceeded to enact a series of necessary ordinances, including one levying taxes. As might be expected, the general approach of the town fathers to spending money was decidedly conservative. As a result, village improvements at municipal expense were slow in coming. When the 1919 budget was established in October 1918, for example, only $1,000 was allocated to the street and alley fund, $500 to the sewer fund, and $700 to the contingency fund to take care of everything else including emergencies.[47] Where money was not an issue the council was quicker to respond. At their second meeting on June 11, 1917, J. E. Macdonald introduced an ordinance prohibiting animals and fowls from running at large within the town limits that was immediately and unanimously passed.[48] The largest expense that first summer was a contract with J. Sidney Williams to supervise street sprinkling eight hours a day, seven days a week, at a rate of $125 per month.[49]

At an early date the town began to require building permits for new additions to homes and businesses and instructed offending property holders to clean up their properties.[50] But when it came to such matters as replacing board sidewalks with concrete ones, it was the property owners who paid for—and directed—the improvements, albeit with town approval. The first request for a sidewalk came in May 1921 from residents on the north side of Elkhorn between Anderson Lane and Fall River who asked the town council for permission to build six-foot-wide concrete walk.[51] This request was followed a month later by a similar one from property owners on the south side of Elkhorn between Moraine and Riverside who asked to be allowed to install an eight-foot walk that October.[52]

These improvements, although lacking uniformity, were greeted enthusiastically by the *Estes Park Trail*, which on June 10, 1921, took note of the new walkways on upper Elkhorn and immediately lobbied for more:

> [This] still leaves the street 63 feet in width from curb to curb, which we
> are informed is wider than Broadway in Denver. It is time also that the
> old board walks were remove and concrete laid. It will add greatly to
> the appearance of our little village and to the comfort of our visitors
> and townspeople. There are places where there is no walk of any
> description and our visitors are compelled to meander down the street
> dodging cars on every hand. This ought not to be and we are sure those
> who have not put in walks would be glad to do so if the town would
> establish the proper place for them and a uniform grade.[53]

The suggestion struck home. In the months that followed cement replaced boardwalk throughout the village and by the time John Baird completed work on a new sidewalk in front of his store just up from the Service home in May 1923, the last boardwalk in the village had disappeared.[54]

The issuance of uniform standards for building setbacks, uniform curblines, and grades for sidewalks followed. Although it would take almost seven years to complete the project, by spring 1922 the council was routinely notifying individuals who requested permission to build new sidewalks that they must be prepared to remove them "at any time the Town see [sic] fit to order sidewalks off the said street or to order them built to grade."[55] Within three years both sides of Elkhorn had been lined with curbs and gutters and, with

9.9 *Lower Elkhorn Avenue in the 1920s: J. Edward Macdonald store; the Josephine Hotel; William Tallant's shop; transportation company garage and offices; and original Hupp Hotel. Courtesy Estes Park Museum*

the installation of ornamental lighting and new regulations regarding signs and awnings in place, the *Estes Park Trail* approvingly commented that "Estes Park is daily taking on a more attractive appearance."[56] In fall 1925 that appearance was further improved when the Stanley Power Company began to remove the light and power poles from the street curbs on Elkhorn, where they had become an increasingly unsightly (and dangerous) nuisance, and to relocate them to the rear alleys.[57] The following May, Mountain States Telephone was notified by the town that, because of changes in the curbing, its poles would also have to be relocated.[58] The irony, of course, was that while all these improvements helped and gave the illusion of progress, they did little to address the things that most bothered people like Marie Richmond.

The extent to which the town fathers and others shared those concerns became clear, however, in the years that immediately followed the publication of her letter—years that marked Estes Park's first, and indeed only, concerted attempt before the Lawn Lake flood of 1982 to significantly alter and improve the appearance of Elkhorn Avenue. These efforts began with the street itself, which had been slowly but irregularly enlarged over two decades to accommodate automobile, truck, and bus traffic. As a result, as the 1926 Sanborn maps clearly show, many of the original buildings on Elkhorn now extended into the street, making uniform sidewalks and curbs impossible. This problem necessarily took precedence over virtually all others, and by 1927 the village trustees finally acted. That February they notified some eleven property owners that by May 1, 1928, their buildings must be moved back approximately eight feet to accommodate the construction of uniform sidewalks, curbs, and gutters.[59]

The greatest offenders were the Loveland–Estes Park Transportation Company at the head of Elkhorn, whose buildings covered some six lots; the Rocky Mountain Parks Transportation Company; and the J. Edward Macdonald house and store, which occupied three. Also on the trustees' list were the Continental Oil Company, which owned six lots (including those occupied by the Grubb and Stanley liveries); the Homer James property; the Hupp Livery, whose log barn stood at the upper end of Elkhorn across from the Osborn garage; and artist William Tallant's Pine Cone Inn directly east of the Transportation Company offices.[60]

To complement this effort the trustees instructed town engineer Frank Bond to draw up plans, specifications, and a schedule of costs to complete the installation of uniform concrete curbs and gutters on both sides of Elkhorn. On September 26, 1927, with Bond's report and his estimate that the project would cost some $3,304.55 to complete, the trustees passed an ordinance creating "Estes Park Improvement District Number One," giving the town authority to assess property owners their pro rata share of the costs. Some fifty properties were affected, the largest number on the south side of Elkhorn in the two blocks from Riverside to the Fall River Bridge and on the north side of Elkhorn in the block west of Anderson Lane.[61]

During the meeting three of the notified property owners showed up with attorneys to object. Of these, two eventually withdrew their complaints while the third, the owners of the Osborn garage, reached a compromise a week later that allowed the installation of two gasoline pumps in front of their premises provided they did not extend into the street more than six inches.[62]

Work to bring Elkhorn Avenue into conformity with the town's new mandates began in September and continued during fall and winter 1927. The front of Sam Service's store was moved back eighteen inches. Across the street, Ed Macdonald went to work remodeling, removing some eight feet from the fronts of home and store to allow for the prescribed sidewalk and curbing. Macdonald also used the occasion to remove one of the store's two entrances and install a new plateglass front.[63] Other businesses made

9.10 *Upper Elkhorn Avenue: Fred Clatworthy's store, the Sherwood Hotel, and the Community Church are the three most visible buildings. Courtesy Estes Park Museum*

similar changes. Lige Rivers's Stanley Livery and Roe Emery's Rocky Mountain Parks Transportation Company office building were both moved back to the new line, while Ralph Macdonald followed his father's example and cut off the front of his building and replaced it with a "modern" one. To meet the new curbline requirements whole sections of sidewalk were removed and replaced.[64]

The spirit of remodeling, once unleashed, became contagious. Sam Service cut off some two and a half feet from the front of his building and installed a new façade of brick and glass.[65] Further up Elkhorn, Lawrence Grace went to work on the building he had recently purchased and divided what had once been a meat market into shops. He also lowered the floor to conform to the new street grade and added a new "Indian pueblo type" front. "These changes will be a big improvement in the property," the *Estes Park Trail* reported with clear understatement, for "the old front was not a thing of beauty."[66]

Grace was not finished. He also began renovating his two-story Gemcraft Shop, the business he had opened shortly after his arrival in Estes Park in 1913. Again he chose an Indian adobe motif, although of a far more elaborate order. After putting in a flagstone walk in front, he painted the doors of his shop blue and orange and placed a strip of wood decorated with red, blue, orange, and yellow Indian designs above the lintel. Hanging from log beams, which extended several feet from the building, were strings of peppers. To add to the effect at night Grace illuminated the small front second-floor window above the doorway. "One can almost imagine," editor A. B. Harris enthused, "that a real Pueblo Indian lives there, it is so realistic." Adding to the realism were the footprints of deer that wandered up to inspect Grace's handiwork, only to leave their trail in the freshly poured concrete walkway leading to the flagstones.[67]

Although it had taken the better part of a decade, by the time the 1928 tourist season opened Elkhorn Avenue had a decidedly different look. "There is a wonderful improvement in the general appearance of most of the stores and shops along the street," the *Trail* editorialized in early March,

> Many of them have added improvements to their fronts, paint, etc. Some of them have aligned with the property line along their block. This has wonderfully added to the appearance of the street. It gets us away from the appearance of trying to hog the attention of the street by crowding out beyond the line others have established.
>
> Another improvement that will be made is that of removing all poles from the street. Both light poles and telephone poles will be moved from the street and ornamental lighting installed.[68]

This was in March. By the end of the year the *Trail* was able to announce that only one building, William Tallant's Pine Cone Inn, was not in conformity with the "village improvement program."[69]

The new ornamental lighting on both sides of Elkhorn, stretching from near the bridge over the Big Thompson at the lower end of town west to the Fall River Bridge, was in place by early May 1928. Strung on a copper cable suspended by guy wires were sets of streamer lights, stretching across the street at intervals. Each set of streamers consisted of between twelve and fifteen individual lamps, depending on the width of the street, anchored at both ends by 100-watt lights. The system, installed by power plant superintendent Byron Hall, was connected by feed line to a clock and central switch at the plant. The power company and the town jointly shared the $800 cost.[70] By early July traffic lights and stop signs had also come to Elkhorn, making "the traffic much safer during the summer months when the large crowds are here."[71]

Although Elkhorn Avenue received its first hard surfacing in 1926 when a layer of pulverized granite was laid down for automobile traffic, dust and dirt continued to be "a bugaboo of the businessmen along the street," especially on summer afternoons when livery horses, turned loose by their riders, trotted up and down Elkhorn on the way back to their stables. In October

1929, this surfacing was improved by applying several inches of crushed material mixed with heavy content asphalt oil, creating a roadway said to be smoother and "more solid" than cement and "unexcelled of its kind anywhere."[72] Unfortunately, the much-applauded job turned out to be "a cheap piece of work." Less than three years later, in spring 1932, it was replaced by a new macadamized surface, consisting of three distinct layers of crushed rock, gravel, and sand, each with its own coat of oil—a surface reportedly better than concrete and with a life of twenty-five years.[73]

By the late 1920s, the village of Estes Park had reached its maturity. Growth and change would continue over the next two decades and beyond, but not at the pace or with the problems that had marked the previous two. What is remarkable about the 1926 Sanborn maps is how closely they mirror the town of today. To be sure, the liveries are gone from Elkhorn and many of the buildings present in 1926 have different faces and have been turned to other uses. In retrospect, these improvements of the late 1920s were accomplished in the nick of time. Colorado and the nation were even then slipping into depression and a year or two later many in the decidedly conservative business-oriented community might well have argued that the public funding of civic improvements should be postponed until better times.

Chapter 10

~~

Hard Times Come to Colorado: Estes Park in the 1930s

For many in Colorado, the Great Depression of the 1930s seemed like more of the same, only worse. Mining and agriculture, the state's first and third sources of income, after prospering during the World War I, limped through the 1920s when commodity prices fell. Manufacturing and trade, Colorado's other economic mainstays, did better, but not well enough to compensate for the poor performance of the other two. As a consequence, Colorado entered the Depression after a decade of stagnation during which its growth rate lagged that of the nation for the first time since the 1860s. Conditions continued to deteriorate. By mid-1933 when unemployment peaked, "economic activity in the state had staggered almost to a halt" and nearly one of every five Coloradans was out of work and in needed of relief.[1]

In a state still half rural, farmers were particularly hard hit. Not only did agricultural prices and land values remain depressed, but the prolonged and unprecedented drought that began in 1931 brought with it the most serious incursions of grasshoppers since the 1870s, followed by dust storms that intensified in severity. Periodic droughts on Colorado's warm, dry eastern plains had been seen before. By the 1930s, however, much of the original prairie grass had been stripped away by dry-land farming, subjecting the land to severe erosion. Despite brief respites, dust bowl conditions continued throughout the 1930s, destroying millions of tons of precious topsoil and creating "black blizzards," great swirling clouds of dust that lasted for days, hid both sun and mountain top, obliterated roads, and brought traffic to a halt. So dense at times was the residue of dust and grit that towns along the Front Range were forced to turn on streetlights at mid-day. During a rain-storm in April 1935, beads of mud were showered upon Denver.

Economic problems were exacerbated by the state's traditional values of individualism and self-help and by tight fiscal policies reinforced by a consti-tutional prohibition against deficit financing. Not until January 1934 did the Colorado legislature and its governor, Edwin C. Johnson (1933–1937), agree to pass statewide relief measures for the needy and provide matching funds for Federal Emergency Relief Administration (FERA) grants by impos-ing a gasoline tax and diverting highway dollars. Even then Johnson, a Demo-crat who prided himself on his independence from his party, remained at loggerheads with Roosevelt's relief director Harry L. Hopkins over the ad-ministration of federal aid funds in Colorado. Nor did Johnson stand alone. His opposition to the New Deal generally mirrored the business and political leadership in Colorado and throughout the West, where state money was spent only in aid of private enterprise and muddling through was a virtue.[2]

Colorado's difficulties persisted throughout the decade under Johnson's two equally conservative successors, Democrat Teller Ammons (1937–1939) and Republican Ralph Carr (1939–1943). Despite an upturn in the state's economy in late 1936 and early 1937, recessionary decline had returned by 1938. In Colorado, as in much of the nation, it took the economic stimulus that followed the outbreak of World War II in Europe in September 1939 to reduce unemployment significantly and set the state on the road to recovery. After 1941, thanks to defense spending and the psychology of a nation at war, "few if any visible traces of the Great Depression remained in Colorado."[3]

Although Estes Park coped well with the stagnation of the middle and late 1920s and in fact used the period to improve the infrastructure of its tourist economy, it was not exempt from the Great Depression. When tour-ism suffered, so did the "gem of the Rockies." Yet even in these uncertain times, which climaxed locally in spring 1933, Estes Park enjoyed a resiliency and degree of prosperity that set it apart from Colorado and the nation.

A homegrown spirit of self-sufficiency, the legacy of pioneer days, helped. So too did the seasonal isolation. Living in a mountain town where many businesses closed down for the winter in September, residents were able to focus their attention on problems close to home. Of greatest help, of course, was the continuing presence of tourist dollars. Thanks to the automobile and a culture increasingly focused on leisure and consumption, vacationing in the United States had become a well-promoted and widely endorsed rite of summer for white collar and blue collar families alike,[4] and throughout the 1930s Estes Park remained an attractive tourist destination. Although many other well-known vacation spots, including Yellowstone National Park, reported a decline in visitors during the early and middle years of the decade, Estes Park did not. After a slight drop in the number of people entering Rocky Mountain National Park in 1930 and 1931,[5] those numbers once again began to climb until 1938, when almost 660,000 visitors were counted— more than two and a half times the number of seven years before.

The fortunes of Estes Park in the 1930s did not rest on tourism alone. Thanks to the very New Deal programs that many Coloradans found so offensive, the decade brought the Estes Park Valley and its adjacent national park an unprecedented level of federal activity, beginning with the construction of Trail Ridge Road in the late 1920s and culminating with the massive Colorado–Big Thompson transmountain irrigation project that lasted into the 1950s. Many of the dollars that these programs provided immediately found their way into the local economy, providing Estes Park and its residents with income that other Colorado and U.S. communities did not have. State dollars also had a role to play, particularly in the latter part of the decade when, after years of neglect and legislative inaction, Colorado finally took advantage of federal help to launch the largest road-building program in its history. By 1939 the three highly traveled and much complained about roads leading from the gateway towns of Lyons and Loveland to Estes Park had been totally rebuilt, turning narrow, unpaved, dusty, and often dangerous mountain roads into modern tourist highways.

If the number of New Deal dollars coming to Colorado was less than it might have been because of the state's political leadership, Estes Park was not affected. During the 1930s and 1940s Estes Park received more federal funds on a per capita basis than almost any other similar-sized community in the nation, while also receiving an infrastructure of roads; power, water, and sewer systems; buildings; and an expanded economic base that others could only envy. As a result the attitude of the valley's residents remained upbeat and positive if not quite as euphoric as in the two decades before. How this happened and why is the story of Estes Park during the 1930s.

Although the number of year-round residents more than doubled between 1930 and 1940—from 417 to 980—the face of the village did not substantially change. In 1940 Estes Park looked much as it had a decade before or, for that matter, as it had looked on the Sanborn maps of 1926. In a town where seasonal businesses came and went, ownership and cosmetic appearance of course changed as the decade progressed, even affecting establishments that by the 1930s had gained a certain air of venerability. These changes began in 1931 when Mrs. William Burgess and her brother Carl Porter purchased the old Tallant building near the transportation company on Elkhorn Avenue and moved it four feet to the south to accommodate a new nine-foot front sidewalk. Extensively remodeled, it reopened as an immediately popular restaurant with the unlikely name of the "Plantation." Other new and remodeled buildings of the decade included Monaghan's Garage, built by Paul J. Monaghan in March 1932 on the site of the original William Parke–Sam Service store just west of the Stanley Livery; the Red and White chain grocery that opened in J. E. Macdonald's old building in 1935; and the store operated by a young man from Lyons named Ron Brodie, that replaced Harry Boyd's market next to the bank in 1936. (Brodie, who had originally worked for Boyd, would later relocate his business to the lower end of Elkhorn Avenue where he successfully did business until the Lawn Lake Flood of 1982.) The next year, 1937, Forrest Williamson moved his Toggery down the street into the old E.M.A. Foot building, John Baird's venerable gift shop was torn down and replaced by a modern two-story brick building with living quarters above, and Harriet Byerly purchased Anna Wolfrom Dove's "Indian Shop" and used the site to construct a new bowling alley and store to the east of her National Park Hotel. There was little to lament about any of these changes other than the fact that, as some old-time residents were aware, the inexorable hand of history was involved.

These years also saw alterations and new construction involving community and public buildings, beginning in 1935 when a new Sunday school, auditorium, and other facilities were added to the Community Church at a cost of more than $25,000, and a small wing was added to the library in Bond Park, containing a room funded and named by Eleanor Hondius in memory of her husband. That August a new football field was graded and installed behind the town auditorium, bordered on the north by the cliff containing the ruins of Al Birch's bungalow and by Black Canyon Creek (a field ten yards short of regulation because of space). The town's largest civic project, however, came three years later, in August 1938, when thanks to a federal grant of $47,045 from the Works Progress Administration and funds matched by a local bond issue, construction began on a new junior-senior high school building located some hundred feet south of the auditorium and containing fourteen classrooms and a variety of activity rooms, including a music room and library. The building was needed. School enrollment in the decade had grown from 146 to 285 and the Bureau of Reclamation, by now a significant local presence thanks to the Colorado–Big Thompson Project, asked the town to accommodate at least 100 new students on behalf of its increasingly large workforce.

The new building causing the biggest stir, however, was Estes Park's first genuine night club, the Chez Jay, built at the close of the decade by Miami, Florida, radio entrepreneur Jesse H. Jay. Jay had come to Estes Park in 1936 and a year later purchased and remodeled the Somers building, the original Hupp Hotel at the corner of Elkhorn and Moraine, behind which he immediately began construction of a lavish two-story restaurant and bar. Clearing the site required the removal of John Cleave's original post office (now known as the Close Building) that had been moved there when the Hupp was built in 1906. Jay was fanciful in the extreme, choosing an art deco design inspired by the Frank Capra film adaptation of James Hilton's 1933 novel of Tibet, *Lost Horizons*. Opened with great fanfare on July 1, 1938, as the "Shangri La of the Rockies," the Chez Jay brought an aura of eastern sophistication and architectural chic to the western town, not to mention an excitement to nightlife along Elkhorn not seen (or heard) since the opening of Ted Jelsema's Riverside fifteen years before. Jay was not finished. In order to give the Chez Jay a large dance floor and increase the size of both dining room and kitchen he immediately began construction of an addition with an entrance directly on Elkhorn Avenue.

Work progressed quickly and on July 4, 1939, Jay threw open his "Shangri La Club" for dinner and dancing in a room featuring Oriental walnut wall panels; custom-built coral, ivory, and blue upholstered furniture; wrought iron seventy-pound lighting fixtures; and an arched ceiling painted coral and lit by "indirect neon shades of alternating rose fluorescent and daylight white." The visual center of Jay's new establishment was the back of the glass-brick bar, where artist and printmaker Lyman Byxbe, a summer resident since the early 1920s, created a black-and-white reproduction of a Tibetan Lamasery across six wine-colored panels. The re-opening of the "most beautiful night club west of Chicago" was accompanied by considerable fanfare. Those who attended had the privilege of dancing to the music of Willie Hartzell and "his famous broadcast band" on a rubber-backed parquet dance floor said to be "the finest in the state."[6]

There was further excitement that summer when in June L. F. Flower of Baird, Nebraska, provided competition for the now-venerable Park Theatre by opening a new 300-seat motion picture house in Sam Service's old warehouse, which he had spruced up considerably by adding a coat of stucco and installing a sidewalk leading from Elkhorn to its entrance on Virginia Drive.

The liveries, however, did not change until late in the decade, continuing to clutter an already traffic-clogged street. The longevity of these establishments was hardly surprising. The horse population during summer 1930 numbered some 1,600, and horses were so much a part of the local tourist industry and the "western" experience that for years their barns and corrals seemed quite impervious to continuing complaints about appearance and cleanliness. "The old barn on Elkhorn Avenue opposite the Post Office is getting a coat of paint," the *Trail* groused in June 1937 about Frank Grubb's old livery, now owned by his son-in-law Don Kilton, "that looks as though it might be manufactured from a bad dream (nightmare to you). It seems a little like a great-grandmother putting on false eyelashes."[7] The new and offensive paint job, coupled with the pressing need for downtown parking, finally signaled the end. The very next year "the eyesore of the Region" was sacrificed for a parking lot, leaving the Hupp and Stanley Liveries to anchor the east and west ends of Elkhorn.

Perhaps the most significant change of the decade was far less dramatic and obvious. This was the generational change in local leadership that came with the retirement or death of many of the individuals who had played a critical role during the town's first three decades. By 1936, C. H. Bond, Pieter Hondius, Joe Mills, Howard James, James Stead, J. Edward Macdonald, Albert Hayden, Frank Crocker, Richard Tallant, Charles Lester, Mary Belle King Sherman, and F. J. Francis were all dead. By 1938 they had been joined by Sam Service, Julius Schwartz, George Johnson, Al Cobb, and Clem Yore. Most of the other remaining "old-timers"—with perhaps the exception of the seemingly ageless F. O. Stanley, Abner Sprague, and Charles Reed—had ceased to be active in village affairs, leaving their roles to other younger men, many of whom lacked the family ties and sense of place and history of those they followed.

The loss of these individuals was keenly felt. "The hard part of the work was done by those old pioneers," the *Estes Park Trail* noted editorially in September 1936, speaking of Joe Mills, Pop Francis, and J. D. Stead, "—now someone is needed to do the much easier job of keeping the Park in its place of grace. . . . The old men have worked long and hard, and now they are handing down the building and selling of Estes Park to younger hands."[8] The problem was, as the *Trail* repeatedly reminded its readers during the 1930s, that these "younger hands" were slow to emerge. The previous September, in fact, a crisis had been reached. When only 27 of 102 members of the chamber showed up for its regular meeting, the *Trail* concluded in a front-page editorial that the community had become "more or less . . . demoralized" and "apathetic."[9] Two months later, in November, chamber president Fay Brainard openly chastised fellow members for their failure to shoulder the task of promoting Estes Park: "The sad part," Brainard noted, "is [that] we have no Chamber of Commerce, no officers, merely a board, none of whom will head up the organization."[10] Fortunately, there were others to fulfill the needs of the times.

~

Leadership of the sort that Stanley, Bond, and Hondius had once provided was particularly critical during the first years of the decade. The years 1931 and 1932 were difficult ones for Estes Park, as for tourist towns generally and by 1933, when conditions again worsened, residents found themselves having to prepare, without much in way of precedent, for an uncertain future. For a community that generally lacked acrimony or even marked disagreement in its public discussions the times proved to be particularly turbulent.

Not surprisingly, it was the town's economically sensitive business establishment, acting through the Chamber of Commerce, that forced the debate over how best to cope with declining incomes and a deteriorating tax base. The first real sign of the tension caused by contracting tourist activity had surfaced the previous summer when resort owners, angered over advertisements in the Denver papers touting the low price of accommodations at the YMCA Camp, took their complaints to the county commissioners and were successful in having the Y's tax-exempt status revoked, an action that unintentionally brought that financially troubled organization to the verge of bankruptcy.[11] In much the same spirit the town trustees passed an ordinance in summer 1932 to prevent outsiders from soliciting business on village streets. These were "cream skimmers," the *Estes Park Trail* told its readers, who paid no taxes, assumed no burden of gift or charity, "but who dart in for a little time, make a profit, and dart away again."[12]

Having flexed its muscle at the expense of the Y Camp, the chamber turned its attention to more pressing matters. That fall, apparently in the belief that the town's elected leaders were slow in responding to current realities, the chamber appointed a Tax Reduction Fact Finding Committee, chaired by shopowner Lawrence Grace. The committee report, released in January 1933, recommended a series of immediate belt-tightening measures to decrease town spending. These included reducing the number and wattage of street lights, forcing firms selling gasoline to the town to do so at less than retail prices or through competitive bidding, requiring all but emergency work to be bid, combining the offices of clerk and water commissioner, and cutting all salaries by 20 percent. The savings, the committee predicted, would reduce the town's annual $9,000 budget by nearly 17 percent.[13]

Grace and his colleagues then offered a similar series of suggestions to the local schools, "not in a spirit of criticism but in a conscientious effort to help you and the community to lower operating costs" without "a lowering of standards" or eliminating "any classes or studies." Their major recommendation, however, was not nearly so disarming: the appointment of an "expert educator" who would "study the current curriculum and revise it in a way that increases teacher load and cuts cost." Producing a series of charts demonstrating that the Estes Park schools were more expensive than their counterparts in the valley towns of Wellington and Berthoud, the committee suggested that the position of superintendent and principal be combined, that teacher salaries be cut to the level "of similar districts elsewhere," and, to avoid the kind of unfair competition some chamber members felt from the Y, that "no person in the employ of the schools compete with other tax paying citizens in housing and feeding teachers."[14]

Prodded into action, town and schoolboard soon responded. Each had ideas of its own. Mayor Frank Bond, on behalf of the trustees, politely assured chamber president F. J. Francis that suggestions for "reducing the expenses of government are welcome" and that those found "sound and workable" after study "will be implemented." But he also pointedly reminded Francis and his fellow businessmen that the Town Board (and, by implication, not the Chamber of Commerce) "has a duty" to efficiently maintain the various functions such as water supply, sewerage disposal, and fire protection. . . . The peace, health, and safety of the community depend on this." Estes Park had a number of critical infrastructure issues to address, Bond continued, and unless other ways to fund such projects could be found, "I doubt if any considerable reduction of the present real estate tax bill for town purposes can be made."[15]

Having offered its recommendation and framed the discussion, the chamber committee disbanded and retired from field, leaving the *Estes Park Trail*—whose editor, Dean Kirby, had been a committee member—to carry on, at least in public, what had now become a community debate on how best to meet current economic realities. Although on the job for less than two years, Kirby was not willing to let Bond have the last word. He and the *Trail's* senior partner and business manager William G. Jackson had dedicated their paper "first and last" to "be for the things that current local opinion thinks are best for the community,"[16] and Kirby now used his position to pursue the issue editorially. "There are probably no business men in the region," he noted in the same issue carrying Bond's response, "who have not taken what amounts to substantial salary or business income reductions since the palmy days of 1929." By implication Bond and the trustees would do well to follow the plan set forth by the committee for the local schools.

The *Trail's* willingness to help manage the school budget had in fact only begun. Two months later, in April, when the school board let it be known that it was considering an austerity program that included doing away with music, athletics, shop, and domestic sciences, it drew the immediate ire of editor Kirby. He editorially responded that the *Trail* found the board's suggestion about eliminating music "incredible" since a number of parents had purchased instruments for their children the previous fall. The "proper" way to curtail expenses was to follow the suggestion of the now-discharged Chamber of Commerce committee and reduce salaries. He cited the example of Loveland where teachers had taken large reductions and were still on the job.[17]

By now the *Trail* was clearly confident that it spoke for the community. Within a month after school board president Charles Chapman released a "tentative plan" that involved closing the auditorium to save on maintenance, discharging two teachers, and reducing the salaries of those remaining by one-twelfth, the *Trail* registered its objection. "The value of the auditorium to the community is obvious. The band, all athletics, the community players, and other organizations center there." It was, in short, of "paramount importance" that the auditorium remain open. The board should achieve the needed savings by eliminating the position of school superintendent and reducing teachers' salaries across the board by 21 percent. Even at that, the *Trail* told its readers, such a reduction was "probably not as great as the average cut for Colorado teachers and certainly not as great as the average business man on Elkhorn Avenue or any other Colorado Main street has taken." Moreover, the curriculum should remain unaltered. "The unqualified advantage of offering a full course [of study] to local students is manifest."[18]

Caught squarely in the middle of what was now a serious disagreement between the local school board and a significant segment of the Estes Park community was school superintendent Walter Early, whose job the *Estes Park Trail* now found unnecessary. Within two weeks of the editorial, Early resigned to work on his master's degree at Columbia University. He had been in Estes Park for only two years. His successor, Jess Caldwell, acted promptly. He gave local teachers a $50 raise and then cut their salaries by ten percent.[19]

That spring, summer, and fall, making use of available civil works program money and giving local residents preference when it came to jobs, Frank Bond and his fellow trustees moved along with the public improvements program to which he had previously alluded. This included resurfacing Elkhorn Avenue, laying new sewer and water lines, and reconstructing roads. The availability of federal funds, although certainly not great by the subsequent standards of the New Deal, managed to get the town and its residents through what turned out to be the worst months of the Depression and position them for the coming winter. By November the town could report that there was "ample work in the offing to take care of all families this winter."[20] There was even better news at year's end. Thanks to access to federal monies and deferring the purchase of new equipment, taxes could be cut by 8 percent. Editor Kirby once again had the last word: "The *Trail* has always insisted that the village was fortunate in having seven men in charge of its affairs who are attempting to run things with the same care and foresight they exhibited in their own business."[21]

～

Although the outline of the history of Estes Park during the Depression is generally clear, actual joblessness and extent of economic dislocation within the community is difficult to establish with precision. The *Estes Park Trail*, although ready enough to give its opinion on most issues, was reticent about matters that might negatively impact local reputation and affect summer business. The paper routinely reported the progress of federal and state New Deal projects but for the most part had relatively little to say about general unemployment conditions or individual economic deprivation.

Available evidence suggests that a number of local families found themselves, at least periodically, struggling against hardship and poverty. Poaching incidents found their way into local papers more or less regularly. And there is every reason to suspect that many residing in or near the mountains where hunting was part of historical tradition found the temptation to bring down a deer or other small game to feed one's family too great to resist and that much of this illegal hunting went undetected and unreported. In less than a week in 1932, for example, county water inspector Herbert McFaren buried nine deer that he found shot in the Big Thompson Canyon. On other occasions wild ducks left behind by hunters were found in Horseshoe Park and park rangers periodically reported the taking of elk, deer, and mountain sheep, some clearly the work of experts who used spotlights and high-powered rifles to paralyze and kill their prey. Jack Moomaw recalled how during these years he and fellow ranger Harold Ratcliff trailed a poacher on skis for two days through deep snow and heavy timber all the way to Grand Lake by way of Spruce Canyon only to find that the man they sought had "left for parts unknown."[22] When poachers were apprehended, fines were assessed, but in many cases local efforts to thwart culprits were hampered by the unwillingness of citizens to cooperate by sharing what they knew, at times, no doubt, because a hungry neighbor was involved.

Much of the evidence of local need tends to be similarly anecdotal. Events, such as the American Legion Rodeo of August 1933, became the occasion to raise money for the relief of area families. Foodstuffs from a Fort Collins commissary were periodically distributed by the county to needy families, including those in Estes Park where in late November 1935 recipients queued up at the town hall to receive sugar, potatoes, ham, and canned goods.[23] That December, with a cold winter ahead, the town made arrangements with the Forest Service to identify a woodlot west of the road between the Estes Park Chalets and Baldpate Inn where the unemployed could cut firewood. Later that same month Ted Jelsema opened his Darkhorse restaurant to serve some forty to fifty people a free Christmas dinner, while the Community Chest distributed sixty-three baskets of foodstuffs and members of the Estes Park Fire Department gave out toys to those who would otherwise go without.[24] The following spring the American Legion began a program to provide health treatment for underprivileged Estes Park children.[25]

The most reliable barometer of the local economy's state with respect to jobs and joblessness is found in the monthly reports of Rocky Mountain National Park's superintendent. Under the direction of Secretary of the Interior Harold Ickes, who enjoyed a close relationship with President Roosevelt, the National Park Service was given an important role in New Deal attempts to cope with the Depression, and as part of that effort park superintendents were required by Washington to describe the local work situation. These reports indicate that a major problem faced by those in Estes Park looking for work, as well as by those who had jobs to offer, was the influx of men from Denver and the valley towns. "Job seekers are in the park office each day asking about work," Edmund Rogers noted in his report for May 1932, "and at times it is extremely trying as some of the men feel that insofar as this is a government bureau they should be taken care of."[26] That June, as the Depression entered its worst summer, more than five hundred men showed up to apply for the fifty jobs doing trail work that Rogers had to offer. The issue of outsiders coming into the village because of rumors "that Estes Park takes care of its own" was considered serious enough to be discussed at a meeting of the Chamber of Commerce that October where the consensus was that proof of residency should be required before help was provided by local organizations.[27] This influx of transients continued to ebb and flow depending upon the labor situation in Denver and the valley towns. When times were particularly hard, many men, hearing of work projects in Estes Park, came to the mountains, only to leave disappointed. The problem became particularly severe as the Colorado–Big Thompson Project finally got underway, forcing the Bureau of Reclamation, the Park Service, and the *Estes Park Trail* to issue a series of warnings that there were few if any jobs in Estes Park and that job-seekers should stay away.

As one would expect, the monthly labor reports of Superintendent Rogers and his successors Tom Allen and David Canfield track almost exactly available jobs on road and public works projects funded by federal and state dollars. The winter and spring of 1932–1933, which followed two summers when tourist activity declined for the first time in park history, marked a low point. "There is no activity in the town of Estes Park," Rogers told his superiors in Washington that January. " 'Old Timers' say it is the quietest year in the history of the region. Business and hotel men are going about with long faces, realizing of course, that the coming summer will be a gamble. It is our opinion that the community has just begun to feel the sting of the depression."[28]

Through spring 1933, Rogers's prediction seemed to be accurate. In April job-seekers continued to clog the Park Service office on a daily basis. Larimer, Boulder, and Grand Counties—the three counties from which the park recruited most of its seasonal workers—had more than four thousand men on its unemployment roles as aid recipients,[29] and in May, with the 1933 summer season about to begin, some ninety men in Estes Park village alone could be identified as unemployed and on relief.[30]

By mid-summer, however, the situation had begun to change. Tourists returned in record numbers to Rocky Mountain National Park, construction work on Trail Ridge Road "absorbed many local men," and thanks to the influx of tourist dollars and the increased federal spending on public works projects in and around the national park, all of which gave preference to local men, a measure of normalcy had returned. These moderating times continued into the fall, bringing with them renewed confidence and good news as reflected in Rogers's monthly reports. "A few men are still idle in and around the village of Estes Park," he wrote in February 1934, echoing his comments of the preceding month. "Conditions are vastly improved over the previous four years. Only two families are 'on relief' in this vicinity."[31]

Although the situation temporarily worsened once again in winter and spring 1936, when the *Trail* reported that at least 110 local men were out of work and 52 families were receiving county and federally provided foodstuffs, the worst of the Depression was over in Estes Park.[32] Jobs made possible through funds provided by the Works Progress Administration (WPA), the New Deal agency established in April 1935 that enabled towns and cities to address infrastructure needs and to construct new educational and municipal buildings, certainly helped. WPA projects in Estes Park, which began that September and lasted into 1939, allowed the town to install water and sewer lines in several new subdivisions, lower existing water mains to prevent winter freeze-up, resurface streets, improve Devils Gulch Road, and construct a new water storage tank on Little Prospect Mountain. WPA funding in 1938 also underwrote much of the cost of the town's new high school building. By that summer, when the village was filled with Bureau of Reclamation personnel preparing to begin construction, and work on the three access highways to the valley had been completed or nearly so, depressed times in Estes Park were all but over. A record number of visitors—nearly 660,000—entered the park, an increase of more than 40 percent from three years before, half from out of state. "Business has been good!" the *Estes Park Trail* editorialized that September. "Estes Park is probably one of the few places in the country that can make that statement with any degree of accuracy."[33]

Rocky Mountain National Park more than did its part in providing jobs. Thanks to $46,805 in special public works funds made available through the Civil Works Administration, men from Estes Park and the valley towns were able to find work during winter 1933 on a variety of road, trail, construction, and brush removal projects contributing to park improvement. Beginning in normally quiet December, and lasting through April 1934, some 170 men—75 of whom were from Estes Park—were employed under the direction of park service personnel, earning $13.50 for a 30-hour workweek, much of which was spent locally. "The men appreciate the opportunity to work," Superintendent Rogers noted in his December report, "and the results received have been gratifying."[34]

Emergency federal funding for park projects continued to be available until 1940 and was particularly significant in helping to alleviate local labor problems during the fiscal years between 1934 and 1937. Despite the fact that Rocky Mountain National Park, like all government agencies, saw its regular annual appropriations reduced beginning in 1933, which limited, among other things, the number of seasonal rangers, such losses were more than offset by this special funding, which totaled $589,039 in 1934, $395,695 in 1935, and $409,480 in 1936, allowing the park to make significant progress in addressing many of its long-term needs.

Rocky Mountain National Park's Civilian Conservation Corps camps, two of which were on the east side of the Divide, also contributed jobs and dollars to the Estes Park economy, beginning in May 1933 when the first contingent of 159 enrollees established a summer tent camp in Little Horse-shoe Park. A second and permanent camp for 200 men was set up on Mill Creek in Hallowell Park the following May. Enrollees were paid $30 a month, of which they usually sent $25 home to their families. Some of the remaining money found its way each month into the shops and tourist attractions of Estes Park, which the young men were permitted to visit on a regular basis.

Mindful of the need to establish a good working relationship with the communities located near its camps, the CCC early on established a policy of giving them preferential treatment when jobs were available and supplies were needed. In the case of Estes Park, the task of establishing and maintaining the camps provided short-term jobs for a number of local men, and some had the benefit of longer employment. Dr. Jacob Mall, who held a reserve Army commission, got the contract to oversee medical care at the two camps, and veteran mountain guide Shep Husted closed out his long and colorful career by serving as foreman at the CCC camp on Mill Creek and later at a camp across the Divide. Superintendent David Canfield estimated in March 1940 that CCC enrollees were spending $2,000 a month from their personal allowances in the local economy, most of it in Estes Park, and that during the past two years the CCC had spent some $69,918 for skilled labor, much of it "a source of revenue for Estes Park village."[35] A year later, Eugene Lamb, writing an article for the *Estes Park Trail* specifically on the impact of the CCC camps on the local economy, noted that in addition to direct expenditures by recruits local purchases of food, lumber, paint, canteen, and other supplies amounted to about $60,000 per year.[36]

~

The most significant new source of jobs and dollars for the economy of Estes Park and the surrounding areas were the five major construction projects of the late 1920s, 1930s, and 1940s: the building of Trail Ridge Road; the reconstruction of the three roads from Loveland and Lyons to Estes Park (today's Routes 34, 7, and 36); and the even more ambitious Colorado–Big Thompson Project to bring water from the Western Slope for irrigation and power. Each of these undertakings was a major achievement, posing unique obstacles and challenges to their engineers and workers, and each, in turn, became a watershed event in Estes Park history. Staggered across more than a decade, these projects not only helped to support the economy of town and region at a time when that economy most needed help but were instrumental in addressing transportation, power, and water needs for the twentieth century and beyond.

~

The construction of 28-mile Trail Ridge Road across the tundra to link Estes Park and Grand Lake was but one of a series of major highway projects pushed forward by the National Park Service during the early 1930s. Good roads, Stephen Mather had insisted, would encourage tourism and, despite the fears of Horace Albright and others that too many roads and automobiles might overwhelm the nation's parks, had been one of the reasons for creating a landscape and engineering department division within the National Park Service as early as 1917. This division made certain that both new and reconstructed roads blended harmoniously with the setting. Although Mather was now gone, his belief in accommodating the automobile to create park boosters remained and, thanks to Congressional generosity, this period saw the completion of not only the "million dollar road" in Rocky Mountain National Park but also Wawona Road and tunnel in Yosemite, Going-to-the-Sun Highway in Glacier, Zion–Mount Carmel Highway with its mile-long tunnel in Zion National Park, and the Red Lodge–Cook City approach to the northeastern corner of Yellowstone, to name the most prominent in the West.

Given prevailing faith in the automobile, Trail Ridge Road was badly needed. By the mid-1920s the road up Fall River, after less than a decade, had become increasingly obsolete, difficult, and costly to maintain. In fact, Fall River Road had never been satisfactory. For all the enthusiasm of its builders and first users and its popularity as the centerpiece of Roe Emery's "Circle Tours," the road was difficult for cars and busses to negotiate because of its steep grade, dangerously narrow stretches, tight and blind curves, and sixteen switchbacks. Some vehicles could not negotiate the road at all because of low gear ratios and gravity-fed fuel systems. More than one traveler found the eight-mile trip up Fall River Road to be little short of terrifying.

With double-tracking virtually impossible because of terrain and the expense involved and with the chronic need for repair and improvement, as early as 1922 Roger Toll suggested building a new road to Grand Lake, one that would begin at High Drive and ascend Trail Ridge to Fall River Pass, thus eliminating many of the problems of the existing road.[37] Although it was agreed that Toll's plan had merit, nothing was done until 1925 when funds for road construction became available within the national park system. That year resident Park Service engineer George A. Gregory began a survey of what would eventually become the Hidden Valley section of a new road, extending westward from High Drive, and before the year was out a new road had been constructed connecting Deer Ridge with Fall River Road in Horseshoe Park.

Planning for the balance of the route, designed to provide a free flow of traffic east and west without dominating or destroying the fragile landscape, began in earnest during summer 1926, when a party of ten men, including Superintendent Toll, conducted a comprehensive inspection by horseback. The route followed was the "Ute Trail," identified in 1914 by the Arapaho brought to Estes Park to recall Indian names and connections as the gentlest of the three routes used by their ancestors to cross the peneplain from Estes Park to Middle Park.

The party was led by Stephen A. Wallace, locating engineer of the Bureau of Public Roads, which now had overall responsibility for planning and constructing roads within the national parks. A skilled surveyor who had earned a reputation with the Santa Fe Railroad for his ability to locate roads through difficult terrain, Wallace ranged ahead of the others, using his experience to establish the control points for the road's projected centerline. Ground rules specified a ruling grade of 5 percent over the 3,400 feet of elevation gain, a maximum grade of 7 percent for short sections, and minimum radiuses for curves. The party took special care to make note of scenic points along the proposed route. Completed the following spring, the Wallace report was enthusiastic:

> The surveyed route via Trail Ridge is one of unsurpassed mountain scenery, high mountains, deep canyons, many lakes and perpetual snow, alpine flower gardens and wooded areas all combining to make a trip over not to be forgotten. . . . This route is needed to better the snow conditions and provide a road that will be open to traffic a longer period of the year, reduce the cost of maintenance, and most of all to relieve traffic congestion.[38]

Politically speaking, however, the time was not yet right. Plans were put on hold for two years to wait the outcome of Colorado's decision on ceding the roads in Rocky Mountain National Park to the federal government.

Although Governor Ammons did not sign the final cede bill until February 1929, plans for the new road's construction had been advanced the previous fall when the project was pre-advertised to give would-be contractors an opportunity to review plans and site before winter snows closed the area. The formal advertising for bids began in August 1929 for the first 17.2-mile section from Deer Ridge to Milner Pass. The lowest of nine came from

W. A. Colt & Sons of Las Animas with bid of $393,674. The company had good credentials. Its principal, seventy-three-year-old William A. Colt, was a pioneer builder who had come to Colorado in 1887 to lay the three hundred miles of rails needed to bring the Missouri Pacific from Kansas to Pueblo. In more recent years he had successfully built roads over high mountain passes, including Wolf Creek Pass in the San Juans.

Colt was ready. Having just completed resurfacing the new Bear Lake Road and in anticipation of a successful bid, Colt had maintained a base camp at Glacier Basin campground, which he shifted to Hidden Valley in late September. There he installed a cookhouse, bunkhouse, and office and erected the first of a series of small wood-frame buildings with tar-paper roofs, each capable of housing eight workers and of being moved by truck without being dismantled.

Colt, who personally supervised the entire project, began work in early October using steam-powered shovels capable of moving as much as five thousand pounds of rock, and crews totaling some one hundred men, equipped with trucks, horses, graders, compressors, and drills. The road generally followed the existing pack trail from Deer Ridge westerly along Hidden Valley Creek and its beaver ponds. At the mouth of Hidden Valley it made a broad curve to the left and started up Trail Ridge to the lateral moraine separating Hidden Valley from Fall River Valley with its views of the Mummy Range. Further ahead there was another switchback at the scenic overlook called Many Parks Curve. From here the road continued up the shoulder of Trail Ridge to Forest Canyon Pass.

Specifications called for building an eighteen-foot road over a twenty-two-foot roadbed, doing as little damage to the high tundra as possible. Colt's workers were highly skilled men who knew how to control solid rock blasting. Salvaged timber was used lattice-fashion as cribbing to shield rock outcroppings adjacent to the blasting areas, while at the bottom of steep slopes logs or rocks were installed to keep debris and loose excavated materials within the staked-out areas. Future drainage was carefully anticipated with the use of corrugated metal culverts, ranging in size from eighteen to thirty inches, whose openings were then concealed with wing-walls built of cement and stone rubble.[39]

By January 1930 most of the clearing along the first five-mile section above Deer Ridge had been finished. The men worked on through the winter despite a brief shutdown in February because of weather and a three-week delay in mid-March. Work began again in April with the addition of new equipment, and good progress was made during summer and fall when, with some 185 men in the field, the timbered sections of the new road were entirely cleared. Drilling and blasting work, on the other hand, were appreciably slowed above timberline in August at the area later known as the Rock Cut where high winds, cold weather, and altitude all compounded the difficulty of the task. One of the blasts at the Rock Cut involved 178 separate shots of explosive wired together and detonated simultaneously. Despite the challenges, by the end of September when work was curtailed at the higher elevations, Colt could report that more than 50 percent of the project had been completed.

On October 8, 1930, work on the second 10.2-mile section of the road, extending from the end of Colt's project at Fall River Pass to the upper Kawuneeche Valley, began under the direction of L. T. "Bill" Lawler of Butte, Montana, who had won the contract with a bid of $437,138. A small construction camp and headquarters consisting of twelve cabins and a blacksmith shop were set up at Phantom Valley Ranch (Squeaky Bob Wheeler's old resort), from where a crew set to work clearing the right-of-way, taking special care, as on the east side, to burn the slash and stack salvageable timber for future use. A second and smaller camp with five cabins was later established near the Poudre Lakes. Lawler's work for 1930 ended in late November and began again the following May after two more power shovels had been brought in from Lyons.

Rather than follow the old route of Fall River Road over Forest Canyon Pass to Milner Pass by way of a series of steep switchbacks, the road built by Colt and Lawler ran eight miles above timberline, making use of a single long switchback at Medicine Bow Curve (located just past Fall River Pass and its future visitor's center). From there the road descended to the Cache la Poudre Valley on a new roadbed located half mile further down the ridge. This section of road paralleled the river until it reached the northeast side of the Poudre Lakes and the Continental Divide where it rejoined the old road just beyond Milner Pass. (Unlike the old road, which approached the Poudre Lakes and Milner Pass from the south, the new one came from the north.) At Farview Curve, overlooking the point where Beaver Creek enters the Kawuneeche Valley, old and new roads again divided. The old road had continued west from Farview Curve to descend to the Colorado River valley by seven steep (and for many unsettling) switchbacks. The new road, by contrast, swung to the northeast to curve down over a longer but less steep grade. Old and new roads then followed the same general alignment south toward Grand Lake, twelve miles distant.

The year 1931 proved to be a good one for both contractors. By the time he closed down for the winter, Lawler had completed fully 75 percent of his share of the project in only 45 percent of the allotted time. This included

10.1 *Construction at the Rock Cut on Trail Ridge Road, August 1932. Courtesy National Park Service–Rocky Mountain National Park*

half of the masonry work on the retaining walls and box culverts, the stone
for which was quarried on the south side of Little Sheep Mountain near
Milner Pass and then brought down an incline to a platform on the old Fall
River Road to prevent scarring of the terrain. Colt was equally productive.
Although he was unable to resume work until mid-June because of weather
and was slowed by large boulders requiring excavation near the Rock Cut, by
year's end his task was 95 percent complete.

Trail Ridge Road, "the eighth wonder of the modern world," was officially open for travel as far as the summit of Fall River Pass on Saturday, July
16, 1932. On August 23 travel was allowed to proceed on to Poudre Lakes
and Milner Pass. The old Fall River Road remained open as far as Fall River
Pass to allow for a circle trip by those not wanting to go on to Grand Lake.
As expected, the road was enormously popular with tourists from the beginning, particularly after it received its final surfacing. During summer 1933
some four hundred cars a day were making use of the road. On weekends and
holidays as many as one thousand were counted.[40] That year a contract was
awarded to a Denver contractor to build the remaining stretch of road, some
eight miles beginning near Phantom Valley Ranch and stretching along the
floor of the Colorado River. Until 1942 the road along the Colorado continued to follow the old alignment. That year a new road was completed to the
park's Grand Lake entrance.

The final cost for the twenty-eight miles of completed roadway approxi-
mated $950,000, or about $34,000 per mile, on which Colt claimed he made
no profit other than what he acquired in the way of new equipment.[41] In
retrospect, the accomplishment of Colt, Lawler, and their tough, skilled,
and resourceful crews had been little short of heroic. Working almost con-
tinuously under difficult and unpredictable conditions of sleet, snow, electrical storms, and for the most part thin air above 11,000 feet, they had successfully built the longest and highest continuous paved highway world and
had done so within budget, with a minimum of serious accidents, and without the loss of a single life.

⌒

The roads from Loveland and Lyons each presented drivers with similar
problems: well into the 1930s they were at best narrow and dusty and at
worst far too susceptible to damage from winter snows and spring floods that
caused rock- and mudslides, wiped out bridges, and halted traffic. These
problems were exacerbated after 1915 by the yearly increase in automobiles
to and from the new national park. By 1917 the situation had become seri-

10.2 Early view of the Big Thompson road. Courtesy Estes Park Museum

ous enough to bring Larimer and Boulder county commissioners together in an unprecedented meeting to discuss the possibility of "compelling all traffic to enter Estes Park by one route and leave by another."[42]

Causing the greatest problem because of the volume of traffic it carried was the road up the Big Thompson Canyon, completed and opened with great fanfare in 1904. So great was local pride in the new road that in October 1907, following its first summer of use by Osborn's auto company, Loveland boosters posted a sign at the canyon mouth proclaiming "Loveland Grand Canyon. The Gateway to Estes Park"—a name that, to the consternation of the Loveland Chamber of Commerce, was soon rejected by the U.S. Geographical Survey in Washington.[43] For all the initial enthusiasm, there were immediate problems, and by the 1930s the road had a long history of frustrated efforts at improvement, beginning in March 1917 when plans were first announced to double-track the entire road.

By December 1918, $90,000 in federal and state funds had been identified to reconstruct the road.[44] The survey, completed early in 1919, was encouraging: it called not only for a double-tracked, guttered roadbed averaging twenty-two feet in width, but for relocating several dangerous curves, eliminating two bridges, and raising the roadbed as high as four feet in places to reduce the chance of flooding. It also called for reducing the grade on the steeper hills to less than 7 percent, including the hill beyond Drake known as The Rapids ("a dread to every man who had to make the trip"). Work began in April 1919, only to come to a halt on the evening of July 31, when a severe cloudburst hit the canyon, tearing out four bridges and doing so much damage that it took nearly ninety men to reopen the road.[45] Finally finished the following spring, the road was opened for use on May 31, 1920, following a ceremony held at the Mont Rose Inn a short distance up the canyon.[46] That day an estimated fifteen hundred cars were counted traveling up and down what one of the day's speakers proclaimed was "perhaps the finest automobile road in any mountainous section of Colorado today [and] . . . a veritable boulevard." The final cost was $270,000, three times the amount projected just two years before.[47]

Additional "improvements," many of the stop-gap variety, continued periodically throughout the 1920s. These included replacing a number of the canyon's old bridges with new steel ones and, at the Estes Park end of things, widening, raising, and relocating the section of the roadbed between where it left the canyon and wound east to join the North St. Vrain and Fish Creek Roads near the old Dunraven Ranch. Sections of the roadbed in the canyon itself were also raised at points where floods periodically blocked the road. One problem mentioned but not resolved was the steep grade on Rapids Hill above Drake, although for a time in 1928 there was talk of eliminating the hill entirely by rerouting the road on a lower grade to the north side of the canyon.[48]

Despite such efforts, the road up the Big Thompson remained a source of frustration for drivers, who by 1930 were routinely referring to its grades and roadbed as "a fright" and "a disgrace to the state." In some places the road's gravel surface was all but gone, leaving sharp rocks and ruts to damage tires and chassis. There were also the ever-present clouds of choking dust. "Why I wouldn't drive up that dusty, dirty Big Thompson canyon if they gave me Estes Park," one New Yorker reportedly told another in the privacy of their club. "When are those backwoodsmen going to sprinkle a little oil on that filthy road?"[49] At times during summer months it was claimed, "you could follow the canon's [sic] course from a high point by the dust haze rising along it."[50] By summer 1926, the condition of the first two bridges east of Estes Park had deteriorated so badly that they had to be propped up to prevent sagging and posted with signs reading "Danger! This bridge is condemned by order of the county commissioners."[51]

By now the long-term remedy was clear enough: as long as county and state remained responsible for maintenance and repair, the road would never receive the attention it needed and deserved. What appeared to be a breakthrough came in September 1930, when after a year of agitation the Big Thompson road, now carrying as much as 60 percent of the summer traffic to Estes Park, was declared a Federal Aid Highway, making it eligible for government funding. The first improvements to what was now U.S. Highway 16 began two years later in summer 1932 on the section of road between Loveland and the mouth of the canyon, where seven new bridges were constructed and a number of curves eliminated, shortening the trip. Again, however, there were delays, this time because of the State of Colorado's inability to arrange constitutionally for its share of the financing.

Petitions and direct appeals to Washington seemingly did little good. "Without a doubt," Edmund Rogers noted in his monthly report for February 1934, "this Park has the worst assortment of approach roads that a Park could have the misfortune to possess. . . . The fact that travel holds up as well as it does is a source of amazement to us."[52] That spring renewed efforts by civic and business organizations in Estes Park, Loveland, Fort Collins, Greeley, Fort Morgan, and Sterling resulted in the formation of the Northern Colorado Highway Association. This well-funded and well-publicized group, galvanized by the desire to improve northeastern Colorado's tourist economy while providing jobs for local workers, played a central role in successfully lobbying over the next four years for the reconstruction of the Big Thompson road.

During spring 1934 there were, in fact, signs of progress. Following the completion of a new survey of the road from Estes Park east in April and using state and local funds, work began on the three-mile section from the Big Narrows at the mouth of the canyon to Mont Rose Inn. At the canyon's mouth a sharp turn and hill were literally blown away. From there west a wider and straighter road was constructed further up the canyon wall, a task that required cutting down the granite cliffs above the river with jackhammers and dynamite in order to raise and secure the new roadbed. While the road was closed traffic to Estes Park was diverted to a tedious six-mile detour over Rattlesnake Hill and down through Dixon Gulch.

By April 1935 the first section of road from the Dam Store west, although still incomplete, was opened for traffic, and by early July the entire stretch of road from the Loveland city limits to east of the Mont Rose Inn had received its first coat of dust-eliminating oil. Work on the road in the lower canyon resumed that October on a stretch connecting the already completed section through the Narrows to the Mont Rose Inn, a distance of a little more than a mile and a half. This work, although clearly less difficult than that near the canyon's mouth, required replacing two existing steel bridges, one of which—measuring a full 22 feet wide—was dismantled, moved to Estes Park, and re-installed in place of the old bridge across the Big Thompson below the Crags Hotel.

Again, however, there were agonizing delays, for Governor Johnson, despite making the road's completion an election priority, still needed to find a way for Colorado to match the federal dollars available for road construction. Held hostage to protracted negotiations that continued into 1936 was the Big Thompson road to Estes Park, now ridiculed as "the Gaston and Alfonse fiasco in Colorado road construction."[53]

In May 1936 with $25 million dollars in state funds finally at his disposal, Johnson announced that the Big Thompson road would be completed in time for the 1937 tourist season. By the end of July bids were authorized for the two-mile stretch between the Mont Rose Inn and Loveland's municipal power plant, and the next month Governor Johnson ordered the state highway engineer to obtain bids for the remainder of the road. Significant new construction began west of the Mont Rose Inn, where the road was redirected away from the Big Thompson River and over a saddle to a place just above Cedar Cove. By September one hundred men were working on the road, including the three-mile section east of Drake, and by mid-November work had begun at the Estes Park end.

In early 1937 Johnson's June 1 completion date still seemed possible, and plans were initiated by the Northern Colorado Highway Association for two celebrations to mark the occasion: one at the mouth of the Big Thompson to be coordinated with Loveland's sixtieth anniversary as an incorporated town; the second in Estes Park.[54] Within days of their announcement, both plans were called into question. Four of the new bridges above Drake had yet to be bid out and, even once in place, could not be safely used for another month. Although the road was actually opened for use over the Fourth of July weekend, making use of detours and temporary bridges, the date for the celebration was pushed back twice, ultimately to summer 1938 to allow for final oiling and larger and better-publicized events.

The long-awaited celebration of the new $1.8 million Big Thompson road took place over three days, beginning with a formal dedication on Saturday, May 28, 1938, at the Loveland end of the canyon attended by Colorado's new governor Teller Ammons, who had come into office the previous year when Ed Johnson resigned to become a U.S. senator. Johnson, who understandably took much of the credit, was on hand as well by means of an amplified telephone hookup from Washington over which he congratulated state highway officials on the completion of such a scenic road. Following a salute fired by a National Guard battery, Governor Ammons declared the road formally open.

10.3 Parade in Estes Park celebrating the completion of the Big Thompson Highway, May 29, 1938. Estes Park Library and Auditorium in background. Courtesy National Park Service–Rocky Mountain National Park

Things were considerably more elaborate the next day in Estes Park, where a crowd of 20,000 turned out to watch a two-mile parade, led by Governor Ammons on horseback and containing vehicles and floats depicting the role of transportation in developing the West. The parade, broadcast over Denver's NBC affiliate from a reviewing stand in front of the Chamber of Commerce, consisted of vintage buggies, stage coaches, surreys, wagons, and automobiles, some of them "ancient," carrying passengers in period costumes. They were accompanied by a series of floats sponsored by local businesses and other organizations. The young men from the local CCC camps used their floats to depict various conservation tasks, while Rocky Mountain National Park's chosen theme, the evolution of the tourist, was presented in nine stages, each on a separate float.

Estes Park's authentic pioneers, Abner Sprague and Charles Reed, were both on hand, riding in a Stanley Steamer dressed in the cutaways they had worn to their weddings. F. O. Stanley, the third member of Estes Park's reigning triumvirate of old-timers, was less fortunate. When the boiler of his Stanley Steamer sprung a leak, a chagrined Mr. Stanley, "the Grand Old

Man of Estes Park," was forced to ride down the new canyon road in a modern vehicle.

~

The reconstruction of Estes Park's two other access roads, South St. Vrain Highway (Route 7) and the North St. Vrain Highway (Route 36), although equally protracted, was somewhat less eventful. The South St. Vrain Highway from Lyons to Estes Park by way of Raymond, Allenspark, and the Tahosa Valley, had originally been constructed before the turn of the century to bring out timber from the St. Vrain watershed and to reach the mines of western Boulder County. Improved in 1906 to allow for automobile use, the picturesque road was immediately popular with travelers, particularly at its lower end above Lyons where it passed by a series of granite rock formations with such imaginative names as "Elephant Rock," "Andy Gump," "Wolf's Head," "Monk's Hood," and "Barking Dog."It remained for a decade, however, little more than a good mountain road, too narrow and steep in many places to accommodate heavy traffic. Then came the years of World War I when increased summer use and renewed interest in mining throughout Boulder County combined to make reconstruction and double-tracking imperative. "This road should be made as wide and as safe as the two present roads into the park," park superintendent L. C. Way was quoted as saying in July 1919. "If it could be improved, . . . all passenger travel could be routed over this new road, and out by the Big Thompson road, leaving the old road by way of Lyons to the handling of freight."[55]

The first improvements of the South St. Vrain were begun by Boulder County in March 1919 using convict labor and completed in stages over the next eight years with state funds under Forest Service supervision. These efforts widened the road to sixteen feet from Lyons to the Boulder county line beyond Allenspark, eliminated all but two bridges below the cottage colony of Raymond, and routed the road to the north side of the river. Above Raymond at Stanley Hill, always a trial, the road was re-directed, providing excellent views up Peaceful Valley and of the Arapaho Peaks and Mount Audubon.[56] Just before Allenspark, the hill at Ferncliff was cut down. By the mid-1920s this "new" double-tracked road was being vigorously promoted by Stephen Mather and the Park Service and by boosters throughout the state as an integral part of the "Park-to-Park" system of mountain roads linking all the national parks in the Rocky Mountain West.

Between 1927 and 1929, double-tracking continued from Copeland Lake at the entrance to Wild Basin through the Tahosa Valley to just south of Lily

Lake. Concrete culverts were installed to take care of the slough created by Aspen and Inn Brooks just north of Longs Peak Inn, which for years drivers had forded without a bridge. Beginning in summer 1932 and extending into 1933, the entire sixteen-mile road from Lyons to Wind River Ranch at the northern end of the Tahosa Valley, now widened to thirty feet, was given a coat of bituminous oil and crushed rock.

Work on the last but critical section of the South St. Vrain, from the hydrographic divide at Lamb's Notch at the north end of the Tahosa Valley to Estes Park village, began in summer 1934. Plans drawn up by the Bureau of Public Roads called for a 7.5-mile road, much of it new, to descend the east side of Lily Mountain to the floor of the valley just east of Marys Lake, skirt the slope of Prospect Mountain, and run on past the golf course to enter the town of Estes Park. Below the Stanley Hotel east of the village it would link up with the road coming up the Big Thompson, which now followed its own route on the north side of the river before entering the canyon. The decision to bring the road down Lily Mountain ended talk of a plan discussed periodically by the Forest Service and others since about 1910 to shorten the distance between Moraine Park and the popular Longs Peak area with a road down Aspen Brook and Wind River Trail that would connect with Wind River Road above the YMCA entrance.[57]

The most difficult part of the new road was the stretch from below Lily Lake to the head of Fish Creek, where the original Lamb Road built in 1875–1876 turned east to ascend the flank of Twin Sisters Mountain. Here, in places, the roadbed was located 600 to 700 feet above the valley floor, providing motorists with "some of the most breathtaking views that can be seen anywhere in the entire region."[58] Heavy blasting was required near what is now the Lily Lake Trailhead, creating the large rock cuts that in postcard photographs were soon being used to illustrate the scenic beauty of the new road. Work, done under the supervision of the Bureau of Public Roads, progressed without incident and by the end of July 1935 the entire road was open for use. Oiled and paved the following summer, the South St. Vrain became the first completely dustless highway from the valley to Estes Park.

The North St. Vrain, the earliest road to Estes Park, was the last to be modernized. Although rebuilt twice by Stanley, from 1915 on it suffered from the same limitations as the other two. Because the road was located in both Boulder and Larimer Counties, maintenance of the North St. Vrain posed a particular problem, giving rise to periodic charges that the commissioners

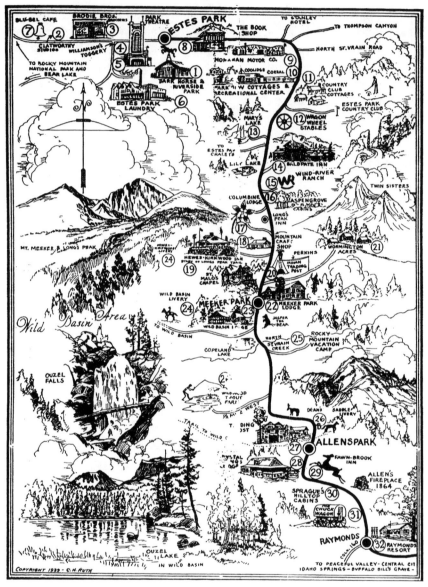

10.4 Map of the new South St. Vrain Highway, 1939. James H. Pickering Collection

of Larimer County were neglecting their section above Pinewood Springs to make sure that Loveland and its Big Thompson route served as the gateway to the national park.[59]

Nature did not help. A cloudburst on the afternoon of July 30, 1919, "said to be the most terrific . . . ever experienced in Northern Colorado"[60] sent a wall of water down the canyon, tearing out all bridges along a five-mile stretch, before rushing through Main Street in Lyons doing extensive damage. New storms, almost equally severe, followed over the next two days, cutting off Estes Park from the east and evoking comparisons to the famous Cherry Creek flood of 1864, which had all but wiped out a fledgling Denver.[61] So severe was the destruction that the North St. Vrain remained closed until mid-September while a crew under Byron Hall's leadership removed debris and installed temporary bridges, repairs that only made obvious how much additional work was required to bring the road to modern standards.

This work took two decades. Though some $25,000 in state highway funds was committed in 1920 to complete the repairs begun by Hall, by the end of 1923 there was once again talk of "sad neglect" on the part of Larimer commissioners "more interested in improving the Big Thompson road to the Park."[62] Despite complaints throughout the remainder of the decade, the road received little additional attention until June 1933, when the Estes Park Chamber of Commerce hosted a regional meeting to talk about roads.

Thanks in part to support of the recently formed Northern Colorado Highway Association, whose efforts on behalf of the Big Thompson road were to prove so decisive, by fall 1934 plans had been finalized and announced for rebuilding the North St. Vrain, now State Highway 66. They called for the road west of Lyons to be rerouted for 3.6 miles along the north side of the river on high ground to a point skirting Steamboat Rock, shortening the distance from Lyons and eliminating the meanderings of the old road through Apple Valley and the dangerous turn over the bridge east of the Hall homestead. From the mouth of the North St. Vrain Canyon the road was engineered to follow its current course on a widened and straightened roadbed as far as the Welch resort (today's Shelleys). The route west into the mountains, financed by a combination of federal, state, and county funds, required a right-of-way through the Welch property in order to eliminate the steep hill on the current road, and here there was a problem. The proposed road came within thirty feet of the resort's main building, and owners William and Sally Welch insisted this proximity would be detrimental to business. When the Welches rejected Boulder County's offer of $500, condemnation proceedings followed.[63]

Work on the first three-mile section from the Welch resort to the "Big Hill" eight miles west of Lyons began in late April 1935. Here the road was built to follow a more scenic route on easier grade, climbing without sharp turns to the top of Mines Hill. This involved heavy blasting. One explosion,

set off in July by workmen who drilled the holes for the charges from a
catwalk in order to remove part of a granite mountain, required two and a
half tons of powder—said to be "one of the largest charges ever to be set off
in Northern Colorado."[64] The danger of such work was dramatically underscored on Friday, September 13, 1935, at about 5 P.M., when tragedy struck a
group of workers placing an electric-timed blasting cap. It failed to detonate
and the men were in the process of setting another, when the first cap exploded a fifty-pound charge of dynamite, sending tons of rock and gravel
into the air and down the 250-foot embankment onto the original roadbed.
The blast killed three men and injured nine others, leaving a scene resembling
"a battlefield." The explosion was so great that it hurled one badly mangled
victim six hundred feet from the blast site where he grotesquely lay in the
full moon's light for some four hours while a rescue party of seventy-five
blinked and jerked their flashlights across the hillside searching for him.[65]

Despite the accident, work quickly resumed. By the end of that month a
twenty-eight-foot-wide road had been completed to Pinewood Springs, a
half mile beyond the Boulder county line, where it was rerouted over a new
right-of-way through what had been the old Meining ranch. Above the Welch
property the new road in many places simply followed the same hillside as
the old, although higher on the hill and on a wider grade, allowing the
current road to remain open to traffic as the project moved west. Late that
fall work also began on the two new sections of road between the Welch
property and Lyons, and by October 1936 the entire eight-mile stretch had
been completed and oiled.

Beyond Pinewood Springs there were fewer problems. From there the
new road followed a relatively easy grade down into and across the drainage
of the Little Thompson and ignored the winding, circuitous route of the old
road as it ascended Muggins Gulch. At the top of Park Hill, the road passed
through a new opening, veered left, and came down the side of the mountain
into the Estes Valley by a shorter and straighter route than its predecessor.
The most difficult section lay just west of Pinewood Springs where the roadbed descended toward the river and crossed the road built by Stanley in
1907. In order to construct a bridge over Little Thompson Creek (thereby
avoiding having to follow the creek bed as the old road had done) it was
necessary to divert the creek into a new channel by blasting through fifteen
feet of solid rock. This work began in spring 1937 and continued into winter
in the hope that the entire road would be ready for use by the beginning of
the 1938 tourist season. Although the road was not yet graveled and oiled,
the goal was met. In early May 1938 the new North St. Vrain Highway from
Lyons to Estes Park was formally accepted by the U.S. Bureau of Roads.

10.5 Parade celebrating completion of North St. Vrain Highway, June 4, 1939. Transportation company building in background. Courtesy National Park Service–Rocky Mountain National Park

When it came to celebrating highways, Lyons, Longmont, and Boulder were not to be outdone by Loveland. The festivities of June 4, 1939, attended by a crowd of four to five thousand, took place on a picture-perfect Colorado day. They began with a baseball game, band concert, and free barbecue dinner at Meadow Park in Lyons, followed by a brief dedication ceremony at the bridge just west of town. There a group of dignitaries led by Colorado governor Ralph Carr and state highway engineer Charles Vail addressed the crowd with remarks broadcast live over the radio. "They often compare us with Switzerland—and I don't like it!" Carr told the crowd, forgetting perhaps just where he was for the sake of his comparison. "Switzerland has nothing to compare with our Fall River road."[66]

The ceremony concluded, Carr threw open a gate, and a long caravan of cars started up the canyon. In Estes Park the governor again spoke, after which a crowd of five thousand watched more than six hundred riders parade down Elkhorn Avenue followed by an old-fashioned horse-roundup that brought saddle horses from the winter range back to their stables in the village to begin the summer season. The day, like the road itself, was a success.

10.6 Parade, June 4, 1939. Reviewing stand in front of Jay Building. Courtesy National Park Service–Rocky Mountain National Park

"'Forty minutes to the Park,' is the way one Longmonter put it approvingly. 'And in my time it used to take a day by spring wagon.'"[67]

The Colorado–Big Thompson Project dominated the final years of the 1930s. The largest and most far-reaching event in the life of Estes Park, it had a long history.[68] Agriculture along the arid Front Range depended on the availability of water, and Colorado's early settlers became adept at building dams, canals, and reservoirs and tapping mountain watersheds to fill them. As far back as the 1860s during their first years in the Big Thompson Valley, Abner Sprague and his father had listened to talk among the farmers of a day when water would be brought across the Continental Divide. And given the irrigation and power needs of northeastern Colorado, it was only a matter of time before that possibility would become a concern of the state legislature as well. That involvement began in August 1884, when the State Engineer's Office dispatched a reconnaissance party to Middle Park "to determine . . . the feasibility of turning the waters of Grand Lake eastward into the St. Vrain and Boulder Creeks." On the basis of a "rough triangulation" the surveyors concluded that such a plan would require a fourteen- to seventeen-mile tunnel costing millions of dollars, an "impracticality [that] may be considered as a settlement of the question."[69]

Impractical or not, in the two decades that followed, irrigation schemes in the Estes Park region seemingly came and went with the seasons and, although a tunnel through the mountains was considered visionary, the concept itself became more or less a part of the accepted long-term solution. One of those who needed no convincing was Louis G. Carpenter, the first professor of irrigation engineering in the United States, who in the summers between 1898 and 1905 gave his students from the agricultural college in Fort Collins practical experience by having them survey the route for a twelve-mile tunnel from Moraine Park to Grand Lake to bring water into the Big Thompson.

Some schemes collapsed under their own grandiosity. In 1893 and again in 1905, rumors circulated that Willow (Moraine) Park would be turned into a large reservoir. The first of these, said to be backed "by the Earl of Dunraven and others," called for the construction of a 1,200-foot-long dam, 400 feet thick at the bottom and 300 feet at the top, in order to build a reservoir two miles wide and three-quarters of a mile long at a reported cost of $245,000.[70] In fall 1907, attention briefly shifted to the area directly east of the new village of Estes Park, where Greeley irrigationist Burton D. Sanborn enlisted the help of Stanley and others in plans to build a 125-foot-high dam to impound water and generate electric power, creating a lake extending from the Dunraven Ranch at the foot of Park Hill into the Big Thompson Canyon to within a mile of the summer enclave of Loveland Heights. Such a reservoir, Sanborn predicted, would "prove a valuable feature for the park," providing a large body of water "on which launches and row-boats might be placed."[71] The visionary Sanborn was talking about Lake Estes—forty years too early.

Most early attempts to impound and redirect mountain water were of necessity more realistic in scope and design. The most ambitious was the Grand Ditch on the eastern slope of the Never Summer Range, begun with hand labor using wheelbarrows and burros in 1890 and gradually expanded between 1891 and 1936. The Grand Ditch intercepted a series of creeks from Baker Gulch north and carried their water some fourteen miles across the Continental Divide at La Poudre Pass (or Mountain Meadow Pass as it was then known) to Long Draw Reservoir where it could be drawn down by Fort Collins farmers.[72]

Closer to Estes Park, on Flattop Mountain, running northwest to empty into the Big Thompson at Sprague Pass was the Eureka Ditch, begun in summer 1902 by Henry J. Heinricy of Loveland with the financial support of

Burton Sanborn and a group of Greeley men. Although the original survey called for a series of ditches 13.4 miles long, only a mile was built before the $2,000 raised by Sanborn ran out, and no one else seemed interested in pursuing a project whose location, inaccessible for most of the year, made construction and maintenance difficult. Other early diversion efforts within the future Rocky Mountain National Park included a ditch from Specimen Creek on the western flank of Specimen Mountain to the Cache La Poudre begun in the 1890, a never-completed 6.3-mile ditch at Milner Pass filed on in 1903, and a less ambitious project at Icefield Pass, which transferred water from the Cache la Poudre drainage to the Big Thompson drainage rather than across the Divide.[73] By the early twentieth century dams had been established at Pear Reservoir and at Blue Bird and Sandbeach Lakes within Wild Basin to impound water from the St. Vrain watershed for use in and around Longmont.

The 1902 establishment of the Reclamation Service, predecessor of the Bureau of Reclamation, marked the beginning of federal involvement in solving Colorado's water problems, particularly with respect to building large storage reservoirs to capture additional drainage. In 1904–1905 the bureau turned its attention to the Grand Lake watershed for a series of studies that included bringing water through a twelve-mile tunnel into the Big Thompson or St. Vrain River.[74] Although nothing came from these efforts other than the bureau's decision to withdraw land from public entry near Grand Lake for future storage sites, they were sufficient to insure that a provision was inserted in the bill creating Rocky Mountain National Park giving the Bureau of Reclamation the right to enter the park for the development of any federal reclamation projects. Twenty years later, much to the consternation of the National Park Service, this stipulation helped provide legal justification for the Colorado–Big Thompson Project.

The "Grand Lake Project" as it came to be called, making use of the general plan developed by the Bureau of Reclamation studies of 1904–1905, came to life in Greeley in late summer 1933 under the leadership of Charles Hanson, publisher of the *Greeley Tribune* and head of the unemployment agencies in Weld County, who in response to an invitation from the PWA called a meeting of irrigation interests to suggest projects that would provide both long-term economic benefit and short-term relief for the region. The result was a group calling itself "The Grand Lake Committee," which set out to gain support among prospective user groups in the Poudre, Thompson, St. Vrain, and South Platte Valleys and to raise funds for a new tunnel survey and feasibility study. The report of Royce J. Tipton, a well-known Denver consulting engineer, released in December 1933 not surprisingly reaffirmed what others had been arguing for decades: that it would be both practical and possible, although costly, to bring water by tunnel under the Continental Divide and into the Big Thompson somewhere west of the Brinwood Hotel in Moraine Park. By April 1934 tunnel proponents in Greeley and their growing list of allies had a new name, the Northern Colorado Water Users Association (NCWUA), an organization that began to rally public opinion and political muscle behind the Grand Lake Project.

Although most of the state's political leadership came on board early, there was major opposition from farmers and ranchers across the Divide. This was led by veteran congressman Edward Taylor, the powerful chair of the House Appropriations Committee, who raised the traditional argument that any and all available water was needed in the west. Taylor and those he represented were ultimately willing to cooperate but only on the basis of the "acre-by-acre and foot-by-foot" provision, which guaranteed additional water storage capacity on the Western Slope in compensation for water diverted east. Strenuous objection also came from in and around Grand Lake, the area most immediately affected by any plan involving the Colorado River, where there was concern about the loss of tax revenues from lands converted into reservoir sites and the reduction in the recreational value of a sizable portion of the North Fork Valley. This agitation, coupled with Taylor's insistence on "compensatory" parity, required protracted negotiations that delayed the project for some three years.

Equally reluctant was the National Park Service, which like the Bureau of Reclamation was part of the Department of the Interior. Citing its opposition to any plan that would "ruin Moraine Park" and "impair the natural beauty" of other park land, new Park Service director Arno Cammerer rejected out of hand the request of the Grand Lake Committee to enter the park for a preliminary survey of a tunnel route. Cammerer's opposition was immediately supported by his conservation-minded boss, Secretary of the Interior Harold Ickes, who telegrammed Colorado governor Ed Johnson that surveyors would not be allowed in the park. For those who had argued a decade earlier that ceding control of the roads in Rocky Mountain National Park would set a precedent endangering the future irrigation development of northern Colorado, the chickens seemingly had come home to roost.

Park superintendent Edmund Rogers followed orders. When Louis L. Stimson, Burgess Coy, and their eight-man party arrived at Grand Lake to begin their survey, chief ranger John McLaughlin was there to intercept them, bar their entry, and force them to complete their survey west and east by taking triangulations from points beyond park boundaries. In the course of nine days, making use of a baseline on Eagle Cliff and the High Drive on the east, they somehow managed to locate both ends of a thirteen-mile tunnel. With results in hand, Hanson and other project leaders opened negotiations with the Bureau of Reclamation, by now transformed under Ickes's leadership into a major instrument of Roosevelt's New Deal.[75] In January 1935, helped by political pressure from Colorado's congressional delegation, the bureau authorized $150,000 for a complete feasibility study and survey covering more than thirty principal components of a large integrated irrigation and power project.

By this date two important legal decisions had been reached in Washington: the first was that the project qualified for federal support under the Reclamation Act; the second, that the Park Bill of 1915 gave the Bureau of Reclamation the right to enter Rocky Mountain National Park. Closer to home the NCWUA, now encompassing more than sixty water districts, incorporated itself as a mutual stock company. Two years later in summer 1937 following the approval of the Colorado legislature, the NCWUA transformed itself once again, this time into the Northern Colorado Water Conservancy District (NCWCD), a seven-county taxing unit with authority to negotiate a contract with the federal government to repay half of the project's estimated $44 million cost. That contract was overwhelmingly approved by voters in June 1938 by a margin of better than 17 to 1.

The new survey, under the general direction of Weld County irrigation engineer Louis Stimson, got under way in late July 1935. Because of the season's lateness in the high country where much of the work had to be done, it was agreed that Stimson's crew of thirty would concentrate its efforts largely on surface topography in order to prepare geologic reconnaissance maps of two different routes from Grand Lake—one that would bring the tunnel into one of the branches of the St Vrain, the other into the valley of the Big Thompson above Estes Park. The much more controversial—and still undecided—question on where and how to drill holes for seismic work that might damage park terrain was wisely left to another season.

Work needed to complete the tunnel survey moved ahead during summer and fall 1936. The most difficult part of the task involved seismic analysis to establish the depth of glacial debris in Glacier Basin and the severity of shearing and faulting near Prospect Canyon, both of which lay on or near the proposed route of the tunnel.

These findings were incorporated into the final report submitted to the Secretary of the Interior in April 1937. It recommended the beginning of construction of a complex and ambitious system of dams, reservoirs, hydroelectric plants, tunnels, penstocks, and power stations on both sides of— and linking—Western and Eastern Slopes. In addition to a 13.1-mile transmountain tunnel, its major features included a reservoir and hydroelectric plant at Green Mountain on the Blue River west of Kremmling to impound compensatory water and provide power for the Western Slope; Granby Reservoir, northeast of Granby, to be created by damning the Colorado River; Shadow Mountain Lake, formed by a dam across the Colorado to accept water pumped from Granby Reservoir and send it on to Grand Lake and the west intake of the tunnel; some five miles of buried pipe, siphons, tunnels, and open canal from the East Portal on Wind River to take Grand Lake water to a large power plant on the Big Thompson near the village of Estes Park; four additional power plants in the Big Thompson Canyon; and several new storage facilities in the Big Thompson Valley. Marys Lake Power Plant, Olympus Dam, and the large reservoir that became Lake Estes—three of the most distinctive features in the Estes Park area—were not part of the original design.

With the Bureau of Reclamation's positive report and the creation of the Colorado River Water Conservancy District, there were calls for immediate congressional action in Washington where the outcome was far from certain. The spending mood of Congress had grown conservative, and both houses seemed inclined to cut rather than increase federal spending, especially spending of the magnitude required by the project in Colorado. Friends of the project were not inactive, especially senator Alva Adams, who on June 18, 1937, introduced legislation authorizing construction. Although approved within a week by the Senate, there was considerable controversy once it reached the House, where the Committee on Irrigation and Reclamation held hearings beginning in late June 1937.

Speaking in opposition was Arthur E. Demaray, the veteran assistant director of the Park Service, whose previous experience included work with the Bureau of Reclamation. Sensing that his testimony—which included the argument that an alternate route for the tunnel should be chosen even if more expensive—was unlikely to carry the day, Demaray offered a series of amendments designed to provide the park with free water and electricity and to insure that the Park Service would be allowed to approve plans for construction and debris removal. He was followed to the witness table by a broad array of conservation groups—including the National Park Association, the General Federation of Women's Clubs, the National Association of Audubon Societies, the Izaak Walton League, and the Colorado Mountain Club—all dedicated to wilderness preservation and opposed to the commercial exploitation of national parks.

In their testimony Demaray and the groups that followed him made extensive use of the thirty-seven-page report released in May 1937 by the Park Service's John S. McLaughlin, which insisted that the project would do "considerable irreparable damage" to the national park and might totally drain the alpine lakes located along fracture or shear zones. There was "a particularly serious zone," Demaray noted, "directly under Glacier Creek in close proximity to Bear Lake, the Loch and Mills Lake." Twenty-three additional lakes were also at risk because they were located over or near the proposed bore, among them Lake Nanita, the largest in the park. There would also be "absolutely ruinous" surface damage from the construction of the tunnel's two ventilation shafts and unsightly scarring in Wind River Basin in and around the East Portal.[76]

The key vote came on July 23, 1937, when after impassioned debate, the House approved but by an uncomfortably narrow margin—174 yeas; 154 nays; with 103 abstaining—the Department of the Interior's appropriation bill with its $900,000 to begin the Colorado–Big Thompson Project. Congressional action was completed on August 9, 1937. The final decision, however, belonged to Interior Secretary Ickes, who was sufficiently concerned by the warfare between his two agencies and the genuine dilemma of having to choose between new sources of water and power and his mandate to protect the integrity of park ideals to call a meeting for November 12, 1937, so that both sides might have their final say. Ickes spoke last. A solid conservationist, he chose his words carefully, saying finally that he was reluctant to defy the will of a Congress that had appropriated $900,000 for the project. "I wish the baby had not been laid at my doorstep, but it is there. . . . Pray for me!"[77] On December 21, 1937, President Franklin Roosevelt approved a finding of feasibility, making the Colorado–Big Thompson Project—the first federally funded inter-basin diversion and one of the largest irrigation and power projects in Bureau of Reclamation history—a reality.

In Estes Park the opposition of the Park Service in the face of northeastern Colorado's demonstrable need for additional water had attracted little sympathy beyond core conservationists. Most residents saw the project as providing a new and ongoing source of local revenue, welcome at any time but especially so during the years of the Depression. By late spring 1938 with actual construction about to begin, the verdict, as far as the *Estes Park Trail* was concerned, had become definitive: the Big Thompson–Colorado River diversion project "is the most important factor in the future development of the region."[78]

∼

By late June 1938 the Bureau of Reclamation had established its presence in the village, leasing space for temporary field headquarters in the Boyd Building near the post office. That month it also dispatched a team of fifteen engineers to the national park as part of pre-construction survey to finalize tunnel alignment. Other survey work on the east side that summer included the location of a thirty-two-mile power line from Loveland to the East Portal over Bald Mountain and down through the Crocker Ranch, a route that generally followed the old stagecoach road from the valley. Surveyors also located a new road from above the main entrance of the YMCA up Wind River to the portal of the tunnel, three hundred feet east of the park's boundary. By August 1939, the transmission line was ready for use, allowing electrical power from Loveland to reach the East Portal work site.

On September 1, 1938, with a total of $4,150,000 identified for the first year's work, bids were solicited for construction of Green Mountain Dam. That fall work also began on the construction of Reclamation Village in Estes Park. This complex of buildings, erected at a cost of some $350,000 to house the bureau's engineers and administrative staff, was sited in the triangular area formed by the junction of the North and South St. Vrain Roads just beyond the village (encompassing what are now First to Fourth Streets). The land selected, however, initially posed a problem, for it was part of the fifty-four acres of meadowland that F. O. Stanley had donated to the town in August 1936 "as a public park and recreation grounds." Fortunately, the rather elaborate plans for its improvement existed only on paper, making it possible, with Stanley's agreement and the unanimous vote of residents, to sell the property to the Bureau of Reclamation. Stanley then deeded to the United States the rest of the land needed for the bureau's headquarters and power plant.

By November 1938 the site for the village had been cleared, and work was underway on a series of six duplexes. The central building, erected at the apex of the triangle, was the 45-by-102-foot field headquarters (today's American Legion building), built according to a "modified colonial design" to office as many as eighty engineers. To its rear, between First and Second Streets, plans called for a large dormitory for unmarried engineers, two equally large garages, and a laboratory building. A block of recreational facilities separated the work area from two additional streets of residences, six three-room, twelve four-room, and six five-room permanent houses, all with basements. Both the administration building and the houses were ready for occupancy in October 1939, allowing the bureau's office in Denver to be relocated to Estes Park. Of considerable benefit to the town and the result of the bureau's need for an easement was the September 1939 agreement giving Estes Park the right to purchase five hundred acre-feet of water annually from the completed project.

The completion of Reclamation Village brought a significant change to the face of Estes Park, and old-timers like Charles Edwin Hewes were impressed. "I was startled," he recorded in his journal after his initial visit that October, "at the present expanse of Estes Park village. Beginning about half a mile south of the village on Highway #7, cottages and businesses now line the road on both sides, culminating in the extensive housing project of the U.S. Reclamation service."[79] When the streetlights in the "miniature city" were turned on for the first time on October 13, they were visible as far south as Hewes-Kirkwood Inn in the Tahosa Valley. "Thus," Hewes added the following month, "the changes gradually come on."[80] So important was the bureau's local presence that by early 1940 the *Trail* had a new weekly column, "Reclamation Village News."

Given the number of workers, labor problems east and west were remarkably few. The only major dispute came early, during summer 1939 when, following a strike at Green Mountain Dam over the issue of a "closed" or "union" shop, a group of men, made up of non-union workers, ranchers, and citizens from Kremmling, Granby, and Hot Sulphur Springs, decided to force the issue. Arriving in a caravan of fifty cars, they stormed the picket line, routed pro-union pickets, and then, having been "deputized" by the sheriff of Summit County, stayed on to guard the site. Shots were fired and seven men were wounded, one seriously. Colorado governor Ralph Carr declared Grand and Summit Counties to be in "a state of insurrection" and called in the Colorado National Guard to restore order. Three weeks later, on August 22, 1939, came an agreement calling for a closed shop, giving those who wished to work seven days to join the union.

The greatest challenge, it turned out, was getting companies to bid the critically important tunnel within the $7.3 million budget. Two rounds of advertising, the first in April 1939, produced bids a full 30 percent above the estimate, leaving Ickes and the Bureau of Reclamation with three apparent options: re-advertise for yet another round of bids; drill on a "force account basis" with the bureau hiring and supervising the workers; or agree to meet the higher bids—all of which made the outlook for beginning the tunnel in 1940 uncertain. Ickes and his subordinates found another way. In February 1940, after a winter of frustrating delay, the secretary announced that he would bid the first mile-long section of the tunnel beginning at the East Portal, with the understanding that the remainder of the project would be completed by similar short-term contracts.

Low bidder was the S. S. Magoffin Construction Company of Denver run by Sam S. Magoffin, whose previous experience included building railway bridges, docks, tunnels, and heavy highway construction on the western

10.7 *Ceremony marking the start of drilling at East Portal, June 23, 1939. Courtesy National Park Service–Rocky Mountain National Park*

side of Wolf Creek Pass in the San Juans. Although work was briefly held up until Magoffin agreed to match the closed shop arrangement at Green Mountain, by late May 1939 work on the facilities at the East Portal had begun. A month later, on Sunday June 23, following a ceremony broadcast by radio and attended by a crowd of twenty-five hundred, Charles Hanson, president of the NCWCD, threw an electric switch detonating 144 sticks of dynamite to begin construction of the world's longest transmountain irrigation tunnel. After the fumes cleared, spectators were allowed to enter the tunnel to inspect the result for themselves, a number of whom emerged with pieces of rock to keep as souvenirs. In mid-August work was begun on the first 6,600 feet of tunnel at the West Portal by the Platt Rogers Construction Company of Pueblo.

For the next four years, work on the ten-foot in diameter tunnel went forward, with men working in continuous shifts, each shift normally making two shots during its eight-hour period, then removing the "muck" or rock debris from the area so that the next charge could be placed. It was laborious work, requiring long hours in the underground darkness, always with the risk of cave-in or sudden immersion in underground streams. Miraculously, there was only one fatality, which occurred in September 1941 when a tunnel worker was accidentally crushed to death by a railcar carrying drilling equipment.

Early engineering plans had called for the construction of two airshafts from tunnel to surface, fueling much of the fear among Park Service officials and conservationists that irreparable damage would be done to park terrain. These shafts were made unnecessary with the installation of a novel and highly efficient ventilation system, consisting of heavy duty blowers driven by 100-horsepower electric motors, which required only a single line to bring in fresh air and exhaust the old.

World War II then intervened. With the tunnel—now named unofficially after senator Alva Adams, who had died in December 1941[81]—nearing the halfway point, it was hoped that the major features of the Colorado–Big Thompson Project might be completed by the end of June 1944. This would not happen. For a variety of reasons, including the scarcity of supplies and machine parts, on October 27, 1942, with all but 2.5 miles of the tunnel completed, the War Production Board (WPB) revoked the construction priority of the Colorado–Big Thompson Project along with those of six other irrigation projects in western states. The only exceptions were the dam and power plant at Green Mountain.

Popular construction projects are never dead in Washington, even in time of war. Backstage lobbying, some of which produced congressional appropriations for a project that could not be built, continued and on July 24, 1943, the WPB finally authorized the resumption of construction. Work on the tunnel began at the West Portal on August 24 and at the East Portal on September 17, although labor was initially in short supply and both contractors had to resort to reduced shifts.

The long-awaited "holing through" occurred on Saturday, June 16, 1944, with the successful completion of the last of some twelve thousand separate blasting and mucking operations. At 12:24 P.M., the chief Bureau of Reclamation engineer touched off a charge ripping away the last eight feet of rock, and nineteen minutes later cheering crews from the East and West Portals cleared away the debris and greeted each other. They had drilled more than thirteen miles through granite, yet their bore was off center line by only $7/16$ inch and off grade by only ¾ inch—errors, it would later be pointed out, that could be covered by a twenty-five cent piece. Even with delays, it had taken only four years to complete what some had once argued was impossible.

Much still remained to be done before water from Grand Lake could flow east. Lack of manpower, labor ceilings, and other wartime limitations continued to retard progress until February 1946, when the tunnel's nine-

10.8 "Holing Through" the two ends of the Alva Adams Tunnel, June 16, 1944. Courtesy Estes Park Museum

foot nine-inch concrete lining and "invert" concrete floor were completed. With the lining in place, the mouth of the tunnel at the East Portal was submerged. Beyond its entrance a 245-foot-long reservoir was built to help regulate tunnel flow.

The other elements of the project in Estes Park, like those on the Western Slope, were left for after the war: the completion of Rams Horn Tunnel beneath Gianttrack Mountain in 1946, the completion of Prospect Mountain Tunnel in 1947, and the completion of Olympus Dam and the filling of Lake Estes in 1949. Although the power plants at Marys Lake and near Estes Park village were also completed in 1949, it would be another two years before their turbines could be installed, tested, and placed in operation.[82]

The result was a virtually seamless irrigation and power system. The Rams Horn Mountain section brought water from the East Portal by means of a concrete siphon to the east side of Aspen Brook and from there by tunnel to Marys Lake Power Plant. The natural depth of Marys Lake, once "a little sheet of alkaline water," was enlarged by twenty-five to thirty feet through the construction of large dikes on its east and northeast sides, one of which contained the controls for the Prospect Mountain conduit. Expansion of the lake's holding capacity required rerouting the original road from the south shore around the northern side of the lake across the top of the dikes.

From Marys Lake a conduit, whose intake was submerged five feet to prevent ice buildup, carried water to the Prospect Mountain Tunnel and from there, by means of a long 700-foot penstock, into the three big turbines of the Estes Park Power Plant, the principal power-generating unit on the Eastern Slope. In addition to furnishing power for a power grid in northeastern Colorado, southern Wyoming, and western Nebraska, a portion of the electricity generated at the Estes Park plant was sent back through the Adams Tunnel over a thirty-nine-mile transmission line to the pumping station north of Lake Granby to raise water into Shadow Mountain Reservoir.

Lake Estes, a mile and a quarter long and a third of a mile wide and covering 168 acres of what was then Stanley Meadows, was not part of the project's original design but was added to help regulate the flow of water into the Big Thompson. Its construction required the relocation of the North St. Vrain Road over a short causeway and also meant the removal of the old Dunraven Ranch at the base of Park Hill, a fixture at the entrance to the park near the original site of Joel Estes's cabin since the late 1870s.

Earth fill operations on seventy-foot high Olympus Dam started that May. Six months later, at noon on November 30, 1948, the Bureau of Reclamation began releasing water into dead storage behind the new dam. Lake Estes received its official name on June 23, 1949. That morning in a ceremony at the West Portal, Colorado governor William Lee Knouss turned a valve releasing water from Grand Lake into the Adams Tunnel. Three hours later, preceded by a large cloud of dust, the water arrived at the reservoir at the mouth of the East Portal where, greeted by a large crowd of spectators, it continued its journey toward the Big Thompson. As the enterprising were quick to realize, Lake Estes—the most visible of the changes brought about by the Colorado–Big Thompson Project—made possible new forms of mountain recreation. Even before the lake's dedication Ted Jelsema, sensing opportunity as he had in building Riverside nearly three decades before, along with a partner tied down a boating concession through the 1952 season. Burton Sanborn's dream of 1907 had become a reality.

~

Estes Park was grateful. "The public works and civil works program [of the New Deal]," the *Estes Park Trail* editorialized in early January 1934, "have benefited Estes Park probably as much as any village in the United States and politics are forgotten by citizens here who are loud in their praise of the president's plan to rehabilitate the United States."[83] Later that month more than three hundred residents turned out to dance and play cards in celebration of Roosevelt's birthday, one of five thousand such events held across the nation to raise funds to fight infantile paralysis. Because of the size of the turnout, the following year's event, during which the president greeted the nation by radio, had to be moved to the Stanley Hotel. Attended by "practically everyone in Estes Park," it was, "according to the frequently expressed opinion of those present, . . . one of the most enjoyable events in the history of the region."[84]

Supporting good causes was one thing. When it came to electing public officeholders, however, Estes Park never wavered in its loyalty to party and Republican candidates, with very few exceptions, could count on sizable majorities from local voters. Those traditional sympathies were never more on display than during summer 1936, when two hundred mounted horsemen gaily dressed in "brightly colored shirts" and "super gallon" hats and led by mayor Casey Rockwell rode out to meet and welcome newly nominated Republican presidential candidate Alf Landon, who had decided to make Estes Park and its secluded McGraw Ranch on Cow Creek his temporary campaign headquarters. There, where Peter Pauly's cattle had roamed before the turn of the century, the Kansas governor, wearing a fishing outfit and amidst jokes about using worms for bait like back home, was photographed in ankle-high water proudly holding a twelve-inch trout. Where the favor of politicians, Democrat or Republican, was concerned, Estes Park in the 1930s, it would seem, had the best of all possible worlds.

~

Although the building and construction activities in town and region added to the hustle and bustle of things, summertime in Estes Park during the 1930s was for the most part what it had always been. While most recreational and leisure activity remained focused in and around the hotels and resorts or in the national park, summers were punctuated by community-sponsored activities including Fourth of July fireworks (some years with a parade and other events), the mid-summer ski carnival on Oldman Mountain, and a two-day rodeo with bronco- and steer-riding, calf-roping, and the usual assortment of cowboy stunts alternately sponsored by the American Legion and the Liverymen's Association. For those craving additional excitement, there was always Elkhorn Avenue and its shops, amusements, and other attractions, as well as swimming and dancing at Riverside.

Most summers also had special events, such as the two-day extravaganza of August 1931 staged by actor-turned-promoter Albert Van Antewerp and his Hollywood Amusement Company, which consisted of a "Days of '49" parade on Saturday followed on Sunday by the first—and only—water ski carnival ever held at Sprague Lake.[85] Equally memorable was a "First of the Season Party" in May 1932, for which a crowd of three thousand turned out to watch Mayor Frank Bond lead a torchlight parade down newly macadamized Elkhorn Avenue to Riverside, where Ted Jelsema opened his dance hall for a free barbecue and dance.[86] At the end of the decade there were the celebrations dedicating the Big Thompson and North St. Vrain Roads as well as the Silver Jubilee Celebration in mid-June 1940, celebrating the twenty-fifth anniversary of Rocky Mountain National Park's establishment.

Perhaps most instructive about Depression summers in Estes Park and about the town's established identity as a summer resort community was what was hardly missed at all. Both the publicity-sensitive Chamber of Commerce and the *Estes Park Trail* took note of the success of the nearby Central City Opera, held in the remote and run-down former mining town then but "one step removed from being a civic junk yard."[87] Beginning in 1932, in the very depths of the Depression Anne Evans, the daughter of Colorado's second territorial governor, used her connections, determination, and promotional skills to establish a three-week festival whose opening night in the 1878 gaslit opera house on Eureka Street became a "must" event for social Denver and culture-conscious summer visitors.

Although by 1935, the *Estes Park Trail*, with an eye on Central City, was lamenting the need for "some sort of community entertainment during summer evenings,"[88] the town's response was much in keeping with the tastes and preferences of its tourist visitors. Anne Evans might well win rave reviews for her revivals of *Camille* with Lillian Gish or *The Merry Widow* with Metropolitan Opera stars Gladys Swarthout and Richard Bonelli. But the *Estes Park Trail* was no less complimentary of the American Legion's 1932 production of *Ten Nights in a Bar Room and What I Saw There*, featuring the ubiquitous Clem Yore and local artists Dave Stirling and Richardson Rome,[89] and the musical and dramatic talent put on display by the performers in *The Dixie Blackbirds*, a minstrel show staged in August 1935 with a hometown cast made up of "the Who's Who of Estes Park."[90] If there was a disparity in the quality of summer entertainments in the two mountain towns, no one in Estes Park seemed to sense the irony or to care. A play based on Timothy Shay Arthur's 1854 temperance novel transformed into melodrama and burlesque was a perfectly fine way to pass a summer evening and to forget, if temporarily, the troubles of the time.

Chapter 11

~

The Years After Roger Toll:
Rocky Mountain National Park, 1929–1941

S UCCEEDING ROGER TOLL was not an easy assignment. Toll was the only park superintendent to have a memorial and a mountain named in his honor and his departure for Yellowstone in 1929 concluded a period of considerable activity climaxed by the successful resolution of the controversy over road jurisdiction that had clouded the park's existence for a decade. Ironically, however, it was during the Great Depression of the 1930s after Roger Toll's departure that Rocky Mountain National Park enjoyed its greatest growth and development. Edmund Rogers, Thomas Allen, and David Canfield may well have lacked the polished presence, political adroitness, and easy self-confidence of their predecessor and none, with the possible exception of Canfield who went out of his way to engage the local community, enjoyed Toll's near-universal popularity. Yet thanks to the availability of emergency federal funding and the young men who passed through the park's CCC camps, more progress was made during the dozen years between 1929 and 1941 in road and trail construction, visitor services, scenic preservation, and wildlife management than in any similar period before or since.

These years also brought with them the largest boundary expansion in park history. In July 1930 President Hoover signed a bill adding the Never Summer Range. Containing both the headwaters of the Colorado River and

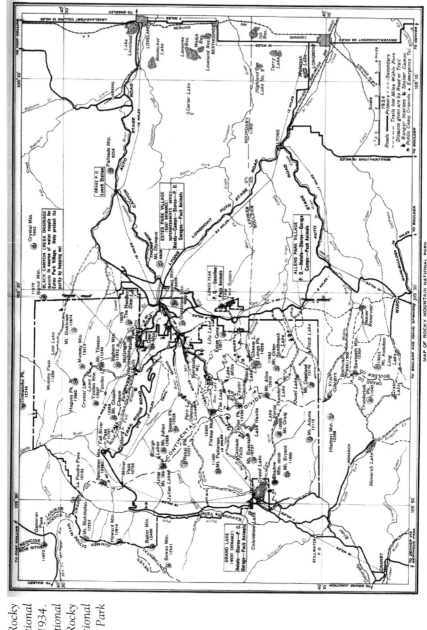

11.1 Rocky
Mountain National
Park in 1934.
Courtesy National
Park Service–Rocky
Mountain National
Park

the old 1879 mining town of Lulu City, this area of just over twenty-two square miles increased recreational activities on the less-visited west side and allowed Trail Ridge Road to be completed entirely within the park over a comparatively easy grade. In 1931 and 1932, federal funding made it possible for the Park Service to eliminate many of the hotels, lodges, camps, and cottages located on privately patented land, adding to the park more than nine thousand acres in Beaver Meadows, Horseshoe and Moraine Parks, and along the drainage of the Big Thompson. Although these purchases would continue beyond World War II, by the end of the 1930s significant progress had been made in returning large sections of the park to their natural condition. All of this made Rocky Mountain National Park in the 1930s a busy place. Added to the normal administrative burden of operating the park with limited resources—resources reduced by a 15 percent mandatory cut in regular appropriations during the early years of the Depression—were the oversight and coordination responsibilities that came with the various New Deal emergency aid programs. Although many of these activities, including roadwork and trail-building, were scheduled for the off-season when the park was relatively free of visitors, there were inevitably times during the summer months when roads and trails were crowded with men and equipment, causing delays and irritation on the part of those who had come to the national park precisely to escape such things. For those capable of a longer view, the activity of these years was exhilarating.

~

Edmund Burrell Rogers (1891–1972), who became superintendent in February 1929, was cut out of the much same cloth as the man he succeeded. Born in Denver and the last of five children of a pioneer surgeon, Rogers was the younger brother of James Grafton Rogers, one of the founding members of the Colorado Mountain Club and the lawyer who drafted the legislation establishing Rocky Mountain National Park. Like the sons and daughters of many well-to-do Denverites, Rogers went east to college, first to Cornell University and then to Yale where he graduated in 1915 with a degree in botany and geology. Following service in World War I as an artillery officer, he came home to Denver, settled into a comfortable career as a trust officer with the Colorado National Bank, and in 1926 married into the prominent Vaille family.

Edmund Rogers also had a long-standing relationship with Rocky Mountain National Park. An avid outdoorsman, Rogers grew up hiking and climbing with the Toll brothers. A charter member and twice president of the

Colorado Mountain Club, Rogers spent many of his weekends tramping the high country around Estes Park often in the company of Roger Toll, to whom he would become related through marriage. In early August 1921, for example, Rogers and Toll climbed Mount Ida to see "whether or not it was practicable to follow the Continental Divide from Fall River Road to the Flattop trail" and "whether it was practicable to reach shelter at Fern Lake or Bear Lake, in one day, starting from a high point on the Fall River Road."[1] They also shared companionship during the CMC's winter and summer outings to Fern Lake and other places.

Edmund Rogers, it turned out, was no more suited for banking than his friend had been for engineering. Handpicked by Toll to be his successor and nominated for the post by Colorado's two senators, Rogers did not take long to accept, although it meant a cut in pay. National parks had become a "sort of hobby," and the challenge offered by a superintendency so close to home seemed at the time "just another adventure." Although the bank held his position open, thinking he would return, Rogers did not turn back. When he retired from the National Park Service in 1961 after thirty-two years, Edmund Rogers had served as superintendent at Rocky Mountain National Park for seven years and as superintendent at Yellowstone National Park, where he again replaced Toll, for nearly twenty-one more. Edmund Rogers may have lacked the stature of Roger Toll, but as the last "civilian" to be recruited to head the nation's most popular western park, he came remarkably close.

Rogers quickly discovered the importance of public relations. Some of the antagonisms of the recently concluded transportation controversy remained, perhaps most visibly in the ever-confrontational Clem Yore, who warned the new superintendent shortly after his arrival that if he had his way Rogers would be fired.[2] Rogers's tenure as superintendent, in fact, was marked by more or less constant tensions with local residents over a series of legislatively proposed extensions of park boundaries. The first two, in 1930, involved land along Fall River and Black Canyon Creek and a plan to turn the hydrographic divide between the two into a park boundary, and an even more ambitious proposal to extend the park two miles east to the edge of the village to create a new approach road over a 500-foot right-of-way between park headquarters and the current Big Thompson entrance near the Y turnoff.

The construction of the "Parkway," as this road came to be called, was designed to create a scenic entrance to the park and allow for the removal of billboards, gas stations, livery stables, and other unsightly tourist enticements along the Big Thompson, a stretch that David Canfield bluntly de-

11.2 Superintendent Edmund B. Rogers, 1929–1936. Courtesy National Park Service–Rocky Mountain National Park

scribed in 1938 when the proposal was raised again as a "public disgrace." The new entrance made particular sense after the 1934 completion of a new road from Deer Ridge to Moraine Park, making it possible for motorists using the Big Thompson entrance to turn left toward Glacier Basin and Bear Lake or right toward Trail Ridge Road or Horseshoe Park, from where they could return to the village over Fall River Road. On each occasion there was vocal opposition and controversy, much of it from property and business owners and the local schoolboard, the latter objecting to having valuable property removed from the tax rolls. A similar flap occurred in May 1932, this time over legislation calling for the addition of nearly six thousand acres to the park's eastern boundary, a proposal inadvertently drafted to include both the Stanley Hotel and the Estes Park Chalets.

Simmering throughout the decade as well was the proposed addition of the area to the south containing the Arapaho Glacier, which had been included in Robert Marshall's original 1913 report but excluded from the final park bill because of opposition from mining, ranching, and irrigation interests. When the idea resurfaced in 1925, in 1935, and again in 1938 (in 1935 as Secretary Ickes's well-intentioned attempt to compensate the park for the feared incursions of the Colorado–Big Thompson Project), there was an immediate storm of protest. On each occasion the current superintendent found himself drawn into the dispute.

Rogers's superiors in Washington tried to help by providing their new superintendent with a new leadership team. It included assistant superintendent John C. Preston, a native of Longmont who had been serving since 1927 as Toll's chief ranger, and John S. McLaughlin, a 1928 forestry graduate of the agricultural college at Fort Collins, who was transferred down from Yellowstone in April 1930 to take Preston's place. Two years later in June

1931, Rogers's permanent staff of fourteen was joined by a talented twenty-nine-year-old naturalist named Dorr Yeager, also from Yellowstone, who brought vigor and direction to the park's educational programs.

~

The elimination of patented lands within the park, particularly those containing lodges and resorts, had been among the earliest objectives of Stephen Mather's Park Service. Private holdings "seriously hamper" the administration of national parks, Secretary of the Interior Franklin Lane wrote in his now-famous letter of May 1918, outlining broad management principles for the new bureau. "All of them should be eliminated as far as it is practicable . . . in the course of time, either through congressional appropriations or by the acceptance of donations of these lands."[3] In the case of Rocky Mountain National Park these inholdings originally consisted of something over 11,000 acres, to which another 2,000 acres were added through subsequent boundary changes. On the west side of the park, private lands extended roughly from the site of Lulu City on the Colorado south to Grand Lake; east of the Continental Divide they were mostly concentrated in Beaver Meadows and in Moraine, Horseshoe, Tuxedo, and Hallowell Parks. Donors willing to give their property to the government outright were, not surprisingly, slow to emerge, and it was not until late 1929 that Congress finally made funds available for direct purchase. Even then there was a troublesome proviso: at least half of each property's fair market value had to be contributed by the owner or a private donor.

This requirement provided little encouragement, particularly during bad economic times. When the National Park Service began to acquire inholdings, it was later charged that it did so by resorting to a subterfuge: by doubling the appraisal price with the understanding that half the doubled value would be considered a "contribution" to the federal government.[4] The first inholding purchased in Rocky Mountain National Park came in October 1931 when for $32,500 the Park Service acquired from C. C. Patrick the 120-acre tract in Horseshoe Park containing Horseshoe Inn. This was followed in spring 1932 by additional purchases, including the John Griffith home on the Bear Lake Road, Allens High Drive Inn, the Chapman and Sprague homesteads and the Moraine Park Lodge in Moraine Park, Abner Sprague's lodge in Glacier Basin, and Jack Woods' cabin camp in Tuxedo Park near the park's Big Thompson entrance.

By the end of 1932 the Park Service had concluded some twenty separate transactions and acquired 4,414 acres of land at a total cost of $435,316 with an additional 240 acres of meadowland along the Big Thompson drainage under contract. The largest of these purchases, concluded in February 1932, was with Pieter Hondius for 1,762 acres in Beaver Meadows and Horseshoe Park for which he was paid $140,720 and with the Reed family who received $56,585 for the 297-acre tract containing their Brinwood Hotel in Moraine Park. The most significant purchase on the western side of the park did not occur until September 1940, when for $12,372 the Park Service obtained the Harbison estate with its 226 acres of meadow and timberland and water rights on the Colorado. The property, located not far from the Grand Lake entrance, had once been the adjacent 1895 homesteads of sisters Annie and Kitty Harbison, where by 1905 tourists were being taken in and served legendary Sunday dinners.

Most of those approached were glad enough to sell. "As far as I can learn," resort owner Charles Edwin Hewes noted in his journal in December 1931 at a time when a number of purchase contracts were still pending,

> most of those who have sold so far, are quite happy about the situation; and I presume for the following reasons: most of the properties are more or less encumbered, the resort and hotel business is on the decline, the owners are considerably advanced in age, and the Government officers enable them to liquidate their debts, retain whatever residue there is as their fund for old age, and if they wish to continue operating the Govt. gives them a 20 year lease without taxes.[5]

There were exceptions. For Emporia, Kansas, journalist William Allen White the thought of giving up the cabin in Moraine Park where he and his family had spent many summers was "heart breaking." "If it is necessary for us to move," he stoically wrote Edmund Rogers in January 1932, "we will have to move, though it will end one of the happiest periods of my life. . . . But of course the beauty of the Park for coming generations should not be weighted against my own feelings in the matter."[6] The Whites did not sell.

The only voice of concern came from the *Estes Park Trail*. With its eye clearly on Yellowstone, Yosemite, and Glacier National Parks where concessionaires within the park were firmly entrenched, the newspaper worried that an active program of property acquisition was but a prelude to new park-owned hotels and recreation services, turning the village into "a back alley" and ruining businesses and eroding property values.[7]

Where lodge and resort owners sold outright rather than take advantage of the twenty-year leases that Hewes mentions, the Park Service almost immediately razed the buildings and began to obliterate their footprints. Within months Horseshoe Inn and its artificial lake, a fixture at the mouth of Endovalley for more than two decades, had disappeared, as had Moraine Park Lodge, where only the recreational hall was preserved to later become a museum. Those who could afford to accept the offered lease and stay on at best postponed the inevitable. One by one, as their leases ran out or through subsequent purchase, the historic old wooden lodges, many now badly in need of repair, began to disappear: Bear Lake Lodge and Camp Woods in 1958; Forest Inn at the Pool and Fall River Lodge in 1959; the Brinwood Hotel, Deer Ridge Chalet, and Sprague's Lodge in 1960; Stead's Ranch in 1963; and Fern Lake Lodge in 1976. Their removal marked the end of a historic period in park history. It was, as Hewes concluded in a 1931 journal entry, "a portentous change."

In addition to providing new meadowland for the winter forage of elk and deer, these sales, together with an infusion of federal relief funding, made possible the construction of two new and important roads within the park. The first, built in summer and fall 1933, was a road from the Fall River entrance up into Horseshoe Park, rerouted through the open area known as Hondius Park and then on a curve up the moraine on an easy grade, eliminating Cascade Hill, to join the old road near what was then Cascade Lodge. From there the road ran west into Horseshoe Park on a bed along the northern edge of the valley. Although this new road avoided the soft marsh along Fall River, it had the unhappy consequence of cutting off Sheep Lakes from adjacent Bighorn Mountain, making generations of shy bighorn sheep have to cross the road on their journey to the mineral-rich lakes.

The second of these roads, built in 1934 at a cost of $90,000, was the short road connecting Deer Ridge and Moraine Park. This began at Deer Ridge Junction, where connecting roads lead up Trail Ridge and down into Horseshoe Park, then curved east down Deer Mountain through a portion of Beaver Meadows and ran over the lateral moraine north of Stead's Ranch into and through Moraine Park to the junction of the Bear Lake Road. That summer, following completion of the upper portion of this new road, the section of the High Drive within the park was closed. Later, the old roadbed was obliterated and the land returned to its natural contour.

∿

Much of the progress made by Rogers and his two successors was the result of the men of the Civilian Conservation Corps who served in Rocky Mountain National Park between 1933 and 1942. A centerpiece of Roosevelt's famous "hundred days," this widely popular New Deal initiative, which blended conservation with character building, education, and job training, was authorized by Congress on March 21, 1933, and signed into law ten days later as a way of addressing the needs of youth in a society grown increasingly urban. The program was just as quickly implemented and underway. On April 17, 1933, just thirty-seven days after Roosevelt's inauguration, the first CCC camp opened in Virginia's George Washington National Forest.

The first of the more than 170 CCC camps in Colorado opened at Trout Creek, northeast of Buena Vista, on May 9, 1933. Three days later, the CCC era began in Rocky Mountain National Park, when an advance party arrived from Fort Logan to establish Camp N.P. 1-C, the first in a national park west of the Mississippi.[8] The site selected because of its privacy and relative ease of access was the former Willard Ashton homestead in Little Horseshoe Park. Preparations began at once. By 6 P.M. that Friday a group of local men had been hired to serve as foremen and crew bosses, and with the arrival of a truckload of camp equipment from Fort Logan, a detail began to shovel aside twelve to eighteen inches of frozen snow to create a level campsite. They also set up a field kitchen, laid down pipe to bring water from a diversion on nearby Hidden Valley Creek, and began to erect tents. By Monday, May 15, the camp with its 24 khaki-colored pyramidal Army tents and three 24-bed hospital tents was ready for the arrival of the first recruits—four dozen young men enlisted from northern Colorado. They were joined the next day by 111 more enrollees brought in from Greeley and, shortly after, by 50 others from Fort Logan, CCC's administrative headquarters for Colorado and Wyoming camps east of the Divide.[9]

L. R. Douglass, who served as superintendent at Camp N.P. 1-C from May to November 1933, described the scene they encountered:

> The camp was laid out in semi-military fashion, with a single company street, with the tents perfectly aligned on both sides. Seven men were placed in each tent. At the upper end of the street on one side were the administration or office, infirmary, and officers' mess tents. Opposite was the kitchen and men's mess hall. At the foot of the street was the bath house and lavatory with hot and cold water and showers. South from the head of the street and at right angles thereto was a single line of tents housing the official family of army officers and park service officials. North and west from the head of the street were located the supply storage building, tool tent, and gasoline and oil station tents for servicing the busses, trucks, and other transportation equipment. A larger recreation tent, with reading tables, magazines, a traveling library, cards and other games, to say that nothing of the crowning glory of a mechanical piano and a radio, was situated in the rear of the south tent line about half way down the street. To the rear of the north line of tents was a 5-KW lighting plant.[10]

11.3 CCC Camp in Little Horseshoe Park, May 1933. Courtesy National Park Service–Rocky Mountain National Park

Unfortunately for these first recruits spring was late. Superintendent Rogers's observation in June that "weather conditions were far from ideal for establishing of the camp"[11] was, in fact, an understatement. It was bitter cold with blinding snow, supplies had not yet arrived, and many of the young men were without coats and sweaters. Army and park officials coped as best they could. Fires were built, hot coffee served, and one of the vacant buildings of Moraine Park Lodge was pillaged for bedding. Some of the new recruits had to be quartered for a week in the park's utility area.

By Friday, May 19, with the arrival of supplies and equipment, the recruits were finally able to settle in. Each received blankets, a cotton-stuffed mattress, two khaki shirts, one blue-denim hat, six pairs of socks, two pairs of boots, a toilet kit, and an aluminum mess kit and canteen.[12] Within weeks the young men had been dubbed by park staff and Estes Park residents the "woodpecker army," because, as one observer noted in a July 1933 letter to *Time* magazine, "Aside from a common habitat there is a further resemblance, for the uniformed men migrate from work-spot to work-spot in old, red, sight-seeing busses [of Roe Emery's transportation company] from which they descend with a clatter to do their busy-work."[13] "The boys in the camps resented it at first," Edmund Rogers noted in his report for June 1933, "but have recently adopted the name and apply it to themselves frequently."[14]

On May 22, the day when fifty young men were sent out into the field for the first time to work on insect control, winter returned once more. Blizzard-like winds hit the tents in Little Horseshoe, tearing some "to ribbons," collapsing others down around the heads of their young occupants, blowing part of the mess tent "into Kansas," and scattering pots and pans over a wide area. For those not used to the waywardness of the mountains it was an unsettling, if instructive, beginning.[15]

A daily routine was soon established. As one of the early recruits, Battell Loomis, an unemployed magazine writer, explained in an article titled "With the Green Guard," published in April 1934,

> Up at six o'clock in the morning. Breakfast—hot and plenty of it—at seven. Camp police from seven thirty to eight. Then off to work for four hours. Lunch at twelve—plenty of it (we get a pound of bread and a pound of meat per man per day, as well as eggs and plenty of vegetables)—followed by four more hours of work. Back in camp by four thirty. The rest of the day is on our own time, except for camp details.
>
> Each day a few of us get leave to go to town, and week-end leave to visit families is also handled in rotation.[16]

That first summer the work program, carried out under the direction and watchful eye of district rangers, included a variety of utilitarian insect and fire prevention, erosion control, trail maintenance, obliteration, and landscaping projects. The attempt to arrest the damage caused to ponderosa pine by the Black Hills pine beetle—a problem noted in the Estes Park area as early as 1914[17] that had severely infected various areas in the park—was particularly critical. The only way to prevent the spread of the larvae was to cut down the infested trees and burn the slash and bark. It was tough work, particularly for those not used to such strenuous activity, but by June CCC workers had completed the first phase of "delousing the forest" by cutting down and peeling some twelve hundred trees.

That same season a much-needed 2.75-mile fire trail, built to the Park Service's new eighteen-inch standard, was constructed to link the ranger station in lower Wild Basin with the village of Allenspark, making use of an outcamp and a crew of twenty-two men. About half of the work took place along a steep and rocky hillside, which introduced the recruits to air compressors, jackhammer drills, and explosives. Whenever possible, electronic detonators were used as a safety precaution because of the inexperience of the young workers, who labored well into September to give "the park more control over the travel coming in from the village of Allenspark."[18] On the park's west side, the CCC built two new trails: the short Red Mountain Trail from Phantom Valley to the service road at the lower end of the Grand Ditch and the first half of a longer 6.5-mile trail from Phantom Valley north to La Poudre Pass. Early in the season CCC workers were given the responsibility for opening the principal hiking trails on the eastern side of the park.

Being detached and alone in Wild Basin, more than twenty miles from the customary, if spartan, amenities in Little Horseshoe Park, proved to be an eye-opening experience. "This is teaching us something about the wilds," Battell Loomis wrote.

> We cleared the ground and pitched our own tents, dug a latrine and set up our own camp kitchen. . . . It's a two-months job, this trail building in Wild Basin. Many of us were afraid of the night, if alone in it, when we first arrived in camp. When we heard a cowardly coyote whoopee-larruping the mountain echoes, some of the boys trembled and seated in their shoes. And when a hoot owl went off suddenly, the roots of their hair prickled. One lad feared redskins—but the only redskin in the district is a courteous college lad of the Montana Blackfeet. . . . The only thing to fear out here is loss of courage.
>
> Up in these mountains the boys of the Green Guard are becoming self-reliant. Whatever we are doing to the forests, they are teaching us how to save ourselves.[19]

Battell Loomis's statement about the CCC as a rite of passage, changing adolescents into men, was widely shared. In the years that followed many veterans of the CCC, looking back, would come to regard their days in the forests of North America as among the happiest and most formative of their lives.

Roadside cleanup to visually improve the park and as a fire protection measure was carried out on Trail Ridge Road from timberline at Fall River Pass down to Horseshoe Park, along the Bear Lake Road beginning in Moraine Park, and along the High Drive, then still in use to connect Deer Ridge Junction and the park boundary. Much of this activity was tedious rather than difficult and involved working debris to the roadside to be picked up by truck or hand-carried to a burn site. More effort was required to hand-saw downed timber into manageable logs and to remove stumps—some 2,400 in all that summer. Erosion control also went on along the lower end of Bear Lake Road, where the Park Service's landscape architects mandated that cut slopes be reduced and rounded, sometimes requiring the blasting of large boulders. Although some in biological circles within the Park Service were beginning to argue, even then, that such efforts affected animal habitat and that zealous insect control and the cutting and removal of dead trees did not

11.4 Robert Fechner, founding director of the CCC, addressing recruits in Little Horseshoe Park, 1934. Courtesy National Park Service–Rocky Mountain National Park

aid long-term forest growth, those voices were muted with so much labor conveniently at hand.

Before mid-November, when Camp N.P. 1-C was moved to Boulder for the winter, CCC workers had also built trout sizing ponds on Mill Creek and in Horseshoe Park; obliterated some four miles of old and abandoned road in various places, including the old Fall River and Moraine Park Roads; completed landscaping work around the administration building in the village; and helped to raze the buildings of Moraine Park Lodge and then fill in the excavations. Similar work was carried out on the old Hondius ranch on Beaver Creek. This program of activities was repeated, with variation, throughout the CCC years,[20] a routine interrupted by emergency work fighting forest fires or participating in search and rescue operations, where their help invariably proved invaluable.

Rocky Mountain National Park also became home for five additional CCC camps. On June 22, 1933, Camp N.P. 3-C, the first of three seasonal camps across the Continental Divide, was established near Beaver Creek in Phantom Valley, some twelve miles north of Grand Lake, with the arrival of 180 men, the majority "flatlanders" from the Texas Panhandle.[21] The park's other two camps, N.P. 4-C and its sister camp N.P. 11-C, were both located in Hallowell Park on Mill Creek, not far from David Primrose's Rocky Mountain Boys Camp, the first in May 1934, the second in November 1939 during the waning years of the CCC, when the camp in Little Horseshoe Park was closed.

The camps in Hallowell Park were designed as permanent, year-round facilities. Nestled out of sight off the Bear Lake Road against a lateral moraine with Steep Mountain to the west, the site offered much the same geographic advantages as its predecessor in Little Horseshoe. Construction of N.P. 4-C began in April 1934 and continued in stages. The work required minimal grading and tree removal, and by June the camp was ready. When the recruits arrived, most of them from Arizona, they were housed in large hospital tents. The only permanent buildings then on the site were the bathhouse and mess hall, both of them altered that September when the Army began to build winter quarters consisting of a headquarters building, recreation hall, five barracks, latrine, garage, and tool house. Most of the materials were either brought in from other places or purchased locally from the Estes Park Lumber Company under a contract said to be worth $12,000.[22] Over the next year with the camp in use, CCC recruits helped complete a variety of other projects, including landscaping and installing walks, rails, and steps, giving a look of permanence to what was otherwise starkly utilitarian.

Surviving photographs suggest that Camp N.P. 4-C, despite its picturesque setting, was hardly a glamorous place. Many of its buildings were portable prefabs, designed to be removed as easily as they were installed; all were drab and functional and built to specification. Although no military training went on in the CCC camps, everything else about them smacked of regulation Army. Each of the enlistee barracks was built to house fifty men, with each man assigned a steel-framed Army bed and simple set of shelves. Those who wished more privacy were permitted to purchase a foot locker. The only heat came from wood-burning Army stoves, and warm water was limited. Compared to the sparse creature comforts on Mill Creek, the rustic buildings of David Primrose's adjacent boy's camp and the cottages and amenities just over the hill at the YMCA Camp must have seemed luxurious indeed.

The coming of the CCC was warmly greeted in the Estes region. As soon as Roosevelt's CCC program (or Emergency Conservation Work program, as it was initially known) was announced, village leaders actively lobbied for a camp of their own, clearly with an eye on the economic advantages it would bring the community. Within weeks of the establishment of the first camp in Virginia in April 1933, mayor Frank Bond had telegrammed congressman Fred Cummings, touting Estes Park "because of the proximity

11.5 CCC Camp in Hallowell Park. Courtesy National Park Service–Rocky Mountain National Park

to [the] national park and four national forests" and the immediate availability of housing for five hundred men. Cummings responded at once: he would press the matter in Washington with CCC director Robert Fechner—"you may be assured that I will do all in my power to bring any business that is possible to the second congressional district."[23] Cummings's intercession proved both necessary and effective. Although Estes Park was not among the first fifteen Colorado sites announced on April 22, 1933, when the first contingent of CCC enrollees arrived in Denver on May 6, one of their three destinations was Rocky Mountain National Park.

Although Roosevelt's conservation program was decidedly popular in Estes Park, this was not universally the case. Many American towns greeted the CCC camps in their neighborhoods with apprehension if not hostility, especially those that drew their recruits from the city.

Accustomed to hosting strangers and having taken the initiative to secure a CCC camp, Estes Park residents went out of their way to make the recruits feel at home. Within days of their arrival, Ted Jelsema opened Riverside for a "smoker," an informal program of vocal and instrumental music and boxing and wresting exhibitions, sponsored by the Chamber of Commerce to raise money to buy sporting goods for the camp. Estes Park's welcome, it turned out, was staged a bit prematurely. The recruits had just been subjected to complete physicals and vaccinations and, although there was no lack of volunteers for the boxing and wrestling matches, "Many of the contestants from the camp had to withdraw on account of sore arms . . . and were unable to compete." The event nonetheless netted $20.[24] The next month residents responded equally well to a request for magazines for the camp's recreation hall, quickly gathering up some two hundred pounds, including the collection of *National Geographic* magazines that Homer James had saved over ten years. Another resident emptied out his library and single-handedly brought in more than one hundred pounds of reading material.[25]

In part these good relations were the result of the CCC's policy of opening its camps to public inspection and encouraging camp leadership to make itself available to speak to local civic organizations about ongoing activities and accomplishments. Care was also taken to instruct recruits visiting the village that they were to be courteous and carry themselves with military deportment. To celebrate its fifth anniversary on April 7, 1938, Camp N.P. 4-C held an open house attended by more than four hundred people from Estes Park and the valley towns. This event included a late afternoon job inspection, an insect control demonstration, and transplanting a large ponderosa pine, followed by a dinner and a dance, with music provided by an orchestra from Longmont. "All visitors to the camp appeared to be very well impressed," David Canfield wrote in his monthly report, "not only with the cleanliness and healthfulness of the camp but with the usefulness of the work being accomplished. A great many favorable comments were heard, and several very complimentary new stories appeared in the papers."[26] This open house became an annual event. In May 1940, the day's activities and demonstrations included planting a tree and installing a commemorative plaque in memory of the recently deceased Robert Fechner, founding director of the CCC, who had toured the camp in 1934. As efforts at public relations, these open houses were hugely successful. "Easily understood after a visit in the local camp," the *Estes Park Trail* commented following the 1939 event, "is the fact that while an emergency experiment in the beginning, the CCC has proved so worthwhile that it promises to attain a permanent position in our national set up."[27]

Remarkably few incidents clouded relations between Estes Park's CCC camps and the local community. Part of this was the result of location. Because the camps were comfortably out of sight within the national park, officers were able to head off and control the kind of incidents that inevitably occurred when groups of young men were away from home. Camp au-

11.6 Noted guide Shep Husted, foreman at Camp NP-4-C. Courtesy National Park Service–Rocky Mountain National Park

thorities, of course, had the upper hand. Not only were the camps run along semi-military lines with experienced Army officers in charge, but there was always the threat of dishonorable discharge, the CCC's ultimate penalty, which not only ended the monthly stipend on which many families back home had come to rely but permanently stigmatized the offender. Most enrollees clearly found Rocky Mountain National Park a congenial place. As Battell Loomis put it, "Instead of holding down a park bench or pounding the pavements looking for work, today I have work, plenty of good food, and a view of the sort that people pay money to see."[28]

Strikes and walkouts were the common form of rebellion in most CCC camps, where protesting enrollees resorted to tactics imitating those used so effectively by their parents' generation in confronting the labor problems of the 1930s. Estes Park had its first and only strike in October 1935 at the camp on Mill Creek. Unlike its sister camp in Little Horseshoe, there had been problems at Camp N.P. 4-C from the beginning. Within weeks of its organization in May 1934 and long before its permanent facilities had been completed, low morale had led to a change in camp commanders.[29] The situation improved, in part perhaps because the entire camp was soon quarantined with a measles outbreak, allowing for acclimation to the discipline of camp life. Nevertheless lingering problems, some apparently caused by inexperienced foremen, continued to ferment. By summer and early fall 1935 these had risen to the level of "antagonism."

The triggering event at Mill Creek was innocuous enough: an order came from the camp superintendent that CCC truck drivers should do manual work when not engaged in driving or maintenance activities. On Saturday, September 29, led by twenty-five-year-old Kenneth Burke of Loveland, CCC members refused to work until the new rule was rescinded. After Park Service personnel and Army officers from Fort Logan attempted without success to mediate the dispute, Edmund Rogers personally drove to Fort Logan and returned with a ranking officer. Both men addressed the strikers, the general reminding the enrollees of the oath they had verbally sworn and then signed upon enlistment to follow CCC regulations or face "expulsion therefrom."

When the men still refused to work, the recalcitrant drivers were taken to Denver and given administrative discharges. The remaining strikers became incensed. Assembling as a mob outside superintendent George Carlson's barracks, order was restored only after Carlson was escorted from the camp. In the aftermath, some ninety CCC enrollees were given administrative discharges.[30] The camp was quickly re-supplied with enlistees from Kentucky and normalcy returned. Notwithstanding occasional complaints about the "cleanliness" and lack of "gentlemanly conduct" in the village on the part of a few "misfits," the only other serious incident during the CCC years—one underscoring the generally good behavior of camp members—occurred in August 1939 when three enrollees were caught shoplifting. Each received a ten-day sentence in county jail and a dishonorable discharge.[31]

The coming of World War II dramatically affected the CCC. Reserve military officers in the camps were called to active duty, and the camps' programs began to reflect job skills thought vital to national defense. Although enrollment in the three camps during summer 1940 totaled six hundred, the largest in history, by year's end it had become hard to recruit young men to the CCC. Those not in military service were attracted to the well-paying jobs offered by the now-booming defense industry. By March 1941, the park's camps had one hundred vacancies. Many of those who left Estes Park for jobs elsewhere did so with regret. "You will remember a 'CCC Punk' who did a little typing and a little microfilming around the office in 1940, last year," wrote recruit Robert Varney from Washington where he was working in the War Department as a result of the training and education he had received in the park.

> Time has fled so fast that I can hardly remember those days but when I do recall them it is not without much sorrow. . . . But I do remember Mr. Canfield, Mr. Moomaw and a few of the rest of the NPS staff. . . . I owe all of this to you and the National Park Service in Estes Park.[32]

Given the circumstances of a nation on the brink of war, a reduction in the number of CCC camps was inevitable. Between September and November 1941, some 133 camps were closed, and after December 7, 1941, the only CCC projects continuing in national parks were those that could be directly related to wartime needs. The first camp closure in Rocky Mountain National Park occurred in early July 1941 with the abandonment of Camp N.P. 4-C on Mill Creek, the park's oldest permanent CCC facility. Camp N.P. 11-C in Hallowell Park and Camp N.P. 12-C, the last of the three temporary camps across the Continental Divide, continued to operate into summer 1942, with a combined enrollment of about 350. That October, after a summer in which Congress refused to authorize further appropriations, the camps were closed and the Civilian Conservation Corps came to an end.

National Park Service policy required that the remaining CCC buildings in Little Horseshoe Park and on Mill Creek be used or torn down. Those in Little Horseshoe were dismantled in October 1942 and the remaining scrap metal was hauled to the village as a donation to the war effort. Camp N.P. 11-C remained in place until January 1943, when its portable buildings and equipment were transferred to Fort Logan. By late spring clearing and obliteration removed its final traces, and the CCC in Rocky Mountain National Park passed into history.[33] "Needless to say," the *Estes Park Trail* editorialized, "the CCC enrollees will be missed by all Estes Park especially on evenings when they had their 'nightout' to come to the Village to see the movies or invest in soft drinks, personal supplies and novelties. And now the Villagers hope that perhaps the boys will be back again when the war is won. There will be a hearty welcome awaiting."[34]

Quite apart from its lasting effect on the enrollees themselves, the impact of the CCC and other emergency programs of the New Deal in developing the nation's park system proved incalculable. According to one estimate, Roosevelt's "Woodpecker Army" advanced park development by as much as two decades beyond where it otherwise would have been.[35] That impact was perhaps best seen in the two decades that followed, for with the departure of the CCC and the manpower it provided, building and maintenance activities within the parks, including Rocky Mountain National Park, declined dramatically.

Among the visible reminders of the hard work and ingenuity of the CCC in Rocky Mountain National Park are the outdoor amphitheaters at the Aspenglen, Glacier Basin, and Moraine Park campgrounds, as well as much of the stonework along the park's trails and roads. The most enduring legacy of the CCC years, in fact, was the final development and improvement of the park's 300-mile trail system, which by 1937 was being used by a record number of summer visitors and some 2,000 saddle horses. Most of this trail work was accomplished by CCC crews, although they were aided at various times by workers hired to do special projects with public works monies. New technology in the form of jackhammers and lightweight gasoline drills helped. But the work was still time-consuming, difficult, and expensive not only because of the remoteness of many sites, but because of rigorous Park Service requirements that abandoned trails be obliterated, cut timber and brush be removed, and weathered rather than cut rock be used for trail aesthetics.

The most immediately visible of this trail work was the so-called "Estes Park Arterial," a giant loop of trails leading from the village to Moraine Park; up Glacier Creek through Tuxedo Park to Glacier Creek Campground, Glacier Gorge Junction, and Bear Lake; and then back again to Moraine Park by way of Odessa Gorge, Fern Lake and the Pool. A hiker could complete the journey to Estes Park by returning to Deer Ridge Junction on a trail beginning near the Brinwood Hotel and the Cub Lake Trailhead, and following Fall River on a trail along the north slope of Deer Mountain.[36] The final leg of this trail terminated on the east side at the Old Man Ranger Station at Oldman Mountain and had branch trails to the Aspenglen Campground and across Little Horseshoe Park where it connected with the trail to Lawn Lake. Built in stages beginning in 1930, this system of trails was completed in 1941 largely with CCC labor.

Other trails of the period owing their existence, or more often their major reconstruction, to the CCC (which brought many of the existing trails to standard) included the trails from Bear Lake to the summit of Flattop Mountain, from Dream Lake to Lake Haiyaha, from Granite Pass to the Boulder Field, and the Cub Lake and Gem Lake Trails. The work on the Gem Lake Trail, which was extended across the ridge to descend to the road above the McGraw Ranch on Cow Creek, completed the job begun in 1923 by Jack Moomaw, who had widened the original trail as far as the lake so that it could be reached by horses. Considerable work was also done in the vicinity of Longs Peak, an area made even more popular with the 1929 opening of the Longs Peak Campground, the park's fifth. The mile of trail from Granite Pass to the Boulder Field was widened and resurfaced. The Storm Pass Trail over the shoulder of Battle Mountain beginning north of Longs Peak Inn was reconstructed, which allowed hikers to descend into Glacier Basin as far as Sprague Lake and provided access to the summit of Estes Cone along the way. Also reconstructed was the trail from the Tahosa Valley to the summit of Twin Sisters Mountain. In Wild Basin the CCC was responsible for building a new trail to Ouzel Lake, which not only passed Ouzel Falls but kept hikers well off the choked valley floor.

There was also considerable CCC activity on the west side of the park, where the trail system was less well developed. In addition to the trails that opened up the Never Summer region, the CCC was responsible for the Timber Creek Trail leading across Beaver and Timber Creeks and through Long Meadows to connect with the existing Onahu and Tonahuto Trails. CCC workers also rebuilt and half-relocated the much longer North Inlet Trail to the summit of Flattop Mountain. Although ongoing throughout the CCC years, trail-building activity in Rocky Mountain National Park reached its peak during summer 1938 when three hundred enrollees spent 3,674 man-days on trail maintenance and 6,825 man-days on trail construction.[37]

The 1930s also saw important developments in the park's increasingly popular interpretive nature program. L. C. Way had made a modest beginning in 1917 when he experimented with women guides to make visitors aware of the park's flora and fauna. Roger Toll, with his scientific background, shared Way's enthusiasm to the extent his limited resources allowed. In summer 1923, he hired Julius M. Johnson, the assistant principal of a New York City school, who had spent summers camping in the area, to organize and offer a naturalist program. Because, as Toll noted, "there is no government building in which a meeting can be held, and no available hall at which large audiences can be obtained on successive evenings,"[38] Johnson held his evening lectures, four nights a week, at various local hotels, a practice continued for many years not only of necessity but because tourists liked the convenience. Over the course of two months, Johnson delivered thirty-one talks before audiences averaging almost eighty, using colored lantern slides to illustrate such topics as "Our Four-footed Friends, and How to Protect Them" and "The Birds of the Park and their Preservation," each popular enough to be repeated throughout the season. Johnson also conducted well-attended field trips on the mornings after his lectures.[39]

Johnson did not return in 1924. In his place Toll hired Perley A. Smoll from Colorado Springs to direct the naturalist program. During the next four summers Smoll repeated and extended the routine that Johnson had established, using stereopticon slides to illustrate lectures on wildlife, with a special emphasis on protection and conservation. Like his predecessor Smoll also offered a program of field study. By 1927 his trips included all-day excursions to Fall River Pass and Chasm Falls that exposed participants to natural history features at various life zones. Although handicapped by the lack of museum space, Smoll prepared an exhibit of trees and flowers for the park's administrative offices. He also condensed his lectures into nature notes for publication in the *Estes Park Trail*, which aided his efforts by publishing a small booklet by local artist and sometime-ranger Dean Babcock titled *Birds and Flowers of Rocky Mountain National Park*.

In 1928 Smoll was succeeded for two seasons by geology professor Margaret "Peggy" Fuller Boos, a summer resident of Estes Park whose Ph.D. dissertation on the geology of the Big Thompson River Valley gave her in-depth familiarity with the region. Following much the same format as her predecessors, Boos did even better, attracting some eight thousand to her programs in 1930, more than three times the number of people served by Julius Johnson seven years before. She also helped prepare a series of mimeographed "Nature Notes" "to give information about natural history matters and scientific facts in the Rocky Mountain National Park region." For all their success, Johnson, Smoll, and Boos were nonetheless temporary summer employees, and once the season ended visitors who wished to learn about the park were left largely on their own.

The appointment in 1930 of a full-time naturalist was one of the first fruits of the reorganization put in place by the Park Service's new director, Horace Albright, who in 1929 had come to Washington from Yellowstone to replace his longtime boss Stephen Mather. Albright was a gifted administrator and brought to his leadership role not only an intimate knowledge of the Park Service and its history and the day-to-day experience of a park manager but a well-developed set of ideas about the way in which national parks should be organized and operated. High on Albright's agenda was the recognition and improvement of educational and wildlife management activities within the park system, and as early as 1930 he obtained funding for a separate administrative branch "to coordinate and supervise all the educational and research work of the service, including nature guiding, lectures, and museum work, plus supervision of publications."[40] Three years later, following the lead of the Forest Service, he moved to improve the caliber of new recruits by requiring permanent rangers to have a college degree. This new regulation, however desirable, was not universally embraced. As the *Estes Park Trail* lamented, it meant the end of "the old time ranger" whose "lore and acute understanding of nature" had been gained over "a life time spent out of doors communing with nature in her various moods."[41]

Albright's new professionalism also brought to an end the practice of appointing new superintendents from outside the Park Service. Roger Toll and Edmund Rogers had been beneficiaries of a system in which general aptitude, local standing, and political strings were sufficient to gain appointment and Roger Toll had been able to handpick his own successor. When Edmund Rogers left Rocky Mountain National Park in May 1936 to take Toll's place at Yellowstone, he would not have the same privilege. The superintendents who followed Rogers would be Park Service veterans who had successfully negotiated their way through the organization, not Denver businessmen schooled in the ways of the mountains by the Colorado Mountain Club. Thomas J. Allen, who succeeded Rogers, was elevated to the position from the superintendency of Hot Springs National Park. When Allen was promoted to the post of regional director in July 1937, his replacement, David H. Canfield, was brought in from Crater Lake National Park in Oregon where he was serving as superintendent.

The park naturalist position remained open until the arrival of Dorr Yeager from Yellowstone in June 1931. As Albright and Rogers had hoped, the Iowa born and raised Yeager, whose credentials included degrees in botany, zoology, and philosophy from Grinnell College, raised the park's interpretive activities to a new level. Yeager, who had been converted from engineering to nature work after a summer spent driving a tour bus in Yellowstone, not

11.7 Park naturalist Dorr Yeager. Courtesy National Park Service–Rocky Mountain National Park

only continued the organized lectures and field trips of his predecessors but expanded them to include all-day and overnight hikes to such remote places as Rowe Glacier and Lake Nanita. The value of having a full-time naturalist was almost immediately apparent. That fall, when a seasonal employee would have returned home, Yeager helped to found the Rocky Mountain Nature Association, an organization that over the years would provide external support for the educational, preservationist, and research objectives of the national park. Its first publication was the three-color 57-page mimeographed pamphlet, "The Animals of Rocky Mountain National Park," which Yeager put together in July 1932 with a foreword by Edmund Rogers.

Yeager served as the association's executive secretary. Joe Mills was the organization's first president; and their working relationship soon took on an added dimension. One of Yeager's lecture sites was the Crags Hotel and it was there that he met and began to court Eleanor Ann Mills, Joe and Ethel Mills's only daughter. Although she vowed that she would never marry one of "them"—by which she meant a ranger—the two were wed on May 18, 1935, just months before Yeager accepted a position with the Park Service's Western Museum Laboratories in Berkeley, California. Fellow ranger John S. McLaughlin ("Johnny Mac") served as best man.

Yeager's most important contribution during his four years at Rocky Mountain National Park was the leadership he provided in developing museum facilities and their exhibits—program-enhancing features, which, as Rogers reiterated in his monthly reports, were absolutely essential to fulfilling the park's educational mission. The park's first real museum, constructed in June 1931, the month of Yeager's arrival, was located in a rustic stone and timber building with open truss ceiling immediately adjacent to park headquarters at the edge of the village. Designed to provide arriving visitors with a better appreciation of the park and its features, Yeager installed a series of exhibits that included a variety of common birds and mammals. In the center of the main room, "given a welcoming touch" by a full-head bearskin spread before the native granite fireplace, stood a bighorn ram—the park's logo—surrounded by walls containing the heads of an elk, deer, mountain sheep, and bison. Other exhibits told the story of the park's geology, human history, and flora and fauna.[42] By the end of the 1932 summer season Yeager had successfully established two more museum sites: a small branch museum at the Bear Lake ranger station and a somewhat larger one in the small stone building at Fall River Pass, built in August 1922 as a shelter cabin. These new facilities stimulated even greater interest in the park's interpretive programs whose needs, Rogers explained that fall, still could not be fully met because of insufficient personnel.

By 1934 it was clear that more museum facilities were needed. The museum at park headquarters was small and could not adequately accommodate day visitors let alone those who packed the building three nights a week to hear illustrated lectures. That fall plans were approved for a new and significantly larger museum space making use of the old recreation hall at Moraine Park Lodge. Federal emergency relief funds made possible the building's conversion, and Yeager set about designing exhibits to complement those at the other museums by emphasizing the human history of park and region. Having decided what he wanted, Yeager spent the winter months of 1934–1935 at the Park Service's Bakersfield, California, field headquarters preparing his interpretive exhibits. Because of delays in completing the building's renovations and the expansion of the adjacent parking lot, by the time the museum opened in summer 1937 Yeager had been transferred to the Western Museum Laboratories in Berkeley to work on dioramas, the next step in a long Park Service career that would take him to Zion, Bryce, and Grand Canyon National Parks. His place was taken by H. Raymond Gregg, who arrived from Hot Springs National Park at the end of the 1936 season.

Yeager's museum displays, which had been installed prior to Gregg's arrival with the help of CCC enrollees adept at museum work, were designed to take advantage of the location. The glacier-carved basin with its two encircling moraines and river lying immediately in front of the two-story building provided an ideal setting to illustrate the geologic and human history of the park. In ancient times the area along the Big Thompson, like other places in the Estes Park Valley, had provided seasonal campsites for Native Americans who came to hunt. Later, the river bottom had been farmed and ranched by means of irrigation ditches and then gradually converted by Abner Sprague and his successor James Stead into a large and popular summer resort, complete with golf course. This was the story that Yeager tried to convey by installing a near life-size display of Arapaho culture containing a twelve-foot tepee made from buffalo hides, as well as horse and dog travois, backrests, hides, meat-drying rack, and domestic implements. The walls with their displays of artifacts completed the valley's story of Ute and Arapaho, the trapper-miner era, the first settlers, and its history as part of a national park. The glassed-in porch on the building's second floor contained a display explaining the glacial features spread out before the viewer. The lower floor of the sturdy 40-x-60-foot log building provided a lobby and offices for the naturalist and the technical staff. Just outside the door was a trail that led to the 200-seat amphitheater recently completed by the CCC for evening programs, a welcome extension of the museum's educational activities.[42]

Also opened during summer 1937 was a new stone museum at Fall River Pass, built to replace the old, poorly lit former shelter cabin by the Rocky Mountain Parks Motor Company, which operated the adjacent concession.

11.8 Arapaho exhibit, Moraine Park Museum. Courtesy National Park Service–Rocky Mountain National Park

Overlooking the immense glacial cirque at the head of Fall River Valley, the site provided a natural vantage point from which to tell the geologic story of uplift and erosion and the struggle for life on the cold and blustery tundra. Occupying the same building was a post office, said to be "the smallest and highest" in the United States.[43] Despite the difficulty of getting there, the museum at Fall River Pass quickly proved to be the most popular of the three.

The opening of the two new museums not only made possible an enlarged schedule of educational programming but resulted in a significant change in park policy. The park naturalist and his three ranger assistants would concentrate virtually all of their lecturing and hiking activity within the park itself—a policy that David Canfield, now the presiding superintendent, noted with obvious relief in his annual report for 1937 drew little objection from hotel and resort owners.[44]

Both Dorr Yeager and Raymond Gregg brought professional expertise and direction to the interpretive programs at Rocky Mountain National Park: Yeager with his museum work and Gregg, who remained on staff into the 1940s, with his immediately popular Junior Nature School, implemented together with a series of fifteen-minute weekly radio broadcasts at the beginning of the 1938 season. It was Yeager, however, who would be longest remembered in Estes Park and Park Service circles. Being the son-in-law of arguably the most popular man in Estes Park helped. But Yeager would also be remembered for his books on wildlife and national parks and as the creator of a fictional ranger named Bob Flame, a literary hero who personified what he believed was best and most admirable in the guardians of the nation's parks.[45]

In each of his four Bob Flame novels—*Bob Flame, Ranger* (1934), *Bob Flame, Rocky Mountain Ranger* (1936), *Bob Flame in Death Valley* (1937), and *Bob Flame among the Navajo* (1946)—Yeager served up a palatable mixture of fact and fiction to showcase the duties, activities, and adventurous life of the modern park ranger and his dedication to the ideals of wilderness conservation. The second of these novels, *Bob Flame, Rocky Mountain Ranger*, a Junior Literary Guild Selection for May 1934, was set in Rocky Mountain National Park and was a semi-autobiographical narrative made all the more realistic by the inclusion of Park Service photographs. In the course of three hundred pages, Bob Flame oversees the establishment of the CCC camp in Little Horseshoe Park, fights a fire caused by careless campers, chases bootleggers and poachers, looks for a lost fisherman, and participates in the search for a missing tourist. Much of what went into *Bob Flame, Rocky Mountain Ranger* seems today old-fashioned and outdated, a product of an earlier and much less complicated era. Yet to his credit Yeager managed to capture the outlines of much of what went on in Rocky Mountain National Park during the 1930s as well as the attitudes of self-conscious professionalism and esprit de corps that Stephen Mather and Horace Albright had worked hard to instill in the men who wore the National Park Service uniform.

~

Despite the fact that Rocky Mountain National Park had originally been conceived of as a vast nature preserve where tourists could safely view animals in their natural habitat, there was little concern during the park's first decade and a half with wildlife management.[46] Superintendents Trowbridge and Way made note in their monthly reports of the number and condition of local herds to the extent they could be observed through field glasses, but it was not until the early 1920s that Mather's deputy Horace Albright requested that park superintendents begin conducting spring and fall game counts.

Although the Park Service mandate of 1916 included wildlife conservation, there was an unspoken assumption during early days that this meant protection rather than scientific study. Wildlife was important, but rather more for its value in attracting visitors than in its own right; and Mather, Albright, and the publicists they employed worked hard to establish the image of national parks as romantic and tranquil places where tourists could safely view wild animals, particularly those that evoked the image of the Old West. In the absence of trained biologists, such views went largely unchallenged. Lean budgets meant limited personnel and choices, and when the Park Service began to build new expertise Mather chose to invest in landscape architecture and engineering, skills needed for the practical matters of infrastructure, particularly roads and trails, rather than to hire biological scientists. To the extent that such expertise was needed, Mather insisted, it could easily be borrowed from other government bureaus.[47]

When it came to wild creatures, the Mather-Albright view, like that of many nature lovers of the day, was dominated by "good" animals—that is, those species "that contributed most to public enjoyment"—which meant turning parks into "a kind of ranching and farming operation to maintain the productivity and presence of favored species."[48] Predators, of course, were automatically excluded. They were to be controlled through extermination, a prejudice widely shared throughout the West including Estes Park, where residents justifiably regarded the park's fledgling elk herd as "its own." As early as November 1914, when a number of newly reintroduced elk were killed by mountain lions, the Forest Service brought in dogs and hunters to protect the herd.[49] Although a year later C. R. Trowbridge indicated that coyotes and mountain lions as yet posed no problem, the next winter his successor, L. C. Way, sent for government hunter A. J. McGlocin, who together with licensed guide Cliff Higby, spent ten days in early January 1917 on snowshoes and skis tracking lions with a pack of trained bloodhounds and high-powered rifles, beginning near the village and working their way toward the Continental Divide.[50]

Later that same year, using the information that McGlocin and Higby had provided, Captain Way decided to initiate a program of predator control. A list of animals considered "detrimental to the use" of parks was put together. It included mountain lions, bobcats, coyotes, wolves, foxes, and lynxes. Between 1917 and 1926 various unsystematic methods of "eradication" and "control" were tried, including tracking, trapping, and poisoning with varying results. Although by the mid-1920s such programs in places like Yosemite and Yellowstone had come under criticism, particularly because of their use of poison and steel traps, this was not the case in Estes Park.

Extermination work was carried out by members of the ranger staff, who were encouraged to augment their salaries by hunting predators in return for

a percentage of the profits from selling their pelts. Local hunters also operated in and near the park under contract. Two of them, lumberman John
Griffith and barber Bob Becker, earned the nicknames "Jack the Giant Killer"
and "Bobcat Bob" for their much-publicized kills. The first systematic predator control effort in Rocky Mountain National Park began in January 1922,
when Roger Toll secured the help of John W. Crook, a hunter from the
Department of Agriculture's Biological Survey, to implement a program to
poison the local coyote and mountain lion populations. To gain community
support and cooperation, Toll called a meeting of the recently organized
Estes Park Fish and Game Association at which he introduced Crook and
predatory animal inspector Stanley P. Young, who explained what they intended to accomplish and how. The tenor of the meeting, as well as the local
attitude, was reflected in the *Trail*'s report of the plan to be followed: "Dainty
morsels of horseflesh will be served Messrs. Coyote and Lion a la Grubb
fresh from Frank's pastures and the local Newhouse wizards Hayden and
'Bobcat' Becker will give Trapper Crook all the necessary pointers. . . . Mr.
Crook has a pack of nine trained dogs and we anticipate there will be fur
flying ere long."[51]

Following the meeting, Crook and a party of local residents, taking advantage of vehicles offered by the transportation company, went over the
most accessible areas of the park to locate sites for poisoning stations. Crook
stayed on for most of the month to watch his plan unfold. It was not a great
success. Although seventeen poison stations were established, all baited with
strychnine, in the weeks that followed only ten dead animals could be clearly
credited to the program. The first nine were "assorted" predators, the tenth
a local resident's dog that died after a poison bait, presumably carried by a
magpie or jay, found its way into the yard where the dog was kept. "Predatory
animals have not been very numerous," Toll was forced to conclude in his
February report. "The coyotes were either poisoned by the meat set out for
them, or have gone elsewhere. Most of the poisoned bait has been eaten, and
the presumption is that the animals have gone off to die."[52]

Predator hunters had greater success elsewhere. Before the season was
over, Toll noted that "Bobcat" Becker had single-handedly taken 20 predators, including 13 bobcats, half of them inside the park, while other hunters
accounted for 47 more, including 6 lions, 30 bobcats, and 8 coyotes.[53] Beaver, while not on the predator list, were considered a nuisance and that
winter they too got their share of attention. In response to complaints from
the owners adjacent to the park, state authorities sent hunter E. A. Teter to
Estes Park to trap on non-government lands. Before he was finished Teter
had trapped a total of 46 beaver, including 9 on the YMCA grounds, 24 in

Moraine Park, 4 in the Black Canyon, and 9 on Cow Creek. Teter got to keep half of the pelts, the state of Colorado getting the rest.[54]

Despite the poisoning campaign's modest results, a number of large predatory animals were killed in the winter months of 1922. The most spectacular kills belonged to John Griffith, who in January during a day-long pursuit with a pack of dogs and accompanied by hunter John Crook tracked a large female mountain lion through the snows in Devils Gulch before cornering and killing the animal on Fox Creek. Five days later the relentless Griffith discovered her three cubs on a rock ledge within two miles of timberline northwest of the Black Canyon and he brought them home in a sack.[55] That same season Griffith bagged another and even larger lion in Cedar Park in the vicinity of Drake after an eighteen-mile chase with dogs through the snow.[56]

The predator campaign continued during the next two years and included another attempt at poisoning, this time using four stations established according to Biological Survey specifications. Despite their somewhat limited success, Superintendent Toll remained convinced of the need for such efforts. "It is my opinion," he wrote in November 1924, "that predatory animal control should be continued in this park. I would consider advisable to reduce the number of mountain lion, coyotes and bobcats to the lowest practicable numbers."[57] The following September Toll estimated that about twenty mountain lions and more than one thousand bobcats remained within the park.

Much of the concern, understandably, had to do with the protection of the two elk herds introduced into the park in 1913 and 1915. Deer remained abundant everywhere, and bighorn sheep, although reduced by hunting and periodic scabies outbreaks, in 1915 still numbered in excess of 1,000, largely concentrated in the area of Specimen Mountain, where as many as 600 were seen that year in a single day.[58]

Without the presence of their natural enemies, both bands of elk continued to thrive, and it is probably no accident that by 1925, after three years of active predator control, Toll first began to register concern about the rapid increase in the number of deer and elk and their impact on the carrying capacity of the park. "The present number of elk is about as large as can be supported within this park without feeding during the winter months. The elk occasionally raid hay stacks and crops of ranchers in this vicinity at times of heavy snowfall."[59] In May 1926 deputy game warden Joe Gray reported considerable damage to a number of fences and heavy concentrations of elk in Moraine Park's meadows.[60] Elk were now increasingly being seen in large herds, as many as one hundred in Beaver Meadows and sixty or more along Fish Creek outside the park. This is "the first year when they could be termed at all tame," Toll emphasized in his report for November 1926; the herd in Beaver Meadows was visited all month by large numbers of Estes Park residents who had no difficulty in getting as close as one hundred feet for their photographs. "The elk showed not the slightest degree of fear of the visitors." The size of the total herd in and adjacent to the park nonetheless remained elusive and, although troubling as an intimation of future problems, Toll's 1925 estimate of between 200 and 400 animals was hardly accurate enough to use as the basis for any long-range plan.[61]

Horace Albright's decision to restructure the Park Service in 1929, which led to the hiring of more wildlife biologists and in 1933 to the establishment of a separate wildlife division, brought an increased awareness throughout the park system of the need for an active wildlife management program. The influence of these biologists, together with the external pressure of public opinion, was evident as early as 1931 in the statement by Albright himself limiting predator control: unless predators seriously threatened other species, they were to be "considered integral parts of the wild life protected within the national parks."[62] The influence of the scientists would continue to grow as the emergency relief programs of the New Deal made more money available to the Park Service.

Edmund Rogers needed no convincing that elk posed a serious problem. The herd was not only growing and in danger of crowding bighorn sheep off parts of their range but, having failed to reestablish its historic migratory patterns, was now leaving the park during the winter months—something it had not previously done—and was doing so in sufficient numbers to become a local nuisance.[63] "Some apprehension is felt for the herd this winter," he wrote in September 1930, his second year in the park, "since the lower altitudes, inside and outside the park, are well grazed by domestic stock during the summer months. It is high time that some provision were [sic] made for winter feeding, else the herd will become a nuisance to nearby ranchers."[64] The following year, after a winter that had seen hungry elk break down fences and destroy haystacks along the North Fork of the Big Thompson River, thereby exposing them to hunters, Rogers became even more insistent:

> The winter range problem of the park elk and deer is rapidly assuming
> serious proportions. . . . The only solution lies in complete control of
> the Beaver Valley, Horseshoe Park, and Moraine Park, and the complete
> elimination of all domestic animal grazing. Regulation of the increase
> in the herds, based on carrying capacity of the range may be necessary.[65]

Most of Rogers's information came from the first systematic study of the issue, an eleven-page typed report prepared in June by Chief Ranger McLaughlin, who candidly admitted that

> game and game problems have been kept in the background by other problems in this park, but the time has come when serious consideration must be given to the wildlife in this section. . . . Last winter, for the first time, the elk began tearing bark off aspen trees. This is the first season this has really been noticeable, although many of the aspen groves have really suffered heavily—in just one season. . . . The range is in generally poor condition. It is overgrazed to the extent that in many places the original ground cover has been destroyed, and the mineral soil has been exposed to erosion, or is rapidly being occupied by undesirable plants and weeds.[66]

Although some relief was provided by the purchase and razing of inholdings in 1931 and 1932, which removed competing cattle from Beaver Meadows and Horseshoe Park and enlarged the range, officials had by now become convinced that the park's carrying capacity had been reached. There were, however, no easy answers. The same problem was evident in other areas of Colorado, but in fall 1931 when state officials considered opening Larimer County, which included the park's winter range, to hunters, there was an outcry from the Estes Park Chamber of Commerce, the Fish and Game Association, and other local groups. The chamber voted to send the county commissioners a strongly worded objection to an open season on elk anywhere in the Estes Park vicinity, and even Superintendent Rogers feared that "the whole herd could be exterminated" if driven to lower elevation by early snows.[67] Compounding the problem was the fact that viewing elk had now become a major tourist activity. "During the entire month," Rogers wrote in his November 1932 report, "elk herds drew more visitors . . . than any other attraction. It was necessary during the early part of the month to barricade many old roads and obliterate the beginning of new ones where visitors in their cars had been running over the parks and meadows in an effort to see, or get closer to, the elk."[68]

Given their value in attracting tourists and local opinion, it was not surprising that the problem of overgrazing as a topic for discussion should remain almost exclusively within official park circles. Behind the scenes, however, McLaughlin initiated a series of detailed field studies to examine what was happening. With the help of park employees and wildlife technicians assigned to the park's CCC camps, over the next two years a series of fifteen enclosures, or "check plots," were erected in different places on the winter range to study the effect of protection on the growth of vegetation as well as the browsing habits of elk and deer. These studies, although far from conclusive because many of the areas sampled had already been over-grazed, confirmed that in places like Horseshoe Park as much as 60 percent of the annual growth had been eaten, that there was little or no aspen reproduction, and that many of the remaining trees were scarred, dead, or seriously infected with fungus. The elk and deer were sufficiently hungry to have grazed, uncharacteristically, on young pine and firs.[69]

Reflecting the rising influence of biologists within the Park Service, McLaughlin's reports had now become an annual event. Although all noted the continuing deterioration of the range, by the mid-1930s much of the attention and blame began to shift from elk to deer. Although this determination made the issue somewhat easier to deal with from a public relations point of view for deer were more numerous and less popular than elk, it did nothing to alter the fact that the elk had outstripped their winter range.

Although both problem and solution had by now been identified—the latter officially endorsed by the National Park Service as part of its management plan for Rocky Mountain National Park[70]—no set course of action was established. Rogers spoke in his 1935 Annual Report of the need to "artificially reduce the number of elk and deer to the carrying capacity for the available range,"[71] but mentioned no timetable. The issue had now become exacerbated by an unexplained decline in the bighorn sheep population and, although internal and external studies showed that the basic situation had not changed, the park continued its wait-and-see attitude for the rest of the decade. One study was the 1939 report of famed biologist Joseph S. Dixon, who was brought in from the Park Service's Wildlife Division headquarters in Berkeley to examine the range. The "main problem," Dixon concluded, is "how to reduce the number of elk to the carrying capacity of the Park and keep it within the limit." He suggested that either areas just outside the park be opened for regulated hunting or yearlings and cow elk be live-trapped and reintroduced into nearby national forests.[72]

In fall 1941, federal funding made possible the first comprehensive scientific survey of the park's elk and deer populations using crews operating both on the ground and from airplanes. Where the rugged and heavily timbered terrain made the work impossible, averages were obtained per known square mile, a methodology that produced results thought to be 97 percent accurate. There were two major findings: that "an elk herd of approximately 1400 head may be carried in the Park, east of the Continental Divide, without over-populating the range," and that the existing range-damage appeared to be caused by "an oversupply of deer rather than elk."[73] The carrying capacity for elk was particularly surprising, for three earlier studies had placed that number at between 400 and 530 head. The study, of course, did not change the fact that the winter range at lower elevations was being dangerously over browsed. That fall, beginning in late November, the State Game and Fish Department in cooperation with park officials authorized a special ten-day hunting season along the park's eastern boundary. Although four hundred permits were issued, the take was disappointing, in part because big game had not yet left the protection of the park in large numbers. Less than one hundred elk were killed, far fewer than had been expected or thought necessary.[74]

On February 22, 1943, during a conference in the office of superintendent David Canfield, the decision to reduce the herd within the park was finally made. The formal recommendation came nine months later on November 20, 1943, in a report to Canfield by park naturalist David Condon, which justified the decision on scientific grounds and indicated that no other solution to the problem could be found. Canfield added a cover letter to Condon's report and sent both on to Washington through the regional director. "To preserve and protect as many and as much of the important natural values of this area," Condon wrote, "in order to attain the optimum for this park, we must put our elk and deer herds on a management basis."[75] Dixon's suggestion that the park live-capture and transport its excess elk was rejected because of the lack of areas to which they could be transplanted and the cost of doing so.

On January 11, 1944, after reaching agreement with the state on how the carcasses would be disposed of, the plan calling for the removal of 300 elk and 200 deer was approved by the assistant secretary of the Interior.[76] During the months that followed, the reduction program and how it would be carried out were carefully explained in a series of articles and news releases provided to the *Estes Park Trail*, the *Denver Post*, the *Rocky Mountain News*, and the valley papers, as well as to the national news services. Aside from what Park Naturalist Condon referred to as "a few local people who apparently mumbled in their beards in a sour grapes manner largely because they had been unsuccessful in their hunting,"[77] there was surprisingly little adverse reaction, even in Estes Park.

The first animal reduction program in Rocky Mountain National Park was quietly carried out away from public scrutiny behind locked gates over a period of two months between January 1, 1945, and February 26, 1945, during which uniformed rangers with the help of Colorado Game and Fish Department members eliminated 301 elk and 113 deer from the winter range using high-powered rifles. Rather than trying to cover the entire park, the decision was made to focus on areas where overpopulated herds were concentrated, including the drainage of Fall River, Black Canyon Creek, Buck Creek,

Mill Creek, Glacier Creek, and the Big Thompson. Fewer deer were taken than planned because their bands were small and widely scattered. Another direct reduction was carried out in 1949 when 340 elk were killed and then on a regular basis until 1962 with the goal of keeping herd size around 700.[78] Transplants were conducted during the 1966 and 1967 winters. Not surprisingly, in a nation now ecologically conscious, these reductions, widely reported by the news media, became increasingly unpopular with the general public.

Perhaps the most telling statement on the subject came from Russell K. Grater, who replaced David Condon as park naturalist during summer 1944, just prior to the program's implementation. Grater, who had the responsibility for announcing its completion and summarizing the results for public consumption in the *Trail's* April 1945 "Vacation Edition," that same year authored a separate in-house report for the Park Service in which he candidly concluded that "from the standpoint of the elk, it is now apparent that no serious problem has existed in the past at Rocky Mountain [National Park] nor had one reached a really serious point at the time of the reduction program. . . . Thus, the present reduction program served to *avert* a range crisis rather than *correct* one already in existence."[79] Grater had one further bit of advice to offer: "Out of all these studies has come one definite conclusion. It seems to me to be vital that our philosophy of wildlife management studies be based on averting a problem before it arises rather than controlling the problem after it is with us."[80] Such counsel, of course, ran counter to human nature and to the political realities of American life. The result of not making wildlife management official Park Service policy where the elk in Rocky Mountain National Park were concerned would become apparent during the decades that followed.

Chapter 12

~

Estes Park and Rocky Mountain National Park:
The War Years . . . and After

The one commodity which we have to sell here is escape.
There is no escape for any of us until it is over.

Estes Park Trail (March 17, 1944)

THE 1941 TOURIST SEASON throughout Colorado had been the best since 1929. Estes Park's hotels and resorts were filled to capacity in July and August, and Rocky Mountain National Park welcomed 685,593 visitors traveling in 208,398 automobiles, nearly 64 percent from out of state. Although the average stay of tourists was somewhat shorter than in the past, their willingness to spend had run far ahead of recent seasons, suggesting that the discouraging days of the Great Depression were finally over. The two-day "Rooftop Roundup" rodeo in August, when Patti Moomaw, daughter of ranger Jack Moomaw, was installed as queen, attracted an audience of 5,000. That summer 994 people climbed to the summit of Longs Peak, and another 35 successfully negotiated the ledges and chimneys of its East Face, including several women. In July Estes Park made national news when Supreme Court justice Harlan Fiske Stone, following a two-week vacation, was sworn into office in front of a cabin at Sprague's Lodge in Glacier Basin. Stone then came down to the village where, standing before a microphone at the Stanley Hotel, he led the nation in an oath of allegiance to the United States following a five-minute radio address by President Roosevelt.

The town exuded optimism. Bank president Charles Hix announced in January that deposits had increased in the previous year, a sure indication,

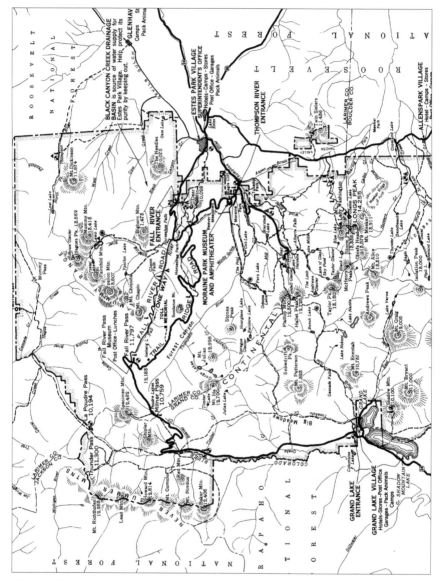

12.1 Map of Estes Park
and Rocky Mountain
National Park, ca.
1950. Courtesy David
Tanton

the *Estes Park Trail* noted, that "prosperity is moving on Estes Park."[1] The *Trail* could also point to other more visible signs of progress: the new sewer disposal plant at the junction of the Big Thompson and North St. Vrain Roads, designed to meet community needs for twenty years; an increased water supply, achieved by installing nearly four miles of pipeline to tap Glacier Creek near the YMCA; and a new post office, nearly tripling the floor and lobby space of the old village park building. Located on Moraine Avenue, just north of the Fall River Bridge, the white stucco, tiled roof post office was designed to match the art-deco exterior of the Jay Building next door. With its opening, the functions of local government were transferred into the old post office building to share newly remodeled space with the Chamber of Commerce. Signaling still more changes to come was the daily flow of men and equipment between Reclamation Bureau headquarters in the village and the East Portal of the transmountain tunnel above the YMCA, where drilling was moving steadily forward.

Missing for the first time in nearly four decades was the "Grand Old Man of Estes Park." On October 2, 1940, Freelan Oscar Stanley, back at his winter home in Newton, Massachusetts, from yet another season in the mountains, stepped outside to pick up the morning paper and collapsed on the front lawn. Brought inside, he died soon afterward. "Ninety-one years of age last June," the *Estes Park Trail* noted its eulogy, "Estes Park's number one visitor was interested in the affairs of the community, intensely aware of world problems and conditions, and yet never lost the ability to enjoy himself hugely. The *Trail* staff will always remember him as he would come into the office during the summer months inquiring if there was any work for a young man."[2] That August there was a memorial service at the Stanley Hotel on "Stanley Night." The man and his contributions were celebrated with a program of music, including some of his own compositions, followed by remarks and reminiscences by mayor Casey Rockwell, Stanley's longtime friend and executor Byron Hall, artist Dave Stirling, and others. As each speaker made clear, with the death of Stanley, one of the most important chapters in the history of Estes Park had come to a close. As a more tangible memorial, that same month plans were made to launch a $15,000 subscription campaign to complete renovation of the park south of the river, which Stanley had deeded to the town in 1936.

$\sim$

If the peaks about Estes Park seemed more serene and beautiful and the Colorado sky bluer and clearer that summer than in other seasons, it was because they stood in stark contrast to increasingly ominous news from Europe and the Pacific and the mounting evidence of America's preparations for war. The previous September, with Germany firmly in control of France, the Netherlands, and Belgium and the Battle of Britain underway, Congress had passed the Selective Service Act, the first compulsory peace-time draft in U.S. history for all men between the ages of twenty-one and thirty-five. Registration sites were established at the Estes Park Public Library, park headquarters, and the two CCC camps, and when the first list of eligible draftees was announced at the end of October it contained the names of local men. That spring and summer Estes Park and its visitors watched with growing concern as German submarines raised havoc with shipping in the Atlantic, Roosevelt signed the Lend Lease Act allowing the United States to send arms to a beleaguered England, and Hitler invaded Greece and Yugoslavia before turning on the Soviet Union. The human dimension of it all was more than evident in the letter from a former summer resident living in Essex, England, who wrote the *Trail* telling of the evacuation of children from London and other British industrial centers.[3]

On December 7, 1941, like the rest of the United States, town and park went to war. Unlike 1918 when Captain L. C. Way and his homegrown militia drilled amidst talk of building a frontier-like armory, thanks to the radio and airplane the world beyond the mountains did not seem far away. The Japanese attack on Pearl Harbor found local sons or relatives in harm's way and for a time unaccounted for. Robert F. Becker, the son of barber Bob Becker, was with the Thirty-fourth Pursuit Squadron in the Philippines; Donald Ross and Donald Miller were aboard ships at Pearl Harbor; and Winston Mills, Roland Reed's brother-in-law, was engaged in defense work at Wake Island. George Swift had two brothers at Pearl Harbor, one working as a defense contractor and the other a sailor aboard the destroyer USS *Phelps*. When reliable news finally arrived, the war quickly came home. Howard Kent, the son of local residents, had been wounded; John Manford's nephew was dead.

Estes Park's proximity to the Army's Lowry Field in Denver and the recently dedicated Remington Ordinance Plant and its thousands of workers west of the city raised immediate concern that the community might be called upon to assist in housing and caring for evacuees in case of attack. There was also the possibility that the transmission lines and substations of the Colorado–Big Thompson Project might become targets for sabotage. With representatives from the National Park and the Reclamation Bureau present, civic leaders, responding to a telegram from Governor Carr, organized the Estes Park Defense Council to coordinate and direct the war effort at home. Before year's end a hundred people had registered to help with civil defense activities; defense bonds and stamps were on sale; the Boy Scouts had begun a paper drive; and the *Estes Park Trail*, with "Remember Pearl Harbor" subheads liberally sprinkled throughout, had embarked on an effort to educate residents on air raid precautions. "Estes Park may be remote from the areas of action," readers were reminded in early January, "but all-out war effort is the role of every citizen in the community."[4] For defense against air attack, the council divided the Estes Valley into twelve zones, each patrolled by an air-raid warden, a system activated by a siren from the village—three rising and falling blasts, repeated four times with 20-second intervals between.

During the four years that followed, Estes Park responded much like any other American town. Local men and women went off to military service, and the town kept track of them through a "With the Armed Service" column in the *Trail*. Seven war bond drives not only met their goals but were over-subscribed. Part of this success was the result of Sam Magoffin's tunnel workers, who pledged 20 percent of their regular paychecks, "the highest percentage of any group of employees in the United States."[5]

There were also annual rubber, paper, and scrap metal drives and Red Cross blood and fund drives, to which the entire community contributed. The largest of these—the October 1942 scrap metal drive—collected 150 tons, roughly 300 pounds for every village resident. The haul included a large amount of salvageable metal brought down by the Park Service from the old Eugenia Mine in the Tahosa Valley. Other relics of the past disappeared as well. Abner Sprague contributed the double-bitted ax that he had used in 1875 to cut logs for his original cabin in Moraine Park and later to build his lodge in Glacier Basin, as well as the ancient maddock that he had used in making some of the area's first roads.

The ninety-one-year-old Sprague made patriotism a personal calling. One morning in April 1942, he arrived at town hall, bringing with him his father's muzzle-loading rifle and powder horn, and insisted that he be registered for the draft. After an argument over his age followed by Sprague's statement that "he was just as good a man as any man one-half his years," he was allowed to sign a card for special call, making him, the *Trail* claimed, "the oldest registrant in the United States." Sprague was photographed in the process in his beaver hat and all, and his story was picked up by the Associated Press and reported in papers from coast to coast, including the *New York Times* and *Boston Herald*.

The whole affair, it turned out, was the work of the Chamber of Commerce and park superintendent David Canfield. Canfield was well aware of Sprague's publicity and advertising value. Three years earlier, in June 1939,

12.2 Scrap drive in Estes Park. Courtesy National Park Service–Rocky Mountain National Park

Canfield himself had been photographed with Sprague and hotel pioneer Charles Reed at the park's Fall River entrance where the two had just flipped a coin for the "right" to be first to pay the newly imposed one dollar annual entrance fee—in effect giving their approval for what for many years had been regarded as unthinkable in a national park.[6]

Rationing of rubber, sugar, coffee, gasoline, and other staples soon became a fact of life to be accepted without complaint. Many did their part through Victory Gardens, emulating the practice of the valley's first settlers who had demonstrated that with water and attention almost any crop was possible, regardless of the altitude and short growing season. Gardens were put in everywhere, including around the Stanley Hotel and Estes Park Chalets. Deer and rabbits, of course, posed a constant menace, and some experimented without much success in trying to keep them out by installing electric wires.[7]

Estes Park's most successful and best publicized fund-raising event of the war occurred in early spring 1943, when residents subscribed $113,000 worth of bonds in only six weeks in response to a challenge by mayor Glen Preston to the Defense Council that Estes Park should buy a fighter plane of its own. On June 14, 1943, Flag Day, a special ceremony was held at the high school auditorium during which the deed to the "Estes Park Avenger" was presented to representatives from Lowry Field. By November 1943 the Avenger was flying missions from a base somewhere in Britain.

12.3 Abner Sprague and Charles Reed, June 1939. Reed has just flipped with Sprague for the "right" to purchase the first annual entry permit for RMNP. Courtesy National Park Service–Rocky Mountain National Park

Estes Park announced its wartime identity early. As the *Estes Park Trail* told its readers in April 1942, "One of the greatest services a resort area can render the national cause is to cater to the needs and desires of weary war workers, thereby building up the nation's morale."[8] "Our patriotic duty," Mayor Preston reiterated a year later in an open letter to the community and its visitors, "is to provide restful, peaceful vacations for overworked war workers and our fighting men home on furlough, and this we intend to do."[9] Although hard-pressed to find adequate summer help and forced by rationing to "streamline" their menus—a euphemism meaning less meat, fewer items, and smaller portions—Estes Park's hotels and resorts stayed open and welcomed all comers, making special efforts to extend their hospitality to soldiers, sailors, and the more than 80,000 defense workers employed in plants and factories within a hundred-mile radius of the village. Morale building, "the first duty of a resort community," meant making sure that the usual program of summertime activities went on with as few interruptions as possible.

The 1942 season turned out to be far better than many had expected. Despite the fact that park admissions decreased from 685,593 to 392,565 because of tire and gasoline rationing, the local economy held up surprisingly well with most operators showing little if any loss, and in some cases even reporting a profit.[10] "In comparison to former summers," the *Estes Park Trail* noted at season's end, "there were longer stays. People rested, relaxed and enjoyed themselves. They spent a great deal of money. Next year and the year following until the war is over will be a different story."[11] The *Trail* was right. In 1943 the park's visitor count plummeted to 130,288 before recovering slightly to 204,253 and 339,928 in 1944 and 1945.

These visitors included a high proportion of servicemen and -women. Beginning in 1942, military personnel were admitted to Rocky Mountain National Park for free, and everyone went to great lengths to make them feel at home. The Service Men's Center, offering a place to sit, magazines to read, and fishing equipment to borrow, was established across the street from the Chamber of Commerce, where visitors usually stopped for information. In June 1943 a similar center was opened in a corner room at the Hupp Hotel further up Elkhorn Avenue. There were regular USO dances at the Stanley, with soldiers brought in from Denver's Lowry and Buckley Fields and from as far away as Fort Warren in Cheyenne, where a renamed Fort Russell had been transformed into a training camp for as many as 20,000 troops. To meet the demand for dancing partners, "truckloads" of girls were "shipped over" from the Y where they were employed for the summer. As one Estes Park resident reminisced, "They'd call everybody and say, 'We've got so many boys, and we want somebody to have dinner for them.' Every Sunday families around town would have dinner for three or four fellows and take them for a ride. We had half of Buckley and Lowry up here for almost two years, and they really loved it."[12]

Estes Park had its share of heroes. The most famous was Colonel Jean R. Byerly, the village's highest-ranking soldier, the son of hotel and resort owners Harriett and Frank Byerly. A veteran Air Force officer, Byerly first earned recognition for his participation in daring daylight raids over German-occupied France where on one occasion he carefully orchestrated the return of his squadron by down-throttling his bomber, "Holy Joe," to protect crippled fortresses on their flight home across the English Channel. In Britain, Byerly was photographed standing by his plane while it was inspected by King George VI. Promoted, Byerly was ordered to North Africa where he once again was photographed, this time for the March 1, 1943, issue of *Life Magazine* by its famous photographer Margaret Bourke-White.

Byerly's greatest fame came in the following months. Reported missing in action after his plane was shot down over Italy on Christmas Day 1943, Byerly turned up in Stalag Luft 1, a prisoner of war camp in Germany, where he made national news reported home in letters from fellow prisoners, by establishing a total community organized by groups and squadrons, that kept the men constantly involved in a program of "collectively inventive" morale- and health-building activities—said to be the first of its kind in a prisoner of war camp. As one letter read, "Rough and ready American humor is ever-present. Everyone contributes something. We have A-1 football and baseball teams, a concert and swing orchestra, a theater troupe now presenting 'The Man Who Came to Dinner,' and a hundred other organizations. . . . How about some air mail letters for the boys?"[13] Released in spring 1945 and honored with the Silver Star and Distinguished Flying Cross, Byerly returned to the village in late May to a hero's welcome.

Other stories had tragic endings. These included the story of another highly decorated pilot, Major Jerald Price, who before the war had been employed for four seasons by the town's public works department and whose seemingly endless wartime exploits the *Estes Park Trail* covered in detail. A member of the celebrated Eighth Air Force based in England, Price flew missions across the Channel and was praised for bringing his badly riddled Flying Fortress safely home under intense enemy fire. After twenty-nine combat missions, the seemingly indestructible Price, on loan to a fighter command, was killed in August 1944 when his plane suddenly crashed west of Cambridge.

Captain Joseph J. ("Junior") Duncan suffered a similar fate. A 1931 valedictorian graduate of the Estes Park schools and a noted skier who had delighted onlookers with his victories on Hidden Valley's slopes, Duncan had enlisted in the newly formed Eighty-seventh Mountain Infantry Battalion and trained at Camp Hale near Leadville. Promoted, transferred, and shipped overseas, Duncan was killed in Italy near the village of Cas Costa on April 17, 1945, while providing artillery support for one of his patrols during a mop-up operation.

Price and Duncan were by no means the only local men to lose their lives in the war effort. That possibility lurked over every American community and was brought graphically home to Estes Park in October 1943 when a B-17 Flying Fortress, on a routine flight from Rapid City, South Dakota, to Lowry Field in Denver, crashed in the vicinity of Signal Mountain just beyond the boundaries of the park, killing its crew of eight. The tangled mass of metal was discovered on a slope at approximately 10,300 feet in terrain impossible for even horses to reach.[14]

Byerly and Price, by letter and while at home on furlough, had been instrumental in promoting the war effort in Estes Park. Both were part of the campaign that made possible the "Estes Park Avenger," and Price, on one of his bombing missions in March 1943, had fulfilled the request of his old boss Lee Tallant, by dropping "a brick on Hitler" during a raid over German submarine yards near Bremen.[15] Later that same summer Price's Flying Fortress, "We the People," dropped a load of bombs with the names of six Estes Park residents hand-painted on them, "purchased" during a special two-week War Bond Drive in June. "Notify the six high bond buyers," Price telegrammed the Estes Park Defense Council, "that their bombs were cashed with interest on Schweinfurt, Germany, August 17, 1943."[16]

Others did important work closer to home. The "Hermit of Horse Creek," radio engineer Siegfried Wagener, a German-born refugee who had served with the kaiser's army in World War I, operated his short-wave "Listening Post," monitoring Nazi propaganda from high up in the Tahosa Valley. For four years beginning in 1939, it was Wagener's self-proclaimed mission to listen in on German broadcasts and then share what he heard in his column "We're Listening—War on Air Waves," which he wrote for the *Chicago Times* and aired through Denver's Mutual Broadcasting System affiliate from Baldpate Inn during a twice-weekly radio program, "Analysis of Propaganda." In October 1943 Wagner himself went to war, working in Europe for the Office of Strategic Services (O.S.S.) and later testifying against American poet Ezra Pound for his pro-Axis broadcasts.

Patriotism also had its ugly side. On July 6, 1943, the Estes Park Board of Trustees met at board members' request with a Mr. Bennison, a representative of the War Relocation Authority, a federal agency established by executive order in March 1942 to oversee the removal and relocation of individuals suspected of endangering national security. The subject of their discussion was Ryoji Kato, who, the trustees told Bennison, was "a Japanese alien, who had recently moved to Estes Park to operate a business on Elkhorn Avenue." The cause of the board's concern, its minutes succinctly note, was "that the public sentiment was strongly against Mr. Kato and that he should be place[d] in some other area." How much subsequent discussion took place is unclear. What is clear, however, is that "Mr. Bennison agreed that he would try and relocate Mr. Kato." Within days Kato, a widower, was gone. His art shop near the Macdonald Book Shop was soon occupied by a new business.[17]

Kato was indeed an alien and as such subject to the Alien Registration Act of June 1940. But it is hardly likely that he posed a danger or was involved in subversive activities. And far from being a "recent" arrival, as the town fathers told Bennison, Ryoji Kato had come to Estes Park in late winter 1927 with his Japanese-born, American-educated wife Yaye, who he had met and married in Denver five years before. Leasing space in the Tallant

12.4 Ryoji and Yaye Kato. Courtesy Estes Park Museum

12.5 Kato Tea Garden on Bear Lake Road. Courtesy Estes Park Museum

Building near the transportation company, the Katos had started an art shop specializing in oriental gifts and novelties. Four years later Mrs. Kato expanded the business by opening the Oriental Tea Garden, offering Chinese and Japanese dishes, in a building rented from Jack Woods in Tuxedo Park on the Bear Lake Road. There, wearing a "beautiful Chinese dress," she greeted her guests next to a doorway adorned with brightly painted Chinese men made by her husband. "This is the first shop of its kind to be opened in Estes Park," the *Trail* noted at the time, and will be the only one serving Chinese food."[18] In June 1929, the Katos had their first and only child. They called her June, a name suggested by "the noted Estes Park author" Clem Yore and validated by the *Estes Park Trail:* "We think June Kiyoko Kato very beautiful and euphonious."[19]

Three years later the *Estes Park Trail* had a sadder story on its front page: "Hundreds of Estes Park visitors all over the United States will grieve with villagers to learn of the death of Mrs. Yaye Kato, who with her husband operated a gift shop and tea room in this region for seven years."[20] Yaye Kato, age thirty-two, was buried in Loveland following a service officiated by Estes Park minister Floyd Kuykendall. Clem Yore was among the pallbearers. Following her death, Ryoji Kato continued to operate his art store, moving its location to a building near the Hupp Hotel, and then back across the street.

In 1939, when Jesse Jay needed oriental décor for the bar of his new night-club, he asked Lyman Byxbe and Ryoji Kato to provide it. Time and circumstance has a way of erasing memory. Announcing Kato's death in August 1965, the *Trail* noted only that he had operated his gift shop "through the summer of 1941 [*sic*]," and then moved to Burbank, California, where he had remarried and made his living in the gift shop business once again and by doing flower arranging.[21]

Such behavior perhaps can be explained by the hysteria of the times and the belief that Japan posed a military threat to the continental United States—a belief that ultimately helped send some 120,000 Americans of Japanese descent to relocation camps in seven western states, including Colorado. Such a threat seemed real enough as late as 1945 when a soldier stationed in the Philippines found a complete map of the Poudre Valley, including the irrigation systems in and around Fort Collins, among the effects of a dead Japanese captain killed in Luzon.[22] Because of such dangers many communities allowed strong public sentiment to be raised against fellow residents. In doing so, some like Estes Park were willing to allow those who surely should have known better to rearrange the facts of their own history for the sake of community peace of mind.

In other matters the village trustees exercised more caution, announcing in spring 1943 that they had adopted a strict wartime "pay-as-you-go" policy that would, for the first time since its incorporation in 1917, leave the town free of debt. This frugality did not, however, preclude projects that would increase the town's self-sufficiency. In September 1944 following a 107 to 1 vote by residents, Estes Park acquired the holdings of the Public Service Company of Colorado by issuing $250,000 worth of bonds, a step that not only returned Stanley's hydro-plant on Fall River with its 1,100 customers to local control but positioned the town to take advantage of the electrical power to be made available with the completion of the Colorado–Big Thompson Project. The old town hall–firehouse building was remodeled to house the new utility department.

Other projects were put on hold for the duration. These included the completion of Stanley Park, which by 1941 had a history stretching back to before the turn of the century when the site had been used to stage rodeo events and other tourist activities. After it was acquired by Stanley when he purchased the Dunraven land, Stanley offered as early as 1913 to give the eighty acres to the town "for an amusement park . . . if the citizens of the

Park will lay off the grounds for polo and baseball, and organize clubs for their use." When no one came forward to take up the challenge, Stanley kept the land, although its rodeo and athletic facilities continued to be used by the community. In the years after 1920, when Stanley erected a hangar to house the Curtiss airplane used that summer to take tourists and residents on sightseeing flights and to places as far away as Denver, it was known as "Aviation Field." Between 1926 and 1929 the land belonged to the Milwaukee syndicate that purchased the Stanley Hotel and they announced their intention to develop the property into a major recreational complex. When they financially defaulted in 1929, the park was reacquired by Stanley.

Six years later on August 14, 1936, the ever-generous Stanley deeded fifty-four acres and its facilities to his adopted town for use "solely as a public park and recreation ground." By then the rodeo had become a fixture of summer, and the town quickly accepted both the property and Stanley's stipulations for its use. The Chamber of Commerce assumed responsibility for the park and hired landscape architect J. Lloyd Fletcher to provide a plan for its development. Fletcher's proposal of January 1938 called for a series of significant renovations designed to bring the grounds into "correct harmony with the rugged mountains that surround the village of Estes Park." These included a landscaped bridle path, natural stone entrance, improved racetrack and athletic fields, and a large north-facing grandstand sited to avoid the sun's glare. Fletcher's plan also contained picnic facilities; a rock shelter house with fireplace; grounds for tennis, croquet, archery, shuffleboard, and horseshoes; children's playground equipment; as well as space for the town's first historical museum.

Nothing further was done about the park and its facilities until August 1941, nearly a year after Stanley's death. That month, following a meeting attended by representatives of nearly every local civic and social organization, the project was revived, although on a more modest scale than the one that Fletcher had outlined. A $15,000 budget was established, to which the town added the Stanley Memorial Park Fund, consisting of most monies received from the Reclamation Bureau in exchange for the twenty-three acres of Stanley's land that the bureau needed for its offices, housing, and power plant. The new plan was strengthened by the generosity of adjacent property owners Carl Sanborn and John Manford, who together donated slightly more than twenty-four acres to the town, in effect restoring Stanley Park to its original size. Private fund-raising, it was decided, would take care of the rest.

On September 23, 1941, with subscriptions of more than $4,500 in hand, long-time summer resident William Allen White, whose years in Estes

Park surpassed even those of Stanley himself, turned the first shovel of dirt for the new Stanley Memorial Park. It was hoped that the facility, to be completed according to plans drawn up by an architect whose services were donated by Reclamation Bureau contractor Sam Magoffin, would be ready for dedication nine months later on July 4, 1942. Magoffin's architect, brought in from Delaware, delivered a set of plans calling for the completion of "Stanley Stadium," a large oval $5/8$-mile track enclosing a football and polo field, as well as for a large 50-by-16-foot clubhouse building with social room at one end and rest rooms at the other, separated by a covered porch. Two large log blockhouses, recalling Estes Park's frontier heritage, were to flank the park's south entrance, replacing the entryway of native rock that Fletcher had envisaged for the park's north side.

Pearl Harbor brought fund-raising and construction largely to a halt, although by summer 1943 the track and rodeo field had been graded, the existing grandstand moved south to make room for a new track, and one of the blockhouses was in place, built with logs that the Forest Service donated and brought out from behind the Twin Sisters. The second blockhouse and the rest of what turned out to be rather pedestrian facilities—a concession to post-war financial realities—were not completed until the early 1950s.

The only major new public facility completed by the town during the war years was Estes Park's first public airfield, bringing commercial aviation back to the valley for the first time since the 1920s. Although Stanley's short-lived romance with the airplane ended badly with the accident involving Alberta Yore, followed three years later in August 1923 by a second crash, this time resulting in a fatality, the old hangar in Stanley Park remained as a symbol of the technology that would lead to the 1929 opening of Denver's Stapleton Field, a short 35-minute flight away. From that time on a commercial airport, as a means of stimulating tourist travel, was sufficiently high on the town's wish list to generate periodic rumors and discussion, the most recent in 1936, when it was reported that plans were afoot to build a federal airfield with a mile-long, 500-foot-wide runway on land straddling the Storer Ranch and Stanley property near the hotel. Again, in 1941 there was talk of establishing an airport, this time somewhere in the Estes Valley to train pilots for high altitude flying.[23]

Estes Park finally got its commercial airport in August 1944 when in just seventeen days land adjacent to the golf course, now being leased to the town, was cleared of rocks and trees to make way for a north-south 3,000-foot runway of hard-packed granite. The field was placed in service by Scenic Air Line, a company owned by Massey and Ransom Flying Service of Fort Collins. Making use of single-engine planes capable of carrying a pilot, three or four passengers, and a modest amount of luggage and freight, Scenic Air Line offered scheduled flights to Denver and other Front Range towns. However exciting and briefly newsworthy, this experiment, like its predecessor, was short-lived. The vagaries of the wind made safe takeoffs and landings problematic and difficult, and the planes themselves were too small to make commercial travel any more than a novel convenience for the wealthy. Air transportation would in time revolutionize vacation travel in Colorado and elsewhere and Estes Park would be one of its beneficiaries, but getting to Denver and the valley would remain much as Stanley had visualized when he rebuilt the North St. Vrain Road up from Lyons for his Mountain Wagons.

In mid-June 1940 village and park sponsored the Silver Jubilee Celebration, a day and a half series of events commemorating the twenty-fifth anniversary of the national park's establishment, featuring a parade and "Jubilee Ball." "Old-timers say it was the best thing that the village of Estes Park had ever staged," David Canfield wrote in his monthly report. "The entire northeastern section of the state participated in the celebration, and the park has reason to be proud for the spirit with which the adjoining communities entered into the celebration."[24] Such enthusiasm was particularly gratifying and "surprising," Canfield noted, "in view of the years of bickering and disagreement."[25]

The celebration was, in retrospect, a moment to be savored, for World War II brought to an end the progress in Rocky Mountain National Park made possible by the New Deal's money and programs. It also decimated the Park Service's staff and budget. Before Pearl Harbor the Park Service had 5,963 full-time employees and an annual budget of $33.5 million. By June 30, 1944, the number of employees had shrunk to 1,573, and its budget had been reduced accordingly, severely affecting such areas as resource management and scientific research. In 1942, to make room in Washington for the infrastructure of war, the Park Service's central offices, like other "nonessential" agencies, were moved out of the capital. When the Park Service returned to Washington from Chicago after five years of being out of touch with Congress, it too in the words of its director Newton Drury had become one of the "victims of war." One of the chief casualties was the Wildlife Division and the research and monitoring activities it had inspired during the 1930s. The few scientists who remained were assigned to the Division of Interpretation and scientists within the Park Service were reduced, in the words of one historian, to "a troubleshooting force" in an organization where "resource-management problems were dealt with only when they became too large or too politically sensitive to be ignored."[26] In the years that followed, the absence of their influence would become evident in a Park Service poorly equipped to contend with criticism from an increasingly ecology-conscious nation, academic scientists, and conservation groups that it was ignoring basic environmental issues or addressing them in the wrong way.

The years 1942 through 1945 saw the nation's parks operating on what Drury called "a maintenance and protection basis." "The primary objective of the National Park Service during the war," Superintendent Canfield noted in a letter published for the 1943 tourist season, "is to protect the forests, watersheds, wildlife, and scenic values . . . with the minimum expenditure of funds so that, when the return is made to normalcy, following the war, that part of the national heritage represented in the national parks will be intact for a war-worn Nation to enjoy."[27] Fortunately, fewer visitors reduced the pressure on now clearly insufficient park resources. That Rocky Mountain National Park and other parks managed to survive the war years so well was the result of lack of use, not upkeep and care.

Rocky Mountain National Park lost both chief naturalist Raymond Gregg and superintendent David Canfield to military service. Gregg left to become a Navy recruiter after the 1942 season, which had seen the permanent ranger naturalist staff reduced from five to three despite continuing demand for its services. After Gregg's departure and until his return in 1945, the naturalist staff was eliminated altogether and its activities turned over once more to temporary rangers. In April 1943, Canfield accepted a Navy commission and was "furloughed from Service." His place was taken by George W. Miller until the arrival from Chicago of John E. Doerr, who would head the park until Canfield returned in January 1946. In 1943 alone, seven regular members of the park staff joined the armed services, further depleting its expertise. Others left by way of transfer, including district ranger Harold M. Ratcliff, who with Ranger Jack Moomaw was the park's senior ranger in terms of service. In August 1941 Ratcliff was made custodian of Dinosaur National Monument. Moomaw, although in increasingly poor health, stayed on until June 1945, when he retired after a career of twenty-one years. The popular Moomaw was especially missed. A ranger who embodied many of the talents and values of Dorr Yeager's fictional Bob Flame, Moomaw had joined the park staff on July 1, 1924, during the Toll years and over the next two decades had been responsible for building or supervising the building of nearly every trail east of the Continental Divide. The last of the all-purpose old-time rangers, his departure signaled the end of an era.

Those who stayed on in the park, in addition to contributing the mandatory Victory Tax from their pay, worked side by side with the local community in its scrap drives, civil defense activities, and other wartime projects. In 1943 alone, park personnel gathered up more than 143 tons of metal, much of it coming from along the Grand Ditch in the Never Summer Range.

With the closing down of the park's CCC camps in 1942, all but the most essential maintenance and protection work came to an end. The reduction from twenty-two to fifteen seasonal rangers that summer further limited such activities. John Doerr succinctly summarized the situation in the annual report that he filed shortly after his arrival: "The year represented a period of retrenchment in the administration, maintenance and improvement in Rocky Mountain National Park in keeping with the Nation's all out war effort. It was marked by changes in personnel, decline in travel, reduced or curtailed work programs and activities, and with essential functions carried out by fewer employees with greater responsibilities for the preservation of the area."[28] It was a refrain that would be repeated until summer 1946, when with the cessation of hostilities and the end of gas rationing a record 808,155 tourists flooded the park. And two years later the number of tourists would exceed one million. Under such circumstances it is hardly surprising that the only new trail constructed during these years should be outside the park—one built to the top of Prospect Mountain by members of the Summer Resident's Association and the Liverymen's Association—opening to hikers the panoramic view of the Front Range first photographed by William H. Jackson during his 1873 visit to Estes Valley.

~

The news of V-J Day arrived in Estes Park by radio on August 15, 1945, where it was greeted by the ringing of bells from the Community Church and followed by a quickly arranged but nearly packed thanksgiving service. That evening a victory program was sponsored by the town and the Chamber of Commerce in what was now Bond Park, attended by as many as a thousand persons. It was publicized in advance by George Hix, the banker's son, who "with his sound truck went through the streets announcing the evening's entertainment," making use of a novel system of metal speakers put together by his brother Frank to play recorded dance music at Riverside. After a welcome by mayor Glen Preston, there was "an impressive talk on Victory," given by Dr. Alfred H. Nickless, a Presbyterian pastor from Iowa who was much in demand as a public speaker, and "closed with a prayer of thanksgiving." If anyone needed further reminder that the war was over, it was signaled by the free entertainment that followed, including "musical numbers by Miss Jean McNichols, . . . Tex Brown with his singing and roping buckaroos, Tate's trained dogs, and Pat Henry with his trained horse. . . . Dancing followed the program until the rain scattered the crowd. Sheer joy seemed to be the keynote of the celebration."[29] The rain scarcely mattered: the war as over; it was summer; and this was Estes Park.

~

There is of course a great deal more to the story of Estes Park and its national park. Even before V-J Day, the town had begun to look ahead "to be ready for post-war business." For the first time there was talk of zoning. In December 1944 the town's planning commission brought in Denver consultant Walter Pesman to explain its purposes and advantages. "The encouragement of the better type of tourist trade," Pesman told the members, "is the direct result from encouraging the better type of business establishment in logical locations only."[30] In a town historically not given to such foresight, these words suggested a new level of awareness about the future and the opportunities and responsibilities it would bring.

Since then more than half a century of history has passed. Estes Park now has a population within town limits in excess of 6,000, almost double the number of the 1990 census; and an estimated 9,700 others live in the surrounding valley. As might be expected, the most recent demographic figures reveal that the population of both town and valley is on average better educated, more affluent, and more racially homogenous than the population of Colorado and the nation. Because of the presence of a significant number of retirees (some only summer residents) this population is also somewhat older. Many of these retirees were attracted to Estes Park by a cost of living thought far more reasonable than that of trendier mountain communities like Breckenridge, Vail, and Aspen. With this group, as with those for whom Estes Park is a second seasonal home, has come a new measure of affluence, which has increased home prices, exacerbated the traditional housing shortage for summer workers and town employees, and made new demands on local services. Those who can vote, not surprisingly, have decided preferences on how their tax dollars should and should not be spent. Land for new construction, thanks in part to the very restrictions that Pesman helped introduce, is in increasingly short supply. It has been further reduced by the success of the Estes Valley Land Trust, which over the past decade and a half, through donation and purchase, has permanently limited the type of development that can take place on some 5,000 acres throughout the valley—about as much land as the Earl of Dunraven himself directly controlled. Included is a conservation easement on land in the Tahosa Valley containing the homestead cabin of Enos Mills.

⁓

The economy of Estes Park in the new century remains the economy of a tourist town, sensitive to the ebb and flow of sales tax dollars and the spending and vacationing habits of more than three million visitors annually. Although improved in appearance since the Lawn Lake Flood of 1982, which created a taxing entity in the Estes Park Urban Renewal Authority, the core downtown and what it has to offer (save for the absence of Riverside Amusement Park, public school buildings, and auditorium) does not fundamentally differ from the Estes Park that welcomed the end of World War II. The challenge for those guiding town affairs also remains substantially unchanged: how to sustain a tourist economy that encourages manageable growth, fosters local employment, and improves infrastructure, while protecting the values and lifestyle of a small community and preserving the environment. This is, of course, no easy task. Yet, even in the absence of individuals such as F. O. Stanley, C. H. Bond, Pieter Hondius, and Joe Mills whose dominating presence and paternalism once ordered and directed village affairs, and the presence of a population far larger and more diversified in background, interest, and values than four decades ago, most would agree that Estes Park has so far done well.

Such is not always, or inevitably, the case in tourist-oriented towns, even those whose historical traditions and commitment to place are strong. During the last half century many resort communities, new and old alike, have embraced tourism as an economic panacea and encouraged the influx of outside capital to underwrite its development, only to discover that they have struck something of "a devil's bargain." The result, all too often, is a new coalition of interests that shifts power away from local decision makers and brings "unanticipated and irreversible" economic, social, and political consequences for which those communities and their residents are unprepared. When this happens, writes historian Hal Rothman, the bonds of community become pulled apart, tensions "buried in the fictions of social arrangements" surface, and "the impact of change throws the soul of the place, any place, up for grabs."[31] Such pressures exist within any resort community, and Estes Park is no exception. In recent years they have bubbled to the surface over any number of local issues involving development, including proposals to bring in an outlet mail and build an IMAX theater. Although the "soul" and identity of Estes Park is still its own, Rothman's warning should be taken seriously lest the historian, looking back a century hence, have a decidedly different story to tell.

Change is perhaps more striking in Rocky Mountain National Park. Gone are the last of the lodges that for many were a central part of the "park experience." New buildings have replaced the old. Thanks to "Mission 66," a ten-year program of large-scale construction and renovation announced in 1956 by park service director Conrad L. Wirth to end fifteen years of neglect and "meet the needs of a much greater number of visitors," Rocky Mountain National Park has been able to construct the Alpine Visitors Center at Fall River Pass (1966); the east-side administration building and visitor center at Beaver Meadows, known as Park Headquarters (1967); and the west-side administration building (Kawuneeche Visitor Center) near Grand Lake (1968). The site for the Estes Park building was deliberately chosen. Rejecting sites in Horseshoe Park and at Deer Ridge Junction, the Park Service located its new facility, designed by a firm staffed by disciples of Frank Lloyd Wright, outside park boundaries. This was done with the hope of improving the sometimes strained relationships between park and town—even though the new building was, as more than one critic pointed out, "on the wrong side of the road." Its opening made it possible to construct a new park entrance linked to Estes Park by an approach road through Beaver Meadows below High Drive—a project on the drawing board since 1932—and to close the old entrance near the YMCA.

Even with these new facilities, Rocky Mountain National Park, like all national parks, has continued to struggle to meet the contradictory expectations mandated by the original Park Service charter of 1916 to promote the freest possible use of what it for years promoted as a "playground" while "conserving . . . the scenery and the natural and historic objects and the wildlife therein." The park has had some advantages. Thanks to the successful resolution of the transportation controversy of the 1920s and the equally successful program of eliminating inholdings, including the facilities at Hidden Valley, it has largely escaped the problems involving concessions and concessionaires that have vexed successive administrations at Yellowstone, Yosemite, Glacier, and elsewhere.

Rocky Mountain National Park, to be sure, has had challenges uniquely its own, many of them resulting from its geographic proximity to the population centers of a fast-growing state. These include the now-perennial problem of overgrazing by elk and deer herds that have been allowed to grow unchecked since the institution in 1969 of a policy suspending active management within the park. The dilemma over elk was highlighted in 1995 by

12.6 The Y-junction: Big Thompson entrance to Rocky Mountain National Park. Courtesy National Park Service–Rocky Mountain National Park

the death by poacher's arrow of "Sampson," a magnificent 1,000-pound bull elk who roamed the grounds of the YMCA. The death of Sampson and the sentencing of his killer became a nationwide news story. Sampson's presence is still felt. A large statue funded by the community at the junction of Highways 36 and 7 and a dedicated website declaring that "we visit the park often and the loss of these animals hurts us all," only underscores the intractability of an issue over which local public opinion seems firmly settled. What to do about the size of the elk herd, given the carrying capacity of the park, has now been subjected to endless study and debate without definitive resolution or timetable. Similarly, there are now those who wonder if, given the number of visitors and a road and trail system that has not been expanded since the 1930s, Rocky Mountain National Park has not reached its human "carrying capacity" as well. How this and other issues can be addressed and solved in an era of reduced resources and increased expectations and within a local, state, and national arena that has become politicized where Park Service matters are concerned is far from clear.

In 1944 the Denver consultant counseled the town fathers to "avoid mistakes rather than trying to rectify them after they have been made." Although Estes Park and Rocky Mountain National Park have clearly tried, the record of the last half century is a decidedly mixed one. No one, let alone this historian, can predict what the future will bring. But we can find comfort in the thought that for now at least Joel Estes's valley and its national park—as in the day that inspired the Earl of Dunraven to make as much of it as possible his own—still remains "America's Switzerland," one of the nation's "last best places."

Notes

～

CHAPTER 1

1. *Fort Collins Express*, 42 (September 5, 1915): 1; *Loveland Daily Herald*, 6 (September 6, 1915): 1. The estimates varied considerably. F. O. Stanley suggested 500; local resort manager Charles Lester "thought there were nearer 700." *Longmont Ledger*, 36 (September 10, 1915): 4.

2. *Denver Times*, 45 (September 4, 1915): 1.

3. Quoted in Robert Shankland, *Steve Mather of the National Parks* (New York: Alfred A. Knopf, 1954), 79.

4. *Fort Collins Weekly Courier*, 37 (September 3, 1915): 5.

5. For studies about the impact of automobile transportation on tourism in general and within of national parks in particular see, for example, Warren Belasco, *Americans on the Road: From Autocamp to Motel, 1910–1945* (Boston: MIT Press, 1979); John Jakle, *The Tourist: Travel in Twentieth-Century North America* (Lincoln: University of Nebraska Press, 1985), 101–170; Hal K. Rothman, *Devil's Bargains, Tourism in the Twentieth-Century American West* (Lawrence: University of Kansas Press, 1998), 50–112; David Louter, "Glaciers and Gasoline: The Making of a Windshield Wilderness," *Seeing and Being Seen: Tourism in the American West*, David W. Wrobel and Patrick T. Long, eds. (Lawrence: University of Kansas Press, 2001), 248–270.

6. *Denver Times*, 45 (September 3, 1915): 1.

7. *Loveland Reporter*, 36 (September 6, 1915): 1.

8. Ibid.

9. Horace M. Albright and Marian Albright Schenck, *Creating the National Park Service: The Missing Years* (Norman: University of Oklahoma Press, 1999), 96. This should not be confused with *The Birth of the National Park Service*, cited in Chapter 3, note 88.

10. *Longmont Ledger*, 36 (September 10, 1915): 4.

11. *Fort Collins Weekly Courier*, 37 (September 10, 1915): 5.

12. *Longmont Ledger*, 36 (September 10, 1915): 4.

13. *Estes Park Trail*, 1 (June 15, 1912): 4.

14. *Rocky Mountain News*, 5 (September 23, 1868): 2.

15. Abner E. Sprague, "My First Visit to Estes Park," (typescript, Colorado Historical Society), 4.

16. Ibid., 5.

17. *Larimer Press*, as subsequently published in the *Greeley Tribune*, 3 (August 27, 1873): 2.

18. Abstract, Estes Park Company, Limited, Articles of Incorporation, August 17, 1876, Larimer County Abstract Company, Estes Park Museum (hereafter EPM).

19. *Estes Park Trail*, 18 (April 22, 1938): 28.

20. Information on most of the resorts listed here, including those built between 1905 and 1915 may be found in my earlier book, *"This Blue Hollow": Estes Park, the Early Years, 1859–1915* (Niwot: University Press of Colorado, 1999). See also Henry F. Pedersen Jr., *Those Castles of Wood: The Story of Early Lodges of Rocky Mountain National Park . . .* (Estes Park, CO: Henry F. Pedersen Jr., 1993).

CHAPTER 2

1. *Lyons Recorder*, 5 (April 13, 1905): 1. This article cites April 20 as the date on which "possession is to be given."

2. The problem that Bond and his partners did not anticipate was John Cleave's lack of clear title. Working through Dunraven's Denver lawyer, Frank Prestige, Bond made two trips to England and reportedly spent some $3,000 to work out the arrangements that in late May finally gave him ownership. *Loveland Register*, 11 (May 31, 1905): 1.

3. Flora Stanley, "A Tenderfoot's First Summer in the Rockies," *Stanley Museum Quarterly*, 16 (June 1997): 15. The original manuscript is in the Frank Normali Collection, Stanley Historic Foundation, Estes Park (hereafter SHF).

4. *Longmont Ledger*, 16 (January 27, 1905): 1.

5. *Loveland Register*, 11 (March 29, 1905): 1.

6. *Loveland Reporter*, 26 (April 6, 1905): 10.

7. Ibid., 26 (July 6, 1905): 8.

8. Quoted in William Wyckoff, *Creating Colorado: The Making of a Western Landscape, 1860–1940* (New Haven, CT: Yale University Press, 1999), 61.

9. *Mountaineer* (August 6, 1908): 6.

10. *Longmont Ledger*, 16 (June 2, 1905): 1. The *Ledger* cites the *Denver Republican* as its source. See also *Loveland Register*, 11 (May 31, 1905): 1.

11. Fred Payne Clatworthy, "Pioneer Business Men Made Estes Park History," *Estes Park Trail*, 23 (April 23, 1943): 36.

12. *Loveland Reporter*, 26 (September 28, 1905): 13.

13. Ibid., 28 (June 27, 1907): 1. Unfortunately, as is the case of a number of the early businesswomen of Estes Park, we know all too little about the enterprising Josie Hupp (1857–1932), who at one time owned four downtown hotels: the Hupp, the Manford, the Josephine, and the Sherwood. Born in Michigan, she came to Loveland as the bride of August Blinn in 1877, where she operated a tent boarding-house. Blinn died in 1891, and two years later Josie married Henry A. Hupp, the son of Estes Park pioneers John and Eliza Hupp. Moving to Estes Park, Josie built the Hupp Hotel in 1906. Two years later, in December 1908, within months of its completion, she purchased John J. Manford's new hotel, the Manford House, for a reported $16,000. She promptly changed the name to the Hupp Annex, both to signify her ownership and to differentiate her new property from the original hotel across Elkhorn Avenue. In 1913, Josie Hupp sold the Hupp Annex to Cornelius Bond, who, in turn, sold it in March 1917, to William and Anna May Derby "for something less than $17,000." The Derbys kept the hotel for a number of years, exchanging its exterior wood for stucco and in 1926–1927 adding a large addition on the north side.

Josie Hupp built the two-story Josephine Hotel, further down Elkhorn, in 1916. Four years later she sold the building to the Lewiston Hotels of Estes Park, only to repurchase it again in 1926. In 1930 it was sold to Ted Jelsema who owned the adjacent Riverside amusement complex. Jelsema renamed it the Riverside Hotel. The top floor burned in December 1956.

Josie Hupp's final hotel venture, the Sherwood Hotel, located on upper Elkhorn just east of the village church, began as the Brown Teapot Inn, a refreshment business operated by a woman named Lil Norton, who in 1915 had a three-story building erected on the property. The Sherwood soon passed into other hands, first to Nebraskans who renamed it the "Aksarben" (Nebraska spelled backward), and then, in 1921, to owners who changed the name to the Sherwood, a name Josie Hupp retained after she assumed ownership in July 1923. Sold by Josie Hupp in 1926, the Sherwood burned on Valentine's Day of 1956 and was not rebuilt. For additional information on these hotels see Pedersen's *Castles of Wood*.

14. Florence Shoemaker, "The Story of the Estes–Rocky Mountain National Park Region" (M.A. Thesis, Colorado State College of Education, Greeley, 1940), 78; *Loveland Register*, 12 (May 31, 1906): 3.

15. *Loveland Register*, 12 (May 24, 1906): 8.

16. Sam Service (1860–1937) came to America in 1883, and in 1890 married Sadie Boyd (1869–1931) of Sterling, Colorado, the sister of blacksmith Jim Boyd, who followed her to Estes Park in 1902. They had eight children. Service operated his store in Estes Park until 1927, when he sold it to his son Frank and his son-in-law Marshall Stith. In 1929 it was purchased by Honor Bright Grocery, a Greeley chain. Sam Service served as Estes Park's mayor from 1925 to 1929, as well as president of the Estes Park Bank.

17. The photograph is produced in Harold Marion Dunning, *Over Hill and Vale*, II (Boulder, CO: Johnson Publishing, 1962), 125.

18. *Longmont Ledger*, 29 (May 15, 1908): 8.

19. *Lyons Recorder*, 18 (June 7, 1919): 1; *Estes Park Trail*, 9 (May 24, 1929): 1. In 1932, this building was taken down to make way for a tile and stucco building to house the Monahan Motor Company. Estes Park Trail, 11 (February 26, 1932): 2.

20. Minutes of the Board of Trustees of the Town of Estes Park, Colorado (hereafter MBTEP), October 27, 1919, 55.

21. *Lyons Recorder*, 7 (June 28, 1906): 3.

22. *Loveland Register*, 12 (June 28, 1906): 8.

23. *Loveland Reporter*, 26 (February 1, 1906): 1.

24. Ibid., 28 (February 22, 1907): 5.

25. The Estes Park fire department was organized on January 29, 1907. Its first elected fire chief was Dr. Homer James. Other resident-volunteers were divided into two teams, the "plugmen "and the "nozzlemen." The first firehouse, built for a small hose cart which blacksmith Jim Boyd put together, was located behind the Estes Park Bank. The first fire alarm was a circular saw blade, which was soon replaced by a fire bell atop a small wooden tower (clearly visible in early photographs of the village). *Estes Park Trail*, 25 (April 27, 1946): 47.

26. Letter Al Birch to Albert C. Edwards, dated July 31, 1969. Quoted in *Estes Park Trail Gazette*, 18 (December 18, 1987): 2. Birch's recollections about the circumstances of the fire do not quite square with the note that appeared in the July 3, 1908, issue of the *Longmont Ledger*: "Mr. Birch, whose house was burned down last winter after he had sold it, has a judgment against the buyer and received his place back and $7,000." *Longmont Ledger*, 29 (July 3, 1908): 8; *Mountaineer* (June 25, 1908): 1.

27. Unsigned manuscript, EPM.

28. *Mountaineer* (June 11, 1908): 1.

29. *Mountaineer* (June 4, 1908): 1.

30. Ibid. (June 11, 1908): 3; *Loveland Herald*, 2 (May 1, 1908): 1.

31. *Loveland Herald*, 2 (August 13, 1908): 8. Johnson's Laundry may have been open during the 1907 season. The young woman quoted above notes that a new laundry was already under construction in May 1907, and the June 11, 1908 issue of the *Mountaineer* quotes Julian Johnson as saying "We did a good business last year and this year will do even better." *Mountaineer* (June 11, 1908): 1.

32. *Longmont Ledger*, 29 (May 8, 1908): 8.

33. The Presbyterian Church of Estes Park was organized on December 31, 1907. Its first minister was John Knox Hall, pastor-at-large for the Boulder Presbytery.

34. *Loveland Reporter*, 29 (May 14, 1908): 1. The Manford House was built on the original site of the house that John Cleave built in 1888. During 1905 and 1906 the Cleave property was occupied by the Bond family. When John J. Manford acquired the property as the site for his hotel in 1907, reportedly paying $3,000, the Cleave house was moved to the rear of the lot where over the next two decades it was occupied by various people and provided quarters for hotel help. It was removed in 1947.

35. *Fort Collins Evening Courier*, 7 (June 8, 1908): 3.

36. *Loveland Register*, 11 (May 31, 1905): 6.

37. As early as spring of 1909 it was reported that Bond had taken an option "on a number of elk he is going to try to get parties interested in and have them kept in a private preserve here in the park." *Loveland Register*, 15 (April 15, 1909): 6.

38. *Mountaineer* (June 4, 1908): 1.

39. *Loveland Reporter*, 27 (December 6, 1906): 2; *Longmont Ledger*, 29 (October 25, 1907): 2. Lester's figure of 500 no doubt includes residents of the valley as well as the village and workers who stayed through the winter because of the Stanley Hotel project. *Longmont Ledger*, 29 (February 28, 1908): 8. The 1910 census figures show 396 residents.

40. *Longmont Ledger*, 29 (June 19, 1908): 8.

41. Ibid., 29 (June 5, 1908): 8.

42. *Mountaineer* (August 27, 1908): 8; ibid. (August 20, 1908): 6.

43. *Estes Park Trail*, 1 (September 14, 1912): 12. It should be noted that there are two separate newspapers with the title *Estes Park Trail*. The first was published during the summers of 1912, 1913, and 1914. When the first year-round newspaper began to publish in 1921, it also took the name *Estes Park Trail*.

44. David M. Steele, *Going Abroad Overland: Studies of Places and People in the Far West* (New York: G. P. Putnam's Sons, 1917), 130–131. The comment about "traffic regulations" and "bonded indebtedness" was in error; in 1916 Estes Park had yet to be incorporated.

45. Estes Park School District, District 30, dates from November 19, 1883, when local residents petitioned the Larimer County Superintendent of Schools, indicating that there were some fifteen children of school age needing formal education. During its first three years as a district, school was held in a three-room cottage at Elkhorn Lodge. In 1886 a new frame schoolhouse was built near the Corners—the site later occupied by the Estes Park Bank. This building, which also served for a number of years as church and meeting hall, was later moved and converted into a studio by photographer Fred Clatworthy. Between 1891 and 1906 school was conducted at different locations. When the town was platted in 1905, it seemed logical to erect a permanent building in a central location, and in 1907 the corner of Park Lane and MacGregor was chosen. That log schoolhouse, one large room and a library to which another room was added in 1910, was replaced in 1916 by the brick building in the photograph. See Louise Reed Hayden's "The Itinerant School," *Little Nature Studies* (Estes Park: Estes Park Woman's Club, n.d.), 19–25.

46. The church was named St. Walter's in memory of Walter Walsh, the son of the Walsh family from Davenport, Iowa, who sometime after 1910 began to invite priests to share their home and hosted the first temporary chapel. A rectory behind the chapel was added in 1932.

47. *Longmont Call*, 17 (July 23, 1915): 10.

48. See, for example, *Trail Talk* (July 20, 1920): n.p.

49. By 1921, the stone and wood post office building, built by Carl Piltz and designed by Henry Rogers, once regarded as "very spacious," was too small to meet community needs. Overcrowding was relieved through a rear addition, completed in the fall of 1924, which enlarged the lobby and added a workroom and fireproof vault.

50. Ralph Macdonald bought Johnson's laundry in 1914 and later opened a second facility on Moraine, south of what was then the telephone office.

51. Shoemaker, "The Story of the Estes–Rocky Mountain National Park Region," 78.

52. J. L. Jackson began construction of the Park Theatre in 1913, and it was completed by C. H. Bond the following year. Bond, in turn, soon sold the building to Fred Jackson. In 1922 Ralph Gwynn became owner. Gwynn added the distinctive tower in 1926 and neon lights in 1938. On June 14, 1984, when the building was added to the National Registry of Historic Places, it was said to be the oldest motion picture theater west of the Mississippi still operating.

53. *Loveland Reporter*, 30 (January 27, 1910): 3.

54. *Loveland Herald*, 3 (September 23, 1909): 7.

55. Ibid.

56. Homer James earned a medical degree but did not formally practice in Estes Park.

57. *Loveland Herald*, 5 (January 19, 1911): 1.

58. *Fort Collins Morning Express*, 42 (September 23, 1915): 1.

59. *Loveland Daily Herald*, 6 (September 22, 1915): 1.

60. Ibid., 6 (September 24, 1915): 2.

61. *Loveland Reporter*, 36 (September 24, 1915): 1.

62. Ibid.

63. Ibid., 2.

64. *Fort Collins Express*, 43 (April 4, 1917): 8.

65. MBTEP, June 25, 1917, 8.

66. Ibid., 13.

67. Ibid.

68. *Loveland Daily Herald*, 9 (January 5, 1918): 1.

69. MBTEP, February 25, 1918, 19. At their April meeting the trustees asked Stanley to "contribute" $1,000 toward the construction of the Imhoff sewerage tank—presumably because his hotel would be among its heaviest users and because it was being installed on his property. MBTEP, April 22, 1918, 27.

70. Ibid., 20. To save money the bonds were sold directly by the town.

71. Ibid., 26.

CHAPTER 3

1. Enos Mills, *The Story of Estes Park* (Longs Peak, CO, 1914), 91–93. Although Stanley's first trip went unreported, subsequent ones did not. "Mr. Stanley rode down from the park in his little machine, 120 minutes from postoffice to postoffice," the *Lyons Recorder* noted in June 1911, "and coasted 5 miles of the way." *Lyons Recorder*, 12 (June 29, 1911): 1.

2. A full account F. O. Stanley and his relationship to Estes Park can be found in my book *Mr. Stanley of Estes Park* (Kingfield, ME: The Stanley Museum, 2000) (hereafter referred to as MSEP).

3. At his death in 1940, F. O. Stanley's assets consisted of little more than his homes in Estes Park and Newton, Massachusetts, and their contents. His Colorado

assets were valued at slightly more than $53,000.

4. J. B. Hall, letter to F. O. Stanley, January 17, 1905, SHF.

5. *Lyons Recorder*, 7 (March 7, 1907): 1.

6. *Longmont Ledger*, 28 (March 22, 1907): 1.

7. *Longmont Call*, 9 (March 23, 1907): 1.

8. *Longmont Ledger*, 28 (August 23, 1907): 1.

9. *Lyons Recorder*, 7 (April 18, 1907): 1.

10. *Longmont Ledger*, 28 (August 23, 1907): 1.

11. Ibid., 28 (June 14, 1907): 1; *Lyons Recorder*, 7 (April 4, 1907): 1.

12. *Longmont Ledger*, 28 (August 23, 1907): 1.

13. *Loveland Reporter*, 8 (June 27, 1907): 2.

14. *Longmont Call*, 9 (August 24, 1907): 1.

15. *Longmont Ledger*, 28 (January 25, 1907): 5.

16. *Longmont Ledger*, 30 (December 11, 1908): 8.

17. In July 1908, Rogers and a concrete worker named Charley Spencer got into some kind of disagreement that ended with Spencer leaving for Denver, "taking his two helpers with him." Ibid., 29 (July 17, 1908): 8.

18. Donald L. Griffith, "Homestead Trails and Tales," unpublished typescript, Estes Park Public Library, Colorado Collection (hereafter referred to as EPPLCC), 35–39.

19. The figure $150,000 was reported in the *Longmont Call* (10 [September 28, 1907]: 1), $1,000,000 in the *Loveland Herald* (3 [March 18, 1909]: 1). A figure of $500,000 was reported by both the *Rocky Mountain News* (50 [June 23, 1909]: 7) and the *Longmont Ledger* (37 [June 30, 1911]: 1). The variation suggests guesswork. To complicate the matter, the *Denver Post* reported the cost to be $250,000 [(June 24, 1909): 6], as did both the *Greeley Tribune* (38 [October 7, 1908]: 3) and the *Loveland Reporter* (29 [October 15, 1908]: 1). F. O. Stanley was hardly cooperative: "No one ever counts the cost, when they are getting what they want." *Denver Republican*, 31 (June 20, 1909): 23. Even half a million dollars may be low. On March 11, 1909, the *Loveland Herald* estimated that the Stanley's furniture alone would cost $200,000. *Loveland Herald*, 3 (March 11, 1909): 1.

20. *Loveland Reporter*, 29 (July 16, 1908): 1.

21. *Longmont Ledger*, 29 (August 14, 1908): 8.

22. *Mountaineer* (August 13, 1908): 6. See also *Loveland Reporter*, 29 (October 15, 1908): 1; *Loveland Reporter*, 29 (August 27, 1906): 1.

23. *Mountaineer* (August 27, 1908): 1.

24. *Loveland Reporter*, 29 (October 15, 1908): 1.

25. Quoted in, "A Week in Estes Park, Colorado," *Hotel Monthly*, 18 (July 1910): 37. The buckskin is in the collections of the Estes Park Museum.

26. The original hotel elevators operated by means of water pressure.

27. *Boulder Daily Camera*, 19 (June 24, 1909): 2.

28. *Denver Post* (June 24, 1909): 6.

29. The syndicate of purchasers, which on March 27, 1926, incorporated itself as the Stanley Corporation, was headed by Fred Bond, youngest son of C. H. Bond, not yet thirty years of age. They immediately embarked on a series of improvements

that included a significant expansion of electrical service and the refurbishing and repainting of the hotel.

The price was $800,000 and to consummate the sale Stanley was given three mortgages, on which the payments were soon in arrears. On September 24, 1929, Stanley won a judgment of $511,394.39 and costs against Bond and reclaimed the hotel. Thirteen months later, in October 1930, he sold the Stanley to Roe Emery, who immediately merged it with the Estes Park Chalets, which he also now owned, into a new subsidiary, the Estes Park Hotel Company. For the complex story of Stanley's dealings with Bond and the Stanley Corporation, see MSEP, 232–249.

30. From a 1919 hotel brochure reproduced in the *Stanley Museum Quarterly*, 18 (December 1999): 17–19.

31. *Denver Post* (August 8, 1919): 1.

32. Ibid. (July 16, 1920): 5; ibid. (August 20, 1920): 3; *Fort Collins Courier*, 48 (August 17, 1920): 1.

33. Roger W. Toll, letter to Pieter Hondius, December 7, 1928, EPM. The source of the account was Hondius. Toll attached to his letter a brief memorandum, dated November 28, 1928, which asks for Hondius's approval and signature.

34. *Loveland Herald*, 2 (March 31, 1908): 1.

35. Floyd Clymer, *Floyd Clymer's Steam Motor Scrapbook* (Los Angeles: Clymer Motors, 1945), 14.

36. *Longmont Ledger*, 29 (March 13, 1908): 1.

37. *Loveland Reporter*, 29 (December 3, 1908): 2. The Osborns' permanent garage in Estes Park was finally completed in 1909 on lots purchased from the Estes Park Town Company for $1,000 in fall 1908. *Loveland Reporter*, 29 (November 12, 1908): 6.

38. *Longmont Call*, 17 (July 23, 1915): 1.

39. F. O. Stanley, letter to William E. Sweet, October 1, 1928, Enos Mills Cabin Collection, MSEP, 123.

40. Golf was played at the Elkhorn Lodge as early as summer 1899 (*Longmont Ledger*, 20 [August 11, 1899]: 2), and Stanley had a nine-hole course laid out at the hotel shortly after its opening, open for play all year. By 1916 the Stanley course could no longer meet demand, and Stanley joined with two of his fellow summer residents, Frank L. Woodward and Thomas B. Stearns, to purchase 120 acres from Carl Sanborn for $20,000 to lay out a new eighteen-hole course. The tract selected encompassed most of the nine-hole course, which the Earl of Dunraven had established shortly after opening his hotel in 1877. Purchase completed, Stanley and the others turned the responsibility over to Joe Mills, Homer James, and Albert Hayden, who organized the Estes Park Country Club and sold $15,000 worth of stock to finance the building of an eighteen-hole, 6,000-yard, par 73 course and a large log clubhouse with a stone fireplace. *Loveland Daily Herald*, 8 (November 7, 1917): 1. The new course opened for play on July 4, 1918. The golf course remained a private corporation until 1944, when it was leased (and later then sold) to the town of Estes Park. Until the early 1950s, the greens were sand and the fairways lacked grass.

41. *Mountaineer* (June 4, 1908): 1. Sherman and his wife Jennie purchased four lots for $400. Ground was broken on June 6—the Shermans' thirteenth wedding

anniversary. The cornerstone was laid on June 12, inside of which the family deposited a small tin box containing mementos, including a photograph of Estes Park. The Sherman house survived until the 1930s, when it was torn down to make way for a new telephone company building. The box and its contents were recovered and are now property of the WestStar Bank in Estes Park (the successor of the Estes Park Bank). *Longmont Ledger,* 29 (May 29, 1908): 8; *Longmont Ledger,* 29 (June 19, 1908): 8; *Mountaineer* (June 11, 1908): *Mountaineer* (June 18, 1908): 8.

42. Charles F. Hix, "History of the Estes Park Bank," undated typescript, EPPLCC, 2–3.

43. Sherman purchased twenty shares on June 2, 1908, and an additional twenty-one shares between July 6, 1908, and May 13, 1910, at a total cost of $2,100. Sherman sold all these shares in 1911 for $4,100, recouping his entire investment. The Estes Park Bank Stock Book is the property of the WestStar Bank in Estes Park.

44. *Loveland Reporter,* 28 (February 27, 1908): 1; *Longmont Ledger,* 29 (February 28, 1908): 1. Minutes of the third meeting of the Board of Directors, March 9, 1908, EPM, 11.

45. *Mountaineer* (June 18, 1908): 8.

46. Ibid. (August 13, 1908): 8.

47. Lewis (?–1957) arrived in Estes Park in 1912, where he became the cashier of the Estes Park Bank. By 1922 he was president and a year later became the town mayor.

48. *Loveland Reporter,* 29 (July 16, 1908): 1.

49. Incorporation Records, State of Colorado, Denver, Colorado (hereafter IRSC), Book 131, p. 108.

50. *Loveland Reporter,* 29 (November 12, 1908): 6.

51. *Loveland Reporter,* 29 (September 24, 1908): 1. The new waterline from the Black Canyon Creek paralleled the existing two-inch line installed by Stanley in 1904.

52. The reason for the sale had little to do with Stanley's wishes. The town fathers had stepped into the breach to prevent "outside parties from securing a controlling interest" and raising water fees exorbitantly. The "outsider" was a newcomer named Charles Salit, the thirty-two-year-old president of Denver's Ice & Storage Company. Having purchased the Woodward property in Devils Gulch, Salit decided to establish a business interest by purchasing the water company. What apparently was disturbing was Salit's approach: he hired a Denver agent to send out a letter offering to buy all the outstanding shares for $100 each. Rather than let Salit have his way, the local men, with backing from a Denver bank, purchased the company themselves. Less than a month later the four sold the water company to the Town of Estes Park for $73,260, a purchase financed by the issuance of $75,000 in bonds. *Longmont Daily Call,* 24 (December 18, 1928): 1; ibid., 24 (June 12, 1928): 1; ibid., 24 (December 24, 1928): 1; *Estes Park Trail,* 8 (April 5, 1929): 1; MBTEP, December 29, 1928, 307; ibid., February 11, 1929, 308–309.

53. That Estes Park would have electricity was taken for granted. "Most of the hotels are wired for electric lights," the *Mountaineer* noted in June 1908, "which

goes to show that the builders believed lights would be here before long." *Mountaineer* (June 25, 1908): 1.

54. IRSC, Book 131, p. 117.

55. The incorporation papers made the larger purposes of the company clear: to acquire and hold "the necessary property to carry on the business of generating and distributing electricity for light, heat and power purposes and to carry on said business with the public." IRSC, Book 131, p. 117. The *Loveland Reporter* indicated as early as October 1908 that Stanley's new plant "will supply every building in Estes Park with light." *Loveland Reporter*, 29 (October 15, 1908): 1.

56. *Loveland Herald*, 2 (October 23, 1908): 1.

57. *Loveland Reporter*, 29 (October 15, 1908): 1.

58. "General Survey of The Stanley Power Company of Estes Park, Colorado" (n.p., March 23, 1927), courtesy Frank Hix.

59. *Loveland Reporter*, 30 (June 10, 1909): 8.

60. *Loveland Herald*, 3 (June 24, 1909): 1. Electricity at the Elkhorn Lodge was turned on June 30, and the next day the *Loveland Herald* predicted that "In a few days the city will be lighted with street arc lamps." Ibid., 3 (July 1, 1909): 2.

61. John Willy, "A Week in Estes Park, Colorado," *Hotel Monthly*, 18 (July 1910): 37.

62. John Willy, "Hotel Stanley of Estes Park, Colorado," Ibid., 18 (August 1910): 39, 41, 42.

63. *Electrical World*, 56 (December 1910): 437–438.

64. *Estes Park Trail*, 12 (April 7, 1933): 20, 35.

65. *Loveland Reporter*, 30 (January 27, 1910): 3.

66. *Estes Park Trail*, 4 (April 18, 1924): 1.

67. *Loveland Reporter*, 42 (September 16, 1921): 2.

68. *Estes Park Trail*, 1 (June 10, 1921): 5.

69. *Estes Park Trail*, 1 (November 11, 1921): 4.

70. At the time that the Public Service Company of Colorado bought the Stanley plant it considered tying it in with its Valmont plant near Boulder to link Estes Park with other PSC-served cities in northern Colorado. In deciding to invest in improvements at the Estes Park plant PSC engineers concluded "the flow of Fall River to be ample with recent and contemplated improvements to provide current for the community for many years to come and . . . for about half the cost of a tie-in to the valley system." *Longmont Daily Call*, 25 (March 19, 1930): 1. In fall 1928 and spring 1929, the company rebuilt the transmission system in order to provide the village with steady voltage.

71. *Estes Park Trail*, 11 (November 6, 1931): 1; ibid., 11 (November 20, 1931): 1.

72. *Longmont Times Call*, 60 (February 16, 1933): 5. The lessons of that winter could not be overlooked and in October 1933 plans were developed to add a second diesel unit. Because of a recovering winter water supply and the Depression, the 300-horsepower engine and its generator were not acquired and placed in service until 1938. *Estes Park Trail*, 12 (April 7, 1933): 35.

73. *Estes Park Trail*, 13 (November 3, 1933): 1.

74. Ibid., 16 (January 29, 1937): 1.

75. Interview with C. Byron Hall, cited in Shoemaker, "The Story of the Estes–Rocky Mountain National Park Region," 49–50.

76. *Estes Park Trail,* 1 (September 7, 1912): 1.

77. Ibid., 1 (September 14, 1912): 12.

78. F. O. Stanley to Dorothy F. Schwartz, letter of June 9, 1913, SHF.

79. *Estes Park Trail,* 2 (June 21, 1913): 10.

80. *Lyons Recorder,* 17 (November 16, 1916): 1.

81. *Boulder Daily Camera,* 26 (December 26, 1916): 1.

82. *Denver Post* (December 3, 1916): Want Ad Section, 13.

83. *Fort Collins Morning Express,* 43 (September 10, 1916): 7.

84. Ibid., 43 (November 11, 1916): 1; *Lyons Recorder,* 17 (November 16, 1916): 1.

85. L. Claude Way to Robert. B. Marshall, letter of October 16, 1916. Copies of this document as well as the others that relate to the 1917 administration building project may be found in the Colorado Collection Pamphlet File at the Estes Park Public Library. See also MSEP, 206–211.

86. J. Edward Macdonald, Pieter Hondius, and Samuel Service to Robert B. Marshall, letter of October 26, 1916, EPPLCC.

87. L. Claude Way to Robert Marshall, letter of October 30, 1916, EPPLCC.

88. Robert Cahn, *The Birth of the National Park Service: The Founding Years, 1913–1933,* Horace M. Albright as Told to Robert Cahn (Salt Lake City, UT: Howe Brothers, 1985), 48–49.

89. L. Claude Way to Robert B. Marshall, letter of November 30, 1916, EPPLCC.

90. T. Robert Wieger, undated handwritten letter, EPPLCC.

91. T. Robert Wieger, four-page undated typescript, "Administration Building and Residence in the Rocky Mountain National Park for the Department of the Interior Describing the Drawings Submitted by T. Robert Wieger, Architect, Denver, Colorado," EPPLCC.

92. Undated one-page typescript, "Schedule of Costs Main Building–Stable and Garage," EPPLCC.

93. Robert B. Marshall to L. Claude Way, letter of December 4, 1916, EPPLCC.

94. L. Claude Way to F. O. Stanley, letter of December 11, 1916, EPPLCC.

95. *Fort Collins Express,* 43 (January 25, 1917): 1.

96. *Estes Park Trail,* 5 (September 18, 1925): 4; ibid., 5 (October 16, 1925): 1, 3; Larimer County Registry of Deeds, Fort Collins, Book 514, p. 251.

97. Larimer County Registry of Deeds, Fort Collins, Book 680, p. 305.

98. The original headquarters building remained on Elkhorn Avenue until late 1924 or early 1925 when it was moved to a location on Riverside to make way for Jim Boyd's new block of stores. In 1987 the Estes Park Museum began a fund-raising campaign to relocate the building to the museum grounds and restore it to its original 1915 appearance. The building was rededicated on June 2, 1990, in connection with RMNP's seventy-fifth anniversary.

99. *Loveland Reporter,* 30 (October 7, 1909): 6.

CHAPTER 4

1. *Estes Park Trail Gazette,* 13 (April 20, 1983): 5.

2. Perhaps the best example was the family of Sam and Sadie Service, which became related through marriage to the Macdonalds, Tallants, Scotts, and Stiths.

3. *Fort Collins Weekly Courier,* 25 (February 11, 1903): 6.

4. *Loveland Register,* 14 (May 17, 1908): 8.

5. Enos Mills, *The Story of Estes Park, Grand Lake and Rocky Mountain National Park* (Longs Peak, CO, 1917), 93. First published in 1905 as the previously cited *The Story of Estes Park,* Mills's small volume grew by accretion over the years.

6. Ibid., 97; Frank Bond, recollections; *Estes Park Trail Gazette,* 7 (September 28, 1977): 7. See also Eleanor E. Hondius, *Memoirs of Eleanor E. Hondius of Elkhorn Lodge* (Boulder, CO: Pruett Press, 1964), 18.

7. *Rocky Mountain News,* 22 (August 23, 1881): 2.

8. William H. McCreery, letter to the *Estes Park Trail,* 3 (November 7, 1923): 3.

9. *Fort Collins Express,* 27 (June 24, 1899): 6.

10. Mills, *The Story of Estes Park,* 93.

11. "The Women's Association of the Community Church of the Rockies: The Early Years," undated typescript, EPPLCC. The association's annual bazaar was sufficiently successful to pose a threat to the one put on by the Woman's Club. In early 1912, to resolve the dilemma the Woman's Club offered the church ladies $300 if they would refrain from fund-raising during the tourist season that year and the next. After 1914 this agreement was replaced with a simple understanding that the Presbyterian women would sell their items at the Women's Club Bazaar in return for a percentage of the profits.

12. *Longmont Ledger,* 16 (June 21, 1895): 2.

13. Ibid., 18 (July 16, 1897): 3.

14. This date is provided by the "Statements and Stipulations of the Estes Park Protective and Improvement Association," adopted September 22, 1906, copy EPM.

15. *Estes Park Trail,* 1 (September 7, 1912): 2–3.

16. Crocker (1846–1932) took an active part in community affairs. His money came from Denver where he established the Crocker Cracker Company (later the National Biscuit Company), and for a time was a business associate of the legendary David Moffat. In 1895 he served as president of the Denver Chamber of Commerce. By summer 1897 Crocker was leasing (and subsequently purchased) the ranch at the base of Mount Olympus originally homesteaded by hunter Israel Rowe and acquired in 1888 by John R. Stuyvesant of New York, a descendant of the famous Dutch governor.

17. "Statements and Stipulations of the Estes Park Protective and Improvement Association," adopted September 22, 1906, copy EPM.

18. Pieter Hondius, *Estes Park Trail,* 1 (August 24, 1912): 2–4; ibid., 3 (August 1, 1914): 3.

19. *Estes Park Trail,* 1 (August 24, 1912): 5.

20. Ibid., 1 (July 6, 1912): 2.

21. J. C. Garrett writing in the *Longmont Call* on September 28, 1907, notes that "Such men as Stanley, Hendrie, Hondius, Crocker and others have given liberally of their time and means." *Longmont Call*, 10 (September 28, 1907): 1; Laurence Thomson, "An Interview with Laurence Thomson," April 30, 1972, EPPLCC, 9.

22. Minutes, Estes Park Protective and Improvement Association, Town of Estes Park (hereafter referred to as MEPPIA), 96–97.

23. *Longmont Ledger*, 28 (May 17, 1907): 4.

24. *Estes Park Trail*, 1 (August 24, 1912): 2.

25. *Longmont Ledger*, 28 (May 31, 1907): 8.

26. Ibid., 28 (July 5, 1907): 1. The use of spring water was not accidental. Unlike river water, its temperature did not substantially vary during the year and it was generally cleaner.

27. Ibid., 29 (October 25, 1907): 4.

28. *Longmont Call*, 10 (September 28. 1907): 1.

29. *Estes Park Trail*, 1 (August 24, 1912): 2.

30. Ibid., 8 (November 16, 1928): 1.

31. See, for example, the *Loveland Reporter*, 29 (August 4, 1908): 1. See also *Trail Talk*, 1 (July 16, 1920): 1–2.

32. *Loveland Reporter*, 36 (October 8, 1915): 4; *Rocky Mountain News*, 56 (October 24, 1915): 23.

33. *Fort Collins Courier*, 48 (August 20, 1920): 1.

34. *Estes Park Trail*, 7 (October 27, 1927): 4.

35. Ibid., 1 (October 14, 1921): 1.

36. Superintendent's Monthly Report, Rocky Mountain National Park (hereafter referred to as SMR), June 1922, 3.

37. *Estes Park Trail*, 7 (October 28, 1927): 4. See also *Estes Park Trail*, 8 (November 16, 1928): 1; ibid., 8 (December 14, 1928): 8; *Longmont Daily Times*, 34 (November 20, 1928): 3; *Longmont Daily Call*, 25 (March 14, 1929): 3.

38. *Estes Park Trail*, 9 (December 4, 1928): 8.

39. *Loveland Register*, 15 (April 17, 1909): 6.

40. Abner Sprague, writing at the time of Hondius's death, notes that the effort to restock the park with elk "was accomplished mainly through his efforts." *Estes Park Trail*, 13 (March 16, 1934): 2.

41. Neal G. Guse Jr., "Comprehensive Report: Administrative History of an Elk Herd," M.S. Thesis, Colorado State University, Fort Collins, 1966, 14. See also *Longmont Ledger*, 34 (March 14, 1913): 4; ibid., 34 (May 16, 1913): 4.

42. *Estes Park Trail*, 2 (June 21, 1913): 4.

43. Guse, "Administrative History of an Elk Herd," 15.

44. F. O. Stanley, letter to Pieter Hondius, March 20, 1913, EPM.

45. Herbert N. Wheeler, "Memoirs of Herbert N. Wheeler," typescript copy, Boulder Public Library, 55.

46. See *Loveland Reporter*, 29 (October 15, 1908): 1; *Greeley Tribune*, 38 (October 7, 1908): 3.

47. *Longmont Call*, 11 (June 19, 1909): 1.

48. MEPPIA, 50–51.

49. *Estes Park Trail*, 1 (August 24, 1912): 3. This followed a reimbursement of $200 that the EPPIA voted Mills at its meeting of February 24, 1911. MEPPIA, 53.

50. *Estes Park Trail*, 2 (September 6, 1913): 10.

51. Ibid., 1 (September 7, 1912): 9.

52. *Denver Times*, 45 (June 26, 1915): 1–2.

53. Mary Belle King Sherman, "Unique Among 1,500 Clubs," 2, 3. A copy of this unpublished typescript, dated by hand June 1914, is found in EPPLCC. Mrs. Sherman, who for a number of years was an Estes Park resident, became heavily involved with wilderness preservation efforts of General Federation of Women's Clubs, of which she became president in 1924. The surviving minutes of the EPPIA are less clear on the role played by women than the memories of individual participants. It is most directly acknowledged in the minutes of the meeting of September 10, 1910, where a "request was made . . . that the Secretary of the Estes Park Protective and Improvement Assoc. notify all the ladies of the Park that they are all members and will be expected to participate in the future work of the Association." MEPPIA, 53.

54. Sherman, "Unique Among 1,500 Clubs," 4; Hondius, *Memoirs*, 40. See also MSEP, 203.

55. *Estes Park Trail*, 3 (August 1, 1914): 24; ibid., 3 (August 15, 1914): 16.

56. *Mountaineer* (August 13, 1908): 1.

57. Sherman, "Unique Among 1,500 Clubs," 4.

58. Hondius, *Memoirs*, 40. C. H. Bond's minutes of the EPPIA for August 17, 1912, contain no hint of controversy. They indicate that the women reported they had collected $152.01 "for the use of roads & trails," but simply note that a motion was made to defer their report until after the annual meeting of the auxiliary.

59. In the concluding paragraph of his August 1912 "statement" reciting the accomplishments of the EPPIA, Pieter Hondius had dutifully applauded the "public spirit" and "influence" of the ladies of Estes Park. "To their ability to raise the necessary money," Hondius wrote, "has been due in great part the good that this association has accomplished."

60. Helen McCracken, "Early History of the Estes Park Woman's Club, 1912–1919," unpublished typescript, copy EPPLCC, 2.

61. *Estes Park Trail*, 2 (August 18, 1922): 1, 13.

62. J. Edward Macdonald, *Estes Park Trail*, 1 (September 7, 1912): 6.

63. Ibid., 7.

64. Ibid., 1.

65. Ibid., 1 (July 6, 1912): 10.

66. Ibid., 3 (July 11, 1914): 18.

67. Ibid., 9.

68. *Estes Park Trail*, 5 (June 5, 1925): 10.

69. MBTEP, April 28, 1920, 68.

70. Glen H. Preston, edited six-page typescript dated by hand April 19, 1943, courtesy, Frank Hix.

71. *Estes Park Trail*, 15 (March 20, 1936): 1.

72. Ibid., 13 (February 2, 1934): 2.

73. *Rocky Mountain News,* 59 (June 30, 1918): 9.

74. *Lyons Recorder,* 18 (June 22, 1918): 1.

75. *Rocky Mountain News,* 59 (June 30, 1918): 9.

76. *Longmont Ledger,* 39 (August 2, 1918): 1.

77. *Rocky Mountain News,* 59 (June 30, 1918): 9.

78. See, for example, *Loveland Daily Herald,* 9 (March 12, 1918): 1; *Loveland Reporter,* 38 (July 3, 1918): 3, 4; *Fort Collins Express Review,* 45 (September 18, 1918): 2; *Loveland Reporter,* 39 (December 4, 1918): 3.

79. *Loveland Daily Herald,* 9 (June 28, 1918): 1.

80. Laurence Thomson, "An Interview with Laurence Thomson," 4, 6.

81. *Loveland Reporter,* 38 (June 3, 1918): 3.

82. Frank and George Hix Collection.

83. *Denver Post* (July 6, 1919): Section 2, p. 4.

84. *Lyons Recorder,* 17 (March 30, 1918): 1.

85. *Fort Collins Express,* 44 (April 10, 1918): 4; see also Helen McCracken, "Early History of the Estes Park Woman's Club," 10.

86. *Lyons Recorder,* 17 (March 30, 1918): 1.

87. *Longmont Ledger,* 39 (June 28, 1918): 1.

88. *Rocky Mountain News,* 59 (June 30, 1918): 9.

89. *Estes Park Trail,* 3 (May 25, 1923): 10.

90. *Lyons Recorder,* 17 (April 20, 1918): 4.

91. *Denver Post* (July 6, 1919): Section 2, p. 4.

92. *Loveland Daily Herald,* 10 (June 27, 1919): 1; ibid. (July 5, 1919): 1; ibid. (July 7, 1919): 1.

CHAPTER 5

1. When early in 1914 the Department of the Interior set up an office to inspect the nation's parks and make plans for their improvement, its head, Mark Daniels, was given the title "General Supervisor." One of his first acts was to change the title of the superintendents reporting to him to "Supervisor." This annoyed many of the existing superintendents because it seemed to put them on a par with those in charge of the national forests who were also called "Supervisors." The title was soon changed back to "Superintendent."

2. *Rocky Mountain News,* 57 (July 15, 1916): 6; Lloyd Musselman, *Rocky Mountain National Park, Administrative History: 1915–1965* (Washington, D.C.: National Park Service, 1971), 78. The sum of $3,000 was to carry the park through the end of the 1915 fiscal year. Musselman's book and Curt W. Buchholtz's *Rocky Mountain National Park: A History* (Boulder: Colorado Associated University Press, 1983) are the two best current sources of information on the history of Rocky Mountain National Park. Invaluable to an understanding of the evolution of the park's road and trail system is William C. Ramaley's "Trails and Trailbuilders of the Rocky Mountain National Park," undated typescript, National Park Service, RMNP, Estes Park, Colorado. This unfinished manuscript exists in several copies and its unclear pagination makes accurate citation impossible. For an overview of the

history of the U.S. park system and the National Park Service see John Ise, *Our National Park Policy: A Critical History* (Baltimore: Johns Hopkins University Press, 1961), and Richard West Sellars, *Preserving Nature in National Parks: A History* (New Haven: Yale University Press, 1997). For the development of landscape design and road and trail construction within the park system see Linda Flint McClelland, *Building the National Parks: Historic Landscape and Design* (Baltimore: Johns Hopkins University Press, 1998), and Ethan Carr, *Wilderness by Design: Landscape Architecture and the National Park Service* (Lincoln: University of Nebraska Press, 1998).

Trowbridge's appointment was controversial. As soon as the park bill was signed, the *Denver Post* began to "boom" Enos Mills for superintendent. "So far as is known," the *Loveland Daily Herald* reported on April 9, 1915, "Mr. Mills has made no application for the place but it is thought that he could be prevailed upon to accept it in that it would not greatly interfere with his other duties." When the position was created, Richard E. McCracken of Denver and Estes Park was recommended by the Department of the Interior for the position but "without consulting the Democratic senators." "A big howl went up," the *Loveland Reporter* noted, "and the Interior Department placed Trowbridge on the job. McCracken is now in the park, and it is believed Trowbridge was merely named temporarily until the ill-feeling dies down, when McCracken will probably get the permanent position." The McCracken referred to was the father of Richard T. "Dixie" McCracken, the park's first ranger (see below). *Loveland Daily Herald*, 6 (April 9, 1915): 1; *Loveland Reporter*, 36 (July 2, 1915): 1.

3. Cahn, *Birth of the National Park Service*, 64–65.

4. U.S. Congress, House of Representatives, Rocky Mountain National Park, Colorado, S. Rept. 1275 to Accompany S. 6300, 63D Cong., 3d session, 1915, 231.

5. *Longmont Ledger*, 36 (March 26, 1915): 1.

6. Superintendent's Annual Report, Rocky Mountain National Park (hereafter referred to as SAR), 1915, 4–6.

7. Louisa Ward Arps and Elinor Eppich Kingery, *High Country Names: Rocky Mountain National Park* (Estes Park, CO: Rocky Mountain Nature Association, 1977), 130–131. See also Richard H. Quin, Historic American Buildings Survey, Fall River Road, Rocky Mountain National Park, HAER No. Co-73, 1993. Copy, Rocky Mountain National Park Library (hereafter referred to as RMNPL).

8. The commissioners had acted under a new state law allowing half the resident owners to petition for a road through a forest reserve. *Fort Collins Farmer*, 2 (August 5, 1913): 1; ibid., 2 (July 22, 1913): 3. Earlier that summer the commissioners, accompanied by county surveyor James M. Edwards, had taken a trip over the proposed road. The *Estes Park Trail* reported on July 19 that "the consensus of opinion between the commissioners, backed up by the report of the engineer, is that the road is entirely feasible." *Estes Park Trail*, 2 (July 19, 1913): 5.

9. The plaintiffs argued that the resources of the Poudre Valley greatly exceeded the area tributary to Fall River in terms of available timber and land for grazing cattle and provided a significant source of income for county residents. *Fort Collins Farmer*, 2 (July 22, 1913): 3.

10. The 1907–1909 Biennial Report to the Governor, quoted in Thomas J. Noel, "Paving the Way to Colorado: The Evolution of Auto Tourism in Denver," *Journal of the West*, 26 (July 1987): 44.

11. *Fort Collins Farmer*, 2 (September 9, 1913): 1; ibid., 2 (September 16, 1913): 4.

12. Ibid., 2 (December 23, 1913): 1. Tynan's convicts spent the 1913–1914 winter with its unprecedented snowstorm in their Endovalley cabins.

13. Ibid., 2 (December 30, 1913): 6.

14. Ibid., 2 (February 10, 1914): 3.

15. Ibid., 2 (March 24, 1914): 7.

16. *Estes Park Trail*, 3 (July 25, 1914): 3.

17. *Fort Collins Farmer*, 2 (June 30, 1914): 4.

18. SAR, 1915, 3–4.

19. Ibid., 4.

20. Ibid., 33.

21. McClelland, *Building the National Parks*, 130. These longer trails included the two trails from Grand Lake, one 18.5 miles over Flattop Mountain, the other 12.5 miles by way of Milner Pass, which joined the county road 12.5 miles north of Grand Lake; the 6-mile Longs Peak Trail to the Boulder Field, which entered the park a mile above Longs Peak Inn; the 6-mile trail from Horseshoe Park to Lawn Lake; the 15-mile Tomb Stone Ridge Trail from Moraine Park through Windy Gulch to the Poudre Lake; the 6-, 7-, and 9-mile trails in Wild Basin to Sand Beach Lake, to Ouzel Falls and Ouzel Lake, and to Thunder Lake; the 15-mile Poudre River Trail from Pingree Park to the South Fork of the Poudre and then up the river to its source at the Poudre Lakes; and the 9-mile trail along the North Fork of the Big Thompson to Lost Lake. SAR, 1915, 7–10.

22. *Rocky Mountain News*, 57 (January 29, 1916): 11.

23. SAR, 1915, 24.

24. Ibid., 17.

25. Ibid., 18.

26. Ibid., 25, 27. The Eugenia (or Cudahy-Norwall) Mine on Battle Mountain was discovered on September 23, 1905, and reported the following month. The site was identified as Camp Norwall after Carl P. Norwall, who was working the property on behalf of his wealthy partner Edward A. Cudahy of Omaha. In June 1910, it was reported that the mine's tunnel had reached 1,500 feet with "lots of ore in sight." The hoped-for lode proved elusive, and although the mine operated through the summers of 1911 and 1912, within a few years the site had been abandoned.

27. Interview with Richard Thompson McCracken, July 5, 1959, EPPLCC. See also *Rocky Mountain News* interview with McCracken (Larry Pearson, "First Park Ranger Relives Service," *Rocky Mountain News*, 106 [November 29, 1964]: 56–57).

28. SAR, 1915, 20.

29. SAR, 1915, 21.

30. *Rocky Mountain News*, 56 (October 31, 1915): 1.

31. Ibid., 56 (November 1, 1915): 1.

32. Ibid., 57 (July 9, 1916): Section 2, p. 3.

33. Cahn, *Birth of the National Park Service*, 31, 65.

34. Buchholtz, *Rocky Mountain National Park*, 149–151.

35. *Denver Post* (July 14, 1918): 3. See also Albright and Schenck, *Creating the National Park Service*, 119.

36. *Denver Times*, 46 (November 28, 1916): 7.

37. Franklin Lane to Stephen Mather, May 13, 1918. Quoted in Ise, *Our National Park Policy*, 194.

38. *Denver Times*, 46 (November 28, 1916): 7.

39. *Fort Collins Express*, 43 (December 21, 1916): 2.

40. *Rocky Mountain News*, 57 (May 16, 1916): 6.

41. Ibid., 57 (May 28, 1916): 1.

42. Ibid., 57 (May 28, 1916): 8.

43. SAR, 1916, 3.

44. Ibid., 1918, 8.

45. *Denver Post* (December 2, 1917): Section 4, p. 9. See also Lela McQueary, *Widening Trails: Narratives of Pioneer Days in Middle Park on the Western Slope of Colorado's Rocky Mountains* (Denver: The World Press, Inc., 1962), 130–136.

46. SMR, September 1918, 3.

47. Ibid., 5.

48. *Report of the Director of the National Park Service to the Secretary of the Interior for the Fiscal Year Ended June 30, 1918* (Washington: Government Printing Office, 1918) (hereafter cited as RDNPS), 64.

49. Ibid., 65.

50. Undated clipping (1918), RMNPL.

51. Secretary of the Interior Franklin Lane to Colorado governor Julius C. Gunter, November 16, 1918. Quoted in *Rocky Mountain News*, 59 (December 8, 1918): Motor Section, 4.

52. *Larimer County Democrat*, 13 (December 26, 1918): 1.

53. SAR, 1919, 12.

54. *Lyons Recorder*, 20 (September 23, 1920): 1.

55. *Loveland Reporter*, 41 (October 1, 1920): 1.

56. *Loveland Daily Herald*, 10 (September 20, 1920): 1.

57. *Longmont Ledger*, 43 (July 22, 1922): 1, 4.

58. On September 3, 1915, the Reverend Thornton R. Sampson, the sixty-three-year-old founding president of the Austin (Texas) Presbyterian Seminary, left Grand Lake to cross Flattop Mountain to attend the park's dedication. His remains were not discovered until 1932. See James H. Pickering, "Vanished in the Mountains: The Saga of the Reverend Thornton R. Sampson," *Colorado Heritage* (Summer 2000): 14–19, 24–29.

59. SAR, 1917, 8.

60. See, for example, Eldon Jessup, *The Motor Camping Book* (New York: G. P. Putnam's Sons, 1921); J. C. Long and John D. Long, *Motor Camping* (New York: Dodd, Mead and Company, 1923); and F. Everett Brimmer, *Autocamping Facts* (Chicago: The Outfitters' Book Company, 1924).

61. Noel, "Paving the Way to Colorado," 47. Denver's most famous autocamping facility, however, was 160-acre Overland Park opened in 1920. Located along the Platte on the site of what had once been a golf course and country club, Overland Park, with its 800 free campsites, paved streets, stores, restaurant, dance hall, and motion picture theater, became one of the showplaces of the city.

62. *Rocky Mountain News*, 57 (January 1, 1916): Agricultural Section, 10.

63. *Longmont Ledger*, 38 (August 10, 1917): 1. The Arbuckle Reservoir Company was organized by a group of Longmont businessmen in 1903 or 1904 and acquired the claims on the five reservoirs in Wild Basin filed on by Emma Arbuckle; her son Frank; and her caretaker, Jabez Billings in 1902. They were sold in 1933 to the City of Longmont. *Longmont Ledger*, 55 (September 22, 1933): 1.

64. SAR, 1917, 8–9; *Denver Post* (July 13, 1917): Section 2, p. 1.

65. SMR, September 1918, 5.

66. *Loveland Daily Herald*, 9 (March 19, 1918): 1.

67. SAR, 1919, 13–14.

68. SAR, 1920, 17.

69. In 1926 the eastern boundary of the park was relocated to eliminate some 12,100 acres of inholdings, most of them adjacent to the village of Estes Park. A year later the gate was moved near the junction of the High Drive and Fall River Roads in Horseshoe Park. In 1933 it was moved to its present site adjacent to the Big Horn Ranger Station, in what was then known as Hondius Park.

70. C. R. Trowbridge noted in his annual report for 1915 that E. A. Brown was operating a camp at Bear Lake with capacity of fifty. It was soon acquired by Frank Byerly, who first became a partner with Brown and later purchased the property. The first building, near the eastern shore of the lake, was constructed in 1916, followed the next year by a 16-by-20-foot recreation hall. Other buildings were gradually added, including a main lodge in 1922 and a large, two-story building housing the lodge's offices and gift and soda shops. Electricity for illumination was furnished by a diesel boiler, which Byerly had installed in 1920. Bear Lake Lodge continued to operate into the 1950s, when the Park Service closed the facility and removed the buildings.

71. SMR, August 1920, 9; SAR, 1920, 14.

72. SMR, June 1923, 6.

73. SAR, 1919, 1–2.

74. The Lewiston Hotel was quite literally built up around the original bungalow home that A. D. Lewis and his wife began opening to summer guests in 1914 and then expanded by adding a guesthouse to the east in 1915. The guesthouse was enlarged two years later, giving it a capacity of seventy. Other enlargements followed, making the building a full three stories high. In its heyday many found the Lewiston with its mountain views a grander place to stay than the Stanley. It was destroyed by fire on September 4, 1941.

75. The Estes Park Chalets was begun by Charles Robbins and his partner Clarence Nevins as a small tourist hotel, the Rockdale, which opened on September 13, 1913. It was purchased in 1915 by Claude Verry, A. D. Lewis's half brother, who managed it until winter 1919 when it was damaged by wind. The site was then

sold to Lewis, who rebuilt a greatly enlarged new hotel, the Lewiston Chalets, further up the hillside, incorporating in its central structure the old Rockdale. In January 1923 the Chalets was purchased by Roe Emery and his Rocky Mountain Parks Transportation Company. Emery changed the name to the Estes Park Chalets and expanded its facilities to the point where it could handle some three hundred guests, many of whom arrived by bus on one of his "Circle Tours" out of Denver. A third of the original structure was destroyed by fire on July 6, 1978. It has since been rebuilt and is now known as Marys Lake Lodge.

76. Built and opened in 1914 as a small 21-room frame hotel, the Crags was enlarged in 1917 and again in 1923–1924, when the lobby and dining room were expanded and additional guest rooms and cottages added. A recreation building was constructed west of the lodge in 1920. The Crags was operated by Joe Mills until his death in 1935 and then by his widow until 1946.

77. SMR, May 1920, 4. Grand Lake Lodge opened with a ball on July 3, 1920, and during the decade that followed more than thirty cottages were added above the lodge. A. D. Lewis sold the lodge to Roe Emery in late 1922 or early 1923, together with the Lewiston Chalets at Marys Lake, for a reported price of $75,000. *Estes Park Trail*, 2 (January 5, 1923): 1.

78. SMR, April 1920, 5.

79. SAR, 1920, 2.

80. Ibid., 1921, 2.

81. Ibid., 1922, p. 3.

82. Louter, "Glaciers and Gasoline," 260–261.

83. Ibid., 257.

CHAPTER 6

1. *Rocky Mountain News*, 57 (July 14, 1916): 6.

2. See, for example, "Interior Department Plan to Develop Rocky Mountain National Park," a full-page feature article written in late 1915 by Yard for the *Denver Post*. *Denver Post* (December 26, 1915), Prosperity Edition, n.p. For a discussion Mather and Yard's success, see Peter Blodgett's "Selling the Scenery: Advertising and the National Parks" in Wrobel and Long's *Seeing and Being Seen*, 270–298.

3. *Fort Collins Morning Express*, 43 (November 18, 1916): 3.

4. *Loveland Daily Herald*, 8 (December 11, 1917): 1; ibid., 9 (January 29, 1918): 1.

5. *Longmont Ledger*, 38 (February 9, 1917): 5.

6. C. W. Buchholtz, "Paradise Regained: The Beginnings of Rocky Mountain National Park," *Colorado Heritage* 1 (1984): 2; *Denver Post* (July 29, 1917): 10. In October 1915 and again in January 1916 Birch's *Post* had run stories about Mr. and Mrs. Walter Estes of Gray, Maine, the "New Adam and Eve," who made two separate trips into the woods "prepared to wrench subsistence from the earth." See *Denver Post* (October 10, 1915): 4; ibid. (January 5, 1916): 3.

7. *Denver Post* (July 29, 1917): 10.

8. Ibid. (July 30, 1917): 1.

9. Ibid. (July 31, 1917): 1.

10. Ibid. (August 1, 1917): 1.

11. Ibid. (August 4, 1917): Section 2, p. 1.

12. Ibid. (August 6, 1917): 8.

13. Ibid. (August 7, 1917): 5.

14. Ibid. (August 8, 1917): 13.

15. Ibid.

16. Quoted in Gene Fowler, *Timberline: A Story of Bonfils and Tammen* (New York: Covici Friede Publishers, 1933), 429.

17. *Denver Post* (August 10, 1917): 17.

18. Ibid. (September 23, 1917): Magazine Section, n.p.

19. Ibid. (September 30, 1917): Magazine Section, n.p.

20. Ibid.

21. *Fort Collins Express*, 44 (August 29, 1917): 6.

22. Quoted in Buchholtz, "Paradise Regained," 16.

23. Oral Interview with Richard (Dixie) McCracken, 1961, EPPLCC; Interview of July 3, 1963, cited in Musselman, *Rocky Mountain National Park*, 31n.

24. *Lyons Recorder*, 17 (August 18, 1917): 1; *Longmont Ledger*, 38 (August 24, 1917): 1; ibid., 38 (August 31, 1917): 1.

25. *Loveland Daily Herald*, 8 (August 31, 1917): 4.

26. For the history of winter sports in Colorado see James Whiteside, *Colorado: A Sports History* (Niwot: University Press of Colorado, 1999), 89–143; Abbott Fay, *A History of Skiing in Colorado* (Ouray, CO: Western Reflection, 2000); and Jack A. Benson, "Before Aspen and Vail: The Story of Recreational Skiing in Frontier Colorado," *Journal of the West*, 22 (January 1983): 52–61.

27. Quoted in an unsigned article, *Denver Times*, January 16, 1904, Enos Mills Papers, Denver Public Library.

28. Quoted in Alexander Drummond, *Enos Mills: Citizen of Nature* (Niwot: University Press of Colorado, 1995), 238.

29. *Trail and Timberline*, 43 (April 1922): 4.

30. *Denver Post* (January 9, 1916): Section 2, p. 9.

31. Ibid. (January 23, 1916): Section 3, p. 2.

32. Clifford Higby, "Winter Sports in Estes Park," *Estes Park Trail*, 2 (March 2, 1923): 6.

33. *Rocky Mountain News*, 57 (February 2, 1916): 3.

34. Ibid.

35. Ibid., 57 (February 16, 1916): 7.

36. *Longmont Call*, 18 (February 18, 1916): 1. Fern Lake Lodge was built by William Workman (1852–1943), a physician, who first visited Estes Park in 1898 and two years later purchased a five-acre tract in Moraine Park from Abner Sprague. A mountaineer, Workman extensively explored the Forest Canyon–Fern Lake area, named many of its features, and about 1910 began work on the lodge that he completed and opened the following year. In 1915 Workman sold it to the Higby brothers. During the heyday of the CMC the lodge was operated by Frank Byerly and then by Mrs. Edna Bishop. It was used sporadically until 1958. Vandals and deterioration led to the decision to burn the facility in March 1976.

37. *Fort Collins Morning Express*, 42 (March 15, 1916): 3.

38. *Rocky Mountain News,* 57 (February 27, 1916): Local Feature Section, pp. 2–3.

39. *Denver Post* (February 18, 1916): 11.

40. *Rocky Mountain News,* 57 (December 5, 1916): 7.

41. *Fort Collins Express,* 45 (January 31, 1917): 6; *Larimer County Democrat,* 12 (February 8, 1917): 1. Although remote, the area had been used for winter sports by the young people of the village since at least 1910, when Gaylord Thomson made available the ponds at the fish hatchery for evening skating parties. *Loveland Reporter,* 30 (January 15, 1910): 3.

42. *Fort Collins Express,* 43 (February 13, 1917): 8.

43. SAR, 1917, 8.

44. *Estes Park Trail,* 2 (March 2, 1923): 6.

45. *Fort Collins Express,* 43 (March 8, 1917): 6.

46. William C. Ramaley, "Ski Trails of Rocky Mountain National Park," undated unpublished typescript, RMNPL.

47. Quoted in *Trail and Timberline,* 18 (March 1920): 2.

48. *Denver Post* (February 21, 1918): 10.

49. *Estes Park Trail,* 1 (March 17, 1922): 1.

50. SMR, March 1922, 5.

51. *Estes Park Trail,* 5 (December 11, 1925): 1.

52. *Denver Post* (February 23, 1918): 8.

53. *Fort Collins Express,* 50 (June 21, 1923): 8.

54. SMR, March 1917, 2; ibid., April 1917, 3.

55. Journal of Charles Edwin Hewes (hereafter cited as Hewes Journal), March 16, 1922, unpublished typescript, EPM. For a brief history of skiing in Allenspark, see Lorna Knowlton, *Weaving Mountain Memories: Recollections of the Allenspark Area* (Estes Park, CO: Estes Park Area Historical Museum, 1989), 161–173.

56. *Longmont Ledger,* 44 (November 17, 1922): 1; *Longmont Daily Times,* 28 (November 20, 1922): 1.

57. *Longmont Ledger,* 44 (March 16, 1923): 1.

58. Ibid., 4.

59. *Fort Collins Express,* 50 (November 11, 1923): 9; *Estes Park Trail,* 3 (November 16, 1923): 1.

60. *Estes Park Trail,* 3 (February 1, 1924): 1.

61. Ibid.

62. Ibid., 3 (February 8, 1924): 1.

63. *Fort Collins Courier-Express,* 50 (February 14, 1924): 5.

64. *Estes Park Trail,* 3 (February 15, 1924): 1.

65. Deer Ridge Chalet began as a lean-to from which Orville W. Bechtel, a semi-professional photographer who had homesteaded the land, sold postcards and lemonade beginning in summer 1917. Deer Ridge was then effectively the end of the road into the national park, from which rough trails led west and north to Hidden Valley and Horseshoe Park. In 1918 he completed a small log store and expanded over the next decade by adding a restaurant, six or seven rustic cabins, and a filling station. In 1926 Bechtel sold the business to the Gustave Shubert family, who relocated most of the business to the north side of the road and con-

structed the large lodge called the Deer Ridge Chalet and a variety of other structures, including cabins. Because of traffic congestion—to which the Shubert business and a small adjacent livery contributed—the Park Service made an attempt to purchase the 227-acre property as early as 1931. It was finally condemned in December 1960, and the following year the Shuberts received $308,000 in compensation.

66. *Estes Park Trail*, 3 (February 8, 1924): 1; ibid., 3 (February 22, 1924): 1.

67. Ibid., 4 (November 21, 1924): 1.

68. Ibid., 3 (January 18, 1924): 1.

69. Ibid., 3 (January 4, 1924): 4.

70. *Rocky Mountain News*, 65 (March 17, 1924): 1.

71. *Fort Collins Express*, 50 (March 13, 1924): 5.

72. *Estes Park Trail*, 3 (March 21, 1924): 3.

73. Ibid., 4 (January 30, 1925): 1.

74. Ibid., 5 (February 12, 1926): 1.

75. *Longmont Daily Call*, 24 (February 27, 1928): 1.

76. *Estes Park Trail*, 10 (March 1931): 1.

77. *Longmont Ledger*, 52 (June 19, 1931): 1; *Estes Park Trail*, 11 (July 3, 1931): 1.

78. *Estes Park Trail*, 11 (January 15, 1932): 1; ibid., 11 (February 28, 1932): 1; *Longmont Times-Call*, 59 (February 22, 1932): 4.

79. *Longmont Times-Call*, 60 (June 28, 1932): 1; ibid., 61 (June 21, 1933): 3.

80. *Estes Park Trail*, 13 (June 30, 1933): 1; ibid. 15 (July 5, 1935): 5. The *Longmont Times-Call* had noted on June 22 of the previous year that preliminary costs for staging the 1932 event were about $1,000 and the expected gate receipts $1,500, suggesting that the profit margin, at best, was a slender one. *Longmont Times-Call*, 60 (June 22, 1932): 1.

81. In 1932 and 1933 Superintendent Rogers considered establishing a winter sports course in Moraine Park, using the north face of Gianttrack Mountain for a 600-foot ski jump and the top of the eastern terminal moraine for a bobsled run with a series of hairpin turns leading to the valley floor. That idea was rejected in fall 1933 in favor of the less visible and more remote Hidden Valley, where old logging cuts could be developed into ski runs. From 1934 to 1938, when the Park Service stopped promoting competitive events, Hidden Valley was periodically used for national and regional tournaments, including regional Olympic trials in 1935. Between 1935 and 1937 new ski runs were constructed from Trail Ridge Road and upper Hidden Valley to lower Hidden Valley, and warming shelters were installed at both places. For many years Hidden Valley was considered one of the better ski areas in Colorado. When it officially closed in 1991, it was the oldest continually operated ski area in the state. See Bob Bradley, "Historic Hidden Valley," unpublished typescript dated November 11, 1993, EPPLCC.

82. *Estes Park Trail*, 18 (October 7, 1938): 1; RMNP Information Bulletin (October 4, 1938), copy RMNPL.

83. *Estes Park Trail*, 19 (March 8, 1940): 6.

84. "The tow is not the most elaborate in the world," the *Estes Park Trail* editorialized, "but it works, and the enthusiastic skiers, who use it each weekend, are ample proof of its success." Ibid., 30 (March 28, 1941): 4.

85. See ibid., 29 (June 24, 1949): 1; ibid., 29 (July 1, 1949): 1; ibid., 30 (June 23, 1949): 8; ibid., 31 (August 17, 1951): 10.

86. *Trail and Timberline*, 12 (April 1919): 2.

CHAPTER 7

1. Letter, L. C. Way to Director of National Park Service, August 16, 1919, RMNPL.

2. For other accounts of the cede jurisdiction-transportation controversy in Rocky Mountain National Park, see Musselman, *Rocky Mountain National Park*, 29–75; Drummond, *Enos Mills*, 267–290; Hildegarde Hawthorne and Esther Burnell Mills, *Enos Mills of the Rockies* (New York: Houghton Mifflin, 1935), 223–251; and MSEP, 251–261.

3. Cahn, *Birth of the National Park Service*, 46. For background on the history of concessions at Yellowstone, see Richard A. Bartlett, "The Concessionaires of Yellowstone National Park, Genesis of a Policy, 1882–1892," *Pacific Northwest Quarterly*, 74 (January 1983): 2–10; and Mark Daniel Barringer, *Selling Yellowstone: Capitalism and the Construction of Nature* (Lawrence: University Press of Kansas, 2002), 8–83. The history of concessions at Yosemite is well treated in Stanford E. Demars, *The Tourist in Yosemite, 1855–1985* (Salt Lake City, Utah: University of Utah Press, 1991).

4. Ise, *Our National Park Policy*, 175.

5. Cahn, *Birth of the National Park Service*, 48.

6. *Rocky Mountain News*, 56 (September 10, 1915): 2.

7. Ibid., 57 (December 4, 1916): 1, 2.

8. *Rocky Mountain News*, 57 (December 5, 1916): 6.

9. *Denver Times*, 46 (December 6, 1916): 4; ibid., 46 (December 7, 1916): 4.

10. *Denver Post* (December 19, 1916): 7.

11. Ibid.

12. See, for example, *Larimer County Democrat*, 12 (December 14, 1916): 1; ibid., 12 (December 21, 1916): 1.

13. *Denver Post* (December 19, 1916): 7.

14. Beginning with 26 motor vehicles in 1916, by 1928 Emery's company owned 326, had a payroll in excess of $450,000, tangible assets of $1,678,252, a capital structure of $2,250,000, and facilities in Denver, Estes Park, Lyons, and Loveland. In 1927 he told a Longmont audience that his company handled "in the Rocky Mountain National Park 36,248 people," traveling over 14 million tire miles. Over the years Emery absorbed still more companies, including the operator of Denver's yellow cabs. In May 1927, when all these holdings were consolidated under the name Rocky Mountain Motor Company, Emery owned the largest transportation company of its kind in Colorado. Interview with Walter Emery, August 20, 1998; IRSC, Book 174, p. 197; *Rocky Mountain News*, 68 (June 12, 1927): Magazine Section; *Longmont Daily Call*, 24 (April 28, 1928): 1; ibid., 24 (June 4, 1928): 3; *Longmont Daily Times*, 34 (June 8, 1928): 1; *Rocky Mountain News*, 90 (October 30, 1949): 22; David Walter and John R. Mcdonald, "Historic Resources

Study, Glacier National Park and Historic Structures Survey," 89–80, unpublished typescript, Museum and Archives, Glacier National Park.

15. RDNPS, 1919, 89.

16. "Rocky Mountain National Parks, Estes Park, Colorado," Union Pacific brochure, 1922, 26.

17. Louter, "Glaciers and Gasoline," 250.

18. *Denver Post* (May 21, 1919): 1.

19. SMR, May 1919, 5.

20. *Denver Post* (June 17, 1919): 16. See also *Loveland Daily Herald*, 10 (June 17, 1919): 4.

21. Donald Swain, *Wilderness Defender: Horace M. Albright and Conservation* (Chicago: University Press of Chicago, 1970), 56–57.

22. Enos A. Mills, *Your National Parks* (Boston: Houghton Mifflin Company, 1920), 279, 264.

23. *Loveland Daily Herald*, 6 (October 28, 1915): 1; *Denver Times*, 45 (October 2, 1915): 12.

24. Albright and Schenck, *Creating the National Park Service*, 194.

25. Cahn, *Birth of the National Park Service*, 62.

26. Quoted in Swain, *Wilderness Defender*, 86.

27. Quoted in Cahn, *Birth of the National Park Service*, 77.

28. Quoted in ibid.

29. Quoted in Swain, *Wilderness Defender*, 94.

30. Albright and Schenck, *Creating the National Park Service*, 220.

31. Ibid.

32. Ibid., 306.

33. See, for example, SAR, 1919, 22–25.

34. Quoted in William Sherman Bell, "The Legal Phases of Cession of Rocky Mountain National Park," *Rocky Mountain Law Review*, I (1928): 44.

35. Letter, Enos A. Mills to L. C. Way, August 14, 1919, Mills vs. Way correspondence, RMNPL.

36. Undated newspaper clipping, RMNPL.

37. Telegram, L. C. Way to Director of the National Park Service, August 16, 1919, RMNPL.

38. Letter, L. C. Way to Director of the National Park Service, August 16, 1919, Mills vs. Way correspondence, RMNPL.

39. Telegram, Arno B. Cammerer to L. C. Way, August 18, 1919, RMNPL.

40. Letter, Arno B. Cammerer to L. C. Way, August 26, 1919, RMNPL.

41. Letter, Enos A. Mills to L. C. Way, August 20, 1919, RMNPL.

42. Telegram, L. C. Way to Director of the National Park Service, August 25, 1919, RMNPL.

43. Letter, L. C. Way to Director of the National Park Service, September 1, 1919, Mills vs. Way correspondence, RMNPL.

44. *Longmont Ledger*, 40 (September 5, 1919): 1; *Loveland Daily Herald*, 10 (September 5, 1919): 4.

45. Clem Yore (1875–1936) was born in St. Louis, the son of a Mississippi boat

pilot said to have worked with Mark Twain, and his early life, as he told it, was fully in keeping with the persona he presented to his neighbors. Running away from home at twelve, at fifteen he somehow joined the Texas Rangers and then spent time as "a cowpuncher, packer, and stage driver." Returning to St. Louis and earning a law degree, Yore briefly practiced in the Klondike before taking up journalism as a reporter in the goldfields. After serving in the Spanish American War, Yore returned to newspaper work in Chicago where he became city editor of the *Chicago American*. By 1912, Yore had embarked on yet another career as a writer of poetry and fiction. His *Songs of the Underworld* appeared in 1912, followed by a lengthy list of popular western novels. Yore came to Estes Park on his honeymoon in 1914 and stayed. In fall 1916 he decided to go into the resort business, making use of a twelve-acre site adjacent to his cottage, "Harmony Hut" (located on the lower slope of Prospect Mountain east of the Big Thompson). Yore's Big Thompson Hotel consisted of cottages, a dining room, and a large "lounging pavilion," designed to appeal "to people of aesthetic tastes." In fall 1918 Yore tried politics, running for congress as a Democrat. Decisively defeated, Yore presented himself in Boulder within a week and at age forty-four attempted to join the army.

Yore's Big Thompson Hotel was not a success, and although he sold it in January 1923, his financial difficulties did not end. Debts went unpaid, and a court judgment followed. The Big Thompson Hotel was purchased by Roe Emery in May 1925, sold again a year later, and razed. See "Clem Yore," unpublished autobiographical typescript, EPPLCC; *Larimer County Democrat*, 11 (October 19, 1916): 10; *Loveland Daily Herald*, 9 (September 17, 1918): 4; *Loveland Reporter-Herald*, 43 (January 17, 1923): 1; *Estes Park Trail*, 4 (July 11, 1924): 16; ibid., 10 (April 10, 1931): 1; *Fort Collins Express-Courier*, 5 (May 5, 1923): 8; *Estes Park Trail Gazette*, 22 (April 3, 1992): 2.

46. Letter, Enos A. Mills to John E. Raker, November 12, 1919, Mills vs. Way correspondence, RMNPL.

47. Letter, L. C. Way to Director of the National Park Service, September 9, 1919, RMNPL.

48. Letter, L. C. Way to Director of the National Park Service, December 13, 1919, RMNPL.

49. SMR, September 1919, 4.

50. L. C. Way, memorandum, October 29, 1919, Mills vs. Way correspondence, RMNPL.

51. RDNPS, 1919, 90.

52. *Loveland Daily Herald*, 10 (January 16, 1920): 1; see also *Loveland Reporter*, 40 (January 14, 1920): 1: ibid. (January 16, 1920): 1; *Fort Collins Courier*, 28 (January 17. 1920): 1. In the meeting's aftermath a number of the organizations represented, including the Loveland and Greeley Chambers of Commerce and the Lyons and Allenspark Commercial Clubs, debated the issue and did precisely that. See: *Loveland Reporter*, 40 (June 21, 1920): 1; *Lyons Recorder*, 19 (February 14, 1920): 1; ibid. (March 6, 1920): 1.

53. *Loveland Daily Herald*, 10 (January 20, 1920): 4.

54. SMR, January 1920, 5–6.

55. *Lyons Recorder*, 19 (February 7, 1920): 1; ibid. (February 28, 1920): 1.

56. *Lyons Recorder*, 19 (March 20, 1920): 1.

57. SMR, March 1920, 4.

58. L. C. Way, memorandum, February 20, 1920, RMNPL.

59. SMR, June 1920, 8.

60. Memorandum, no date, Robbins vs. McDaniel correspondence, RMNPL; letter, L. C. Way to Director of the National Park Service, July 17, 1920, RMNPL.

61. Letter, L. C. Way to Director of the National Park Service, July 17, 1920, Robbins vs. McDaniel correspondence, RMNPL.

62. "Complaint," Robbins vs. McDaniel correspondence, RMNPL.

63. Maye M. Crutcher, memorandum, July 20, 1920, Robbins vs. McDaniel correspondence, RMNPL.

64. Maye M. Crutcher, memorandum, July 22, 1920, RMNPL.

65. Telegram, Arno B. Cammerer to L. C. Way, July 24, 1920, RMNPL.

66. Memorandum, L. C. Way, July 25, 1920 RMNPL.

67. Ibid.

68. "Statement by Mrs. John P. Thomey and Mrs. George W. Howell," July 26, 1920, Robbins vs. McDaniel correspondence, RMNPL. See also *Loveland Daily Herald*, 10 (July 29, 1920): 1.

69. See, for example, letter, Arno C. Cammerer to L. C. Way, August 16, 1920, State of Colorado vs. McDaniel correspondence, RMNPL.

70. Letter, L. C. Way to Director of the National Park Service, August 11, 1920, State of Colorado vs. McDaniel correspondence, RMNPL. Much of the local press, of course, disagreed. For the *Lyons Recorder* it was but the "National Park Service's latest bonehead." *Lyons Recorder*, 20 (August 28, 1920): 4.

71. Letter, L. C. Way to Director of the National Park Service, August 11, 1920, State of Colorado vs. McDaniel correspondence, RMNPL.

72. Letter, Arno C. Cammerer to L. C. Way, August 13, 1920, Robbins vs. McDaniel correspondence, RMNPL.

73. Enos A. Mills, "The Kingdom of National Parks," *Estes Park Trail Talk*, 1 (August 27, 1920): 5–6.

74. *Fort Collins Express*, 47 (May 28, 1921): 8.

75. SMR, May 1921, 9. The association appointed a committee to conduct a "painstaking investigation" of Mills's charges. Its report that November—which it gave to the press and published in its magazine, *The Denver Commercial*—was unequivocal: "every one of the specific charges made by Mills has been disproven." It also pointedly noted that Mills had refused "to substantiate his charges or give facts upon which he based them" and had brusquely dismissed the committee's request to do so with the statement that "to fully answer your questions will not touch the main issue or throw any light upon it." The lengthy report accused Mills of "irresponsible conduct" and of "vituperation, vindictiveness, fabrication, [and] deliberately misleading statements and untruths," in the name of "promoting his own selfish business interests." Reprint from *The Denver Commercial*, November 10, 1921, RMNPL; *Denver Post* (November 4, 1921): 23.

76. *Denver Post* (March 1921): 3, 6.

77. *Estes Park Trail*, 1 (September 30, 1921): 1.

78. Ibid., 1 (October 7, 1921): 1.

79. Ibid.

80. Not everyone, of course, shared these sentiments. "It is hardly necessary to tell you," Horace Albright wrote a colleague, "that I was considerably relieved when I heard that the undertaker was attending to him instead of a doctor." Roe Emery was even more direct: "Enos Mills died last night," he telegrammed Albright; "Ain't nature grand?" Quoted in Albright and Schenck, *Creating the National Park Service*, 306, 221.

81. Interview with Dixie McCracken, July 3, 1963, cited in Musselman, *Rocky Mountain National Park*, 47.

82. *Estes Park Trail*, 1 (October 28, 1921): 1.

CHAPTER 8

1. Toll's mother, Katherine, was the sister of U.S. senator Edward O. Wolcott and Henry Roger Wolcott, two of the wealthiest and most prominent men in Colorado. Toll's father specialized in irrigation law and had as clients some of the city's largest corporations.

2. Roger W. Toll, "Foreword" in *Mountaineering in the Rocky Mountain National Park* (Washington, D.C.: Government Printing Office, 1919), 10.

3. *Estes Park Trail*, 8 (January 18, 1929): 1.

4. Cahn, *Birth of the National Park Service*, 93.

5. See, for example, "Roger Toll," *Trail and Timberline*, 209 (March–April 1936): 27–28.

6. *Estes Park Trail*, 1 (October 21, 1921): 5.

7. *Denver Post* (December 4, 1921): 6. See, for example, *Fort Collins Express*, 48 (December 11, 1921): 12; *Fort Collins Courier*, 47 (December 12, 1921): 10.

8. Roger W. Toll, letter of July 29, 1922, to the Director of the National Park Service, RMNPL; *Longmont Times-Call*, 28 (August 1, 1922): 1.

9. Roger W. Toll, letter of July 29, 1922, to the Director of the National Park Service, RMNPL.

10. Paul W. Lee, "Litigation Concerning the Rocky Mountain National Park," in *The Rocky Mountain National Park*, Enos A. Mills (Garden City, N.Y.: Doubleday, Page & Company, 1924), 237.

11. *Loveland Reporter-Herald*, 43 (August 9, 1923): 1; *Fort Collins Courier*, 45 (August 9, 1923): 1.

12. *Loveland Reporter-Herald*, 43 (August 23, 1923): 1; ibid., 43 (September 3, 1923): 1.

13. Roger W. Toll, letter to the Director of the National Park Service, June 23, 1925, RMNPL.

14. Roger W. Toll, letter to the Director of the National Park Service, May 30, 1925, RMNPL.

15. Arno B. Cammerer, letter to Roger W. Toll, June 17, 1925, RMNPL.

16. Roger W. Toll, letter to the Director of the National Park Service, June 23, 1925, RMNPL.

17. *Rocky Mountain News*, 67 (January 9, 1926): 1; *Denver Post* (January 9, 1926): 2; *Estes Park Trail*, 5 (January 15, 1926): 1; *Fort Collins Express Courier*, 52 (January 10, 1926): 1.

18. *Rocky Mountain News*, 67 (December 24, 1926): 1.

19. Ibid., 67 (December 23, 1926): 1.

20. *Boulder News-Herald* (February 5, 1927) quoted in Musselman, *Rocky Mountain National Park*, 63. See also *Denver Post* (February 22, 1927): 11.

21. *Rocky Mountain News*, 68 (February 7, 1927): 7.

22. *Boulder Daily Camera* (March 19, 1927) quoted in Musselman, *Rocky Mountain National Park*, 70; *Rocky Mountain News*, 68 (March 2, 1927): 4.

23. *Rocky Mountain News* (March 6, 1928), Cede Jurisdiction Scapbooks, RMNPL.

24. *Longmont Daily Times*, 34 (March 6, 1928): 3; Musselman, *Rocky Mountain National Park*, 71.

25. Unidentified Denver newspaper clipping, February 7, 1928, Cede Jurisdiction Scrapbooks, RMNPL.

26. *Longmont Daily Times*, 34 (January 28, 1928): 1.

27. *Rocky Mountain News*, 70 (January 4, 1929): 6.

28. *Longmont Daily Call*, 24 (February 18, 1929): 3; *Rocky Mountain News*, 70 (February 17, 1929): 1.

29. SAR, 1927, 1.

30. RDNPS 1924, 43–44.

31. RDNPS 1923, 58.

32. Quoted in Musselman, *Rocky Mountain National Park*, 86.

33. RDNPS 1925, 32.

34. Typescript copy, "Memorandum to the Estes Park Trail," October 8, 1926, RMNPL; *Estes Park Trail*, 5 (June 4, 1926): 3; *Fort Collins Express-Courier*, 52 (January 31, 1926): Section 2, p. 1.

35. SMR, July 1925, 2.

36. *Estes Park Trail*, 5 (May 15, 1925): 1.

37. SMR, April 1931, 3.

38. *Estes Park Trail*, 4 (October 24, 1924): 5; *Longmont Ledger*, 46 (October 31, 1924): 7.

39. *Longmont Ledger*, 46 (May 29, 1926): 2; *Estes Park Trail*, 5 (May 29, 1925): 1.

40. SMR, July 1926, 2.

41. SMR, June 1926, 2–4.

42. RDNPS 1923, 58.

43. Toll, *Mountaineering in the Rocky Mountain National Park*, 33–34.

44. *Estes Park Trail*, 1 (August 19, 1921): 1.

45. Ibid., 2 (August 11, 1922): 15.

46. *Longmont Ledger*, 46 (June 12, 1925): 8. The story of Longs Peak's most famous tragedy, based on the account dictated in December 1931 by Vaille's companion, Walter Kiener, to Charles Edwin Hewes, is found in James H. Pickering, "Tragedy on Longs Peak: Walter Kiener's Own Story," *Colorado Heritage*, 1 (1990): 18–31.

47. Jack C. Moomaw, *Recollections of a Rocky Mountain Ranger* (Longmont, CO, 1963), 40. Moomaw (1892–1975) grew up on the St. Vrain between Lyons and Allenspark, exposing him to the nearby mountains. After spending time as a cowboy from Wyoming south to Mexico, as a stevedore in Galveston and San Francisco, and as a sailor aboard the battleship *Oregon*, Moomaw still in his twenties came back to the Estes Park region, where he finished high school in 1915, married, and pursued a number of jobs before joining the National Park Service in 1921. He became a ranger the following year—a career he pursued until his retirement in 1945. Moomaw had literary aspirations, and his several volumes of published poems—including *By the Winding St. Vrain* (1919), *Poems of a Mountain Guide* (1924), and *Rhymes of the Range* (1930)—earned him the title "Poet of the St. Vrain." Something of a renaissance man, Moomaw also painted.

48. SMR (June 1925): 7.

49. Moomaw, *Recollections*, 45.

50. Arps and Kingery, *High Country Names*, 72.

51. Dunning, *Over Hill and Vale*, vol. 1, 236–237.

52. Quoted by Curtis K. Skinner, unidentified newspaper article dated May 27, 1928, RMNPL.

53. Dunning, *Over Hill and Vale*, vol. 1, 237.

54. Dorothy Collier was the sole female member of a party of four that on August 30–31, 1931, made the first recorded nighttime climb of the East Face.

55. Merrill J. Mattes, "The Boulderfield Hotel: A Distant Summer in the Shadow of Longs Peak," *Colorado Heritage*, 1 (1986): 37–38.

56. Ibid., 70.

57. A copy of the guides' questions and answers is in the EPM.

58. Mattes, "The Boulderfield Hotel," 38.

59. *Estes Park Trail*, 13 (August 17, 1934): 1.

60. Mattes, "The Boulderfield Hotel," 39–40; *Longmont Ledger*, 50 (July 2, 1929): 1.

61. *Estes Park Trail Gazette*, 32 (October 10, 2001): 1–2. These are the reported findings of geologist Jonathan Archuff. They are not, however, new. Merrill Mattes in his 1986 article writes, "It seems the Boulderfield Plateau is a 'rock glacier' resting on a substratum of ice. Its slow but inexorable shifting fractured the cabin's walls." Mattes, "The Boulderfield Hotel," 40.

62. Dunning, *Over Hill and Vale*, vol. 1, 237.

63. Enos Mills's report is in Toll, *Mountaineering in the Rocky Mountain National Park*, 53–54. The June 1903 descent was reported the following year by journalist Earl Harding, who met Mills as he was returning to Longs Peak Inn. See Earl Harding, "Climbing Longs Peak," *Outing*, 44 (July 1904): 461–468.

64. Willard T. Day in Toll, *Mountaineering in the Rocky Mountain National Park*, 54.

65. Roger Toll in ibid., 55.

66. Moomaw, *Recollections*, 26.

67. Ibid. James Alexander (1888–1971) would go on to enjoy a distinguished career as both a topologist and a mountaineer. The following year, 1923, Alexander

made nine additional ascents of the East Face before moving on to Europe and the Alps where he completed some eighty-five climbs. According to Longs Peak historian Stephen Trimble, Alexander may have been beaten in his ascent of the East Face by more than three years. Trimble cites the August 23, 1919, entry on the summit registry by one Werner Zimmerman of Bern, Switzerland, who wrote "Alone. Traverse east west by abyss chimney 20 yards south." Trimble speculates that Zimmerman, who never claimed the honor, reached the summit by way of Alexander's Chimney or a route further to the south making use of the saddle between Longs Peak and Mount Meeker. See Stephen Trimble, *Longs Peak: A Rocky Mountain Chronicle* (Estes Park: Rocky Mountain Nature Association, 2000), 78.

68. William M. Buehler, *Roof of the Rockies: A History of Colorado Mountaineering* (Evergreen, CO: Cordillera Press, 1986), 113.

69. See ibid., 113–117. See also John D. Gorby, *The Stettner Way: The Life and Times of Joe and Paul Stettner* (Golden: Colorado Mountain Club Press, 2003), 57–74.

70. Arps and Kingery, *High Country Names*, 33–34. The Arbuckle Reservoir Company was sold to the City of Longmont in October 1933.

71. *Longmont Ledger,* 31 (July 29, 1910): 1; ibid., 32 (July 28, 1911): 4.

72. RDNPS, 1926, 36; *Longmont Ledger,* 47 (July 2, 1926): 8.

73. *Estes Park Trail,* 12 (April 7, 1933): 26. This despite the fact that a parking area at the Mills Lake–Loch Vale Trailhead had been completed in June 1929, further opening the area to hikers.

74. SMR, July 1922, 30; ibid., August 1922, 5–6; SAR, 1922, 27.

75. By 1916 the Y could advertise in its brochure that it had a physical plant on 500 acres containing "upwards" of 70 buildings, including 55 cottages capable of sleeping 400 guests. In addition to the administration building and dining hall, the camp boasted a "general store, barber shop, baths and toilets, gymnasium, assembly hall, six tennis courts, a baseball diamond, and an athletic field. "The Estes Park Conference of the Young Men's Christian Association Season of 1916," EPM.

76. Jack B. Melton and Lulabeth Melton, *YMCA of the Rockies: Spanning a Century* (Estes Park, CO: YMCA of the Rockies, 1992), 90. This book remains the best source of information on Y history.

77. *Estes Park Trail,* 3 (May 4, 1923): 12.

78. Ibid., 1 (August 12, 1921): 11.

79. Ibid., 3 (June 29, 1923): 9.

80. Ibid., 3 (July 27, 1923): 19.

81. Ibid.

82. Ibid., 4 (November 21, 1924): 1.

83. "The Rocky Mountain Boys Camp," brochure, c. 1928, copy, RMNPL.

84. *Estes Park Trail,* 3 (June 8, 1923): 1. The most detailed historical information on the Olinger Highlander organization and RMNP is found in Marjory Busse, "A Concise History of the Highlander Boys Camp, Glacier Basin Campground, Rocky Mountain National Park," typescript report, February 1949, RMNPL.

85. Quoted in Busse, "A Concise History of the Highlander Boys Camp," 4.

86. *Longmont Times,* 28 (June 19, 1922): 2.

87. Reprinted in Jack Cheley, "Cheley Colorado Camps," undated typescript, copy EPPLCC.

88. Oral anecdote, Ernest Petrocene to James H. Pickering, Summer 2000.

89. These included Camp Ekelela ("Ever Growing") in the Tahosa Valley near Katherine Garetson's Big Owl Tea Room, which opened in 1923 and operated for seven seasons under the direction of Agnes Dawson of Madison, Wisconsin; Camp Dunraven, operated by the Camp Fire Girls of Northern Colorado, which in 1923 leased and then purchased and remodeled the Earl's old cottage on Fish Creek; the Estes Park Camp for Girls ("Camp Eloise"), established during the mid-1920s by Nellie Eloise Boyd on the east side of Prospect Mountain; and the Rocky Mountain Camp for Girls and the Allsebrook Camp for Girls, both begun in 1928. The Rocky Mountain Camp for Girls, located on Fox Creek near Glen Haven, was run by William S. Cord, principal of the fashionable Lockwood School in Webster Groves, Missouri. Camp Allsebrook was founded by Bertha Gillette Allsebrook, who initially converted her own cabin, "Will o' the Wisp" on Sheep (Rams Horn) Mountain, into camp facilities and added four sleeping cabins and a bathhouse. In 1934 she had the largest of the cabins and the bathhouse moved to the side of Emerald Mountain west of the Y, where she leased Morningside Lodge, the three-story log and stone building erected by the reverend John Timothy Stone as a summer home about 1920. She continued to use that site for her small camp—there were never more than thirty-six campers—through the 1939 summer season. Elaine Allsebrook Hostmark, "Allsebrooks in Estes Park," unpublished typescript, 23–40, EPPLCC.

90. Beginning in 1911 the Y offered a successful, if relatively unprofitable, summer school, a series of training programs for those involved in Y work that attracted students from around the world. See Melton and Melton, *YMCA of the Rockies*, 47ff. For a number of years the normal school at Greeley offered college-level courses at Camp Olympus, near the entrance to the Big Thompson Canyon.

91. "Roger Toll," *Trail and Timberline*, 209–210 (March–April 1936): 28.

CHAPTER 9

1. The Sanborn Map Company was founded in New York City in 1867 by D. A. Sanborn, a former surveyor from Somerville, Massachusetts, who had become convinced of the utility of such maps while working for the Aetna Insurance Company. By 1937 Sanborn maps covered more than 13,000 towns and cities, each drawn to strict standards at a scale of fifty feet to an inch on sheets measuring 21-by-25 inches. Copies of these maps are housed in a special collection at the Library of Congress.

2. These insurance records are contained in two bound volumes titled "Fire Insurance Rates for Estes Park (Larimer County) Colorado, October 1924," EPM.

3. The telephone came to Estes Park by way of Loveland in fall 1900, when local residents, frustrated by Colorado Telephone Company's refusal to provide service, began to construct a line of their own. These efforts attracted the attention of the company, which agreed to take over and complete the project. The first telephone—the one from which F. O. Stanley made his famous phone call to Billy

Welch announcing his arrival in Estes Park—was installed in William T. Parke's store on lower Elkhorn Avenue. The arrangement with Colorado Telephone lasted until May 1907, when a group of local businessmen formed a company with Pieter Hondius as president and James Stead as vice president and purchased the exchange to protect local service after the company claimed that there was not enough "work to be done" to justify keeping an employee in Estes Park. In 1911, the company was merged into Mountain States Telephone. By 1923, some 423 telephones were connected to the Estes Park exchange. From 1924 until 1960 the telephone company occupied a building on Moraine Avenue whose foundations incorporated the house built by Sidney Sherman in 1908. When the building was demolished in 1960, the tin box and its artifacts placed there by Sherman were recovered. See *Longmont Ledger*, 13 (August 1, 1902): 2; *Loveland Reporter*, 28 (May 9, 1907): 1; and *Estes Park Trail Gazette*, 40 (August 5, 1960): 10.

4. *Estes Park Trail*, 7 (June 10, 1927): 19.

5. The Estes Park Library had its beginnings in October 1916, when the Woman's Club approached the school board and offered to take care of the school library in exchange for space in the school for a public library to be open two afternoons a week. The board agreed, and the following spring the committee gave a "Book Social," gathering 192 books and $11.50 in donations for the new facility. This arrangement lasted until fall 1920 when the library was forced to vacate its space because of crowded conditions in the school. Planning then began for a library building in the village park constructed on land donated by the town. When the new library opened in September 1922, some 1,478 books were transferred. See Alma Bond, "A Short History of the Estes Park Library," *Estes Park Trail*, 6 (November 11, 1926): 3.

6. MBTEP, April 28, 1919, 46.

7. *Estes Park Trail*, 4 (May 16, 1924): 1; ibid., 4 (April 8, 1925): 1; *Fort Collins Express-Courier*, 51 (October 8, 1924): 7. The building itself cost $6,324.40, which was paid for as part of a $14,000 bond issue approved by voters in April 1925.

8. *Estes Park Trail*, 5 (January 8, 1926): 4.

9. Ibid., 4 (March 20, 1925): 1; ibid., 4 (May 1, 1925): 1; *Estes Park Trail Gazette*, 13 (March 14, 1984): 12.

10. *Estes Park Trail Gazette* 13 (May 17, 1984): 2. Mrs. James was the former Jennie Chapin, who before her marriage in 1905 spent four seasons, beginning in 1901, as a partner with Emma Foot in the store that Miss Foot had opened in 1891.

11. *Estes Park Trail*, 3 (June 8, 1923): 8; ibid., 3 (June 8, 1923): 5; ibid., 4 (April 11, 1924): 1; ibid., 4 (May 1, 1925): 1; ibid., 6 (January 7, 1927): 4.

12. For the life and achievements of Joe Mills see James H. Pickering's "Introduction" in *A Mountain Boyhood* by Joe Mills (Lincoln: University of Nebraska Press, 1988), ix–li.

13. The first organizational meeting of the Estes Park Rotary took place at the Elkhorn Lodge on May 6, 1926. The installation ceremony came a month later. *Fort Collins Express Courier*, 53 (June 8, 1926): 2.

14. *Estes Park Trail*, 2 (June 16, 1922): 1; ibid., 3 (May 4, 1923): 1.

15. Ibid., 2 (June 30, 1922): 1.

16. Ibid.

17. Ibid., 3 (May 4, 1923): 1; *Loveland Reporter*, 43 (May 17, 1923): 1.

18. *Estes Park Trail*, 3 (May 18, 1923): 1.

19. Ibid., 3 (May 25, 1923): 1.

20. See, for example, *Fort Collins Courier*, 45 (June 12, 1923): 6.

21. *Estes Park Trail*, 3 (June 1, 1923): 1.

22. Ibid., 3 (June 10, 1923): 5.

23. Ibid., 3 (August 10, 1923): 11.

24. Ibid., 3 (September 14, 1923): 1.

25. Ibid., 3 (October 19, 1923): 6.

26. *Fort Collins Express-Courier*, 50 (October 29, 1923): 6; *Estes Park Trail*, 3 (October 19, 1923): 6.

27. *Estes Park Trail*, 4 (May 16, 1924): 1; ibid., 4 (May 30, 1924): 1.

28. *Fort Collins Courier-Express*, 51 (July 31, 1924): 2.

29. *Estes Park Trail*, 4 (August 15, 1924): 1.

30. Ibid., 5 (April 2, 1926): 9.

31. *Fort Collins Courier-Express*, 52 (June 19, 1925): 2.

32. *Estes Park Trail*, 5 (June 19, 1925): 1.

33. Ibid., 5 (October 16, 1925): 4, 5.

34. Wilma Glendenning, unpublished typed transcript, "Business on Elkhorn, An Oral Interview," April 17, 1986, EPPLCC, 3.

35. *Estes Park Trail*, 1 (September 23, 1921): 4; ibid., 1 (November 11, 1921): 2.

36. Harriet Rogers Byerly (1879–1955), a native of Nebraska, came to Estes Park in 1912 to attend a conference at the Y Camp. In 1916 she returned to stay, having married photographer Frank W. Byerly who she later divorced. That same year, apparently with the help of family money, she began the construction of the Pine Cone Tea Room on Elkhorn Avenue just west of Sam Service's house and store. In fall 1919, the Tea Room was moved to the rear of the property to allow for construction of her ten-room National Park Hotel. In 1926 the hotel underwent a major renovation with the construction of a two-story, thirty-bedroom addition, bringing the number of rooms to forty. The building in more recent times has undergone a number of transformations, one of which converted the hotel into a Ripley's "Believe It or Not Museum." It is now a mall of shops.

37. *Estes Park Trail*, 3 (May 25, 1923): 11.

38. Ibid., 3 (October 26, 1923): 8. Historical information on Riverside is found in the special "Farewell to Riverside" souvenir program put together to commemorate its closing in January 1970. Copy, EPPLCC.

39. *Mountaineer* (August 6, 1908): 6.

40. *Estes Park Trail*, 18 (April 29, 1938): 1.

41. Ibid., 10 (June 27, 1930): 9.

42. Riverside Amusement Park continued to be a fixture in Estes Park through the 1930s and into the 1940s and 1950s. In December 1933 after prohibition ended, Jelsema added the Dark Horse Tavern, a bar using for barstools the wooden horses of a merry-go-round that he purchased but could not operate. It was such an immediate success that for the 1935 season Jelsema had it enlarged. In January

1946, Jelsema sold Riverside. Soon afterward the swimming pool was closed, covered with flooring, and converted to a roller skating rink. Between 1958 and 1969 the Dark Horse Theater offered theatricals on a stage built over the pool. In October 1969 the town entered into a lease-purchase agreement, with the understanding that the site would be used for a badly needed parking lot. After a farewell dance on January 31, 1970, Riverside was razed.

43. *Estes Park Trail*, 6 (November 5, 1926): 3, 10.

44. See, for example, ibid., 4 (April 10, 1925): 4; ibid., 5 (January 8, 1926): 4; ibid., 5 (February 26, 1926): 4.

45. *Denver Post* (April 4, 1917): 13.

46. *Longmont Call*, 19 (June 15, 1917): 4.

47. MBTEP, October 18, 1918, 44.

48. Ibid., June 11, 1917, 4.

49. Ibid., June 14, 1917, 6.

50. On March 15, 1921, Byron Hall (Rocky Mountain Parks Transportation Company), Charles Masters (meat market), Fred Clatworthy (general merchandise store), Estes Osborn (garage), and the Estes Park Bank were cited for allowing piles of ash and rubbish to accumulate on their properties. Ibid., March 15, 1921, 84.

51. Ibid., May 23, 1921, 93.

52. Ibid., June 13, 1921, 95.

53. *Estes Park Trail*, 1 (June 10, 1921): 6.

54. Ibid., 2 (April 10, 1923): 6. Baird's store had originally been built by photographer William T. Parke.

55. MBTEP, June 5, 1922, 31.

56. *Estes Park Trail*, 5 (May 8, 1925): 4.

57. Ibid., 5 (December 4, 1925): 12.

58. MBTEP, May 24, 1926, 247.

59. Ibid., February 28, 1927, 251.

60. Ibid., May 9, 1927, 265. As required by law the proposed ordinance, containing a list of the properties affected, was published in the *Estes Park Trail*. See *Estes Park Trail*, 7 (August 26, 1927): 4, 17.

61. MBTEP, September 26, 1927, 273.

62. Ibid., October 3, 1927, 275.

63. *Estes Park Trail*, 7 (September 16, 1927): 1; ibid., 7 (September 30, 1927): 1.

64. Ibid., 7 (October 7, 1927): 10.

65. Ibid., 8 (April 20, 1928): 1.

66. Ibid., 8 (April 27, 1928): 6.

67. Ibid., 8 (July 6, 1928): 14.

68. Ibid., 7 (March 9, 1928): 2.

69. Ibid., 8 (January 18, 1929): 7.

70. Ibid., 8 (April 27, 1928): 7; ibid., 8 (May 4, 1928): 11.

71. *Longmont Daily Call*, 24 (July 2, 1928): 1.

72. *Estes Park Trail*, 9 (October 18, 1929): 1. See also *Longmont Daily Call*, 25 (October 11, 1929): 2; ibid., 25 (October 24, 1929): 1.

73. *Estes Park Trail*, 12 (May 6, 1932): 1.

CHAPTER 10

1. James F. Wickens, *Colorado in the Great Depression* (New York: Garland Publishing, 1979), 50, 61. Other useful studies of Colorado during the Depression include Stephen J. Leonard's *Trials and Triumphs: A Colorado Portrait of the Great Depression, With FSA Photographs* (Niwot: University Press of Colorado, 1993).

2. Carl Abbott, Stephen J. Leonard, and David McComb, *Colorado: A History of the Centennial State* (Boulder: Colorado Associated Press, 1982), 264.

3. Wickens, *Colorado in the Great Depression*, 379.

4. See Cindy S. Aron, *Working at Play: A History of Vacations in the United States* (New York: Oxford University Press, 1999), particularly 236–257.

5. The park's visitor count was 255,874 in 1930 and 265,663 in 1931, as compared to 274,408 in 1929. The number of automobiles actually rose in both years, from 67,682 in 1929 to 73,100 in 1930, and 75,429 in 1931.

6. *Estes Park Trail*, 17 (July 7, 1937): 1.

7. Ibid., 17 (June 18, 1937): 4.

8. Ibid., 17 (September 3, 1937): 4.

9. Ibid., 15 (September 27, 1935): 1.

10. Ibid., 15 (November 15, 1935): 2.

11. As the Meltons make clear in their history, the late 1920s and early 1930s were characterized by insufficient cash flow, rising debt, and a lack of stable and decisive leadership, particularly following the departure of director Ira Lute in 1927. By July 1930 association president William Sweet was on record stating that "unless sources of greatly increased revenue can be found . . . it is only a question of time before the Conference grounds will have to be permanently closed." Only vigorous action by Sweet and his fellow board members allowed the Y to survive. After imposing a series of draconian measures for summer 1933, the YMCA actually ended the season with a small surplus. See Melton and Melton, *YMCA of the Rockies*, 105–109, 114–121.

12. *Estes Park Trail*, 12 (July 28, 1932): 4.

13. Ibid., 12 (January 13, 1933): 1.

14. Ibid., 12 (February 10, 1933): 1.

15. Ibid.

16. Ibid., 11 (May 15, 1931): 2.

17. Ibid., 13 (April 21, 1933): 4.

18. Ibid., 13 (May 5, 1933): 4.

19. Ibid., 13 (May 26, 1933): 1.

20. Ibid., 13 (November 24, 1933): 4.

21. Ibid., 13 (December 8, 1933): 1, 4.

22. Moomaw, *Recollections*, 131–136.

23. *Estes Park Trail*, 15 (November 29, 1935): 1.

24. Ibid., 15 (December 13, 1935): 1; ibid. (December 20, 1935): 1, 4; ibid. (December 27, 1935): 1.

25. Ibid., 15 (April 10, 1936): 2.

26. SMR, May 1932, 2.

27. *Estes Park Trail*, 12 (October 7, 1932): 1.

28. SMR, January 1933, 1.
29. Ibid., April 1933, 2–3.
30. Ibid., May 1933, 2.
31. Ibid., February 1934, 3–4.
32. *Estes Park Trail*, 15 (January 31, 1936): 4; ibid. (February 14, 1936): 1.
33. Ibid., 18 (September 16, 1938): 4.
34. SMR, December 1933, 1; *Estes Park Trail*, 13 (December 22, 1933): 1; SAR, 1934, 15. Time cards for this CWA project are part of the RMNP archives. They record such familiar local names as Baldwin, Bishop, Grace, Griffith, Hyatt, Low, McGraw, Peck, Reed, Scott, and Wilson.
35. *Estes Park Trail*, 19 (March 22, 1940): 2.
36. Ibid., 20 (January 24, 1941): 8.
37. SAR, 1922, 16. Other sources of information on the building of Trail Ridge Road may be found in Richard H. Quin, "Historic American Buildings Survey", Trail Ridge Road, Rocky Mountain National Park," HAER No. Co-31, 1993, RMNPL; "United States Department of Agriculture Bureau of Public Roads . . . Final Construction Report (1929–30–31–32) on Fall River Pass National Highway, Trail Ridge Section (1933), RMNPL; Daniel C. Harrington, "The Trail Ridge Saga," unpublished typescript of talk given at RMNP, July 17, 1982, RMNPL; and Musselman, *Rocky Mountain National Park*, 89–94.
38. S. A. Wallace, Chief of Survey, "Report of Surveys, Rocky Mountain National Park, Colorado" (Denver: U.S. Department of Agriculture, Bureau of Roads, 1928), quoted in Quin, "Historic American Buildings Survey, Trail Ridge Road" 8.
39. See Anna L. Newsom, "Trail Ridge Road . . . in Rocky Mountain National Park," *Highway Magazine*, 27 (March 1936): 76–78.
40. "United States Department of Agriculture Bureau of Public Roads . . . Final Construction Report," 26.
41. Ibid., 20–21.
42. *Denver Post* (March 25, 1917): Section 3, p. 2.
43. *Loveland Reporter*, 28 (October 24, 1907): 1; ibid., 28 (November 21, 1907): 1.
44. *Loveland Reporter*, 39 (December 20, 1918): 1; *Loveland Daily Herald*, 10 (December 28, 1918): 1.
45. *Loveland Daily Herald*, 10 (August 1, 1919): 1; (August 2, 1919): 1.
46. Named after its builders Monty and Rose Tucker, the Mont Rose Inn at Dixon Gulch with its dance pavilion and cottages was for many years a popular canyon destination. It was destroyed by fire in February 1938.
47. *Loveland Reporter*, 40 (June 2, 1920): 1; *Loveland Daily Herald*, 10 (June 1, 1920): 1.
48. *Longmont Daily Call*, 24 (March 14, 1928): 2.
49. *Longmont Ledger*, 52 (August 4, 1931): 2.
50. *Longmont Times-Call*, 43 (October 22, 1935): 2.
51. *Fort Collins Express Courier*, 53 (November 8, 1926): 1.
52. SMR, February 1934, 2.

53. *Longmont Times-Call*, 44 (July 9, 1936): 1.

54. *Estes Park Trail*, 16 (January 22, 1937): 1; *Longmont Times-Call*, 44 (January 22, 1937): 4.

55. *Denver Post* (July 13, 1919): Section 2, p. 2.

56. Subsequent work in 1931 eliminated Stanley Hill entirely by building a new mile and a half section of road above Raymond.

57. The route, to be located on the southwest slope of Lily Mountain, was one preferred by the Park Service in part because it could be opened earlier in the season. It was along the lower section of the proposed road, known as the Wind River Trail, that Anna Wolfrom homesteaded in 1907 and later opened her Wigwam Tea Room and Gift Shop. Mentioned as a possibility in the superintendent's annual report for 1919, the route was surveyed and staked by the Bureau of Public Roads late in 1924 as an alternative to the road on the east side of Lily Mountain. See *Estes Park Trail*, 1 (July 6, 1912): 1; ibid., 3 (September 5, 1914): 3.

58. *Estes Park Trail*, 15 (June 21, 1935): 1.

59. *Loveland Daily Herald*, 12 (July 27, 1921): 1.

60. Ibid., 19 (July 31, 1919): 1.

61. *Lyons Recorder*, 19 (August 2, 1919): 1; ibid. (August 9, 1919): 1.

62. *Fort Collins Courier-Express*, 50 (December 9, 1923): 15.

63. *Boulder Daily Camera*, 44 (January 16, 1935): 1; *Longmont Times-Call*, 42 (December 28, 1934): 1.

64. *Boulder Daily Camera*, 45 (July 19, 1935): 2.

65. *Longmont Times-Call*, 43 (September 14, 1935): 1; ibid. (September 16. 1935): 1.

66. Ibid., 47 (June 5, 1939): 1.

67. *Longmont Times-Call*, 47 (June 4, 1939): 2.

68. The standard study of the Colorado–Big Thompson Project is Daniel Tyler's comprehensive *The Last Water Hole in the West: The Colorado–Big Thompson Project and the Northern Colorado Water Conservancy District* (Niwot: University Press of Colorado, 1992). See also Donald B. Cole, "Trans-mountain Water Diversion in Colorado," *Colorado Magazine*, 25 (March–May 1948), 49–65; and Musselman, *Rocky Mountain National Park*, 111–124.

69. *Report of the State Engineer to the Governor of Colorado for the Years 1883 and 1884* (Denver: Collier and Cleaveland, 1885), 66, 68. See also F. H. Newell, *Fourth Annual Report of the Reclamation Service, 1904–1905* (Washington, D.C.: Government Printing Office, 1906), 126–127.

70. *Longmont Ledger*, 14 (March 17, 1893): 3; *Loveland Reporter*, 26 (August 31, 1905): 2. See also C. E. Tait, *Storage of Water on Cache La Poudre and Big Thompson Rivers* (Washington, D.C.: Government Printing Offices, 1903), 87.

71. See MSEP, 86–88.

72. For a history of the Grand Ditch in relation to RMNP see Jeffrey S. Hickey, "An Uneasy Coexistence: Rocky Mountain National Park and the Grand River Ditch," M.A. Thesis, University of Colorado, Boulder, 1988, copy RMNPL.

73. Patrick McKnight, "The Water Rights of Rocky Mountain National Park: A History," unpublished typescript manuscript, RMNPL, 35–35; *Fort Collins Evening*

Courier, 7 (September 20, 1902): 1. In September 1940, the City of Loveland officially abandoned the Eureka Ditch.

74. Tyler, *Last Water Hole in the West,* 31–32.

75. See Donald C. Swain, "The Bureau of Reclamation and the New Deal," *Pacific Northwest Quarterly,* 61 (July 1970): 137–146.

76. John S. McLaughlin, "Colorado–Big Thomson Diversion Project and Its Relationship to Rocky Mountain National Park," May 26, 1937, unpublished typescript, RMNPL, 16.

77. Quoted in Tyler, *Last Water Hole in the West,* 88.

78. *Estes Park Trail,* 18 (June 10, 1938): 4.

79. Hewes Journal, October 17, 1939.

80. Ibid., November 10, 1939.

81. Announced at the time of a memorial service for Adams, the name was made official by legislation signed by Roosevelt on December 21, 1944.

82. Construction on elements of the Colorado–Big Thompson Project continued into the 1950s. As in the case of the decision to build Lake Estes, some of the final components were added once engineers were in the field and actual construction got underway; the design and location of some of the original components were revised for the same reason. On the Eastern Slope the Marys Lake and Lake Estes Reservoirs were added to allow the Estes Park Power Plant to operate efficiently without disturbing the flow of water from the Adams Tunnel and to aid power generation below Estes Park.

83. *Estes Park Trail,* 13 (January 8, 1934): 4.

84. Ibid., 14 (February 1, 1935): 1.

85. *Estes Park Trail,* 11 (August 14, 1931): 1; ibid. (August 28, 1931): 1, 14.

86. Ibid., 12 (May 27, 1932): 1.

87. Charles A. Johnson, *Opera in the Rockies: A History of the Central City Opera House Association, 1932–1992* (Central City, CO: Central City Opera Association, 1992), 1.

88. *Estes Park Trail,* 15 (June 15, 1935): 4.

89. Ibid., 12 (August 19, 1932): 1.

90. Ibid., 15 (August 23, 1935): 1.

CHAPTER 11

1. Roger W. Toll, "Mountain Trail Trips in Rocky Mountain National Park and R.M.N.P. Quadrangle," vol. 1, unpublished manuscript notebook, RMNPL, 1.

2. Interview with Edmund Rogers, July 13, 1964, cited in Musselman, *Rocky Mountain National Park,* 89.

3. Quoted in Cahn, *Birth of the National Park Service,* 70. The statement had been drafted by Horace Albright for Lane's signature at the request of Park Service director Stephen Mather.

4. Just who authorized, was involved in, or knew about the practice or its implementation remains unclear. In 1939, after an investigation by the General Accounting Office of a transaction in General Grant National Park resulted.in a federal indictment of a number of individuals, including former Park Service di-

rector Horace Albright, Harold Ickes conducted his own inquiry. His attempt to get to the bottom of what was then a nearly decade-old practice resulted in only denials and finger-pointing. See Harold L. Ickes, *The Secret Diary of Harold L. Ickes* II (New York: Simon and Schuster, 1954), 582–584. Of those in Estes Park involved in such transactions, only Abner Sprague chose to write about his experiences with the government—one that left him with a tax liability and decidedly negative feelings. See Abner Sprague, *My Pioneer Life: Memoirs of Abner E. Sprague* (Estes Park: Rocky Mountain Nature Association, 1999), 229–232. The agreements signed were explicit. Pieter Hondius, for example, agreed to sell his lands for a price of $281,440 "but with the understanding that he shall accept in full payment thereof one-half of said amount, thereby in effect donating to the United States the remaining one-half purchase price as herein set forth." "Agreement" between Peter Hondius and the United States, December 30, 1931, 9. Courtesy Pieter Hondius.

5. Hewes Journal, December 31, 1931.
6. William Allan White to Mr. and Mrs. Edmund Rogers, January 4, 1932, RMNPL.
7. *Estes Park Trail*, 8 (February 2, 1929): 1.
8. Organized administratively into districts, the letters and numbers assigned each CCC camp represented (in order) the government agency that supervised the camp, the number of camps supervised by that agency in order of their founding, and the state in which the camp was located. N.P. 1-C thus identified the first camp in Colorado under National Park Service supervision. For historical background on the CCC in the West, including RMNP, see I. A. Gleyre and C. N. Alleger, *History of the Civilian Conservation Corps in Colorado* (Denver: Press of the Western Newspaper Union, c. 1936); L. R. Douglass, "The Civilian Conservation Corps in Rocky Mountain National Park," *Colorado Engineer*, 30 (March 1934): 49–51; Richard Melzer, *Coming of Age in the Great Depression: The Civilian Conservation Corps Experience in New Mexico, 1933–1942* (Las Cruces, NM: Yucca Tree Press, 2000); and Musselman, *Rocky Mountain National Park*, 95–110.
9. Musselman, *Rocky Mountain National Park*, 97–98; SMR, June 1933, 1.
10. Douglass, "The Civilian Conservation Corps," 49.
11. SMR, June 1933, 1.
12. Musselman, *Rocky Mountain National Park*, 11.
13. Letter copied verbatim, SMR, June 1933, 12.
14. Ibid.
15. *Estes Park Trail*, 13 (May 26, 1933): 1; Buchholtz, *Rocky Mountain National Park*, 186.
16. Quoted in Musselman, *Rocky Mountain National Park*, 98–99.
17. *Estes Park Trail*, 3 (August 8, 1914): 6.
18. SMR, October 1933, 6.
19. Battell Loomis, "With the Green Guard," *Liberty* (April 1932): 41. The reference to a "lad of the Montana Blackfeet" is undoubtedly to Charles Eagle Plume Burkhart (1910–1992), then working at O. S. Perkins's store in the nearby Tahosa Valley.
20. Douglass, "The Civilian Conservation Corps," 50–51.

21. Camp N.P. 3-C was a seasonal, temporary camp. It operated in Phantom Valley during the 1933 and 1934 summers. It was replaced in 1935 by Camp N.P. 7-C, also a temporary camp, which was disbanded during spring 1936 and activated once more in summer 1938. Two years later in 1940, Camp N.P. 12-C was established as a permanent camp near Grand Lake. It was abandoned in summer 1942.

22. *Estes Park Trail*, 14 (September 7, 1934): 8.

23. Quoted, *Longmont Times-Call*, 60 (April 19, 1933): 5.

24. *Estes Park Trail*, 13 (May 26, 1933): 1.

25. Ibid., 13 (June 2, 1933): 7.

26. SMR, May 1938, 1, 8.

27. *Estes Park Trail*, 19 (April 28, 1939): 4.

28. Quoted in Musselman, *Rocky Mountain National Park*, 101.

29. Ibid., 22–23; SMR, June 1934, 1.

30. *Estes Park Trail*, 15 (October 4, 1935): 1, 7.

31. Ibid., 19 (August 23, 1939): 6.

32. Reprinted in ibid., 20 (April 18, 1941): 5.

33. Ibid., 23 (May 28, 1943): 3.

34. Ibid., 22 (July 31, 1942): 9.

35. Sellars, *Preserving Nature in National Parks*, 101.

36. The present trail from Moraine Park to the Pool was built by the CCC between 1935 and 1938. Beyond the Pool the trail leading up to Fern Lake has had many locations and at one time two were in use. The trail as it existed before the CCC reconstruction did not pass either Fern Falls or Marguerite Falls. The present trail, which passes both, was built in 1937–1938. Between 1933 and 1936 the trail from Fern to Odessa was rebuilt to swing east of Fern and then follow the creek between the two lakes.

37. *Estes Park Trail*, 18 (August 19, 1938): 8.

38. SMR, July 1923, 10.

39. Ibid., August 31, 1923, 8.

40. Cahn, *Birth of the National Park Service*, 270.

41. *Estes Park Trail*, 13 (July 14, 1933): 4.

42. H. R. Gregg, "Museums in Rocky Mountain National Park," *Estes Park Trail*, 17 (April 23, 1930): 11, 30.

43. RMNP News Release, October 4, 1938, RMNPL.

44. SAR, 1937, 13.

45. Yeager also wrote a number of animal novels, including *Scarface: The Story of a Grizzly* (1935), the story of the last grizzly in the Estes region.

46. For background on wildlife management efforts by the National Park Service and in RMNP, see Sellars, *Preserving Nature in the National Parks*; R. Gerald Wright, *Wildlife Research and Management in the National Parks* (Urbana: University of Illinois Press, 1992); Joseph S. Dixon, "The Elk Problem at Rocky Mountain National Park," unpublished typescript report, RMNPL; Guse, "Administrative History of an Elk Herd"; Daniel Howard Henning, "National Park Wildlife Management Policy: A Field Administration and Political Study at Rocky Mountain

National Park," Ph.D. dissertation, Syracuse University, 1965, copy RMNPL; Robert F. Buttery, "Range Conditions and Trends Resulting from Winter Concentrations of Elk in Rocky Mountain National Park," M.S. thesis, Colorado Agricultural and Mechanical College, 1955, copy RMNPL; and Musselman, *Rocky Mountain National Park*, 125–146.

47. Sellars, *Preserving Nature in National Parks*, 69–70.

48. Ibid., 70.

49. *Longmont Call*, 17 (November 27, 1914): 2.

50. *Fort Collins Express*, 43 (December 29, 1916): 6.

51. *Estes Park Trail*, 1 (January 6, 1922): 1. Grubb refers to liveryman Frank Grubb; Hayden to one of the Hayden brothers, Al or Julian, local surveyors and real estate men.

52. SMR, February 1922, 2.

53. Ibid., May 1922, 61; SAR, 1922, 21.

54. SMR, February 1922, 3.

55. *Estes Park Trail*, 1 (January 27, 1922): 1; *Longmont Ledger*, 43 (February 3, 1922): 1.

56. *Longmont Ledger*, 42 (February 10, 1922): 5.

57. SMR, November 1924, 2.

58. Fred Mallery Packard, "An Ecological Study of the Bighorn Sheep in Rocky Mountain National Park, Colorado," *Journal of Mammalogy*, 27:1 (1914): 8; Musselman, *Rocky Mountain National Park*, 135.

59. Quoted in Guse, "Administrative History of an Elk Herd," 21.

60. *Fort Collins Express Courier*, 53 (May 23, 1926): 7.

61. SMR, December 1926, 3; Guse, "Administrative History of an Elk Herd," 21.

62. Quoted in Sellars, Preserving Nature in National Parks, 74.

63. Packard, "An Ecological Study of the Bighorn Sheep," 9.

64. SMR, September 1930, 5.

65. SAR, 1931, 20.

66. Quoted in Guse, "Administrative History of an Elk Herd," 27.

67. SMR, September 1931, 10.

68. Ibid., November 1932, 7.

69. Musselman, *Rocky Mountain National Park*, 132–133; Buttery, "Range Conditions and Trends," 83–84.

70. Guse, "Administrative History of an Elk Herd," 31.

71. SAR, 1935, 8.

72. Dixon, "The Elk Problem at Rocky Mountain National Park," 29, 41.

73. Quoted in Guse, "Administrative History of an Elk Herd," 35.

74. *Estes Park Trail*, 21 (December 12, 1941): 1.

75. David D. Condon, "Recommendations and an Outline for Management of the Elk and Deer Population in Rocky Mountain National Park," unpublished typescript report, November 20, 1953, RMNPL.

76. Daniel Henning, cited in note 46, this chapter, provides the best account of how the decision to reduce the herd was made and implemented. Henning had access to notes made during the February meeting and later interviewed a number

of the principals involved. See Henning, "National Park Wildlife Management Policy," 128–140.

77. Quoted in Guse, "Administrative History of an Elk Herd," 37.

78. The elk reduction program in Rocky Mountain National Park continued until 1969, when a natural regulation policy involving no active management within the park was instituted in the belief that hunting in adjacent areas would control the elk population in and near the park.

79. Quoted in Guse, "Administrative History of an Elk Herd," 38–39.

80. Quoted in Musselman, *Rocky Mountain National Park*, 139–140.

CHAPTER 12

1. *Estes Park Trail*, 20 (January 17, 1941): 1.

2. Ibid., 20 (October 4, 1940): 4.

3. Ibid., 20 (November 1, 1940): 20.

4. Ibid., 21 (January 9, 1942): 4.

5. Ibid., 22 (May 8, 1942): 1.

6. Despite the fact that other parks had entrance fees, the Estes Park business community resisted the idea for fear it would discourage tourists. When the new fee was announced, officials braced themselves for "a local furor." "Almost the opposite has been the case," Canfield noted with relief in his March 1939 monthly report. "The public's reaction on the whole has been favorable." SMR, March 1939, 1.

7. "The Forties in Estes Park," Oral History transcript, July 15, 1979, EPPLCC, 8.

8. *Estes Park Trail*, 22 (April 24, 1942): 2.

9. Ibid., 23 (April 23, 1943): 3.

10. SMR, May 1943, 9.

11. *Estes Park Trail*, 22 (September 11, 1942): 4.

12. "The Forties in Estes Park," 28.

13. *Estes Park Trail*, 24 (June 16, 1944): 24.

14. Ibid., 23 (October 22, 1943): 1, 5.

15. Ibid., 23 (April 30, 1943): 1, 5.

16. Ibid., 23 (August 9, 1943): 1.

17. MBTEP, July 6, 1943, 341.

18. *Estes Park Trail*, 11 (May 8, 1931): 1.

19. Ibid., 9 (June 21, 1929): 15.

20. Ibid., 12 (June 3, 1932): 1.

21. Ibid., 45 (August 20, 1965): 7.

22. Ibid., 44 (March 2, 1945): 3.

23. The 1923 accident was a freak one. It involved a tourist, who fearing the plane was about to crash shortly after takeoff, climbed to its wing, jumped, and broke his neck. *Loveland Reporter-Herald*, 43 (August 8, 1923): 1. See also *Estes Park Trail*, 15 (August 2, 1935): 1; ibid., 15 (August 9, 1935): 1; ibid., 15 (August 30, 1935): 4; ibid., 20 (March 7, 1941): 1.

24. SMR, July 1940, 1.

25. Ibid., June 1940, 1.

26. Wright, *Wildlife Research and Management*, 22.

27. *Estes Park Trail*, 23 (April 23, 1943): 4X.

28. SAR, 1943, 1.

29. *Estes Park Trail*, 25 (August 17, 1945): 1.

30. Ibid., 24 (December 15, 1944): 3.

31. Rothman, *Devil's Bargains*, 11.

Selected Bibliography

~

PRIMARY SOURCES

Albright, Horace M., and Marian Albright Schenck. *Creating the National Park Service: The Missing Years*. Norman: University of Oklahoma Press, 1999.

Cahn, Robert. *The Birth of the National Park Service: The Founding Years, 1913–1933*. Horace M. Albright as Told to Robert Cahn. Salt Lake City, UT: Howe Brothers, 1985.

Colorado Collection. Estes Park Public Library.

Dixon, Joseph S. "The Elk Problem at Rocky Mountain National Park." Unpublished typescript, Rocky Mountain National Park.

Frank Normali Collection, Stanley Historic Foundation, Estes Park.

Hewes, Charles Edwin. Journal of Charles Edwin Hewes. Unpublished typescript, Estes Park Museum.

Hondius, Eleanor E. *Memoirs of Eleanor E. Hondius of Elkhorn Lodge*. Boulder, CO: Pruett Press, 1964.

McLaughlin, John S. "Colorado–Big Thomson Diversion Project and Its Relationship to Rocky Mountain National Park." Unpublished typescript, May 26, 1937. Rocky Mountain National Park.

Mills vs. Way correspondence. Rocky Mountain National Park.

Minutes of the Board of Trustees of the Town of Estes Park, Colorado. Town of Estes Park.

Minutes of the Estes Park Protective and Improvement Association. Town of Estes Park.

Moomaw, Jack C. *Recollections of a Rocky Mountain Ranger*. Longmont, CO, 1963.

Quin, Richard H. Historic American Buildings Survey, Fall River Road, Rocky Mountain National Park, HAER No. Co-73, 1993.

————. Historic American Buildings Survey, Rocky Mountain National Park Roads, HAER No. Co-78, 1993.

————. Historic American Buildings Survey, Trail Ridge Road, Rocky Mountain National Park, HAER No. Co-31, 1993.

Robbins vs. McDaniel correspondence. Rocky Mountain National Park.

Rocky Mountain National Park. Superintendent's Annual Reports. Typescripts. Rocky Mountain National Park.

————. Superintendent's Monthly Reports. Typescripts. Rocky Mountain National Park.

Sprague, Abner E. "My First Visit to Estes Park." Typescript. Colorado Historical Society.

State of Colorado vs. McDaniel correspondence. Rocky Mountain National Park.

Toll, Roger W., comp. *Mountaineering in the Rocky Mountain National Park*. Washington, D.C.: Government Printing Office, 1919.

————. "Mountain Trail Trips in Rocky Mountain National Park and R.M.N.P. Quadrangle," 2 Vols. Unpublished manuscript. Rocky Mountain National Park.

United States Department of the Interior. *Report of the Director of the National Park Service to the Secretary of the Interior for the Fiscal Year Ended June 30, 1917*. Washington, D.C.: Government Printing Office, 1917 (and for subsequent years).

Wallace, Stephen A., Chief of Survey, U.S. Department of Agriculture, Bureau of Public Roads. "Report of Surveys, Rocky Mountain National Park, Colorado." Denver, CO: Bureau of Public Roads, 1928.

Yeager, Dorr G. *Bob Flame, Rocky Mountain Ranger*. New York: Dodd Mead, 1935.

SECONDARY SOURCES

Aron, Cindy S. *Working at Play: A History of Vacations in the United States*. New York: Oxford University Press, 1999.

Arps, Louisa Ward, and Elinor E. Kingery. *High Country Names: Rocky Mountain National Park*. Estes Park, CO: Rocky Mountain Nature Association, 1977.

Barringer, Mark Daniel. *Selling Yellowstone: Capitalism and the Construction of Nature*. Lawrence: University Press of Kansas, 2002.

Bartlett, Richard A. *Yellowstone: A Wilderness Besieged*. Tucson: University of Arizona Press, 1985.

Belasco, Warren. *Americans on the Road: From Autocamp to Motel, 1910–1945*. Boston: MIT Press, 1979.

Buehler, William M. *Roof of the Rockies: A History of Colorado Mountaineering*. Evergreen, CO: Cordillera Press, 1986.

Buchholtz, Curt W. *Rocky Mountain National Park: A History*. Boulder: Colorado Associated University Press, 1983.

Buttery, Robert F. "Range Conditions and Trends Resulting from Winter Concentrations of Elk in Rocky Mountain National Park." M.S. Thesis. Colorado Agricultural and Mechanical College, 1955.

Carr, Ethan. *Wilderness by Design: Landscape Architecture and the National Park Service.* Lincoln: University of Nebraska Press, 1998.

Demars, Stanford E. *The Tourist in Yosemite, 1855–1985.* Salt Lake City: University of Utah Press, 1991.

Drummond, Alexander. *Enos Mills: Citizen of Nature.* Niwot: University Press of Colorado, 1995.

Dunning, Harold Marion. *Over Hill and Vale.* 3 vols. Boulder, CO: Johnson Publishing Company, 1956–71.

Fay, Abbott. *A History of Skiing in Colorado.* Ouray, CO: Western Reflection, 2000.

Gleyre, I. A., and C. N. Alleger. *History of the Civilian Conservation Corps in Colorado.* Denver: Press of the Western Newspaper Union, c. 1936.

Gorby, John D. *The Stettner Way: The Life and Times of Joe and Paul Stettner.* Golden: Colorado Mountain Club Press, 2003.

Guse, Neal G., Jr. "Comprehensive Report: Administrative History of an Elk Herd." M.S. Thesis. Colorado State University, Fort Collins, 1966.

Henning, Daniel Howard. "National Park Wildlife Management Policy: A Field Administration and Political Study at Rocky Mountain National Park," Ph.D. Dissertation. Syracuse University, 1965.

Ise, John. *Our National Park Policy: A Critical History.* Baltimore: Johns Hopkins University Press, 1961.

Jakle, John. *The Tourist: Travel in Twentieth-Century North America.* Lincoln: University of Nebraska Press, 1985.

Leonard, Stephen J. *Trials and Triumphs: A Colorado Portrait of the Great Depression, With FSA Photographs.* Niwot: University Press of Colorado, 1993.

Louter, David. "Glaciers and Gasoline: The Making of a Windshield Wilderness." In *Seeing and Being Seen: Tourism in the American West.* Ed. David W. Wrobel and Patrick T. Long. Lawrence: University of Kansas Press, 2001.

McClelland, Linda Flint. *Building the National Parks: Historic Landscape and Design.* Baltimore: Johns Hopkins University Press, 1998.

McKnight, Patrick. "The Water Rights of Rocky Mountain National Park: A History." Unpublished typescript. Rocky Mountain National Park.

McQueary, Lela. *Widening Trails: Narratives of Pioneer Days in Middle Park on the Western Slope of Colorado's Rocky Mountains.* Denver: The World Press, 1962.

Melton, Jack B., and Lulabeth Melton. *YMCA of the Rockies: Spanning a Century.* Estes Park, CO: YMCA of the Rockies, 1992.

Melzer, Richard. *Coming of Age in the Great Depression: The Civilian Conservation Corps Experience in New Mexico, 1933–1942.* Las Cruces, NM: Yucca Tree Press, 2000.

Mills, Enos. *The Story of Estes Park.* Longs Peak, CO, 1914.

Musselman, Lloyd. *Rocky Mountain National Park, Administrative History: 1915–1965.* Washington, D.C.: National Park Service, 1971.

Pedersen, Henry F., Jr. *Those Castles of Wood: The Story of Early Lodges of Rocky Mountain National Park and Pioneer Days of Estes Park, Colorado.* Estes Park, CO: Henry F. Pedersen Jr., 1993.

Pickering, James H. *In the Vale of Elkanah: The Tahosa Valley World of Charles Edwin Hewes.* Estes Park: Alpenaire Publishing and the Estes Park Area Historical Museum, 2003.

———. *Mr. Stanley of Estes Park.* Kingfield, ME: The Stanley Museum, 2000.

———. *"This Blue Hollow": Estes Park, The Early Years, 1859–1915.* Niwot: University Press of Colorado, 1999.

———. "Tragedy on Longs Peak: Walter Kiener's Own Story." *Colorado Heritage*, 1 (1990): 18–31.

———. "Vanished in the Mountains: The Saga of the Reverend Thornton R. Sampson." *Colorado Heritage* (Summer 2000): 14–19, 24–29.

———. *The Ways of the Mountains: Thornton Sampson, Agnes Vaille, and Other Tragedies in High Places.* Estes Park, CO: Alpenaire Publishing and the Estes Park Area Historical Museum, 2003.

Ramaley, William C. "Trails and Trailbuilders of Rocky Mountain National Park." Undated typescript. Estes Park, CO: National Park Service, Rocky Mountain National Park, n.d.

Rothman, Hal K. *Devil's Bargains, Tourism in the Twentieth-Century American West.* Lawrence: University of Kansas Press, 1998.

Sellars, Richard West. *Preserving Nature in National Parks: A History.* New Haven, CT: Yale University Press, 1997.

Shaffer, Marguerite S. *See America First: Tourism and National Identity, 1880–1940.* Washington, D.C.: Smithsonian Institution Press, 2001.

Shankland, Robert. *Steve Mather of the National Parks.* New York: Alfred A. Knopf, 1954.

Shoemaker, Florence. "The Story of the Estes–Rocky Mountain National Park Region." M.A. Thesis. Colorado State College of Education, Greeley, 1940.

Swain, Donald. *Wilderness Defender: Horace M. Albright and Conservation.* Chicago: University Press of Chicago, 1970.

Toll, Giles. "'Now We Are Entering That Other World': Roger Wolcott Toll and Rocky Mountain National Park." *Colorado Heritage* (Autumn 2004): 17–31.

Tyler, Daniel. *The Last Water Hole in the West: The Colorado–Big Thompson Project and the Northern Colorado Water Conservancy District.* Niwot: University Press of Colorado, 1992.

Whiteside, James. *Colorado: A Sports History.* Niwot: University Press of Colorado, 1999.

Wickens, James F. *Colorado in the Great Depression.* New York: Garland Publishing, 1979.

Wright, R. Gerald. *Wildlife Research and Management in the National Parks.* Urbana: University of Illinois Press, 1992.

Wrobel, David M., and Patrick T. Long, comps. and eds. *Seeing and Being Seen: Tourism in the American West.* Lawrence: University Press of Kansas, 2001.

Wrobel, David. M. *Promised Lands: Promotion, Memory, and the Creation of the American West.* Lawrence: University Press of Kansas, 2002.

Wyckoff, William. *Creating Colorado: The Making of a Western Landscape, 1860–1940.* New Haven, CT: Yale University Press, 1999.

Index

Page numbers in italics indicate illustrations

Adams, Alva, 317, 322
Adams, Fred, 35
Adams, John (Johnny), 91, 106
Adams, William, 216, 218
Adams Tunnel, 322–23, 324
Adam the Apostle. *See* Desouris, George.
Advertising, 148–50, 201, 287
Agriculture, Front Range, 312–14
Airfield, at Stanley Hotel, 62–63, 376
Airport, 377–78
Alberta Falls, 228, 239
Albizzi, Lieutenant Marquis d', 167
Albright, Horace M., 9, 82, 128, 134, 170, 181, 185, 211, 251, 349, 358, 414(n80), 425–26(n4); on game management, 354, 355; on Mount Evans, 190–91; on roads, 218, 295
Alderdyce, Frank, 28
Alexander, James Wadell, 234–35, 416–17(n67)
Alien Registration Act, 372
All-Colorado Tournament, 172, 174
Allen, Thomas J. (Tom), 170, 218, 292, 327, 349
Allens High Drive Inn, 332
Allenspark, 169–70, 175, 306, 337

Allenspark Chamber of Commerce, 217, 238
Allenspark Commercial Club, 200
Allenspark Ski Club, 169
Alpine Visitors Center, 383
Altick, Ernest, 249, 250
American Expeditionary Force, 114, 115
American Legion, 92, 325, 326
American Legion Rodeo, 291
American Red Cross, 115
American Travel Development Association, 200
Ammons, Elias M., 123, 132, 151
Ammons, Teller, 282, 296, 304
Amphitheaters, 346
Anderson, Harrison Ray, 243
Anderson, Joseph R., 23, 29, 33, 70
Andrew, John, 264
Andrews, Ed, 100
"The Animals of Rocky Mountain National Park," 351
Annual Mid-Summer Ski Meet, 175
Apache, 14
Apple Valley, 309
Arapaho, Northern, 13–14, 296, 352
Arapaho Peaks, 306
Arapaho Glacier, 189, 331

Arapaho, Mount, 189
Arbuckle Reservoir Company, 121, 237,
    405(n63)
Arizona, CCC recruits from, 340
Arps, Harold, 86
Arthur, Timothy Shay, 326
Ashton, Willard H., 20, 125, 171, 238, 335
Ashton Flats, 171
Aspen Brook, 307, 323
Aspenglen Campground, *139*, 241, 346, 347
Auditorium, 259–60, 289, 305; fund raising
    for, 262–64; plans for, 264–65
Audubon, Mount, 306
Autocamping, 138–139, *139*, 240–41,
    405(n61)
Automobiles, 9–10, 41, 92, 146; Stanley,
    55, 63–65
Auto stage lines, 56
Aviation Field, 376

Babcock, Dean, 140, 142, 226; *Birds and
    Flowers of the Rocky Mountain National
    Park*, 348
Bache, Charles, 98
Baird, John, 274, 284
Baker, Dr., 54
Baker, John, 114, 117
Baker Gulch, 313
Bakersfield (Calif.), 352
Balanced Rock, 165
Bald Mountain, 319
Bald Mountain–Pole Hill road, 26, 96, 319
Baldpate Inn, 128, 141, 291, 372
Bands: at Chez Jay, 285; at Riverside
    Amusement Park, 267–68
Banking, 68–70
Barnard, George, 163–64, 251
Bartholf Park, 139
Bath house, 35
Battle Mountain, 125, 226, 228, 347
Bazaars, 105–6
Bear Lake, 19, 93, 108, 125, 131, 140, 168,
    318, 331; improvements to, 219–20;
    road to, 121, 143; trails at, 142, 219,
    346, 347
Bear Lake Lodge, 143, 219, 248, 249, 250,
    334, 405(n70)
Bear Lake ranger station, 351
Bear Lake Road, 143, 177, 220–21, 297,
    332, 334, 338, 374
Bear Lake–Sprague Lake Road, 140

Bear Lake Trail School, 242, 243, 248–49
Bears, 106, 125
Beautiful Estes Park, Colorado, 148, *149*
Beaver, 125, 356–57
Beaver Creek, 339, 347, 358
Beaver Creek Road, 121
Beaver Meadows, 14, 92, 96, 329, 383; elk
    herd at, 357, 359; inholdings in, 332, 333
Beaver Point, 263
Bechtel, Orville W., 171, 408–9(n65)
Becker, Bob (Bobcat Bob), 356, 366
Becker, Robert F., 366
Beckfield, William, 23, 33
Belleau Woods, 114–15
Bennison, Mr., 372
Berthoud Pass, 186
Bethel, Ellsworth, 251
Beust, Herman von, 166
Bible Point, 140
Bierstadt Lake, 19, 59, 93, 124
Bierstadt Moraine, 220, 239
Big Drift, snow removal on, 222–24
Big Hill, 309–10
Bighorn Mountain, 334
Bighorn sheep, 125, 358, 360
Big Narrows, 303
Big Red Barn, 41
Big Thompson Canyon, 25, 290, 313, 317
Big Thompson Canyon Road/Highway, 26,
    55, 63, 64, 121, 135, 326; bridges on,
    303–4; construction of, 301–3; dedica-
    tion of, 304–6; reconstruction of, 303–4
Big Thompson Hotel, 154, 411–12(n45)
Big Thompson River, 2, 18, 74, 95, 241,
    329, 331, 348, 352, 362; inholdings
    along, 332, 333; and sewage system, 45,
    46, 47; water diversion into, 313, 315,
    316, 317. *See also* Colorado–Big
    Thompson Project
Big Thompson Valley, 13, 48, 312, 314, 317
Billings, George (Many) S., 258
Billings, Norton, 172, 175
Bintner, Harry, 20
Biologists, wildlife, 358, 360, 378
Birch, Al, 34, 44, 78, 258, 284, 390(n26);
    publicity hoax of, 150, 151–52, 154, 155,
    156
*Birds and Flowers of the Rocky Mountain
    National Park* (Babcock), 348
Bishop, Edna, 248, 407(n36)
Black Canyon, 17, 70, 92, 357

Black Canyon Creek, 29, 284, 330, 361; water supply from, 70, 71, 395(n51)
Black Hawk, 27
Black Lake, 131, 239
Blacksmith and wagon repair shop, 41
Blasing, Bert, 152
Blue Bird Lake, 121, 237, 238, 314
Blue Lake, 131
Blue Ribbon Livery, 86
Blue River, 317
Boating, 324
Boatright, William L., 215
Bobcats, 356
Bob Flame novels (Yeager), 354
Bond, Cornelius H., 18–19, 23, 24, 25–26, 29, 41, 69, 72, 81, 103, 111, 112, 154, 260, 266, 286, 382, 388(n2), 391(n37), 400(n58); businesses of, 35–36, 392(n52); on park concessions, 195, 196, 198, 201, 212; and Protective and Improvement Association, 94, 95, 98, 101; residence of, 33–34; on water and sewage system, 45–47, 50, 70; on wildlife, 36–37
Bond, Frank, 111, 265, 266, 276, 326; on CCC, 340–41; and Depression-era finances, 288, 289
Bond and Company, C. H., 258–59
Bond Park, 27, 380
Bonfils, Frederick, 157
Boos, Margaret (Peggy) Fuller, 348
Boosterism, 170–71; Loveland's, 10, 301
Boulder, 17, 188, 199
Boulderado Hotel, 61–62
Boulder Brook Trail, 228
Boulder County, 216, 292, 301, 306; and road maintenance, 55, 56, 57, 307
Boulder Creek, 312
Boulder Field, 416(n61); shelter cabin on, 229–230, 230, 233; trails to, 226, 227–28, 347
Boulderfield Shelter Cabin (Boulderfield Hotel), 229–30; Collier's operation of, 231–33; guides at, 232–33
Boulder Grand Pass, 238
Boulder Municipal Band, 177
Boulder News-Herald (newspaper), 216
Bowles, Samuel, 1
Bowling alley, 284
Boyd Building, 28, 318–19
Boyd, Fannie, 91

Boyd, Harry, 35, 284
Boyd, Jim, 30, 33, 41, 90–91, 258, 389(n16), 390(n25)
Boynton, Charles, 12–13, 60, 97, 120, 136–37
Brainard, Fay, 286–87
Bridges, in Big Thompson Canyon, 303–4
Brinwood Hotel, 20, 65, 167, 168, 315, 333, 334, 346
Broadway, 235, 236
Brodie, Ron, 284
Brown Tea Pot Inn, 41
Brown, Tex, 381
Bruns, Colonel, 235
Bryson, Charles, 240
Buck Creek, 96, 241, 361
Buckley Field, 370
Buhl, Elmira, 235
Building permits, 274
Building setbacks, 276
Buildings, fireproof, 258, 259
Bureau of Public Roads. *See* U.S. Bureau of Public Roads
Bureau of Reclamation. *See* U.S. Bureau of Reclamation
Burgess, William, 284
Burke, Kenneth, 344
Burlington Railroad, 101, 148, 182, 245; and road projects, 55, 56
Buses, White Motor, 42, 185
Businesses: in Estes Park, 28–30, 33, 34–36, 43–44, 48, 49, 51, 69, 275, 284; transportation, 63–64, 65–66. *See also by name*
Business Men's Association, 76, 82
Byerly, Frank, 143, 148, 168, 219, 248, 370, 405(n70), 407(n36), 420(n36)
Byerly, Harriet Rogers, 33, 144, 266, 284, 370, 420(n36)
Byerly, Jean R., 370–71
Byers, William, 14
Byrd, Amanda Blocker, 250
Byxbe, Lyman, 285, 375

Cache La Poudre River, 122, 314, 403(n21)
Cache la Poudre Valley, 298, 314, 402(n9)
Caldwell, Jess, 289
Calypso Cascades (Calypso Falls), 236, 238
Cammerer, Arno B., 193–94, 202, 315
Camp Chief Ouray, 248
Camp Chipeta, 249, 250

Campgrounds, 138–39, 141, 142, 145, 221, 236, 240, 241, 254. *See also by name*
Camp Haiyaha, 249, 250
Camping, 93. *See also* Autocamping; Camps
Camp N.P. 1-C, 335–36, 339, 426(n8)
Camp N.P. 3-C, 339, 427(n21)
Camp N.P. 4-C, 340, 342, 344–45
Camp N.P. 11-C, 340, 345–46
Camp N.P. 12-C, 345, 427(n21)
Camps, 405(n70); boys and girls, 241–50, 418(n89); CCC, 294, 335–36, 339–40, 341, 426(n8), 427(n21)
Camp Ski Hi, 250
Camp Woods, 334
Canfield, David, 177, 292, 294, 327, 330–31, 342, 349, 353, 361, 378, 379, 429(n6); during World War II, 367, 368
Cañon City, 122
Cantwell, Frank, 25
Capra, Frank, *Lost Horizons*, 285
Carlson, George, *12*, 344
Carpenter, Louis G., 313
Carr, Ralph, 282, 311, 320, 366
Carruthers, Hattie, 114
Cascade Hill, 334
Cascade Lake, steam power plant and, 74–75, 76
Cascade Lodge, 334
Catholic Church, 40
Catlett, Edward, 179, 193
Cattle/Cattle raising,92, 96, 98, 178, 201, 325, 359
CCC. *See* Civilian Conservation Corps
Cedar Cove, 304
Celebrations, 90–91
Central City, 27, 326
Central City Opera, 326
Chalets at Marys Lake. *See* Estes Park Chalets
Chapin, Mount, 225
Chapin Creek, 133, 134
Chapin Pass, 133, 134
Chapman, Arthur, 104
Chapman, Charles, 289
Chapman homestead, 99, 332
Chasm Falls, 123, 219, 348
Chasm Lake, trail to, 227, 228
Cheley Colorado Camps, 242, *244*; operations of, 248–50
Cheley, Frank Howbert, 219, 245; camp operations by, 242–43, 248–50

Cheley, Jack, 250
Cheleyville, 250
Cheyenne, 14
Chez Jay, 285
Chicago, campers from, 243, 245
Childs, Harry W., 182
Christian, Jacob, 249
Churches, 35, 40, 284, 390(n33)
Citizens Party, 112, 113
City Park (Denver), 138
Civic issues, 92–93
Civilian Conservation Corps (CCC), 177, 293–94, 334, 426(n8), 427(n21); and Estes Park, 340–43, 345; in Rocky Mountain National Park, 335–42, 344, 346–47, 359–60
Civil Works Administration, 293
Civil works programs, 289–90
Clarabell Mine, 169
Clatworthy, Fred Payne, 27–28, *29*, 34, 148, 242, *277*, 391(n45), 421(n50)
Cleave, John, 18, 29, 33, 42, 285, 388(n2), 390(n34); ranch of, 23, 25, 26
Clerc, Fred, 106
Climbers, on Longs Peak, 233, 234–36
Close Building, 285
CMC. *See* Colorado Mountain Club
Cobb, Al, 40, 43, 286
Collier, Dorothy, 231, 233
Collier, Robert, Jr., 164, 229, 231–32
Colorado, State of, 91, 99, 189, 198, 335; Depression economy and, 281–83; road jurisdiction of, 212, 215–18; road projects of, 56, 121, 123, 132
Colorado and Southern Railroad, 65
Colorado–Big Thompson Project, 22, 283, 285, 292, 294, 365, 425(n82); construction of, 320–24; history of, 312–18; Reclamation Village, 319–20; during World War II, 366, 375
Colorado Campfire Club, 154
Colorado Fish and Game Commission, 100
Colorado Game and Fish Department, 361
Colorado Mountain Club (CMC), 219, 317, 330; and Longs Peak, *230*, 235; Roger Toll and, 210–11; trail registers of, 225–26; winter sports promotion by, 161–62, *163*, 163–65, 167–68, 178
Colorado National Guard, 320
Colorado Pharmacal Association meeting, 62
Colorado River, 123, 300, 315, 317, 327

Colorado River Water Conservancy District, 317

Colorado Ski Club, 170, 171–72, 174

Colorado Springs, 17

Colorado State Highway Commission, 192, 193

Colorado State House of Representatives, 216

Colorado State Prison, 122

Colorado Supreme Court, 46

Colt, William A., 297, 300

Colt & Sons, W. A., 297–98, 300

Columbines Lodge, 20, 65

Communication system, 137–38

Community-building, 90–91

Community Chest, 291

Community Church, 284, 380

Concessions, 324; national park, 180–82, 200–206, 333; opposition to, 189, 199–200; in Rocky Mountain National Park, 179–80, 183–84, 187–88, 191–96, 198–99, 211–12, 214–15, 231–32, 413(n75)

Condon, David, 361

Continental Divide, 2, 9, 77, 102, 121, 122, 133, 137, 144, 160, 166, 167, 171, 219, 224, 238, 293, 294, 298, 312, 313, 314, 315, 330, 332, 335, 339, 345, 355, 360, 379

Continental Oil Company, 276

Conventions, attracting, 260, 262–64

Convicts, road construction by, 121, 122, 123, 124

Cony Creek, 131, 236, 238

Cook, Hull, 233

Copeland, Mount, 238

Copeland Lake, 121, 139, 157, 237, 306

Copeland Lake Lodge, 20, 159

Copeland Moraine, 237–38

Corbelle, Louie, 30

Cordeau, 222, 224

Corners, 18, 19, 25

Cottages, 33, 145

Coulter-Boettcher Plumbing Company, 35

Council of Defense, 114

Cowbell Hill, 169

Cowboy Dance, 269–70

Cow Creek, 347, 357

Coy, Burgess, 315

Coyotes, 125, 355, 356, 357

Crags Hotel, 20, 51, 52, 144, 162, 164, 165, 259–60, 351, 406(n76)

Crocker, Frank W., 69, 94, 95, 98, 126, 286, 398(n16)

Crocker Ranch, 319

Crook, John W., 356, 357

Crutcher, Maye M., 202, 203

Cub Lake Trail, 346, 347

Cummings, Fred, 340, 341

Curry Company, 198

Dalpes, Lewis, 172, 175

Dams, 238; for electrical power, 75, 76; for water supply, 70, 71, 237, 241, 313

Dances: at Riverside Amusement Park, 268–70; at Shangri La Club, 285

Dark Horse Tavern, 269, 291, 420–21(n42)

Davis Hill, 86, 107, 162, 168

Day, Willard T., 234

Days of '49 parade, 326

Deer, 125; managing, 358, 360, 361, 383

Deer Mountain, 12–13, 96; ski and toboggan runs on, 168, 171; trails on, 239, 346

Deer Mountain Trail, 107

Deer Ridge, 221, 239, 296, 297, 331

Deer Ridge Chalet, 171, 334, 408–9(n65)

Deer Ridge Junction, 346

Deiterich, L. H., 169

DeLux Studios, 151, 152, 159

Demaray, Arthur E., 190, 317, 318

Denver, 9, 10, 55, 161, 282; autocamping in, 138, 405(n61); boys camp and, 245–47; and Estes Park, 1–2, 17; park concessions, 183, 200; road jurisdiction and, 217–18

Denver Civic and Commercial Association, 132, 141, 217; Fall River Road and, 133–34; and Rocky Mountain National Park concessions, 183, 205

Denver Motor Club, 9

Denver Post, 212; publicity hoax of, 150–59; on Rocky Mountain Parks Transportation Company, 187–88

Denver Ski Club, 172

Denver Tourist Bureau, 148, 183

Department of the Interior, 107, 124, 134

Depression: boys camps and, 247, 250; economy and, 281–82; Estes Park finances during, 287–88; federal jobs during, 291–92; poaching during, 290–91; Rocky Mountain National Park and, 327–29; tourism and, 175, 177, 282–83

Desouris, George (Adam the Apostle), 155, 156–57, 158
Devils Gulch Road, 293
Dings, Mac, 226
The Dixie Blackbirds, 326
Dixon, Joseph S., 360
Dixon Gulch, 303
Doerr, John, 380
Douglass, L. R., 335
Dove, Anna Wolfrom, 33, 214, 263, 284, 424(n57)
Draft, World War II, 366, 367–68
Drake, 64
Dream Lake, 347
Drought, 281–82
Drury, Newton, 378, 379
Duncan, Joseph J., 112, 204, 205–6
Duncan, Joseph J. (Junior), 371
Dunning, Harold, 229, 230–31, 234
Dunraven, Earl of (Wyndam-Quin, Windham Thomas), 15, 16, 17, 18, 20, 61, 89, 93, 313, 388(n2)
Dunraven Glade, 250
Dunraven Ranch, 18, 92, 313, 324
DuPont Powder Company, 222
Dust storms, 281–82
Dyer, John L., 160
Dynamite, used in snow removal, 222, 224

Early, Walter, 289
East Face (Longs Peak), climbs on, 167, 227, 234–35, 363, 416(n54), 417(n67)
East Inlet Trail, 238
Eastman, George, 55
East Portal, 317, 318, 319, 320, 321, 324, 365
Eaton, Bruce, 98
Economy, 240; Great Depression and, 281–83, 287–89, 332; World War II, 369–70
Eddins, Tex, 226
Education, 243; Rocky Mountain National Park program, 332, 347–54. *See also* Schools
Ehrhart, Thomas J., 132
Eighmy, Hazel (Agnes Lowe), as Eve of Estes, 151–59
Elections, in Estes Park, 112–13, 205–6
Electricity, 38, 67, 278, 395–96(nn53, 55, 60); generation of, 71–75, 324, 396(n72); Public Service Company and, 75–76

Elk, 125; management of, 357–62, 383–84, 429(n78); reintroduction of, 37, 101–102, 102, 355
Elkhorn Avenue, 26, 27, 40, 41, 80, 290, 311, 325; businesses on, 28, 29–31, 35, 51, 65, 69, 221; changes to, 254–55; improvements to, 274–78; residences on, 31–32, 33; Sanborn maps of, 252, 255–57; surfacing, 278–79
Elkhorn Lodge, 20, 51, 52, 65, 71, 101, 394(n40); electrical system for, 73, 396(n60); trails from, 106–7
Ellison, Mark, 136
Else, Hub, 269
Emerald Mountain, 140
Emery, Roe, 41, 42, 66, 144, 145, 170, 295, 405–6(n75), 406(n77), 414(n80); park concession and, 200–201; and Rocky Mountain Parks Transportation Company, 179, 185, 186–88, 192–93, 198, 253, 277, 410(n14)
Emmons, Dorothy, 86
Endovalley, 20, 122, 241
English Hotel. *See* Estes Park Hotel
EPPIA. *See* Estes Park Protective and Improvement Association
Erosion control, 338
Ervin, William F., 235
Estes, Joel, 13, 14, 16, 18, 324
Estes, Lake, 22, 317, 323, 324, 425(n82)
Estes Cone, 347
Estes family, 14
Estes Park, 1–2, 3, 8(map), 89, 113, 116, 128, 186, 260, 303, 311, 312, 323, 391(n45), 418(n3); airport, 377–78; appearance of, 283–84; assault and battery trial in, 204–5; auditorium for, 262–65; beautification of, 76–81, 85; Big Thompson Canyon Highway dedication, 305–6; buildings in, 258–59, 285–86; Bureau of Reclamation and, 318–20; businesses in, 28–30, 34–36, 266–70, 284; and CCC, 340–42, 344; civic problems in, 92–93; and CMC, 161, 163; as community, 382–83; construction in, 37–38; criticism of, 270–73; during Depression, 282–83, 287–89, 293–94; development of, 18–19, 38; development restrictions in, 381–82; elections in, 205–6; electric power and, 73–75, 395–96(nn53, 55, 60, 72); federal projects

and, 324–25; growth of, 20, 22, 39, 40–44, 45; 1930s activities, 325–26; public improvement projects, 289–90; standardized improvements to, 273–78; and Stanley Memorial Park, 375–77; incorporation of, 50–51, 85, 104, 110; infrastructure development of, 67–68; land sales in, 26, 28, 29; local government in, 111–12; maps of, 252, 253, 255–57, 364; mid-summer skiing in, 175–77, 178; 1982 flood, 86–87, 238; organization of, 23–25; and park concessions, 183–84, 188, 192–93, 195–96; and park dedication, 7, 10–11, 12; promotion of, 148–50; public buildings in, 284–85; residences in, 33–34; sanitation and water in, 44–50, 70–71, 365; social activities in, 90–92; street front improvements in, 274–78; street surfacing in, 278–79; summer activities in, 17–18; tourism in, 363, 365; town layout in, 26–27; wind in, 32–33; winter in, 90–91; winter sports, 161, 162, 163–64, 165–68, 170–75, 178; during World War II, 366–69, 371–75, 377–78

Estes Park Arterial, 346–47

Estes Park Auditorium, 259–60

Estes Park Auditorium Company, 262, 263, 264

"Estes Park Avenger," 368, 371

Estes Park Bank, 34–35, 41, 272, 363–64, 391(n45), 394–95(nn41, 43, 47), 421(n50); formation and management of, 68–70

Estes Park Board of Trustees, 111

Estes Park Business Men's Association, 81, 92, 105, 110, 239; organization and activities of, 107–9

Estes Park Chalets, 74, 143–44, 145, 186, 393–94(n29), 405–6(n75)

Estes Park Chamber of Commerce, 110, 217, 233, 254, 260, 286–87, 291, 309, 326, 359, 376, 380; and convention business, 262, 263, 264; and town appearance, 271, 272

Estes Park Company, Limited, 16, 17

Estes Park Defense Council, 366–67, 368

Estes Park Development Company, 240

Estes Park Electric Light and Power Company, 71–75

Estes Park Fire Department, 34, 291, 390(n25)

Estes Park Fish and Game Association, 99–100, 356, 359

Estes Park Fish Hatchery, 94–95, 96, 100, 105; construction of, 97–98; expansion of, 99–100; renovation of, 100–101; support for, 98–99

Estes Park Group of the Colorado Mountain Club, 168, 170

Estes Park Guard, 114

Estes Park Hotel, 16, 17, 20, 31, 258

Estes Park Hotel Association, 242

Estes Park Hotel Company, 394(n29)

"Estes Park Improved" (Richmond), 270–71

Estes Park Improvement District Number One, 276

Estes Park Lumber Company, 340

Estes Park Post of the American Legion, 92

Estes Park Power Plant, 324, 425(n82)

Estes Park Protective and Improvement Association (EPPIA), 10, 76, 92, 93, 104, 124, 400(nn53, 58, 59); auxiliaries, 105–6; Business Men's Association and, 108–9, 110; elk reintroduction in, 101–2; fund-raising for, 96–98; and Rocky Mountain National Park, 102–3; role and activities of, 94–95; support for, 95–96

Estes Park Public Library, 27, 254, 284, 305, 366, 419(n5)

Estes Park School District, 265, 391(n45)

Estes Park Sewage Association, 45–46

Estes Park Sewer Company, 47, 49, 52

Estes Park Steam Laundry, 35, 41, 47, 390(n31), 392(n50)

Estes Park Town Company, 18–19, 23, 26, 31, 33, 35, 44, 70; aesthetic considerations, 76–77

Estes Park Trail (newspaper), 258, 320, 326, 333, 348, 391(n43); on Depression-era economy, 288–89, 290

Estes Park Transportation Company, 65–67, 70, 164

Estes Park Urban Renewal Authority (EPURA), 87, 382

Estes Park Water Company, 70–71, 259

Estes Park Woman's Club, 10, 77, 86, 92, 105–6, 109, 110, 164, 206, 254; and Long's Peak Trail, 227–28; during World War I, 115, 116

Estes Valley, 2; early settlers in, 13–15; land acquisition in, 15–16

Estes Valley Land Trust, 381

Eugenia Mine, 125, 367, 403(n26)
Eureka Ditch, 313–14
Evans, Anne, 326
Evans, Griff, 15, 16
Evans, John, 162
Evans, Mount, 189, 190, 191
Eve of Estes, as publicity hoax, 150–60

Fall, Albert, 206
Fall River, 2, 17, 18, 49, 125, 221, 240, 330, 334, 346, 361; flood on, 86, 238; hydropower plant on, 72, 73, 74, 75–76; park entrance on, 142–43
Fall River Canyon, 137
Fall River Lodge, 20, 334
Fall River Pass, 122, 133, 222, 338, 348, 383; museum at, 351, 352–53; summer skiing at, 168, 175; Trail Ridge Road and, 298, 300
Fall River Road, 7, 11–12, 20, 141, 145, 146, 177, 192, 193, 201, 241, 295, 296, 331, 339; completion of, 135–137, *137*; construction of, 121–23, 124, 130, 131–34; fish hatchery on, 94–95; improvements to, 219, 221–22; jurisdiction over, 202, 205; snow removal on, 222–25
Fall River Valley, 297, 353
Fan Slide, 225
Farmers Irrigating Ditch and Reservoir Company, 238
Farming, 113, 281
Fechner, Robert, *339*, 341, 342
Federal Aid Highway, 303
Federal Emergency Relief Administration (FERA), 282
Federal government, 425–26(n4); Depression-era projects, 283, 289–90; jobs, 291–94; public works projects, 324–25, 346–47; road jurisdiction, 215–18; road reconstruction, 300–12; Trail Ridge Road construction, 295–300; water diversion, 314–18
Fellowship Park, 242
FERA. *See* Federal Emergency Relief Administration
Ferber, Edna, 128
Ferguson, Horace, 20, 93
Ferguson, James, 93
Ferguson family, 16, 17
Ferncliff, 306
Fern Creek, 165

Fern Lake, 95, 131, 168, 140, 246; Colorado Mountain Club at, *163*, 164–65; trail to, 219, 346, 427(n36); winter festival at, 166, 167
Fern Lake Lodge, 162, 219, 248, 334, 407(n36)
Fern Lake Trail, 124, 125, 142
Fifth American Expeditionary Force Regiment, 114
Filling stations, 32
Finances: Depression-era, 287–89; Rocky Mountain National Park, 120–21, 129, 141–42, 401–2(n2)
Finch Lake, 237–38
Fires, 34, 93, 258, 390(n26); in Rocky Mountain National Park, 126–28
Firewood, 291
Fireworks, on Longs Peak, 233
First of the Season Party (1932), 326
Fish Creek (Willow Creek), 13, 16, 249, 307, 358
Fish Creek Road, 302
Fish hatchery. *See* Estes Park Fish Hatchery
Fishing, 93, 100
Flattop Mountain, 13, 137, 141, 161, 162, 313, 347, 403(n21), 404(n58)
Flattop Trail, 125, 130, 142, 330
Fletcher, J. Lloyd, 376
Floods, 237, 309; Lawn Lake, 86–87, 101, 238, 284, 382
Flower, L. F., 285
Food distribution, during Depression, 291
Foot, Elizabeth Ann (E.M.A.), 29, 30, 41, 43
Football field, 284
Forest Canyon Pass, 297
Forest Inn at the Pool, 334
Forks Hotel, 64, 259
Fort Collins, 10, 33, 185, 313; and park concession policy, 188, 199; roads from, 122, 133, 134
Fort Collins Chamber of Commerce, 217
Fort Collins Commercial Club, 158
Fort Collins–Estes Park Transportation Company, 66
Fort Logan, 335, 344, 346
Fort Morgan, 303
Fort Warren, 370
Fourth National Parks Conference, 189
Fourth of July celebrations, 91, 109, 116–17, 233, 325; Lily Lake fire and, 127–28
Fowler, Gene, 157

Fox Creek, 250
Fox Movietone News, 175
France, World War I, 115
Francis, F. J. (Pop), 32, 286, 288
Fried egg route, 226
Friends of Our National Parks, 214
Front Range, 2, 189; water supply for, 312–13
Front Range Lodge Company, 248
Frontier Days Rodeo (Cheyenne), 243, 270
Frozen Lake, 239
Fulton, Walter, 33
Funding, fund raising: for civic improvements, 107, 217, 219–21, 242, 262–64, 291, 368, 400(n58); EPPIA, 96–98, 400(nn58, 59)

Garett, J. C., 97, 98
Gem Lake, 128
Gem Lake Trail, 347
General Electric, 71–72, 75
General Federation of Women's Clubs, 127, 317
Genessee Mountain, 162
Geology, 2
Gianttrack Mountain, 323, 409(n81)
Gifford, Alderman, 48–49
Glacier Basin, 219, 226, 316, 331, 332; campground in, 139, 141, 221, 241, 297, 346; lodge in, 20, 239; Olinger Highlanders at, 246–247, 247; trails, 124, 347
Glacier Basin Road, 139, 140, 142
Glacier Creek, 121, 125, 220, 221, 318, 362; trails through, 124, 239, 346; water supply from, 71, 365
Glacier Creek Campground, 346
Glacier Creek Hill, 220
Glacier Gorge, 93, 131, 140, 238, 239
Glacier Gorge Junction, 239, 346
Glacier Knobs, 239
Glacier National Park, 181, 185, 219, 295, 333
Glacier Park Transportation Company, 185
Glaciers, 350; Arapaho, 189, 331; Boulder Field, 233, 416(n61); Mills, 235, 236
Going-to-the-Sun Highway, 295
Good Roads Committee, 132
Glover, Grant, 66
Golf courses, 16, 62, 67, 116, 253–54, 301, 352, 377, 394(n40)

Gordon, J. N., 60
Grace, Lawrence E., 112, 114, 201, 203–4, 277–78, 287
Gracecraft Shop, 201, 277–78
Granby, 320
Granby Reservoir, 317, 324
Grand Circle Tour, 146, *187*, 295, 405–6(n75)
Grand Ditch, 313, 338, 380, 424(n72)
Grand County, 121, 292
Grand Lake, 186, 300, 324, 383, 427(n21); road to, 12, 121, 123, 135–36; trails, 238, 403(n21); water from, 312, 313, 315, 317
Grand Lake Chamber of Commerce, 217
Grand Lake Committee, 314, 315
Grand Lake Lodge, 144, 145, 186, 406(n77)
Grand Lake Project, 314; final report for, 316–17; opposition to, 317–18; survey for, 315–16
Grand Lake Village, 136
Granite Pass, 226, 227, 228, 347
Grater, Russell K., 362
Gray, Joe, 357
Great Depression. *See* Depression
Greeley, 185, 199, 303, 313, 314, 335
Green Lake, 239
Green Mountain, 317
Green Mountain Dam, 319, 320, 321, 322
Gregg, H. Raymond, 352, 353, 379
Gregory, George A., 295–96
Griffith, Albin, 59, 141
Griffith, John (Jack the Giant Killer), 332, 356, 357
Grubb, Frank, 33, 41, 71, 101, 259, 286
Guides, Longs Peak, 231–33
Gunter, Governor, 134, 135
Gymnasium, 265

Haberl, Frank, 170
Haiyaha, Lake, 347
Half Mountain, 239
Hall, Chester Byron, 76, 86, 111, *150*, 258, 278, 365, 421(n50); and road construction, 56, 57, 309; and water plant construction, 72, 73
Hall, Henry, 166, 171, 172
Hall, John B., 56, 57
Halloween, Hidden Valley fire, 126–27
Hallowell Park, 220, 243, 332; CCC camps in, 294, 340, *341*, 345

Hanson, Charles, 314, 316, 321
Harbison, Anne, 333
Harbison, Kitty, 333
Harbison estate, 333
Hardin, Charles, 235
Harris, A. B., 278
Harter, S. B., 33
Hartzell, Willie, 285
Haugen, Andres, 162, 168, 169, 171, 172
Haugen, Lars, 162, 167, 168, 169, 171, 172, 174
Hayden, Albert, 71, 85, 110, 111, 112, 170, 259, 286, 394(n40)
Hayden, Julian, 114, 259
Heinricy, Henry J., 313
Helene, Lake, 124
Henry, Pat, 381
Hewes, Charles Edwin, 20, 80, 169, 238, 320, 333, 334
Hewes, Steve, 20, 80, 238
Hewes-Kirkwood Inn, Hotel, Ranch & Store, 20, 80, 169, 226, 234, 238, 255, 320
Hidden Valley, 59, 239, 296, 297, 408(n65); fire in, 126–27; winter sports in, 175, 177, 409(n81)
Hidden Valley Creek, 297, 335
Higby, Clifford, 125, 162, 166, 170, 226, 236, 245, 355, 407(n36)
Higby, Lester, 125, 162, 407(n36)
Higby, Reed, 125, 126, 162, 407(n36)
High Drive, 74, 96, 205, 221, 241, 296, 334, 338
Highland (Denver), 245
Highlands Hotel, 20
Hill, Louis, 185
Hillyer, Granby, 214
Hix, Charles, 71, 111, 115, 170, 363, 365
Hix, Frank, 380
Hix, George, 380
Hollywood Amusement Company, 326
Homestretch, 237
Hondius, Eleanor James, 96, 106–7, 166, 284
Hondius Park, 334, 405(n69)
Hondius, Pieter, 92, 94, 95, 103, 106, 124, 205, 241, 286, 333, 382, 394(n33), 400(n59), 418–19(n3), 425–26(n4); elk reintroduction, 101–2; fish hatchery and, 96, 97, 98
Hondius ranch, 339
Hondius Water Line, 96

Hoover, Herbert, 327
Hopkins, C. L., 169
Hopkins, Harry L., 282
Horse Creek, 23
Horseshoe Inn, 20, 221, 332, 333–34
Horseshoe Park, 7, 10, 20, 86, 92, 96, 131, 142, 148, 175, 205, 241, 329, 331, 334, 408(n65); CCC work in, 338, 339; elk herd in, 101, 358, 359, 360; inholdings in, 332, 333; roads in, 122, 221, 296; trails into, 106–7, 238–39, 403(n21)
Hotel Men's Association, 198
Hotels, 16–17, 20, 35, 40, 40–41, 131, 186, 348; construction of, 37, 38, 57–61; in national parks, 148, 183–84; resort, 61–62
Hot Springs Hotel, 186
Hot Sulphur Springs, 160–61, 162, 320
House Committee on Federal Relations, 216
House Committee on Irrigation and Reclamation, 317–18
Housing, 17–18, 38
Howell, Mrs. George, 203, 204
Howelsen, Carl, 161, 162
Huebner, Al, 178
Hunting, 93, 359; as predator control, 355–57
Huntington, Frank, 133
Hupp, Charlie, 97
Hupp, Ellen, 30
Hupp, Henry (Hank), 30, 33, 97, 389(n13)
Hupp, Josephine (Josie), 29, 30, 32, 33, 270, 389(n13)
Hupp family, 16
Hupp Hotel, 20, 29, 31, 32, 41, 42, 46, 47, 162, 258, 275, 285, 370, 389(n13)
Hupp Livery, 41, 51, 276, 286
Hutcheson, Henry H., 237
Husted, Shep, 148, 294, 343
Hyde, A. A., 242
Hydropower plant, 71–74, 75–76
Hygiene, 30

Icefield Pass, 314
Ickes, Harold, 291, 315, 316, 318, 320, 331, 425–26(n4)
Ida, Mount, 330
Idaho Springs, 186
Imhoff tank, 51–52, 392(n69)
Incorporation, of Estes Park, 50–51, 85, 104, 110, 273

Indian Shop, 284
Inholdings, 330, 332–34, 405(n69)
Inn Brook, 307
Irrigation systems, Front Range, 312–14
Izaak Walton League, 317

Jackson, William G., 288
Jackson, William H., 380
Jacob's Ladder (house), 34, 44
James, Ella, 93
James, Homer, 43, 45, 142, 262, 276, 342, 394(n40)
James, Howard, 70, 97, 98, 103, 172, 254, 286
James, Jennie, 259
James, Eleanor Estes. *See* Hondius, Eleanor James
James, William E., 93
James family, 16, 17
Japanese, in Estes Park, 372–75
Jay, Jesse H., 285, 375
Jay Building, *312*, 365
Jayhawks, 269
Jelsema, Ted, 177, 265–66, 270, 291, 324, 341; and Riverside Amusement Park, 266–68, 269, 326, 420–21(n42)
Jim's Grove, 125, 226, 227
Jobs, Depression-era, 291–93
Johnson, Ben, 35
Johnson, Charles, 28
Johnson, Edwin C. (Ed), 28, 282, 304, 315
Johnson, George, 30, 35, 286
Johnson, Julian, 35, 41, 390(n31)
Johnson, Julius M., 348
Josephine Hotel, 41, 44, *275*, 389(n13)
Junior Nature School, 353

Kandy Kitchen, 35
Kato, June Kiyoko, 374
Kato, Ryoji, 372 75
Kato Tea Garden, 374
Kato, Yaye, 372, *373*, 374
Kawuneeche Valley, 298
Kawuneeche Visitor Center, 383
Kennedy, Frank, 158
Kent, Howard, 366
Kent, William, 189
Keyes, Victor, 212, 213
Keyhole, 229–30, 233
Kiener, Walter, 227, 228
Kilton, Don, 286

Kirby, Dean, 288–89, 290
Kirchoff, Frank, 58, 59
Kirchoff Lumber Company, 58, 59
Kitchell, Ed, 270
Knouss, William Lee, 324
Knowles, Joe, 151, 152
Koenig, Frank, 126
Kremmling, 320
Kuykendall, Floyd, 374

Labor organization, during Colorado–Big Thompson Project, 320
Ladies Aid, 115
Ladies' Auxiliary. *See* Estes Park Woman's Club
Ladies Improvement and Development Society, 77
Lady Washington, Mount, 2, 227
Lake Placid, 172, 175
Lamb, Carlyle, 226
Lamb, Elkanah J., 33, 226
Lamb, Eugene, 294
Lamb, Jane, 33
Lamb family, 16, 17, 20
Lamborn, Alfred, 49, 75, 112, 199, 201
Lamb Road, 307
Lamb's Notch, 307
Lancaster, Thomas, 122, 123
Land, 71, 425–26(n4); Earl of Dunraven and, 16, 388(n2); Estes Park lots, 23–24, 26, 28, 29, 35–36; in Estes Valley, 15–16, 18, 381–82; Hondius's, 95–96; inheld, 330, 332–34; for Rocky Mountain Park headquarters, 80–81, 82; F. O. Stanley and, 85, 375–76
Landon, Alf, 325
Land O'Peaks Ranch, 250
Lane, Franklin, 131, 134–35, 181, 182, 185, 190, 332
La Poudre Pass, 313, 338
Larimer County, 26, 63, 69, 85, 172, 193, 292, 359, 391(n45); road construction in, 122, 132, 301; road maintenance in, 307–8
Larimer County Court, 202
Larimer County Fair, 10
Larimer County Grand Jury, 52
Laursen, Lars, 229
Lawler, L. T. (Bill), 298, 300
Lawn Lake, 125; flood, 86–87, 101, 238, 284, 382

Lawn Lake Trail, 11, 238–39, 347
Lawsuits, concessions-related, 202, 204–5, 212, 213–15
Laycock, Barney, 172
Leases, in Rocky Mountain National Park, 333, 334
Lee, Paul, 212, 213, 214, 215
Lend Lease Act, 366
Lester, Charles E., 38, 69, 115, 201, 286
Lester's Hotel, 65, 115
Levings, Charles, 262, 265
Lewis, A. D. (Gus), 20, 70, 144, 198, 405(n74), 406(n77); boosterism, 170–71
Lewis, Robert E., 195, 214
Lewiston Chalets, 20, 405–6(nn75, 77). *See also* Estes Park Chalets
Lewiston Hotel, 20, 143, 172, 186, 405(n74)
Lewiston Hotel Company, 143–44
Liberty Loan program, 116
Liebman, Joseph, 171
Liebman Hill, 171
Lighting, ornamental, 275, 278
Lily Lake, 127–28, 306–7
Lily Lake Trailhead, 307
Lily Mountain, 307, 424(n57)
Lindley, Ed, 111
Literary society, 91
Little Elk Park, 56
Little Horseshoe Park, 171, 222, 239, 294, 347; CCC camp in, 335–36, 337, *339*, 345
Little Prospect Mountain, 40, 171, 293
Little Sheep Mountain, 300
Little Thompson Creek, 56, 310
Liveries, 33, 34, 35, 41, 49, *51*, 52, 62, 78, 79, 86, 101,108, 259, 273, 276, 277, 278, 279, 284, 286, 330, 409(n65)
Liverymen's Association, 325, 380
Loch Vale, 93, 108, 124, 140, 142, 238, 239, 318
Lodges, 20, *21*
Lodging, availability of, 143–45
Long Draw Reservoir, 313
Long Meadows, 347
Longmont, 17, 65, 185, 199, 237, 312, 314, 405(n63)
Longmont Chamber of Commerce, 217
Longmont Lions Club, 200
Longs Peak, 2, 14, 17, 137, 141, 307, 347,

363; cable system on, 228–29; climbs on, 234–36, 416–17(nn63, 67); guides on, 231–33; shelter cabin on, 229–31; trail system on, 125, 225–28, 403(n21); winter climbs on, 167, 174
Longs Peak Campground, 347
Longs Peak House, 33, 226
Longs Peak Inn, 65, 128, 154, 207, 214, 226, 307, 403(n21)
Longs Peak Road, 221
Loomis, Battell, 337, 338, 344
Lost Horizons (film), 285
Loveland, 2, 17, 74, 185, 241, 260, 311, 319; boosterism in, 10, 301; Estes Park sewage and, 46, 47, 48–50, 52; and park concessions policy, 188, 199; road from, 121, 283, 294, 300–304
Loveland Chamber of Commerce, 301
Loveland–Estes Park Transportation Company, 63–64, 65, 66, 70, 276
Loveland Heights, 313
Loveland Stage Company, 30
Low, Clyde, 111
Low family, 423(n34)
Low, Oscar Peter (O.P.), 240, 254
Lowe, Agnes (Hazel Eighmy), as Eve of Estes, 151–59
Lowe, Mrs. H. R., 157
Lowry Field, 366, 370
Lulu City, 123, 329, 332
Lumpy Ridge, 58
Lute, Ira, 241–42, 422(n11)
Lyons, 2, 10, 17, 25, 30, *67*, 185, 237, 311; and park concessions, 199, 200–201; roads from, 55, 56–57, 65, 283, 294, 300–301, 306–7, 309–10
Lyons Chamber of Commerce, 217
Lyons Commercial Club, 200–201

McClure, L. C., 148
McCollister, Johnny (Mack), 169
McCracken, Richard T. (Dixie), 125, 126, *127*, 159, 164, 401–2(n2)
McCracken, Robert, 125–26
McDaniel, Dwight S., 202, 203, 204–5
McDaniel, Lloyd, 226
Macdonald, J. Edward (Ed,) 33, 42, 116, 262, 268, 274, 276, 286; Business Men's Association, 107–9, 110; stores of, 43–44, 48, 49, *275*, 284
Macdonald family, 254

Macdonald, Ralph, 41, 43, 47, 71, 277, 392(n50)
Macdonald Book Shop, 43, 372
Mace, Charles, 128
Mace, Gordon, 128
McFaren, Herbert, 290
McGlocin, A. J., 355
McGraw family, 423(n34)
McGraw Ranch, 325, 347
MacGregor, Alexander, 70
MacGregor, Clara, 70
MacGregor, Donald, 70, 71, 201
MacGregor family, 16, 17, 20, 92; Black Canyon, 70, 71
McLaughlin, John S. (Johnny Mac), 315, 317–18, 331, 351, 359, 360
McMahan, Harry, 202
McMullen, James, 47
McNichols, Jean, 381
McPherson, Mary Imogene, 20
McQueary, Richard W., 133, 136
Magoffin, Sam S., 320–21, 367, 377
Magoffin Construction Company, S. S., 320
Mail service, 25, 92
Majestic Building (Denver), 9
Mall, Jacob, 294
Manford, John, 366, 376, 389(n13)
Manford House/Hotel, 20, 35, 37, 41, 389(n13), 390(n34)
Manitou, 17
Many Parks Curve, 297
March, Daniel (Dan), 20, 122, 240
March, Minnie, 20, 122, 241
Marguerite Falls, 165
Marshall, Robert B., 83, 121, 331; and new park headquarters, 81–82, 84, 85
Marys Lake, 17, 20, 95, 307, 317, 323–24, 406(n77), 425(n82)
Marys Lake Power Plant, 317, 323
Massey and Ransom Flying Service, 377–78
Mather, Stephen T., 9, 10, 11, 82, 83, 131, 138, 170, 251, 332, 355; and concessions, 180–82, 184, 185, 187, 188, 196, 198; and Enos Mills, 189, 195; and National Park system, 147–48, 189–90; on road construction, 132, 134, 135, 295, 306; on Rocky Mountain National Park development, 182–83; on transportation, 186, 198–99
Mattes, Merrill, 231–32, 233
Mattox, Steve, 38

Medicine Bow Curve, 298
Medicine Bow Mountain, 243
Meeker, Mount, 2, 14, 141, 234
Meeker Park, 237
Meining ranch, 310
Mercantile Company, Elizabeth Foot's, 30
Merriman, Bert, 97, 98
Mesa Verde National Park, 189, 216, 217
Middle Park, 296, 312; roads to, 12, 121, 122, 134
Middle Slide, 225
Military, during World War I, 113–14
Mill Creek, 220, 339, 362; CCC camp on, 294, 340, 344, 345–46
Mill Creek Basin, 27, 121, 177, 243
Mill Creek Ranger Station, 168
Mill Creek Road, 140, 141
Miller, Donald, 366
Miller, George W., 379
Miller Fork, 128
Mills, Eleanor Ann, 351
Mills, Enos A., 2, 11, 12, 13, 18, 33, 53, 54, 91, 92, 94, 112, 161, 180, 196, 226, 382; on concessions policy, 192–95, 198, 199, 200, 201, 202, 204, 205, 213, 215, 413(n75); death of, 207, 414(n80); and *Denver Post* publicity hoax, 152, 153, 154, 155, 157, 158; and Longs Peak climbs, 234, 416(n63); and National Park Service policies, 188–91; and Rocky Mountain National Park, 102, 103, 120, 121, 125, 134, 179; and winter sports, 160, 166
Mills, Esther Burnell, 214, 227, 406(n76)
Mills, Enoch Josiah (Joe), 20, 91, 100, 114, 144, 148, 164, 166, 198, 261, 286, 351, 382, 394(n40), 401–2(n2), 406(n76); and auditorium project, 259–60, 262–64
Mills, Ethel, 261, 351
Mills Glacier, 235, 236
Mills Lake, 238, 239, 318
Mills Moraine, 226, 227
Mills vs. Way, 204
Mills, Winston, 366
Milner Pass, 121–22, 125, 133, 300, 314, 403(n21); road over, 218, 296
Mines Hill, 309–10
Mission 66, 383
Mitchell, John, 101
Model Z Stanley Mountain Wagon, 64
Monaghan, Paul J., 284

Monaghan's Garage, 284
Monroe's Livery, *51*
Mont Rose Inn, 302, 303, 304, 423(n46)
Moomaw, Jack, 235, 290, 363, 379,
    416(n47); and Boulder Field shelter, 229–
    30; and Longs Peak Trail, 227, 228, 237;
    trail building by, 238, 347
Moomaw, Patti, 363
Moraine Park, 13, 17, 25, 50, 65, 74, 226,
    329, 331, 338, 357, 358, 407(n36),
    409(n81); fish nursing pond in, 99–100;
    inholdings in, 332, 333; resorts in, 140,
    164; roads in, 221, 307; trails in, 124,
    346, 403(n21), 427(n36); water diversion
    into, 313, 315
Moraine Park Lodge, 20, 332, 334, 336,
    339, 352
Moraine Park Road, 141, 263
Morgan, Dr. J. H., 50, 51
Morley, Clarence J., 215–16
Motion picture house, 285
The Mountaineer (newspaper), 36
Mountaineering, 209, 210; on Longs Peak,
    225–26, 234–35, 416–17(nn63, 67)
*Mountaineering in the Rocky Mountain
    National Park* (National Park Service),
    210–11
"Mountain Home," 33
Mountain lions, 139; hunting of, 355–56,
    357
Mountain Meadow Pass, 313
Mountain registers, 210, 225–26
Mountain States Telephone, 275
Mount Rainier National Park, 211
Mudslides, on Fall River Road, 222
Muggins Gulch, 15, 56, 310
Mummy Range, 2, 297
Munson, John Yale, 23, 70, 72, 109; on
    Estes Park aesthetics, 76–77
Museums, in Rocky Mountain National
    Park, 351–53
Mutual Broadcasting System, 372

Nakoni Lake, 138
Nanita Lake, 138, 318, 350
National Association of Audubon Societies,
    317
National Guard, 114
National Park Association, 317
National Park Auto Company, 201
National Park Hotel, 33, 144, 420(n36)

National Park Service, 82–83, 85, 128, 134,
    138, 177, 226, 291, 292, 295, 345, 352;
    concessions policy of, 180–82, 193–94,
    200–206, 214–15, 413(n75); Enos Mills
    and, 188–91; and Grand Lake Project,
    315–16; inholding acquisition by, 332–
    34; road construction and, 220, 295; road
    jurisdiction and, 212, 216–17, 218; and
    water diversion projects, 317–18; wildlife
    management by, 354–55, 358, 360;
    during World War II, 378–79
National Parks Portfolio, 147, 148
National park system: concessions in, 180–
    82, 200–206, 214–15; expansion of,
    189–90; publicity for, 147–48
Native Americans, 13–14, 352
Natural history, interpretation of, 139–40,
    347–54
Naturalists, park, 349–54, 361, 362, 379
"Nature Notes," 348
NCWCD. *See* Northern Colorado Water
    Conservancy District
NCWUA. *See* Northern Colorado Water
    Users Association
Nebraskans, 267–68
Never Summer Range, 313, 327, 347
New Deal, 282, 316; CCC in, 334–35;
    federal projects in, 283, 290, 291, 293,
    346
New Year's Day, 90
Nickless, Alfred H., 380
Night club, 285
Norcross, T. R., 48, 49
North Chimney, 235
Northern Colorado Highway Association,
    303, 304, 309
Northern Colorado Water Conservancy
    District (NCWCD), 316
Northern Colorado Water Users Associa-
    tion (NCWUA), 315, 316
North Face (Longs Peak), 228–29, 234
North Fork, Billy Welch's resort at, 53, 56,
    57
North Fork Big Thompson, 250, 403(n21)
North Fork Colorado River, 133
North Fork Valley, 315
North Inlet Trail, 347
North St. Vrain River, 236, 237, 309
North St. Vrain Road/Highway, 54, 56–57,
    65, 131, 302, 324, 326; reconstruction
    of, 306, 307–12

North Longs Peak Trail, 226, 228
Nugent, James, 15

Odd Fellows Lodge 163, 92, 116
Odessa Gorge, 219, 346
Odessa Lake, 124, 165–66, 219, 427(n36)
Old Faithful Slide, 225
Oldman Mountain, 117, 325, 347; ski runs on, 171–72, *173*, 174, 178; summer skiing on, 175, *176*, 325
Old Man Ranger Station, 347
Olinger, George, 246, 248
Olinger Highlander Boy's Band, 246
Olinger Highlanders, 168, 245–47
Olympus Dam, 317, 323, 324
Onahu Trail, 347
Oriental Tea Garden, 374
Osborn, David, 63, 65, 70, 301
Osborn Garage, 276
Osborn, Estes, 63
Osborn, Otto, 63
Osborn, Will, 63
Outdoor Club of Estes Park, 162–63, 166, 168
Ouzel Falls, 238, 347, 403(n21)
Ouzel Lake, 238, 403(n21)
Ouzel Lake Trail, 236, 347
Overgrazing, by elk herd, 359–60
Overlooks, on Trail Ridge Road, 297

Pangborn, J. G., 23
Pan-Hellenic Ball, 269
Park Bill, 316
Parke, William T. (Billy), 30, 103, 418(n3), 421(n54)
Park Hill, 18, 310, 313, 324
Park Hotel, 41, 162
Park rangers, 126–27, *127*; naturalists, 349–54
Park superintendents, 349, 401(n1). *See also by name*
Park Theatre Mall, 41–42, 65, 272, 392(n52)
Parkway, 330–31
Pathe Studios, 11
Patrick, C. C., 332
Patriotism, 114–15, 148
Patterson, George, 265, 273
Pauly, Peter J., 98, 325
Peaceful Valley, 306
Pear Lake, 121, 237

Pear Lake Trail, 236, 237–38
Pearl Harbor, 366
Pear Reservoir, 314
PEO sisterhood, 92
People of the State of Colorado vs. the Hupp Hotel, 46
Pesman, Walter, 381
Phantom Valley, 338, 339, 427(n21)
Phantom Valley Ranch, 298
Phipps, Lawrence, 215, 218
Pikes Peak, 189
Piltz, Carl, 34, 391(n49)
Pine Cone Inn, 276, 278, 420(n36)
Pineledge Campground, 241
Pinewood Springs, 56, 308, 310
Placer Inn, 186
Plane crashes, 371, 429(n23)
Plantation restaurant, 284
Platt Rogers Construction Company, 321
Poaching, 290–91, 384
Poisoning, as predator control, 355, 356, 357
Pole Patch, 27, 121, 126, 141
Pollution, Big Thompson system, 45–52, 241
Ponderosa pine, removal of infested, 337, 338–39
Pool, the, 125, 140, 165, 168, 334, 346, 427(n36)
"Popular Shop," 43, *48*
Porter, Carl, 284
Post office, 25, 27, 28, 29, 31, 34, 38, 41, 46, 79, 80, 84, 104, 154, 240, 286, 319, 365, 391(n49)
Poudre Canyon Road, 123, 134
Poudre Lakes, 122, 125, 133, 138, 298
Poudre River. *See* Cache la Poudre River
Poudre River Road, 133
Powell, John Wesley, 14
Powell, C. B., 136
Power lines, survey for, 119
Power plants, 54; hydro, 72–73; steam, 74–75; water diversion and, 317, 322, 323, 324
Predator control, 355–56, 357, 358
Presbyterian Church, 35, 92, 258, 390(n33). *See also* Community Church
Presbyterian Women's Association, 92
Preston, Glen H., 112, 170, 368, 369, 380
Preston, John C., 331
Price, Jerald, 371–72

Primrose, David, 245
Private property, 241; in Rocky Mountain
    National Park, 330, 332
Professionalism, National Park Service, 349
Prospect Canyon, 316
Prospect Inn, 20, 40, 40–41
Prospect Mountain, 18, 20, 95, 162, 171,
    185, 253, 259, 307, 380, 412(n45),
    418(n89)
Prospect Mountain Tunnel, 323, 324
Prospectors, 14
Publicity: *Denver Post* hoax, 150–59; Estes
    Park area, 148–50; for National Parks,
    147–48; Van Den Enden hoax, 159–60
Public Service Company of Colorado, 75,
    375, 396(n70)

Radio, 353, 372
Railroads, 148, 185–86, 222
Raker, John E., 196
Ramsey, Hugh, 238
Rams Horn Tunnel, 323
Ranches, 13, 23–24, 92
Ranger stations, 124–25
Rapids, The, 302
Ratcliff, Harold M., 290, 379
Rattlesnake Hill, 303
Raymond, 306
Real estate, town, 23–24, 26, 28, 29, 35–36
Rebekas, 92
Reclamation Act, 316
Reclamation Service, 314
Reclamation Village, 319–20
Red and White grocery, 284
Red Lodge–Cook City road, 295
Red Mountain Trail, 338
Reed, Charles, 69, 198, 286, 305, 368, 369
Reed family, 333, 366, 423(n34)
Relocation camps, Japanese, 375
Remington Ordinance Plant, 366
Rent-car drivers, concessions policy and,
    201–3, 205
Republican party, 325
Reservoirs, 70, 71, 121, 237, 313,
    405(n63), 425(n82). *See also by name*
Residences, 42–43, 241; on Elkhorn
    Avenue, 31–32, 33–34
Resort industry, 18, 20, 35, 121; hotels and,
    61–62; Stanley Hotel and, 58, 62–63
Resorts, 21; inside Rocky Mountain
    National Park, 125, 140, 333–34

Resource management, 379
Restaurants, 284
Retaining walls, on Fall River Road, 222
Retirees, 381
Reunion Dinner, 91
Richmond, Marie, 272; "Estes Park
    Improved," 270–71
Riley, Barney, 172, 174, 178
Rivers, Elija (Lige), 41, 111, 277
Riverside Dance Hall and Amusement Park,
    177, 265, 272, 325, 326, 420–21(n42);
    attractions at, 266–70; CCC and, 341–42
Roads, 7, 9, 11–12, 17, 26, 54, 67, 339,
    402(n8); condition of, 218–19; double-
    track, 306–7; as federal projects, 283,
    294; jurisdiction over, 202, 205, 212,
    214, 215–18; park entrance, 330–31;
    reconstruction of, 300–312; in Rocky
    Mountain National Park, 121–24, 130–
    41, 192, 220–22, 295–300, 334; F. O.
    Stanley and, 55–57, 63. *See also by name*
Roadside cleanup, 338
Roaring River, 86, 238
Robbins, Charles, 201, 202, 204, 212, 214,
    405–6(n75)
Rock Cut, 298, 299
Rockdale Hotel, 20
Rockefeller Foundation, 242
Rockside cottage, 54, 58, 106
Rockwell, Casey, 111, 325, 365
Rocky Mountain Boys Camp, 243, 245, 340
Rocky Mountain Lodges, Inc., 144
Rocky Mountain National Park, 2, 3, 4,
    161, 252, 319, 363, 401–2(n2), 429(n6);
    administration building for, 107, 130,
    206, 220, 239; boys and girls camps in,
    241–50; budgets for, 120–21, 129, 141–
    42; campaign for, 102–3; campgrounds in,
    138–39; CCC in, 335–47; changes to,
    383–84; communication system in, 137–
    38; concessions in, 179–80, 182–84, 185,
    187–88, 191–96, 198–206, 211–12,
    214–15; dedication of, 7, 9, 10–11, 12,
    148, 404(n58); Depression-era jobs, 291–
    92, 293–94; expansion of, 327–29; Fall
    River entrance of, 142–43; Forest Service
    and, 190–91; fires in, 126–28; headquar-
    ters, 41, 85–86, 397(n98); inholdings in,
    332–34, 405(n69); natural history
    interpretation in, 139–40, 347–54; new
    headquarters for, 78, 80–85; organization

of, 119–20; poaching in, 290–91; publicity hoaxes in, 150–60; rangers in, 126–27; ranger stations in, 124–25; roads in, 121–24, 216–17, 215–21, 295–300, 334; Rogers as superintendent, 330–32; trails in, 130–31, 225–29; utility area in, 239–40; visitation in, 144–46, 422(n5); water diversion projects in, 315–16; Way's management of, 128–37; wildlife management in, 354–62, 429(n78); winter sports in, 165–66, 175, 177; during World War II, 369, 370, 378–80

Rocky Mountain National Park Ski Club, 174, 175

Rocky Mountain Nature Association, 351

Rocky Mountain News, on road jurisdiction, 217, 218

Rocky Mountain Parks Transportation Company, 41, 66, 144, 171, 198, 214, *221*, 222, 249, 253, 276, 277, *311*, 352, 405–6(n75); as concession, 179, 185, 191–93, 200–201; operation of, 186–88, 410(n14)

Rodeos, 92, 325, 363

Roenfelt, Al, 59, 70

Rogers, Edmund Burrell, 161, 164, 291, 292, 293, 303, 327, 329–30, 333, 349, 351, 409(n81); and CCC, 337, 344; elk herd management, 358–59, 360; as park superintendent, 330–32, 336; Grand Lake Project and, 315–16

Rogers, Henry (Lord Cornwallis), 25, 33, 59, 98, 391(n49)

Rogers, James Grafton, 103, 161, 214, 329

Rollins, Frank, 254

Romancers, 268

Romans, Ab, 49

Rome, Richardson, 326

Rooftop Roundup rodeo, 363

Roosevelt, Franklin D., 291, 318, 334, 366

Ross, Donald, 366

Rotary International, 260, 262, 263–64, 419(n13)

Rowe family, 16

Rowe Glacier, 350

Rowell Hill, 56, 57

Ruple, Fluta Ann (Flutie), 33

Rustic Hotel, 65, 115

Rutledge, Warren, 91

Ryan, Joe, 28

St. Vrain River, 312, 316

St. Vrain Valley, 314

St. Walter's Catholic Church, 40

Sampson, 384

Sampson, Thornton R., 137, 404(n58)

Sanborn, Burton D., 18, 19, 98, 313, 314, 324

Sanborn, Carl, 376

Sanborn, Carrie, 105

Sandbeach Lake, 237, 314

Sanitation, 44–45; Loveland and, 46, 48–50; septic tanks, 51–52; sewer system, 47, 50, 392(n69)

Santa Fe Railroad, 148

Saw mills, 59; fires in, 126–27

Scenic Air Line, 377–78

Schools, 40, 391(n45); Depression-era finances for, 288–89, 293; junior-senior high, 284–85

Scilly, Hugh, 260

Scott's Heights, 249

Scrap metal drives, 367, 368, 380

Schwartz, Dorothy, 77

Schwartz, Julius, 33, 111, 286

Secor & Secor, 273

Selective Service Act, 366

Septic tanks, 50, 51–52

Service Block, 259

Service family, 254, 389(n16)

Service Men's Center, 370

Service, Samuel, 45, 53, 103, 111, 154, 286, 389(n16); businesses of, 30–31, 35, 38, 41, 285; residence of, 31–32, 33

Sewer system, 44–46, 47, 54, 266, 290, 293, 365, 392(n69); Imhoff tanks and, 51–52; Loveland and, 48–50

Shadow Mountain Lake/Reservoir, 317, 324

Shafroth, Morrison, 164

Shangri La of the Rockies, 285

Shaw, George, 212, 213, 214, 215

Sheep Lakes, 334

Shelley's resort, 309

Shelter hut, on Longs Peak, 229–30

Sherman, John King, 165, 190

Sherman, Mary Belle King (Mrs John D.), *12*, 105, 106, 127–28, 190, 286, 400(n53)

Sherman, Sidney Willis, 72, 254, 418–19(n3); and Estes Park Bank, 68–69, 70, 394–95(nn41, 43); residence of, 33, 42

Sherwood Inn, 20, 389(n13)

Shoshone, 14

Shoup, Oliver H., 198, 212–13
Sidewalks, 274
Signal Mountain, 371
Signs, regulation on, 275
Silver Jubilee Celebration, 326, 378
Simpson, Harry, 228, 229
Skating, at Hidden Valley, 177
Skiing: mid-summer, 175–78, 325;
    recreational, 160–61, 162, 165–66, 167–
    68, 169, 171–75, 409(nn81, 84)
Skinner, Curtis, 227
Smith, Guy, 69
Smith, J. Gordon, 37
Smith, Lansing F., 248, 249, 250
Smoll, Perley A., 348
"Snow-Go," 222
Snow plows, 222
Snow removal, on Fall River Road, 222–25
Snowslides, 225
Social activities, 90–92; as fund raisers,
    105–6, 116
Somers building, 285
Sommers, Elmer E., 135
Sortland, Herbert, 227
South Platte Valley, 314
South St. Vrain Road/Highway, 169, 306–7
Specimen Creek, 314
Specimen Mountain, 314
Speer, Robert, 132
Sprague, Abner, 13, 14, 15, 17, 20, 125,
    170, 239, 286, 305, 312, 332, 352, 369,
    407(n36), 425–26(n4); and Protective
    and Improvement Association, 93, 94;
    road layout by, 56–57, 121, 122; town
    layout by, 24, 26–27; and World War II
    draft, 367–68
Sprague, Alberta, 239
Sprague family, 16, 17, 20, 332, 334
Sprague, Fred, 226
Sprague Lake, 226, 239, 326, 347
Sprague, Mary, 13, 17
Sprague Pass, 313
Sprague's Lodge, 334, 363, 367
Sprague, Thomas, 13
Sprague Trail (North Longs Peak Trail), 228
Spruce Lake, 168, 246
Stanley, Flora, 18, 25, 54, 92, 105
Stanley, Francis Edgar, 54–55
Stanley, Freelan Oscar, 2–3, 11, 12, 18, 19–
    20, 41–42, 62, 64, 69, 86, 87, 92, 102,
    103, 240, 242, 254, 263, 286, 305–6,

319, 375–76, 377, 382, 418(n3);
    beautification programs of, 77–81; death
    of, 365, 392–93(n3); electric power and,
    72, 73, 74, 76; EPPIA and, 95, 97, 98;
    Estes Park infrastructure and, 67–68; and
    park concessions, 195, 196, 198, 201,
    212, 213; and road construction, 55–57,
    307, 392(n1); career of, 54–55; and
    Rocky Mountain Park headquarters, 80–
    81, 83–85; and sewage system, 45, 51,
    392(n69); and social events, 105–6;
    summer house of, 53–54; and town
    improvement, 272–73; transportation
    venture of, 65–67; and water system, 70,
    71
Stanley Corporation, 259, 393–94(n29)
Stanley Dry Plate Company, 55
Stanley Hill, 306
Stanley Hotel, 20, 40, 54, 65, 71, 72, 186,
    259, 272, 325, 393–94(n29); airfield at,
    62–63; construction of, 37, 38, 57–61,
    391(n39), 393(n19); winter sports and,
    170, 172
Stanley Livery, 41, 277, 286
Stanley Meadows, 324; sewer system and,
    47, 50, 51, 52
Stanley Memorial Park, 375–77
Stanley Model F touring cars, 63
Stanley Motor Carriage Company, 55, 66,
    85
Stanley Mountain Wagons (Stanley
    Steamers), 9, 37, 42, 62, 63–65, 67, 68,
    101
Stanley Power Company, 275, 396(n70)
State Board of Health, 51
State Highway Commission, 134, 135
Stead, James D., 20, 69, 94, 97, 100, 110,
    264, 286, 352, 418–19(n3)
Stead's Ranch, 50, 65, 74, 164, 221, 334
Steamboat Rock, 56
Steamboat Springs, 161, 162
Steam shovel, for snow removal, 224
Steele, John, 172, 175
Stephan, George, 214–15
Sterling, 303
Stettner, Joe, 235–36
Stettner, Paul, 235–36
Stevens, John H., 245
Stimson, Louis L., 315, 316
Stirling, David, 326, 365
Stone, John Timothy, 242, 243, 418(n89)

Stop signs, 278
Storer Ranch, 377
Storm Pass Trail, 124, 347
Stover, Frank W., 98
Street front improvements, 274–78
Streets, surfacing of, 278–79, 293
Strikes, 320, 344
Strom, Erling, 174
Summer Resident's Association, 380
Summit County, 320
"Sunbeam," 99
Sundance Mountain, 251
Sweet, William, 242, 422(n11)
Swift, George, 366
Symes, J. Foster, 214

Tahosa Valley, 17, 20, 33, 65, 141, 306,
    307, 347, 382, 418(n89)
Tahosa Valley Trail, 226, 228
Tallant, Lee, 372
Tallant, Louise, 91
Tallant, Richard, 286
Tallant, William, 30, 33, *275*, 276, 278
Tallant Building, 372, 374
Tammen, Harry, 157
Taxpayer Party, 112–13
Tax Reduction Fact Finding Committee,
    287–88
Taylor, Edward, 9, *12*, 120, 217, 218, 315
Telephones, 92, 137, 168, 227, 418–19(n3)
Telluride, 72
*Ten Nights in a Bar Room and What I Saw
    There*, 326
Teter, E. A., 356–57
Texans, in CCC camps, 339
Thanksgiving dinners, 91
Theater, 41
Third Colorado Infantry, 114
Thomey, Mrs. John F., 203, 204
Thomson, Clarence, 114, 115
Thomson, Gaylord, 95, 98–99, 100, 101,
    114, 408(n41)
Thomson, Homer, 114
Thomson, Laurence, 114–15
Thrift Stamp dance, 116
Thunder Lake, 152, 154, 157, 159, 236,
    238, 403(n21)
Thunder Lake Trail, 236, 238
Timber Creek Trail, 347
Timber cutting, 121
Timberline Cabin, 125, 226, 227, 229, 236

Timberline Road Camp, 224
Tipi-Waken, 248
Tipton, Royce J., 314–15
Toboggan runs, 162, 164, 167, 168–69, 177
Toggery, 284
Toll, Charles, 210
Toll, Charles Hanson, 210
Toll, Henry, 210
Toll, Oliver, 210
Toll, Roger Wescott, 100, 140, 145, 161,
    167, 170, 210–11, 231, 241, 251, 295,
    296, 327, 330, 348, 349, 414(n1);
    lawsuits against, 213–14; mountaineering
    of, 209, 234; as park superintendent,
    211–12, 217, 218, 219, 220–29, 236–40;
    on wildlife management, 356, 357, 358
Toll Memorial, 251
Tonahuto Trail, 347
Touring cars, 9–10
Tourism, 3–4, 15, 28, 89–90, 92, *142*, 148,
    162, 355, 359, 363; changes in, 145–46;
    Depression-era, 175, 177, 282–83, 287,
    292; hotels, 16–17; housing, 17–18;
    lodging and, 143–45; roads and, 12, 295,
    303; transportation and, 9–10, 186, 192;
    vacation habits and, 240–41; winter,
    168–69, 171; during World War I, 115–
    16, 140
Tourist and Publicity Bureau (Denver), 141
Town hall, 254
Town Ordinance #9, 52
Traffic lights, 278
Trail registers, 210, 225–26
Trail Ridge, 13
Trail Ridge Road, 121, 218, 251, 283, 329,
    331, 338; design and construction of,
    292, 294, 295–300
Trails, 95, 108, 168, 380, 403(n21),
    424(n57), 427(n36); CCC construction
    of, 337–38, 346–47; improvements to,
    219, 225–29, 236–39; Rocky Mountain
    National Park, 124, *142*, 225–29,
    427(n36); Woman's Club of Estes Park
    and, 106–7
Trails End Ranch for Boys, 250
Trails End Ranch for Girls, 250
Transportation: to Estes Park, 54, 56, 63–
    66; in Rocky Mountain National Park,
    179–80, 184, 186–88, 192–96, 198–204,
    211–12, 214–18
Travel, 3–4

Trout, 36, 99–100
Trout Creek, 335
Trowbridge, Charles Russell, 128, 354, 355, 401–2(n2); as acting supervisor, 119–120, *120*, 121, 126, 127, 405(n70); on park development, 124–25; on road construction, 123–24
Tschudin, Cesar, 171
Tunnels, Colorado–Big Thompson project, 320–24
Turner, George E., 10
Turner Moving and Storage Company, 10
Tuxedo Park, 220, 240, 332, 346, 374
Twentieth Colorado Company, 114
Twin Owls, 58
Twin Sisters Mountain, 128, 141, 249, 307, 347, 377
Typhoid, 48

Unaphone touring car, 9–10
Unemployment, 292
Union Pacific, 148, 206
U.S. Bureau of Biological Survey, 101
U.S. Bureau of Public Roads, 220–21, 296, 307, 310, 424(n57)
U.S. Bureau of Reclamation, 285, 292, 293, 314, 366; and Colorado–Big Thompson Project, 318–19, 365; in Estes Park, 319–20, 376; and Grand Lake Project, 316, 317
U.S. Circuit Court of Appeals, on road jurisdiction, 212, 214
U.S. Congress, 219
U.S. Department of Agriculture, 220
U.S. Department of the Interior, 315, 316–17, 401(n1). *See also* National Park Service; U.S. Bureau of Reclamation
U.S. Forest Service, 27, 33, 59, 124, 125, 190, 236, 291, 349; elk reintroduction by, 101–2; road construction and, 123, 306, 307
U.S. Railroad Administration, 140
University of Nebraska, 267
Upper Horseshoe Falls, 123
USO, 370
Utes, Northern, 13–14, 352
Ute Trail, 296
Utility Area, 241; construction of, 239–40

Vacations, family, 240–41
Vail, Charles, 311

Vaille, Agnes, 164, 167, 174, 227, 233
Vaille, Frederick O., 229
Vaille, William N., 215
Van Antewerp, Albert, 326
Van Den Enden, Prof., 159–60
Varney, Robert, 345
Victory Gardens, 368
Victory Tax, 380
V-J Day, 380–81
Volunteerism, 93, 96–97

Wagener, Siegfried (Hermit of Horse Creek), 372
Wagner, George, 35
Walker, Glenn, 228, 229
Wallace, Stephen A., 296
War Relocation Authority, 372–73
War Savings Stamps, 116
Water diversion schemes: Eureka Ditch, 313–14; Grand Lake Project, 314–18; Western Slope, 312–13. *See also* Colorado–Big Thompson Project
Watersheds, 237, 312–13
Water skiing, 326
Water system, 28–29, 54, 67, 70–71, 241, 290, 293, 365, 395(nn51, 52). *See also* Colorado–Big Thompson Project; Sewer system
Wawona Road, 295
Way, Louis Claude, 80, 81, 82, 83, 84, 114, 185, 190, 207, 239, 306, 366; and campgrounds, 139, 141; and concessions policy, 179–80, 183–84, 189, 194–95, 196, 198, 200, 200–206; on lodging, 143, 144–45; and nature guides, 140, 347–48; as park superintendent, 128–40; and publicity hoax, 150–60; on wildlife management, 354, 355; winter sports promotion by, 160, 165–66, 169; on transportation issues, 188, 191–92, 193–94
Way, Mrs. Louis, 129–30
Welch, William (Billy), 53, 56, 57, 309, 418(n3)
Welch, Sally, 309
Welch resort, 309
Weld County, 316
West brothers, 28
Western Conference of the YMCA, 65, 241–42, 250
Western Electric, 72

Western Museum Laboratories, 352
Western Slope, 133; water from, 312–13, 315, 317
Westinghouse, 71
West Portal, 321, 322
Wheeler, Herbert N., 102
Wheeler, Squeaky Bob, 298
White, Walter, 186
White, William Allen, 333, 376–77
White Motor Company, 186
Whyte, Theodore, 15, 16, 17, 89, 92
Wieger, T. Robert, 58, 83–85
Wiest, Roy, 30, 35, 45, 51, 92, 154, 155, 262
Wigwam Tearoom, 263, 424(n57)
Wilbur, Ray Lyman, 175
Wild Basin, 20, 125, 131, 152, 157, 159, 314, 338, 405(n63); roads in, 121, 306–7; trails in, 236–38, 337, 347
Wild, Raymond, 35
Wildlife, 94, 125; introduced, 36–37; management of, 354–62, 429(n78)
Wildlife Division, 378
Will, Burns, 20, 214
Williams, J. Sidney, 274
Williamson, Forrest, 284
Willow Creek (Fish Creek), 13, 177
Willow (Moraine) Park, 13, 313
Wilson, Woodrow, 7, 85, 113–14
Wind, in Estes Park, 32–33
Wind River, 33, 226, 317, 318
Wind River Lodge, 242
Wind River Ranch, 127–28, 307
Wind River Road, 307
Wind River Trail, 263, 307, 424(n57)
Winter, 90–91
Winter sports, 131; in Allenspark, 169–70; in Estes Park, 166–68, 170–78, 408(n41), 409(n81); promotion of, 160–61, 162–65; in Rocky Mountain National Park, 165–66
Wirth, Conrad L., 383
Woman's Club of Estes Park, 398(n11), 419(n5); and Business Men's Association, 109–10; organization and activities of, 106–7
Women's Defense Club of Estes Park, 114
Woods, Jack, 332, 374
"Woodpecker army," 336–37

Woodward, Frank L., 143, 394(n40)
Work, Hubert, 215, 216–17
Works Progress Administration (WPA), 284–85, 293
World War I, 85, 113–14, 306; tourism during, 115–17, 140
World War II, 250, 282, 322, 345; Estes Park during, 366–75, 377–78; Rocky Mountain National Park, 378–80; V-J day, 380–81
WPA. *See* Works Progress Administration
Wren, Gordon, 178
Wright, Frank Lloyd, 383
Wyndam-Quin, Windham Thomas. *See* Dunraven, Earl of
Wyoming, 189

Yard, Robert Sterling, 10–11, *12*, 147, 148, 189, 190
Y Camp. *See* Western Conference of gthe YMCA; YMCA
Yeager, Dorr, 239, 332; as park naturalist, 349–52, 353, 354
Yeager Eleanor Ann Mills, 351
Ye Little Shop, 28, *29*
Yellowstone National Park, 83, 219, 245, 251, 283, 295, 355; concessions in, 181, 182, 333
Yellowstone Park Transportation Company, 182
YMCA, 65, 76, 121, *140*, 356, 384; camp operations, 241–42, 248, 287, 417(n75), 418(n90), 422(n11)
Yore, Alberta, 63, 377
Yore, Clem, 112, *148*, 154, 195–96, *197*, 199, 201, 269–70, 286, 326, *330*, 374, 411–12(n45)
Yosemite National Park, 181, 219, 295, 333, 355
Yosemite National Park Company, 198
Young, Stanley P., 356
Youth: summer camps for, 242–50, 418(n89)
Ypsilon, Mount, 238
Ypsilon Lake, 95

Zion–Mount Carmel Highway, 295
Zion National park, 295
Zumwalt, Clerin (Zumie), 235